# FRANCE
## IN MODERN TIMES

# FRANCE

## IN MODERN TIMES

## From the Enlightenment
## to the Present

### FOURTH EDITION

## GORDON WRIGHT

*Stanford University*

W · W · NORTON & COMPANY · NEW YORK · LONDON

Published simultaneously in Canada by Penguin Books Canada Ltd., 2801 John Street, Markham, Ontario L3R 1B4.

Printed in the United States of America
All Rights Reserved
W•W•Norton & Company, Inc. 500 Fifth Avenue, New York, N.Y. 10110
W•W•Norton & Company, Ltd. 37 Great Russell Street, London WC1B 3NU

Library of Congress Cataloging in Publication Data
Wright, Gordon, 1912–
  France in modern times.

  Includes bibliographies and index.
  1. France—History—18th century.   2. France—
History—1789—   •  I. Title.
DC110.W7   1981      944      81–38395
                         AACR2

ISBN 0-393-95582-6

1 2 3 4 5 6 7 8 9 0

# Table of Contents

IV

*CONTEMPORARY FRANCE: CRISIS AND RECOVERY*
*1919–1986*

## MAPS

# Preface to the Fourth Edition

In the preface to the original edition of this book, published twenty-seven years ago, I attempted to assert the validity of the subject and to explain my approach to it. At the time, it was not quite intellectually respectable to write national history—to analyze and narrate the evolution of a single nation. The best minds held that nations were ephemeral entities, already in process of absorption into some broader category such as Europe or Western society. Such a historian as Arnold Toynbee would admit guardedly that "France perhaps approaches nearer than any other national state to being co-extensive and co-central with the whole of Western Society"; but he rejected nevertheless the practice of studying individual nations. This point of view is by no means dead, and time may eventually vindicate it. Yet present reality and the foreseeable future suggest that there is still a case to be made for national history. No one can cross the Channel or the Rhine without becoming quickly aware that real cultural differences survive, even where peoples have lived side by side (or back to back) for centuries. And one soon begins to suspect that those differences must be the product, not of "race" or "blood," but of history.

Some Frenchmen believe (as Jacques Fauvet has put it) that "France, like a microcosm, reproduces the problems of all humanity." There is a touch of cultural chauvinism here: from such a belief it might follow that studying French history is a convenient shortcut to understanding all of Europe or even Western culture as a whole. But if the idea seems bizarre, it is no more so than its mirror image—the belief that one needs only to study the history of Europe or of Western culture to understand France. The French share many traits with the peoples of other Western nations, but there are distinct differences too; and it is the differences that justify singling out France for separate study. Without national history, France's particular contours fade into a blur.

That being said, I shall add a word about my approach to the subject. The writing of history is a subjective process, involving selection and interpretation rather than simply exhuming "facts." I have not hesitated to inject my own judgments into the text, but I have also tried to introduce the changing and contradictory interpretations that scores of historians past and present have offered us. This book took shape in my mind as what might be called a "non-textbook" (though that may be unfair to the genus). Textbooks are held to be dull and lifeless, crammed with facts at the expense of ideas, often didactic in tone—products, in short, of some sort of bloodless machine rather than of a human mind. My hope was to produce a book that might not only be informative but that might actually be read for pleasure, whether or not in connection with a formal university course. If some teachers of French history were to assign it for class reading, I thought, then so much the better.

Over the past quarter-century the book has indeed been so used, and that fact has encouraged me to try to keep it up to date. No doubt if I were to begin again from scratch, I would change it somewhat, reducing the emphasis here and increasing it there. Yet it still contains what I view as the basic elements for an understanding of France's development over the last two centuries. Many specialists, I am sure, would like to see greater emphasis on other facets of the past—popular culture and mores, "high culture," foreign and colonial policy—whereas my central focus has been the evolution of France's political system and social structure. Some would also like an ideological slant considerably different from mine (which might be described as that of an old-fashioned unapologetic liberal). My own view, however, is that a "non-textbook" is more useful if it provokes some dissent, and if it supplements rather than echoes what a lecturer has to say.

In this fourth edition, I have brought the last few chapters up to date, and have added a full chapter on France since de Gaulle. It seemed essential to take account of the Socialist experiment from 1981 to 1986, and the early stages of the subsequent return to conservative rule. I have also put the four chapters entitled "The Varieties of History" through extensive revision, both to update the bibliographical references and to prune back the content drastically. I had originally conceived of these chapters as readable commentaries on some of the controversial aspects of French history, extending or supplementing the ideas contained in the text. In subsequent revisions, however, they became increasingly cluttered with titles and bibliographical paraphernalia, to the point that they became indigestible. Some readers may find that the pruning has been too brutal, and that their favorite books have been omitted. If so, I would suggest that they refer to the third edition of this book (W. W. Norton, 1981), which contains extensive bibliographies of works published before that date. The "selective lists of readings" in this fourth edition emphasize recent books, controversial issues, and a few older classics.

I am grateful to Robert E. Kehoe and Sandy Lifland of W. W. Norton and Co. for their expert editorial suggestions. I also owe a continuing debt to several readers of earlier editions—notably the late Val Lorwin, Nathanael Greene, John M. Merriman, and Charles H. O'Brien.

*Stanford, California, January 1987*

# I
# ENLIGHTENMENT AND
# REVOLUTIONARY FRANCE
## 1750–1814

ENGLAND

ENGLISH CHANNEL

HOLY ROMAN EMPIRE

Rhine R.

FLANDRE AND HAINAUT

ARTOIS

PICARDIE

METZ AND
VERDUN

Varennes

Seine R.

NORMANDY

ILE DE
FRANCE

CHAMPAGNE
AND
BRIE

LORRAINE

ALSACE

Versailles

Paris

BRETAGNE

MAINE

Orléans

ORLÉANAIS

FRANCHE-
COMTÉ

ANJOU

NIVERNAIS

SWISS
CONFEDERATION

TOURAINE

BERRY

Loire R.

BOURGOGNE

SAUMUROIS

BOURBONNAIS

POITOU

AUNIS

MARCHE

SAVOY

Lyon
LYONNAIS

K. OF SARDINIA

ATLANTIC

SAINTONGE AND
ANGOUMOIS

LIMOUSIN

AUVERGNE

OCEAN

DAUPHINÉ

Rhône R.

Bordeaux

GUYENNE

AND

GASCOGNE

PROVENCE

LANGUEDOC

Marseille

BÉARN

Garonne R.

SPAIN

FOIX

ROUSSILON

MEDITERRANEAN
SEA

CORSE

## FRANCE UNDER
## THE OLD RÉGIME

# CHAPTER 1

# *The Nation's Heritage*

It is commonly said that in this fertile country, on this territory so well marked out by nature, the emergence of a great people was to be expected. Such a statement confuses result and cause.... France is the work of man's intelligence and will.

JACQUES BAINVILLE

France in 1750 had almost attained its modern territorial limits. The duchy of Lorraine was still a border enclave, but its absorption was only a matter of time; it was quietly annexed sixteen years later. The island of Corsica, under Genoese rule, was to be purchased in 1768; while along the Alpine frontier, the province of Savoy and the city of Nice were not to come under the French flag for another century. If France had a territorial destiny, it was largely fulfilled two hundred years ago, much in advance of most European nations.

The phrase "territorial destiny" might have meant little to Frenchmen of 1750, but "natural limits" would have had a more familiar ring. It harmonized with the more general concept of natural law, so basic to Enlightenment thought. That each state had its natural limits was taken as an axiom by Montesquieu, Turgot, Rousseau. Though none of these *philosophes* chose to define just where France's proper frontiers ran, the politicians of the revolutionary era promptly leaped to an obvious conclusion. "The boundaries of France," cried Danton in 1793, "are marked out by nature. We shall reach them at their four points, the Ocean, the Rhine, the Alps, the Pyrenees." The legend was to be a powerful and enduring one. Frenchmen of the nineteenth century applauded Michelet's lyrical phrase that asserted France to be "not the work of men, but of Providence" and Albert Sorel's dictum that French foreign policy through the centuries had been "dictated by geography." Even as late as the Paris peace conference in 1919, the concept was far from dead.

3

The curious thing is that the natural frontiers doctrine gained currency and significance only after French territorial unity had been largely achieved. The kings and statesmen who had pushed French sovereignty out from the Île de France toward Rhine, Alps, and Pyrenees had done so as empirical rather than as doctrinaire expansionists; even Richelieu acted thus, despite the legend that he originated the natural frontiers concept. It is just as well that the territorial builders of modern France did not rely on so dubious a theory, for the case against France's alleged natural limits is overwhelming. It may have become a convenient fiction to justify expansionism in the modern era, it may have seemed consistent with common sense, but, in fact, it rested on no valid base in geography or economics.

Frenchmen also leaped much too readily to another conclusion: that nature had dictated the formation of a single state rather than several states in the area bounded by Rhine, Alps, and Pyrenees. Undoubtedly, geography had contributed something to French unity; but the natural forces for unity had been fairly well balanced by opposite forces working for division and diversity. The great river basins of the Seine, Loire, and Rhone were semidetached regions, neither isolated nor fused by nature. The fact that Burgundy became attached to France rather than to the Low Countries or to no neighbor at all was certainly not the work of geography. Despite Michelet, French unity was the work of men, not of natural forces; and it was a heterogeneous rather than a homogeneous unity, within which regional diversities stubbornly survived.

One other geopolitical theory may have more merit. Some scholars have found in topography, location, and climate a set of factors that contribute to shaping a nation's social and political structure, its attitudes, its "national character." This kind of geographical determinism has more often been applied to Germany or Russia than to France; yet a plausible case can be made for the effect of location on the structure of France and the behavior of Frenchmen. No other major state opens out in three directions: on the Mediterranean world, on north central Europe, and on the Atlantic. It is at least a reasonable hypothesis that the impact of varied ideas and cultures over the centuries produced a uniquely cosmopolitan and diversified culture in France, and that French governments were faced with a variety of alternative national policies as well as with a wide choice of friends and enemies. The critical significance of geography for France may lie in the very fact that too many choices were open—that no clear path was dictated by nature. The new nation-state of France might have become a land power, with a strong army and a continental destiny; or it might have become a maritime power, with a strong navy and merchant marine and a world destiny. The two alternatives implied quite different social structures, political systems, and even psychological frameworks. During the formative centuries, it was France's fate to hesitate or straddle rather than to be drawn ineluctably into a consistent course of development. Indeed, down to our own day there remains a certain ambiguity about France's proper nature—an ambiguity that conflicts with the passion of Frenchmen for coherence, clarity, and logic.

❖❖❖❖❖❖❖❖❖❖❖❖❖❖

Some Frenchmen in 1750, and in the two succeeding centuries as well, found the factor of "race" to be more important than geography in the shaping of the nation. The eighteenth-century aristocracy took for granted that its members were set off from the masses by a difference in blood; that they were descended from the conquering Franks who had overrun the indigenous Gauls twelve centuries earlier. Some commoners accepted this thesis, too, and viewed the great revolution as a kind of massive, if delayed, revenge of the Gauls at the expense of the "Goths." As late as 1871, so notable a scholar as Ernest Renan was to find in race an explanation for France's defeat at the hands of Bismarckian Germany: the warlike and courageous Frankish strain, wrote Renan, had been too·much diluted by Celtic blood, with its hereditary taint of effervescence and weakness.

Racial theories, however, have not had much political or psychological significance in France's modern history. Frenchmen of our era have readily admitted that they are hybrids in origin, as mixed as almost any people in Europe. From prehistoric times until the end of the first Christian millennium, invasion brought a series of injections of "new blood." Over the next eight or nine centuries, a rather complete blending process occurred; then, from the later nineteenth century onward, France was again to become the melting pot of Europe. Most of the components of the mixture are known; only the proportions, and the real significance of these proportions, remain unclear. Even "our ancestors the Gauls" (the stock phrase that used to introduce French grade-school textbooks in history) were not indigenous, but constituted a fusion of Neolithic stock with early Celtic invaders. Then were added, in turn, Roman immigrants, Franks, Burgundians, and Normans. On the northern plains, each wave of invasion rolled over the previous one and merged with it. In remote regions like the Auvergne highlands and the Basque country, a more nearly pure variety of the Neolithic or Neolithic-Celtic stock survived.

Modern Frenchmen have made a virtue of their mixed origin. "We are a race of half-breeds," wrote the republican historian Charles Seignobos, "but mongrels are often more intelligent than pure-breds." "France," declared the monarchist Jacques Bainville, "is better than a race; it is a nation." And André Siegfried summed up the case in this fashion: "To the Latins the French owe their gift for expression and their intellectual lucidity; to the Celts their artistic nature as well as their individual anarchism; to the Germans what they possess of seriousness and constructive capabilities."[1] There is a curious flavor here of racism in reverse—a variety of racism, it ought to be added, that is far less dangerous than the usual narrowly exclusive or "tribal" sort.

In one fasion, however, France's heterogeneous origins may have made a genuine contribution to France's present. Whatever the significance (or lack of it) of the ethnic factor, no one can doubt the importance of a nation's cultural heritage; and it is clear that each wave of invaders in the early centuries brought its peculiar institutions and folkways. The components of the resultant blend have produced violent (and perhaps useless) controversy. The most violent dispute of all, the echoes of which persisted well into the twentieth century, was the product of the nineteenth-century Celtic revival. Until a century ago, the traditional view of Frenchmen had been that the Gauls were benighted barbarians who needed the civilizing influence of Roman rule in order to permit the building of a strong state and a brilliant culture in Gaul. A new school of historians passionately challenged this tradition; it argued that the Roman conquest had been one of the worst crimes and tragedies in all French history, involving the destruction of a culture even more advanced than Rome's and the systematic creation of a false legend by the official propagandists of the Roman state. Vercingetorix, leader of the Gallic resistance movement, became the tragic hero of this pro-Celtic school, the victim of " ...the baldheaded Caesar, the wan proconsul ... [who] rejoiced in the ...morbid pleasure of blasting and trampling under foot human destinies ...."[2] Whatever the validity of the case, it is hard to deny the profound effects of the Romans' language, law, religion, and architecture on the subsequent development of France.

A controversy of somewhat less intensity surrounds the Frankish conquest. To what degree were Germanic institutions and folkways blended with, or superimposed on, the Gallo-Roman culture found by Clovis and his successors? Modern scholars have, in the main, rejected the older thesis of predominant Frankish influence and have concluded that the Gallo-Roman fusion survived under a Germanic veneer. Some Frankish law was introduced, but it was grafted onto a Roman root. In religion, the Roman influence prevailed completely. In the same fashion, the ethnic contribution of the Franks seems to have been rather slight. But in the gradual process of fusion of Frankish and Gallo-Roman institutions and "blood," the already existing differences between northern and southern Gaul were increased. More Franks intermarried with the Gallo-Romans north of the Loire; the Frankish accent gradually converted the northern ver-

---

[1] In E. M. Earle (ed.), *Modern France* (Princeton: Princeton Univ. Press, 1951), pp. 4–5.
[2] F. Funck-Brentano, *The Earliest Times* (New York: Putnam, 1928), p. 106.

nacular into the ancestor of modern French, while a purer southern vernacular developed into the quite distinct language of Provençal or *Langue d'Oc*.

By the year 1000 the phase of racial and cultural mingling through violent irruptions of invaders from east or south was over. The last such group, the Normans, added little or nothing to the cultural amalgam, though blond Nordic types still appear today in the valleys of northern France. For several centuries the process of cultural fusion went on, never in complete isolation from neighboring cultures, but never again through sudden submersion. In the course of events there emerged quite early both a French state and a consciousness of French nationality, primitive in nature yet none the less real.

❖❖❖❖❖❖❖❖❖❖❖❖

The French state, according to the classic formula of Jacques Bainville, was the work of its forty kings. One need not be a monarchist like Bainville to admire their work, even though it might be argued that Frenchmen were no better off within a powerful unitary state than they would have been within a decentralized structure like that of the Germanies or the Low Countries. At any rate, a single dynasty ruled France, in either the direct or the indirect line, from 987 to 1789; and while there was the normal quota of weak or contemptible kings, the dynasty was fortunate in producing a great man or a clever man at most of the right times. The early Capetians were thoughtful enough to provide, without exception, a male heir; and they were shrewd enough not to waste their substance, as certain German princes did, in chasing phantoms like the crown of the Holy Roman Empire. They concentrated, rather, on building up the family's personal domain from its tiny original nucleus around Paris, until their holdings exceeded those of any other French feudal prince, and they could overawe all potential rivals.

According to an old and romantic theory, the kings were aided in the process of building national unity by an obscure but deep longing of the masses for strength, authority, and an embodiment of their instinct toward nationhood. Such a theory may have satisfied Michelet, but it no longer finds many defenders. If anyone helped the kings break down feudal weakness and build royal authority, it was not the mass of Frenchmen but rather the rising bourgeoisie and the Catholic clergy. From the thirteenth through the seventeenth century, French holdings were gradually pushed out in all directions, and royal agents were invested with a growing share of power. There is both paradox and truth in the remark that absolutism was the product of the crown's weakness rather than of its power; that "...absolute monarchy was...no more than a gigantic system of bribery of those whom the crown found it worth while to bribe."[3] But if the methods used by French kings were not always admirable ones, they were none the less effective. By the seventeenth century, the way was open for Cardinal Richelieu to consolidate the work of his forerunners and to hand on to Louis XIV a functioning royal absolutism.

Although the record of the French kings was a remarkable one in certain ways, it had its seamy side as well. The trend toward centralization and absolutism was not accompanied by either steady or adequate progress toward the creation of an efficient and enlightened despotism. Royal institutions grew up gradually, haphazardly, with a barnacle-like encrustation of overlapping functions and useless sinecures. Never—not even under Richelieu—was there a thorough house cleaning. By 1750 the administrative structure resembled a palace that had been built piecemeal by adding rooms and wings without any renovation of the original structure or any attempt to harmonize the whole. One source of the trouble had been the state's constant need of money and its inability to establish an effective mechanism for getting what it needed. In the later Middle Ages the monarchy had hit on the easy device of selling government offices; and as time went by, the temptation was great to expand the bureaucracy in order to increase the royal income. There was another reason, too, for this bureaucratic inflation. From time to time, when a set of officials had become so solidly entrenched as to bridle at royal authority, the monarchy had brusquely superimposed a new set and had transferred to the latter the functions (but not the perquisites) of the first group. This old Capetian device had proved useful at times, but it was hardly a way to build an efficient bureaucratic system. Worse still, certain office-holders eventually demanded (and got, in 1604) a hereditary vested interest in the posts they held; such posts could be willed to an heir, sold outright, or used as security for loans. The monarchy, deprived of the right to resell offices to each new generation, was driven to subdivide functions and create sinecures in order to replenish the treasury.

The absolute monarchy failed also to carry centralization to its logical conclusion. Richelieu took the longest step in that direction when he appointed intendants to enforce the royal will in the various provinces; but these officials, despite their extensive powers, could not challenge many traditional practices and institutions. A tangled undergrowth of local rules, trade restrictions, and special law codes seriously hampered domestic commerce and made travel a test of patience. Even the scale of weights and measures varied in different parts of the country. A few provinces had retained a special kind of local autonomy in

---

[3] M. Prestwich, in J. M. Wallace-Hadrill and J. McManners (eds.), *France: Government and Society* (London: Methuen, 1957), p. 121.

the form of provincial "estates," which were deliberative bodies representing the privileged orders. Deeper still, provincial loyalties and folkways stubbornly survived, along with some linguistic variations. If France in 1750 was a centralized despotism with a conscious sense of nationhood, there was a curious patchwork quality about both state and society.

Undoubtedly, the regime's greatest weakness was in the sphere of public finance. There persisted even in the eighteenth century something of the medieval idea that the king should support himself from his own private domains, like any lesser feudal lord, and should levy taxes on his fellow lords only on a temporary basis, in times of grave national emergency. Kings and ministers tried periodically to impose a direct permanent tax beyond the traditional *taille* and *gabelle* (from which most members of the privileged orders were partly or completely exempt), but always gave way before the storm of outrage that resulted, and turned to devious schemes or, more often, to borrowing at high interest rates. More than any other single factor, it was the failure to construct an adequate structure of public finance that eventually destroyed the monarchy.

True, building such a structure would have required real statesmanship and strength of will. While the Bourbons and their ministers had gradually tamed the old aristocracy and had stripped it of much of its onetime power, they allowed two institutions to retain a special power role; and both institutions used their advantage to challenge royal attempts at reform. The first of these obstacles was the Catholic hierarchy; the second was the *parlement* of Paris, buttressed by the lesser provincial *parlements*. Both agencies were major pillars of the monarchy; both, in the end, contributed to its downfall.

In appearance, the king had brought the church to heel in 1516; the concordat of that year was a compromise worked out by king and Pope at the expense of the high French clergy. The concordat ensured for the king the right to select bishops and archbishops and to dominate church affairs, while it ensured for the Pope a steady income from the French faithful. The concordat was Gallican in spirit, for it placed control of the French church in Paris rather than in Rome; but this was not the kind of Gallicanism that French churchmen had so longed wanted. They had hoped to free the French church of papal control in order to place it under the authority of a church council, not of the king. The hierarchy was never fully reconciled to the new system, and in consequence, its loyalty was always rather grudging. Yet no king dared challenge the clergy too directly, for the church's annual "free gift" was essential state revenue, and the clergy's corporative spirit and spiritual influence made it a dangerous opponent.

The twelve *parlements,* led by the one in Paris, were agencies of medieval origin that combined judicial, administrative, and political functions. During early modern times, they had buttressed the kings' efforts to assert royal authority throughout the kingdom, especially in dispensing justice. By approximately 1500, that royal authority had been solidly established—whereupon the relationship between the king and the *parlement* of Paris began to change. The *parlement* now defined its role as a restraining one; it claimed the right to police the arbitrary and excessive use of the royal power, and to protect the privileges and immunities of the king's subjects. Those privileges it saw as antedating the royal authority, and as limiting the latter in legal or even constitutional fashion. It held that the loss of these basic rights of groups and individuals would transform authoritarian rule into despotism. From 1500 onward, as successive kings sought to shake off traditional limits on their authority, a sporadic contest developed between king and *parlement*. The *parlement*'s chief weapon was the function of registering royal edicts, and issuing "remonstrances" if it could show that the new edict violated long-established customs and privileges. In the end the king could always enforce his will by holding a royal session of the *parlement* (called *lit de justice*) and ordering that the edict be registered. But most kings preferred to avoid such confrontations whenever possible, and the uneasy relationship continued well into the eighteenth century.

By 1750, matters seemed to be approaching a crisis. The need for fiscal and administrative reform was obvious to some of the king's ministers, who saw the *parlement* of Paris as the chief obstacle to basic change. They were right; more stubbornly than ever, the *parlement* asserted its right to make the king respect the law. Both sides in the conflict claimed high-minded motives, and both may well have been sincere. Still, the judges of the *parlement* were defending something more than an ideal, or an abstract principle; they were also defending special privilege, vested interests, in which they had an important personal stake. As members of the highest echelon of the *noblesse de robe,* they shared with the old aristocracy a set of important rights and immunities that were threatened by the schemes of the royal reformers. These material concerns, however, were veiled under a cloud of fine words, so that the *parlement* increasingly achieved a distorted public image as protector of the ordinary Frenchman against despotism. A forceful and prestigious king might have challenged these defenders of the traditional system, and might have won for himself the kind of popular support that was needed to achieve fundamental reform. It was the rapid decline in royal prestige during the eighteenth century that gave the *parlement* its opening. In seizing the opportunity, the judges were shortly to destroy not only the monarchy but their own cherished institutions as well.

❖❖❖❖❖❖❖❖❖❖❖❖❖

France in 1750 was precariously at peace. This was something of a novelty; since 1667, when Louis XIV embarked on his lifelong campaign to dominate

Europe, France had been engaged in a series of six major wars, broken only by armistices improperly described as peace settlements. True, there had been one long interlude of almost uninterrupted peace from 1713 to 1741, when the king's chief minister, Cardinal Fleury, had managed to repress the war hawks of the day. Then the almost irrepressible conflict had resumed once more, to be interrupted again by a shaky peace settlement in 1748.

England was the principal enemy; and the crux of the Anglo-French conflict was the contest for overseas empire in India and North America. But the English were also concerned with the continuing threat of French domination in Europe. France probably could not have avoided the colonial aspect of the struggle, except by abandoning any ambition to expand its holdings in America and Asia. On the Continent, however, a policy of caution and restraint would not have injured France's national or dynastic interests. But the king unwisely let himself be drawn into dangerous ventures; intriguing courtiers at Versailles persuaded him to make a strange alliance with France's traditional rival Austria. The French stood to gain little and to lose much; and lose they did, in the Seven Years' War that broke out in 1756. By the humiliating peace settlement of 1763 they were forced to give up almost all of their overseas holdings. Their fleet was decimated, their influence in Europe weakened. But gravest of all were the financial consequences. "Of the hundred years that elapsed between 1689 and the Revolution, nearly half were spent in wars with Britain. They involved the French government in continually mounting costs. They overburdened the economy and reduced the system of taxation to chaos. They were one of the main obstacles in the way of reform, because most of the projected reforms would have involved a temporary loss of revenue, and this could never be afforded."[4] The matter could hardly be put more succinctly.

Since the death of Fleury in 1743, Louis XV had been vainly trying to serve as his own chief minister. The vanity of the effort sprang partly from the size of the task he faced and partly from his own limitations. Louis had inherited a realm as rich and populous as any in Europe, but one with an empty public treasury and a ramshackle administrative system. At court and within the bureaucracy, political factionalism exceeded that of twentieth-century France at its worst. A domineering ruler like Louis XIV had been able to overawe the factions; a shrewd manipulator like Fleury could somehow manage to keep them balanced. For a well-intentioned but weak man like Louis XV, the problem was insoluble.

The Louis of popular tradition was pure cynic and profligate, indifferent to the imminent disaster so long as it did not interfere with the chase after game and women. As a matter of fact, if Louis really said anything like "After us, the deluge" (and he probably did not), it would have been in a spirit of gloomy

---

[4] C. B. A. Behrens, *The Ancien Régime* (New York: Harcourt, Brace, 1967), pp. 160–62.

resignation rather than cynicism. There is an opposite legend—of more recent origin, in this case—that has sought to rehabilitate Louis and to make him an able king overwhelmed by the force of circumstance. But the evidence offered in support of this thesis does more to prove Louis's good intentions than his capacity for crisis leadership. It is true that when he chose to rule directly after 1743, he was guided by higher motives than a thirst for personal power. But he lacked the strength of will, the intelligence, and the character to shape a wise policy and to risk his crown in an effort to push it to completion. By the later years of his reign he was discouraged and disillusioned, and he no longer seemed capable of offering much resistance to the factional pressures that surrounded him.

The strongest pressures were quite naturally exerted by those who were personally closest to the king: the queen's faction on the one hand, that of the official mistress Madame de Pompadour on the other. From 1745 until her death in 1764, "la Pompadour" and her favorites were to exert direct though sporadic influence on public policy. In certain respects that influence was relatively enlightened: Pompadour's common birth and her fancy for being considered an intellectual made her susceptible to the reform ideas of Enlightenment thinkers. But she was also a charming and emotional woman who impulsively played favorites and thought of policy in terms of personality; her recommendations to the king were sometimes disastrous. Through the queen, on the other hand, was channelled the influence of the church hierarchy and the aristocracy—especially the more selfish, narrow-minded, and bigoted elements of the old elites.

Also impinging upon the king were pressures from within the administration. The chief career bureaucrats were eager to keep aristocratic factions and court favorites out of positions of power and to run the government themselves as direct agents of a royal despot. Some of them were sincerely moved by a concern for efficiency and continuity of policy, while others were merely ambitious self-seekers; but among them a statesmanlike king might have found the kind of agents who could have helped him shore up and reform the decadent regime. Just before mid-century, one of these bureaucrats made a valiant effort. The new controller-general, Machault, persuaded Louis XV to confront the fiscal crisis head-on. A royal decree instituted a new five per cent tax on income from land, called the *vingtième,* and imposed it on all property-owners, including even the largely tax-exempt privileged orders. Unlike most earlier tax proposals, this one was designed to be a permanent reform rather than a temporary wartime expedient. Three years of violent controversy ensued, with the *parlements,* the nobility, and the clergy challenging the measure as an infringement of vested rights. In this instance the church hierarchy leaped forward with such energy to lead the fight that the *parlements* could remain in the background and confine themselves to moral support. In 1751 the enemies of reform prevailed, thanks to the help of the queen's faction at court. Church property was exempted from the *vingtième,* and noble property also relieved of much of its impact. The government once more fell back on a variety of fiscal expedients, barely adequate in time of peace and hopelessly inadequate in time of war.

Monarchist historians of France have commonly dwelt on those bits of evidence that show the later Bourbons' awareness of the need for sweeping change. Their suggested conclusion is that the kings, despite their deplorable lack of backbone, were more to be pitied than censured. The real troublemakers, according to this version of history, were the selfish bureaucrats of the *parlements,* whose narrow recalcitrance undermined the monarchy while it opened the way to abstract theorists and political fanatics. This much can be said for the monarchist viewpoint: it serves to offset the legendary thesis of a simple two-way struggle in the eighteenth century, with king and nobility on one side and the rest of the nation on the other. The power struggle of the time was, rather, a three-cornered one, and the protagonists were the conservative vested interests, the advocates of reform, and the crown. By 1750 the tensions among them were severe, yet they did not make a violent revolution "inevitable." True, the crown and the reformers failed to join forces to avert revolution, and it would not have been a simple matter for them to do so. Still, the possibility of doing so did exist, and a different kind of king—or a king surrounded by different pressures—could have seized the opportunity. The English monarchy reconciled itself with changing times and opened the way to a long era of peaceful evolution. The eighteenth-century kings of France, whatever may be said in their defense, failed to do what needed to be done.

# CHAPTER 2

# Society and Economy: Structure and Trends, 1750–1789

Whether we analyse the Revolutionary age in terms of social forces or of ideas, it appears more and more clearly as the child of the eighteenth century and only to be understood in terms of the society out of which it emerged.

**ALFRED COBBAN**

France in 1750 was the most populous of European states. Louis XV's subjects totalled approximately 22 million, which meant that one of every six Europeans west of the Russian frontier was a Frenchman. Ever since the Middle Ages, Frenchmen had outnumbered Englishmen, Germans, Spaniards, Italians, even Russians; and only the tsar's vast realm seemed capable in 1750 of catching and surpassing France.

For several centuries the French population, like that of Europe generally, had not grown very much; a harsh nature had provided its own correctives for the high birth rate. No Frenchman in 1750 could know that the nation (and Europe generally) stood at a major demographic turning point and that the century from 1750 to 1850 would bring an unprecedented population explosion. By 1789 the total had already reached 26 million; by 1850 it would rise to 36 million. Even in retrospect, the reasons for so dramatic a change are not entirely clear. Improved sanitation and medical science, a more varied diet, and a general rise in living standards certainly must have contributed to it. The single fact that infant mortality in 1750 was 250 per 1000 births and that it had fallen to 160 a century later suggests one explanation for the population increase. Paradoxically, this century of France's most rapid population growth was to bring the first serious challenges to the nation's numerical predominance in Europe and the first anticipatory signs of a slowdown in the birth rate. Other nations were meanwhile experiencing an even more rapid population growth, while the French after 1800 took the lead in voluntary birth control.

Of Louis's subjects, barely two per cent belonged to the socially and legally privileged nobility and clergy. The First Estate, which included members of the monastic orders as well as priests and bishops, numbered about 130,000; the Second Estate, the hereditary nobility, is usually estimated at about 300,000 (of whom 80,000 belonged to the "old" nobility). All the rest were commoners: either members of that ill-defined category called the bourgeoisie, or ordinary peasants, artisans, workers—*le menu peuple,* as they were usually called. Nine out of ten lived by agriculture, either on isolated farms or in small village clusters. Few of them ever saw a city; at most, they might look forward to a rare visit to the nearest *bourg,* a commercial town of five or ten thousand people. Paris, with a population of a half-million, was the only metropolis; no other city except Lyon exceeded a hundred thousand.

In the hierarchical society of the eighteenth century, the court aristocracy stood at the apex of the pyramid, just below the royal family itself. Since the unsuccessful revolt of the great lords against royal absolutism in 1648–53—the so-called Fronde rebellion—the nobility had been forced to acquiesce in a position of prestige without much power. Generous royal pensions lessened the sting, and so did the pleasures of life at Versailles, where the court nobles filled their time with the pursuit of pleasure or with intrigue. The support of this leisure class put a considerable burden on the public treasury, although compared to other expenditures (such as interest on the public debt) it was a minor item. A more serious consequence was the atmosphere of factionalism that hung like a fetid miasma about the court, choking and stifling those who sought to give France a vigorous and efficient administration. Only the notables of the aristocracy lived at court; the vastly greater number of lesser nobles remained on their provincial estates, often in isolation from both the course of events and the main stream of ideas. Some of them enjoyed the comfortable life of the country gentleman in a society that retained much of its feudal tone (though almost nothing of feudalism's formal structure); others barely managed to maintain themselves in a style not much above that of a prosperous bourgeois. Not all of the old aristocrats were drones; many served as officers in the king's crack regiments, and some held high bureaucratic posts (e.g., in the provincial *parlements*). Nor was it unusual for nobles to engage in certain acceptable forms of industrial enterprise, or to invest in such ventures.

The nobility in 1750 was not a closed caste, nor had it ever been one. Over the centuries, there had been a slow but steady upward flow into its ranks, through royal action or through the purchase of government offices that carried noble status. For a long time the newcomers who bought such offices (the *noblesse de robe*) had been treated disdainfully by the old aristocrats. By 1750, however, most of them had gained acceptance if not full equality of status with the oldest families. Some could now boast of several generations of aristocratic rank; they no longer smelled of the counting house. Besides, the new nobility had quickly forgotten its bourgeois origins and had adopted the mores and standards of the old aristocracy. By 1750, it was the *noblesse de robe* that furnished some of the ablest spokesmen for aristocratic privilege.

It may seem curious that the aristocratic elite in a society still strongly tinged by feudal attitudes felt any need for spokesmen or defenders. In part, that was because the aristocracy wanted to protect the *status quo,* some aspects of which (its partial or complete tax exemption, for example) were under sporadic attack. But it was also because a segment of the eighteenth-century nobility was increasingly inclined to challenge the *status quo.* The goal of these malcontents was a return to a semimythical medieval system—to an unwritten constitution that had allegedly been torn up by the absolutist kings and their bourgeois ministers. The aristocrats talked of decentralization, of the restoration of provincial rights, of an end to royal and bureaucratic despotism, of a "return to legality." Under the same banner they sought to resuscitate old feudal dues that had long since lapsed, and claimed a monopoly of appointments to certain high ranks in the army, church, and government. The aristocrats' motives combined social snobbery with economic pressure; in an era of rising prices and competitive extravagance, every possible source of income had to be tapped if they were to "live nobly," as tradition required them to do. One effect of this pressure to return to a medieval system was to nurture the resentment of those commoners who would pay the price for such an aristocratic reaction.

Alongside the aristocracy as a privileged order stood the clergy, whose label "First Estate" seemed to suggest even greater pre-eminence. Although there was a clear line distinguishing the clergy from the other estates, its members by no means constituted a class, in any sense of the word, or even a homogeneous stratum of society. It was, rather, a professional category enjoying certain social privileges; its upper ranks came almost entirely from the nobility, its middle and lower ranks from the bourgeoisie and the peasantry. Although a strong corporative spirit—and in some cases a common intensity of faith—held these diverse elements together, the gulf between hierarchy and parish priests was growing steadily wider and more obvious during the eighteenth century. Many village curés resented the contrast in income between the upper and lower ranks—a contrast roughly of 140 to 1. The village priests were, however, better off than the average peasant or wage earner, and they enjoyed greater social prestige. Dissatisfaction was sharper in the middle ranks of the church hierarchy—the cathedral chapters, for example, and the seminary teachers. Many of these posts were held by bookish young men of bourgeois origin, who chose the clerical career for reasons similar to those that inspire their modern successors to become university teachers. There had been a time when the able and ambitious ones might hope to rise to so distinguished a post as a bishopric; but the increasing difficulties of advancement in the eighteenth century were producing a sense of exasperated frustration among them.

High standards of morality and fervency could hardly be expected of a hierarchy that had come to be (in Alfred Cobban's phrase) a system of unemployment relief for sons of the aristocracy. It is easy to cite such cases as that of Talleyrand, who lived at court and visited his bishopric only once—his sole purpose then being to gain election to the Estates-General; or the Cardinal de Rohan, key figure in the squalid Diamond Necklace scandal; or the Prince of Bourbon-Condé, abbot of four monasteries, whose nearest approach to a spiritual act was the construction of a marble tomb for his pet monkey, McCarthy. The surprising thing is that the clergy contained so many pious and sincere men and so many who managed to combine faith with enlightened tolerance. A century later, Alexis de Tocqueville went so far as to write: "I am not sure whether, in spite of the crying faults of some of its members, there was ever a more remarkable clergy than that of France in 1789." Even the members of the Jesuit order, singled out by Voltaire for his bitterest sarcasm and invective, sometimes displayed a breadth of interest and an open-mindedness that contrasted sharply with Voltaire's inverted bigotry. To regard the clergy as a solid reactionary bloc fanatically committed to the defense of dogma and special privilege would be vastly unfair. If the Great Revolution ultimately united the bulk of the First Estate under the standard of reaction, the fault was at least partly that of the church's critics.

❖❖❖❖❖❖❖❖❖❖❖❖❖❖

The line that separated the nobility and clergy from the ninety-eight per cent of Frenchmen who made up the Third Estate was not, strictly speaking, a line between privilege and non-privilege. Historians of the period keep reminding us that privilege, in the sense of vested legal rights or special dispensations granted to certain groups, was varied and widely shared in the hierarchical society of the old regime. Not only the nobility and the clergy, but many well-to-do commoners, many cities, whole provinces, were exempt from direct taxation; while on the other hand even the nobility in certain provinces had to pay the direct land tax called the *taille*. The idea of equality of treatment for all citizens was still in the future. The fact remains that some Frenchmen were clearly more privileged than others, and that the nobility and clergy as a whole bore a far smaller share of the tax burden than did the commoners. To speak of them, then, as the privileged orders may not be technically correct, yet it does convey the deeper reality that marked the system.

Among the unprivileged, the great bulk of Frenchmen lived and worked on the land. With rare exceptions, these peasants were free men who had long since shaken off all but a few annoying remnants of feudal servitude. It is not easy to reconstruct the rural life of that time; travellers' accounts are sketchy and full of contradictions, and statistics are remarkably inadequate. Some of the evidence suggests an almost incredible degree of degradation and misery: mud-floored huts, ragged clothing, undernourishment, frequent famine. Other testimony supports the view that, however primitive the existence of the French peasantry, conditions had improved over the previous century and were probably better than anywhere else on the continent.

Most peasants were tenants, sharecroppers, or day laborers on estates owned by the privileged orders or the bourgeoisie; but a great many—perhaps half of all the peasants—had achieved virtual ownership of at least a bit of land. A few of these, the so-called *laboureurs,* were on the way to becoming a kind of rural middle class; they were expanding their holdings, acquiring herds of stock, even hiring field-hands and lending money. The great mass of *manouvriers,* on the other hand, lived at a precarious subsistence level, supplementing their meager crops by working part-time on the large estates or taking employment in the rural textile industry, which allowed them to spin or weave at home. Their eagerness to acquire land amounted to a passion; but they were even more dedicated to preserving such remainders of the medieval rural structure as the right to graze animals and collect firewood on the common land of the village. The bulk of the peasantry was clearly precapitalist and intensely traditionalist in outlook—except that it wished to free itself from the tag-ends of feudalism.

It was in the cities and towns, not in the countryside, that the ferment of social change was at work. The bourgeoisie, an amorphous and varied category that included industrial and commercial enterprisers, financiers, professional men, bureaucrats, shopkeepers, and some independent artisans, had been making steady economic gains during the eighteenth century. Some of this new wealth was plowed back into business expansion, but more of it was used to purchase town houses, country estates, government bonds, government or church offices, or army commissions. This was, on the whole, a professional rather than a business bourgeoisie; the capitalist urge to innovate and expand was not its dominant trait. Its goal, for the most part, was to gain social status, to broaden out its share of special privilege within a society of inequality, to "live nobly" after the pattern of the aristocracy. To view the social conflict of the old regime as one that pitted a rising capitalist class against a medieval feudal class is tempting, in an age so strongly marked by Marxist ideas as ours, but it is also more misleading than it is accurate. Classes were much less clearly defined, and their value systems much less clearly in conflict, than the Marxian model would require.

If France had possessed a rigid and impermeable caste system, no such idea as sharing aristocratic privilege and adopting the aristocratic value system would ever have occurred to the bourgeoisie. But over the centuries there had been opportunities to rise: difficult and devious perhaps, but always available to the opportunist. Some bought office that carried noble status; some married their daughters to an impecunious aristocrat (who might speak contemptuously of the need to "manure his land," but who nevertheless gave noble status to his half-bourgeois sons); some were content to move a few steps up the ladder by the purchase of a minor army commission or a middle-rank church post. Enough opportunities had been available in the past to keep the bourgeoisie generally satisfied with the system and to make them want to share its advantages. To what degree did the situation change in the mid-eighteenth century? On this crucial point, recent years have brought an active historical debate. Many historians have argued that a drastic change did occur—that an "aristocratic reaction" saw the old nobility embark on a successful campaign to monopolize all high offices in the state, thus blocking the upward channels of mobility against the ambitious bourgeoisie. By the 1780's, they point out, Jacques Necker was the only remaining top-level bureaucrat who was of common birth. There had been twenty non-noble bishops in 1740; the last one disappeared in 1783. By a royal decree of 1781, officers' commissions in certain elite army regiments were reserved to men who could show four generations of noble lineage. The result, as these historians see it, was the gradual alienation of much of the bourgeoisie. Forced to abandon its aristocratic aspirations, it began to adopt the views of the reforming *philosophes,* either in a mood of bitter frustration or in the hope that criticism might make the aristocracy retreat. By the 1780's—so goes the argument—Enlightenment ideas were in general circulation in bourgeois salons and publications. Like Molière's doctor, the French bourgeois was becoming a revolutionist in spite of himself.

Although this thesis is neat and attractive, it has clearly been pushed too far. More than a century ago, Alexis de Tocqueville made the puzzling comment that even though the pre-1789 nobility was becoming more of a caste, entry into the nobility had never been easier. Many recent studies suggest that there was in fact no conscious campaign to block the rise of ambitious members of the bourgeoisie and, indeed, that ennoblement through wealth may have become even more common after 1750 than before. The old nobility's campaign for monopoly seems to have been confined to a few of the very highest posts in the bureaucracy, the church, and the army, and it was apparently aimed more against recently-ennobled aspirants of great wealth rather than against the bourgeoisie generally. Recruitment of bourgeois candidates into the lower and middle echelons of state service does not seem to have slowed at all. If this is so, the attraction of Enlightenment ideas for a certain number of bourgeois Frenchmen would have to be found in some other motive than selfish, frustrated ambition. It should probably be traced to a spreading awareness of something wrong in the state of France—an awareness, shared by a minority of the privileged orders as well, that many aspects of the old regime's government and society desperately needed to be reformed.

One other segment of eighteenth-century society remains to be mentioned. At the very bottom of the social pyramid, marked off from the petty bourgeoisie by no clear line of division, was the small but growing category of urban wage earners. Only Paris and Lyon contained sizable groups of this sort. Most of them were skilled artisans or handicraftsmen who worked in small shops, in intimate association with a bourgeois employer. Frequently they crossed the line that separated them from bourgeois status simply by setting up shop as independent enterprisers, with one or two assistants. Below them, ranging down into a kind of urban underworld that lived by its wits, was an almost submerged category of unskilled laborers who worked irregularly at menial or rough tasks. Many of them could not have survived without regular recourse to charity; in periods of economic stress, half of them—indeed, half of the skilled workers as well—might be unemployed. Early in 1790, according to official records, one Parisian in five was on some kind of relief roll, public or private. Even in prosperous times, the line between human and subhuman conditions in the urban slums would have been hard to draw.

❖❖❖❖❖❖❖❖❖❖❖❖❖❖

France's favorite historian, Jules Michelet, believed (as did most of his contemporaries a century ago) that the Great Revolution was at bottom the product of generalized misery—of conditions that had grown steadily worse throughout the eighteenth century until they finally reached the limit of tolerance. Many historians since Michelet's time have rejected his thesis and have argued that the mass of Frenchmen were not only better off than the subjects of any other continental monarch, but were also making some significant gains as the century moved on. They have found it easy to prove that the bourgeoisie, spearhead of the revolution, was a long way from being miserable in the generation before 1789; and they have contended that the peasant masses as well enjoyed greater prosperity and freedom than any other peasantry in Europe. Indeed, Alexis de Tocqueville could write in 1856 that the revolution was the outgrowth not of increasing misery but of the very opposite condition—the steady improvement in living conditions and the growth of France's national wealth during the eighteenth century.

The story of the prerevolutionary era, as recent economic historians have been reconstructing it, is too complex to coincide with either the Michelet or the Tocqueville position. Paradoxically, these recent researches suggest that both versions have some validity and that the revolutionary situation came at a moment when hope and despair were strangely compounded. Most of the long-term statistical trends support the Tocqueville thesis; they show that the half-century before 1789 was an era of prosperity and economic growth. Price studies indicate a long upward price swing from 1733 to 1817. From the second to the fourth quarter of the century, French industrial production doubled in value and French foreign trade tripled. Furthermore, this was not a case of artificial economic growth produced by fiduciary inflation. The French monetary unit, stabilized in value in 1726 after the disastrous experiment of John Law, was to remain steady from that date until 1914 (save for a brief interlude during the revolutionary era). France's business expansion of the eighteenth century was a healthy one, based on such solid factors as a rapid increase in both the supply of precious metals and in population.

In an era of long-term price rise and business boom, profits tended to increase and new opportunities opened out before those who knew how to take advantage of them. The chief gains went, quite naturally, to that enterprising minority of the bourgeoisie engaged in industry, commerce, or finance. Business expansion would have been even more rapid if so much capital had not been siphoned off into government bonds, elegant town houses, and rural estates. Large-scale factories remained exceptional though not unknown in the years before the revolution.

Rising prices and a growing population did not, however, work to the benefit of all Frenchmen. While the bourgeoisie gained, the wage earners of the cities clearly lost ground, for prices far outstripped money wages and buying power dropped markedly. That the eighteenth century brought increasing misery to this submerged segment of the nation seems undeniable. A plausible conclusion might be that this misery constituted one of the principal driving forces of the revolution, and that it stimulated the emergence of an embryonic proletarian class consciousness directed against the bourgeoisie. If the shock troops of the revolution after 1789 had been composed primarily of these depressed wage earners, the hypothesis would be hard to refute. But the evidence strongly controverts it: the revolutionary crowds were made up, rather, of the next higher social category—the skilled artisans, the shopkeepers, the petty bourgeoisie of Paris. To the extent that the wage earners joined the action, they were inclined to follow the lead of bourgeois agitators and to direct their joint hostility against the "aristos" who were believed to be responsible for food shortages and high prices. There is little evidence of emerging class tension between wage earners and bourgeoisie, either before or during the revolution.

Rising prices and a growing population meant a gradual increase of fifty to sixty per cent in the price of foodstuffs—an increase from which the landowners were likely to benefit. Who owned the land in prerevolutionary France? No sure answer can be given, though widely varying estimates have been made. If one ignores local variations, the rough average was probably something like this: the nobility a quarter of the total area, the church about ten per cent, the bourgeoisie thirty per cent, and the peasants thirty-five per cent. The most obvious gainers from rising food prices were the nobility, the bourgeoisie, and the clergy, for much of their crop went onto the market. Not only did they receive more for what they sold, but the cost of production tended to drop as the rapid growth in rural population made more and cheaper labor available. The nobles and the bourgeoisie profited also by the rising pressure of the population on the land, as a result of which land rentals roughly doubled in value during the eighteenth century. The clergy shared the foregoing advantages with respect to church-owned land and enjoyed a special advantage of its own: rising food prices gave it a steadily larger income from the tithe *(dîme)* on non-church lands, amounting to about one-thirteenth of the gross harvest.

The peasants, although they owned more of the soil than any other social group and rented or sharecropped much of the remainder, rarely benefited from the economic expansion of the prerevolutionary era. On the contrary, most of them probably lost ground. Only a few had anything left to sell after making provision for family consumption, the next year's seed, church and feudal dues, and taxes. In difficult years, a great many had to buy some food to get through the winter, so that even rural villages were the scene of frequent food riots. The pressure of population growth made matters even worse, for neither the amount of land in cultivation nor productivity per acre increased very much. A tiny minority of the peasantry managed to pull itself up by its bootstraps and to prosper in the era of rising prices; but the economic trends of the century worked against most of the peasants, whether they were small-owners, tenants, or share-croppers.

The over-all impact of a half-century of economic growth, then, was to bring about a gradual but significant redistribution of wealth. The rich on the whole grew richer and the poor poorer, while in the middle ranges there was continuous opportunity for a vigorous and imaginative minority of peasants, artisans, and bourgeoisie to rise in the economic scale. The general effects of this evolutionary process were mixed; but on balance, dissatisfaction and despair probably out-weighed confidence and hope. Within the Third Estate, a majority became in-

creasingly hostile toward the semifeudal social order and the ineffective bureaucratic monarchy that perpetuated such a system.

Any analysis confined to long-term economic trends is certain to be unrealistic unless it also considers the short-term fluctuations in the general curve. Concealed beneath the long-range rise in prices and in national wealth after 1730 was
a zigzag pattern of boom and slump. About every ten years, on the average, came
a cyclical crisis, originating almost always from a poor harvest and spreading
rapidly to all parts of the economy. The first stage was normally a food shortage
that drove grain prices up, severely affecting the mass of urban and rural consumers; then the domestic market for such items as textiles dried up temporarily,
leading many manufacturers to curtail or suspend production and to throw their
workers out of jobs. Food riots followed in many cities and villages, with popular
passions directed against grain speculators, the aristocrats, or the government.
A rash of bankruptcies increased the uneasiness of the bourgeoisie.

The last of these cyclical crises in the old regime began in 1787 and was
inaugurated, as usual, by a bad harvest. What made this crisis worse than most
was the fact that it struck an economy already weakened and undermined by a
decade of recession or stagnation. A whole series of difficulties had converged to
produce this recession; some of them were accidental, like the interruption of
cotton imports during the American Revolution. Since about 1778 French economic life had been suffering from this "persistent languor." The poor harvests
of 1787 and 1788 therefore produced effects even more rapid and severe than was
normally the case. Grain prices doubled in a year; textile production was reduced
by half; a wave of bankruptcies occurred; unemployment among the wage
earners in the major cities probably reached a figure of fifty per cent. Few
Frenchmen understood the nature of the crisis, but this did not restrain their
bitterness. They found it easy to load the blame on the government, which, in
1786, had lowered protective tariffs against British goods in the so-called Eden
Treaty and had removed restrictions on the export of grain from France. Their
complaints had at least some validity; French manufacturers did face increased
English competition under the Eden Treaty, and grain exports did rise fourfold
in 1787, sixfold in 1788. The government's decision to turn toward freer trade
was undoubtedly a farsighted one for France's long-run prosperity and strength,
but it came at an unfortunate moment when readjustments in the economy were
especially painful. There can be little doubt that the economic stress of the 1780's
contributed to the outbreak of the Great Revolution. But to describe it as the
major contribution would be risky and probably inaccurate. Without the pervasive influence of new ideas since mid-century, without the political crisis that
culminated in 1788, the downward business cycle of 1787 might have passed like
its predecessors, leaving behind it the usual jumble of economic wreckage and
the usual memory of temporarily intensified misery.

# CHAPTER 3

# Temper of the Age, 1750–1789

Between the social or economic fact and the historic event it is necessary for the mind of man to intervene if the first is to lead to the second.

GEORGES LEFEBVRE

Social change, most historians agree, is the product of multiple causes. But when scholars begin to assign relative weights to these multiple factors, controversy begins. Historians with left-wing tendencies have usually been inclined to stress the role of conditions as fundamental; historians with right-wing leanings, the role of ideas and of individual men. The contrast is sharpest when the origins of a great political-social revolution are being sought. To an especially rigid variety of Marxist, the dominant ideas of eighteenth-century France were little more than an intellectual secretion of the bourgeoisie, a by-product of the rise of that class to power and self-consciousness. To a conservative like Hippolyte Taine, those ideas were "...the central motor of events; the morbid germ which, introduced into the blood of a...profoundly sick society, produces the resultant fever, delirium, and revolutionary convulsions."[1] Rightists from Edmund Burke to Pierre Gaxotte have held that the doctrines of the Enlightenment gradually corroded the old order by breaking down respect for authority and for established institutions and by proposing as a substitute a "natural" order based on reason. Some of these rightists have even found in Freemasonry a subversive underground network that served to spread and popularize the new ideas.

It is clear enough that the eighteenth century brought a basic change of

---

[1] A. Aulard, *Taine, historien de la révolution française* (Paris: Plon, 1907), p. 57.

outlook among educated Frenchmen and that one product of this mental transformation was that familiar process known as the alienation of the intellectuals. The importance of an intellectual elite in the maintenance of social stability or the furtherance of social change has often been questioned or even ridiculed, yet there seems to be a remarkable correlation between the alienation of such a group and the outbreak of revolution. Perhaps the most important development of the period 1750–1789 was the progressive transformation of France's educated elite from loyal supporters into hostile critics of the old regime. Chateaubriand was to remark in retrospect that "the revolution had been accomplished before it occurred." He meant, of course, that many men's minds had been conditioned in advance for the upheaval that began in 1789.

If it was the generation of 1770–1789 that turned potentially subversive, that same generation absorbed most of its ideas from the thinkers and publicists of mid-century. Montesquieu's *Spirit of the Laws* was published in 1748; Rousseau's prize essay that brought him sudden fame appeared in 1750, and his major theoretical works (*The New Héloise, Emile,* and *The Social Contract*) came in a rush from 1760 to 1762; the first volume of Diderot's great *Encyclopedia* came off the press in 1751, and the last in 1772; almost all of Voltaire's writing was done before 1770. Thereafter, there were few new works of basic importance. From the 1760's, the Enlightenment spirit was gradually spreading outward and seeping downward: outward into certain segments of the privileged orders, downward through the various strata of the bourgeoisie. This was also the period that brought the progressive disillusionment of those intellectuals who had been the earliest converts to the Enlightenment view of man and society, and who had devoted a generation to propagandizing that view. In 1750 they had assumed that an enlightened political leadership, once it understood the new doctrines, would willingly make the necessary alterations in society and politics. By 1789 they were determined to see the changes accomplished in spite of the existing political elite, if there should be no other way.

Enlightenment doctrines had their roots in the seventeenth century, perhaps even in the Renaissance. By 1700 the works of John Locke had crossed the Channel and were offering Frenchmen a startling new concept of the nature of man—as a creature not of immutable inborn traits but of vast, almost unlimited potentialities. The writings of Pierre Bayle, exiled along with his fellow Huguenots to the Netherlands, arrived in France soon after the turn of the century and produced an even greater impact. In the personal libraries of educated Frenchmen of the eighteenth century, Bayle's *Historical and Critical Dictionary* appeared more frequently than any other book; it became a kind of arsenal of ideas for the *philosophes* and buttressed their growing skepticism of authority. Voltaire's and Montesquieu's first political writings were published soon after 1720, and after mid-century the trickle grew into a torrent. The themes of the *philosophes* clustered about the somewhat ambiguous concept of humanism. Man—individual man—became the central figure in the universe. He was viewed as basically (though not purely) rational in nature; he was essentially good and almost infinitely perfectible, if provided with the proper education and institutions; he had the right to expect freedom from arbitrary rules and restrictions and to develop his capacities to their ultimate limit.

Such a set of beliefs was not subversive in the sense that it dictated the overthrow of the monarchy, the repudiation of the church, or the destruction of the social order. A society without a king, a god, or an elite of birth was almost inconceivable to most intellectuals before 1750. Mably and Morelly might question the validity of private property, or even preach a kind of utopian communism; Holbach might denounce all religion as mere superstition; an anonymous agitator might look forward to the day when "the last king would be strangled with the entrails of the last priest"; but these were exceptions, men of the lunatic fringe. The Enlightenment temper as a whole retained its loyalty to the dynasty, its deep-rooted faith in God (if not always the God of the Catholic church, or even the Christian deity), and its conviction that social distinctions were natural and necessary things. Yet in a deeper sense, Enlightenment concepts were far more subversive than its proponents knew; they could scarcely be reconciled with the dominant ideas on which the old regime rested. The institutions of eighteenth-century France were still based on authority and tradition, not on any rational or utilitarian test; the old ideal of an organic society could not be harmonized with the new concept of an atomistic one made up of autonomous individuals. The post-1770 generation of intellectuals became increasingly aware of the irreconcilable differences between the Enlightenment temper and the basic assumptions of the old regime.

Although most of the major Enlightenment thinkers shared the same general outlook—a rational, individualistic humanism—the writings of Rousseau introduced a number of new concepts that were less easily absorbed into the Enlightenment world-view. One such novelty was the idea of equality—the most ambiguous and potentially the most explosive concept produced in the eighteenth century. The meaning of equality in practice, the possible contradictions between equality and individual liberty—these were problems that did not begin to emerge clearly until after 1789, and they were to weigh heavily upon the subsequent course of French history. A second accretion was Rousseau's emphasis on emotion and sensibility rather than on reason, suggesting a fundamentally different psychological base for the new order. Still a third novelty was Rousseau's concern for community as well as for the individual—a concern that would eventually force French intellectuals to consider the unavoidable but insoluble problem of reconciling the rights of the group with those of the citizen in the new free society. Many of Rousseau's ideas had little resonance in the prerevolutionary years, but after 1789 they strongly influenced at least some of the Revolutionary leaders.

The precise impact of ideas on men's minds is difficult to measure even in the most favorable conditions. For eighteenth-century France, which had not yet come to know the blessings of public opinion polls, the task becomes almost impossible. Illiteracy (measured by a man's ability to sign his own name) ranged from twenty to ninety-five per cent of male Frenchmen in various parts of the country, and it is a safe guess that some of those who could read did not very often do so. Yet there is enough scattered evidence to suggest that most thoughtful Frenchmen of the pre-1789 generation, whether literate or not, had been exposed to the new doctrines, and that a great many of them had absorbed some of the effects of those doctrines almost as unconsciously as modern man absorbs radioactive fallout. In the age of Voltaire and Rousseau, as in the later ages of Darwin and Freud, it was not always necessary to read the masters in order to pick up the catchwords, slogans, and simple ideas that were explicit or implicit in their systems. Gradually, indirectly, those ideas permeated the mood or temper of the era.

The peasants were undoubtedly least affected, for there still existed no channel for the diffusion of ideas outside the cities and *bourgs*. The impact on the aristocracy, on the other hand, was direct and widely felt, though variable in its effects. Some nobles, like the young Marquis de Lafayette, were promptly subverted by the new doctrines. Others reacted strongly against them and found an antidote in religious faith or in the idea of a return to the old feudal monarchy. For most of the court nobles, however, Enlightenment ideas seem to have been picked up as amusing topics for modish conversation in the salons. Montesquieu's writings were taken more seriously, for they could easily be adapted to support the aristocratic campaign against bureaucratic despotism. There is no way to be sure whether the aristocracy's flirtation with the new ideas of the age seriously affected its capacity to resist revolutionary change. What is much more certain is that only a minority of nobles were very deeply infected. For the others, the revolutionary crisis was to peel off the Enlightenment veneer, revealing in most of the aristocracy a deep commitment to the defense of an old order that its own errors had done much to undermine.

The largest group of dedicated adherents to the Enlightenment temper was undoubtedly drawn from the bourgeoisie (including the middle and lower levels of the bureaucracy) and the middle ranks of the church hierarchy. The Abbé Sieyès, whose career after 1789 was to make him the most prominent of these frustrated church intellectuals, was by no means an isolated case. Even that eminent revolutionary terrorist, policeman, and cynic, Joseph Fouché, had begun his career as a teacher in a church school. As for the bourgeoisie proper, its more reflective members were quite naturally attracted to the new currents of ideas that had been sweeping into western Europe during the past century. True, a great many bourgeois clung to the idea of a hierarchical society of unequals, and sought to rise in it through the traditional methods. But for those whose ambitions were frustrated—and that was true of many lesser bureaucrats—the idea of advancement through merit rather than through wealth and influence was bound to be appealing.

One important agency in the diffusion of Enlightenment ideas was Freemasonry, which came to France from England in 1725. By 1789 there were about 600 lodges in France; scattered through their predominantly bourgeois membership were a number of aristocrats and even some churchmen. The rituals of Freemasonry were permeated with the humanist doctrines of the Enlightenment. But to call Freemasonry an organized international conspiracy working for revolution is a grotesque distortion. The members were loyal monarchists and had to swear to a belief in a supreme deity in order to be initiated. Freemasonry's violently republican and anticlerical tinge was to be acquired much later, in the mid-nineteenth century. Indeed, when the whirlwind of revolution struck after 1789, the lodges assumed no role of leadership. On the contrary, they were quickly swept out of existence and disappeared for a generation or more.

❖❖❖❖❖❖❖❖❖❖❖❖❖❖

Modern France and the modern Western world as a whole are in large measure products of the Enlightenment temper. Yet that temper has never won universal acceptance in a pluralistic and fragmented nation like France. From the very outset, a hard core of conservative critics rejected most of its premises and found in this set of ideas the source of France's gravest problems. The twentieth century has brought new recruits to this little anti-Enlightenment army and has added new variations to the attack. Alongside the traditional conservative position, with its emphasis on society's organic nature, on man's inherently evil tendencies, and on rationalism's evasion of reality, there has emerged a series of hostile views sprung in part from the Enlightenment tradition itself.

One such view, Marxian in inspiration, characterizes Enlightenment ideas as the reflection of bourgeois class interest. The ideas themselves are seen as natural products of changes in Europe's economic structure; the *philosophes* are viewed as class-bound propagandists. That the bourgeoisie seized upon the new outlook and used it, consciously or unconsciously, for its own ends, is taken to be the normal and inevitable behavior of a rising class. Exponents of this thesis single out as partial exceptions Rousseau, the theorist of egalitarianism, and a few lesser *philosophes* who were materialists and atheists. Their argument combines some validity and much plausibility—enough to permit its widespread acceptance, usually in a more muted form, by non-Marxians. But this premise that ideas must always be rigidly class-bound, that the Enlightenment temper was associated with bourgeois interests alone, has too often been accepted without careful examination. The Enlightenment temper was produced by other factors besides the rise of capitalism; it was shared by other groups besides the bourgeoisie; and it was broad and rich enough to fertilize much of European political and social thought for the next two centuries.

A second line of attack on the men of the Enlightenment has charged them with naive credulity, with the unconscious substitution of a new set of superstitions for the old discarded ones. The *philosophes,* according to this thesis, prided themselves on putting enlightened reason in the place of blind faith, but in actuality they only built themselves a new heavenly city based on little more than the will to believe. Their new faith rested on the untested premise that men would make rational choices if given free access to the truth; that man was basically good and was rendered evil only by bad institutions; that progress was a kind of law of human development, an inevitable process if the artificial roadblocks could be cleared away. The *philosophes* scoffed at people who believed in miracles, yet they built their whole system on faith in the miracle of human perfectibility.

Closely related to the foregoing criticism is the charge that the *philosophes* preached tolerance but neglected to practice it. Voltaire is the most vulnerable target of this school of critics, who insist that his scurrilous vilification of his opponents (especially the Jesuits) made the replies of the latter seem eminently fair-minded by contrast. Voltaire and other leading *philosophes* engaged in a concerted attack on one Catholic journalist that wrecked his reputation and his career; at one point these defenders of free speech called on the governmental censors to suppress his newspaper. On controversial issues of the time, the *Encyclopedia* was often more bigoted than the leading Jesuit journal.

There is a good deal of validity in this case against the intellectual leaders of the Enlightenment. Like crusading reformers of other eras, they often displayed a curious kind of inverse fanaticism, distorted the motives of their opponents, and showed signs of persecution mania. As a matter of fact, Enlightenment thinkers and publicists were rarely molested for their ideas after mid-century; and if the official censorship continued to operate right down to the revolution, it functioned sporadically and ineffectively. Frenchmen of the generation after 1750 were surprisingly free in both thought and action; it was the annoying remnants of regimentation that lent color to the continuing fears and accusations of the Enlightenment intellectuals.

Whether this reform generation really substituted a new blind faith and dogma for the old is a more questionable charge. Few of its thinkers really believed in the unmixed rationality or the unlimited perfectibility of men; they were aware that irrational motives were intertwined with rational ones in human beings. Nor is it certain that they were mere ideologists, abstract system-builders, drafters of rationalistic blueprints largely unrelated to the facts of life. Defenders of the *philosophes* make a strong case for the empirical, utilitarian spirit of these thinkers and contend that most of them were, in fact, breaking the chains of abstract rationalism.

One other variety of modern anti-Enlightenment thought has directed its criticism at individual theorists of the eighteenth century. The two most common targets have been Montesquieu on the one hand and Rousseau on the other.

Montesquieu's critics have portrayed him as a kind of wolf in sheep's clothing—a concealed enemy of Enlightenment principles masquerading as a spokesman for these principles. Montesquieu belonged to that judicial aristocracy whose interests had become intertwined with those of the old nobility; his real purpose, so the argument goes, was to protect those interests by substituting an aristocratic for a bureaucratic monarchy. His masterpiece *The Spirit of the Laws* is supposed to have been designed as a kind of handbook for those who would restore France to the pre-Richelieu system; his praise of English government is alleged to have sprung not from its liberal character but from the aristocracy's continuing power role across the Channel.

This much can be said in support of Montesquieu's critics: he did adopt some of the traditionalists' arguments against royal despotism, the aristocracy and the *parlements* did rely heavily on his book, and many *philosophes* of the next generation did find his ideas uncongenial. But the assumption that Montesquieu's motives were hypocritical is purely conjectural. It is just as plausible to regard him as a man of moderate, pluralist temper who sensed the danger of concentrating power in any one man or group of men, and who aimed to lessen this risk by a check-and-balance system of distributing power. No other thinker of the Enlightenment so completely eschewed pure reason in favor of the empirical spirit; his system was built not on logic but on the study of real examples chosen from history. If it is true that the aristocracy seized upon Montesquieu's arguments, so did other more forward-looking reformers. His ideas, more than those of any other Enlightenment thinker, seem to have inspired France's new political elite during the most constructive phase of the Great Revolution—the moderate phase from 1789–92.

No other figure of the Enlightenment has drawn such frequent and such vindictive attacks as Rousseau. One school of critics has denounced him for exalting the non-rational impulses of man and for allegedly preaching a kind of flamboyant self-indulgence; they find in him "...clashing phantasms in the guise of reason and a deadly virus oozing from a sick soul in lieu of moral principle."[2] A more recent manifestation of anti-Rousseau thought is that which condemns him as an ancestor of modern totalitarianism.

Rousseau not only shifted his emphasis from reason to sensibility and emotion, but he also added the doctrine of equality to the liberty and tolerance preached by his predecessors. When he chose to become the advocate of equality and democracy, Rousseau went out looking for trouble, for these were concepts that were inherently ambiguous. According to his critics, Rousseau worsened that natural ambiguity by introducing the concept of the general will, one of the most easily corrupted phrases ever coined by a political thinker. If Rousseau never adequately defined the general will, he did specify that it was not synonymous with the will of all or with the will of a majority. He seems to have conceived it in a moralist's sense, as the spirit that would inspire all men if they were rightly and fully informed, and if no distorting factors existed to mislead them.

Some of Rousseau's disciples could conclude, therefore, that pending the arrival of those utopian conditions, the general will might be embodied temporarily in a minority of men—even a small handful of them. That minority alone would know what all men would desire if they were not misled by evil institutions and by the psychological distortions produced by those institutions. The duty of such a vanguard would be to seize and hold power, if necessary in spite of the majority; to make men happy and virtuous by setting up new institutions and carrying out a thorough process of re-education; to "force men to be free," in Rousseau's own phrase. Rousseau's modern critics find in the climactic phase of the Great Revolution the earliest examples of this fanatical, crusading application of Rousseauan doctrine: first with Robespierre and his faction, then with the futile scheming of Babeuf. They find, too, a continuing current of Rousseauan influence in a series of exalted thinkers and activists of the nineteenth century, and a modern embodiment of the theory in Lenin's and Stalin's Russia.

Rousseau's defenders are appalled at this version of Rousseauan thought and brand it as sheer distortion. They insist that Rousseau's writings show a hatred of despotism of all kinds and an unwillingness to sanction the use of brutality to drive men even toward a desirable goal. By his phrase, "force men to be free," he meant only to create the kind of social environment in which no one would be tyrannized and in which man's native goodness would blossom naturally. These defenders see the general will as a kind of moralist's ideal, a symbol of the goal to be attained; they insist that for Rousseau a regime founded on tyranny and corruption could never, even in transitory fashion, embody the general will. Some of these Rousseauans prefer to regard the general will as no more than a

---

[2] E. H. Wright, *The Meaning of Rousseau* (London: Oxford Univ. Press, 1929), p. 3.

bit of jargon to represent the generous social tendencies within each man, as opposed to his selfish tendencies.

The defenders of Rousseau probably have the stronger case. But they are not always ready to admit that Rousseau's ambiguity did leave his ideas open to distorted interpretations. His disciples and readers, left to wrestle with the meaning of the general will as well as with the more basic ambiguities of equality and democracy, almost inevitably divided into two factions and ended as polar opposites: on the one hand, as liberal, empirical democrats like Gambetta, Jaurès, Léon Blum; on the other, as totalitarian democrats such as Robespierre, Blanqui, and Maurice Thorez. Both of these streams might have risen out of Enlightenment thought and eighteenth-century conditions had Rousseau never lived. The fact is that he did live and write and shape men's thinking, that he did provide an intellectual pedigree for divergent democratic dogmas throughout the course of modern French (and Western) history. Certainly Rousseau was one of the most effective pamphleteers of all time; and "unfortunately," as one of his critics has ironically remarked, "he had a first-class mind."

From Edmund Burke's time to our own day, men have debated the validity of Enlightenment thought and the practical impact of those concepts on French society and politics. Recent criticism of the eighteenth-century temper has sometimes tended to obscure its admirable side. Perhaps the *philosophes* and their disciples were sometimes simple and naive; perhaps they put too much trust in man's natural goodness and rationality; perhaps they indulged in some self-deception and unwittingly furnished a theoretical foundation for a worse kind of tyranny than the sort they were trying to destroy. Yet the Enlightenment spirit also helped to break men free from arbitrary controls, gave them a chance at fuller self-development, and encouraged the introduction of humanitarian reforms. If the Enlightenment image of man's true nature was too simple to fit the reality, the older image against which it was set was surely even less adequate. If totalitarian democracy sprang from Enlightenment thought, it was neither the inevitable product nor the only product of that thought. Alongside it emerged the enduring stream of liberal, empirical democracy as well: the kind of undoctrinaire doctrine that inspires men to work in skeptical and cautious fashion, via trial and frequent error, toward a more humane society; the kind that doubts the imminence of any utopia, yet never abandons utopia as a theoretical long-term goal. For good or ill, the next two centuries of French history were to be pervaded by the ideas of Enlightenment.

# CHAPTER 4

# The Decadent Monarchy, 1750–1789

> ... Experience teaches us that, generally speaking, the most perilous moment for a bad government is when it seeks to mend its ways.
>
> ALEXIS DE TOCQUEVILLE

In the late spring of 1774 a disgraceful scene occurred in the streets of Paris. As the funeral procession of Louis XV passed on its way to the royal tomb in Saint-Denis, the route was lined not with weeping mourners but with tipsy celebrants shouting "Tally-ho!" Fifty years earlier, when the boy-king had begun his reign, he had been Louis the Well-Beloved. He had long since used up his credit and his popularity, though the fault was not entirely his own. Louis's mistakes and his character flaws had contributed much to the disintegration of his prestige; but he was burdened from the outset with almost insoluble problems inherited from his brilliant predecessor, and he faced growing and convergent pressures during his reign—pressures that even a greater man might have found overwhelming.

Part of the king's unpopularity at his death stemmed, ironically enough, from the wisest and most courageous act of his reign. In 1771 he had finally lost patience with the obstructionist *parlements* and had moved to break their power once and for all. His principal adviser at the moment was a minister named Maupeou, a career bureaucrat dedicated to the ideal of an efficient bureaucratic monarchy and known to be capable of ruthless action. Maupeou purposely goaded the *parlement* of Paris into resisting a decree that reduced its powers. When the *parlement* struck back by refusing to transact business, Maupeou exiled the magistrates to the provinces, stripped them of their powers, and transferred some of those powers to new courts with more restricted authority. Then he plunged without delay into the pressing task of fiscal reform. The long struggle, it appeared, was over, and the worst obstacle to efficient government was cleared away.

Maupeou's action (which had the king's firm support) was not a popular one, however urgent it may appear in retrospect. A few prominent intellectuals like Voltaire and Turgot approved it, but the great bulk of opinion was outraged at what seemed to be a case of despotic repression. The *parlements* profited by the false public image they had built up in recent decades, which had won them the sympathy of some new Enlightenment reformers as well as of the old aristocracy. Which of these two quite incompatible factions they really represented was not yet clear in 1771; the *parlements,* by using ambiguous and emotion-loaded phrases, somehow managed to combine the opposites as they talked of constitutional rights and essential liberties. The king's initial decision, therefore, was much to his credit, and so was his stubbornness in supporting Maupeou after 1771 against the latter's almost hysterical critics.

French monarchist historians believe that the death of Louis XV at this critical juncture was the old regime's greatest disaster; that "only then did the Revolution become inevitable."[1] Their case rests on the assumption that the old king, had he lived another decade, would have pushed ahead with further reforms and would have managed to win the country's support for his program. They insist that the monarchy was still sound in 1774; that the discontent revealed at Louis's funeral was superficial and narrowly restricted, and that it indicated no real revolutionary spirit. Their thesis is plausible even if unprovable. Ten years of firmness might have given the new institutions time to take root; Frenchmen might have tired of the *parlements'* outcries, especially if the king had countered with his own public relations campaign. Whether Louis possessed the requisite vigor and imagination is, of course, highly doubtful. His prior record as king hardly suggests it, and the monarchy had never shown much talent for explaining its program to the people. True, the popular welcome given to his successor, Louis XVI, in 1774, supports the view that the monarchial institution was still solidly rooted in the public affection. At least part of that enthusiasm, however, may have stemmed from a hope or belief that the new king would reverse rather than continue the policy of his grandfather and would resuscitate the suppressed *parlements.*

That, in any case, is what Louis XVI promptly did. His good intentions were epitomized in the remark he is supposed to have made on his accession: "What I should like most is to be loved." Some of his initial actions were remarkably enlightened: he reduced royal expenditures, talked of the need to

---

[1] J. Bainville, *Histoire de France* (Paris: Fayard, 1924), p. 291.

bring bread prices down, and made some of the best ministerial appointments in many years. But his most popular decision was undoubtedly the dismissal of Maupeou. The *parlements* were restored to their old status, much to their own satisfaction and that of the public; someone enthusiastically chalked on the statue of Henry IV, most popular of all French kings, the Latin phrase "He is resurrected."

Two years sufficed to prove the lack of wisdom of Louis's act. The king's most significant new appointment had been that of Turgot as controller-general. Turgot was both an eminent economic theorist (the most notable spokesman of the physiocratic school) and a career civil servant with a reputation as a practical reformer. During his term as royal intendant at Limoges, he had made notable progress in cleaning up abuses and invigorating the economy of a backward province. His nomination caused a sensation, and Turgot lost no time in embarking on an equally sensational new deal. His goal was to strengthen royal absolutism by making it efficient and enlightened. In the process, it was necessary for him to restore public credit and to clear away a thicket of outmoded economic restrictions. His program, if accomplished, would undoubtedly have revolutionized the old regime; for it involved abolition of tax exemption for the privileged orders, abolition of the restrictive guild system, drastic cuts in sinecures and pensions, and the creation of a national elective body empowered to deliberate on taxes (though not to legislate).

Turgot's failure has usually been attributed to his rashness, his lack of tact, his eagerness to get things done in a hurry. Such a view has at least some validity, for, as Turgot remarked, "in my family we die of the gout at fifty." But gradualism and tact might have been no more effective in furthering a program that directly challenged almost every powerful vested interest in France. Turgot's only chance of success lay in the unlimited and undeviating support of the king, buttressed perhaps by a direct appeal to the urban middle class and the peasants for mass support. Turgot doubted the feasibility of a massive public relations campaign; he believed that time was of the essence, and that it would take a generation or two of enlightenment to bring the masses around. He relied, unfortunately, on the king alone. For two years Louis held up remarkably well against the powerful convergent pressures that bore down upon him from the vested interests, from the circle of reactionary aristocrats around Queen Marie Antoinette, even from certain reform ministers who were offended by Turgot's tactlessness and his domination of policy. In the end Louis succumbed, with the disillusioned remark that "only Turgot and I love the people." The new deal was swept away in 1776, leaving scarcely a trace of effect.

Turgot's successor in the controller-general's office was a man of quite different qualities. Jacques Necker, a Swiss Protestant banker who had settled in Paris and had made a fortune in speculation, was generally believed to be a financial wizard. Besides, he had friends among the *philosophes* and the physiocrats and was reputed to share some of their ideas of enlightened reform. Historians have not been kind to Necker, and probably with good reason. Though he was incorruptible and a man of moral courage, his self-image was a highly inflated one. He thought of himself as France's greatest statesman since Colbert, and unfortunately, many Frenchmen came to share his view. Although he embarked on a program of well-conceived and necessary administrative reforms that made the treasury far more efficient, he hesitated to mount a major challenge to the powerful antireform interests, and continued to "live on borrowed time and capital."

A policy of expediency has its limits. By 1781 the enthusiasm for Necker was being offset by rising dissatisfaction. One principal source of trouble was the financial drain resulting from France's participation in the war of the American colonies against England. Foreign Minister Vergennes, with Necker's support, plunged into the war in 1778, primarily in the hope of getting revenge against England and recovering the colonial possessions lost in 1763. As a foreign policy gamble the venture proved reasonably successful, but the impact on the French treasury was disastrous. By 1781 Necker felt it necessary to take drastic action at last. The financial statement that he proceeded to publish was both unprecedented and shocking. For the first time, Frenchmen were given a glimpse into the mysteries of public finance; they could get a rough idea of how much tax money was being wasted in futile expenditures. Any good that might have been accomplished by this act was undone, however, by Necker himself; he juggled the figures to show an excess of income over expenditure and thus concealed the desperate need for tax reform. Necker's dramatic action brought his prompt downfall; there was an outcry from all the vested interests, and the king shortly found an occasion to ask for Necker's resignation. Necker left office a public hero, in the opinion of "enlightened" Frenchmen. His exaggerated reputation was to have unfortunate results several years later when crisis leadership was required; for Necker was mistakenly assumed to have the necessary qualities.

After a brief interlude of drift, Louis found an able successor for Necker in the career bureaucrat Charles Calonne. The new controller-general was more intelligent than Necker and more diplomatic than Turgot; what he lacked was a stiff backbone. As a former intendant in the provinces, Calonne understood as well as Turgot what was wrong with the royal finances. Past extravagances, and especially past wars, had saddled the treasury with such a heavy public debt that the interest on it consumed half of the government's total revenue. There were only two ways out of the impasse: the first, a repudiation of the public debt, openly or through the concealed method of inflation; the second, a broadening of the tax base to place a fair share of the burden on the privileged orders. For several years Calonne avoided either solution. Instead, he set out to restore public confidence by borrowing heavily and by embarking on a major public works program. His methods produced a brilliant surface prosperity but did nothing to correct past evils. By 1786 Calonne had come to the end of his rope; he was forced to approach the king with a proposal to broaden the tax base and a scheme by which the aristocracy and clergy might be persuaded to accept it. Instead of the usual futile attempt to bully the *parlement,* Calonne suggested that Louis convoke an Assembly of Notables, a handpicked body of aristocrats, churchmen, and bureaucrats, summoned to hear their sovereign's needs and to grant him financial aid.

Louis accepted the idea with enthusiasm, thanks to Calonne's confident assurance that the privileged orders would welcome the plan and would hail the king as a public savior. When the Assembly met in February, 1787, Calonne appeared before it with an intelligent (though not entirely frank) exposé of the government's financial situation and with a well-conceived program of reform. But for once his remarkable powers of persuasion failed. The Notables stubbornly refused to vote any funds to the king unless the latter would first agree to revolutionize the governmental system. They wanted the conversion of bureaucratic despotism into aristocratic monarchy, with both central and local decision-making controlled by a national assembly and a series of provincial assemblies drawn from the privileged classes. Calonne, with the king's support, stood surprisingly firm against these demands; but pressure from the queen and her advisers (who belonged to the most bigoted element of the aristocratic caste) finally led Louis to repudiate and dismiss Calonne. The Notables adjourned shortly with nothing accomplished, except that the session had stimulated widespread discussion of the fiscal abuses that had brought France to the verge of crisis. A flood of pamphlets inundated the country, many of them only distantly related to the issues discussed by the Notables, but all of them revealing a deep undercurrent of dissatisfaction.

Calonne's successor, Archbishop Loménie de Brienne, owed his appointment to the faction around the queen. Whether the archbishop believed in God was a matter of sardonic discussion among his contemporaries. Whether he was competent in financial matters could arouse no debate at all. His talents were those of the consummate courtier; his standing as a financial technician was strictly amateur. Even an amateur, however, could not evade the fact that every easy solution had been used and that only drastic and painful ones remained. The baffled minister promptly adopted the central idea in Calonne's program—a new land tax, to be levied against all classes without exception. But he decided to resort to the old-fashioned method of putting it into effect: an edict by the king, followed by due registration of the edict by the *parlement* of Paris. Now, at last, Louis was to suffer the consequences of his earlier error, the re-establishment of the *parlements.* Not only did the *parlement* of Paris refuse to register the edict, but it continued to balk even when the king appeared before it in formal *lit de justice* session. For a year the deadlock went on, the *parlement* clothing its motives in the usual disguise of righteous phrase. New taxes, it declared, could not be levied without the consent of the nation through its duly chosen representatives; only the Estates-General, an institution dead since 1614, could give validity to the king's decree.

In calling for an Estates-General, the *parlement* was merely repeating a suggestion made by the Assembly of Notables when it adjourned in 1787. In retrospect, it is easy to see that this proposal opened the door to revolution in France, and that it was the French aristocracy, not the unprivileged Third Estate, that took the fatal initiative. The aristocrats assumed that they could control the Estates-General and use it as a device to transform the monarchy, after which they would vote the king enough money to save the government from bankruptcy. Their long campaign for a revolution in reverse, for a return to the quasi-feudal monarchy of pre-Richelieu days, seemed to be reaching its point of culmination.

The king, however, had one other alternative. It was still in his power to return to the Maupeou policy of 1771–74 and sweep the *parlements* out of existence. In 1788 he chose that course, though only in limited form. Instead of abolishing the *parlements,* he stripped them of much of their power, including their right to register royal edicts. The popular outcry that followed was spontaneous and overwhelming; it far exceeded the protest caused in 1771 by Maupeou's more drastic measures. The contrast indicated the change of mood in France in only seventeen years, though it may also have reflected the economic stress of the late 1780's. The public clamor confronted Louis with a risky decision: he must either carry his policy to its logical conclusion by dissolving the *parlements,* or else he must capitulate to the opposition. The tougher course he dared not try; the *parlements* had succeeded in making themselves too widely popular. Besides, he had no able and forceful adviser to bolster his determination; at court he was surrounded by critics of his new policy, and the queen's faction kept up a constant drumfire of misguided counsel. Reluctantly, Louis capitulated in July, 1788; he issued an edict convoking the Estates-General for the following spring, restored the rights of the *parlements,* and recalled Necker in a desperate attempt to stave off bankruptcy through the winter.

This time the edict was registered promptly and enthusiastically by the *parlement* of Paris. But the magistrates added a kind of postscript of their own: they shortly ruled that the Estates-General must be organized in the same manner as its predecessor of 1614. By that act, the magistrates cast off their disguise as defenders of Enlightenment doctrines. The 1614 assembly had been dominated by the privileged orders; the representatives of the three estates had sat as separate houses, and any action had required the approval of all three branches. The *parlement's* ruling outraged those bourgeois intellectuals who, since an Estates-General was first mentioned, had been urging and expecting that the new model would sit as a single house, in which the unprivileged Third Estate would possess the dominant influence. Overnight the *parlements* lost most of their popular following; it became clear that their cause was that of the aristocracy. The advocates of reform, who had hoped till now that the magistrates would speak for them, began to seek out other champions to challenge inefficiency and privilege.

The winter of 1788–89 brought the first signs of active political organization by the men of the Enlightenment. The story remains obscure, but a mysterious Committee of Thirty seems to have assumed a directing role in the election campaign. It sent agents to the provinces, circulated pamphlets (like the Abbé Sieyès' *What is the Third Estate?*) as guides to the voters, and furnished interested groups with model grievance petitions (*cahiers de doléances*). The Committee's composition showed that the movement for reform was more than merely a class affair. Its most notable members were not drawn from the bourgeoisie but were maverick aristocrats like Lafayette and Condorcet, or unorthodox churchmen like Talleyrand and Sieyès. Whether or not the Committee received subsidies from the Duc d'Orléans, the ambitious and scheming cousin of the king, remains uncertain; but Orléans undoubtedly was involved in the election campaign through his own separate network of agents.

It was still not too late for the king to regain the initiative. If his chief adviser at this juncture had been a Turgot rather than a Necker, he might have won the enthusiastic support of the reformers by issuing his own reform program and embarking on a personal electoral campaign to get a majority committed to that program. Such a strategy would have required a kind of alliance between king and Third Estate, buttressed by the pro-reform minority within the privileged orders; it would have required the king to accept the Third Estate's demand for a one-house Estates-General in which the commoners would have as many seats as the aristocracy and clergy combined. Not very much reform would have been needed to win the support of the educated elite; no more, certainly, than the restored Bourbons were to have to accept in 1814. Unfortunately, neither Necker nor the king perceived the possibilities of such a plan. Instead, Necker wasted those critical weeks in elaborate, too-clever schemes designed to get a tax reform through the Estates-General while leaving all other issues in the king's control. Eventually the king and Necker did authorize double representation for the Third Estate, but they evaded any clear decision on the vexing problem of one versus three houses, and they neither announced nor prepared a program of reforms. Opportunity knocked at the door of Versailles palace; it produced little more than empty, reverberating echoes within.

Early in 1789, after much delving into ancient documents to discover proper election procedures, the voters met in the chief town of each district to choose their representatives. Both the First and Second Estates used a system of direct election, with an equality of suffrage that enabled parish priests and lesser nobles to outvote their hierarchical and caste superiors. Two-thirds of the clergy's elected representatives were parish priests of common social origin; only a handful were bishops, among them being Talleyrand. Most of the Second Estate's representatives were drawn from the country nobility or the *noblesse de robe* rather than from the great court aristocrats; a handful of liberal nobles like Lafayette also managed to win election. The Third Estate, though granted almost universal suffrage for male citizens aged twenty-five or over, chose its delegates by an indirect process involving two, three, or even four stages. Partly because of this screening process, the Third Estate's representatives were drawn from its educated elite rather than from the mass of commoners. Most of the delegates came from the middle or upper bourgeoisie; the bulk of them were lawyers or career bureaucrats. There were almost no peasants, and no wage earners at all. The Third Estate was also represented by a few renegade priests like Sieyès and a few renegade nobles like the Comte de Mirabeau (neither of whom could hope for election by his own privileged order). If the resulting body of delegates necessarily lacked experience for its imminent task, it certainly did not lack talent. Some historians believe that the level of ability in the Estates-General exceeded that of any elected body in French history.

Each group of electors, after choosing its representatives, performed a second traditional task: it drafted a *cahier* or grievance petition designed to call to the king's attention the abuses that needed correction. None of the *cahiers* of 1789 challenged such basic institutions as the monarchy, the church, or private property. Those of the Third Estate were, however, filled with phrases from the *philosophes* about natural rights and social equality. All three estates agreed in condemning such obvious abuses as the *lettre de cachet,* which permitted indefinite imprisonment without formal charge; and they spoke often of such practical reforms as the unification of weights and measures and the abolition of internal tariffs. They called, too, for more local autonomy and for some kind of constitution that would limit royal power and ensure to the nation a voice in taxation. On these latter issues, however, the privileged and unprivileged classes used similar words but meant quite different things. The aristocratic idea of a constitution and of increased local autonomy implied a transfer of power from king and bureaucrats to privileged classes, not to the nation. Nor was there the least sign that the nobility was prepared to grant the commoners' demands for social equality.

Perhaps the most remarkable aspect of the *cahiers* was their moderate tone. The winter preceding the election had been a terrible one: food had been scarce, prices high, and the weather unseasonably severe. Unemployment in the major cities probably reached a figure of fifty per cent, and the meager charitable facilities of the time were overtaxed. Yet little of this misery was reflected in either the *cahiers* or in the choice of representatives. The dominant mood was not one that presaged revolution; it was rather a mood of buoyant enthusiasm, of confidence that at last something was about to be done and that a new and better future was in prospect for France.

# CHAPTER 5

# Upheaval, 1789–1792

Whoever wishes to avert a revolution must desire it enough to carry it out himself.

RIVAROL

The historian Crane Brinton once observed that in the greatest of American university libraries, there are as many books on the French Revolution as on all the rest of French history combined. As tourists flock to Niagara rather than to Mud Creek Falls, so historians and readers of history have naturally been attracted to an episode that contains in concentrated form all the action, passion, color and drama that can be found in man's past. Excitement alone, however, does not explain the appeal of this monumental upheaval. As one of the few great political-social revolutions in modern history, it constitutes a rare laboratory for analysis and comparison. And by its very scope and depth, its impact was to shape the course of French development from that day to this.

Yet it may be pertinent to remark at the very outset that both the uniqueness of the Great Revolution and its enduring effects are matters of some controversy. Certain historians in recent years have argued that the French upheaval was only the culminating phase in a long process of social, economic and ideological change that affected both shores of the Atlantic. Out of that process, they contend, came both the American and the French revolutions, as well as the somewhat milder pressures for change throughout much of western Europe. Events in France from 1789 to 1814 are thus merged into a "world revolution of the west," or an "Atlantic revolution," introducing an age of liberalism and democracy. The argument clearly has some merit; the forces at work in the eighteenth century were not confined to France alone. Yet it would be a mistake to reduce the French upheaval to the lowest common denominator of revolutionary pressures and events in the western world. Something special, different in degree and perhaps in kind, did happen in France; social and ideological conflict reached a point of greater intensity than in any other part of the Atlantic world, and thus foreshadowed revolutionary changes of the future.

Even more controversial is the thesis that one can find in the Great Revolution a simple key to the understanding of all French history ever since. It is tempting, but misleading, to accept the dictum of the historian who declared that "as a consequence of the Great Divide created by the French Revolution, a chasm yawned between the two Frances, so deep and so wide that all attempts to bridge it failed. . . ." It is easy to believe that France's modern problems stem from an almost congenital conflict between defenders and enemies of the revolutionary heritage. There is this much truth in the thesis: France's Great Revolution, unlike those of England and the United States, did produce an enduring heritage of division rather than a powerfully-unifying national myth. But that this particular division has been the only one, or even the most essential one, from 1789 until our day is a doubtful proposition. Possibly it *was* the basic issue dividing Frenchmen for a generation or two after 1814—until the mid-nineteenth century, perhaps even until 1875. But in more recent times the defenders of the revolutionary tradition have far outnumbered its enemies, and other divisive issues of far greater importance have been superimposed upon the original one or have cut diagonally across it. France during the past century has become much too complex to fit into the easy set of categories provided by the doctrine of the "two Frances."

And yet, one can still find in the revolutionary experience an important key for understanding the evolution of modern France. The real source of instability and division stemming from the Great Revolution has not been the conflict between its enemies (a shrinking faction) and its defenders (a vast majority) but rather the conflict within the revolutionary tradition itself. Georges Clemenceau might contend a century later that "the Revolution is *un bloc*," to be accepted or rejected as a whole; the fact is that it was never a monolithic and homogeneous unity, and no objective viewer could ever see it as such. Clemenceau failed (or refused) to see that the revolutionary myth might have different meanings to different Frenchmen. Some of them looked back to the revolution of Mirabeau—to a constitutional monarchy rooted in the older tradition. Some were inspired by Danton's revolution—moderate, bourgeois, empirical. Others meant by the revolution the Robespierrist system and spirit—egalitarian, uncompromising, filled with crusading zeal. Still others found their model in Napoleon's revolution—in an efficient "authoritarian democracy," with the end justifying the means. To some extent, these different branches within the revolutionary tradition were to remain in agreement on ideology or values; they simply differed concerning techniques, on how best to achieve a commonly held goal. But there was a deeper division as well—one that concerned the goal itself, the nature of the future good society. The conflict might be summed up as one that brought into sharp contrast the libertarian and the egalitarian ideals: the one giving free play to individual talents, with little restriction by government or society; the other ensuring the rights of the weak as against the strong, through the agency of powerful, positive government action. Both attitudes could quite convincingly claim to find their origin in the revolutionary tradition, but they could not easily be reconciled in a nation whose intellectual formation did not incline its members to empirical compromise.

Temperamental differences were to reinforce, and at the same time complicate, this ideological division within the revolutionary heritage. The libertarians often (though not always) were men of the type that Lenin once labelled "softs": men of moderate, empirical, tolerant temper, inclined to favor gradualist methods and to doubt the imminence of the millennium, content to grope by trial and error toward a utopia without ever believing that it could be wholly achieved. The egalitarians often (though again not always) were the kind of men Lenin called "rockhards": fanatical, convinced of the oneness of truth, dedicated to the achievement of a perfect society without compromise or delay, willing to sacrifice the happiness of one or more generations for the sake of all those to come.

This complex set of inner contradictions involving techniques, ideologies, and temperaments suggests why there was never to be a single, unified revolutionary heritage in France during the nineteenth and twentieth centuries. All of them stemmed in one way or another from the experience of the Great Revolution, and, somewhat less distinctly, from the Enlightenment doctrines that preceded it. In that sense, the significance of the revolution as an enduring divisive force is real enough. But the study of the revolutionary episode would be a far less complex task if one could cling to the stubborn legend that classifies all Frenchmen as for or against the revolution *en bloc*.

❖❖❖❖❖❖❖❖❖❖❖❖❖

Early in May 1789, the delegates to the Estates-General straggled into Versailles for the opening session. The atmosphere was cordial and full of hope. The American ambassador, who heard the king's welcoming address, found himself choking with emotion at the warm applause and cheers that repeatedly interrupted Louis's remarks. The king spoke well, but, unfortunately, said nothing; once again he had missed his historical cue. What he provided was a vacuum, and the more vigorous and imaginative representatives of the Third Estate promptly rushed in to fill it. Their strategy was remarkably shrewd; instead of turning to violent demagoguery or noisy complaints, they quietly announced their determination to do nothing at all until the king would agree to fuse the three estates into a unicameral assembly. They knew that unless they could win that initial victory, the privileged orders would block any reform program except that of the aristocratic faction.

The war of nerves lasted for six weeks. The delegates of the Third Estate met daily but refused to elect officers or conduct formal business. Their strategy began to show results in June when a few parish priests deserted the meeting hall of the First Estate and joined the Third. To hasten the process, the Third Estate on June 17 voted to call itself the National Assembly and urged the privileged orders to join it. The king meanwhile had been subjected to intense pressure from aristocratic leaders and from the queen's faction, who wanted him to break the general strike. At last Louis gave in to their demands and scheduled a new joint session of the three orders for June 23.[1] This time, in the course of a long-winded speech, he went so far as to express his support of a whole series of reforms; but in the end he asserted that the vested rights of the privileged orders must remain intact and that the three estates must meet as separate houses. When the king had retired and the First and Second Estates had gone off to their meeting halls, the delegates of the Third Estate refused to budge. This was the occasion that won for Mirabeau his first fame as the revolution's spokesman; he rose and thundered at a royal official in his stentorian voice: "We will not leave except by force of the bayonet!" The stalemate lasted for four more days; then it was the king, not the Third Estate or the aristocracy, that gave in. On June 27 Louis reluctantly ordered the three estates to meet as one house; and the privileged orders even more reluctantly obeyed. No adequate explanation of Louis's capitulation has ever come to light. The most plausible explanation is that the motive was fear: rumors had reached the court that a Parisian mob was being organized to march on Versailles, with a view to forcing action. Whatever the reason, popular enthusiasm was mingled with relief. The English traveller Arthur Young, who had been waiting about the Paris region in anticipation of trouble, went off to the provinces, noting in his diary: "The whole business is now over, and the revolution complete."

The new unicameral body at Versailles could now properly call itself the National Assembly, and it set out at once to provide the monarchy with a constitutional base. The road seemed clear at last; but the next four months were to

---

[1] In order to prepare the hall for the royal session, the king's officials on June 20 locked out the delegates of the Third Estate who had been meeting there. The angry delegates, suspecting that the Estates-General was about to be dissolved and sent home, met in a nearby covered tennis court and swore a solemn oath to remain in session—against the king's will, if necessary—until they had given France a constitution. The episode had little effect on the course of events, but it caught the public imagination and became an important part of the revolutionary myth.

bring a whole series of unexpected obstacles. Most of them were put there by the privileged orders, which had awakened at last to the fact that their harassment of the king and their demands for an Estates-General had opened the way to a quite unexpected kind of revolution. Indeed, the shortsightedness of the reactionary faction during the years before 1789 was to be matched only by its glaring lack of leadership in the tumult. Its spokesmen now urged the king to stop what they themselves had started; they wanted the National Assembly broken up, by force or threats, and sent home without delay. Whether they won Louis over to their plan is not quite certain; at any rate, he behaved in such a way as to make him appear a convert. Fresh mercenary troops began to arrive in Versailles early in July, and when the Assembly protested, only lame excuses were offered by the court. Then on July 11 Necker, still a theoretical symbol of reform within the government, was brusquely dismissed and replaced by a reactionary.

Nothing else in Necker's career produced such consequences as his dismissal. It crystallized the suspicion and resentment of the Assembly's leaders and brought the active elements of the Third Estate in Paris into action for the first time. The origins of the disorders that promptly developed, and that led to the mob attack on the Bastille on July 14, are still obscure. Whether there were paid agitators at work behind its apparent spontaneity, it is impossible to say; but there is at least some reason to suspect that the Duc d'Orléans was involved, and possibly a group of financiers who feared that the king might be preparing to repudiate the public debt. The crowd—made up primarily of artisans and shopkeepers rather than wage earners and unemployed—initially went into the streets in search of arms to defend Paris against the rumored plots of the "aristos." This was its motive when it converged on the Bastille on July 14; the attack on the fortress was accidental rather than premeditated.

The fall of this symbol of tyranny (which had long since been virtually abandoned as a place to incarcerate political prisoners) had repercussions far out of proportion to the incident itself. Its long-term effect was to produce a revolutionary myth of spontaneous popular action against despotism and injustice—a myth so appealing that the French republic a century later made July 14 its national holiday. Its short-term effect was to unnerve the king and cause him to reverse his policy. Louis's reactionary advisers tried to persuade him to strike hard against the rioters of Paris; they proposed that he leave for the provinces to rally loyal citizens and the army, and that he then lead a march on the capital to dispense awful justice. After some hesitation, the king decided on appeasement rather than force. He restored Necker to office, made a personal visit to Paris to show that he held no grudges, and assured the National Assembly that there was no truth in the rumors of an impending royal coup d'état. "From this moment," wrote the British ambassador, "we may consider France a free country, the King as a very limited monarch." Many of the leading court aristocrats, led by the king's younger brother the Comte d'Artois, packed up and left the country in disgust to wait until this foolishness should blow over. Unfortunately, the queen and some members of her faction did not join this first phase of the emigration. Had she, too, departed, there might still have been a faint chance for a workable alliance between king and National Assembly.

Louis's capitulation enabled the National Assembly to settle down to its long task of converting France into a constitutional monarchy. But the next three months were to be marked by a sporadic continuation of the violence that had erupted on July 14. The first and gravest problem was posed by the disintegration of public order in many rural districts—a disintegration that reached the point of near-anarchy by August 1789. Rural riots had begun to occur several weeks before the Bastille affair; a kind of mass hysteria brought them to a climax in the latter part of July. Confused rumors circulated that the "aristos" were planning some kind of reactionary coup or were hiring bands of unemployed vagrants to roam the countryside, raid granaries, and disrupt the public peace. The aroused peasants, assembled by tocsin to deal with the mythical invaders, found release for their fury by attacking local chateaux and burning records of feudal obligations.

The National Assembly, disturbed at this spontaneous insurrection, talked of appealing to the peasants for patience until their demands could be taken up in due form. Some members realized, however, that further delay might bring general chaos and decided on immediate action to calm the countryside. The upshot was the dramatic night session of August 4, when the Assembly voted by acclamation to sweep away the remnants of feudalism. Most of the aristocratic members went along with the decision in the hope of saving something from the wreckage; the next day the Assembly voted that the feudal dues should be commuted in the form of a cash payment. In reality, the peasants paid no such indemnity; the progress of the revolution was too rapid. But the reform of August 4 proved to be one of the most durable of all the revolutionary changes. The wave of rural anarchy subsided, never to recur on such a scale during the next decade. The peasantry was converted from a potentially revolutionary into a conservative force. A year or so later, many peasants were to gain further satisfaction when church lands and some noble estates were made available for purchase. The poorer peasants were pacified, meanwhile, by being assured continued use of their traditional rights in the common land of each village—the right to graze animals, gather firewood, and so on.

No sooner had the countryside been quieted than the Paris crowd went on the move again. By the end of summer, economic stress in the cities was severe: bread was scarce, prices high, and unemployment general. Besides, Paris now had a new set of tabloid newspapers and a collection of popular agitators whose warnings of dastardly plots at court kept suspicions aroused. Such men as Camille Desmoulins and Jean-Paul Marat were gaining notoriety as self-appointed guardians of the public welfare. Early in October rumors again spread that the court was plotting a coup against the National Assembly. The evidence to support the accusation was much less convincing this time than it had been just prior to Bastille Day; but the Paris crowd no longer needed much evidence.

The great riot of October 5, like its predecessor in July, seems to have been produced by a mixture of spontaneity and *sub rosa* planning, in undetermined proportions. A crowd of women demonstrating for cheaper bread was somehow diverted into marching on Versailles and was accompanied by a mixed group of agitators and curiosity-seekers. The unruly crowd spent the night in the palace courtyard and was in so ugly a mood by morning that the king capitulated to its demand. Court, government, and National Assembly, he announced, would all be transferred at once to Paris, presumably to remove them from the dangerous reactionary influences at work in Versailles. The Tuileries palace in Paris was hastily cleared of its occupants to make room for the royal family, and the Assembly shortly took up quarters across the street. Some members of the Assembly, angry or fearful at these events, resigned their seats and returned home. Perhaps they foresaw that the atmosphere surrounding the government would be quite different in Paris, where public opinion could no longer be ignored, and where the possibility of direct crowd pressure would be a constant threat.

Paradoxically, however, this October riot was to mark the end of violence for the next two years and the beginning of the longest period of quiet in the whole revolutionary decade. By 1790 a gradual improvement in economic conditions had relieved the worst stress among the masses. The most determined enemies of reform had emigrated or had gone back to the provinces. The formation of rival political factions in Paris, though it had begun, had still not reached the point where factional leaders could call out their followers to threaten or to attack their opponents. The Assembly was able to proceed in leisurely fashion with its task of drafting a constitution and with the even more pressing task of clearing up the financial mess which it had inherited. The king, though he had sacrificed some of his independence by moving to Paris, remained popular and respected. The time had passed when he might hope to reverse the revolution, but he was still in a position to guide its course through intelligent action.

This first phase of the revolution was to be its most constructive period, in the sense that many of its reforms were to endure.[2] The principal change was the creation of a political system that may or may not have been inspired by Montesquieu's writings, but that certainly harmonized with some of his ideas. It was a system replete with checks and balances, based on the concept that power ought to be distributed in order to avert its abuse. The constitution (pro-

---

[2] It is true that many of these reforms were interrupted during the years 1792–1814, but they reappeared thereafter in somewhat modified form.

mulgated in 1791) provided for a balance between king and legislature and between central and local authority. Attached to it as a preamble was a declaration of rights—not of the rights of French citizens, but of "man." It was a classic statement of the Enlightenment's natural-rights ideal, and it was permeated by the libertarian spirit. Historians have often been cynical about the allegedly class-bound bourgeois spirit that produced this declaration and made the possession of property one of the sacred rights of man. But if the tone of the document seems today to place excessive stress on liberty, on rugged individualism, that was probably natural enough at a time when men were reacting against an arbitrary, caste-bound system that still contained many outmoded restraints. If equality received less attention than liberty in this first declaration of rights, it was not ignored; social equality, the end of legal privilege, was asserted without equivocation.

The most controversial action of the National Assembly was the series of decisions concerning the church—decisions that stripped away its special privileges, confiscated its landed wealth, and converted the priesthood into a kind of branch of the governmental bureaucracy. The law establishing the new church organization was labelled the Civil Constitution of the Clergy. It provided that men of the cloth, bishops as well as priests, were henceforth to be paid like postmen by the state, according to a fixed salary scale. More startling still, all church officials were to be chosen by popular election in the parish or diocese. A subsidiary change was the Assembly's decision to sell church lands to private buyers. The gradual disposal of these lands, most of which went to well-to-do peasants or bourgeois speculators, speeded the expansion of the small-owning peasantry and committed it strongly to revolutionary principles.

The church settlement was closely interlinked with the Assembly's attempt to solve the problem of public finance. As the presumed value of church lands approximately equalled the public debt, the Assembly issued certificates (called *assignats*) based on the church lands as security. The *assignats* would presumably be retired as fast as the lands were sold. Instead, they promptly began to circulate as paper currency; and the Assembly (along with subsequent legislative bodies) could not resist the temptation to issue more and still more of them. They were eventually to lose more than ninety-nine per cent of their value; succeeding governments sank deeper into the financial swamp, until Napoleon at last dictated a solution. The inflation of the 1790's had one hidden virtue, however. It wiped out much of the public debt inherited from the old regime, for the government could repay its creditors with ever cheaper money.

Among the National Assembly's reforms, some were so ill-conceived as to be totally unworkable. The church settlement was undoubtedly the worst example; it brought down the Pope's anathema upon the revolutionary leaders and turned most of the clergy into stubborn opponents of the new system. After only a few years the arrangement had to be abandoned in favor of complete separation (1795) of church and state. Still, one can understand the Assembly's mistakes even if one does not condone them. The traditional role of the church in France was such that no conceivable reform could have worked smoothly; the Assembly's plan was merely the worst of several bad alternatives. As for the financial problem, it had become too grave for any government except a ruthlessly authoritarian one. A decade or two of peace and prosperity might conceivably have allowed a solution less drastic than Napoleon's; it was not the National Assembly's fault that France plunged into a generation of war instead.

*****************

On the whole, the reforms worked out during this initial phase of the revolution fitted together to form a coherent pattern, a system that ought to have functioned successfully. Why, then, did the new constitutional monarchy break down almost at once? Inaugurated in 1791, it was in ruins only a year later. Its collapse seems all the more regrettable when one considers that the next seven years, from 1792 to 1799, were to contribute little in the way of permanent reforms (though much in the way of revolutionary mythology). Most of the durable changes of the revolutionary generation were the work of the National Assembly (1789–91) or of Napoleon's early years in power (1799–1804). If the situation could somehow have been stabilized in 1791, Frenchmen might have been spared twenty years of domestic strife and foreign war.

The problem thus posed is one that arises in the study of almost any great social upheaval. It can be argued that the failure of the moderates results from a kind of law of revolution, from a dynamic process which, once begun, develops its own irresistible momentum and runs its natural course from moderation to radicalism to extremism to reaction. The theory is bolstered by the fact that moderates are not always good crisis leaders, since they lack the fanatical determination that would enable them to override opponents and doubters. Once in power, they are subject to the onslaught of the reactionaries, on the one hand, and of the "rock-hard" extremists, on the other. Caught in this fashion between ruthless elements on both right and left, moderate leaders may be doomed by their own moderation.

A less deterministic theory would trace the failure of the moderates in all great modern revolutions to individual human shortcomings—to a lack of adequate leadership at the critical moment or to an unlucky turn of chance that prevented the emergence of the right man at the right time. It has been argued, for example, that the fatal factor in the French Revolution was the death of Mirabeau in 1791, at the early age of forty-two. He has been described as the only moderate possessing the requisite ability and charisma to make the new system succeed and to mediate between king and popular assembly. So great was his prestige that the National Assembly entombed his body in the Pantheon; he was the first Frenchman to achieve that honor. The case for Mirabeau is seriously weakened, however, by the fact that the king refused to trust him as a potential chief minister, and by the further fact that Mirabeau's real ambition was to serve an autocratic rather than a constitutional king. Toward the end, Mirabeau privately urged Louis to repudiate the almost-completed constitution and to leave for the provinces to rally loyal support there.

There is an easier and more convincing explanation for the failure of the constitutional monarchy: it puts the blame primarily on the king himself. Although Louis was well-meaning and showed occasional flashes of insight, his narrow mind had a stubborn and devious quality about it, too. The king did little to consolidate the new system, even though it left him a role of real importance. His most flagrant attempt at open sabotage was his attempted flight with the royal family in June 1791. His purpose was to rally loyal supporters near or beyond the frontier and to march on Paris at their head. Such a scheme had been urged by the queen's faction as early as July 1789; it was much less likely to succeed by 1791. Apprehended and brought back under guard before he could reach the border, Louis was nevertheless forgiven for his escapade and was shortly installed as constitutional monarch. But the king's indiscretions were not to stop there. During the subsequent months he used his legal power to veto far too often and much too unwisely; and he topped it off by repeated secret appeals to his fellow monarchs to intervene in his behalf.

This was curious behavior for a king who before 1789 had shown an inclination to challenge the vested interests and to carry out essential reforms. The explanation may lie in the constant pressure of the queen and her advisers, which weakened Louis's resolution and changed his flabby mind. Or it may be that this pious king had serious pangs of conscience at some of the reforms built into the new system—notably the reforms affecting the church. Or again, perhaps the course of events brought out his own true character as an irritable, small-minded, stubborn man who built up a neurotic resentment at his loss of initiative after 1789. It is true that even if Louis XVI had been ideally suited to his new role, the system might have broken down nevertheless. The reformers of 1789–91, immersed in the general theories of the Enlightenment, had groped in rather empirical fashion for ways to convert those theories into a precise and workable mechanism of government. Differences of opinion over both ends and means had begun to emerge early; the National Assembly had begun to divide into factions, each of them linked with one or more of the emerging political clubs in Paris. Still, these differences were not yet overwhelming, and the unavoidable clashes between factions might still have been kept within the bounds of peaceful discussion if the king had made a sincere effort to play his assigned role.

The crisis that wrecked the system was brought on by the outbreak of war against Austria and Prussia in April 1792. Tensions had been building up for several months, partly through the machinations of French émigrés in the German states. No issue was involved that was serious enough to require war to resolve it; but both Louis and the dominant faction in the new French legislative body (now called the Legislative Assembly) wanted war, though for different reasons. The king favored war because he expected it to bring disaster; he believed that the French army, deprived of its aristocratic officers, would collapse before the invader and that the French people would call on Louis to save the country. The controlling faction in the legislature, the so-called Girondins or Brissotins, wanted war because its leaders expected victory. An aroused sense of patriotism, they believed, would solidify the nation behind the government. Besides, they had begun to suspect the king of treasonable foreign contacts, and they hoped that war might smoke him out. There was also an ideological side to this warmongering attitude. Some French politicians thought that the rest of Europe would eagerly welcome a libertarian crusade by French troops, who would serve as midwives in the birth of constitutional systems everywhere. This illusion contained just enough truth to make it attractive; it was fostered by political refugees (like the eccentric Dutchman Anacharsis Cloots), who flocked to Paris and assured Frenchmen that the Continent was panting for freedom. Only a few skeptics spoke out in opposition as the Assembly enthusiastically adopted its declaration of war. Not even those skeptics had any idea that the war would drag on for a quarter-century; but they did believe that it might play into the king's hands and destroy the constitutional experiment.

In this latter expectation, they were quite right. The French armies near the frontier disintegrated on the approach of the invaders. Ministers, generals, and king bickered angrily over responsibility for the disaster. In the end the king dismissed the leading ministers (who represented the dominant Brissotin faction) and substituted pliable nonentities. This rash act produced a series of disorders in Paris that culminated in what has been called "the second French revolution." On August 10, 1792, a crowd led by some of the new radical politicians and club orators of Paris moved against the royal palace and took it by storm, after a bloody fight with the Swiss guards assigned to protect it. The royal family escaped just before the crowd arrived and sought the temporary security of the Legislative Assembly's meeting hall across the street. The Assembly, unwilling to resist this mob action, voted the deposition of the king and the immediate convocation of a National Convention to decide France's future. The royal family was placed in custody pending a later decision about its fate; the Assembly handed over interim authority to a small executive committee drawn from its own membership and from the Parisian radicals. On this note of violence and improvisation, with foreign armies on French soil and with all the gains of the revolution gravely threatened, the experiment came to a jarring end.

# CHAPTER 6

# Climax and Relapse, 1792–1799

A "revolution" is an ambiguous entity. In any single "revolution" there may in fact be one, two, or several, each treading on the heels of the one before and kicking viciously at the one behind.

DAVID CAUTE

No phase of the revolutionary epoch was so complex or so controversial as the climactic period between the fall of Louis XVI (1792) and the fall of Robespierre (1794). For almost the first time in European history, a major nation tried the experiment of government without either a monarch or a hereditary governing class. That nation quickly became involved in war against most of Europe and, at the same time, in civil war. Class tensions and ideological conflict rapidly grew more severe. They were embodied in the emergence or the consolidation of a whole series of factions and organized political groups. Of these organizations, the most remarkable was the network of Jacobin clubs—some two thousand of them, linked together under a tight central leadership, and anticipating in many ways the totalitarian parties of the twentieth century. Under Jacobin leadership, France was to try a series of economic and social experiments almost unprecedented in Europe and was to resort to outright terror and the purge as instruments of government. Throughout these two climactic years, a constant factor in the background or the forefront of affairs was the Parisian crowd, acting either spontaneously or through manipulation to shape the course of events. So tumultuous a period is bound to produce a wide variety of sharply contradictory historical interpretations. Not only the significance of the events, but some of the events themselves have been the subjects of bitter controversy.

Within a month after the suspension of the king, the citizens of France were once again summoned to the polls, this time to elect a National Convention whose sole purpose was to frame a new governmental system for France. The Convention gathered in September, but so pressing were the issues facing France that constitution-making was postponed for a time. Even when a new constitution was hastily adopted in 1793, the Convention voted to put it on ice until the end of the national emergency. For three years the Convention governed the country on an *ad hoc* basis, unhampered by constitutional limitations of any kind; it simply made its own rules as it went along. Absolute power rested in its hands; there was no check or balance in this system of government by assembly.

The Convention, elected by universal and direct manhood suffrage (though nine out of ten voters had not taken the trouble to go to the polls), was a more radical body than either of its predecessors. It no longer contained any professed monarchists but only different varieties of republicans. The two most important organized factions were the moderate Brissotins and the radical "Mountain" (so called because its members sat in the upper tier of seats in the Convention). The bulk of the Convention's membership fluctuated between these two poles. The Brissotins, who had dominated politics during the brief constitutional period, were coming to be known by the newer label of "Girondins," from the fact that several of their leaders came from the Gironde region near Bordeaux. Whether the Girondins really existed as a coherent organization is open to some question; the men so labelled varied rather widely in their views, and some of them (including their original leader Brissot) actually belonged to the Jacobin club. Still, they thought and acted in common enough of the time to be regarded by contemporaries as a loosely articulated group or party. "The Mountain" was coming to be known as the Jacobin party, even though its membership did not coincide exactly with that of the Jacobin club of Paris. Its most notable leaders were, however, prominent members of the latter organization. The Jacobin club had first been formed in 1789 by certain representatives in the National Assembly as a forum for political discussion. Over the years its structure had become more rigid and its ideology more coherent. In addition, local branches had sprung up in hundreds of provincial cities and towns. Speaking broadly, the Girondin outlook was strongly libertarian, and its leadership was drawn from the prosperous middle bourgeoisie; the Jacobin world-view contained a stronger dash of egalitarianism, and its leaders came from a slightly lower stratum of the bourgeoisie. The difference between Girondin and Jacobin was more often one of temperament than one of class or doctrine.

The Convention lost no time in involving itself in an all-out war against most of Europe. The French armies had already checked the invading Prussian forces at Valmy, on the very day in September when the Convention had first met. By the end of the year French forces had pushed across the frontier into

Savoy, the Rhineland, and the Austrian Netherlands; and the Convention enthusiastically announced that it would go on crusading for freedom so long as there were peoples in Europe who thirsted for liberation. To make sure that the already conquered territories would remain free, the Convention decreed their annexation to France. These measures alone would have been enough to arouse Europe; but the Convention promptly added another—the execution of Louis XVI. The margin in favor of the death penalty was narrow; most of the Girondins would have preferred to banish the ex-king to the United States.

These defiant acts ensured a foreign war; they also ensured the outbreak of civil war at home. Those friends of the martyred king who had not emigrated rose up now to defy the regicides and to resist government agents sent to draft their sons and to tax their purses for the conduct of the war. The Convention's new foreign policy, active and ideological in spirit, required a large army; its decision to conscript 300,000 men aroused far more hostility than did the execution of the king. Much of western France was soon aflame with revolt; it was easy for fervent patriots of Jacobin temper to suppose that royalist agents were at work everywhere.

A crisis so serious quite naturally played into the hands of the more fanatical element in the Convention and in the reorganized Paris municipality (now called the Commune). The Mountain, aided by pressure from the Paris crowd, hounded the Girondin leaders out of office in June 1793; the mob besieged the Convention for three days running and refused to leave until the Girondins were arrested or agreed to resign. A few were imprisoned; the rest went off to their provincial homes and in some cases joined the spreading rebellion against the Convention's rule. By midsummer half of France was affected by insurrection. Meanwhile, the foreign war took a serious turn for the worse; the French armies were driven out of the Low Countries and their commanding general, Dumouriez, deserted to the enemy.

The threat of disaster abroad and at home opened the way to unrestricted authoritarian rule. The Convention had already established two potentially powerful executive organs: the Committee of General Security, to deal with police matters; and the Committee of Public Safety, to shape general policy. Although the committee members were elected for terms of only a month, the Convention gradually abdicated power into their hands, and re-election became an empty formality. The twelve-man Committee of Public Safety quickly became the effective governing authority; it was composed of "... perhaps the ablest and most determined men who have ever held power in France."[1] Within it, Maximilien Robespierre and his henchmen emerged as the dominant faction. Robespierre, a young and impecunious lawyer from northern France, had been

---

[1] A. Cobban, *A History of Modern France* (London: Penguin, 1957), I, 213.

an obscure member of the National Assembly from 1789 to 1791 and an active figure in the Jacobin club from the outset. He had made his way upward not by charm or brilliance or oratorical power, but by sheer persistence, dogged consistency, fanatical conviction in the rightness of his own ideas. A man of little warmth, lightness, or humor, "priggish on a heroic scale," he nonetheless managed to win the admiration and respect of his fellow Jacobins and of the lower middle-class elements of the Parisian population. To these disciples, he was the Incorruptible, the voice and conscience of the revolution, the spokesman for the egalitarian spirit of Rousseau. Backed by his handsome, brilliant, and absolutely ruthless young lieutenant Saint-Just, Robespierre embarked on a policy of repression and regimentation that dimly foreshadowed those of twentieth-century totalitarian regimes. The new ruling clique mobilized the nation's manpower and resources for war; it imposed strict economic controls, including price ceilings; it sent special agents to the provinces to enforce its will; it developed large-scale purge machinery to deal with "bad patriots." The provincial rebellion was ruthlessly repressed, though not extinguished; the tide of foreign war began to turn again in favor of the French. By the spring of 1794 the most critical moment had passed.

But Jacobin unity could not long stand so severe a test. Signs of dissension began to appear within the Jacobin leadership; one faction, headed by Georges-Jacques Danton, hinted that it was time to soften the regime and slow the machinery of terror. Conflict developed, too, between the Committee of Public Safety and the Committee of General Security over rival claims to police power. At the same time new threats were emerging to the left of the Jacobins. Various factions of extremists, notably the followers of a Parisian demagogue named Hébert, demanded an intensification of the terror, more rigid economic controls, an all-out attack on religion, and a transfer of real power to the activist citizens of Paris, organized in the forty-eight wards called *sections*.

Robespierre struck back ruthlessly against his critics. In March the Committee arrested and guillotined the Hébertist leaders; in April it was the turn of the Dantonists to be "shaved by the national razor." It seemed that the Robespierrists had cleared the path of all possible rivals and that no one could now stand in the way of their determination to establish utopia on earth, to create the Republic of Virtue. At that triumphal point, the Robespierre faction itself began to show signs of internal dissension. Simultaneously, many Convention members who had hitherto supported the Robespierrists developed an acute attack of nerves; there were rumors that sweeping new purge lists would include even those suspected of tepidity and doubt. A Robespierrist decision in June to step up the terror machinery by adding more courts and by stripping accused citizens of even the forms of judicial protection seemed to confirm the fears of those who were not intimate members of the power group. The outcome was a plot within the Convention itself, with the ex-terrorist Joseph Fouché as its key figure. Late in July 1794 (the month of Thermidor in the revolutionary calendar), the plotters challenged the man whom they now secretly called "the dictator." They howled him down on the floor of the Convention and voted the arrest of the whole Robespierrist group. In the midst of a night of confusion, during which the Robespierrists vainly tried to mobilize the Paris crowd to save them, the leaders were captured; and at dawn they were carted off to the guillotine.

The victims of Thermidor were Jacobins; but so were most of the victors. The purpose of these victors was not to slow the course of the revolution, nor to stop the Reign of Terror that had already sent almost twenty thousand citizens to the guillotine, nor to return to a system of moderation and compromise. Yet their action produced all of these results. Thermidor marked the climax of the terror and the beginning of a gradual relaxation. Most Frenchmen were tired of the tension and violence that had gripped the country for a year; they began to realize, too, that the threat of foreign invasion and of internal upheaval was no longer great enough to justify emergency measures. Robespierre's successors responded to the country's changing mood and the new conditions. They hobbled the Committee of Public Safety, gradually dismantled the purge machinery and the economic controls, and drafted a new constitution. The rump Convention adjourned at last in 1795, making way for the Directory—a structure of government that strongly resembled the one built in 1789–91, save for the fact that it provided for no king,[2] and that the church was cut adrift from the state to enjoy the uncertain blessings of freedom.

The surviving members of the Robespierrist faction made one last attempt in 1795 to block this return to moderate government. The removal of price ceilings by the Thermidoreans had brought a sharp jump in food prices and severe distress among the underprivileged urban groups. The resultant discontent produced renewed mob action; in April and May, crowds repeatedly went on the march or invaded the Convention's meeting hall. But, for the first time since 1789, the mob failed to get its way. Instead, the Convention used the National Guard to break up the riots by force. These incidents gave clear proof that the pendulum was no longer moving jerkily toward the left but had begun to swing back to the right. Indeed, the trend of events encouraged the royalists to take their turn at attempted insurrection. In Ocober 1795, as the Convention was preparing to adjourn, royalist agitators led a mob into the streets. This time the Thermidoreans called on the regular army to break up the threat to the regime: a young unemployed general named Bonaparte received the assignment and scattered the attackers with a whiff of grapeshot. The incident ominously fore-

---

[2] Some Thermidoreans hoped to restore the monarchy in 1795, with the ten-year-old son of Louis XVI as king. They presumed that a regency council of good revolutionaries could raise the child as a constitutional monarch. The boy's death in prison in June, 1795, wrecked the scheme.

shadowed the emergence of a new force in French political life: the army, and its crop of revolutionary generals.

❖❖❖❖❖❖❖❖❖❖❖❖❖❖

Historians by the dozen have analyzed and narrated the French Revolution's climactic years; but somehow the story emerges in a wide variety of quite different forms. Here, as always, the facts do not speak for themselves; or at least they fail to speak with the same voice to all men. Although the various interpretations shade into one another, most of them can be fitted into four major categories: conservative or monarchist, liberal, radical, Marxian.

To conservative and monarchist historians, it was logical and almost inevitable that the revolution should reach a climax in dictatorship and terror. If fanatical extremists achieved power and bathed the country in blood, it was because the so-called sensible moderates had opened the way to them, and because the *philosophes* had even earlier subverted the legal order. Enlightenment thinkers, ignoring the facts of history in favor of the attractions of pure reason, corrupted the nation's intelligentsia and undermined a legitimate system that was capable of being reformed. Edmund Burke had warned as early as 1790 that to uproot a social and political system and to seek to create a brand-new substitute was certain to bring disaster. Once the first steps had been taken in 1789, only one uncertainty remained: how much bloodshed and anarchy would be needed to produce a healthy revulsion among decent people? At what point would the nation call on a strong man to step in and clear up the wreckage?

In the conservative view, Robespierre was the disciple of Rousseau, the first in a long line of demagogues capable of translating Rousseau's ideas into action. The motive of this fanatic was not so much thirst for blood or power as for perfection; this zealot was prepared, for the good of mankind, to destroy wrongheaded people and to force men to be free. He found (or thought he found) in Rousseau the lesson that in times of crisis the general will may be embodied in a small minority, a vanguard, whose members can and must make decisions for a whole people. To attain his end, Robespierre built his vanguard into a disciplined organization, a kind of totalitarian party. He gradually converted the Jacobin clubs from free debating societies into a regimented clique of rigidly orthodox believers, imbued with a sense of duty to make men virtuous and free.

The conservative analysis of the revolution rarely pays much attention to class tensions or to economic and social forces. The decisive factors shaping the course of events are seen as psychological, temperamental, ideological; the explanation of terror is found in the distorted mind of the neurotic or the psychotic leader. When the revolution attained its paroxysm under "the sea-green Robespierre" and that "icy monster" Saint-Just, it had come to depend on outcasts "...recruited from that human trash that infests capital cities, from the epileptic and scrofulous rabble that...imports into civilization the degeneracies, the imbecility, the defects of...its retrogressive instincts and its ill-formed heads."[3]

The liberal view of the revolution begins with a quite different set of preconceptions. It sees the old regime as hopelessly outmoded, far too weak and too rotten to reform itself. The revolution, therefore, was necessary, and most of its early leaders were admirable and high-minded men. Some liberal historians have singled out the Girondins for special praise and have described them as the cream of France's educated elite, honestly seeking a middle way. More commonly in recent years, the liberal interpretation admits that the Girondins were not much good at anything but making speeches and getting elected; it finds the real hero of the epoch in Danton, spokesman for the more moderate wing of the Jacobins. Here was a man who could act as well as talk; here was a charismatic figure, a crisis leader, and above all a master of the political art of compromise. Danton more than any other revolutionary politician was equipped to unify all French patriots and to find a true middle way.

If this estimate is sound, then why did Danton fail to hold power for more than a few months? The liberal answer is likely to be that Danton was destroyed by the villainous, scheming Robespierre, "the most hateful character in the forefront of history since Machiavelli...."[4] Danton's defenders see Robespierre as a small-minded, jealous man who thirsted for power but possessed no talent for managing men, and who could not even comprehend Danton's statesmanlike policy of conciliating rival groups. The selfish plot of the Robespierrists disrupted revolutionary unity at the worst moment of national crisis and made that crisis far more serious than it needed to be. If it is true that Danton flaunted his weaknesses of character—his lack of integrity in financial matters, his lax personal habits—these were minor sins, the personal idiosyncrasies of a great man. In Victor Hugo's phrase, "Danton [was] venal but incorruptible. He took bribes but didn't deliver the goods."

The liberal interpretation of the revolution, like the conservative, subordinates or oversimplifies the economic aspect and the issue of class conflict. The whole revolutionary era is seen as a two-way struggle between the privileged caste and the Third Estate; by implication at least, it seems that all commoners, from millionaire to beggar, joined forces to build and defend a new system. There is not much sign of a clash of interest between bourgeoisie and masses or of any

---

[3] H. Taine, *Les origines de la France contemporaine: la révolution* (Paris: Hachette, 1890), II, 471.

[4] Lord Acton, *Lectures on the French Revolution* (London: Macmillan, 1910), p. 300.

conscious attempt by one social group to use another as a tool for achieving its aims.

When one moves from the liberal to the radical or "common man" view of the revolution, one crosses a kind of historiographical divide. Beyond that barrier, the emphasis shifts to the theme of class conflict. Individuals and ideas take on significance only as they reflect class interests; such factors as psychology and temperament are relegated to a secondary position. To the radical historian, it was the upper bourgeoisie that inaugurated and carried forward the revolution. Its aim was to take over the place of the aristocracy as the privileged class in the state and to combine with privilege a share of political power even greater than the nobility had possessed. Bourgeois leaders used the common man, consciously and even cynically, as the cannon fodder of the revolution; the *sansculotte* crowd was persuaded to do the fighting and dying that was needed to attain bourgeois ends. The conversion of the bourgeoisie to republicanism was a piece of sheer opportunism, when bourgeois leaders found that the king would not accept their domination.

But in the process of winning its fight (so runs the radical thesis), the bourgeoisie found itself threatened by two new dangers. The common man grew vaguely dissatisfied at being exploited and developed a tinge of antibourgeois class consciousness. On top of that, fissions began to occur within the bourgeoisie itself; some bourgeois leaders developed a sympathy for the condition of the underprivileged and became committed to a kind of primitive concept of social justice. The most notable examples of this conversion were Robespierre and Saint-Just, the real heroes of the revolution. Their aims were high-minded and pure, their methods were dictated by the seriousness of the crisis. The Reign of Terror was essential to break the selfish resistance of reactionaries and profiteers and to save the nation from its foreign enemies; the economic measures of the Robespierre era were not mere wartime expedients, but part of a conscious plan to build a welfare state. If Robespierre purged such social reformers as the Hébertists, that was because their dangerous demagoguery was frightening the bourgeoisie, arousing the animal instincts of the still unenlightened dregs of society, and endangering the great experiment of the Robespierre faction. But the liquidation of the Hébertists did not suffice to allay the fears of the bourgeoisie, whose selfish interests were threatened by the Incorruptible's plans for a welfare state. At Thermidor the class that had launched the revolution regained the initiative once more.

The Marxian view of the revolution, at one time almost undistinguishable from the radical view, has more recently diverged somewhat from it. Orthodox Marxists find the origins of the revolution not in the aristocrats' misguided activities nor in the decreased social mobility of the eighteenth century, but in the increasing tension between dynamic forces and static forms. The forces were those of capitalism; the forms (of both state and society) those of feudalism. Part of the upper bourgeoisie had been absorbed into the feudal system, but those who had not been bought off in this fashion were driven by class interest to challenge all feudal limitations on emergent capitalist production. One after another, the various strata of the bourgeoisie assumed leadership in the revolution, always directing their efforts toward the same general end.

Until 1791 the upper bourgeoisie clung to power and to the futile hope that the feudal aristocracy might agree to a compromise. From 1791 to 1793 a slightly lower stratum of lawyers and commercial capitalists (the Girondins) took over; but they were doomed by a spirit of "class egoism" that made them incapable of appealing for popular support in the anti-aristocratic struggle. Power therefore passed in 1793 to the Jacobins or *"moyenne classe"*—an ambiguous and not entirely homogeneous group, yet one that was bound together by class ties rather than by temperament or ideology. Jacobin aims seemed sufficiently like those of the *sanculotte* masses to make them natural collaborators. The *sansculottes* as a group were even more ambiguous than the Jacobins; they were not an embryonic proletariat, or even a coherent social class at all, but rather a mélange drawn from the petty bourgeoisie, artisans, and wage earners. Together, Jacobins and *sansculottes* became the "essential motor" of the revolution. But there could be no real mutual comprehension or compromise between them once the aristocratic threat was destroyed. For their class aims were completely contradictory: the Jacobin bourgeoisie wanted to break all chains on capitalist enterprise, while the *sansculottes* wanted to set up a network of new controls guaranteeing the survival of the small independent enterpriser, relic of the precapitalist era. Although the *sansculottes* were admirable men with progressive political ideas, their economic doctrines were retrograde, and they had inevitably to be pushed aside by the triumphant bourgeoisie.[5] Robespierre himself shared responsibility for destroying the momentum and the cohesion of the *sansculottes,* by paralyzing their chief agency of political action (the *sections* or wards of Paris) and by putting a ceiling on wages. He could not do otherwise, given his lack of real contact with the masses, his ignorance of economic and social issues, and his position as spokesman for a bourgeois-dominated government. That the masses lost confidence in him and failed to save him at Thermidor is, therefore, hardly surprising. Yet in

---

[5] According to the Marxians and near-Marxians, a similar conflict had been developing in rural France, but it had a somewhat different outcome. The rural parallel to the urban bourgeoisie was the emergent group of prosperous small-owners called *laboureurs;* they, too, wanted to break all traditional shackles on individual enterprise. The rural equivalent of the *sansculottes* was the mass of poorer peasants, who clung to all the ancient regulations (such as the right to use the village common land) that would protect the marginal family farm. The poor peasants, unlike the *sansculottes,* got at least part of what they wanted and managed to preserve some aspects of the precapitalist rural structure for another century.

spite of his natural defects, he remains the hero of the period, "incorruptible animator of the revolutionary government . . . , artisan of national independence."[6]

The radical interpretation of the revolution and some aspects of the Marxian interpretation have won widespread acceptance in recent decades. Both views are plausible ones, and their special value is that they have given greater depth to the study of the crisis by their concern for social forces and relationships. The older liberal view of the Third Estate as a solid bloc, almost undifferentiated within by social or economic variations, is no longer tenable. On the other hand, the Marxian view forces the facts into a much too rigidly deterministic framework of theory and reads far too much into the minds of bourgeois leaders. The very concept of "class" itself remains too indistinct, and the boundaries between classes in that epoch too ambiguous, to serve as an adequate model for a thorough understanding of the revolution. The liberal thesis may be outmoded, yet, in fact, the various segments of the Third Estate had a great deal in common throughout the revolutionary upheaval. All commoners had much to gain by preserving the major achievements of 1789. No doubt the bourgeoisie profited most by the revolution, both at the time and over the succeeding century. Yet in the even longer run, it is hard to believe that the common man did not gain just as much as the bourgeoisie from the Great Revolution, or that these gains for the common man were not implicit in the Enlightenment doctrines accepted by the bourgeoisie.

❖❖❖❖❖❖❖❖❖❖❖❖❖

With the establishment of the Directory in 1795, France embarked for the second time on an experiment in balanced constitutional government. This time

---

[6] A. Soboul, "Maximilien Robespierre (1758–1794)," *Cahiers du communisme*, XXXIV (1958), 820. In 1958 (the bicentenary of Robespierre's birth), the Communists in parliament proposed that the state erect a monument to Robespierre in Paris. The bill failed to reach the floor for discussion. Robespierre remains, therefore, one of the few first-rank figures in modern French history who has neither a statue in Paris nor an important street bearing his name. He also remains the only revolutionary leader about whom Frenchmen are still deeply divided. According to a recent opinion poll, Robespierre-admirers and Robespierre-haters are almost evenly balanced in France.

There is a second Marxian version of the revolution—Trotskyite in spirit—that views the *sansculottes* as an embryonic but genuine proletariat, whose incipient class-consciousness was, by 1794, beginning to be directed against the bourgeoisie. According to this version, the real heroes of the epoch were such left-wing extremists as Jacques Roux, spokesman for a faction called the *Enragés* or Wild Men. Robespierre, on the other hand, is regarded as nothing more than a hypocritical demagogue engaged in a contest for personal power against other bourgeois politicians. After he had tricked and betrayed the *sansculottes*, Robespierre was in turn mercilessly betrayed by powerful bourgeois interests that no longer needed him, and that resented his refusal to pursue an expansionist foreign policy designed to conquer new seaports and markets for the business class. When the bourgeoisie a few years later again needed protection against the resurgent masses, they turned to a military dictator rather than a politician.

it was to last for four full years—an endurance record in that revolutionary decade. Yet in the end it, too, failed; and that failure raises once again the question of responsibility. Was the breakdown of the Directory traceable to a bad constitution, to ineffective leadership, to moral corruption, to class conflict, or to sheer bad luck? Was the regime wrecked not by its own shortcomings but by an overwhelming set of convergent problems, combined with the fateful appearance of a power-hungry genius?

Napoleon himself, like most of his admirers since, always insisted that his coup d'état of 1799 really destroyed nothing except a rotten facade; that his seizure of power merely averted other dangerous alternatives—the rise of a new Robespierre, or rapid disintegration into anarchy, or the resurrection of the old monarchy. Perhaps one ought to be skeptical of such a justification, since it resembles the excuses commonly offered by men who destroy constitutional systems. Yet many of Napoleon's enemies and critics, men of republican and liberal temper, have agreed that the Directory was a futile and contemptible regime. They have described it as rotten and impotent; as a system shot through with graft and controlled by a licentious ruling group whose appropriate symbol was the Director Barras, an unparalleled cynic "surrounded by crooked men and fallen women." These critics have called the regime a failure in economic policy, since the government constantly skated on the thin ice of bankruptcy; a failure in foreign policy, since it could neither win the war against Europe nor get out of that war by negotiation; a failure in domestic politics, where its leaders zigzagged between enemies of left and right and repeatedly saved themselves by openly violating the constitution and by gradually abdicating into the hands of the military.

Few kind words have been said by historians about the Directory. Yet perhaps there is a case to be made for it, as for some other weak and short-lived regimes in modern history—Weimar Germany, for instance, or the Second and Fourth French republics. Such a case would not rest on a denial of the regime's shortcomings but rather on an affirmation of the difficulties inherent in representative government in times of stress and crisis, when a nation is deeply divided over both aims and methods. In circumstances of that sort, a middle-of-the-road group possessed of a bare majority and belabored by extremists of right and left is not likely to be effective, or even to survive, unless it is fortunate enough to turn up remarkably statesmanlike leaders and to profit by an upward economic trend. Perhaps flabby moderate republics like the Directory fall not because of their own internal weaknesses, but because they have the bad luck to be challenged by a strong, ambitious, unscrupulous critic—by a man who can make the system appear worse than it is, who can persuade the citizens to overlook its virtues and to concentrate on its faults, who can convince them that authority and efficiency are more to be desired than liberty combined with weakness.

If this hypothesis has any validity at all, it would follow that without a Napoleon Bonaparte the Directory might have survived for years or decades; or, more probably, that it might have given way to a modified monarchy something like that of 1791, with a king committed this time to accept his role as constitutional monarch. France was eventually to arrive at that kind of solution in 1814, but only after experiencing the fifteen years of glory and tragedy that were Napoleon's gift to Frenchmen.

The constitution of 1795, like that of 1791, put the government into the hands of an educated and well-to-do minority. More than a million Frenchmen were deprived of the right to vote, though they kept the juridical equality won in 1789. A five-man board of Directors elected by the bicameral legislature took the place of the king. In an effort to ensure stability, both executive and legislative terms were staggered; one Director and one-third of the members of the legislative councils were to go out of office each year.

The group in power—men of Thermidor, for the most part—was faced from the outset with constant sniping by the revived Jacobins and with backstage intrigues conducted by the royalists (who enjoyed British subsidies). Hardly a year passed from 1796 to 1799 when the Directors were not confronted by a serious threat from one side or the other. Sometimes the threat took the form of a conspiracy, as in the case of Babeuf's egalitarian plot in 1796 and General Pichegru's royalist intrigue in 1797. Such a danger could be handled rather easily as long as the political police remained alert. The threat was more serious when it took the form of an electoral victory by the left or right opposition, which could then disrupt or hamstring the government. "Third force" governments in such circumstances have few real alternatives. They can try for a coalition with one extremist faction, in the hope of absorbing its dynamism. Or they can cling to power without a clear majority, in the hope that the two extremes will balance each other. The Directors usually chose to follow neither course. Instead, they resorted to flagrant violations of the constitution in order to retain a majority; they invalidated the election of opposition legislators and suppressed their newspapers. Such tactics are risky ones, even when based on a sincere conviction that the opposition's purpose is to use its constitutional foothold for anticonstitutional purposes. They are doubly risky when the government must depend on army support to accomplish its ends, for at some point decisive power passes from the civilian to the military authorities. By the later 1790's the revolutionary army of volunteers, conscripts, and old-line officers had shaken down into a career force whose members remained in uniform because they chose to do so. Most of these troops had been continuously on campaign for several years, and much of that time had been spent outside France. The soldiers lost touch with events at home; they grew increasingly dependent on and loyal to their commanding officers. Among these officers there were some who were developing a sense of intrigue and a taste for politics—partly, it must be said, because certain Paris politicians tempted them to indulge that taste. In the end, Bonaparte himself was to strike for power not on his own initiative, but at the invitation of a political faction in Paris.

The Directors' increasing dependence on the military proved fatal in the end. Yet even in retrospect it is not easy to suggest alternatives that might have ensured the survival of the regime. A really first-rate set of leaders would have been needed to find and follow such an alternative; and the Directory turned up no statesmen of that caliber. A vigorous, coherent attack on the worst problems of the time—notably on the problem of inflation, inherited rather than created by the Directory—was essential. By 1795, a flood of *assignats* was in circulation, so many that they had become almost valueless. The Directory was no more capable than the old monarchy of setting up and enforcing a rigorous system of tax collection. Nor could it find new revenue through borrowing from its own citizens; bond issues found few takers. The Directors' only feasible solution was a kind of concealed declaration of national bankruptcy. The *assignats* were repudiated in piecemeal fashion, slowly enough to give clever speculators a chance to buy up much property with the nearly worthless currency. By the end of 1797 they were out of circulation, and the Directors could proceed to a masked repudiation of about two-thirds of the state's internal debt. These measures, though unavoidable, were painful to many Frenchmen and added to the unpopularity of the regime. Besides, there was no guarantee that the bankruptcy procedure would not be followed by a new inflationary spiral, for the government was still spending more than it took in.

The chief reason for the continuously unbalanced budget was France's persistent war. Like the inflation, it was not the Directors' war; they had inherited it from previous regimes. But they failed to understand that domestic problems were simply insoluble so long as the war that had begun in 1792 dragged on. Their most disastrous mistake, therefore, would seem to have been in the sphere of foreign policy, where for reasons of obtuseness or weakness they did not face facts.

The Convention's armies had managed to conquer virtually all the territory up to the Rhine, thus rounding out the so-called natural frontiers. Several smaller states had withdrawn from the war, leaving only Austria, England, and Russia in the coalition. Might the Directors have negotiated peace at that point, retaining the revolutionary acquisitions? The issue has been bitterly debated by historians. Some of them argue that the English would never have agreed to let France keep conquered Belgium with its excellent seaports. They contend that since no patriotic Frenchman could think of giving up the natural frontiers once they had been attained, the Directory had no choice but to carry on the war. Other historians insist that both the English and the Austrians were war-weary and financially hard pressed and that both governments might have been persuaded to accept a *status quo* peace. They point out that in 1797 Pitt's government actually put out feelers indicating that it might be willing to see a trustworthy French government keep the Rhine frontier. What the English meant by "trustworthy" was not defined, but it probably implied a restored monarchy.

Pitt's suggestion came at an opportune time. The royalists in France had just made important gains in the legislative elections of 1797; it seemed possible that the Directors might join forces with the royalist faction, re-establish the constitutional monarchy, and get out of the war. They seriously considered the prospect but unwisely elected to challenge the royalists and continue the war. Most of the new royalist legislators were excluded from parliament; Pitt's agents went home empty-handed. It was not mere chance that one of the generals who urged and actively supported continuation of the war was Napoleon Bonaparte.

Here, it would seem, was a crucial example of bad judgment and weakness on the part of the Directors. Their critics believe that they misunderstood British war aims and exaggerated British weakness. They assumed that English business interests, aroused at the loss of profits caused by wartime trade disruption, would soon force Pitt out of office and would allow the French to dictate terms. In defense of the Directors, it has been argued that they had no way of penetrating the real mood and motives of the English and that they simply took the wrong calculated risk. Their task was complicated, too, by the behavior of General Bonaparte, who exceeded his orders in Italy and set up satellite states there well beyond the natural frontiers. Finally, as the Directors weighed the prospect of a peaceful return to constitutional monarchy, they received little help from the exiled Bourbons. On the contrary, the pretender had recently issued an untimely manifesto announcing his determination to restore the old regime intact. Nothing could have been better calculated than this Bourbon manifesto to wreck the hope of stabilizing France and Europe through compromise.

By 1799 the English, aided by the Directory's unwise and unpopular policy of plunder in the new satellite states (Holland, Switzerland, and northern Italy), had managed to organize a new anti-French coalition and to invade the French sphere of influence. Meanwhile the Jacobins won enough legislative seats in 1798 and 1799 to challenge the faction that had controlled the government since 1795. Through pressure and manipulation, they succeeded in replacing four of the five Directors. The Jacobin club was once again legalized, and it embarked on a noisy propaganda campaign in favor of a return to the Robespierrist system. At the other political extreme, royalist intrigues rose to a new pitch of intensity. Still a third variety of intrigue developed at the very heart of the government. The ex-Abbé Sieyès, relegated to obscurity since the early phase of the revolution, had re-emerged as one of the Directors in June 1799. Sieyès promptly began to plan a coup d'état that would, he hoped, frustrate both the right- and the left-wing threats. He proposed to draft a new constitution that would give the republic a strong executive (in which role he probably hoped to serve). He counted on the threat from the new English-led coalition to arouse Frenchmen to the necessity for unity and strength; but he needed also an excuse to act and a general to over-awe possible opposition. The excuse was easily trumped up: an alleged Jacobin conspiracy would serve the purpose. The general was less easily found; it was only after a couple of false starts that Sieyès hit on Bonaparte as the right man and got his consent to participate.

The coup of the 18th Brumaire (November 9, 1799) came near misfiring. The legislative body, called into emergency session at St. Cloud outside Paris, re-fused to swallow General Bonaparte's story of a Jacobin conspiracy against the regime. Some legislators called instead for a vote to outlaw and arrest Bonaparte and his fellow schemers. Quick action by the general's younger brother Lucien, president of the lower house of the legislature, saved the day. Lucien refused to allow a vote on the outlawry proposal, called in the contingent of troops waiting outside, and persuaded them to clear the hall of the protesting legislators. A de-pendable rump faction of the lower house was then convened, and promptly voted full powers to the Sieyès-Bonaparte clique. The constitutional system was once again swept away—this time, as it turned out, in favor of a barely-concealed military dictatorship.

The coup of 1799 was bloodless and was met with general indifference in the country, even on the part of those sectors of society upon which the regime had been based. The evidence is unmistakable that the Directory, whatever its modest virtues, had failed to win the affections of any important group of Frenchmen. Most citizens were tired of protracted civil unrest and political chicanery; they were ready to pay a considerable price for stability at home and security against foreign enemies. Even so, it was not this lack of public support that in the end doomed the Directory. Bonaparte probably could not have succeeded if some of the system's own leaders had not opened the way to him. The political elite of the time had, for the most part, lost confidence in the system and was ready to aban-don it as unworkable. Such is often the fate of weak compromise regimes—not only in the eighteenth century, and not only in France.

CHAPTER 7

# *Dictatorship, 1799–1814*

> There will always be Frenchmen who subordinate social and spiritual needs to power and glory, to authority and order.
>
> **PIETER GEYL**

In all the history of modern France—indeed, of modern Europe—few men have aroused more controversy than Napoleon Bonaparte. Passions in the debate run strong even after a century and a half. To his bitterest critics, he was a grasping, cynical, power-hungry despot, a distorted genius whose taste for brutality and tyranny grew more intense with the years. These critics see him as essentially a counterrevolutionary who diverted France from its proper course of absorbing and consolidating the revolution's gains; as a ruler who chose to govern through the twin devices of propaganda and terror, and who crushed out liberty as thoroughly as any of history's dictators. To his admirers, he was the national hero who preserved the essential achievements of the revolution, who brought their blessings to the rest of Europe, and who came nearer than any other political leader of modern times to solving the problem of government in France. "He was not [wrote one fulsome admirer] ... for the Revolution of Marat and Saint-Just, for the Revolution of assassination and plunder. With all his earnest fiery heart he was for the Revolution of liberty and justice, for the Revolution of national honor.... But when the Revolution became a sewer of anarchy, a dung-hill of ferocious demagoguery ..., he reared against it, brushed it aside with the flat of his sword, bent over a France that lay prostrate in the gutter, lifted her to her feet and held her there with arms that had suddenly grown strong enough and proud enough to support his country."[1]

To summarize even the high points in Napoleon's career as it impinged on the history of France is a formidable task. Born in Corsica just thirty years before his seizure of power, he became a Frenchman and a career soldier largely by accident. Corsica had become a French territory only a year before his birth; and the royal decree that enabled young Bonaparte to obtain a scholarship at a French military school was issued in the 1770's, just in time to make him eligible. In 1789 he was an obscure lieutenant in the royal army, with slight prospect of advancement but with a restless urge to action. The revolutionary era suddenly opened new vistas. For a time Bonaparte seemed inclined to plunge into the maelstrom of Corsican politics, but the broader opportunities in France brought him back to the mainland. His Jacobin friendships and his talents as artillery commander brought him rapid distinction during the Robespierre era, and near-disaster after Thermidor. Imprisoned briefly, dropped from the active army, he spent an obscure year or two in Paris remaking his fortune. His acquaintance with Barras opened the way to a command in the armies of the Directory; in 1796 he took over the army of northern Italy, one of three French contingents assigned to converge on Vienna. His brilliant campaign of 1796–97 enabled him to dictate peace to the Austrians and to convert part of northern Italy into satellite republics. This he did without orders from the Directory.

The Directors, unnerved yet impressed at Bonaparte's talents, next assigned him to lead an invasion of England. Bonaparte persuaded them to let him sail instead to Egypt, whence he might cut English trade routes, threaten England's control of India, and begin the construction of a new French empire in the Middle East. Cut off in Egypt when Admiral Nelson destroyed the French fleet that had landed his troops, Bonaparte spent almost a year in futile and costly desert expeditions, awaiting his chance to return to the European scene. Bad news from Paris strengthened his conviction that his star would soon lead him out of the Egyptian trap that threatened to wreck his career. A new European coalition had been formed, and its armies were not only overrunning the French satellite states but seemed to be threatening France itself. Seizing upon this excuse, Bonaparte secretly embarked for France in August, 1799, leaving his Egyptian army to its inevitable tragic fate.

The French public, unaware that the Egyptian adventure had turned into a disaster, welcomed Bonaparte as a national hero and as a potential savior from the menace of invasion. Many Frenchmen did not know that they had already

---

[1] O. Aubry, *Napoleon, Soldier and Emperor* (Philadelphia: Lippincott, 1938), p. 17. The power of the Napoleonic legend was demonstrated by the findings of a French public opinion poll in 1969. Asked to name the most important individual in all of France's history, 35 per cent of the respondents chose Napoleon. No competitor even came close.

been saved; that French armies in Holland and Switzerland had won notable victories, and that in Italy the enemy coalition had begun to quarrel over the spoils. What the nation wanted was security and peace; and it was beginning to think that only a general could achieve them. Against this background, Bonaparte received and accepted Sieyès' proposal to sweep away the flabby Directory and to replace it with a firm authoritarian republic. Though Bonaparte almost bungled the job on the crucial day, he made no false moves once power had fallen into the hands of the conspirators. Sieyès' new constitution provided for a powerful executive board of three consuls. Bonaparte, by a few deft suggestions, persuaded the other plotters to alter the draft in such a way as to vest virtually unlimited powers in the hands of the First Consul—Bonaparte himself. The other two consuls promptly faded into obscurity, as did the kingmaker, Sieyès. So great was the enthusiasm for Bonaparte's leadership that a national plebiscite produced a majority of 99.999 per cent in favor of the new system. "What's in the new constitution?" one citizen is supposed to have asked another. "Bonaparte," came the simple and accurate answer.

For several years the nation's confidence seemed to be well justified. By luck and shrewdness, Bonaparte managed to get the Russians to withdraw from the war; by a victorious though costly new campaign into northern Italy, he restored the French satellite states there and forced the Austrians to surrender. Once again, England alone remained as an active enemy; and this time the English were ready to negotiate. By the Treaty of Amiens in 1802, France attained peace for the first time in a decade. True, the treaty left many critical points unsettled; but France retained control of the Rhine frontier as well as of northern Italy. So great was popular enthusiasm that Bonaparte's puppet senate proposed to lengthen his ten-year term as consul to twenty years. The First Consul modestly suggested that he would prefer to be consul for life; and almost without dissent the nation again approved his action by referendum.

Peace gave Bonaparte an opportunity to channel his overflowing energies into domestic reform. He had already moved, in 1801, to restore the tie between church and state; he persuaded the Pope to accept a concordat recognizing Catholicism as the religion of the majority of Frenchmen, placing priests once again on the state payroll, and providing for state nomination of bishops. The Vatican formally abandoned any claim to church property lost during the revolution. By this shrewd device, Bonaparte cut the ground from under clerical opposition to his regime. It was, as a royalist bitterly remarked, "a business arrangement between Christians and philosophers, made in the name of a government that was neither philosophic nor Christian."[2] A second set of reforms tightened and further centralized the governmental bureaucracy. A network of

---

[2] J. M. Thompson, *Napoleon Bonaparte: His Rise and Fall* (Oxford: Blackwell, 1952), p. 172.

prefects, subprefects, and centrally-appointed mayors wiped out the last remnants of real federalism introduced by the revolution and carried the decisions of Paris into every hamlet. In the capital itself, a series of refurbished agencies like the Council of State and the Inspectorate of Finances provided vigorous, efficient bureaucratic leadership.

Authoritarian rule at last made possible a rigorous program of financial reform. Bonaparte found the treasury virtually empty and the government desperately dependent on loans from private bankers. He encouraged his experts to revamp the system of direct taxation, and, through his new nation-wide bureaucracy, he succeeded in enforcing collection. To stabilize the currency and to ease the problem of government borrowing, he established the Bank of France and gave it control over the nation's credit system. The bank was owned and controlled by the leading financiers of France, who had a vested interest in checking inflation and restricting the issue of paper money; for the next century the franc was to become one of the most stable monetary units in Europe.

The law code that bears Napoleon's name also emerged during the era of the Consulate. Although the task of legal codification (like a number of other reforms attributed to Napoleon) had been begun by the Convention, it had dragged on until the First Consul inspired its rapid completion. Written into the code were some of the fundamental achievements of the Great Revolution—notably the principle of equality before the law. Another durable creation of this period was the Legion of Honor, designed to recognize achievement in every sphere and to harness the loyalty of an elite of talent. Education also drew Bonaparte's attention, though not so much because of his love of learning as because of his belief that educational discipline would produce good subjects and well-trained officers. He aimed to create a teaching hierarchy as rigid and obedient as the cadres of his army and a curriculum marked by absolute uniformity. A powerful board of education in Paris controlled the system, and Napoleon might have boasted (as did a later minister of education) that in every *lycée* in France every student at a given hour would be poring over precisely the same passage in the same book. The budget provided almost no funds for primary education (which was left to the local communes) or for girls' schools; Bonaparte was concerned with training a leadership elite, not with bringing literacy to the masses or diverting females from what he considered to be their proper functions. "What we ask of education," he wrote, "is not that girls should think, but that they should believe."

Bonaparte's only serious failure during the early years was the frustration of his colonial plans. His ambitions ranged to every continent, but only in America did he embark on a practical program. His attempt to reconquer the rich sugar island of Haiti from the ex-slaves who had seized control there ended in disaster; guerrilla warfare and fever decimated his troops. The renewal of war with England made communications impossible; Bonaparte withdrew the remnants of his expeditionary force and cut his losses by selling Louisiana territory (destined to be the granary for his West Indian sugar islands) to the United States.

The fragile peace between France and England broke down in 1803, after little more than a year. Superficially, the fault was England's for refusing to evacuate Malta in accordance with the peace terms. England's stubbornness, however, was inspired by the obvious fact that Bonaparte was not ready to rest content with the share of Europe he already controlled. During the year of peace he annexed Piedmont outright, tightened his domination of satellite Switzerland, embarked on a series of intrigues in the German states, and sent an agent to the Near East to explore possibilities for extending French influence there. It was not the kind of behavior to persuade the British that France was ready for peaceful coexistence.

With the renewal of war, Bonaparte threw himself into plans for a cross-Channel invasion. The British retaliated by occupying France's remaining colonial outposts and by smuggling agents into France to create a monarchist fifth column. The plot was detected just in time, and its leaders executed; but Bonaparte seized the excuse to convert the Consulate into an Empire. By founding a dynasty, he could assure France of long-range stability; even if an assassin were to destroy the emperor, a successor would be assured and the regime would survive. A plebiscite produced the usual massive majority, though there were graver reasons this time to doubt the integrity of the proclaimed results. On December 2, 1804, the coronation occurred in the cathedral of Notre Dame. The Pope, who had come all the way from Rome for the ceremony, was not even permitted to set the crown on the new emperor's head; it was Napoleon himself who did the crowning.

Through the early months of 1805 Napoleon waited anxiously for news that his Mediterranean fleet had sailed into the Atlantic, where it was supposed to decoy the English fleet into leaving the Channel unprotected for a few days. The cautious French admiral preferred to duck into a Spanish port and ignored the emperor's furious orders to come out at once.[3] By summer the moment for a Channel crossing had passed, for England had managed to organize a new coalition against France. Napoleon, unable to risk an attack on England when Austria and Russia were again in the war, switched his plans with lightning speed and set off on the most brilliant of his campaigns. After his victory at Ulm in southern Germany, Vienna was taken without a fight, but the Austro-Russian forces fell back toward the east. The emperor caught them near the village of Austerlitz where, on December 2, 1805, he won his most famous single victory. The disaster left the Austrians no choice but to beg for peace. For the third time

---

[3] It was not until after Napoleon had abandoned his plans for a channel crossing that the French fleet ventured out to sea, where Nelson promptly destroyed it in the battle of Trafalgar.

Napoleon dictated terms, this time much more severe than had been the case in 1797 or 1800. His foreign minister Talleyrand strongly urged a policy of generosity in order to win and keep Austrian friendship and to convert the Hapsburg empire into a bulwark against Russian encroachment into Europe. Napoleon unwisely ignored Talleyrand's counsel; he preferred to teach the annoying Austrians a lesson and to return home a triumphant conqueror.

England and Russia remained in the war, but the Russian forces had been so badly decimated that they withdrew from central Europe. As for England, Napoleon tried once more for peace based on the *status quo;* but the emperor's tightening grip on Europe made the *status quo* steadily more unacceptable to London. Late in 1806 the English persuaded Prussia, for the first time in a decade, to join the anti-French coalition. Once again Napoleon's armies went on the move; at the double battle of Jena and Auerstaedt, Prussian resistance was shattered and the road was opened to Berlin. Only a small fraction of the Prussian forces escaped to the east, along with the Prussian court.

By this time Russian armies were again in the field, thanks in part to English subsidies; and Napoleon's troops had to continue eastward despite the approach of winter. A bloody, icy, and inconclusive campaign ended at last in the summer of 1807, when the French managed to win the battle of Friedland. An even greater victory promptly followed: Russia was transformed by personal diplomacy from enemy into partner. At a meeting between Napoleon and Tsar Alexander on a raft moored in the middle of the River Niemen, the two sovereigns were reconciled and agreed to divide most of Europe (as well as parts of the Near East) between them.

By one of the clauses of the Treaty of Tilsit, the Russians agreed to close their ports against English goods. Napoleon thus plugged the largest single gap in his so-called continental system, his scheme for the economic strangulation of England. The system had been in effect since 1806, though certain earlier measures had anticipated it. Napoleon believed that by closing the Continent to British goods, the nation of shopkeepers would be driven to sue for peace. His commercial blockade lasted for eight years and severely damaged the British economy, but it failed to achieve its ultimate purpose. To some extent, leaks in the blockade were responsible; much contraband trade with England continued, and Napoleon himself eventually gave a quasi-legal base to this trade by granting licenses for the smuggling of certain British products. Far more important, however, was England's success in finding new markets (mainly in the New World) to compensate for its European losses. England's total exports therefore remained fairly stable throughout the period. But moral as well as economic factors wrecked Napoleon's scheme; the English will to resist at heavy cost was something that he had not anticipated and could never quite understand.

One fatal by-product of the continental system was a French expedition to Portugal in 1807 to force Portuguese participation in the trade blockade. Napoleon's armies got permission to cross Spain for this purpose, but some of them settled down on Spanish soil and refused Spanish requests to withdraw. Napoleon's intentions were obviously not honorable; he intended to convert Spain into a new satellite. By intrigue and threats, the weak Bourbon king was forced to abdicate and was replaced by a French puppet, Napoleon's brother Joseph. A spontaneous uprising of the Spaniards followed, with young army officers and the church hierarchy as the backbone of the rebellion. More and more French troops were poured into Spain in a vain attempt to repress the insurgent nation. Meanwhile the Spaniards received help from England; an army under Wellington landed in Portugal and crossed the frontier.

Napoleon's difficulties in Spain inspired a generalized unrest in Europe. The Austrians restlessly sought an occasion to get revenge; the Pope, increasingly discontented with the way Napoleon had interpreted the Concordat, was becoming obstreperous. Even in Paris itself, shrewd politicians like Talleyrand were engaged in devious intrigues aiming at a possible palace revolution. Reports of these intrigues brought Napoleon rushing home from Spain. In a whirlwind of furious action, he dismissed Talleyrand as foreign minister and ordered the annexation of the Papal States to France. The Pope himself was virtually abducted and was held a kind of prisoner near Paris. When the Austrians suddenly declared war in 1809, Napoleon eagerly marched off to the slaughter. For the fourth time the Austrian armies were crushed (this time at Wagram), and large chunks of Austrian soil were carved off for the benefit of neighboring states allied with France.

In 1810, at the end of his first decade in power, Napoleon's fortunes had reached their zenith. His domination of Europe was almost complete, and his position at home seemed unassailable. Annexations had carried the frontiers of France well beyond the Rhine and the Alps, all the way to Hamburg in the north and to Rome in the south. A series of satellite states, several of them ruled by Napoleon's brothers or brothers-in-law, adjoined all of France's land frontiers; there were outposts of this satellite empire as far distant as Poland and southern Italy. Most of the German states were fused into the so-called Confederation of the Rhine and subjected to the domination of Paris. Prussia was a mere shadow of its old self, Austria a landlocked empire shorn of much territory and prestige, Russia an ally. Only the stubborn resistance of England and the irritating guerrilla war in Spain remained to plague the emperor. It is not surprising that he foresaw the early capitulation of the British, whose morale was threatened by the long strain of war.

At home, the system seemed to have attained stability at last, after the constant upheaval of the revolutionary decade. The last of the royalist plots had been crushed in 1804, and so had a renewed peasant outbreak in the west in support of the royalist cause. Gradually, many of the émigrés had drifted back to France, to be given positions of prestige at court or, in some cases, ministerial posts of real responsibility. A new Napoleonic nobility was gradually created, and it mingled awkwardly with the old: most of the emperor's marshals became dukes or princes, and so did such ex-revolutionaries as Talleyrand and Fouché. Only the question of the imperial succession remained unresolved. In 1809 the emperor, eager for an heir, divorced his childless wife Josephine and persuaded the Austrian court to furnish him with a Hapsburg bride. In due course Marie Louise presented him with a son, thus apparently ensuring the perpetuation of the dynasty in a direct line.

Nothing, it seemed, was lacking; the regime had given France stability, efficiency, prosperity, glory. A vast building program in Paris stimulated business and added to the beauty of Europe's most beautiful capital. Government encouragement to industry through cheaper credit, better technical education, and productivity propaganda fostered the growth of factories; the blockade cut off English competition, and the needs of Napoleon's armies provided a huge market. For a decade business had been good (except in the hard-hit seaport cities); industrialists and bankers were content, and so were the workers, who had steady work at rising wage levels. The streamlined administrative system was operated by the most efficient bureaucracy France had ever known. Bonaparte had come to power without an organized faction of supporters; in filling key posts he had sought talent and energy alone and had ostentatiously ignored the political backgrounds of those who served him. It had been a shrewd gamble; the bureaucracy served him faithfully and well. Napoleon himself set the example for his officials by his almost inhuman capacity for sustained work. "Come, come, gentlemen, let's wake up!" he told his ministers at a night session, "It's only two o'clock; we've got to earn the salaries the French people pay us." The price of all these achievements—increasing regimentation and unceasing war—seemed to many Frenchmen well worth paying. If equality of status and the fraternal unity of all Frenchmen survived from the revolutionary triad, liberty disappeared in all but name. The number of political journals in Paris was reduced from seventy-three in 1800 to four in 1811, and the content of those four was rigorously censored. A network of police agents under Fouché's orders unearthed subversives before they had gotten much beyond thinking dangerous thoughts. Napoleon's increasingly autocratic temper gradually turned his ministers into little more than errand boys; his unwillingness to share military glory led him to omit from the list of victories on the Arc de Triomphe the battle of Auerstaedt, where Davout had saved the day for his hard-pressed sovereign.

If Napoleon's power reached its peak about 1810, one can see in retrospect that the forces of disintegration were already at work. His continental system had not only failed to wreck Britain's economy, but it had also aroused European resentment toward France. Napoleon eventually had to depose his brother Louis as king of Holland because Louis could not and would not check the Dutch smuggling trade with England. There were other reasons, too, for the growth of dissatisfaction in the satellite states. Napoleon imposed heavy exactions in men and money for the conduct of his wars. When his stepson Eugène de Beauharnais wrote from Italy to protest this rapacious policy, the emperor replied brutally: "My principle is *France first.*" By 1812 non-French conscripts made up almost half of Napoleon's forces. The flickering guerrilla war in Spain helped to keep discontent aglow everywhere and encouraged the hope of eventual resistance to the iron rule of the French. There were some faint signs of an emergent sense of nationalism in the Italian states, the Germanies, and the Austrian realm, though it probably affected only a rather small educated elite. Not even France itself was immune from the growth of discontent. A severe business recession that set in during 1810–11 cooled the enthusiasm of the bourgeoisie, which had been a solid pillar of the regime.

The signal for the revolt of Europe was given by Tsar Alexander. Whether he had really fallen under Napoleon's personal spell at Tilsit is an insoluble question; at any rate, by 1810 the friendship was fading fast. Napoleon made an effort to patch things up at a summit meeting at Erfurt in 1808, but the fundamental conflict was only deferred. Late in 1810 the tsar withdrew from the continental system and opened his ports to neutral ships carrying the goods of England or any other nation. Napoleon at once began to move men and supplies eastward to the Russian frontier. By early summer of 1812 he had collected the largest force ever to serve under his command, and the fateful invasion of Russia was launched. The retreating Russian forces evaded a pitched battle and scorched the earth as they withdrew, forcing the invaders to depend entirely on their own elaborate but inadequate supply system. Smolensk fell after two months, but Napoleon decided against going into winter quarters there and gambled on a lightning march toward Moscow. Early in September the Russians made their stand at Borodino and were beaten after a bloody all-day conflict. A week later the emperor rode into Moscow to dictate peace terms. But he found no one to hear his terms; tsar and court had withdrawn behind Moscow with the remaining Russian forces. Within twenty-four hours Napoleon, too, had left the city; fires, set intentionally or accidentally by the Russians, were whipped into fury by a high wind, and before rain fell to check the holocaust three-quarters of the city was destroyed. Deprived thus of winter quarters and supplies, unable to make contact with a Russian government that refused to ask for terms, Napoleon set out in October on the retreat to Smolensk. But by the time that city was reached, discipline had begun to disintegrate. The supply system, already over-taxed, broke down completely; soldiers roamed through the city looting or fight-ing over food and vodka. The weary forces headed westward again in mid-November, dragging their cannon and their booty, harassed by Cossack raiders, pierced by the incredibly severe cold. On December 14 Marshal Ney and three hundred and fifty half-frozen, half-starved men marched in good order across the border into Poland—the remnants of the Grand Army that had contained, only six months earlier, about a half-million men.

Napoleon had already abandoned his men in his haste to get back to Paris. Optimistic and cheerful in spite of the disaster, his central idea was to raise and train a new force for a second Russian invasion in 1813. This time, however, the task was to be far more difficult. There was open dissension in France and dangerous restlessness in Europe. For the moment, however, only the Prussians dared risk an open challenge to Napoleon by joining Russia and England in the war. By the late spring of 1813 Napoleon had recruited and trained a fresh army numbering a quarter of a million men, most of them French this time; and he set out once more toward the east "with his young guard and his long boots." He met the enemy in central Germany but was no longer strong enough to follow up his two inconclusive victories. From Vienna came disturbing indica-tions that even his father-in-law, the Hapsburg emperor, might join the coalition against him. He spent a month in a desperate attempt to keep Austria neutral, but it was already too late. Secretly, Metternich had committed Hapsburg power to the enemy coalition and was only awaiting a safe moment to intervene. In August the Austrians cast off the cloak of neutrality; for the first time since his earliest campaigns, Napoleon faced a coalition whose armies outnumbered his own. His victims had learned at last, after far too much delay, that cooperation was the only way to defeat their oppressor. In October, in the Battle of the Na-tions near Leipzig, the French army was decimated, and its remnants forced to retreat. Word of disaster came from Spain as well; the last French forces were driven across the Pyrenees into France, and Wellington's army followed close behind. The Confederation of the Rhine collapsed, and its members joined the coalition; the Dutch called back the House of Orange; even King Joachim of Naples—Napoleon's brother-in-law—went over to the enemy.

Back in Paris, Napoleon could no longer ignore the threatening wave of discontent and weariness. He proceeded nevertheless to comb the country once more for troops. This time he could turn up nothing better than a meager force of teen-agers, untrained and appallingly outnumbered. Nevertheless, the armies of the coalition waited prudently along the Rhine in the hope that a full-scale campaign in France might be avoided. In November, 1813, the allied governments offered peace if Napoleon would agree to stay within France's natural frontiers. Napoleon was both too proud and too suspicious of allied sincerity to accept this proposal; he turned instead to a vigorous diplomatic campaign designed to split the shaky coalition, and when that failed, to defensive war on the soil of France itself. His brilliant campaign of 1814 was, however, a hopeless one; the coalition armies crunched straight on toward Paris while the small French army buzzed angrily about them like a hornet before a tank. The city capitulated on the last day of March; on April 4 most of Napoleon's marshals abandoned his cause as futile and informed the emperor that they intended to surrender. The disillusioned ruler promptly abdicated in favor of his son, but the victors demanded (and got) an unconditional abdication instead. As a bitter joke they named him Emperor of Elba, a barren island of eighty-six square miles off the Italian coast. Two weeks later he left Paris for his new realm. On the way southward through France he was met with apathy, taunts, or threats from his former subjects. In the whole country, no voice was raised in his behalf except in the army, where most of the noncommissioned officers stubbornly asserted their loyalty to the commander they had served so long.

The fate of France lay in the hands of the coalition. A Bourbon restoration had not been one of the allies' war aims; the victors were not at all sure that such a solution would ensure a stable and peaceful France. The tsar had been inclined to favor promoting the Swedish crown prince, former Marshal Bernadotte of France, to the French throne. The Austrians had been tempted by the prospect of perpetuating the Empire, with Napoleon's little son on the throne and the Austrian-born empress, Marie Louise, acting as regent. The English had leaned toward the Bourbons, but they doubted the country's enthusiasm for a restoration. They were right in being skeptical; Frenchmen had lost their enthusiasm for anything except peace. The resultant vacuum provided a tiny organized faction of royalists with its opportunity. In an empty room small voices reverberate loudly; so it was with the Chevaliers de la Foi, a *sub rosa* organization of Bourbon supporters founded in 1810 to work toward an eventual restoration. As the invasion proceeded, the Chevaliers had managed to stir up royalist demonstrations that impressed the allied statesmen. Just after Paris fell they won an important new recruit—Talleyrand, still one of the highest dignitaries of the Empire. Talleyrand's effective lobbying converted the tsar and then the dominant faction in the imperial senate, which voted on April 6 to call the Bourbon pretender to the throne of France. Without much enthusiasm, the allied rulers concurred in the only course that now seemed open. If any one man can be called the author of the restoration, that man was Napoleon. By his stubborn determination to fight to the bitter end, he had ruled out the only workable alternative—a perpetuation of the Empire, with his child-son on the throne.

Across the Channel in exile, an aide burst in upon the pretender with the joyous news: "Sire! You are king of France!" Coldly the new sovereign replied, "And when have I been anything else?"[4]

✤✤✤✤✤✤✤✤✤✤✤✤✤

"What a romance my life has been!" These were Napoleon's words as he reflected at St. Helena on his own career. Historians from his day to ours have looked back on that career and have found no aspect of it upon which they could all agree. "History," remarks Pieter Geyl, "can reach no unchallengeable conclusions on so many-sided a character, on a life so dominated, so profoundly agitated, by the circumstances of the time."[5]

Napoleon's right to be called a military genius probably draws the greatest degree of consensus. Even if it is true that he was the last of the eighteenth-century commanders rather than the first of the moderns, he was, after all, still fighting an eighteenth-century war. Results count in war; and Napoleon was rarely beaten. Few commanders in history can point to so perfect a masterpiece of strategy and tactics as the battle of Austerlitz—second only, perhaps, to Cannae in the whole history of warfare.

Yet even in this sphere the critics have been severe. They have pointed out that Napoleon faced few opponents of first-rate ability; that the coalitions opposing him put as much energy into jealous squabbling as into the common effort; that his forces in the field usually outnumbered those of the enemy. They have observed that he made no original contribution to the art of war but was content to use a set of principles worked out by eighteenth-century strategists and taught to him at school; that his talent for handling armies grew less as his armies grew larger; that he was guilty of serious carelessness in his later years. They have charged that he sometimes made grievous mistakes and had to be saved by the heroism of a subordinate; that he would rarely share credit for any victory, unless one of his generals had been killed in action and was thus removed as a rival; that he consciously built up a false legend of his concern for the common soldier and his intimate knowledge of the men who fought for him; that, in fact, he had no more interest in his soldiers than a good workman has in his tools.

To Napoleon's admirers, his greatest and most durable achievement was in the sphere of domestic reform. The list of major reforms dating from the Con-

---

[4] G. de Bertier de Sauvigny, *La restauration* (Paris: Flammarion, 1955), p. 72.

[5] P. Geyl, *Napoleon: For and Against* (New Haven: Yale Univ. Press, 1949), p. 15.

sulate cannot be matched in any other brief period in French history; the administrative structure and the legal system have survived to this day. Napoleon's defenders insist that his actions preserved rather than destroyed the revolutionary achievements—notably civil and social equality and the revolutionary land settlement. They contend that a resurrection of the monarchy in 1799 or soon after would have meant a brusque return to the old regime; that by postponing the Bourbon restoration for another fifteen years, Napoleon provided time for the essential changes to take firm root. Some admirers even believe that by 1810 the emperor had virtually completed the difficult but all-important task of fusing the two traditions of old regime and revolution into a workable middle way.

An effective case can be made for this view. Napoleon was, in many respects, a son of the revolution; the great upheaval made his success possible, and he did preserve some of the revolutionary gains. More uncertain is the thesis that those gains would have been lost without him, and that a restored monarchy in 1800 or soon after would have been capable of resurrecting the old regime intact. The Bourbons undoubtedly nursed such illusions at the time; but they might have been forced to compromise once they tried to put their program into effect. It is true, too, that the planning for most of Napoleon's reforms had been begun by the Convention or the Directory, and that his most striking personal contribution —the Concordat with the Vatican—was not an unmixed blessing for France. The Concordat replaced the Directory's experiment in the separation of church and state which, given time, might have won general acceptance in France. Eventually the French were to return to such a system; but only after a century of bitter conflict over the clerical issue, much of which might conceivably have been avoided had Napoleon not restored the tie between church and state. Perhaps, however, it was too early for separation to succeed in a country with France's Catholic heritage and in an era when the phrase "a free church in a free state" still had little meaning.

No aspect of Napoleon's career is more controversial than his foreign policy. To one school of historians, he was an aggressive expansionist incapable of being satisfied with what he had conquered; a man whose belief in his star meant that there could be no limits to his ambition and who therefore doomed Europe to a generation of war. To another school, he was no more than a patriotic Frenchman concerned with achieving national security and France's natural frontiers; this worthy goal was frustrated by self-seeking rival nations, notably England. Most of Napoleon's admirers insist that, if he pushed his territorial conquests beyond the natural frontiers and established there a cordon of satellite states, the purpose was purely defensive; he sought nothing more than buffers against enemies who would never be content to let France border on the Rhine and the Alps. Some of them add that the buffer-state policy was not Napoleon's creation but was inherited by him from the Directory. General Bonaparte, they say, merely helped to set up these satellites on orders from Paris, and once having taken power, could not abandon what the previous regime had passed on to him. Thus the whole epic of the Empire may be summed up as a defensive struggle to keep the conquests of the revolution—conquests that the kings of France had sought for centuries to achieve and that represented the fulfillment of France's historic destiny.

Napoleon's critics contend, on the contrary, that it was he who initially dragged the Directory into the buffer-state policy. They offer impressive evidence that the Directors intended to keep no territory beyond the Rhine and the Alps and that, if they ordered the conquest of northern Italy, it was only in order to trade that region for Austria's acceptance of the Rhine frontier. Napoleon, they insist, willfully ignored his instructions and conquered additional Italian territory. So glamorous were his victories, and so profitable the booty that the general sent home, that the Directors dared neither to challenge Bonaparte nor to abandon what he had taken. They were therefore trapped into a policy of conquest that ensured the hostility of the rest of Europe.

Many of Napoleon's critics further challenge the thesis that there were limits to his expansionism. It is true that until about 1805 he gave no clear indication of wanting to move beyond a buffer strip in Europe. After that date, however, he cast off any limitations. Much of the buffer area he annexed outright or handed over to some member of the Bonaparte clan. The rest of the Continent west of Russia gradually came into his grip in one fashion or another. Napoleon's critics conclude that this had always been his purpose, and that he had concealed his aims until his strength was great enough to let him move eastward. France, ringed about by a security cordon of buffer states, was simply too small for his vaulting ambition and vanity. His real dream was the domination of all of Europe—the construction of a new-model Roman empire ensuring peace, prosperity, and stability, with himself as heir of the Caesars.

There are a few admirers of Napoleon who accept this latter thesis, and who contend that the conquest of Europe was a high-minded and defensible program. France, they argue, was so far ahead of the rest of Europe that it was the duty of Frenchmen to speed the Continent's evolution by their benevolent rule. Both France and Europe, they suggest, would have had a happier and healthier future if Napoleon had managed to keep his conquests consolidated for at least a generation or two. The result in France would have been to ensure a permanent fusion of the revolutionary gains with a tradition of strong and efficient government. The result in the rest of Europe would have been to lay the foundations for a more nearly unified Continent. The next half-century was to be an era of critical importance, when the middle class everywhere was rising to power and liberal and national ideas were taking root. If these developments had occurred within a Napoleonic Europe rather than within separate and widely divergent political and social systems, the new governing class would have been more European than national. Its members would have found themselves constantly working on common problems, getting used to European-wide collaboration, and receiving their training in the most efficient of governmental bureaucracies. The hypothesis is an intriguing one; but it leaves open the question of Napoleon's willingness (or that of his successors) to relax his authoritarian grip as the new liberal and national forces gained strength.

Most of Napoleon's admirers have been somewhat more restrained than this. They have defended his purposes and actions prior to the fatal date of 1805, at which time they believe he made a disastrous error by pushing beyond the buffer region essential to France's security. The mistake, as they see it, was comprehensible; Napoleon can hardly be blamed for wanting to teach the Austrians a lesson after the latter had twice broken earlier treaty agreements with France. Besides, Corsican clan loyalty was deeply ingrained in Napoleon, and he was urged on to further conquests by his grasping brothers and sisters. But even though his motives were understandable, the conquest of Europe was pragmatically impossible to achieve.

These defenders-turned-critics point out that Napoleon's foreign minister Talleyrand warned him and sought to restrain him, arguing for a generous peace in 1805 that would have converted Austria into a grateful friend and an anti-Russian buffer. This policy, in turn, would have diverted Russia's attention eastward toward Asia, where a clash between Russia and England might have followed. In Talleyrand's mind was a complex balance-of-power arrangement that might have ensured to France the dominant role for decades to come. Perhaps it was sheer bad judgment that led the emperor to reject Talleyrand's advice; or perhaps it was Napoleon's excessive ambition and self-esteem. No man who believed so intensely in his star was likely to think that his star would lead him no farther than the Rhine. If Napoleon had some of the sense of balance and moderation so typical of the classical age, he also possessed the instincts of a gambler, an opportunist, a fatalist, unwilling to let himself be bound by a blueprint of long-range goals.

If Napoleon had really wanted peaceful coexistence within a balance-of-power system, he might have achieved it on two other occasions as well. The first was in 1802, after the English had agreed to peace. The English archives offer considerable evidence that both public and government were ready to try "appeasement," to let France keep the so-called natural frontiers, if Napoleon in turn would offer some guarantees of good behavior. Instead, the First Consul blandly proceeded to intrigue in the affairs of the rest of Europe and to disclose his further ambitions. A second possible opportunity came toward the end of 1813 when the allied sovereigns offered to let France keep the natural frontiers in return for appropriate commitments. Pride and suspicion combined to make

Napoleon reject the offer. In this case, perhaps he was right to be suspicious; and probably it was as well for France and Europe that the drama was played out to the end.

One of the dogmas of Napoleon's admirers is that the emperor fell victim at last to the "awakening of Europe"—to the masses and nations of the Continent that rose against foreign rule, moved by a spirit of nationalism that they owed in large part to the French example. Napoleon was successful (the legend goes) so long as he fought against kings; he was beaten only when he had to fight against peoples—the peoples whom he had helped to free from their feudal chains. Napoleon himself contributed to this romantic legend after his downfall. It suited his ego to argue that no sovereign or combination of rulers could ever match him; that he could be overwhelmed only by the great elemental force of the masses in motion. Napoleon's critics have offered persuasive evidence that the alleged awakening of Europe in the years before 1814 had scarcely begun. In the long run, French conquests doubtless inspired some growth in national sentiment everywhere; but there was little sign of it by 1814. The soldiers who destroyed Napoleon's system were almost all drill-hardened conscripts rather than volunteers. The crucial factor in Napoleon's defeat was the decision of Europe's monarchs to join forces, to suspend their jealous rivalries and cooperate for the duration of the war. Napoleon himself, by his ruthless and self-centered policies, had forged the iron ring of sovereigns that eventually choked and crushed his ambitions.

To judge the greatness of any eminent man of the past is a hazardous venture. If success and accomplishment are the tests of greatness, it must be admitted that Napoleon put his mark on French and European history to a degree seldom equalled by others and that he left behind a durable myth which, like so many myths, has had powerful effects. No one can question his charismatic qualities, his quick and keen intelligence, his capacity for sustained effort. Yet the flaws in his character were almost startling by contrast, for they were often so petty in nature. Napoleon was convinced that, as a man of destiny, he stood above any law; that he was not bound by ordinary moral standards in either his political or his personal life. His career was marked by a cynical realism, by a conviction that the end justifies the means. Was the end the greatness of France, the good of Europe, or the personal glory of Napoleon? Selfish and high-minded motives can rarely be disentangled in any man. One may best conclude with the perceptive phrase of Tocqueville: Napoleon Bonaparte was as great as a man can be without virtue.

CHAPTER **8**

# *The Varieties of History,*
# *1760–1814*

In one of Agatha Christie's whodunits, a disillusioned young lady fresh from her first year in college sagely remarks: "Such a lot of things seem to me such rot. History, for instance. Why it's quite different out of different books." Her comment represents a long step toward historical understanding. Sometimes, as J. H. Hexter reminds us, "a loss of certainty stands at the beginning of knowledge." If written history is viewed not as a cut-and-dried series of indisputable "facts" but rather as a highly controversial set of judgments about past events, then its varied character can be taken as a matter of course, and history becomes (as Pieter Geyl once put it) "an argument without end." The purpose of this chapter, and of similar chapters terminating each section of this book, is to provide some guideposts through the historiographical maze.[1] The focus will be on changes in interpretation over time, and on certain issues that have recently provoked controversy.

The Great Revolution—its causes, course, and consequences—has been analyzed and dissected more often and more passionately than any other phase of French history. Two centuries of these changing historical fashions have been surveyed by Alice Gérard in her essay *La révolution française: mythes et interprétations, 1789–1970,* and by William Doyle in *Origins of the French Revolution.* As early as the 1820's young liberal historians were beginning to refurbish

---

[1] For the convenience of American readers, books that have been translated will be cited in the English-language version.

the image of the revolution as a constructive episode; by the 1840's Louis Blanc, Lamartine, and Michelet were extolling some of its leaders as heroes and martyrs. Alexis de Tocqueville in 1856 published one of the most influential and enduring of all interpretations; his essay *The Old Regime and the Revolution* argued that the revolution, instead of changing the course of French history, served to hasten and complete the process of building centralized power already begun by the monarchy. Tocqueville regretted the aristocracy's failure to block this process, and the decay of traditional local institutions that, in his opinion, might have permitted France to move toward democracy without sliding into tyranny. Subtle and complex, Tocqueville's analysis has offered subsequent scholars of various political colors the opportunity to draw from it the ideas that will strengthen their separate causes. Nineteenth-century conservatives were more attracted to Thomas Carlyle's or Hippolyte Taine's version of events. Carlyle's *French Revolution* (1837) implanted in the minds of generations of Englishmen the legend of the revolution as a long reign of terror, a bloodthirsty orgy. Taine, in his *Origines de la France contemporaine* (1878–84) took a similar view; the revolution was an adventure in anarchy and criminal subversion, ". . . the insurrection of donkeys and horses against men, under the leadership of monkeys with parrots' tongues."

By the 1880's the revolution's defenders were firmly established in power and set out to challenge Taine by shaping a quasi-official version of the great upheaval. Alphonse Aulard's *Histoire politique de la révolution française* (1901) was a sober, carefully documented analysis that glorified the moderate republicans of the early revolutionary years and elevated Danton to the role of hero. The great Socialist tribune Jean Jaurès promptly countered with a more populist version, inspired, he said, by Marx and Michelet. His *Histoire socialiste de la révolution française* (1901–1904) gave lyrical expression to his faith in the wisdom of the masses.

After the First World War Aulard's disciple, Albert Mathiez, broke with his mentor on the ground that Aulard's interpretation was both too narrowly political and too bourgeois. Mathiez developed his own more radical and quasi-Marxian version, shifting the emphasis to class conflict, attacking Danton as a corrupt bourgeois opportunist, and substituting a new hero—Robespierre. His three-volume synthesis *La révolution française* appeared in 1922–27, and from it flowed the mainstream of French revolutionary historiography for the next generation. The dominant figure in the Mathiez succession was Georges Lefebvre, whose *The French Revolution* and *The Coming of the French Revolution* portrayed the upheaval as "the culmination of a long social and economic development which has made the bourgeoisie the masters of the world." Lefebvre ordered and simplified the complexity and confusion of the period through the use of Marxian class analysis. The aristocracy, he contended, started it all by a concerted challenge to royal absolutism; the bourgeoisie then moved in to take control of events and to shape the future in its own interests. To achieve its aim, the bourgeoisie took advantage of peasant and urban mass discontent. The peasantry, like the bourgeoisie, was eager to throw off the shackles of feudalism, and its more prosperous stratum shared with the bourgeoisie the spoils of victory. The urban masses, exploited but not yet class-conscious, provided the physical force the bourgeoisie needed to overthrow the old regime. Lefebvre's disciples, led by Albert Soboul, have carried forward his work without altering the basic schema (as in Soboul's *The French Revolution, 1787–1799* and *Comprendre la révolution*).

Although the Lefebvre version attained a kind of orthodoxy from the 1930's onward, it never attained a total monopoly, and it has been sharply challenged in recent decades. Royalist historians such as Pierre Gaxotte continued the Taine tradition; American liberal scholars like Crane Brinton and Robert R. Palmer wrote in the spirit of Tocqueville, insofar as they shared the latter's balanced judgments and urbane skepticism. But the real confrontation with the Lefebvre school came from London, where Alfred Cobban and his followers challenged the champions of orthodoxy. In a provocative series of essays (notably *The Social Interpretation of the French Revolution*), Cobban urged historians to "escape from the rigid patterns of system-makers who have deduced their history from their theories." The revolution, he asserted, was not bourgeois either in its leadership or in its outcome. Coherent classes of the modern sort, conscious of some sort of class interest, simply did not exist at the time. Instead of a "revolutionary bourgeoisie," there was only a loose collection of disparate middle classes. They were not incipient capitalists breaking the shackles of feudalism, for feudalism (except for a few vestiges) no longer existed in 1789. If any group led and profited by the revolution, it was a stratum of office-holders and lawyers who desired both reform and power. Cobban's work, buttressed by monographs published by some of his students and by other English or American scholars, has been paralleled in France by the revisionist writings of François Furet. His *Interpreting the French Revolution* and Furet's and Denis Richet's *The French Revolution* identify the revolutionary leadership as an innovating segment of the ruling elites, drawn from both the aristocracy and the precapitalist bourgeoisie of the time.

❖❖❖❖❖❖❖❖❖❖❖❖❖❖

Interpretations of the crisis of the old regime are intertwined with the broader question of the revolution's nature. Conservatives from Taine to Gaxotte, confronted by the question "Was this revolution really necessary?," have usually answered with a vigorous negative and have stressed the role of subversive ideas in undermining a social and political order that needed to be reformed rather than destroyed. Taine's was the classic statement of this view. More recently, royalist historians like Gaxotte and Jacques Bainville have argued that the eighteenth-century monarchy could have reformed itself had it not become infected with "political Fénélonism" (i.e., the limited-monarchy ideas of the old aristocracy). They seek to rehabilitate Louis XV as an intelligent, farsighted statesman who was hamstrung by vested interests, misunderstood by doctrinaires, and weakened by his own self-doubts.

Republican historians, on the other hand, have traditionally emphasized conditions rather than ideas as the principal causes of the revolution, and have pictured the old regime as a decrepit and venal system headed by cynical or incompetent despots. They have scoffed at the monarchists' conspiracy theory and have, on the whole, defended the *philosophes* as constructive and innovative thinkers. In recent decades, however, the outworn debate over the relative importance of conditions versus ideas has given way to more serious inquiries into social structure, economic trends, the royal bureaucracy's role as a force for reform, and the precise impact of Enlightenment ideas.

For the Lefebvre school, the key factor was the rise of a capitalist bourgeoisie, and its adoption of Enlightenment slogans as weapons to use against the privileged aristocracy. Meanwhile the aristocracy was digging in behind the barriers of feudal privilege, in an effort to block both bourgeois ambitions and the centralizing reforms of the king's advisers. Lefebvre's *Coming of the French Revolution* gave wide currency to the thesis that an "aristocratic revolution" against the monarchy in 1787–89 preceded and paved the way for the bourgeois revolution. Again, the most direct challenge to this view has come from Alfred Cobban and François Furet, with support from some American historians. George V. Taylor, for example, has demonstrated that if a bourgeoisie existed in prerevolutionary France, it was nothing like a modern capitalist class; and Elizabeth L. Eisenstein has raised serious questions about the thesis of an "aristocratic revolution" just before 1789.

Another long-disputed aspect of the prerevolutionary era has to do with economic conditions. Were Frenchmen prosperous or miserable? Was their lot improving or growing worse? Michelet's was the classic statement of the thesis that increasing misery caused the revolution; Tocqueville first argued the contrary view that France's prosperity, rather, contributed to the great upheaval. The most important scholarly contribution to this debate has been made by C.-E. Labrousse: *Esquisse du mouvement des prix et des revenus en France au XVIIIe siècle*. His study of eighteenth-century price trends shows a significant long-term rise, reflecting real economic growth. But it also reveals a cyclical pattern of boom and slump, with bad harvests setting off periodic depressions; and it shows that the decade preceding 1789 was one of those periods of slump. The Labrousse schema has drawn some criticism on grounds of methodology, but it has now been generally accepted.

The nature and appeal of Enlightenment ideas continue to be subjects of some controversy. From the time of Edmund Burke to our own day, conservatives have disparaged the *philosophes* as fuzzy-minded ideologues whose taste for abstract speculation made them ignore practical reality. Marxists, on the other hand, have condemned most of them as mouthpieces of the rising bourgeoisie, while singling out for praise a few advanced thinkers who anticipated socialism. Even the liberal center has produced its critics: Carl Becker, in *The Heavenly City of the Eighteenth-Century Philosophers*, argued that the men of the Enlightenment were in fact "true believers" rather than coolly objective men of reason, and that they were blind to their own myth-building proclivities. J. L. Talmon, in *The Origins of Totalitarian Democracy*, went still further, branding Rousseau as the fountainhead of left-wing totalitarian doctrines which would inspire tyrants from Robespierre to Stalin. The counterattack in defense of the Enlightenment has been led by Peter Gay, in *The Party of Humanity* and *The Enlightenment: An Interpretation*. Gay extols the eighteenth-century thinkers as pioneers who challenged outworn ideas and opened the way to modernity in the western world.

On the events of the revolutionary decade 1789–99, most general syntheses fall into either the Lefebvre or the Cobban pattern. To a lesser degree, the same is true of most specialized monographs, whose number is legion. An interesting exception is Lynn Hunt's *Politics, Culture, and Class in the French Revolution*, which draws upon current techniques of literary criticism and insights from the social sciences to analyze the use of rhetoric and symbols by the revolutionary leaders, and which investigates the social origins of the new elite in several provincial cities. A number of probing studies of the rival political factions and leaders (notably the Girondins and the Jacobins) have appeared recently; several of them are listed at the end of this chapter. One novelty of late has been the attention given to the revolutionary masses, notably by such scholars as Richard Cobb, Albert Soboul, and George Rudé. Soboul's major work, *The Parisian Sans-Culottes and the French Revolution*, has drawn special attention. He argues that these militant activists upon whom Robespierre and the Jacobins based their power constituted neither a mindless mob nor a class-conscious proletariat.

Rather, they were a phenomenon of the pre-industrial age, a mélange of craftsmen, shopkeepers, and domestic servants, who combined a peculiar blend of political radicalism and economic conservatism. Their role, in Soboul's eyes, was nevertheless progressive; they can be seen as an incipient proletariat. His argument thus remains within the Marxian canon. Cobb's studies of what might be called the underclass during the revolutionary years belong to no canon but his own; he brings to life, in such works as *The Police and the People* and *Reactions to the French Revolution*, the impact of the upheaval on individual Frenchmen and Frenchwomen on the fringes of society.

The period of the Directory (1795–99) has long been neglected by historians, who have seen it as an unsavory interlude between the Terror and Napoleon. Recently, however, it has begun to attract some attention and a bit more sympathy. Notable studies include Martyn Lyons's *France Under the Directory*, and a volume of essays edited by Gwynne Lewis and Colin Lucas: *Beyond the Terror*.

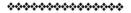

No man in history has been so much written about as Napoleon; someone has recently estimated the number of books on the man and his times at a quarter of a million. Few men, furthermore, have drawn such bitter denunciations or such uncritical praise. The voluminous literature on the subject has been surveyed by Pieter Geyl in his *Napoleon, For and Against*—a book based on lectures the Dutch historian gave to his fellow inmates in a Nazi concentration camp. The differences in viewpoint range over almost every aspect of Napoleon's career: his stature as a military commander, his role as a domestic reformer, his claim to be "the creator of French industry," his hold on French public affections, and so on. But the central foci of dispute are two: Was Napoleon the consolidator of the revolution or its destroyer? Were his expansionist ambitions responsible for the long war that eventually wrecked his empire, or was he merely attempting to hold the legitimate gains won by his predecessors?

The debate over the first issue is probably a futile one, since it revolves in part around semantic difficulties. His detractors cannot deny that Napoleon carried to completion many of the administrative and legal reforms begun by the Convention; his admirers cannot deny that civil liberties were drastically curtailed in this authoritarian police state. The ambiguity lived on in the Bonapartist tradition of the nineteenth century; Bonapartism sometimes seemed to belong on the left, sometimes on the right, and usually it managed to draw considerable support from both extremes.

On the foreign policy issue, the classic defense of Napoleon is that of Albert Sorel in his *L'Europe et la révolution française*. Sorel contended that Bonaparte inherited his policy from the old monarchy, the Convention, and the Directory; that, like any patriotic Frenchman, he considered it his mission to attain and preserve France's "natural frontiers"; and that the only way to protect those frontiers against English greed and incomprehension was by setting up a chain of buffer states beyond the Rhine and the Alps. Critics like Raymond Guyot, on the other hand, charge Napoleon with willfully ignoring the Directory's orders to take no territory beyond the natural frontiers except for bargaining purposes; they hold that he dragged the country at once into a campaign of unlimited conquest (*Le Directoire et la paix de l'Europe*). A middle category of historians follows the lead of Adolphe Thiers (*Histoire du consulat et de l'empire*) who held that Napoleon's aims were honest and defensible until 1805, at which time he made a crucial error by rejecting Talleyrand's policy of restraint and conciliation with Austria.

Among recent biographies of Napoleon, Vincent Cronin's *Napoleon Bonaparte* is compulsively readable; it is an unblushing defense of the emperor, recognizing his human flaws but asserting his greatness as ruler, soldier, and man. New life has recently been breathed into the serious study of the Napoleonic years by the work of Louis Bergeron—notably in his two-volume work *L'épisode napoléonien 1799–1815*.

## A SELECTIVE LIST OF READINGS ABOUT FRANCE 1750–1814

Aulard, Alphonse. *Histoire politique de la révolution française*. 4 vol. Paris: Colin, 1901.
Baker, Keith M. *Condorcet*. Chicago: University of Chicago Press, 1975.
Becker, Carl. *The Heavenly City of the Eighteenth-Century Philosophers*. New Haven: Yale University Press, 1932.
Behrens, C. B. A. *The Ancien Regime*. New York: Harcourt, 1967.
Bergeron, Louis. *L'épisode napoléonien*. Paris: Seuil, 1972.
Bosher, J. F. *French Finances, 1770–1795*. New York: Cambridge University Press, 1970.
Brinton, Crane. *A Decade of Revolution, 1789–1799*. New York: Harper, 1934.
Cobb, Richard. *The Police and the People: French Popular Protest, 1789–1820*. New York: Oxford University Press, 1970.
Cobb, Richard. *Reactions to the French Revolution*. New York: Oxford University Press, 1972.
Cobban, Alfred. *The Social Interpretation of the French Revolution*. Cambridge: Cambridge University Press, 1964.
Cronin, Vincent. *Napoleon Bonaparte, an Intimate Biography*. New York: Morrow, 1971.

Darnton, Robert. *The Literary Underground of the Old Regime.* Cambridge: Harvard University Press, 1982.

Doyle, William. *Origins of the French Revolution.* New York: Oxford University Press, 1980.

Eisenstein, Elizabeth L. "Who Intervened in 1788? A Commentary on The Coming of the French Revolution," *American Historical Review,* LXXI (1965), 77–103.

Forrest, Alan. *The French Revolution and the Poor.* New York: St. Martin's Press, 1981.

Furet, François. *Interpreting the French Revolution.* New York: Cambridge University Press, 1981.

Furet, François, and Denis Richet. *The French Revolution.* New York: Macmillan, 1970.

Gay, Peter. *The Party of Humanity.* New York: Knopf, 1964.

Gay, Peter, *The Enlightenment: An Interpretation.* New York: Knopf, 1966–1969.

Gérard, Alice. *La révolution française: mythes et interprétations, 1789–1970.* Paris: Flammarion, 1970.

Geyl, Pieter. *Napoleon: For and Against.* New Haven: Yale University Press, 1949.

Goubert, Pierre. *L'ancien régime.* Paris: Colin, 1969.

Guyot, Raymond. *Le Directoire et la paix de l'Europe.* Paris: Alcan, 1911.

Hampson, Norman. *A Social History of the French Revolution.* Toronto: University of Toronto Press, 1963.

Hufton, Olwen H. *The Poor of Eighteenth-Century France.* Oxford: Oxford University Press, 1974.

Hunt, Lynn. *Politics, Culture, and Class in the French Revolution.* Berkeley: University of California Press, 1984.

Jaurès, Jean. *Histoire socialiste de la révolution française,* rev. ed. 8 vols. Paris: Ed. de l'Humanité, 1922–1924.

Kaplan, Steven L. *Bread, Politics, and Political Economy in the Reign of Louis XV.* The Hague: Nijhoff, 1976.

Kennedy, Michael L. *The Jacobin Clubs in the French Revolution: The First Years.* Princeton: Princeton University Press, 1982.

Labrousse, Ernest. *Esquisse du mouvement des prix et des revenus en France au XVIIIe siècle.* 2 vol. Paris: Dalloz, 1933.

Lefebvre, Georges. *The Coming of the French Revolution, 1789.* Princeton: Princeton University Press, 1947.

Lefebvre, Georges. *The French Revolution.* London: Routledge & Kegan Paul, 1962–1964.

Lewis, Gwynne, and Colin Lucas (eds.) *Beyond the Terror.* Cambridge: Cambridge University Press, 1983.

Lucas, Colin. *The Structure of the Terror: The Example of Javogues and the Loire.* London: Oxford University Press, 1973.

Lyons, Martyn. *France Under the Directory.* New York: Cambridge University Press, 1975.

Mathiez, Albert. *La révolution française.* Paris: Colin, 1922–1927.

Mousnier, Roland. *The Institutions of France Under the Absolute Monarchy, 1598–1789*. Chicago: University of Chicago Press, 1979–1984.

Palmer, Robert R. *The Age of the Democratic Revolution*. Princeton: Princeton University Press, 1959–1964.

Patrick, Alison. *The Men of the First French Republic*. Baltimore: Johns Hopkins University Press, 1972.

Rudé, George. *The Crowd in the French Revolution*. Oxford: Clarendon Press, 1959.

Soboul, Albert. *The Parisian Sans-Culottes and the French Revolution*. Oxford: Clarendon Press, 1964.

Soboul, Albert. *The French Revolution 1787–1799*. New York: Vintage, 1975.

Soboul, Albert. *Comprendre la révolution*. Paris: Maspero, 1981.

Sorel, Albert. *L'Europe et la révolution française*. 8 vols. Paris: Plon, 1885–1904.

Sydenham, M. J. *The Girondins*. London: Athlone, 1961.

Taine, Hippolyte. *Les origines de la France contemporaine*. 4 vol. Paris: Hachette, 1875–1893.

Talmon, J. L. *The Origins of Totalitarian Democracy*. London: Secker and Warburg, 1952.

Taylor, George V. "Noncapitalist Wealth and the Origins of the French Revolution," *American Historical Review*, LXXII (1967), 469–496.

Thiers, Adolphe. *Histoire du consulat et de l'empire*. 21 vols. Paris: Paulin, 1845–1875.

Tilly, Charles. *The Vendée*. New York: Wiley, 1967.

Tocqueville, Alexis de. *The Old Regime and the French Revolution*. New York: Doubleday, 1955.

Vovelle, Michel. *La mentalité révolutionnaire: société et mentalités sous la Révolution française*. Paris: Ed. sociales, 1985.

# II
# FRANCE IN SEARCH OF
# A NEW EQUILIBRIUM
## 1814–1870

ENGLAND

ENGLISH CHANNEL

HOLY ROMAN EMPIRE

Rhine R.

PAS-DE-CALAIS

NORD

SOMME

SEINE-INFÉRIEURE

AISNE

ARDENNES

OISE

MOSELLE

MANCHE

CALVADOS

EURE

Paris

MARNE

MEUSE

MEURTHE

BAS-RHIN

ORNE

SEINE-ET-OISE

SEINE-ET-MARNE

FINISTÈRE

CÔTES-DU-NORD

EURE-ET-LOIR

AUBE

HAUTE-MARNE

VOSGES

HAUTE-SAÔNE

HAUT-RHIN

ILLE-ET-VILAINE

MAYENNE

SARTHE

LOIR-ET-CHER

LOIRET

YONNE

MORBIHAN

CÔTE-D'OR

DOUBS

SWISS CONFEDERATION

MAINE-ET-LOIRE

INDRE-ET-LOIRE

NIÈVRE

SAÔNE-ET-LOIRE

JURA

LOIRE-INFÉRIEURE

CHER

Seine R.

Loire R.

VENDÉE

DEUX-SÈVRES

VIENNE

INDRE

ALLIER

AIN

HAUTE SAVOIE (1860)

ATLANTIC

CHARENTE-INFÉRIEURE

HAUTE-VIENNE

CREUSE

PUY-DE-DÔME

RHÔNE

Lyon

SAVOIE (1860)

K. OF SARDINIA

OCEAN

CHARENTE

CORRÈZE

LOIRE

ISÈRE

GIRONDE

Bordeaux

DORDOGNE

CANTAL

HAUTE-LOIRE

DRÔME

HAUTES-ALPES

LOT-ET-GARONNE

LOT

AVEYRON

LOZÈRE

ARDÈCHE

Rhône R.

BASSES-ALPES

ALPES-MARITIMES (1860)

LANDES

GERS

TARN-ET-GARONNE

TARN

GARD

VAUCLUSE

BOUCHES-DU-RHÔNE

VAR

Garonne R.

HAUTE-GARONNE

HÉRAULT

Marseille

BASSES-PYRÉNÉES

HAUTES-PYRÉNÉES

ARIÈGE

AUDE

SPAIN

PYRÉNÉES-ORIENTALES

MEDITERRANEAN SEA

CORSE

FRANCE IN THE
NINETEENTH CENTURY

# CHAPTER 9

# The Bourbon Experiment,
# 1814–1830

Louis XVIII has not been restored to the throne of his ancestors: he has simply ascended the throne of Bonaparte.

JOSEPH DE MAISTRE

Restoration periods often strike posterity as tame and colorless. They usually follow upon an era of profound revolution or of prolonged war, and they naturally suffer by contrast. Efforts to return to normalcy, to recover a lost stability and to assure order, are not likely to be exciting. Yet if they are less spectacular than times of upheaval, they are sometimes equally significant in the development of a nation.

French history from 1814 to 1848 is a case in point. Preceded and followed by major revolutions and by dramatic experiments in one-man leadership, that generation seems a dull and prosaic one. Yet specialists in the era are agreed that few periods have been of greater formative influence in the shaping of modern France; some of them even consider that influence more profound than the impact of the revolutionary epoch itself. This was a time of ferment—of intense intellectual and literary activity, of unprecedented richness in social theorizing, of fundamental economic change. It was a time of experimentation, too; France in these years tried out a kind of proto-parliamentary system of government and grew so accustomed to it that the parliamentary principle became an almost permanent fixture. It was an era marked by the attempt to find a stable compromise combining the principles of the old bureaucratic monarchy, the surviving feudal-aristocratic tradition, and the ideals of the revolution. The historian's problem is to judge how nearly the compromisers approached success, and why in the end they failed to create a durable constitutional monarchy.

When the Bourbons returned from almost a quarter-century of exile, they found a France that had been profoundly altered. A new social structure had replaced the old semifeudal system; equality of status had established itself in French law and mores. Juridically at least, special privilege survived only for the male sex, as the Napoleonic code enshrined "the rights of man and the wrongs of woman." True, Napoleon had begun to infringe the new equality by creating his own aristocracy, which clung to its titles after 1814. But these new nobles, like the old, possessed no special juridical status; before the law, all men were equal citizens.

The revolution had brought, too, a considerable redistribution of wealth through the sale of much large landed property. But legend has greatly exaggerated the extent of the social revolution involved. Land transfers did not change France overnight from a nation of large estates to one of small-owners. That process had been proceeding gradually for centuries; the revolution speeded it up, but left it still unfinished. Many small-owners after 1789 got clearer title to the land they already possessed and added more as well. But the great bulk of poorer peasants had no capital with which to make even a down payment on "aristo" land and, in any case, could not hope to bid on land that was not within walking distance of their cottages. Most of the transferred land went to the already well-to-do peasant minority or to the bourgeoisie, who became absentee owners in most cases, and who arranged to have the land worked by small-renters or *métayers* (sharecroppers). Furthermore, a considerable number of large estates survived the revolutionary epoch pretty much intact. Many nobles kept their land by refusing to emigrate; some émigrés found devious means to retain their property or got it back by serving Napoleon; some of the church lands were sold in large undivided tracts. The shift toward rural democracy was therefore relative; the French agricultural structure remained exceptionally varied through the nineteenth century.

A more fundamental change was the highly centralized and relatively efficient administrative structure with which Napoleon had endowed the country. There was some irony in the fact that the revolution had accomplished in this sphere what the kings of France had been groping to achieve for centuries. Even more ironic was the fact that the revolutionists had done it rather in spite of themselves, for their initial program had aimed at decentralized local democracy. The Jacobin leaders had felt it necessary in time of national emergency to create a rigid structure of centralized control, and this, in turn, had been consolidated by Napoleon. New or remodelled administrative agencies in Paris—the Council of State and the Inspectorate of Finance, for example—also proved to be both effective and durable.

France possessed, too, a new and sounder structure of public finance. Napoleon handed on to the Bourbons the privately owned and operated Bank of

France, with control over the nation's credit system. With the bankers rather than the bureaucrats or the politicians in control, a debased or inflated currency was a much less likely prospect. A more curious heritage was the nation's financial soundness despite the drain of a twenty year's war. Much of the old public debt incurred by the monarchy had been liquidated by the inflation of the 1790's, and Napoleon managed to fight his wars without doing very much borrowing. Although the British finally triumphed, they emerged from the war with a per capita public debt twenty times as heavy as that of defeated France.

Still another change for the returning Bourbons was the new relationship between church and state. The clergy had been transmuted from a privileged corporation into a special branch of the bureaucracy, with its salaries paid by the state; and Catholicism now enjoyed a somewhat reduced status as the religion of a majority of Frenchmen, not of all loyal subjects. Church domination of education had also been reduced, though by no means broken. Napoleon's network of *lycées* provided for only a small proportion of young Frenchmen; primary education remained largely in the hands of the church. Finally, the revolutionary era had implanted a tradition now fairly well rooted in the public consciousness— that some sort of elected assembly was a normal and necessary part of the governmental machinery. Although Napoleon had stripped his legislature of most of its power, he had retained the principle of a representative body within his authoritarian system.

If Louis XVIII had felt completely free to follow his basic impulses, perhaps he would have begun his reign by wiping out all of these changes produced by the revolutionary whirlwind. Historians have disagreed sharply about the real character and motives of this complex monarch. For some of them, he was the personification of moderation and statesmanship, the prince who had absorbed the spirit of English institutions during his long exile, and who now set out to reconcile all Frenchmen. For others, he was a narrow and bigoted old man who chose the path of compromise only when he was pushed onto it by necessity. His ministers, according to this theory, made the key decisions of the reign, and Louis in the end got the credit for their wisdom. It is probably true that Louis had developed no real taste for English constitutional monarchy; but at least he was shrewd enough to recognize that, in the current state of France and Europe, an attempt to restore the old order might mean trouble. Whether he was really wiser and more flexible than his late brother Louis XVI is difficult to say; perhaps he was merely older and more cynical. When he failed to get his way, he found it easy to divert himself through other pastimes: gourmandizing, for example, and the platonic company of royal favorites.

Not all of the resurgent royalists were so reconciled to compromise. A faction of extremists, whom their critics called "ultra-royalists," was determined to root out the reforms of the revolutionary epoch and to purge the administration of those who had served the Corsican. Some of the ultra-royalist leaders were returned émigrés; but the faction was made up in large part of the lesser backwoods aristocracy, most of whom had stayed in France throughout the revolutionary epoch. Among them were the organizers of the Chevaliers de la Foi, who had done so much to bring about the restoration. These rural nobles were militant and uncompromising men, tinged by a strain of real fanaticism; they held that any compromise with evil (i.e., the revolution) would be a betrayal of principles. Their symbol and hope was the king's younger brother, the Comte d'Artois. In prerevolutionary days Artois had been a court playboy of scandalous reputation; in his new incarnation he was a fervent and almost blue-nosed religious fanatic. Artois's conversion was not unique, for exile had brought many émigrés back to the church. The eighteenth-century court had been touched by skepticism, even cynicism; the nineteenth century was to bring a new interpenetration of royalism and Catholicism. If there was any Bourbon who resisted the trend and clung to the skeptical eighteenth-century tradition, it was Louis XVIII himself.

Although Louis owed his restoration in part to ultra-royalist propaganda activities, he owed it also to the allied powers and to that large group of Napoleonic peers and bureaucrats that had rallied to the Bourbon cause as the Empire collapsed. His initial policies were designed to satisfy all three groups but to let none of them get dominant influence. Instead of embarking on a major purge of Napoleonic officials, he maintained most of them in their posts. "Union and forgetfulness" was his motto. On the other hand, he brusquely rejected a constitution hastily drafted in April, 1814, by Napoleon's Senate and Corps Législatif; for that constitution was a bald attempt to tie his hands and to perpetuate the Napoleonic legislators in office. He promulgated instead a kind of pseudo-constitution called the Charter, which restored the principle of divine right but absorbed many of the revolutionary changes. His new bicameral legislature was granted more power than the Napoleonic legislative bodies had possessed; and its upper house, the Chamber of Peers, was packed not with loyal ultras but with Napoleonic officials who had climbed aboard the Bourbon bandwagon. It was not surprising that a man of ultra spirit like de Maistre should remark acidly that Louis had not restored the Bourbon throne but had merely taken over that of Bonaparte.

But if some of the new king's actions infuriated the ultras, other decisions alienated the rest of the country. Thousands of army officers were brusquely retired on half-pay, and the crack regiments of the imperial guard were scattered among isolated provincial garrisons. Meanwhile, many émigrés demanded and got their old officers' commissions with appropriate promotions for seniority; almost four hundred new generals were created within a year. A series of public ceremonies in memory of victims of the revolution gave Paris a kind of permanent funereal air. There were indications that the king intended to restore the church to its old privileged role. Most disastrous of all, taxes were increased until they exceeded the exactions of Napoleon.

Before the Bourbons had been back in office for a year, unrest was so general that rumors of it began to reach the exiled emperor on his bucolic Mediterranean island. Bad British puns about Napoleon's lack of Elba-room had some basis in fact. The emperor found it hard to curb his energies; and he was disturbed also at reports that he might be banished to a still more distant island as a security measure. This combination of circumstances suggested to him that his star was rising once more and that destiny called on him to follow it in one last adventure. With a handful of followers, he evaded British surveillance and landed on the southern coast of France in March, 1815. Within three weeks he was in Paris, acclaimed by a hysterical crowd; all along the route northward, cities had opened their gates to him, troops sent to block his progress had fallen to their knees before him. Not a drop of blood had been shed in defense of the Bourbons—not even by Louis himself, despite his brave assertion that he would die if need be on the steps of the throne. Instead, the court had hastily departed to a new place of exile across the border in Ghent.

The failure of the nation to defend the dynasty, and of the dynasty to defend itself, reflected badly on Bourbon rule. On the other hand, the nation's hysterical welcome of Napoleon overlay a generalized mood of antagonism and suspicion. Napoleon sought to appease his opponents by announcing a program of liberal reform that contrasted sharply with his whole authoritarian record. He knew, however, that his only chance of regaining the country's affections would be a quick and cheap military victory. Such a prospect, in the face of an aroused and united Europe, would have seemed dim indeed to anyone without Napoleon's self-confidence; and Waterloo promptly shattered his chimeric dream. Again he was forced to abdicate, and, after a hesitant attempt to escape to America, he threw himself on the mercies of his British captors.

❖❖❖❖❖❖❖❖❖❖❖❖❖

Napoleon's mad gamble left the nation worse divided than before and gravely threatened the Bourbons' chances. For a time, the irritated victors of Waterloo hesitated to permit the dynasty to return; when they finally did so (for lack of a better alternative), Louis XVIII seemed to be the creature of the allied powers rather than the choice of the French nation. Furthermore, the second restoration, unlike the first, was followed by a wave of angry reprisals against those who had served Napoleon. Many high officials had compromised them-

selves during the Hundred Days and could not be forgiven a second time. Alongside the governmental purge, a more spontaneous "White Terror" occurred in
certain monarchist regions; vigilante justice was freely dispensed. Above all, the
episode played into the hands of the ultras, for it seemed to confirm their warnings that a policy of moderation would bring disaster. In the legislative elections
that followed shortly, a large majority of ultras was swept into the Chamber of
Deputies.

At first the king was pleased at this result, for he had feared that the elections
might reveal the monarchy's unpopularity. In an unfortunate phrase, he referred
to the new assembly as the Incomparable Chamber. On second thought, his
pleasure was reduced by his concern at the possible effects of the ultra program;
he chose as ministers, therefore, moderate royalists like the Duc de Richelieu and
Élie Decazes. There followed a year of severe tension between king and ministers
on the one hand and the ultra-dominated Chamber on the other. The ultras
embarked on a drastic purge of regicides, Jacobins, and collaborators of Napoleon.[1] They agitated for the return of all property to the "rightful" owners, and
abolition of Napoleon's administrative bureaucracy, and the return of education
to church control. The long-range goal of the ultras, however, was not merely
the repeal of the past twenty-five years of French history, but the repeal of the
past two centuries. They still clung to the nostalgic program of the eighteenth-
century aristocracy—the destruction of the centralized bureaucratic monarchy in
favor of a quasi-feudal system. If there was anyone who had learned nothing and
forgotten nothing since 1789, it was not the Bourbons but their dedicated ultra
supporters.

The most curious aspect of the contest between ultras and moderates was
the ultras' unprincipled espousal of certain liberal and even democratic ideas.
They argued not only for the adoption of the parliamentary principle of legislative control over the ministry but for universal manhood suffrage as well. Since
the ultras controlled the Chamber of Deputies but not the ministry, their advo-
cacy of the parliamentary principle was at least understandable, if not very
sincere. Their desire to give the vote to the common man may seem more surprising. It rested on the conviction that the "popular classes" were mostly loyal
to their betters and to tradition, while the prosperous bourgeoisie had been tainted
by un-French ideas. The moderate royalists preferred a rigorously limited suffrage, confined to men of high birth or great wealth; and in the end they got their
way. By the system adopted in 1817, the vote was granted to only about ninety
thousand Frenchmen. Some royalist historians contend that the ultras were right
on this point; that universal suffrage would have rooted the monarchy firmly in

---

[1] The dominant figure in a parliamentary committee set up to try suspects was a returned
émigré named Count Robert Joseph MacCarthy, who attained quick but fleeting notoriety as a rabid
hunter of subversives.

the nation. If so, the fatal error of the Bourbons after 1814 (and of the Orleanist dynasty after 1830) was their fearful rejection of votes for the masses. But the hypothesis is not a very convincing one. Although some regions in southern and western France were still intensely royalist in the traditionalist sense, the ultras probably exaggerated the depth and extent of this mass sentiment. Wishful thinking made it easier for them to ignore the changes that had occurred in the outlook of many ordinary Frenchmen since 1789.

Perhaps it was the king's native good sense that led him to resist the ultras; or perhaps it was the rising pressure of the allied powers, whose nervousness increased as the ultras' demands grew louder. Wellington hinted that France might have to be saved from its own folly a third time. The tsar warned bluntly: "Either send your deputies home, or we'll keep all our troops in France." At last, late in 1816 Louis dissolved the Chamber and lent support to his moderate ministers as they manipulated the new elections. This time the moderates swept the major cities and most of northern and eastern France; ultra domination of the Chamber was broken. A few ultra hotheads talked angrily of a palace revolution against "King Voltaire"; but most of them preferred a policy of embittered sniping at Louis and his moderate advisers and warned gloomily that the Jacobins would soon be riding again.

In spite of ultra obstructionism and predictions of disaster, the Bourbon compromise functioned reasonably well from 1816 to 1820. Richelieu and Decazes, the two strong men of the ministry, steered successfully between reactionaries and reviving radicals; if their rule was not glamorous, it was, on the whole, effective. By 1818, thanks to large loans secured from English and Dutch bankers, France's war indemnity was paid and the allied occupation ended. Domestically, there were glimmerings of a true parliamentary system; ministries tended to become more homogeneous and *de facto* Chamber control over the ministry more real. The title *président du conseil des ministres* (the French equivalent of prime minister) came into common use, although Louis disliked it and sought to avoid it. The king had by now fallen almost completely under the influence of his current favorite, Élie Decazes, a shrewd and ambitious politician of bourgeois origin. Louis doted on his "darling Élie" in almost maudlin fashion; when a crisis eventually forced Louis to dismiss Decazes from the ministry, the king not only gave him a dukedom but took down the portrait of Francis I in the royal chambers to make way for that of Decazes. Whether Decazes was merely a scheming opportunist or one of the ablest middle-way politicians of the nineteenth century remains a subject of lively controversy.

The partial revival of representative government after 1814 led to the emergence of loosely organized yet on the whole durable factions or parties for the first time in a generation: ultras on the right, moderates in the center, and liberals on the left. None of these factions was rigid or homogeneous; none could face the test of power without being promptly riven by personal and doctrinal conflict. Such was the fate of the moderates after 1816, and of the ultras during the 1820's; such was eventually to be the destiny of the liberals as well, in 1848.

The ultras, doctrinally speaking, came closest to being homogeneous. Their tendency to divide into two wings derived from differences over means rather than ends; the extremists, the "ultra-ultras," were true fanatics in spirit, while a more restrained element preferred to regain and to hold power by political maneuvering. The ultras' principal theorist was the Vicomte de Bonald; their chief political leader, the Comte de Villèle; their symbol and voice, the eminent literary man Chateaubriand.

The moderate royalists, like most middle groups, were less sharply defined in composition and doctrine. Such theory as they had was worked out by a small group of intellectuals who chose to call themselves the "doctrinaires": the philosopher Royer-Collard and the historian Guizot stood out among them. Royer-Collard as chief doctrinaire spokesman contended that the Charter of 1814 amounted to an ideal compromise, resting as it did on a strong king, a hereditary nobility, and an influential bourgeoisie whose wealthiest leaders were represented in parliament. The whole course of French history, pontificated this Sorbonne professor, had led up to this present pinnacle of perfection. Practical politicians like Decazes paid little attention to the doctrinaires; political realists, they accepted the existing system and adapted themselves to it.

The self-styled "liberal party" on the left was a complex mosaic of elements joined together by little more than common hostility to the Bourbons. Of their three most noted leaders, Lafayette was a republican, Jacques Manuel a Bonapartist, and Benjamin Constant a constitutional monarchist. None of the three possessed the qualities of effective political leadership. The republican element within the liberal faction was small. The very word republican suggested violence and anarchy to most Frenchmen; the republic implied Jacobinism, and "Jacobin" carried with it a flavor like that of "Bolshevik" in our times. The liberal party's ablest spokesmen in this era were the constitutional monarchists, who stood for a parliamentary system like that of Britain, with individual rights protected by the state and suffrage limited to men of property alone. The most curious adherents to the liberal coalition were the Bonapartists. Their presence might seem to suggest a mere marriage of convenience, a hypocritical alliance of authoritarians and libertarians bound together by nothing more than their common desire to destroy the Bourbon compromise. In fact, both Bonapartists and liberals felt a strong common bond when the fundamental achievements of the revolution were thought to be in danger. Not even the harsh experience of the years 1789–1814 had yet fully clarified the fact that within the revolutionary tradition there were potential conflicts as deep as those separating the revolution from its enemies.

Four years sufficed to destroy the Bourbon experiment in moderate autocracy. The moderate politicians faced the same alternatives that normally confront any centrist group possessing no comfortable majority of parliamentary or public support. One possibility was to convert enough adherents of the right and left to give the center a solid majority; a second was to negotiate a firm alliance with either the right or the left. The moderate leaders of 1816–20 achieved neither goal. On the contrary, moderate support in the Chamber of Deputies shrank steadily after 1816; and neither right nor left showed any interest in a compromise alliance with the center.

Some historians have denounced the liberal left as principally responsible for the failure of the moderate experiment. A left-center alliance, they argue, might have opened the way to a gradual reform of the whole system and the emergence in France of a constitutional monarchy as durable as that of Britain. Other critics contend that it was the ultra right, rather, that committed the fatal error. They suggest that a right-center coalition might have developed into a genuine conservative party, the kind of political force that modern France has always lacked, the kind that could have ensured political stability. In fact, it would be hard to choose between the two extreme wings for factiousness and bigotry. This was not to be France's last experience with the distortion of a parliamentary or proto-parliamentary system through the obstructive tactics of large extremist minorities on right and left. A governing center, caught between groups that reject the rules of the system and the possibility of gradualist reform within the system, finds itself driven to abandon rational discussion of political issues and falls back into a position of sheer self-defense. At best, it seeks to defend the system; at worst, it defends nothing more than its personal position. Its shortcomings of leadership are therefore made to appear even worse than they are.

The political trend after 1816 was steadily leftward; at every partial renewal of the Chamber, more liberals gained election. By 1819 it was even possible for a regicide of 1793 to win a seat. The ultras hysterically predicted that a "revolutionary torrent" was about to engulf France; Decazes calmly ignored them and clung to his middle-of-the-road line in the belief that he could gradually convert the milder liberals to his cause. The effort may have been a futile one; perhaps it was the moderates who were on the way to being swallowed up by the left. At any rate, the experiment was wrecked by the assassination, in 1820, of the king's nephew the Duc de Berry. The assassin, a fanatical Bonapartist who had followed his hero to Elba and then to Waterloo, had hoped to wipe out the royal line by killing the last Bourbon still young enough to produce a male heir. He struck too late; seven months later the Duchesse de Berry gave birth to a son, "child of the miracle." What the assassin destroyed instead was the moderate regime. The ultras set out in full cry after Decazes, whose criminal laxity, they alleged, had encouraged the assassin. The king was reluctantly driven to part with Decazes;

the electoral law was altered to weaken the chances of the left; and in the emotional wave that followed the assassination, the ultras swept back into control of the Chamber. They were to govern France, with only a brief interlude, for the entire decade.

One immediate result of the ultras' triumph was a turn to outright subversion on the part of the left. A series of underground plots culminated in the formation of a secret society called the Carbonari, whose name and ritual were borrowed from Italy. But the Carbonari lacked both skilled leadership and mass support. Its members were mostly intellectuals and army noncommissioned officers; it put down almost no roots among the city workers or the common soldiers. A successful uprising might have brought workers and soldiers to the banner of revolution; but the attempts of the Carbonari were ill-planned and futile affairs that gave rise to little more than durable legend. The effect, in fact, was negative; for subversion gave the government an added excuse for repression. The press was subjected to more severe controls and censorship; a dozen Sorbonne professors were dismissed, and a priest was installed as rector of the university. At the same time a stronger foreign-policy line was adopted, partly as a device to weaken the left by competing with the tradition of Napoleonic glory. The device succeeded; a French military expedition into Spain in 1823, designed to restore the Spanish king's full authority which had been undermined by a liberal revolt, culminated in glorious success rather than the disaster that had been predicted by the liberals. The army, mollified by the prestige and promotions that came out of the Spanish affair, became reconciled to ultra rule. For the rest of the decade the liberals had to abandon their plots in favor of a renewed effort at peaceful opposition.

To cap their Spanish success, the ultras in 1824 achieved their greatest electoral victory since 1816; the liberal opposition was reduced from 110 seats to 20. A few months later the last feeble barrier to their complete triumph was cleared away when Louis XVIII at last expired. The aged king had confined himself to a largely inactive role since 1820, seeking diversion in the company of the new royal favorite, Madame du Cayla, an amateur agent of the ultras. He had made no serious attempt to hamper the ultra leaders; but the latter were sure to feel themselves on more solid ground once the Comte d'Artois was elevated to the throne as Charles X. Yet within six years both the ultras and the dynasty itself were to find themselves dislodged from power—and largely through their own mistakes.

✦✦✦✦✦✦✦✦✦✦✦✦✦✦

Charles X has been roughly handled by historians for more than a century, and has gone down in legend as a kind of paragon of bigoted ineptitude. In fact, he possessed almost all of the qualities of kingship except good judgment. There was much to be said for his character and his general comportment; certainly he looked and acted like a king, far more so than his obese and almost immobile predecessor. Nor did he dictate a sharp and sudden shift in policy, or even in the tone of politics, as soon as he took the throne. Yet several incidents early in the new reign seemed to imply a sharp thrust toward reaction and sufficed to arouse the mixed fears and hopes of the left.

One such incident, unimportant except for its symbolic character, was the new king's coronation at Reims. This five-hour ceremony of medieval splendor, climaxed by the anointment of the new sovereign with holy oil miraculously preserved from the revolutionary despoilers, seemed to suggest a will to return to the old regime in both form and spirit. More serious was a series of laws adopted by the Chamber in 1824–25—laws that could easily be viewed by suspicious Frenchmen as inspired by a mood of black reaction. The most notorious of these was a measure to indemnify the émigrés for the loss of their property during the revolution. To pay for the scheme, Finance Minister Villèle worked out a conversion of five per cent government bonds to a lower rate of interest and used the savings to issue new bonds which were handed over to the émigrés in question. The measure produced a bitterly partisan debate in parliament and in the press. The opposition charged that honest bourgeois bondholders were to be victimized for the benefit of a class that had deserted the country in time of crisis; the ultras replied that the émigrés' sole crime had been to run away from the guillotine. Only in later retrospect was it possible to see that the law labelled "the émigrés' billion" (the figure was a considerable exaggeration) was in fact a sensible compromise of a nagging issue. After 1825 there was no more talk of restoring the lost property itself; its new owners at last possessed safe title. The law thus consolidated, at rather low cost, one more important aspect of the revolutionary reforms.

There were other parts of the ultra program that were far less defensible. Such, for example, was a law to punish sacrilegious acts in churches by long imprisonment or even death—a law that an ultra-royalist political theorist, the Vicomte de Bonald, defended with the curious argument that the death penalty was eminently fair because it would send accused persons before the natural judge of sacrilegious acts. The law produced bitter resentment, yet it was never enforced; its only victim, remarks one historian, was the regime. Equally unwise was a severe press law that virtually hamstrung the publishers of newpapers, pamphlets, and circulars—a bill that one minister described, with monumental ineptitude, as "a law of justice and love." Finally, there was a bill to restore (in aristocratic families only) the prerevolutionary rule of primogeniture in the inheritance of landed property. In fact, the measure's effects would have been slight even if it had not been rejected by the Chamber of Peers. But susceptible

Frenchmen feared that it implied a continuing effort to restore the old regime by destroying the revolutionary principle of legal equality.

Not all of the ultras' program after 1824 was so bigoted and dangerous as the left asserted it to be. Neither did the program represent a brusque shift toward reaction, inspired by the accession of the new king. Several of the measures in question (notably the "émigrés' billion") were being drafted before the death of Louis XVIII. The fault of Charles X was a failure to sense the mood of the country and to take seriously enough the growing evidence of discontent. Several times, during or after vindictive debates in the Chamber, Charles made state visits to the provinces and received such a warm welcome that he returned with all his doubts relieved. Convinced that the country stood solidly behind him, Charles in turn stood solidly behind his chief minister Villèle. Unfortunately for the dynasty, Villèle's genuine abilities were balanced by equal shortcomings. His real talent lay in the sphere of public finance; he took a passionate interest in revising the government's accounting procedures and did it so scientifically that those procedures have been used in France ever since. Furthermore, he was more politician than fanatic; unlike some of his fellow ultras, he had at least a marginal propensity to compromise. What Villèle lacked was imagination, color, the indefinable qualities of real statesmanship; he had an accountant's soul. Honest and efficient, but petty and inclined to devious scheming, Villèle and the king together gradually frittered away the almost impregnable political power they possessed at the peak of ultra-royalist strength in 1824.

One might assume that the ultras' decline was the product of their own extremism, of a policy line that drove center and left to cooperate and that brought a revival of the left. To a much greater degree, however, that decline was the product of fissures within the ultra bloc itself. Men of extreme views and of fanatical temperament often find it easier to cooperate when out of power than when faced with the task of governing. Such, at any rate, was the case after 1824.

One source of conflict was Villèle's growing inclination to compromise. The necessities of governing softened his rigid views at least to a degree; he was willing to maneuver within fairly narrow limits. But to his fanatical supporters, the "ultra-ultras," any compromise at all was anathema; and there shortly emerged once again a right-wing opposition group that harassed the ministry and sometimes even collaborated with the left to stir up trouble.

A second divisive factor was a personal feud that developed between Villèle and Chateaubriand. The two men had worked in close harmony during the early restoration years; but once in power, neither of these ambitious egoists was willing to relinquish the spotlight to the other. Chateaubriand had always affected an artist's disdain for politics and had preferred to pose as an observer watching the game in tolerant amusement, when in fact, his passionate interest and his personal ambition were too obvious to conceal. In 1822 Chateaubriand achieved the post of foreign minister, where he upset Villèle's cautious foreign policy and overshadowed Villèle by his flamboyant showmanship. His natural conceit was redoubled by his successes; he became an impossible subordinate. In 1824 he managed, by devious means, to defeat one of Villèle's finance bills. Perhaps he was scheming to upset the president of the council and take his place; Villèle, in any case, thought so and persuaded the king to dismiss him abruptly. Thereafter it was unlimited war between the two men. Chateaubriand embarked on a vindictive antigovernmental campaign in his newspaper, the effect of which was increased by his literary prestige and his ultra-royalist connections. No other man contributed so much to the downfall of the ultra government in 1828 and, eventually, to the fall of the dynasty itself. Too late, Chateaubriand was to realize what he had done. After 1830, as a point of honor, he refused to serve the new dynasty. "I'm still following that carrion [Charles X]," he would explain to questioning friends.

A third source of trouble within ultra ranks was the religious question, which produced a limited revival of the old Gallican spirit of hostility toward Rome. The Gallican mood had seemed well on the way to dying out by 1815. Both king and clergy continued to be Gallican almost by instinct, but the progressive weakening of the papacy had lessened the old fear that Rome might dominate the French church and France itself. Perhaps Gallicanism might have disappeared imperceptibly had it not been for the religious revival of the restoration period. That revival reflected the ultras' sentiment that France had sinned and must repent; that the nation must be brought back from its Voltairean skepticism to the true faith.

Certainly the church needed some kind of revival if it was not to wither away. The clergy was seriously reduced in numbers; recruiting had become extremely difficult after 1789. Most of the bourgeoisie had been weaned away from the faith, and Enlightenment skepticism was beginning to spread downward. An English traveller in 1818 found that "though the churches are still open, the congregations are gone"; and he concluded that French Catholicism was a mere vestige of the past.[2] Only in the aristocracy had the trend away from religion begun to be reversed.

The first step in the effort to renew the faith was the organization of a kind of domestic missionary order in 1814. The Missions de France sent teams of evangelists into the countryside to hold open-air revivals. Some of them resorted to demagogic devices in an effort to stir up mass emotions; crosses were erected, books burned, sermons delivered at night in church cemeteries with weird lighting and sound effects. The campaign converted few apostates; but it did

---

[2] F. Hall, *Travels in France in 1818* (London, 1819), p. 364.

stir up both religious and antireligious fanaticism. A more important development was the rapid growth of extra-legal church schools. The church was permitted to establish a *"petit séminaire"* in each department for the preparatory
training of priests; but the seminaries promptly turned into clandestine secondary
schools, and by 1830 they were enrolling one-third of all the secondary students
in the country. Fantastic rumors spread that the returning Jesuits were infiltrating
everywhere, and that these agents of papal domination were on the way to taking
over the country. Even the king was alleged to have become a secret Jesuit, committed to turning France over to "the men in black." There were, in fact, fewer
than four hundred Jesuits in France, but the order always made an attractive
target for anticlerical suspicions.

Still another legend of the 1820's concerned the Congrégation, which was
alleged to be a kind of Catholic freemasonry controlled by the Pope, with secret
agents strategically placed throughout the government and the administration
making all decisions and destroying any official who defied its will. Most of the
ultras ridiculed the charges as pure left-wing propaganda; the Congrégation,
they said, was no secret society but an inoffensive organization of Catholic laymen dedicated to good works. But even some ultras grew disturbed and began
to suspect their colleagues of responding to secret instructions originating in
Rome.

These converging internal dissensions gradually broke up ultra solidarity
and, at the same time, stimulated a revival of the center and left. When Villèle
gambled on elections late in 1827, the venture brought political disaster. The
liberal left and the moderate royalists (by now called the "right-center") together
won as many seats as did Villèle's supporters, while Villèle's bitter enemies on
the extreme right, the so-called ultra-ultras, held the balance of power. Reluctantly, King Charles had to part with Villèle in order to appease the moderate
element.

The new ministry, a mélange of moderate royalists and Villèle supporters,
was headed by a relative unknown named Martignac. The king made it clear
that he regarded this government as a mere stopgap; he even refused to let
Martignac use the title "president of the council." This lack of royal confidence,
plus the ministry's own heterogeneity, made its task almost hopeless. Martignac's
best chance for survival seemed to be to win the support of the liberal left; he
sought to appease them by such measures as relaxation of the press law and
reinforcement of controls over church schools. But the liberals refused to meet
him halfway; they accepted his concessions, yet systematically opposed him on
every issue that arose. This persistent hostility of both the left and the extreme
right finally gave the king the excuse he wanted to unload Martignac. In 1829
the ministry was dismissed, and Charles restored the ultras to power.

In itself, this decision was not necessarily fatal to the dynasty. The right kind

of ultra might still have saved the system: a Villèle perhaps (despite his unpopularity), or, better still, a Chateaubriand. Whatever his failings, this lion of the
literary salons did possess immense prestige. Instead Charles chose for key
ministerial posts "the three most unpopular men in France": Polignac, the king's
personal favorite; Bourmont, who had deserted to the enemy on the eve of
Waterloo; and La Bourdonnaye, the most bigoted ultra-ultra in political life.
The character of the new ministry transformed the temper of the opposition,
turning it aggressive to the point of outright disloyalty. It brought, too, the
emergence of younger, more vigorous spokesmen on the left. Early in 1830 a new
liberal daily called *Le National* was founded, inspired by Talleyrand, backed by
the liberal financier Laffitte ("the king of bankers and the banker of kings"),
and run by a youthful team whose most remarkable member was Adolphe
Thiers. This brilliant southerner, of common birth but uncommon ambition,
had risen rapidly in Parisian society through sheer ability and energy. For a time
he had grown discouraged at the prospect of political advancement and had
talked of leaving France. The creation of the Polignac ministry gave him new
hope; he and his friends plunged into a press campaign designed to bring about
not a change of ministry but a change of dynasty and of constitution. "We must
either cross the Channel or cross the Atlantic," Thiers asserted. It was clear that
he preferred the shorter crossing, and that his group at *Le National* was committed to the king's cousin the Duc d'Orleans as candidate for the throne.

The best ally of the opposition was the Polignac ministry itself, which managed to commit virtually every possible mistake during its year in office. Some
of the ministers had urged a royal coup d'état at the very outset. Perhaps decisive action in 1829, followed by rigorous repression of the left, might have
succeeded in shoring up the monarchy for a time. But Polignac came round to
such a policy only slowly and reluctantly; and when he finally did adopt it, the
opposition was well organized and dug in. Through the winter of 1829–30, the
ministry debated and marked time, giving no clear indication of a positive policy
or of effective leadership. Polignac toyed with some fantastic schemes in the field
of foreign policy, apparently in the hope that a great diplomatic victory might
arouse the nation's enthusiasm.

When the Chamber met early in 1830, its majority was spoiling for a fight;
it promptly voted an address to the throne denouncing the new ministry. Charles
dissolved the Chamber without delay and ordered new elections in July. The
outcome was ominous: 274 seats for the various opposition groups, 143 for the
ministry. That Polignac was doomed was quite clear. That the Bourbon dynasty
was doomed was much less clear, though its survival now probably would have
required Charles to accept the role of constitutional monarch. Some of his advisers urged another alternative: why not buy off enough members of the opposition to get a majority in the Chamber? "We know the price of consciences—it's

not too high," remarked one minister. But the king, as honest as he was bigoted, would hear of neither bargaining nor retreat. He chose instead a head-on challenge to the left: a royal coup d'état that would alter the Charter beyond recognition.

Ministry and king carefully and secretly prepared a set of decrees (the July Ordinances) that dissolved the new Chamber even before its convocation, altered the electoral system, deprived the wealthy bourgeoisie of the right to vote, and stripped the press of any semblance of liberty. In order to ensure surprise, no troops were moved to Paris to reinforce the small garrison there. King and ministry acted with incredible naiveté in assuming that no disorders would follow; the prefect of police proved his total incapacity by guaranteeing that there would be no trouble. The government was comforted, too, by good news that arrived opportunely from Algiers. A French expeditionary corps sent to punish the Dey (the Moslem ruler of Algeria) had landed and swept to a conquest of the capital in only twenty days. This news was expected to smother discontent in a wave of patriotic fervor. Even so, Charles wavered at the very end and signed the July Ordinances only after some hesitation. Once the decision had been made, he abandoned all doubts and went off to the country to hunt.

During the "three glorious days" that followed, Charles lost his capital and his throne. The insurrection developed gradually: a few small demonstrations on the 27th, bloody street clashes on the 28th, barricades everywhere on the 29th, when the battered royal garrison abandoned the city to the rebels. The street fighting was largely spontaneous and lacked organized leadership. A group of liberal politicians and journalists had been meeting sporadically from the outset of the crisis in an effort to shape and control the course of events; but they could agree on no effective action until the 29th, when the city had been virtually cleared of royal troops. Faced by the prospect that the republicans or the Bonapartists might move into the vacuum, the liberal leaders hastily named a governing commission for Paris. Its members were constitutional monarchists; its aim was to substitute a new dynasty for the old. On the morning of July 30 the walls of Paris were plastered with posters (the work of Thiers and his friends) calling for the transfer of the crown to the Duc d'Orléans.

The duke, however, showed some reluctance in mounting the throne, which had not yet been formally vacated by his royal cousin. Orléans had prudently left Paris for the suburbs when the disorders began, and it took a series of urgent missions by Thiers and others to persuade him to return to the capital. Complex negotiations ensued; the outcome, on the morning of July 31, was an agreement that the duke would accept the interim title of "lieutenant-general" of the kingdom. That afternoon the duke, with the liberal deputies trooping behind, ventured to the Hôtel de Ville through glowering street crowds of Parisian workers, students, and shopkeepers—the pro-republican street fighters who sensed that their revolution was being confiscated. Their hero, Lafayette, had already privately refused a proposal that he become president of a republic; now he publicly reaffirmed that decision by appearing on the balcony with the Duc d'Orléans and, jointly shrouded in a large tricolor flag, embraced the duke as the crowd cheered. On August 2 Charles abdicated in favor of his grandson and called on the new "lieutenant-general" to make way for the legitimate king. The duke professed lack of authority to decide the country's fate; but the next day, when the two chambers of parliament met, the duke baldly announced to them that Charles had abdicated without condition. The ex-king, after some thought of further resistance, ended by accepting his fate and departed for a second exile in England.

Though the Bourbon experiment ended in failure, there is no reason to suppose that it had to end thus. Frenchmen were, on the whole, well governed, prosperous, contented during this fifteen-year period; one historian even describes the restoration era as "one of the happiest periods in [France's] history."[3] It was not an easy task to blend two traditions as incompatible as those inherited from the revolution and the old regime; yet blending them ought not to have been beyond human capacity. Some of the responsibility for the failure of the experiment certainly belonged to the extremists of both right and left—to those elements that had no sympathy for gradualism or compromise. The greater fault, however, must be laid at the door of the king and his advisers—better men, but not wiser men, than they have customarily been described. It has sometimes been argued that the failure of the Bourbon experiment was one of modern France's major disasters; that this failure ruled out the development of a durable constitutional monarchy, one that might have given France the kind of stability based on legitimacy that has distinguished modern England. Perhaps so; but if it is true, the dynasty itself must bear most of the blame. Besides, a second experiment in compromise, less legitimate yet possibly better adapted to changing times, still remained to be made—the Orleanist system.

---

[3] Bertier de Sauvigny, *La restauration*, p. 628.

CHAPTER **10**

# *The Orleanist Experiment,*
# *1830–1848*

Stagnation is perhaps the only practical way of remaining faithful to one's principles.

R. DE JOUVENEL

Some months after the revolution of 1830 a deputy arose in the Chamber to complain that not very much had changed in France. The Charter of 1814 still existed, slightly revised; the suffrage had been broadened only from 90,000 to 170,000 voters; ministers were still not responsible to the Chamber; nothing had even been done to punish that evil man Polignac. Casimir Périer, president of the council, answered bluntly: "The trouble with this country is that there are too many people like you who imagine that there has been a revolution in France."

To men like Périer, there had, in fact, been no revolution but only a change of dynasty, a return to the balanced compromise that had operated in the years 1816–20. They saw no real flaw in the Charter of 1814; all it needed to function successfully was the right sort of king.

Not all of the Orleanist politicians shared this view. It was easier to convert the Duc d'Orléans into King Louis-Philippe than to agree on his proper function once he was on the throne. Two principal factions emerged almost from the outset and came to be known by the ambiguous labels right-center and left-center. The former group, represented by such men as Casimir Périer and the former doctrinaire François Guizot, saw 1830 as a culmination, not as a beginning. The regime, they believed, should be based on the upper bourgeoisie alone; and the king, as an active executive, should govern as well as reign. The

112

left-center, with Adolphe Thiers and Alexis de Tocqueville as representative spokesmen, saw 1830 as the beginning of an evolutionary process. They aimed to broaden the base of the regime to include the middle and lower ranks of the bourgeoisie; and they held the king's role to be (in Thiers' classic phrase) to reign but not to govern.

It was the right-center that dominated the ministry through most of the Orleanist period, partly because the king so largely shared its views of the meaning of 1830. Louis-Philippe, who had played so hesitant a role during the revolution, proved to be a much more complex and positive person than appearances might have indicated. He was the son of that Duc d'Orléans who had flirted with revolution after 1789 but had ended on the scaffold. He himself had passed through a youthful republican phase: at eighteen he had fought in the republican army at Valmy, and he had even joined the Jacobin club for a time. The Terror had driven him into exile, but he had carefully remained aloof from the émigré group. Even during the Hundred Days he had chosen to seek his own place of refuge in England rather than to follow the court to Ghent. After Waterloo the British had seriously considered setting him on the French throne in place of Louis. During the Bourbon era his mansion in Paris had been a gathering place for liberals—but he had played the liberal role with restraint, in moderation. It seemed safer to aspire than to conspire; and so he struck a democratic pose, kept a wide circle of varied acquaintances, and avoided committing himself to any cause.

Transmuted suddenly into king of the French, Louis-Philippe continued to look and act like a typical Parisian bourgeois. He rose early, shaved himself, and put in a long day at the office; he broke royal precedent by sending his sons to one of the public *lycées* founded by Napoleon; he invited business men and their wives to palace functions; he showed a strong instinct for thrift and prudently invested part of his income in British bonds. A certain lack of aristocratic dignity made it easy to scoff at him as "the shopkeepers' king" and to caricature him as the Crowned Pear. Even Thiers remarked acidly that the king's morning prayer began with the phrase: "Oh Lord, give us this day our daily platitude." His accession to the throne was in startling contrast to that of Charles X: instead of the pompous coronation at Reims, there was a simple formality in the chambers of parliament, with the emphasis on the contract between king and people rather than between king and God.

But beneath this unimpressive exterior, Louis-Philippe concealed a stubborn determination to be a king rather than a figurehead. He showed no sympathy for the idea of broadening the suffrage, or for making the ministry responsible to the Chamber, or for permitting the president of the ministerial council to be the real executive. Instead, he assumed an active role in the governing process; he tried when possible to choose ministers who would take orders, and there is even some evidence that he liked to provoke quarrels among his ministers so that he might step in with a dictated solution. Despite appearances, Louis-Philippe had no sympathy with the view of many Orleanist politicians that the institution of monarchy had outgrown its mystical significance and now possessed only a purely utilitarian value. Perhaps it is true that the king suffered from a deep "illegitimacy complex"; that he was determined to establish his right to rule by heredity, as head of the younger branch of the Bourbon family, and not merely by the choice of parliament. In short, the king was not willing to regard 1830 as a French 1688. In some ways, Louis-Philippe was a remarkably astute monarch; but he was not the kind of king who was likely to make a system of constitutional monarchy function smoothly, or who would be inclined to adapt it to the changing needs of society. From the outset the throne rested squarely on a double ambiguity—the source of the king's authority, and the extent of that authority.

The Orleanist period has commonly been described as a completely class-bound era: as "the bourgeois monarchy," run by and for the plutocrats. The label, though not entirely false, is misleading. It is true that the new Orleanist aristocracy created by Louis-Philippe was drawn almost entirely from the upper bourgeoisie, while most members of the old aristocracy withdrew disdainfully to their provincial chateaux or their Parisian town houses in the Faubourg Saint-Germain. It is also true that the mass of the population—peasants, urban workers, middle and petty bourgeoisie—still had no voice in politics. But it would be wrong to conclude that Orleanism was completely identified with the prosperous business and banking community. Some members of the older aristocracy—the Duc de Broglie, for example—rallied to the new monarchy; and some able men of common birth and relatively modest means, like Thiers and Guizot, were able to rise into the governing group. The historian A.-J. Tudesq has shown that the *"grands notables"* who dominated the period included both aristocrats and plutocrats, usually working in close alliance to further their common ends. René Rémond has characterized the Orleanist system as not so much a government of a single class as a "government of elites"—of all the elites, whether of money, birth, or intelligence.[1] The link between the government and the universities has rarely been so intimate, either before or since. A number of high posts went to Sorbonne professors; Guizot was only the most prominent among them, while the philosopher Victor Cousin became a kind of quasi-official theorist of the regime. The Académie Française, that group of forty immortals, became so thoroughly Orleanist that "for half a century it remained an Orleanist salon." Thus the regime possessed an intellectual tone (or perhaps it was only a veneer) that dignified its more crassly materialistic base.

---

[1] R. Rémond, *La droite en France de 1815 à nos jours* (2d ed., Paris: Aubier, 1963), pp. 88–89.

If the Orleanist system had an ideology, a distinctive spirit or outlook, it was best summed up in the phrase *juste milieu,* or golden mean, implying an attempt to find a stable equilibrium between liberty and order. A regime marked by such a mood is an easy target for ridicule; the middle-of-the-road virtues are rarely glamorous, and the ideal itself suggests a fuzzy ambiguity, a tendency toward flabby compromise. "Any regime," it has been said, "faces the threat of degenerating into a parody of its intentions; a middle-of-the-road regime faces it more than most."[2] The Orleanist system has received its full share of such criticism, both from its contemporaries and from posterity. Some of the charges were undoubtedly well founded; but some of them have just as certainly distracted attention from the virtues of the regime. Peace abroad, stability at home, prosperity and at the same time an active intellectual life—these things France enjoyed during the Orleanist era, whether or not it was the Orleanist system that produced them.

❖❖❖❖❖❖❖❖❖❖❖❖❖❖

The political history of the July Monarchy falls naturally into two contrasting periods: the decade of instability (1830–40), when ministries averaged less than a year in duration; and the era of rigidity (1840–48), when the regime's governing personnel and policies became almost petrified.

The ministerial instability of the first decade strikes one as incongruous at a time when the extremes of left and right had little influence in politics, and when the dominant center groups prided themselves on their attachment to the spirit of the golden mean. On the right, the old ultras had withdrawn from political life, and no extreme left was likely to emerge in parliament as long as the suffrage was so narrow. The Chamber of Deputies was filled with men of middle-class virtues, men of education and oratorical talent, men inclined to judicious moderation rather than to demagoguery and political bulldozing. Yet by the end of the decade the Chamber was sometimes torn by tumult as great as in the cruder era of universal suffrage; the deputies bombarded ministerial orators with interruptions and insults, and one speaker who complained of fatigue was even greeted by the unmannerly cry "Drop dead, dog!"

This anomalous condition was the product of the chronic conflict between right-center and left-center, a conflict intensified by the emergence of sharp personal rivalries and ambitions and by the king's habit of interfering in periods of crisis. Because the Chamber contained no well-defined parties but only amorphous factions, clear majorities were rare and homogeneous ministries excep-

---

[2] R. Rémond, *La droite en France,* p. 81.

tional. Right-center domination was broken by occasional interludes of left-center control, but such interruptions were brief. Adolphe Thiers, whose brilliance was exceeded only by his ambition and his conceit, twice managed to attain the post of president of the council, but failed to hold power for more than a few months. Louis-Philippe was not the kind of king to let himself be overshadowed by a politician, even one as clever as Thiers. The right-center, though it controlled the ministry most of the time, produced no really outstanding leader except the banker Casimir Périer, a domineering figure who could overawe both Chamber and king; but Périer fell victim to the 1831 cholera epidemic, much to Louis-Philippe's secret satisfaction.

That first decade brought instability not only within the parliamentary arena but outside it as well. Only a few months after the 1830 revolution some of the ultras (who now began to call themselves Legitimists) attempted to oust the "usurper" from his throne. The Duchesse de Berry, mother of the "miracle child," who was now next in line as the Bourbon pretender, landed in southern France in 1832, expecting to be welcomed by a general insurrection in favor of the Bourbons; but division among the Legitimists, coupled with amateurish planning, turned the affair from drama into farce. The duchess escaped to the Vendée in peasant disguise and again called vainly for a rising, then eluded the Orleanist police for several months before an informer revealed her hiding place. The Legitimist cause, bolstered somewhat by the duchess' daring, was severely shaken a few months later when the duchess (still in custody) was found to be pregnant. Not even the evidence of her secret marriage to an Italian count sufficed to restore her tarnished reputation; the Bourbon cause languished during the rest of the reign.

Meanwhile, republican agitation was raising an even more serious threat. Though the republicans were probably less numerous than the Legitimists, they were more concentrated and, for a time, more united. A whole series of *sub rosa* organizations began to spring up in Paris, with branches in other major cities. New leadership was emerging, too: a younger generation of bourgeois intellectuals and artisans, idealistic and romantic in temper, filled with the doctrine of the common man. Out of this inchoate movement came a series of large-scale riots and insurrections in the years 1831–34. They were usually touched off by labor discontent and took on political overtones as they developed. In the most serious of these affairs, the Lyon insurrection of 1831, fifteen thousand workers engaged in a pitched battle with the National Guard; the casualty figure exceeded six hundred. The fact that the National Guard (a kind of bourgeois honor society) was called out to help repress the disorders gave a strong color of class conflict to these episodes.

The effect of all this unrest was to weaken the republican movement through the arrest of its leading figures and to drive it underground through the adoption of more severe laws on press and associations. Only scattered and small-scale disorders occurred thereafter, as in 1839 when that dedicated conspirator Auguste Blanqui tried one of his many abortive coups in Paris. But the gradual decline of violence on the left did not mean that the republican element was becoming reconciled to the regime and had decided to work within it. Rather, republican leaders were now aware that the time had not come when violence would be effective; and they turned by necessity to a sustained propaganda campaign instead. But as they did so, they began to lose some of their ardent supporters. The urban workers showed signs of swinging away from the bourgeois republican leaders in favor of newer crusaders for sweeping social reform. This cleavage between bourgeois and proletarian republicans was not clearly recognized at the time, but 1848 was to make it dramatically evident.

Alongside the Legitimist and the republican threats to the regime there developed still a third active challenge to the reigning dynasty, in the form of a Bonapartist campaign. By 1830 the Napoleonic legend was taking the form of a vague but widely generalized sentiment. To many Frenchmen, Napoleon was no longer the ruthless dictator who had sacrificed an entire generation of young Frenchmen, but the "Little Corporal" who had made his own way up the steps of the throne and had finally died a martyr to British francophobia and greed. The legend made him always the defender of the common man—the commander who knew each of his soldiers by name, the ruler who gave every citizen a voice at the polls. But while the legend had gained in strength, Bonapartism as an organized political movement had been steadily disintegrating. The leading figures of the Empire were disappearing one by one; the imperial heir presumptive, Napoleon's only legitimate son, died, too, in 1832. It seemed that Bonapartism was on the way to becoming nothing more than a special variety of republicanism; Bonapartists began to resemble the partisans of other defunct dynasties, clinging more stubbornly to their lost cause as its futility became more obvious.

The new pretender, Louis-Napoleon Bonaparte, seemed an unlikely prospect to crystallize this amorphous sentiment. He was alleged to be the son of Napoleon's brother Louis, although doubts about his paternity made it uncertain that he was a Bonaparte at all. Even more doubtful were his qualities of leadership and his potential appeal to the French nation. Louis-Napoleon had grown up in exile; even the French language was to him a foreign tongue that he never learned to speak without a German accent. In his youth he had fought briefly for Italian freedom as a Carbonaro; and in 1831, shortly after his arrival in Paris, he was expelled from France for associating with republican subversives. Frenchmen knew little more than this about the young man until his farcical attempt in 1836 to invade France with a handful of partisans. He appeared dramatically at a barracks in Strasbourg and persuaded its commander (who had served under his uncle) to follow him with troops and band into the heart of the city. There he was promptly arrested, given a trial that made his cause seem ridiculous, and shipped off to exile in the United States. Undismayed, Louis-Napoleon got himself back to England and tried again in 1840. This time he crossed the Channel in a chartered launch with some fifty loyal supporters and a tame eagle. His hope that the army commander at Lille might rally to his cause was disappointed; again he was ignominiously arrested, tried, and this time sentenced to life imprisonment in the fortress of Ham. It was clear now to everyone, even to Louis-Napoleon, that the Napoleonic legend alone was not enough to produce a successful revolution. That legend had somehow to be embodied in a person—in a man distinguished by qualities of leadership and possessed of a program as well as a name. Louis-Napoleon was to use his six years in prison (which he called ironically "the University of Ham") to develop such a program and to publicize it in a series of pamphlets.

None of the abortive insurrections and coups of the 1830's seriously shook Louis-Philippe's regime. More dangerous, in fact, were the attempts at assassination of the king that marked the unstable decade. Ten near misses within that short period constituted a kind of record and led Louis-Philippe to remark philosophically that "there seems to be a closed season on all kinds of game except me." Luck or fate saw him through, and, though some of his escapes were so close as to seem almost miraculous, he survived without a scratch.

By 1840 the regime was settling at last into a kind of torpid stability. The country was prosperous and at peace; if the ruling elite was rigid and narrow, it was not fickle or tyrannical. Under the leadership of François Guizot, France was about to enter upon one of the longest periods of stable government in its modern history. The Orleanist monarch, it seemed, had found the key to success that had eluded the Bourbon dynasty.

Guizot, a talented historian turned politician, has always been a subject of controversy among his fellow historians. Some of them have called him the greatest statesman of the nineteenth century; others contemptuously rate him as "an outstanding mediocrity," or "remarkably second-rate." More than any other Frenchman of his time, he symbolized both the policy of the golden mean and the idea of government by all the elites. Guizot sincerely believed in the principle of equal opportunity; and he believed that the principle was fully operative in France. Every man, he held, was free to get rich; those who failed to seize the opportunity could no longer blame an unjust society but must face the fact of their own limitations. Although Guizot was a Protestant (and one of the first of his creed to rise high in government), he reflected the spirit and ideals of the Catholic bourgeoisie as well—especially that segment of the provincial bourgeoisie that had never turned Voltairean. There was a strong tinge of Jansenism in the outlook of this group—a kind of quasi-Calvinistic view that the upper classes had a moral duty to govern and to protect the lower orders. Jansenism had long since disappeared as an organized sect, yet remnants of it survived as a set of moral and intellectual standards that colored French life for generations, and that pervaded the thinking of much of the provincial bourgeoisie throughout the nineteenth century.

Few nineteenth-century politicians were so unpopular as Guizot or so blandly indifferent to popularity. There was an irritating holier-than-thou quality about this cold and self-righteous man. To his critics in parliament he once remarked, "As for your insults, your calumnies, your venomous attacks, you may multiply them, pile them up as high as you like, yet they will never reach the level of my contempt." If he managed to retain power from 1840 to 1848, that was because the king lent him steady support and because Guizot was a clever practitioner of corridor politics. Louis-Philippe's support was natural enough, for Guizot perfectly embodied the king's doctrine that the ministry should regard itself as the emanation of the monarch and not of the Chamber. Guizot's talent as a political operator may seem more surprising, for he was personally incorruptible as well as cold. There was something of the Robert Walpole about him; Guizot knew English history well and apparently took Walpole as a kind of model. His most effective device was to win the support of wavering or hostile deputies (who drew no salaries) by offering them salaried government posts on the side. At times, as many as one-third of the deputies were on the state payroll in this fashion. Recent scholarship suggests that the legend of Guizot's corrupt tactics has been much exaggerated; yet it is doubtful that he could have held office for eight years if the opposition had managed to push through a bill denying bureaucrats the right to sit as deputies. Eighteen times such a bill was introduced in the Chamber; eighteen times it was defeated.

Guizot's energies during his years in power were devoted mainly to encouraging business expansion (primarily through a hands-off policy, but in some cases through direct governmental aid) and to conducting foreign policy. Only one great legislative act remains associated with his name—and that one dated from an early period, when he was merely minister of public instruction. Guizot's educational reform of 1833 was a landmark in the field; it has been properly called the charter of French primary (i.e., elementary) education. Of the thirty-eight thousand communes in France, fifteen thousand had no school of any kind. Guizot's law obligated every commune to establish a public primary school and provided for expanded teacher-training facilities. The law did not yet guarantee free or compulsory education, nor did it eliminate church influence in the primary schools (though local school boards were to have a majority of laymen). Furthermore, the law was not implemented everywhere—notably in regions where the church had already set up its own primary schools. It was, nevertheless, an important step in the direction of mass education and in the direction of giving the teaching profession more status and better working conditions. By 1848 the number of teacher-training schools had risen from forty-seven to seventy-six, and enrollment in public primary schools had almost doubled.

Guizot's chief rival and most acerbic critic was Thiers, who likewise combined the roles of historian and politician. As one of the principal kingmakers of 1830, Thiers had expected far more than he got in the way of political power under Louis-Philippe; and his wounded vanity drove him almost to the point of opposition to the Orleanist regime. Disappointed in his political hopes, Thiers devoted part of his enormous energy to journalism and to writing a massive history of the Napoleonic era. He had been prudent enough to marry money, which gave him independence and an entree into the best Orleanist society. The salon provided a forum for his sparkling monologues on every subject from Japanese porcelain to differential calculus. But social and scholarly success left him unsatisfied; his ambition was not to write history but to make it. "Just think," he told a friend disconsolately, "how much a man must do to get half a line in a book on world history!" Thiers' neurotic self-esteem may have reflected his small stature (he barely topped five feet in height), or it may have derived from his irregular and humble birth. Whatever its origin, this egotism left little room for generous or humane inclinations. It is hard to avoid the conclusion that he was essentially an *arriviste* concerned with carving out his own career, indifferent to the welfare of less fortunate beings. He lacked both understanding of and interest in social problems and social forces. His phrase for the masses was "the vile multitude"; to him, universal education would be "like building a fire under a great pot that is empty." His world was circumscribed by the halls of parliament and the salons, where his skills at repartee and debate were unsurpassed. No other French statesman of the nineteenth century was to have so long and distinguished a career, or would be remembered with greater admiration. Yet the essential flaw in his character offset his talents and kept him from attaining the highest level of statesmanship. Although he remained an Orleanist until 1872, his harassing tactics during the 1840's contributed much to the downfall of the regime that he had done so much to create.

❖❖❖❖❖❖❖❖❖❖❖❖❖

Religious issues, which had done so much to complicate the French political problem during the revolutionary and restoration epochs, seemed to be losing their intensity in the Orleanist era. It was not that French Catholicism was losing its hold on the nation; on the contrary, one might almost call this an era of Catholic renaissance. Two incidents that occurred in Paris in 1831 and 1848 provide a suggestive contrast. Early in 1831 some ultras arranged to celebrate a Mass in memory of the Duc de Berry. A mob of hostile Parisians broke into the church and dispersed the worshippers, then moved on to the archepiscopal palace, sacked the place, and threw the archbishop's library into the Seine. The Orleanist police made no serious effort to stop the riot; neither did Thiers, who was an interested eyewitness. But at the height of the revolution of 1848, when a mob broke into the royal chapel of the Tuileries palace, its behavior was quite different. Instead of desecrating the place, the crowd reverently carried the crucifix to the nearest church. The old cry *"A bas la calotte!"* ("Down with the priests") was no longer heard; onlookers in 1848 reported cries of *"Vive la religion!"* instead, or even, *"Vive Jésus Christ!"*

A remarkable change had occurred within two decades, and no simple explanation of it will suffice. One contributing factor was the church's loss of special privilege after 1830. In previous years its close tie with the ultras, its commitment to Bourbon reaction, its rapid gains in power and wealth, had made it an object of suspicion and hostility in many quarters. The Orleanists broke the alliance between throne and altar; the new regime took on a mildly anticlerical cast. Louis-Philippe himself was a Voltairean who privately scoffed at religion but attended Mass as a social duty. Thiers was openly contemptuous of religious belief, except for the vile multitude. Victor Cousin held that the clergy would still be useful as "moral policemen and funeral directors," but assumed that the skepticism of the urban bourgeoisie would gradually spread downward as education did its work. Guizot, though a believer, was not a Catholic. At the very outset the regime pruned the state budget for religious activities and expelled some religious orders. In the end, this mild and rather painless persecution benefited the church. Perhaps the Vatican recognized this fact; at any rate, the Pope repeatedly advised the clergy to remain loyal to the Voltairean king.

More significant still was the gradual process of change that had set in within the church. New currents of thought were developing there, currents that seemed destined to rejuvenate Catholicism and that foreshadowed a reconciliation with the modern world. In a word, the church (or an important segment of it) was at last getting round to accepting the revolution of 1789. It may be true (as one impatient French Catholic has put it) that "the church in France is always one revolution behind." At any rate, the Orleanist period did bring the beginnings of what has sometimes been called "neo-Catholicism."

In the church, as outside it, the older generation of leaders was rapidly disappearing; the unreconstructed ultras were being replaced—at least in part—by vigorous young priests and laymen attuned to their times. Some of them, like Frédéric Ozanam, were principally concerned with social problems and the alleviation of misery. Ozanam, while still a university student, brought together six friends to form the new Society of St. Vincent de Paul, an organization that rapidly expanded until it became nation-wide and then world-wide in scope. Ozanam was the fountainhead of the durable current called "social Catholicism" in nineteenth-century France. Although conservative in spirit, it refused to be satisfied with the mere practice of charity but insisted on seeking the reasons for poverty and on working toward greater social justice. Ozanam's was only the best known of a whole series of Catholic social-action groups, which blossomed in unprecedented fashion in this era.

Other Catholics were moving meanwhile toward a new and still hardier doctrine: one that would reconcile the church with political liberalism or even with democracy. In 1830 a little group of priests headed by Félicité de Lamennais founded the first Catholic daily newspaper in Europe, *L'Avenir,* and set out to preach political democracy mixed with some incipient social reform. Modern Catholicism has produced few figures so striking as Lamennais. A crusader whose enterprises always withered, a fanatically fervent believer who eventually left the church, he has been described as "a modern Savonarola," and as the only genius produced by nineteenth-century French Catholicism. Of Breton birth, Lamennais was a kind of "caricature of the Celt": a romantic, mystical, brooding, and undisciplined youth. In the Bourbon era he had been, like his fellow Breton Chateaubriand, an ultra-ultra royalist; but even more intense had been his ultramontane convictions, his hostility toward the Gallican tradition. Gallican kings and bishops, he argued, had long used the church as a tool of national policy; instead, they ought to serve the Pope, who alone could accomplish the regeneration of human society.

By 1830 Lamennais had become totally disillusioned with the Bourbons; he shifted brusquely from his program of "Pope and King" to a new program of "Pope and People." In *L'Avenir* he proposed to regenerate mankind by starting at the bottom, with individual and ordinary men. His fervent crusade, though it made him the idol of many young priests, promptly aroused the hostility of the hierarchy; and Lamennais went off to Rome to appeal his case to the Pope. His hopes were no more than illusions; he should have known that the Vatican could not adopt his cause when almost the entire French hierarchy opposed it, and that the Pope would be unlikely to commit the church to the ideal of political democracy. Instead, he was instructed to recant and to suspend his newspaper. Lamennais submitted, but he stormed and brooded over the outcome; he soon broke with the Vatican as he had broken with the Bourbons. Thereafter he became increasingly isolated; as he moved farther left, he began to anticipate the Christian socialist position of the twentieth century. The revolution of 1848 brought him a brief period of glory—he was elected a deputy in Paris—but he soon slipped back into obscurity once more, to die a lonely old man almost without followers.

There is a dramatic contrast between Lamennais' career of repetitious failure and the long-range success of most of the ideas for which he fought. His ultramontane doctrine gradually gained strength until, by the end of the century, it had virtually wiped out all remnants of the Gallican tradition. His attempt to reconcile the church with political democracy was to be reflected in one of the most important political movements of twentieth-century France and Europe. His Christian socialism anticipated papal doctrine as expressed in the encyclical *Rerum Novarum* (1891), but it was to have an even more direct heritage in the emergence of labor-oriented Catholic movements with a strongly leftist slant. Lamennais and Karl Marx, someone has remarked, were the two greatest visionaries of nineteenth-century Europe.

The failure of Lamennais' campaign in the 1830's did not mean the immediate relapse of French Catholicism into a mood of reaction. Although such disciples as the Dominican Father Lacordaire and the Comte de Montalembert left him, they remained representative of what might be called a moderately liberal Catholic current, seeking to adapt the church to the new society that had emerged from the Great Revolution. Lacordaire's impact was exerted through his powerful sermons at Notre Dame, sermons that attracted thousands of hearers, including many young intellectuals and bourgeois Parisians whose parents were thorough Voltaireans. Montalembert meanwhile turned to politics as the most effective sphere of action. He set out in the 1840's to fuse all Catholics into a single political bloc, dedicated not to an attempt to restore the old regime but to effective political action within the existing regime. The practical issue on which he chose to fight was the school question. Montalembert demanded the right to establish Catholic secondary schools competitive with those of the state and to operate them without state interference. The church already had its network of primary schools and its seminaries for training priests; what it wanted now was legal authority to train the sons of the bourgeoisie, the nation's future governing elite.

Montalembert was shrewd enough to build his campaign around the attractive slogan "liberty of education" and to aim his arguments quite frankly at the literate public rather than at the politicians alone. The emotional impact was great: here at last was the church committed to the principle of liberty, to the principle of equal and fair treatment, rather than to the idea of monopoly or special privilege. Montalembert's campaign was not to succeed until 1850, but it probably contributed to the revived popularity of the church in the later Orleanist period. On the other hand, a tinge of demagoguery crept into the bitter debate between Montalembert's forces and the defenders of state schools; so vindictive were the charges and counter-charges that they intensified the hostility between Catholics and dedicated anticlericals. This was to be the first passage of arms in a century-long conflict over the school question—a conflict whose divisive effects have sometimes verged on the tragic.

If the Orleanist epoch brought fresh currents into French Catholicism, it also brought evidence that the old currents kept much of their force. Indeed, division within the church seemed to be attaining a new pitch of intensity. In 1842 a strange young man named Louis Veuillot took over the editorship of the Paris daily *L'Univers* and established himself over the next forty years as one of the most powerful figures in modern French religious history. Of common birth and Voltairean upbringing, his sudden conversion as a young man had turned him into a superheated fanatic. He was the bitterest enemy of the liberals and the compromisers. Intolerant of error, a master at the art of whipping up emotions, he set out (as Ozanam put it) "not to win back unbelievers, but to arouse the passions of believers." Veuillot possessed remarkable journalistic talent and a flair for speaking the language of the people; he has been called one of the most influential journalists of all time. His tireless activity gave promise that not all French Catholics would slip docilely into the liberal current. And the Vatican, for a generation at least, was to favor the Veuillot position against that of the liberal Catholics.

Statistically speaking, the number of churchgoers in France may not have increased very much during the Orleanist era. There is clear evidence that difficulties in recruiting new priests were increasing. Yet perhaps the turning point in the church's fortunes had already arrived by 1848, in the sense that a segment of the bourgeoisie was beginning to swing back from Voltaireanism to the Christian faith. It has often been alleged that the bourgeois outlook changed only after the traumatic shock of civil war in 1848; that fear of social revolution led the freethinking property-owners to reconstruct Catholicism as a bulwark of the social order. Some Frenchmen undoubtedly did react this way after the June Days. But there is good reason to believe that the Catholic revival was fed by other emotions than fear, and that its roots went deeper than 1848. The first signs of the bourgeois return to the faith can be found in the Orleanist era; and that return was inspired or hastened by the forces of rejuvenation within the church.

❖❖❖❖❖❖❖❖❖❖❖❖❖❖

The revolution that destroyed the regime of Louis-Philippe has sometimes been called a result without a cause. A more appropriate phrase would describe it as a result far out of proportion to the cause. Frenchmen were not being oppressed or tyrannized; the government was not confronted by bankruptcy or undermined by a powerful subversive movement plotting its overthrow. Indeed, one of the two leading republican newspapers in Paris had so small a circulation that it was forced to suspend publication a few weeks before the upheaval. Until the very last moment most of the opposition leaders aimed not at revolution but merely at abdication. Some of them were even less ambitious; they meant only to give the king a scare.

But even if a revolutionary temper was lacking, there was widespread irritation and discontent—so much of it that even court circles were nervous. The king's sons frankly expressed their concern; his widowed daughter-in-law, mother of the heir apparent, was reputed to believe that Louis-Philippe's stubbornness was endangering her son's chances for the succession. The king was subjected to rising court pressure to sacrifice Guizot, chief symbol of the regime's unpopularity. Alexis de Tocqueville, in a prophetic speech delivered in the Chamber in January, 1848, warned that if trouble should occur, it was likely to have repercussions much more profound than a mere change of ministry.

Louis-Philippe complacently ignored the prophets of doom. He sent his dissatisfied sons off to Algeria or to service with the navy; he let it be known that he considered his daughter-in-law dangerously disloyal. He refused even to consider parting with Guizot, whose presence he thought essential for the perpetuation of the system to which he had grown so much attached. A less dependable and pliable chief minister might embark on some risky foreign crusade or demand a beginning of political reform.

If there had been little talk of revolution or republicanism in the years before 1848, there had been much talk of reform. Throughout the decade opposition deputies had been introducing bills designed to broaden the suffrage or to deny deputies the right to hold salaried posts in the bureaucracy. This frustrated desire for reform had gradually corroded the middle and lower ranks of the bourgeoisie and had even found expression in that pillar of the regime, the National Guard. A second source of discontent, more imprecise but even more widely shared, was the regime's lack of glamor. "France is bored," remarked the poet-deputy Lamartine as early as 1839; by 1847 he was bold enough to predict a "revolution of contempt." Even the virtues of the regime were thus turned to its discredit; peace and stability seemed to suggest cowardice and stagnation. Still a third factor endangering public morale was the apparent evidence of dry rot within the ruling elite. A financial scandal in 1847 implicated two ex-ministers, who were charged with accepting bribes and playing favorites in the grant of government concessions. A prominent Orleanist peer, involved in a marital triangle, murdered his wife and then committed suicide. Cases of this sort gave some bourgeois supporters of the regime a bad conscience; they wondered whether the very base of the system was rotting away, and their will to defend it was undermined.

All these sources of irritation affected the bourgeoisie but left the masses largely indifferent. The discontent of the urban workers sprang from other sources: in part from the cumulative impact of socialist propaganda, but in the main from long-endured misery, compounded by the depression that began in

1846–47. This was the gravest economic crisis of Louis-Philippe's reign. The same wave of bad weather that produced the great Irish famine brought a series of crop failures in France as well. Food became scarce and expensive; the price of wheat rose 250 per cent, and the government was driven to import foodstuffs. The agrarian crisis rapidly affected the whole economy; many mines and factories shut down, some of the new railway companies went bankrupt, unemployment spiralled upward.

The 1840's brought, too, a dangerous alienation of the intellectuals. Novelists like Victor Hugo, George Sand, and Eugène Sue were developing a kind of mythology of the common man and were playing with doctrines of democracy or socialism. The biting caricatures of Honoré Daumier stripped the governing elite of its veneer of dignity and respectability and suggested that men in authority ranged from petty frauds to human vultures. Three notable historians —Michelet, Lamartine, Louis Blanc—produced in 1847 three striking new interpretations of the Great Revolution, all of them glorifying some aspect of that dramatic upheaval. Lamartine's heroes were the Girondins; Blanc praised Robespierre; Michelet exalted the people, the revolutionary crowd. "It is said everywhere," wrote Lamartine proudly, "that my book fans the hard fires of revolution, and that it will inspire the people for revolutions to come. May God so will it!"

Dissatisfaction took organized form in the summer of 1847. Opposition leaders, denied the right to hold public political meetings, evaded the law by scheduling a series of banquets in the major cities and indulging in political oratory between courses. The novelist Gustave Flaubert attended one in Rouen that lasted nine hours, and that destroyed his enthusiasm for politics: "What abominable taste! [he wrote to a friend] what wines! and what speeches! . . . I was nauseated." But Flaubert was the exception; most of Guizot's critics wallowed enthusiastically in their opportunity to denounce the government and to drink toasts to reform. A huge banquet scheduled to be held in Paris on February 22, 1848, with a hundred opposition deputies on the invited list, finally broke the government's patience; orders were issued to cancel the affair. Although most of its sponsors were willing to give in, a few hotheads insisted on action and announced that they would appear at the assigned place in spite of the government.

Their stubbornness sparked the crisis that followed. On the 22d, disaffected students and workers congregated in the streets and began to clash with the police. Louis-Philippe showed a serene confidence in his ability to handle the riots, which he thought would be minor in any case. His army garrison in Paris was three times as large as that of the Bourbons in 1830; it was well equipped, possessed carefully laid plans to meet an insurrection, and could depend on the support of the bourgeois National Guard. Indeed, the king's confidence was well founded; and the regime almost certainly would have beaten back the

uprising save for three crucial sources of weakness. One was the virtual desertion of the National Guard, whose loyalty was corroded by the growing desire of
the lesser bourgeoisie for a share of political power. The second was the character
of the army command in Paris; at its head were fourth-rate generals elevated to
their posts for reasons of influence rather than of competence. The third was the
king's own reluctance to be responsible for a blood bath—a reluctance that
led him to suspend the army's prearranged plan at a critical moment, when
the rebels seemed to be on the run and appeared ready to give in without further
fighting.

Toward the end of the second day of rioting, the king reluctantly decided
to sacrifice Guizot. Perhaps that decision might have saved the regime, had not
an accidental clash occurred a few hours later between troops and rioters
outside Guizot's office. Or perhaps that bloody incident only gave the more
dedicated revolutionaries a better excuse for continuing the fight; for by now,
the working-class quarters were speckled with street barricades. In any event,
the situation had become critical; and at midnight on the 23d, Louis-Philippe
turned grudgingly to Thiers as a possible savior. Again, the possible effect of this
gesture was nullified when the king at the same time named Marshal Bugeaud
to be army commander in Paris, for Bugeaud was probably the most hated
general in the service. By morning the revolutionary tide was flooding toward
the royal palace. Thiers, who fancied himself a new Napoleon in the sphere of
military strategy, urged the king to leave Paris, organize an army of sixty
thousand men, and besiege the city until it could be taken by storm. Louis-
Philippe refused to consider such a solution; after a futile attempt to rally the
remnants of the National Guard in defense of the palace, he wrote out his abdication in favor of his grandson and departed by cab for the suburbs, whence he
eventually made his way to English exile. The king's daughter-in-law remained
behind with the ten-year-old heir apparent. While the mob ransacked the
Tuileries and tested the contents of the royal cellar, the duchess and her children
went to the Chamber of Deputies, hoping that the child would be accepted as
king by acclamation. Many of the deputies were willing, but the Chamber was
gradually inundated by waves of rioters who disrupted the proceedings. When
Lamartine finally got the floor, his flamboyant oratory destroyed the dynasty's
last faint hope; only that morning he had tentatively committed himself to the
republic as the sole solution. As the disillusioned duchess and her brood departed in their turn for exile, the crowd and the deputies surged off across Paris
to the Hôtel de Ville, the traditional seat of newly-founded republics.

Thus for the second time in a generation, and for the third time since 1792,
constitutional monarchy had failed in France. Was this proof that such a system,
in essence a pragmatic and somewhat incoherent compromise between rival doctrines, was unworkable for Frenchmen, with their passion for coherence and

logic? Or was it simply the product of ill fortune, of the country's failure to turn up the kind of monarchs and politicians capable of making such a system function? Or, rather, was the heritage of conflict produced by the Great Revolution so intense as to make any kind of stable government impossible until time allowed passions to die down? A case can doubtless be made for an affirmative answer to each of these questions. Yet once again, as in 1792 and as in 1830, shortcomings of statesmanship seem to have been the crucial factor; and the thesis that any of these three experiments in constitutional monarchy was bound to fail in France is hard to defend. To debate whether the Orleanist experiment was better fitted to survive than its Bourbon predecessor (assuming in both cases a somewhat higher caliber of leadership) would be interesting but not very profitable. The Orleanists lacked the Bourbons' aura of legitimacy and some of the authority conferred by ancient tradition. They possessed, on the other hand, a somewhat greater comprehension of the emerging nineteenth-century world; and, potentially at least, they should have been better able to base their rule on all segments of that broad amorphous category called the bourgeoisie. It is tempting to conclude that no other regime in modern French history missed so good an opportunity to perpetuate itself as a durable political system. A little flexibility, a little imagination, a little capacity for self-criticism—only this, and France might have remained Orleanist for another century.

"Any immobile institution is vicious because it ends as privilege and contradicts the real state of the society it serves." The author of this perceptive comment was, strange to say, François Guizot.

# CHAPTER 11

# The Republican Experiment, 1848–1852

Each revolution undertaken by the French people must establish a new philosophical truth in the world.

*From the preamble to a governmental decree of 1848*

"The importance of 1848," Theodore Zeldin tells us, "is that the masses were drawn into politics, and won over to [the republican] movement."[1] It was indeed from this date onward that the modern phenomena of mass politics began to emerge. Universal suffrage, though interrupted at times, became standard procedure; rudimentary parties began to emerge; the electoral map of France took on a pattern that has in certain respects persisted until the present day. Although the Second Republic was to be short-lived, its effects on French development would be more enduring.

Historians writing on the episode have in many cases been strongly influenced by Karl Marx's two short books, published soon after the events they described. Some of these recent analysts have set out to confirm and elaborate on Marx's views, while others have sought to correct and refute the Marxian judgments. It seems useful, therefore, to begin with a stripped-down summary of this Marxist version, as embodied in the works of Marx himself and of his contemporary followers.

The February revolution, in this view, amounted essentially to the overthrow of the older financial bourgeoisie by the newer industrial bourgeoisie. That basic fact was concealed at the time by a brief interlude of confused class relationships, when the deep conflicts within society were temporarily obscured

---

[1] Theodore Zeldin, *France 1848–1945* (Oxford: Oxford Univ. Press, 1973), I, 477.

by a romantic haze of good will (called by Marx the "universal brotherhood swindle"). The bourgeois provisional government made grand gestures, granting universal manhood suffrage and adding a workingman (Albert) and a prominent socialist (Louis Blanc) to the governing body of the new republic. The old feud over the church's proper role seemed to be ended; republicans and Catholics worked together more intimately than they had ever done before, or were to do again until the mid-twentieth century. Parisian workers paraded to the Hôtel de Ville to offer the new republic a gift of a day's wages; during the first few weeks such voluntary contributions from the workers brought the government more income than it could raise through its first bond issue.

Then, according to the Marxian version, came a gradual clearing of the romantic haze, the emergence of suspicion and hostility on both sides, the recognition of true class conflicts. The proletariat and its petty-bourgeois democratic allies, sensing that they were being duped, threw their energies into organizing clubs on the Jacobin model, organizing street demonstrations, and pressing for what they called "the social republic," including a legal guarantee of the right to work. Spokesmen for the workers urged that the election of a constituent assembly be postponed for a year or more, so that proper enlightenment might be brought to the ignorant peasant masses; and they called for an active ideological foreign policy to aid revolutionary regimes in other European countries. This rising tide of mass activism gave substance to the nervous fears of the bourgeois elite, which saw its special privilege threatened. The poet Lamartine served for a time as a kind of lightning rod, diverting mass discontent by his florid and evasive oratory. A few concessions were made to the workers in an effort to keep them quiet. In the Marxian account, the bourgeoisie gradually recovered its self-confidence and abandoned sham. Its leaders resented the concessions that had been forced on them; they were upset at the business crisis caused by the political upheaval; they were angry when some republicans proposed to nationalize public utilities like the railways and the insurance companies; they were frightened at the success of a few producers' cooperatives that the skilled workers had managed to establish. The bourgeois politicians resorted at last to violent confrontation; they consciously provoked a workers' revolt in June, 1848, to provide an excuse for drowning the "reds" in their own blood.

The Marxist version of 1848, in its most dogmatic form at least, regards the bourgeois leaders as dishonest as well as narrow-minded and selfish. A typical example of their hypocrisy was the creation of the so-called National Workshops a few days after the revolution, under pressure from the workers' representatives in the government. The experiment, we are told, was purposely sabotaged from the outset by placing the Workshops under the control of a violently anti-socialist minister. That minister consciously set out to discredit social reform ideas by making the Workshops a ridiculous caricature of the "social workshop" scheme popularized in the 1840's by Louis Blanc. Another discreditable trick was the recruiting of a special armed police force called the "mobile national guard," chosen from the dregs of the Parisian *lumpenproletariat* and entrusted with the task of breaking up street demonstrations by the true proletariat. The same self-serving motives allegedly inspired the government's decision to order the election of a Constituent Assembly without delay, before the partisans of social reform might have an opportunity to "educate" the mass of peasant voters. Similar hypocrisy is seen behind the motivation of the republic's foreign policy: a spate of fine words on behalf of revolutionary movements in Europe, cancelled out by a refusal to lift a finger in support of those revolutionary governments. In the end, the bourgeoisie is charged with opening the way to a political adventurer named Louis-Napoleon Bonaparte, whose system of authoritarian law and order it preferred to the risks of free government.

Some aspects of Karl Marx's original analysis and of the modernized Marxist version are undoubtedly sound. Many members of the bourgeoisie were openly or hypocritically bigoted and subject to panic; too often the leading politicians were shortsighted or confused. Yet the thesis is too neat and schematic to be completely persuasive. The events of 1848 were more complex than that; some of the Marxist assertions stem from doctrinaire beliefs rather than from solid evidence. A few hair-raising quotations from particularly bigoted politicians will not suffice to support generalizations about the outlook of the entire political elite. No one can sensibly deny that the story of the Second Republic was in part a story of emergent class conflict; but it was in some ways less than that, and in some ways more. This chapter, then, will attempt to sketch out an alternative version of the events of 1848–1851: the same events, but viewed from a somewhat different perspective.

❖❖❖❖❖❖❖❖❖❖❖❖❖❖

The provisional government that was patched together in February, 1848, contained some estimable men, but there was no single figure who combined executive ability with charismatic appeal. Only Lamartine seemed to possess a touch of charisma, and he therefore emerged as symbol and spokesman for the government; but Lamartine clearly lacked the qualities of real crisis leadership. Perhaps no man could have managed so heterogeneous a group of ministers; or perhaps the issues of the time were too complex for settlement. Yet if the new republic had turned up an energetic, shrewd, and high-minded group of leaders at the very outset, it is at least possible that the whole history of the period might have been altered.

Except for the workingman Albert, the membership of the provisional government was solidly bourgeois. The bourgeoisie, however, was far from solid in outlook. Within the government two major factions promptly emerged: a moderate wing, dedicated to political reform, and a radical wing, committed to social experiments as well. Both elements did agree on one basic principle—that of universal manhood suffrage, even though such an experiment was almost unprecedented in Europe, and even though more than a third of the prospective voters were still illiterate. The government's action may have been naive; its decision to rush the elections may have been ill-advised. But there is not the slightest evidence that either decision was dishonest or inspired by shrewd class calculation.

Even on the issue of social reform, the basic division within the government did not show up very clearly at first. Both elements agreed to set up a large study commission directed by Louis Blanc to examine and recommend useful social experiments; both elements agreed to establish the agency misnamed the National Workshops. Neither of these decisions represented a clear governmental commitment to sweeping social reform; but neither one seems to have been designed as a hypocritical scheme for discrediting or sidetracking the social issue. It is true that Louis Blanc's Luxembourg Commission did end in total futility and that the National Workshops resembled an emergency relief agency of the leaf-raking variety rather than a revolutionary system of producers' cooperatives, as advocated by Louis Blanc. But there is only meager and shaky evidence for the view that the bourgeois ministers were inspired by ulterior motives. The provisional government was faced on its accession by a severe economic crisis that had gripped the country since 1846, and the upheaval of 1848 quickly made the situation even worse. As unemployment grew and as thousands of jobless workers flocked to Paris from the provinces, some kind of emergency measures had to be taken for both humanitarian and practical reasons. The Workshops provided some relief, however meager and badly administered they may have been. Alongside them, there did emerge a few real producers' cooperatives of the Blanc variety—notably in the shoemaking and clothing trades.

The government's foreign policy, shaped mainly by Lamartine as foreign minister, was the source of sharper dispute between moderate and radical elements as the months went by. The radicals called for a crusade in support of revolutionary governments in central and eastern Europe. Lamartine gave the idea lip service but no material aid. Not even a huge street demonstration organized by the radicals in support of aid to the Poles succeeded in forcing Lamartine's hand. Perhaps this failure to act was really "the first step on the road to Munich";[1] perhaps, in retrospect, it would have been better if Frenchmen had died carrying liberty throughout Europe rather than fighting each other on the barricades in June. Yet the problem is too complicated for such an easy formula; and doubt must greet the charge that Lamartine's foreign policy was motivated by nothing more than a bourgeois fear of spreading social upheaval. It may be

---

[1] A. J. P. Taylor, in F. Fejtö (ed.), *The Opening of an Era: 1848* (London: Wingate, n.d.), p. xxvi.

that Lamartine, instead of being wicked, was simply wrong; indeed, it is even possible that he was partly right. He believed that an ideological crusade might be disastrous, since it might drive the European powers into a new anti-French coalition like that of Napoleon's day. He probably suspected also that the crusading spirit of the noisy radical minority was not shared by Frenchmen in general. Lamartine was evidently misled into believing (as German liberals also believed) that the king of Prussia had rallied to the liberal cause and would be a dependable ally for the French republic. Together, these liberal states of western Europe could then free the Continent from the chief threat to liberalism—armed intervention by reactionary Russia. If Lamartine was wrong in this analysis, his motives would seem to have been above reproach, and his reasoning comprehensible at least.

On Easter Sunday (April 23) Frenchmen went to the polls to shape the destiny of the republic. There had been little time for nation-wide campaigning or for "educating" the nine and a half million new voters. Most of the peasants and villagers, at a loss to make choices among candidates, ended by voting for lists of local notables—landlords, doctors, notaries—whose names were familiar but whose political affiliations were kept ambiguous. Frenchmen turned out on election day in surprising numbers: 84 per cent of the eligible voters cast ballots, a figure rarely matched since then in any French election. The outcome confirmed the fears of the radicals: the rural vote went to moderate or conservative candidates in all but a few regions. Of nine hundred seats in the new Constituent Assembly, fewer than one hundred were won by the radical republicans or socialists. Even in Paris candidates of the extreme left ran well behind the moderate republicans: Lamartine's name led all the rest, while the radical Ledru-Rollin ranked only twenty-fourth, Louis Blanc twenty-seventh, and Lamennais thirty-fourth. Moderate republicans numbered about five hundred in the new Assembly, monarchists three hundred, and radicals only eighty.

The moderate politicians, bolstered by the verdict of the country, unfortunately failed to show much wisdom in the way they used their new authority. When the Assembly met in May, its majority was determined to root the radicals out of the five-man executive council that was destined to replace the provisional government. Lamartine, fresh from an unprecedented electoral triumph that had seen him poll a million and a half votes in ten districts, took it upon himself to resist that pressure; he refused to accept membership in the new executive council unless the Assembly would elect the radical spokesman Ledru-Rollin as well. It may be that Lamartine's motives were demagogic; his angry moderate colleagues thought so, and so have Marxist historians. But perhaps his action stemmed rather from his deep conviction that an open breach between moderate and radical republicans might bring disaster to the republic itself and that his unparalleled influence must be used to preserve the broad coalition between rival ideologies and classes. The Assembly resentfully bowed to his pressure but showed its anger by barely electing Lamartine and Ledru-Rollin to the new executive council.

During the month that followed, Lamartine proved incapable of dominating the new moderate majority. He failed, most notably, in his effort to provide an acceptable substitute for the National Workshops, the cost of which was bitterly resented by most bourgeois and rural politicians and taxpayers. His plan was to convert the uncompleted railway system into a great public works project and to transfer the unemployed from the Workshops to this more constructive enterprise. The Assembly's rejection of this proposal buttresses the Marxian view of the bourgeoisie's class-bound outlook; but it is worth noting that the idea of public works and of nationalization of the railways was accepted by a number of bourgeois politicians.

The outright abolition of the Workshops followed logically and speedily; young men on the state payroll were offered enlistment in the army as an alternative, older ones were faced by the prospect of departing for the provinces to drain pestilential swamps. The almost immediate consequence was the three-day civil war in Paris known as the June Days—next to the Commune of 1871, the bloodiest episode in the history of modern France.

Two grave charges have been made against the men who abolished the Workshops: that they consciously aimed to provoke the Parisian proletarians to revolt, and that they gave the rebels two full days to assemble and build street barricades so that they might then wipe out the reds en masse. Neither charge can be convincingly defended. Beyond doubt, there were a few rabid red-haters who thought in terms of provoking the radicals to a bloody showdown; but there is no proof that this sentiment was strong among the bourgeois politicians in general, or even that this sentiment existed at all among most of the deputies. The principal bourgeois motive, rather, seems to have been a shortsighted impulsion to cut taxes and to end the boondoggling that allegedly marked the operation of the National Workshops. As for the second charge, there is some reason to believe that prompt army action at the very outset of the June Days might have mastered the rebellion quickly without much bloodshed. General Cavaignac, who was charged with the defense of Paris, refused to take such prompt action despite the urging of Lamartine. His motives remain unplumbed; but the most plausible explanation is that Cavaignac's rigid mind had been set by his experience in repressing Algerian disorders. His practice there had been to let the rebels commit themselves to strong positions and then to blast them out with artillery. Such tactics used in Paris had savage results: at least fifteen hundred rebels were killed on the barricades or in the settling of accounts that followed, and unofficial estimates put the figure at three thousand or more. Twelve thousand others were arrested, and many were subsequently transported to Algeria.

The effects of the June Days were calamitous. One immediate result was the replacement of the five-man civilian executive council by a temporary military dictatorship under Cavaignac. The general became the idol of the bourgeoisie, while Lamartine plummeted into political obscurity. The Parisian radical movement was decapitated by the death, imprisonment, or exile of most of its leading figures. Class hostility reached a new pitch of intensity. While bourgeoisie and aristocracy developed an unreasoning terror of the reds, the workers retreated into silent and embittered opposition to the regime. If the June Days did not doom the Second Republic to extinction, they undoubtedly lengthened the odds against the system's survival.

Comparative quiet descended on the country after the catastrophic June crisis. Gone was the constant effervescence of the republic's early months; gone also the euphoria, the enthusiasm, that had been the hallmark of '48. Cavaignac as temporary executive remade the ministry to suit more conservative tastes. Many of the reform decrees of February and March (e.g., the reduction of the working day in Paris factories to ten hours) were repealed. Louis Blanc's Luxembourg Commission had already been abolished in May. By the end of the year the sum total of surviving social reform—despite an unprecedented flowering of proposals— was virtually zero. The Assembly turned meanwhile to its allotted task of drafting a constitution. Six months of discussion produced the inevitable compromise document designed to satisfy a variety of rival factions and theories. In form at least, it was unambiguously democratic, for its unicameral legislature was to be chosen for a three-year term by universal male suffrage and its president for a four-year term by the same voters. For the first time a French republic chose to experiment with a presidential rather than a parliamentary system.

What the constitution of 1848 left unclear was the relationship between president and legislature, both of which were to be emanations of the popular will. One optimistic deputy offered this prediction: "The executive and legislative powers will clash and balance each other under the nightly and daily surveillance of the press. If they are jealous of each other, that's no matter; if they dispute, so much the better. When you hear them squalling, you'll know they're not dead." A strong minority of the constitution-makers was much more skeptical about the benefits of squalling controversy. An obscure young deputy named Jules Grévy even sought to abolish the office of president entirely and to provide no executive except a committee of the legislature. Grévy's fear of a strong executive, that was given consistency a few years later by Louis-Napoleon's coup d'état, was to lend him an appearance of prescience that would eventually carry him to the presidency of the Third Republic in 1879.

Other nations have proved that a constitutional system like that of the Second Republic can be workable—in other nations, at any rate. Perhaps the system was doomed in France by the peculiar political heritage of the country. Or perhaps it might have been workable there except for the presence of a popular presidential aspirant with autocratic ambitions. The constitution-makers were not aware that such an aspirant was at hand (though some of them were suspicious of the aims of Cavaignac and Lamartine). Few of them would have thought of Louis-Napoleon Bonaparte as a serious threat, for his beginnings in politics had resembled farce rather than high drama.

Louis-Napoleon had returned from British exile[2] soon after the revolution, accompanied by a motley group of supporters and subsidized by his blonde English mistress, the actress Miss Howard. He had been elected to the Constituent Assembly in a by-election in June, but his first speech at the tribune had ended in grotesque failure. Some politicians were sensitive to the curious appeal of his name and got early seats on his bandwagon; but few of them believed him capable of aggressive leadership. Indeed, that was precisely why some of them joined him. Thiers, for example, backed him for the presidency in the hope that a weak executive might open the way to the return of the Orleanist monarchy (and the return of Thiers to the ministry). Not even the shrewdest politician could have foreseen the extent of the Bonapartist landslide in the December presidential election: Louis-Napoleon polled 5,500,000 votes compared to 1,500,000 for Cavaignac, 370,000 for Ledru-Rollin, 37,000 for the radical Raspail, and an almost insulting 17,000 for Lamartine. A further shock followed when the new unicameral Legislative Assembly was elected in May, 1849. The moderate republicans who had shaped the new regime were almost wiped out; the big winners were the monarchist right with some 400 seats and the resurgent radical left with almost 200. Although the monarchists controlled a clear majority, their division into hostile Legitimist and Orleanist factions hampered their potential effectiveness. In any case, a republic whose president was a Bonaparte, whose parliamentary majority was monarchist, and whose organized opposition was composed of the so-called *"démoc-socs"* or "reds" seemed predestined to disaster. Disaster was indeed to be its fate—and within three years.

✖✖✖✖✖✖✖✖✖✖✖✖✖✖

Any coherent account of the Second Republic's constitutional phase must depend on a prior judgment of Louis-Napoleon's aims and character. At one extreme, critics have seen him as an unprincipled schemer interested in little except women, race horses, and power and determined from the outset to destroy the republic at the appropriate moment. At the opposite extreme are those who

---

[2] He had escaped from the fortress of Ham in 1846 after serving six years of his life term.

see him as a sincere idealist who sensed the trend of his age and who sought to give France the vigorous leadership it needed. Some of his defenders believe that the president always meant to convert the republic into an empire, but only for high-minded reasons. Others remain convinced that until late in 1851 he remained loyal to the republic and sought only to get the constitution amended so that he might run for a second term. If Louis-Napoleon has been an enigma to historians, perhaps that is because he was an enigma even to those who knew him best. His cousin Princess Mathilde, one of the shrewdest of the Bonapartes, once remarked impatiently: "If I had married him, I think that I would have broken his head open to find out what's inside."

During the early phase of Louis-Napoleon's presidency he seemed inclined to collaborate with the conservative majority in the Legislative Assembly. He catered to conservative views in his foreign policy—notably by sending aid to the beleaguered Pope, driven from Rome by republican revolutionaries—and by his acceptance of a Catholic-sponsored educational reform, the Falloux Law of 1850. He also signed into law bills that deprived one out of three Frenchmen of the right to vote and that restricted the press and the right of political assemblage.

Yet Louis-Napoleon had long since indicated his sympathy for ideas that ran counter to the whole conservative doctrine. During his imprisonment at Ham in the 1840's he had published several pamphlets of vaguely Saint-Simonian flavor—notably a work entitled *The Extinction of Poverty*. Bonapartist candidates, when they ran for the Legislative Assembly in 1849, had usually chosen to stand on a platform of dynamic change rather than one of static defense. Monarchist candidates in that election had been inclined to talk of order, family, property, religion; their Bonapartist rivals preferred to urge the importance of rural roads, railways, canals.

Karl Marx contended (and recent Marxist historians echo his view) that Louis-Napoleon's leftist leanings were mere sham; that he resorted to pseudo-socialist phraseology as a demagogic device to frighten the bourgeoisie. His attempt to win the genuine affection of the propertied class had failed, according to Marx, and so Louis-Napoleon shifted to a kind of blackmail by hinting that he might turn sharply left and use the *lumpenproletariat*, the scum of the cities, to establish a socialist dictatorship. By this tactic, according to Marx, the bulk of the bourgeoisie was not so much won over as neutralized; and the country's fate was left in the hands of the "inert" classes—the most backward and superstitious elements of the peasantry and the petty bourgeoisie. Only after Louis-Napoleon had repressed the proletariat and neutralized the bourgeoisie, argued Marx, did he consider it safe to challenge the conservative majority in the legislature. But the Marxist thesis that Louis-Napoleon looked to the ignorant, the inert, the "troglodytes" of French society for his chief support can hardly be reconciled with what Louis-Napoleon said throughout his life, or with what he did as emperor, or with the kind of support he got from certain dynamic ele ments in the population.

If President Bonaparte went along with the conservative majority until 1851, he did so not by choice but by what seemed to be necessity. He needed funds from the Assembly, and he needed also a constitutional reform that would enable him to run for a second term. He signed the Assembly's bill restricting the suffrage, but with great reluctance; and he was not much more enthusiastic about the Falloux Law in 1850. That law, a major event in the nineteenth-century religious, educational, and political history of France, marked the successful conclusion of a ten-year Catholic campaign to secure greater influence in education. It gave the church the right to operate secondary schools (*collèges*) alongside those of the state, and it increased church influence in the supervision of state primary schools. Similar bills had been defeated four times during the 1840's by the skeptical Orleanist politicians. In 1850 many of those same politicians (Thiers, for example) swung over to join the conservatives in its support.

The motives that produced this change of mind were not all admirable ones. The hysterical red scare produced by the June Days led Voltaireans like Thiers to acclaim the church as "the last bulwark of the social order." "Every Voltairean in France with a few thousand pounds of income," remarked Ozanam bitterly, "wants to send everybody to Mass, provided that he himself doesn't have to go." Thiers even talked of giving the church a total monopoly of primary education. The mood of the moment benefited Catholic reactionaries like Veuillot and led even a mildly liberal Catholic like Montalembert to declare: "There is only one recipe for making those who own nothing believe in property-rights: that is to make them believe in God, who dictated the Ten Commandments and who promises eternal punishment to those who steal." The trend in France was furthered by a swing toward reaction in the Vatican; Pius IX, after recovering his lost throne in 1849, abandoned his earlier liberal inclinations. It was clear by the end of 1848 that the Christian democratic current, so prominent in the early months of the revolution, had in fact touched only a small elite within the church. Not until the twentieth century was it to know a significant revival.

The Falloux Law has been described as the greatest clerical victory of the nineteenth century. Although the confirmed Voltaireans among the bourgeoisie remained skeptics, they nevertheless began to send their sons to Catholic *collèges;* within a generation, half of the secondary students in France were enrolled in Catholic schools. The return to the faith that had revealed itself within the aristocracy after 1814, and that had begun to affect the middle classes in the 1840's, now made rapid progress among the bourgeoisie. This process of rechristianization was to give Catholicism a solid bourgeois base in twentieth-century France. The church's problem henceforth would be to check the trend toward unbelief that had already set in strongly among the urban workers and that was to make serious inroads among the peasantry as well after the mid-nineteenth century.

If the Falloux Law was a victory for the clericals, it was in some ways a costly one. Its effect was to intensify the anticlerical spirit of the left and to infect the whole republican movement with an almost unreasoning suspicion of the church. It was no accident that the next generation saw the conversion of Free-masonry from its mildly deist and liberal outlook to a mood of violent repub-licanism and bigoted anticlericalism, or that an obscure politician in 1863 coined the durable battle cry, "Clericalism, there is the enemy!" Anticlericals became convinced that the church's purpose was to achieve a complete monopoly of education in order to tighten its grip on the state; they believed that church schools were brainwashing machines whose influence would divide French youth into two irreconcilable camps. The Falloux Law became a kind of symbol of the conflict, a bogey to frighten the left. Thus the Second Republic, which at the out-set had brought republicans and Catholics together in a flush of fraternity and good will, ended by making the religious problem a major political issue destined to poison the atmosphere in France for generations. Objectively, the Falloux Law scarcely deserved such opprobrium, for it was a compromise that infuriated Catholic extremists like Veuillot as much as it aroused the anticlericals. The real tragedy for France was that this relatively moderate Catholic victory came at a moment when passions were building up on both sides. During the subsequent generation the loudest Catholic voices were to be those of the Veuillot faction, while the most vocal republicans would be turning to a dogmatic and material-istic doctrine called positivism. Neither faction was inclined toward peaceful coexistence or was ready to let the Falloux Law, in either its original form or a revised version, be given a fair trial.

❖❖❖❖❖❖❖❖❖❖❖❖❖

By the summer of 1851 the relationship between Louis-Napoleon and the Legislative Assembly had reached total stalemate. Despite the president's efforts to appease the conservative majority, it stubbornly refused to grant him the two things he most wanted: a constitutional revision to permit a second presidential term, and a vote of funds to enable him to pay his personal debts. At some undetermined point in 1851 Louis-Napoleon gave in to the pressure of his entourage and, with apparent reluctance, turned to planning a coup d'état.

In this scheming, the army was destined to play a key role. Since 1799 the officer corps had remained aloof from politics and had served each successive regime in docile fashion. Its morale and prestige had fallen sharply since the great days of the Napoleonic empire. If the military life and the ideal of patriotic glory still had defenders in France, they tended to cluster on the left, among Jacobin republicans and chauvinistic Bonapartists. Yet a segment of the officer corps showed signs of abandoning its neutrality after 1848 and ended by participating—for the first time in the nineteenth century—in the overthrow of a regime. Most of the officers, even though the bulk of them were commoners promoted from the ranks, disliked the republic as a regime of squabbling lawyers; they leaned toward a return to the monarchy, and some of them engaged in manipulative intrigues with the monarchist majority in the Assembly. A smaller group of officers—mostly below the top echelon—found themselves attracted to the prospect of a restored empire. Louis-Napoleon quietly shifted these men into key posts and entrusted to one of them, General Saint-Arnaud, the task of ensuring the success of the coup d'état.

Early on the morning of December 2, 1851 (the anniversary of Austerlitz, and of the first Napoleon's coup in 1804), the leading legislators were routed out of bed and arrested, and a drastic revision of the 1848 constitution was announced by the president. It extended the presidential term to ten years and sharply reduced the legislature's powers. The nation was called upon to approve the new authoritarian order by plebiscite and proceeded to ratify the change by a massive majority of 92 per cent of the votes cast. Louis-Napoleon's only disappointment came from the fact that his coup had not been unopposed and bloodless. Despite Saint-Arnaud's military precautions, barricades had gone up on December 3 in the working-class quarters of Paris, and two days of violent fighting followed before the Parisian resistance was quelled. Meanwhile, organized opposition to the coup had been spreading to the provinces—especially to a number of regions in the center and south where the *"démoc-socs"* or "reds" had established bastions of strength since 1848. Most of this provincial resistance was small-town or rural rather than urban; it rallied some one hundred thousand men, which made it by far the largest extra-Parisian insurrection France was to experience in the nineteenth century. Before quiet could be restored, several hundred protesters had been killed and twenty-six thousand arrested, ten thousand of whom were subsequently transported to Algeria. Many others were interned in France, while the leaders of the monarchist opposition were exiled. Students of electoral behavior in France have observed a remarkable continuity in the strength of the left; many of the areas that elected *"démoc-soc"* candidates in 1849 vigorously resisted the coup d'état of 1851, and still vote strongly left in our own day.

The authoritarian republic created in 1851 was obviously no more than a stopgap arrangement. A year later, on December 2, 1852, Louis-Napoleon took note of what he called the nation's desires and transmuted himself from president into emperor. This time there was no trace of open resistance; the decisive step had been taken in 1851. The docile voters once again approved by plebiscite, this time by an increased margin of 97 per cent.

The brief episode of 1848–52, shortest of France's five republics, cannot be explained without an analysis of class antagonisms; nor can the social stresses of the next half-century he fully understood without an analysis of the events of 1848, which intensified those stresses. Class conflict alone, however, furnishes only a partial explanation of this upheaval. Individuals act for other reasons than those of class interest alone; nations are something more than mere congeries of classes. Perhaps, as the historian Ernest Labrousse suggests, the tragedy of 1848 was that a set of twentieth-century problems suddenly confronted a society with an eighteenth-century structure, and that the leaders of the time had no real understanding of the emergent industrial age.

CHAPTER 12

# *The Imperial Experiment,*
# *1852–1870*

> The empress is legitimist, my cousin is republican, Morny is Orleanist, I am a socialist; the only Bonapartist is Persigny, and he's crazy.
>
> Attributed to NAPOLEON III

Only twice since 1815 has parliamentary or quasi-parliamentary government in France been interrupted by frankly authoritarian systems.[1] These two exceptions, the Second Empire and the Vichy regime, both appear to be aberrations from the country's norm, and both were generally denounced as such after their overthrow. In the case of the Second Empire, however, the passage of time eventually brought a revisionist current and suggested to many Frenchmen that there had been unsuspected virtues in Napoleon III's system. Some biographers converted the emperor from an unscrupulous tyrant into an almost visionary reformer and patron of progress. Many economists pointed out that the period of the Second Empire brought the most rapid economic and social change in French history, so that in retrospect it constitutes a kind of watershed between the France of the old regime and the France of the twentieth century. Some historians even suggested that Napoleon's system came nearer than any other to reconciling the diverse traditions—libertarian, equalitarian, authoritarian—left to posterity by the Great Revolution. The new legend has doubtless been exaggerated in some respects, but it does permit a more balanced view than was possible in the years after Napoleon's fall.

---

[1] Charles de Gaulle's Fifth Republic might be considered a third—though much more ambiguous—case.

142

Built into the empire were a number of inconsistencies that have always made it difficult to analyze. The regime's emphasis on glory stood in at least potential contrast to Napoleon's enduring interest in the right of nationalities to self-determination. Its stress on the defense of order and stability seemed incompatible with Napoleon's encouragement of dynamic change. Its authoritarian beginnings are hard to reconcile with its gradual liberalization, a process that eventually turned it into a quasi-parliamentary system resembling that of 1814–48. Perhaps these inconsistencies prove that the imperial regime was nothing more than a haphazard jumble, reflecting the confused welter of ideas within the opportunistic emperor's mind, and prevented by its very nature from arriving at any sort of harmonious fusion. But an even more persuasive hypothesis is that Napoleon III, a man of complex and imaginative temperament, sensed some of the trends of his times and sought, in quite un-Cartesian fashion, to adapt an old and complex nation to those trends. If his course was sometimes illogical and his system hybrid, it can only be said that perfect symmetry and logic have not always been the hallmarks of durable systems.

The Second Empire divides itself into two major periods: the authoritarian phase to 1859, the liberal phase thereafter. The transition from one to the other was closely linked with a change in foreign policy that sharply affected Napoleon's relations with the church, and a change in tariff policy that affected his relations with the business group. The new foreign policy grew out of the emperor's decision to help the Piedmontese prime minister Cavour drive the Austrians out of northern Italy in 1859. The fillip thus given to Italian nationalism endangered the Pope's temporal control of Rome and alienated French clericals who had hitherto supported Napoleon. The new economic policy was embodied in Napoleon's surprise negotiation of a low-tariff treaty with England in 1860. It aroused widespread concern among French manufacturers, who had hitherto applauded the empire's economic policies and had profited greatly from the remarkable boom of the 1850's.

Napoleon's turn toward domestic liberalization that began late in 1859 and continued jerkily throughout the next decade may have been merely an attempt to find a new base of support in place of that lost through his foreign and economic policies. Perhaps the emperor and his advisers slipped into this dangerous current under pressure of circumstances, through mere opportunism or sheer weakness, somewhat against their own preferences and without any clear idea of where the current might carry them. But it is equally possible that the evolution of the 1860's was both planned and desired; that it had been, from the very outset of the empire, the more or less conscious intention of Napoleon and of certain advisers like his half-brother the Duc de Morny; that it was the product of an ambition to reconcile the conflicting political traditions inherited from France's past. A choice between these interpretations depends on an estimate of motives and therefore permits no sure or easy answer. But a second problem is equally crucial. Whatever the motivation of Napoleon and his entourage may have been, was their new course after 1859 a sensible and realistic one? Was it, by 1870, on the way to producing a viable compromise system of government, or was it dragging the regime into a morass of hopeless contradictions? Was this kind of authoritarian system capable of mellowing without destroying itself? Here again, no easy or certain answer is possible; yet some answer must be attempted if the record of the empire is to be judged as well as narrated.

❖❖❖❖❖❖❖❖❖❖❖❖❖

The political system of the authoritarian phase requires only brief analysis. Its institutions were frankly borrowed from those of the First Empire: the façade of legislative organs without much prestige or power, the ministry responsible to the emperor alone, the plebiscite utilized as an occasional device to give the illusion of popular control. Napoleon III justified this attempt to resurrect the past by remarking that for fifty years France had retained the administrative, judicial, religious, and financial structure established by Napoleon I, so that a return to his political institutions was only logical and consistent. In a relatively mild sense, the new empire was a police state. Opposition to the regime was possible, but it was narrowly restricted by controls on the press and on the right to hold public meetings. The modern concentration camp did not yet exist, but there was its primitive equivalent in the penal colonies of Guiana and Algeria. Most of the regime's outspoken critics had chosen exile in preference to prison or deportation: among them were such notables as Thiers, Victor Hugo, and Louis Blanc. Silent but bitter antagonism persisted among diehard republicans, Legitimist aristocrats, and most Orleanist politicians, though some Orleanists were converted by Napoleon's policy of aid to enterprising business men.

Support for the regime during its authoritarian decade came not only from the business class but also from the church hierarchy, from the bulk of the peasantry, and from a considerable minority of the urban workers. Churchmen knew that Napoleon was a freethinker, but they applauded his support of the Pope's temporal power and his defense of social order; some bishops indulged in the most fulsome adulation, publicly comparing the emperor to Constantine and Saint Louis. Napoleon's proletarian support came from those workers who were embittered and disillusioned with the republicans after 1848. Bonapartist candidates who promised vigorous measures of economic expansion caught the fancy of at least some working-class elements, and the boom of the 1850's kept them relatively content. The peasants, save for those few who voted republican or the larger number who remained subservient to local aristocrats, contributed the regime's mass base. Many of them were moved by considerations of glamor and glory, many by a conviction that Napoleon would defend private property against "the reds." But there were some who clearly betrayed quite opposite motives—who voted for Bonapartist candidates as a kind of declaration of independence from the local notables who had dominated them for so long. At least the beginnings of peasant education in the use of the ballot can be traced to the era of the Second Republic and the Second Empire; as early as 1849 peasant voters in certain regions had shaken off the docility that marked their voting behavior in April 1848, and had turned to republican or Bonapartist candidates. This rebellious sense of independence benefited Bonapartism in the early years, but in the long run it was to undermine the regime's support in the countryside. Once a stiff-necked peasant had learned that he could safely ignore the admonitions of the local aristocrat, priest, or notary, he was likely to rebel against the pressures of Napoleon's prefects as well.

The authoritarian empire left only a restricted sphere for active political life. Sessions of the Corps Législatif (the new lower house of parliament) were closed to the public, and only a brief summary of its proceedings was made available in the press. Although the Corps was elected by universal manhood suffrage, Napoleon was careful to space the elections at intervals of six years. "I am prepared to be baptized with the water of universal suffrage," he is supposed to have said, "but I don't intend to live with my feet in a puddle." The plebiscite, a device theoretically designed to indicate the responsibility of the emperor to the people, was actually used only three times: in 1851, 1852, and 1870.

Yet it would be unjust to conclude that the authoritarian empire anticipated the totalitarian system of Hitler, or that the empire was run by a hand-picked collection of Bonapartist fanatics and puppets. In creating the new political class whose function it was to shore up and administer the empire, Napoleon and his advisers did not confine themselves to "pure" Bonapartists, nor did they seek to sweep away the old elites in favor of a new privileged caste. Instead, they drew heavily on the existing elites, in an effort to combine aristocracy with democracy. "Official candidates" for the Corps Législatif—i.e., those who were openly endorsed by the government—were not hand-picked in Paris but were often selected by the imperial prefects from among the local notables whose influence might get them elected and whose support (if it could be won) would be valuable to the regime. Although many of the notables resisted the government's blandishments and remained loyal to a previous regime, a fair number of ex-Legitimists and ex-Orleanists gradually let themselves be converted. The effect was to shunt aside many of the early Bonapartists of more modest social origins who had rallied to Louis-Napoleon's cause in 1848 and had begun to build local party machinery. The Second Empire thus came to be a curious alliance of old and new forces, and it represented neither a total break with France's political past nor a revolutionary change in the locus of power within French society. The lower middle class, which was to be so heavily represented in the political elite of twentieth-century fascist states, got little satisfaction out of Napoleon III's revolution. Not until the middle years of the Third Republic did this segment of society work its way up into the controlling circles of the state.

Napoleon's ministers and high administrative officials also represented a mixture of old and new. Some, like Persigny, were personal henchmen whose loyalty had been tested in the early days of adversity. Some, like the Duc de Morny and Comte Walewski, were kinsmen of the emperor—illegitimate ones, it is true, but kinsmen nevertheless. Some, like Achille Fould, came from powerful banking families. Some, like Eugène Rouher, Jules Baroche, and Michel Chevalier, were ex-Orleanist lawyers, politicians, or intellectuals. Some, like the prefect Haussmann who rebuilt Paris in its modern form, were career bureaucrats who had served both the monarchy and the republic. Critics of the regime alleged that it was run by a band of shady and unscrupulous adventurers whose qualities reflected the shoddy artificiality of the system. There were men around Napoleon who did fit that description; but the empire had a broader and more reputable base than its enemies' charges would suggest. If the regime was not served by all the elites, that was not because the emperor preferred adventurers to solid citizens, but rather because so many prominent Frenchmen remained irreconcilable after 1851.

❖❖❖❖❖❖❖❖❖❖❖❖❖❖

Napoleon's first steps toward softening the authoritarian system in 1859 were relatively hesitant ones. Political exiles were amnestied and allowed to return; the Corps Législatif was given the right to present an annual "address" or set of formal resolutions to the emperor, and its sessions were opened to the public. More important, however, was the fact that additional reforms followed at irregular intervals throughout the decade. The process grew more rapid after 1867: Napoleon relaxed many of the controls on the press and public assembly, and gave parliament the right to interpellate the ministers. The workers, who had been granted the right to strike in 1864, were now told that workers' organizations would be tolerated as well. A significant program of broadened public education was drafted by the emperor's forceful minister of education, Victor Duruy; the curriculum was liberalized, and a feeble gesture was made toward secondary education for girls. Duruy also created the Ecole pratique des hautes études, an advanced training and research institution that was to be one of the most durable and productive innovations of the Second Empire.

This jerky progress toward "liberalized authoritarianism" during the 1860's cost Napoleon much of his conservative support, yet failed to win him an equal number of new converts on the left. Instead, the opposition steadily gained strength at each legislative election. In 1857 opposition candidates had polled only three-quarters of a million votes; in 1863 they got two million, and in 1869 3.3 million, or almost 45 per cent of the total vote cast. Prima facie, the evidence seemed clear that the emperor's liberal gamble had backfired, and that good sense would require a return to a purer form of authoritarianism, supported by the church and the business community. Some of his advisers (notably Persigny) had argued all along against a swing toward a liberalized empire, and they fought a steady rear-guard action to check the liberal trend before it was too late.

Instead, after considerable hesitation, the emperor elected to attempt an even more extreme dose of liberalism. In January 1870 he invited one of the leaders of the liberal opposition, Emile Ollivier, to form a government. Ollivier, a moderate republican, was permitted to staff his cabinet with men of republican or Orleanist background, most of whom had long been advocates of parliamentary government. He then embarked on the drafting of a new constitution which, though hybrid in nature, converted the empire into a quasi-parliamentary regime. The ministers were declared to be "responsible" (though to whom was not entirely clear), and their powers were broadened, along with those of the Corps législatif. At the same time, the emperor retained most of his existing prerogatives, so that in the event of a deadlock between emperor and parliament, the real locus of power would be clouded. A similar ambiguity had existed from 1814 to 1848 but had not prevented a gradual evolution toward a government very similar to a parliamentary monarchy.

The empire's downfall only a few months later might seem to justify the warnings of the Persigny faction, and to suggest that Napoleon III destroyed himself by attempting to graft liberal branches onto an authoritarian stem. Yet those critics who prophesied disaster offered no real alternative except standpattism—a policy that has rarely succeeded for very long in any nation committed to modern and dynamic action. Successful regimes have normally been the ones with enough flexibility to adapt themselves to changing economic, social, and psychological conditions. At any rate, it does seem certain that after 1859 Napoleon was moving in the right general direction so far as the bulk of French opinion was concerned. The most persuasive evidence for this view was given by the voters in May 1870, when they were summoned by plebiscite to approve or reject the new Ollivier constitution. The pro-regime share of the vote, which had been only 55 per cent in the 1869 elections, rocketed to 83 per cent; the opposition total fell by more than half. No greater victory had been won by the regime since the days of authoritarian empire. Even though the persistent hard core of opposition was still disturbingly large, it seemed clear that Napoleon had at last found a formula satisfactory to the bulk of the nation. Seven Frenchmen out of nine were ready to support the quasi-parliamentary experiment of 1870, combining an autocratic monarch with a responsible cabinet. The record of the liberal decade thus suggests that Napoleon III did grope his way toward a workable governmental system: a system lacking in inner logic, yet potentially capable of reconciling and balancing the nation's most important conflicts.

One crucial question remained, however: was Napoleon III capable of heading that kind of regime? A compromise system that lacks inner logic, that combines Caesarism and responsible government, calls for exceptionally shrewd, adaptable, pragmatic leadership. The flaws in Napoleon's character make it doubtful that he could have furnished that kind of adept yet vigorous statesmanship. His intimates knew that he had an indolent streak, that he was inclined to vacillate, that he indulged at times in wishful thinking in preference to facing hard facts. "Napoleon the Well-Meaning," someone sarcastically called him. If there had been time to try the new experiment in quasi-parliamentary government, Napoleon might have been confronted quite soon with a major challenge to his personal authority; for many of his new supporters were determined to complete the process of liberalization by converting the emperor into a British-type monarch, subordinate to parliament's wishes. No one can be sure that Napoleon would have been flexible enough to take that final logical step in a process that he himself had voluntarily begun. Indeed, his next step might possibly have been in quite the opposite direction—a brusque repudiation of the trend of the 1860's, a virutal coup d'état against the liberal empire.

Events were not to permit the testing of the new hybrid regime; only four months after the triumphant plebiscite, it had collapsed, and the emperor was on his way to exile in England. What doomed the empire was not its internal evolution but rather the cumulative results of a series of errors in foreign policy. By 1870 France found itself isolated and confronted by a powerful new rival across the Rhine. Napoleon III had failed to intervene in central Europe in 1866 when it might have been easy to check the growth of Prussian power. He had failed in his subsequent efforts to secure face-saving compensations in the form of territorial gains along the Rhine. He had failed once more when he sought to bolster French military power by introducing a new army bill into parliament in 1867. His proposal, which would have brought a larger annual contingent of draftees into the army and would have increased the cost of preparedness, aroused a political storm; in the end the bill had to be so watered down that it became innocuous. Meanwhile the failure of Napoleon's "great idea"—the building of a Catholic empire in Mexico allied with France—had divided the nation and provided his critics with effective ammunition. Efforts after 1866 to negotiate alliances with Italy and Austria-Hungary produced no result except to arouse false hopes in Paris.

War with Prussia was not the only possible outcome of the crisis that erupted suddenly in July, 1870. Either Bismarck or Napoleon III could have averted a test of arms. Bismarck had no desire to avert it; Napoleon lacked the foresight to do so. Chronic illness during the last years of his reign probably lessened his capacity to devote sustained attention to the developing crisis or to make difficult decisions; he was unwise enough to let authority slip into the hands of his second-rate foreign minister, the Duc de Gramont. The French government, aroused at the news that Spain had secretly arranged to place a Hohenzollern prince on the Spanish throne, put such heavy pressure on the king of Prussia that the latter persuaded the Hohenzollern nominee to withdraw his candidacy. Gramont had thus won a notable diplomatic victory, but he was not intelligent enough to be satisfied with it. Instead, he demanded still further Prussian assurances for the future, and thus gave Bismarck an opportunity to play the picador to "the Gallic bull." On July 19 the French government, angered at Prussia's apparent flouting of French demands, slipped into war—unnecessarily, unwisely, and with inadequate preparation for so severe a test.

Few Frenchmen except Adolphe Thiers (who had been issuing gloomy warnings ever since 1866) fully understood the threat that France faced. Prime Minister Ollivier encouraged the nation's illusions by announcing that he accepted war "with a light heart," and his war minister even more recklessly assured parliament that the army was ready "to the last gaiter button." What the army lacked in 1870 was not gaiter buttons but something far more serious: efficient, vigorous, and imaginative leadership. The officer corps, though honorable and loyal, had slipped into a rut of routine-mindedness and smug complacency that contrasted sharply with the tough and keen mentality of the Prussian staff. France's clumsy and antiquated process of mobilization had not even been completed when the first German troops crossed the frontier. Within a month the great border fortress of Metz was cut off by the invaders, and the army of Marshal Bazaine besieged therein. Napoleon, who had gone to the front to share the perils of war with his soldiers, refused to adopt the one strategic plan that might still have averted defeat—a slow retreat to Paris and a stand outside the walls of the capital. Fearing the political repercussions of such a strategic withdrawal, he accompanied his remaining army under MacMahon in an attempt to relieve Metz. The Prussians cornered MacMahon's force at Sedan on August 31 and broke its resistance in a brief battle fought the next day. Napoleon, aware that the fight was hopeless, sought a hero's death in the front lines, on the theory that his martyrdom might save the throne for his adolescent son. Even that consolation was denied him; and he fell ignominiously into the hands of the Prussians.

The emperor, but not the empire, survived the carnage of Sedan. When the news reached Paris on September 3, the regime's political leaders tried desperately to prop up the imperial system by arranging an interim government under a military leader. Even the republican politicians were willing; most of them were not eager to take power at so gloomy a moment. But it was far too late to save the empire; its prestige had vanished in defeat. On September 4 demonstrating crowds converged on the Corps législatif and demanded the proclamation of a republic. Napoleon's system disintegrated without bloodshed, and almost without regret.

The Second Empire outlasted any other governmental experiment that had been tried in France since 1814. Whether it achieved more than its predecessors and whether it came nearer to producing a durable compromise are controversial issues. For two generations after its fall the empire was bitterly maligned by all good republicans. Yet by the middle 1870's Bonapartism had revived sufficiently to become an important political force in France; in 1877 there were 104 Bonapartists in the Chamber of Deputies. So quick a recovery (even though it proved fleeting) may suggest that many Frenchmen remembered the days of Napoleon III with nostalgia. Some twentieth-century critics of the parliamentary republic were to find a retrospective utopia in the Second Empire: a middle way, they said, between the divisive weakness of multiparty democracy and the oppressive tyranny of modern totalitarianism. Yet it is quite possible that the consequences of the empire were more destructive than constructive; that this interruption in the nineteenth-century trend toward responsible government created as many problems as it tried to solve, and that some of France's contemporary ailments are at least partly traceable to it. Certainly it deepened the neurotic fear of the strong man among French republicans and liberals and reinforced the sentiment that authority must be both suspected and resisted. After 1870 the new republic was shaped, its institutions were built in an atmosphere of violent revulsion against the Second Empire—even against those aspects of it that might have helped France adapt its political, social, and economic structure to the needs of modern times.

# CHAPTER 13

# Economy: Structure and Trends, 1814–1870

> ...Despite a contrary view that has been too long accepted, economic life is in large measure what governments make it.
>
> J.-M. JEANNENEY

The changes wrought in France's economic system by the upheaval of the Great Revolution were probably less sweeping than those effected in the political, the social, or even the psychological spheres. True, the revolution bulldozed away many of the tangled restrictions on domestic trade that had grown up in the old regime and destroyed the remnants of the corporative system that had still hampered production. It thus cleared the way for a fundamental change in economic structure and for the arrival of the industrial age. But not even the faint beginnings of anything like an industrial revolution had occurred in France by 1814, and another full generation was to pass before French enterprisers were to take much advantage of their new freedom.

Napoleon, to be sure, claimed credit for great advances and boasted, "It is I who created French industry." His regime did in fact stimulate some progress toward mechanization, and, by providing a huge protected continental market, it offered French businessmen an unprecedented opportunity for expansion. Some of them took advantage of it; a good many fortunes were founded in the Napoleonic era. Yet the emperor's industrial policy was so narrowly military in purpose that what he achieved was rarely durable; and the business crisis of 1810–12 undid much of what had been done. Furthermore, it was finance rather than industry that attracted the ablest enterprisers during the Napoleonic era. Except in banking, the economic consequences of the revolutionary-Napoleonic years were clearly negative. The technological gap between Britain and France, already serious in 1789, became even wider; the British had increased their productive power and conquered new overseas markets, while French businessmen had been hampered by a loss of capital and manpower, by financial and commercial instability, and by a temporary loss of markets that became, in some areas, permanent.

In theory, the restored Bourbons might have returned to the rigid and hierarchical structure of the old regime, based on gilds or corporations. In practice, such an idea found few defenders, even among the ultras. The obvious alternative was a venture into laissez-faire, freeing French enterprisers from the restrictions of both the old gild system and Napoleon's wartime controls. Logically, such a venture should have included a sharp reduction in tariffs in order to stimulate exchanges with the rest of Europe. Even the old monarchy had established some precedent for such a policy when it negotiated the Eden treaty of 1786 with Britain; and after 1789 the revolutionary leaders had seemed inclined to perpetuate it before they were drawn into a generation of war. At first Louis XVIII and his advisers, urged on by the British, made a timid effort to move back in that direction. They reduced trade barriers moderately, but an influx of British goods followed and quickly forced the government back toward high protection. Pressure in the direction of tariffs was exerted by the two most powerful interest groups in France: the large landowners and the business group. Their vigorous lobbying ensured steadily rising tariff rates after 1816, to the point of total exclusion of some items. The duty on iron goods, for example, eventually reached 120 per cent.

The defensive attitude of French producers of basic items like textiles and iron goods was understandable; British technology had left them far behind. More surprising was the fact that French farm producers joined in the demand for higher tariffs. France in the past had never needed barriers against incoming farm products; the only restrictions, indeed, had been against the *export* of grain. France, as a great agricultural nation, seemed to possess the same kind of competitive advantage that the British now enjoyed in industry. The new defensive stance was the outgrowth of a dual change. First, wartime shortages had driven grain prices up, and agrarian interests believed that protection might keep them there. Second, France faced for the first time the threat of quantity imports from the steppes of Russia. As British landlords got their corn law in 1815, so French landowners won the same kind of victory in 1819; and protection for other farm products followed in series. Even the winegrowers climbed aboard the tariff bandwagon, though they faced no direct foreign competition. Their aim was a high duty on tea, to avert what they described as a threat to the French way of life as well as to their own prosperity. "Tea," declaimed one agrarian deputy, "breaks down our national character by converting those who use it often into cold and stuffy Nordic types, while wine arouses in the soul that gentle gaiety . . . that gives Frenchmen their amiable and witty national character."

Few voices were raised in opposition to the steady spiral of tariff increases, even to suggest that other nations might retaliate and thus injure French exports. Any possible concern on this point was quieted by the customs officials, who annually presented figures that showed a steady growth in both exports and imports, but especially the former. Recent studies suggest that these figures were systematically falsified for political reasons, and that accurate statistics would have indicated a growing stagnation in trade and a disturbing decline in exports. For the protective system not only kept French domestic prices high and slowed up modernization; it also brought reprisals abroad.

By the end of the Bourbon era some Frenchmen were becoming aware of this fact. An economic crisis that set in from 1826 to 1829 caused enough stress to arouse serious questioning of the system, especially on the part of the wine-growers, shipping interests, and other seaport groups. Nothing in the way of change was accomplished under the Bourbons; vested interests were too numerous and too strong. Besides, a governmental study commission rejected the idea of a turn toward lower tariffs on the ground that it would work an injustice to men who had, in good faith, gone into business with the expectation of continuing tariff protection. Here was a classic example of special privilege crystallizing promptly into vested interest. The doctrines of economic liberalism nevertheless began to make serious progress for the first time during the late 1820's. Professor J.-B. Say, the French popularizer of Adam Smith, began to get a hearing at last, even in parliament. The discontent produced by the recession of 1826–29 undermined the nation's previous solidarity on economic policy and doubtless contributed to the unrest that produced the revolution of 1830.

France's economic structure changed remarkably little during the Bourbon restoration. The government's attitude toward business was epitomized in the accountant's outlook of Villèle: his goal was a balanced budget with the lowest possible expenditure. Government aid to industry or agriculture or commerce, except through tariff protection, was almost nil. No French regime has ever offered so perfect an antithesis to the twentieth-century Keynesian ideal. While industrial production and commercial enterprise made slow progress, French bankers consolidated their position as the real business elite of the era; as in Napoleon's day, finance continued to attract the nation's most vigorous enterprisers. Perhaps it was in part their discontent with the regime's narrow lack of imagination that drove a number of wealthy bankers—Jacques Laffitte and Casimir Périer, for example—into the liberal opposition and led some Frenchmen to call the 1830 upheaval "the bankers' revolution."

❖❖❖❖❖❖❖❖❖❖❖❖❖❖

Something resembling an industrial revolution began at last during the reign of Louis-Philippe, though it did not reach its apogee until the Second Empire. It was natural enough that a regime that has often been called a "bourgeois monarchy" should favor the interests of the business community (or what the business group thought to be its interests). That favoritism was reflected in a continuance of high protective tariffs; in a low level of taxation; in a policy of governmental noninterference in business operations; and in a benevolent stance toward private enterprise through governmental concessions and financial guarantees. The Orleanist monarchy also spent more freely than its Bourbon predecessor. Public expenditures were doubled: larger sums were allotted to the army, to agricultural development, to the building of schools, but above all to public works—canals, roads, railways. The public debt increased, since taxes remained almost stationary; but public credit remained sound.

The result of the government's policies was a steady though not spectacular growth in production and trade, particularly after 1840. The Sorbonne historian François Crouzet has calculated the mean rate of industrial growth during the years 1840–60 at 2.4 per cent a year (as against a rate of only 1.6 per cent for the entire century 1815–1913). Coal production tripled, though it continued to lag behind that of Belgium and far behind that of England (the ratio in 1846 was one to ten). Pig-iron output doubled, though it still amounted to only a quarter of England's output. Imports doubled, though exports rose only about half as much. Railway building was begun at last, but it proceeded less rapidly than was the case in several rival nations, including the German states. Some of the first rails had to be imported from England despite the heavy tariff, for most French iron was still being smelted on small charcoal furnaces, inadequate for the purpose. Technological change did begin to occur in some industries (notably in the Alsatian textile mills, where the Protestant entrepreneurs of Mulhouse led the way), but it was slow and spasmodic. France's industrial revolution "was not only belated but incomplete"; a peculiar aspect of it, at least until about 1850, was the parallel growth of large and small-scale industry. More than elsewhere, there was a tendency to dispersal of industry in the countryside rather than to concentration in industrial cities; and there was even a considerable expansion of the eighteenth-century "putting-out" system, especially in textiles, to take advantage of cheap labor in the overcrowded rural districts. "Large lumps of the Ancien Régime economy survived in France;" the modernized sector remained the exception.[1]

---

[1] F. Crouzet, "French Economic Growth in the 19th Century (1814–1914): Data and Interpretation". Mimeographed. Paper read at the annual convention of the Society of French Historical Studies.

This relative lack of dynamism, this curious blend of old and new, has given rise in recent years to a lively controversy among economic historians. Until the coming of the industrial revolution, France had outproduced any other European nation; French enterprise and artisanship seemed capable of facing up to any challenge. Why, then, did France fall behind during the nineteenth century, until by 1914 it ranked a poor fourth among the nations of the world? The debate, someone has put it, has been between "coal-men" and "culture-men"; but these are labels that certainly oversimplify the complexity of the argument.

In the opinion of the first school of historians, France's handicaps in the new era were primarily technical and structural ones: expensive fuel, cheap labor, and inadequate risk capital. Because labor was plentiful and cheap (France then being a crowded country), the introduction of machine methods was no pressing necessity. Because some of France's coal deposits were still undiscovered, part of the nation's fuel had to be imported at high cost. Because commercial capitalism had developed more slowly in France than in England, the impetus to produce in quantity for large overseas markets was less intense, and the amount of liquid capital accumulated by the trading class was more limited. Because French banking developed late, the capital that did exist in France was not properly mobilized for investment purposes until the last half of the nineteenth century.

A second school sees France's relative lack of dynamism as the product of psychological and sociological handicaps rather than technical and structural ones. Its exponents grant that Frenchmen faced some technical difficulties (as in lack of coal and inadequate mobilization of capital), but they contend that the principal missing factor in the new age was a lack of vigor, of the spirit of risk, of entrepreneurial drive on the part of French businessmen, combined with a social atmosphere that was uncongenial to business enterprise. The business tradition in France, according to this thesis, was one of conservatism and caution. The goal was security rather than expansion; the ideal was one of preserving rather than creating wealth; the ethical code favored coexistence rather than competition. The customary business structure was the "family firm," small enough to be operated without any sort of outside interference. Expansion beyond a certain point, or even investment by outsiders, was to be avoided because it would undermine the family's independent control. Furthermore, the idea of seeking to destroy weaker competitors or to monopolize the market would have outraged most French businessmen even if it had occurred to them. During a tariff inquiry in 1832 the large and prosperous Anzin firm of iron-makers actually opposed a reduction in duties on iron on the ground that it would wipe out some of Anzin's weaker competitors.

A contributing factor in this lack of aggressive entrepreneurial drive, according to this school of historians, was the social ethos inherited from the old regime. The businessman had traditionally ranked low in prestige; the way to gain status in prerevolutionary France had not been to succeed in business but to get out of business somehow, or to get one's sons out. "In the bourgeoisie," ran the eighteenth-century maxim, "only the fool remains a bourgeois." Balzac's novels reflect (though in rather distorted form) the persistence of an anticapitalistic atmosphere even in the nineteenth-century era of bourgeois rule. Dislike and contempt for the vigorous enterpriser marked the outlook not only of the old aristocracy but also of the governmental bureaucracy. If an exceptional young man did turn up, full of imagination and aggressive ambition, he was likely to face the massed hostility of the entire business group and to find sources of risk capital (which were meager enough, at best) closed against him. As a result, most business expansion of the era was the work not of new men but of old families gradually expanding their plants through reinvestment of profits (as the de Wendels) or moving out from banking into industry (as the Périers). Successful new operators like the Schneider brothers at Le Creusot, whose iron-works was founded in 1836, were rare exceptions to the rule.

Some light may be shed on the debate by a brief reference to railway development, the most important new field of enterprise in the era of Louis-Philippe. In 1842 the government laid out a plan for a national network and assigned the task of construction to private firms through a system of concessions. Large-scale government aid was provided; the state first took on more than half the construction cost by providing the land, the roadbed, and the bridges, and later shifted to a kind of cost-plus arrangement by which it guaranteed to the private firms a fixed return on their investment. But the decision in favor of private rather than state construction and operation of the railways was not reached automatically, despite the predominant influence of the business group in this era. The ministry leaned at first toward a governmental monopoly of the railroads, and a vocal minority in parliament (headed by Lamartine) fought for that solution on the ground that private control would lead to profiteering and the emergence of a new class of "feudal" tycoons. Such an antibusiness attitude suggests that even some members of the political elite in the bourgeois monarchy reflected the traditional ethos of hostility toward the entrepreneur.

On the other hand, French businessmen lost no time in taking advantage of the opportunities offered by railroad building; there was sharp competition among financial houses for the concessions that seemed most likely to be profitable. In the end the concessions were shared out among the principal financial groups by pragmatic arrangements among the businessmen themselves. No powerful new category of rail tycoons of the Jim Hill type emerged during the railway-building era in France; the old guard of banking divided the spoils.

But the railway age, and the beginnings of industrial expansion, quickly revealed a serious weakness in France's banking structure. The existing banking firms like Rothschild and Hottinguer constituted what the French still call *la haute banque*. These institutions were, in David Landes' phrase, "small, exclusive credit clubs"; they were owned by a family or a small well-knit group of financiers, who contributed all the funds and doled them out to only the safest borrowers. Businessmen without access to the "club" had no recourse except to turn to a usurer at excessive interest rates. The old banks had no machinery by which to mobilize risk capital for the kind of large-scale investment that began to demand huge funds in the 1840's. Besides, most of them preferred smaller and safer operations and concentrated their efforts on buying government bonds. Rothschild, for example, got a near-monopoly of government loans during the Orleanist epoch. Some members of the *haute banque* clique nevertheless wanted to engage in railway and industrial financing, and they sought to set up new credit institutions of the joint-stock variety in an effort to mobilize idle capital. They got little encouragement from the state, and the old banking structure remained largely intact under Louis-Philippe. Of the billion francs invested in French railways before 1848, only four hundred million was contributed by Frenchmen; most of the remainder came from England. Yet even that contribution strained the existing credit resources of the old banks; the growing distortion between an outmoded credit system and an expanding economy contributed to the business crisis of 1846–51 and, indirectly, to the revolution of 1848. Not until the Second Empire was a solution to be found.

Until 1846 the Orleanist monarchy enjoyed economic stability and rather steady growth. The end of the reign, however, brought the most severe depression in a generation. Bad weather was partly responsible; there was a series of crop failures throughout western Europe in 1845–47. The agrarian crisis and the rapid rise in food prices that resulted produced a creeping paralysis of business that sharply reduced production in the nation's factories and mines, that bankrupted several of the new railway companies as well as many small local banks, and that led to widespread unemployment. The revolution of 1848, far from solving the problem, only compounded it; the political upheaval added to business uncertainty and intensified the depression. The Second Republic, after an initial series of expedients to alleviate the crisis, returned to the well-rooted tradition of domestic laissez faire—combined, of course, with a continuing high level of tariffs. The depression dragged on nevertheless, shrouding the whole history of the Second Republic in its gloom. Sizable numbers of Frenchmen turned to overseas emigration as a solution, for almost the only time in the modern history of France; a quarter of a million left between 1846 and 1851.

Although the effects of the mid-century crisis appeared to be most intense in the industrial cities, they were in fact much deeper and more enduring in certain densely-populated rural areas where the "putting-out" system of handicraft production had been combined with part-time farming. For more than a century this combination of activities had supported (at a marginal standard) a rural population far larger than primitive agriculture alone would have allowed.

The depression of 1846–51 hastened the ruin of rural handicrafts, already threatened by the rise of the factory system; and it gave a great impetus to the flow of population out of the depressed rural areas. The crisis thus heralded the end of a whole economic era, an era whose structure had been carried over from the eighteenth century.

❖❖❖❖❖❖❖❖❖❖❖❖❖

It was Louis-Napoleon's good fortune that the business slump was coming to an end at the moment when he seized power in 1851, and that the first decade of his rule coincided with one of the two most remarkable periods of economic growth and change in modern French history. Although the boom was to be checked somewhat in the 1860's, the Second Empire stands out in the nineteenth century as a time of exceptional economic vigor. Statistics, though dull, are revealing. Industrial production doubled between 1852 and 1870; foreign trade tripled, outstripping the growth of any other European nation; the use of steam power rose fivefold; railway mileage was increased sixfold. The intriguing question here is this: To what degree were imperial policies responsible for this growth and for the sudden emergence of a remarkable group of entrepreneurs? Did the empire merely ride the crest of a world-wide boom in the 1850's? Was the appearance of vigorous entrepreneurs nothing more than a fluke, a kind of un-French deviation from a basic norm?

Undoubtedly the European climate was favorable to economic growth in the 1850's. Prosperity was general throughout the world, stimulated in part by a rapid rise in the available gold supply from Californian and Australian mines. New technical methods made their appearance in industry; new kinds of business organizations were emerging, based on the principle of limited liability and favoring the growth of large-scale enterprise. But it is clear that Napoleon would not have been content to relax and enjoy the fruits of general prosperity. He intended to stimulate economic growth; he believed (in his own classic mixed metaphor) that it was the function of government to be "not a necessary ulcer, but rather the beneficent motor of any social organism."

This repudiation of the laissez faire ideal might seem to suggest a kind of state-socialist philosophy. In fact, what the imperial government did was not so much to engage in public spending (though both budgetary expenditures and the public debt did rise) as to encourage private speculation and investment. For example, the regime guaranteed a minimum interest rate on railway securities; it sponsored the merger of many small and shaky railway companies into six large ones; it authorized the creation of the first investment banks (notably the Crédit Mobilier); it stimulated the building trades by a vast state-financed plan to reconstruct Paris, along with lesser plans in most major cities. For the most part, the state avoided direct economic activity, preferring to create a favorable climate for private enterprise.

More significant than the new government's tendency to favor business was the fact that so many Frenchmen took advantage of the opportunities offered. Perhaps this meant that the French as a whole were not so deeply rooted in an older tradition after all and were not so ill-adapted to the demands of entrepreneurship; or perhaps this particular crop of Frenchmen happened to be unique. At any rate, they proceeded to establish not only investment banks but also most of the great deposit banks (like the Crédit Lyonnais) that have endured to this day; they created the first department stores (notably the Bon Marché) and the first chain groceries, selling their own packaged products (Félix Potin); they modernized the bulk of the iron and textile industries; they completed the network of major railways and telegraph lines; they expanded the stock exchange in such fashion as to mobilize the savings of small investors; and they started France on its long career of foreign investment.

It is true that some of the older business families disliked and resisted the new men and the new methods. It is true also that "large lumps of the Ancien Régime economy" survived alongside the new dynamic sector and found ways to protect themselves until the mid-twentieth century. It is true, finally, that many of the new entrepreneurs of the empire were of Protestant or Jewish background, and they may have been naturally inclined to repudiate the standard French cultural heritage and the antibusiness social ethos. But the struggle between old and new was not simply a contest between a dominant national culture and a frustrated, resentful subculture. Among the older business and banking leaders, committed to the traditions of family enterprise and cautious conservatism, there were many of Jewish or Protestant origin; among the modernizers there were at least some members of old Catholic families. Furthermore, the struggle of old against new was less clear-cut than it has often seemed to economic historians. According to the standard legend, for example, the old families of the *haute banque* bitterly opposed the new joint-stock investment banks that mobilized vast sums of idle French capital and poured them into industrial development; and in the end (still according to the legend) they managed to destroy the Crédit Mobilier, bellwether of the new banking system. As a matter of fact, many representatives of the *haute banque* had been experimenting for years with primitive forms of the new investment bank, and after 1852 most of the old firms bought into the new banks as devices to achieve what the old banks could not do. By 1870 France's credit system had been almost completely renovated; a real financial revolution opened the way for the nation to play a major role in industrial expansion both abroad and at home.

Of all the actions of Napoleon III in the economic sphere, the most hotly disputed was his turn toward lower tariffs in 1860. There are Frenchmen still who regard that date as the critical turning point in French economic progress, as the "black day" of the century—just as there are others who see 1892 (the decisive return to high tariffs) as the real disaster. The so-called Chevalier-Cobden Treaty with England, followed by similar pacts with other nations, introduced the only period of relatively free trade in modern French history.

The origins of this sudden shift are somewhat controversial. The new policy was certainly urged on the emperor by Saint-Simonian advisers like the economist Michel Chevalier. Enemies of the treaty charged at the time that Napoleon's purpose was far less idealistic; they held that his aim was to buy back England's cooling friendship through economic appeasement. The emperor's long-standing Saint-Simonian leanings make the former theory more plausible. At any rate, the new policy either caused or coincided with a slackening in France's prosperity and economic growth; a severe slump occurred in 1862, and full recovery was never achieved in Napoleon's time.

Economic liberals could and did argue that the slump was due at least in part to the interruption of American cotton shipments during the Civil War, and to a general world-wide slackening after the boom of the 1850's. Still, they could not deny the fact that the Chevalier Treaty severely affected enterprises like iron and textiles that had to face stiff British competition; and a fair number of marginal firms were forced out of business. The government had foreseen the need for readjustment and had set up a special loan fund to aid the industries affected; but the sum provided was too small to shield all those in trouble. In justification of the turn toward freer trade, it may be said that the policy forced many French businessmen to consolidate, enlarge, or modernize their plants, so that these firms emerged healthier than before. Thus some segments of business were helped, others hurt, by the new liberalism of 1860. There is no easy criterion for judging the over-all results for the nation. If the long-run gains outweighed the immediate pains and stresses of readjustment, it is nevertheless likely that the imperial regime was, on balance, the loser; for much of its support in business circles was alienated by the brusque turn to freer trade.

***************

When one attempts to view the era 1814–70 as a unit and in longer perspective, the general impression is mixed but certainly not negative. If France was outpaced in economic growth by Britain, it remained a strong competitor and one of the world's leading economic powers. Those who have used the term "stagnation" have clearly exaggerated; indeed, if growth is measured per capita rather than in aggregate physical product, the French growth rate was not far behind that of Britain, and ranked near the top in Europe generally. By 1870 an effective new banking structure had been created, and completion of a basic transportation system made a national market possible. Since about mid-century the value of industrial production had at last caught up with and surpassed the value of agricultural production. Textile production was still far and away ahead of any other sector of industry, but the foundations had been laid in metallurgical enterprise as well. Frenchmen in 1870 saw no reason to apologize for their record of adaptation to changing times. In retrospect, their performance seems to justify François Crouzet's judgment: "not brilliant, but quite creditable."

# CHAPTER 14

# Society: Structure and Trends, 1814–1870

The paradox of French history is that a revolutionary settlement was to provide the basis for a profoundly conservative pattern of society.

ALFRED COBBAN

Only one short generation ago, a well-known French historian could still declare that the social history of nineteenth-century France was "terra incognita." No one would risk such a statement today. The past twenty years have been marked by a kind of historians' gold rush into the neglected field of social history; no other aspect of France's modern development has drawn so much serious attention.

The precise boundaries and contours of social history, however, remain somewhat ambiguous. Some see it as "history from below": an attempt to resurrect the daily lives, customs, beliefs, group activities, and cultural product of ordinary people who have enjoyed no more than a shadowy presence in the works of most traditional historians. "Popular culture" has drawn particular attention from the new historians; so have various disadvantaged groups—the poor, the sick, the aged, the insane, criminals, and that quite different category of neglected people, women. For other social historians, however, the central concern is to analyze the overall structure of society: to assess the relationships among various classes or strata, to expose where power lies and the ways in which it is exercised. The Marxist model of class relationships has been the most influential (though not the only) conceptual device for an understanding of social structures over time. Whether valid or not, the Marxian categories and vocabulary have thoroughly infiltrated our thinking about "class" and "power"; even non-Marxists speak almost automatically of bourgeoisie, proletariat, middle classes, as though they were real entities rather than potentially useful heuristic devices. This chapter will attempt to deal with social structure in a somewhat tentative way, by describing the main social categories and their evolving interrelationship.

❖❖❖❖❖❖❖❖❖❖❖❖❖❖

Juridically speaking, France emerged from the revolutionary era a society of atomized equals, with no intermediate groups intervening between the whole society and its individual citizens. In reality, it remained a complex tapestry of classes, groups, and professions, the outlines of which are difficult to distinguish clearly. Many of France's prerevolutionary social distinctions survived in custom if not in law; and superimposed upon them were new distinctions of more strictly economic character. The diversity thus produced was still further increased by persistent regional differences in speech, culture, and outlook. Although the revolution had swept away many artificial barriers to national unity and had intensified the sentiment of nationalism, several generations would still be needed to erode away deeply etched provincial traits. Indeed, that process of erosion has never been completed to this day.

Restored to the top of the social pyramid in 1814 was the old aristocratic caste, undiminished in its pride of birth though no longer privileged in a legal sense. The prerevolutionary gap between the court nobility of Versailles and the lesser provincial aristocracy of the backwoods had been narrowed considerably by the revolutionary experience. The playboys and skeptics of Versailles had been converted into solid pillars of morality and religion; the country nobility had never ceased to be such pillars. Political leadership during the restoration era was shared by both groups; alongside great émigré nobles like the Duc de Richelieu sat obscure country gentlemen like the Comte de Villèle. The old court aristocracy did face serious problems of readjustment, notably of an economic nature. Most of them had lost their prewar estates and—more serious still—the royal subsidies that had once supported them in frivolous leisure at Versailles. They looked to the public treasury for help; what they sought was either compensation for lost properties or some kind of salaried government post, even if it might involve menial duties. In the 1820's many aristocrats moved into such bureaucratic positions as justices of the peace, tax collectors, even postmasters. The fact that they often served honorably and efficiently did not reconcile the sons of the bourgeoisie, many of whom emerged from university or law school to find no official posts left open to them. The resentment of this latter group contributed to bourgeois antagonism toward the Bourbon dynasty.

From the outset the old aristocratic families were forced to share the top rung of society with those members of Napoleon's peerage that had rallied to the Bourbon cause in 1814. As one historian succinctly puts it, "Napoleon I was overthrown but his followers were not. They arranged the Bourbon restoration and were absorbed into the new system."[2] Contempt for these upstarts was general among the "real" aristocrats, who nevertheless had to confine themselves to grumbling about it. Their bitterness was to be even greater toward the new peers named by "the usurper" Louis-Philippe after 1830. Relations between the two branches of the nobility were frigid; the old families ignored these social climbers (most of whom had been promoted from the upper bourgeoisie) and withdrew to their provincial chateaux or to their Legitimist salons in the Faubourg Saint-Germain. The Orleanist peers therefore had Louis-Philippe's court to themselves, and developed their own salons across the Seine in the commercial quarter of Paris. Louis-Philippe's peerage was not intended to be hereditary. It became so, by a curious irony, through the fall of the dynasty that had created it; there was no sovereign after 1848 who could deny to an Orleanist peer the right to hand on his title to his son. Although such titles lacked any juridical base, custom made them as permanent as the titles of the oldest families. After 1852 Napoleon III once again inflated the nobility by elevating his favorites to the peerage. The nineteenth century thus produced a far more complex aristocracy than that of the old regime—one that by 1870 was divided into categories almost as distinct as geological strata.

Until 1830 the aristocracy dominated politics, set the tone of society, and controlled much of the nation's wealth. From 1830 to about 1880, its monopoly was steadily eroded by the bourgeoisie. Under Louis-Philippe and successive regimes, it was the bourgeoisie that began to set the tone, no longer in obsequious imitation of the nobility but in conformity to its own developing set of standards and ideals, a curious blend of capitalist and precapitalist values. It was also the bourgeoisie that now provided the bulk of France's political elite, and that displaced the aristocrats at the top of the economic ladder.

Few terms, however, are more amorphous than the word "bourgeoisie." The range of variation from the millionaire banker or industrialist of Paris or Lyon to the village grocer or postal clerk of Clochemerle renders almost meaningless any label that seeks to classify them in a common category. Nineteenth-century custom tended increasingly to distinguish various subdivisions—usually an upper, a middle, and a petty bourgeoisie; but the three groups shaded imperceptibly into each other, just as the petty bourgeoisie in certain respects merged into the category of workers just below it. To speak of the nineteenth century in Europe as "the bourgeois century," or of Louis-Philippe's regime as "the bourgeois monarchy," therefore begs the essential question: which stratum of the bourgeoisie ruled, and how did it assert its power? Or, to put it another way, from which stratum was the political elite drawn, and which strata were capable of influencing the decisions of that elite?

---

[2] T. Zeldin, *The Political System of Napoleon III* (London: Macmillan, 1958), p. 4.

One fact is clear: during the period from 1815 to 1870 (except for a brief interlude in 1848–49), it was only the upper echelons of the bourgeoisie that moved up into positions of political and social power. These were the wealthy bankers and business men: financiers like the Rothschilds and the Périers, industrialists like the Wendels and the Schneider brothers. For the most part, their rise to wealth and status was recent. "It is scarcely an exaggeration to say that the French *grand bourgeois* ... seemed new-rich alongside the English *grand bourgeois* whose fortune had been made over a period of a hundred fifty years. The roots of the new society developed in the hothouse of imperial protection [i.e., of Napoleon I]."[3] As long as the Bourbons reigned, the upper bourgeoisie was still overshadowed by the aristocracy; but its members did have the right to vote and to sit in parliament, where its spokesmen made up the liberal opposition. After 1830 it moved to the center of the stage, and stayed there (with a partial interruption in 1848) through the next four decades. But its hold on political and social power was not a total monopoly; those landed aristocrats who chose to collaborate with Louis-Philippe or with Napoleon III kept a share of influence, and both Legitimist and Orleanist peers kept much of their local power and social prestige. Furthermore, the distinction between the *grande bourgeoisie* and the aristocracy was somewhat blurred. Both businessmen and nobles invested in industry and owned large tracts of land; as the character of their holdings overlapped, so did their value-systems. The *grands notables* of that era were, in A. J. Tudesq's words, "the ruling group of a society in transition"—a society that was slowly evolving from its ascriptive agrarian base to the capitalism of the industrial age.[4]

Both the Bourbon and the Orleanist regimes drew a quite arbitrary line between those privileged to share political power and those denied it, and that line was based frankly on birth and wealth. Louis-Philippe reduced the entrance fee slightly in 1830; the number of eligible voters at the outset of his regime was increased from 90,000 to about 170,000. As thus revised, the line may serve as a kind of pragmatic dividing point between upper and middle bourgeoisie. This latter stratum was larger and more varied than the upper bourgeoisie. Included in it were the middle-rank industrialists and traders, most members of the liberal professions, and the upper echelons of the governmental bureaucracy. For them as for their betters, landholding remained an important form of wealth; precapitalist values still exerted a powerful attraction. No legal barrier prevented their rise into the upper bourgeoisie: it was primarily to this group that Guizot addressed his famous admonition, "Get rich, by hard work and saving!" Some of them profited by the opportunities that came their way with the business expansion

---

[3] C. Morazé, *Les bourgeois conquérants* (Paris: A. Colin, 1957), pp. 151–52.
[4] A.-J. Tudesq, *Les grands notables en France, 1840–1849* (Paris: Presses Univ., 1964), p. 1227.

of the 1840's and after, though not so many as one might have expected in a regime described as a bourgeois monarchy. For a brief period in 1848–49, the middle bourgeoisie found itself catapulted into the ranks of the ruling elite; the *grands notables* of the Orleanist era were temporarily divided and in disarray. The *grands notables* soon closed ranks again, however, and recovered control, so that the day of the middle bourgeoisie was postponed for another generation.

The petty bourgeoisie was an even more heterogenous category. It included the mass of little independents of city, town, and village—small enterprisers, shopkeepers, artisans, clerks, schoolmasters, petty employees of the state. Some of them inherited an old family tradition of shopkeeping or craftsmanship; their fathers or grandfathers had been the *sansculottes* of the Great Revolution, the partisans of Robespierre and Marat. A far greater number had recently made the transition from what the eighteenth century had called *le menu peuple* or the "popular classes." Those who came of peasant origin usually took two or three generations to penetrate the lower levels of the bourgeoisie; the process of direct promotion from peasant to bourgeois was to remain uncommon until the later nineteenth century, when access to the bourgeoisie became a matter of educational level and achievement. The more common upward route before 1870 was from skilled workman to petty entrepreneur, or from shopkeeper's son to the liberal professions or the state bureaucracy. "The nineteenth century," says Charles Morazé, "is filled with striking examples of shopkeepers' sons arriving at the very highest honors via science or industry."[5] The process was usually a great deal slower, however; and the petty bourgeoisie as a whole was distinguished from the urban and rural masses more by attitude, values, and life-style than by economic status. The frontier between bourgeois and workingman or peasant was mainly psychological, and was jealously guarded by those who defined themselves as bourgeois.

One special source of pride to the petty bourgeoisie was membership in the National Guard, whose origin dated from the Great Revolution. No institution, perhaps, was more representative of the era 1814–48. All citizens who paid a direct tax were automatically enrolled in the Guard and were required to furnish their own uniforms and weapons. Here was the clerk's or the shopkeeper's most glamorous mark of distinction, setting him off from the common people and establishing him as a defender of the social order. The fact that some contemporaries scoffed at these "greengrocer janissaries" detracted nothing from their pride. Charles X infuriated its members in 1827 when he brusquely dissolved the Guard for its lack of discipline and its "subversive" attitude during a review. Louis-Philippe was shrewd enough to reconstitute it in 1831 and to appear on frequent occasions in National Guard uniform. But by 1848 indiscipline and political

---

[5] C. Morazé, *Les bourgeois conquérants*, p. 415.

discontent had again weakened the Guard as an effective defender of the monarchy. It was the Guard's impending defection just outside the Tuileries that led the king, in February, 1848, to abandon his last hope of repressing the revolution. Thereafter it was never again to play a significant role (save for a brief interlude in 1870–71, during the Prussian siege of Paris and the Commune). The regular army and the new uniformed police took over the function of preserving public order.

**❋❋❋❋❋❋❋❋❋❋❋❋❋❋❋**

Whether France possessed a true proletarian class during the early nineteenth century is largely a matter of definition. If one essential aspect of proletarian status is psychological, involving the development of a clear sense of class-consciousness, then one can find little sign of a real proletariat in France before 1848 and virtually no sign at all before 1830. The suggestion has even been made that 1880 would be the most accurate date for the appearance of a self-aware proletariat. If, on the other hand, the test is merely one of economic function—if men who have nothing to sell but their labor are *ipso facto* proletarians—then an embryonic proletariat had existed in the larger French cities for centuries and in rural districts ever since the end of serfdom. Probably the most accurate conclusion would be that the period 1814–70 gradually converted the urban workers into class-conscious proletarians but left the process incomplete.

Labor's heritage from the revolution was a mixed one, combining as it did the liberalism of the men of 1789 with the regimentation of Napoleon. The Le Chapelier law of 1791 had outlawed labor organizations and strikes in the name of liberty; Napoleon in 1803 had reimposed on every worker the obligation of carrying a workbook, a kind of labor passport, in which each change of domicile or of job had to be recorded by employers. A few anemic mutual-aid societies survived the revolutionary period and were tolerated extra-legally after 1814; so did those curious medieval remnants called the *compagnonnages,* which were fraternal societies of skilled artisans. Exclusive in spirit, open only to bachelors, each one had its elaborate rituals, its ancient traditions, its bloody feuds with rival societies. New members normally spent several years in a tour of France, working for a time in each major city. Although these vestiges of a past era were decaying rapidly by 1850, some remnants of them were to endure even into the twentieth century and were to complicate the task of forming modern trade unions.

The artisans of the *compagnonnages* were the aristocrats of labor. In contrast, the domestic handicrafters (who were usually part-time peasants) and the new stratum of factory workers faced an existence that was often subhuman. If Karl

Marx had written *Das Kapital* in the Bibliothèque Nationale rather than in the British Museum, he might have buttressed his argument with French examples just as appalling as those which he drew from official British surveys. In those cities where the factory system was emerging, a working day of fifteen hours or even more was normal during the Bourbon and Orleanist epochs. Wages rarely sufficed to keep a family alive, even if both parents and children worked; a supplement from private charity was common. In the Lille area in 1828 two-thirds of the workers were carried on some kind of relief roll. Only a minority of workers could expect to eat meat more than once or twice a year. From 30 to 50 per cent of a working family's budget went for the purchase of bread; it was quite literally the staff of life. Contemporary descriptions of housing conditions in the slums of Lille or Nantes are almost beyond belief. At Mulhouse about 1830 the average life expectancy for children of the bourgeoisie was thirty-one years; for children of weavers, less than four years. In Louis-Philippe's reign nine-tenths of the army draftees from industrial areas had to be rejected for physical deficiencies. Alcoholism and promiscuity were common; in one representative year, one-third of all births in Paris were illegitimate. Illiteracy among the workers was almost universal. Price and wage studies for the period 1814–48 are undependable, but real wages almost certainly fell during the Bourbon era and barely held their own under Louis-Philippe. Until the 1840's at least, population growth far outstripped economic growth, and the workers of both city and countryside suffered the consequences.

In face of such conditions, the workers behaved with surprising docility. The Bourbon period produced few serious labor disorders, and there were only 382 strikes (most of them minor) during the whole reign of Louis-Philippe. The only major outbreaks were those of the Lyon silk weavers in 1831 and 1834; they produced severe repression and an enduring legend, but nothing in the way of improved conditions. Some historians have seen the Lyon insurrections as nothing more than spontaneous hunger riots; others contend that they embodied a burgeoning class-consciousness and a bitter resentment at the unfair practices of the industrial employers or middlemen. It may be pure legend that the 1831 rioters carried a black flag bearing the phrase "Live working or die fighting"; whether true or not, it eventually became part of labor's myth. The 1834 outbreak had repercussions in Paris as well; there, too, labor protest was repressed in bloody fashion, and the episode was immortalized by Daumier in his powerful caricature entitled "The Massacre of the Rue Transnonain."

Premier Casimir Périer told parliament in 1831, just after the first Lyon insurrection had been put down, "The workers have got to get one thing through their heads: their only remedies are patience and resignation." His statement epitomized the outlook of most political leaders and most industrialists of the time. There were exceptions, however. Some sensitive Catholics, like the Vicomte de Villeneuve-Bargemont, prefect at Lille during the late 1820's, exposed the miserable conditions of life among the workers and asked (as did the archbishop of Cambrai in 1845): "Is it necessary that the worker perish, body and soul, so that the master may climb faster to the summit of opulence...?"[6] Not even a regime committed to laissez faire could ignore forever such evils as slum conditions, absenteeism, and the high rate of draft rejections. In 1837 and 1840 the government conducted investigations of child-labor conditions, and in 1841 it pushed through parliament the only labor reform of the period. This measure outlawed the employment of children below the age of eight and shortened hours for those below sixteen. The bill aroused bitter opposition in parliament, not only from factory owners but also from such notables as the philosopher Victor Cousin and the scientist Gay-Lussac; they declared that it violated the sacred principles of liberty and justice. The opposition managed to attach an amendment that pulled the teeth in the bill; it provided that factory inspectors must be unpaid volunteers, chosen from among retired manufacturers. In consequence, the law had little practical effect. By 1848 France had fallen far behind England in the sphere of social legislation.

The 1848 upheaval seemed destined for a time to reverse the order of precedence and to make France the world's model for social advance. The working day in Parisian factories was reduced to ten hours; several large producers' cooperatives were organized with state aid; a government commission to study labor problems was set up, with two hundred employers and two hundred workers as members and the socialist Louis Blanc as chairman. There was much talk of guaranteeing the right to work and of adding a minister of labor to the cabinet. But by the end of the year the proposals had been abandoned and the reforms repealed. The vanished mirage of a new utopian era left the workers more bitter and frustrated than ever.

In this state of disillusionment, a great many workers could easily be attracted to Napoleon III, who was supposed to be an advocate of Saint-Simonian policies and a friend of the common man. During his first decade in power, however, Napoleon was too dependent on the support of the business community to embark on any startling social reforms. Labor profited indirectly from the remarkable economic expansion of the Second Empire, though not in proportion to the gains of the business group; wages rose a little faster than prices during these years. After 1860 Napoleon turned to more direct measures of social reform as well. In 1862 he provided a subsidy for a workers' delegation to attend the London Exposition and to observe English labor conditions; in 1863 he set up a credit agency to finance cooperatives; and in 1864 he granted labor the right to

---

[6] Quoted in V. Lorwin, "Labor and Economic Development in France" (unpublished manuscript).

strike. The last years of the empire brought a rash of strikes, far more extensive than France had ever known. They brought, too, the first important steps toward the organization of labor. A delegation of French workers helped establish the First International in 1864, and by 1870 the French branch of the International was larger than that of any other nation. More important still, Napoleon let it be known in 1868 that he would permit (but would not legally authorize) the formation of unions, and workers from the skilled trades promptly took advantage of the opportunity. It was only "a blinking and uncertain tolerance," however, that labor got from the Second Empire. French leaders of the International, for example, were repeatedly prosecuted for their activities. This curious mixture of liberty and repression probably had the effect of driving the most active elements of French labor toward more radical doctrines.

One imperial reform that did produce lasting effects on class relationships was Haussmann's rebuilding of Paris in the 1860's. The effect was to produce, for the first time, a kind of generalized social segregation in the capital. Hitherto, in most parts of Paris, workers and bourgeoisie of all levels had resided in the same buildings, with social status in inverse proportion to the floor occupied. Prior to the social revolution introduced by the elevator, the wealthy lived on the lower floors, families of moderate income on the middle floors, and the poor in the garret. Haussmann's face-lifting of the city destroyed large areas of mixed housing and replaced them with new apartment houses far too expensive for the workers. A general exodus toward the suburbs followed: the heart of Paris, largely bourgeois henceforth, was to be surrounded by a largely proletarian red belt. The long-range effects of this segregation on class relationships are difficult to measure, but they probably were very complex and far-reaching.

In some parts of France, on the other hand, the years of the Second Empire brought scattered efforts at paternalistic social reform by certain employers. The Protestant textile magnates of Mulhouse led the way in the 1850's by providing model housing and by pioneering in efforts to prevent work accidents. Some employers, whether through humanity or self-interest, began to establish a variety of social-welfare services. By 1875 a parliamentary committee inquiring into labor conditions could report proudly that France had outstripped all other countries in such employer-sponsored welfare schemes. Yet many employers clung to the idea that short hours and higher wages would only debauch the inherently inferior working man, whose fate it was "... to support with resignation the privations and sufferings which our social conditions are powerless to spare him."[7] Paternalistic reforms, in such an atmosphere, could scarcely suffice to satisfy labor.

There can be little doubt that the position of French workers began to change markedly during the Second Empire, and that by 1870 a considerable

---

[7] Quoted in V. Lorwin, "Labor and Economic Development in France."

nucleus of the labor movement had become self-consciously proletarian. Outward appearances, as well as later studies of price and wage trends, suggest that the workers were also better off: that their living standards had risen a little since 1848, for the first time in the nineteenth century. What is certain is that the urban working class had grown in size, had begun to organize, and was becoming class-conscious by 1870. Unfortunately, its class feeling was "deeper in resentments than in solidarity, better defined in its alienation from other classes than in its own organization."[8] This was a condition that was destined to persist for decades, with serious effects on both social relationships and political stability in France.

❖❖❖❖❖❖❖❖❖❖❖❖❖❖

Nineteenth-century France was still a peasant nation, so far as its mass base was concerned. In 1814 three out of four Frenchmen lived by farming; by 1870 the proportion had dropped, but it was still more than half.

Surprisingly little is known about rural life in that epoch. History, it seems, was made in the cities and bypassed the countryside. There is even a lack of adequate statistics, for agricultural surveys before 1870 were infrequent and incomplete. No accurate estimate can be made, for example, of the number of landless peasants who became small-owners as a result of the Great Revolution. What does seem certain is that the peasantry changed less than any other segment of society in the years 1814–70, and that rural life remained pretty much as it had been in the eighteenth century, save for the legal abolition of some feudal remnants.

If the period was marked by any constant trend, it was the steadily increasing subdivision of the soil, produced in part by the new law codes that required equal shares to all heirs, but produced primarily by the growing pressure of population on the land. France's rural population reached an all-time peak in the late 1840's, and even the drift to the cities that set in thereafter did not suffice to reduce the pressure very much by 1870. The total number of farms operated in France kept growing throughout the period and was to continue to increase until about 1890. Some new land was brought into cultivation, but not enough to prevent a shrinkage in the average size of farms. The bulk of the peasantry remained, therefore, on a marginal standard that permitted little improvement in either living conditions or in agricultural techniques. Millet's famous painting of "The Man with the Hoe" probably represents no grotesque caricature of rural life but a faithful reproduction of an "average" peasant of the time (1862). At

---

[8] V. Lorwin, "Labor and Economic Development in France."

best, that "average" peasant had raised himself one notch economically—from the level of misery to that of poverty. But at least one recent study seems to suggest that the peasantry as a whole was actually worse off at mid-century than it had been in 1789.[9]

In part, the peasants were responsible for their own backwardness. There seems to have been widespread resistance to the idea of change in either techniques or mores. Furthermore, most peasants suffered from what has been called "the proprietary illusion"—the desperate desire to own a piece of land or to add to that already owned. Instead of devoting their meager savings to better housing or improved techniques, they were inclined to scrape and borrow in order to invest in a piece of soil. Nothing was left for raising living standards or experimenting with new methods; and besides, a burden of indebtedness was built up over the years—a load made heavier by the lack of adequate sources of farm credit. Not until Napoleon III's time was an institution set up to rescue peasant borrowers from the usurer, and even then it failed to provide much help. Nothing like adequate farm credit was to become available until the burgeoning of mutual credit associations in the 1890's. Many peasants suffered also from the complex pattern of land division that forced them to farm tiny scattered parcels of land and to spend as much time travelling from one to another as in fruitful labor.

The fault was not entirely theirs, however. Large landowners in France offered much less vigorous leadership toward a modernization of techniques than was the case in England; and successive governments offered scarcely any leadership at all. Until 1848 at least, the politicians appeared to believe that high tariffs on foodstuffs gave the peasants all the help they needed. The Second Republic established at last a chain of schools for specialized agricultural training, but the Second Empire undermined this promising new effort when it reduced the budget for agricultural education by half. The peasantry got little from the state except the right to vote plus slowly improving facilities for basic education. By 1870 the number of children in primary schools had more than doubled since 1830, though 30 per cent of French army conscripts were still illiterate, and most of those were peasants' sons.

Generalizations about the peasantry are, however, likely to be misleading; for the farm population in the nineteenth century certainly did not constitute a single homogeneous class or stratum. Large landowning continued to coexist with small farming; sizable groups of tenants and sharecroppers survived alongside the independent owners; and there was an important population of landless farm laborers. Significant regional variations continued to mark the countryside.

---

[9] J. Vidalenc, *La société française de 1815 à 1848: le peuple des campagnes* (Paris: M. Rivière, 1970), *passim*. For the slightly less gloomy view, M. Augé-Laribé, *La révolution agricole* (Paris: Michel, 1955), p. 181.

Even before 1789 the intensity of religious belief had varied markedly, and the areas that had been least fervent then were the first to show signs of abandoning the faith entirely in the mid-nineteenth century. Likewise, there were old variations in educational level, mores, and habitat. After 1814 a new source of regional differentiation began to emerge. Certain areas in the north and east—notably the region adjoining the Belgian frontier—began to move steadily ahead of the rest of France in the adoption of new techniques. The resulting contrast between dynamic and stagnant sectors was to become a permanent feature of France's agrarian structure and was to be intensified rather than softened during the century after 1870. It was only partially offset by the introduction, after 1850, of the practice of liming the soil in certain infertile regions of the center and west. That practice reclaimed for the plow vast areas of "acid" soil, notably in Brittany, that had never before been cultivated.

Even though no sweeping agricultural revolution had occurred in France by 1870, and even though rural life remained primitive and isolated, events were conspiring to prepare a fundamental change. For one thing, the use of the ballot and the gradual spread of literacy were providing the peasants with a slow course in political education—one that would eventually give them, after 1870, a kind of negative check on the machinery of the state. Meanwhile, the penetration of many parts of the countryside by the new railway network was opening the way to a real social revolution. Most villages until now had been almost hermetically sealed off against the world and had lived largely untouched by outside currents of ideas. Some peasants and village artisans had travelled during the slack season in search of work, but these adventurers were exceptions to the rule. Nine out of ten Frenchmen in the census of 1861 were living in the department where they had been born; it seems a safe guess that seven or eight out of ten had never even journeyed outside their natal region. By 1870, however, the major rail lines were complete, and in the 1880's additional secondary lines were to reach all but the most remote sectors. Men, ideas, products, could at last flow both into and out of the village. Rural France was about to become, not overnight but over a half-century, an active and organic part of the nation.

❖❖❖❖❖❖❖❖❖❖❖❖❖❖

Of all the disadvantaged groups in French society, women constituted by far the largest element. They formed, after all, approximately half of the population; and in theory at least, the Great Revolution's promise of equality was not confined to the male sex. In practice, however, both deep-rooted mores and the Napoleonic Code relegated women to second-class citizenship—a condition that was not, of course, unique in France. French law established the family as the basic social unit, and organized the family in authoritarian, hierarchical fashion. The husband and father was designated as "head of the family," with sole authority to manage all family property, even including that brought by the bride's dowry. Under the marriage contract, a man owed his wife protection, while the wife owed her husband obedience. Divorce was made illegal in 1816, and remained so until 1884. A double standard of moral conduct was reinforced by the law: penalties for adultery were severe for women, merely nominal for men. Education for girls was meager, and was confined mainly to Catholic schools; the first state secondary schools for girls were not established until the late 1860's, and most towns had to await the 1880's to get such a school. In many rural areas, Eugen Weber tells us, women were treated as beasts of burden and breeders of children; they took their meals standing, or after the men had finished; sometimes they were expected to walk several steps behind their husbands. "When the cock sings," ran one peasant proverb, "the hens are silent." [10]

Some Frenchmen and foreign observers contended that in reality French women enjoyed a position of unique influence and high status, and that all but a few were entirely content with that position. The wife, they argued, was the unchallenged mistress of the household: as manager of family finances, as supervisor of the childrens' education and moral training, she was the queenpin of the family, which in turn was the most important of all French institutions. That role was both so demanding and so rewarding, the argument ran, that most women wanted nothing more. No doubt the thesis has some validity, especially for bourgeois Frenchwomen. What we do not know is the proportion of women who were vaguely or actively dissatisfied at their condition, and who yearned for a chance to express themselves as individuals beyond the confines of the family. A great many women did, of course, work for wages either within the home or outside it; but such work was almost always the product of financial need rather than personal fulfillment. Young women of the working class were employed full time until their children were born; then, more often, they worked part time at home in the textile trades. Peasant women, of course, commonly shared the heavy work of the farm with the men.

Recent scholarship has helped to remind us that there were a few crusading Frenchwomen, and a handful of men, who sought to challenge this state of things. There were lonely individuals like Olympe de Gouges, who during the Great Revolution advocated a Declaration of the Rights of Women; or the fiery activist Flora Tristan, who in the Orleanist years agitated for the joint liberation of women and the proletariat; or the schoolteacher Jeanne Derain,

---

[10] Eugen Weber, *Peasants into Frenchmen* (Stanford: Stanford Univ. Press), 171.

who in 1848 insisted on running for elective office, and was jailed for her presumption. In times of upheaval such as 1848 and the era of the Paris Commune, a number of women's clubs were formed to push the feminist cause, and many women became political activists. A few women—notably the novelist George Sand—challenged all convention by espousing free love, wearing trousers, and smoking cigars (though Sand rejected the feminist cause). And among the utopian socialists of the 1830's and 40's, there were some dedicated crusaders for women's equality: notably Fourier and his followers, and the disciples of Saint-Simon. Yet the status of women in fact underwent little change between 1815 and 1870. Such changes as did occur were so gradual as to go largely unnoticed at the time. One was a withdrawal of some women from the labor market into the home, as improved living standards freed those women from the need to supplement the family income. Another was the gradual adoption of elementary birth-control methods that had already come into use in the eighteenth century, but that now became more generalized. Women thus began to exercise at least some control over their own lives.

❖❖❖❖❖❖❖❖❖❖❖❖❖❖❖

France's population in 1814—twenty-nine million—exceeded that of any other European nation save Russia. The figure had increased by more than 30 per cent since 1750; it was destined to grow another 33 per cent by 1870. In retrospect, the century from 1750 to 1850 stands out as unique in French demographic history; it was the only long period that produced a sustained and sizable population increase. Until about 1850 the effects were felt primarily in the country districts, where population density reached a peak about mid-century. A serious threat of overpopulation was checked by the exodus toward the cities that began with the depression of 1846–51, and that was to continue sporadically thereafter. The process of urbanization, exceptionally slow until this time, got under way at last during the Second Empire.

France's remarkable population growth in the early nineteenth century concealed from contemporaries the first signs of an opposite trend, whose full impact was not to be felt until after 1900. The decade of the 1820's was the last one to show a large excess of births over deaths; thereafter, the birth rate declined more sharply than the death rate. The severe depression of 1846–51, complicated by a cholera epidemic in 1849, produced a kind of demographic disaster. Annual population growth fell during those years to 2.2 per thousand, the lowest figure since the French had begun to keep statistics; in a number of regions, population actually declined. The Second Empire brought some recovery; but explosive growth was never again to recur until the years after the Second World War.

In retrospect, the crisis of 1846–51 can be seen as marking the end of one demographic era and the beginning of another. Before 1846 the nation's reproduction rate had rarely fallen below 1.00 (the level theoretically required for a population to replace itself without decline). After 1846 the rate tended increasingly to fall below that figure.[11] In 1814 one of every seven Europeans west of Russia had been French; in 1914 the proportion was to be only one in ten. At midcentury, however, the trend was not yet clear. No Frenchman in 1870 foresaw that the demographic problem would strike his grandchildren as one of the most severe threats to the nation's vigor and greatness.

---

[11] The annual net reproduction rate, which fell below 1.00 during most of the period 1846–59, rose again during the generation 1860–89. But in 1890 it dropped below 1.00, and stayed there almost constantly until 1946.

# CHAPTER 15

# Intellectual and Cultural Currents, 1814–1870

This kind of froth called the fine arts is the necessary product of a certain fermentation. If you are to explain the froth you must explain the nature of the fermentation.

STENDHAL

The years of the revolution and the Napoleonic wars had diverted the minds of most Frenchmen from intellectual and cultural pursuits. But it was not mere contrast with that relatively barren era that made the early nineteenth century seem a time of such intense productivity, of such "prodigious intellectual ferment." No French generation since that of 1660, says the historian Pierre Gaxotte, had been so creative, so rich in artistic and literary genius. "With tame rabbits in the seats of the mighty [remarks Albert Guérard] the age was, intellectually, a glorious jungle."[1] Just as striking was the rapidity of change in mood and taste, in intellectual climate. Rationalism in thought and neoclassicism in the arts had marked the eighteenth century, and ruled almost unchallenged to the end of the Napoleonic era; but by 1830 the romantics had clearly won the battle for predominance. The election of the young romantic poet Lamartine to the French Academy in 1830 symbolized the victory. For a generation thereafter, romanticism was to pervade the modes of thought and sensibility of Frenchmen concerned with ideas and the arts.

The romantic outlook was not, of course, a peculiarly French product. Indeed, it arrived in France later than in either England or Germany, and it was regarded by some old-school Frenchmen as a degenerate foreign import. Yet

---

[1] A. Guérard, *France, A Modern History* (Ann Arbor, Univ. of Michigan Press, 1959), p. 290.

romanticism did have its own French forebears—notably in the person of Rousseau—and it would doubtless have come to dominate the age even if France had been tightly sealed off from dangerous foreign ideas. A generation of revolution and war, of stress and upheaval, had undermined the base of certainty and security upon which the age of reason had rested. Doubts and pessimism now challenged hope and optimism; men felt a deepened concern for the metaphysical problems of existence, death, and eternity. The twentieth-century age of anxiety offers some insight into the *mal de siècle* of early nineteenth-century Europe.

No two scholars would be likely to agree on the precise meaning and content of the term romanticism. Its essential spirit, after all, was one of revolt against an established order of things—against precise rules, laws, dogmas, formulas. A mood or movement whose central characteristic is revolt, and whose stress is on self-expression and individual uniqueness, does not lend itself to precise definition. To the extent that one can generalize about uniqueness, romantics held that men and women are and ought to be guided by warm emotions rather than by cold abstract reason—by the heart more than by the head. The scale of those human emotions was felt to be limitless, ranging from ecstasy to *Weltschmerz*. Nations and races as well as individuals were seen as unique, possessed of an indwelling spirit that was theirs alone, bound up with their past and inseparable from it. The romantics' preferred image of the world was not a static and mechanical thing, a Newtonian machine, but an organism in process of uninterrupted change, growth, evolution. Passionately interested in nature as well as in the self, romantics often felt the need to escape from the ugly and arid reality of the present into some distant time or place: the exotic East or Africa, the mountain wilderness, the Middle Ages, or a future utopia. Yet they were not, for the most part, mere escapists; they wanted to be, and were, an organic part of the life of their times. For the first decade or so after Napoleon, romanticism was linked with political reaction in Bourbon France. Ultra political theorists like Bonald, ultra literary figures like Chateaubriand, could view the restored dynasty as the spearhead of their rebellion against the established order of rationalism and classicism—against an intellectual tyranny that had gripped educated Frenchmen for a century, and that had led (they believed) to illusion and disaster. The early romantics found their utopia in France's distant past; they put their faith in such age-old institutions as monarchy and church, whose appeal was more emotional than rational. "I wept, and I believed"—so Chateaubriand described his reconversion to Christianity. Nations are organisms rather than machines, argued Bonald; therefore "...to ask an assembly to write a constitution is like a patient asking his doctor to make a temperament for him."

Until 1830 the defenders of rationalism and classicism fought back successfully against the new mood. Rationalism found its chief support on the liberal left, among the adherents of the revolutionary tradition. To the liberals, the romantics were permitting themselves to wallow in sentimentality and to indulge in an emotional orgy: "Romanticism is not merely ridiculous," they declared, "it is a disease, like sleepwalking or epilepsy." They tried to sabotage Victor Hugo's play *Hernani* on its opening night; they accused Delacroix of "painting with a drunken broom;" they derided the unconventional bohemianism of the young rebels, their morbid self-pity, their cadaverous heroes and fragile, swooning heroines. The passion of controversy led them to exceed the bounds of reason and to equate all romantic works with modern soap operas.

No one should be much surprised that men of rationalist outlook were unfair toward the romantics. Rationalists were temperamentally unsuited to appreciate the passionate force of a Delacroix canvas; or the lines of a Gothic cathedral restored by Viollet-le-Duc; or the mood of the composer Berlioz, who boasted of loosing "floods of sinister vibrations" in the concert halls of Paris, and who verged on passionate frenzy as he listened to the premiere performance of one of his own works ("It's superb! It's sublime! How monstrous, colossal, horrible!").[2] What the rationalists failed to perceive was the "constructive destructiveness" of the romantic spirit, its clearing away of rules and restrictions that had hampered the free expression of men's imagination and sensibility. With all its excesses and excrescences, romanticism was to have a liberating impact almost unparalleled in modern cultural history.

There was another aspect of romanticism, too, that the liberals overlooked at first. They failed to realize that the central characteristic of the new spirit—its intense individualism and its mood of revolt—might soon lead to a natural alliance between the romantics and the political opposition. Even before 1830 that alliance had begun to develop; a decade had been enough to destroy most of the romantics' illusions about the Bourbon dynasty. Not even Charles's fantastic coronation ceremony in 1825 could do more than create a shoddy façade of ersatz medievalism, behind which could be detected a most mediocre reality. Chateaubriand, the living embodiment of romanticism, was already deep in intrigue with the liberal opposition; Victor Hugo in 1829 executed a complete about-face with his new manifesto that "romanticism is, at bottom, nothing more than liberalism in literature." For the utopia of the past, the romantics began to substitute one in the future—an era of harmony, brotherhood, and universal peace. By the time this literary generation came to an end, some of its leading figures had moved all the way to the extreme left, where they combined republicanism with a variety of socialist doctrines. George Sand, professional novelist and amateur feminist, was the most prominent of these intellectual socialists; but there were many others by the 1840's who were in full rebellion against the bourgeois era. Victor Hugo, though a peer of the realm, preached the brotherhood

---

[2] Bertier de Sauvigny, *La restauration*, p. 492.

of nations and the instinctive goodness and justice of the common man; Lamartine implied a belief in the cleansing virtues of violence; the historian Michelet found the Great Revolution to be a magnificent epic, with its hero "the people"; the best-selling novelist Eugène Sue, who kept Paris on tenterhooks for the next chapter in his serialized romances, crusaded for the regeneration of society through Fourier's brand of utopian socialism. A few romantics resisted the leftward trend and clung to reactionary views or withdrew (like the poets Alfred de Vigny and Théophile Gautier) into an ivory tower of devotion to pure art. But on the whole, romanticism by 1848 was as closely intertwined with democratic and socialist doctrines as the earlier romanticism had been committed to reaction.

❖❖❖❖❖❖❖❖❖❖❖❖❖❖

Even at the height of the romantic age, the rationalist mood of the Enlightenment continued to dominate some French minds. There was an old-fashioned variety of liberal, deeply rooted in the classical and rationalist heritage, who found the romantic temper fundamentally alien whether linked with right-wing reaction or with left-wing radicalism. The liberal outlook, as it evolved into its early nineteenth-century form, still displayed some tendency toward ideological narrowness and rigidity; but just as deep or even deeper was its spirit of moderation and balance. Many nineteenth-century liberals in France as well as in England were put off by impassioned crusading for causes and by immoderate appeals to the heart in defiance of the head. George Sand appalled them as much as Bonald had done. This surviving liberalism made its greatest appeal to the bourgeoisie, but it was far more than just a congealed class dogma, a rationalization of class interest. What separated liberal rationalists from romantic democrats throughout the century seems to have been not self-interest so much as temperament.

French liberals of the early nineteenth century did not form a solid bloc. One variety early became reconciled with the monarchical compromise of 1814–48 and sought to provide a doctrine for this fusion of revolution and old regime. The mark of any such doctrine was inevitably a kind of eclecticism, pragmatic rather than rigorously logical in nature. During the Bourbon period it was the so-called doctrinaires who represented this right wing of liberal thought: men like the philosopher Royer-Collard and the historian Guizot. Under Louis-Philippe, Guizot continued the tradition, but it was the Sorbonne philosopher Victor Cousin, semiofficial theorist of the regime, who provided the most elaborate statement of what he called "enlightened eclecticism." Cousin produced an attractively blended cocktail of ideas borrowed from every kind of philosophical and religious system. "The Good, the True, and the Beautiful"—these were to be the eternal axioms on which the social order should rest.

Alongside the eclectic right wing, a somewhat more rigorously consistent left-wing current of liberal thought persisted throughout the period. Its partisans were less easily satisfied by the monarchical compromise and more inclined to cling to the heritage of the Enlightenment. Cousin's ideological cocktail they found completely unpalatable; but they showed little creative talent in presenting a substitute. Their most notable thinkers were Benjamin Constant and J.-B. Say during the Bourbon era; Adolphe Thiers, Charles de Rémusat, and Frédéric Bastiat in the Orleanist period; Lucien Prévost-Paradol under the Second Empire. Their total intellectual contribution to the development of liberal theory was remarkably meager—especially when contrasted with the richness of French liberal thought in the age of reason and with the vigor and variety of the English contribution in the era of Bentham, Mill, and Ricardo. French liberalism in the nineteenth century could do little more than produce pale imitators or dilettantes. Somehow it seemed that the liberal ideology had gone to seed in France, after its unprecedented flowering before the Great Revolution.

Yet there was one figure of remarkable stature whose contribution seems to contradict these generalizations about the barrenness of French liberal thought. Whether Alexis de Tocqueville truly embodied the liberal temper has been much debated; the twentieth-century neoconservatives have made a concerted effort to claim him as their ancestor. But if Tocqueville, like the conservatives, was deeply concerned at the potential dangers built into democratic thought—the threat of mediocrity, of mass tyranny, of a totalitarian distortion of the democratic ideal—his solution was not to build a barrier against the natural growth of democracy or to return to some kind of organic and hierarchical society. It was, rather, to ensure the survival of liberal values and minority rights in an age predestined to become democratic. Tocqueville claimed to possess no foolproof solution but proposed instead a set of psychological and structural safeguards. He advocated a kind of pluralism—a scattering of authority both within the governmental structure and between the state and private associations. And he warned his contemporaries, in effect, that vigilance is the price of freedom. Few other liberals of his century saw so far into the future or sought so intelligently to ensure the long-range protection of constitutional government and individual rights.

❖❖❖❖❖❖❖❖❖❖❖❖❖

No current of ideas in early nineteenth-century France ran so strongly or as deep as the current of social theory. From 1814 to 1870 an unbroken series of

French thinkers debated the complex problems of social organization and proposed a wide variety of reform programs, unparalleled in any other time and place. This burgeoning of social theory was the more remarkable in the light of France's relatively late and slow conversion to industrialism. If it is rapid social change that produces new currents in social thought, England rather than France ought to have led the way.

The two great precursors, the Comte de Saint-Simon and Charles Fourier, reacted to the impending industrial era in quite opposite ways. Saint-Simon's was a creed of progress, through the application of science and technology to social problems. He combined his gospel of productivity with that of brotherhood; in his hierarchical society of unequals, guided by an elite of engineers and entrepreneurs, classes would collaborate for the common welfare. He foreshadowed, even though in impractical and romantic fashion, such modern concepts as technocracy, the managerial revolution, and "enlightened capitalism." Saint-Simon died in 1825 obscure and almost unknown, and his disciples soon wrecked the tiny movement that survived him. Their effort to win over the workers by persuasion (mainly through courses of lectures) failed dismally; and their attempt to organize a semireligious communal sect only made them seem ridiculous. Saint-Simonianism as an organized movement lacked impact; but its ideas, propagated by individual converts, infiltrated the thinking of a great many Frenchmen over the next generation. Indeed, the ferment produced by the doctrine was almost unique in its effect, for it influenced a wide variety of reformers who rejected or moved on from the Saint-Simonian faith. A number of vigorous entrepreneurs as well as intellectuals were attracted by the gospel of productivity and welfare, and so were a few political figures—notably Louis-Napoleon. Its appeal to the workers, however, was meager. It offered them neither liberty nor equality, but only what struck them as the dubious privilege of being led by a priesthood of dedicated capitalists and technicians. Saint-Simonian ideas have nevertheless enjoyed a considerable revival in post-1945 France.

Fourier's creed was harmony rather than productivity; he combined a reluctant acceptance of the industrial age with a desire to get back to a simpler life. Like Saint-Simon, he stressed the idea of class collaboration, but without a managerial elite to guide the new society. Fourier's idea, rather, was free and voluntary association of capital, labor, and talent. He proposed to check the oppressive growth of large cities and of mass-production methods by scattering industry in small communities where modern techniques might be combined with country life. Fourier's ideal community or "phalanx" was designed to contain 1620 people, or a complete assortment of the 810 different species of male and female temperament that he believed to exist in humankind. Life in these utopias would be so pleasant that the residents would rise at three in the morning and would rush to work with passionate enthusiasm. Labor would no longer be onerous, for there would be a variety of work assignments, and ingenuity would make even the unpleasant jobs seem fascinating. Garbage collection, for example, would be entrusted to hordes of small boys mounted on Shetland ponies and dressed in colorful costumes, with full freedom to indulge their natural propensity to dirt.

Some modern scholars have found in Fourier a precursor of contemporary industrial decentralization, of suburban garden cities, and of neoFreudian themes of individual neurosis as the product of frustration. His doctrines, like those of Saint-Simon, produced no durable organized movement and won him no labor support. All of the experimental communities set up in France and elsewhere eventually failed. Yet the Fourierist doctrine survived and spread, especially among intellectuals and petty bourgeois converts. Fourier's principal disciple, Victor Considérant, who tried to bring his ideas down to earth by linking them with political action, was popular enough to be elected a deputy in both 1848 and 1849.

Of all the utopians, it was Étienne Cabet who came nearest to arousing mass enthusiasm. Some estimates (probably exaggerated) have given him as many as two hundred thousand disciples during the 1840's; one historian attributes to Cabet's influence the fact that there was no violent clash between workers and bourgeoisie in Paris in February, 1848. Cabet was a gentle and harmless socialist of the seraphic school; he preached the ideal of a classless society and complete communal ownership, to be achieved by persuasion and example. His doctrines were in fact neither very consistent nor very original; he had absorbed many of them from the Owenites, while in exile in England. The 1848 episode burst Cabet's bubble; by April he was not even able to win election to the Assembly. Disheartened, he departed with his disciples to establish an unsuccessful utopia across the Atlantic.

Even before 1848 a new mood was beginning to make itself felt within the socialist movement: a mood that was more intransigent and less idealistic. The evils of the early industrial age could not be entirely ignored; the fact of class conflict was growing obvious; the attractions of state action, or even of violence, were becoming more tempting. One representative of this new outlook was Louis Blanc. At the base of Blanc's doctrine was the producers' cooperative—an idea already advanced by such predecessors as Philippe Buchez, a onetime Saint-Simonian turned Catholic. Blanc gave the idea more systematic treatment and suggested a practical mechanism through which the workers might take over ownership of a factory. His device was to be state aid: the government would lend capital to the workers, who would gradually repay it from the profits of the enterprise. His "social workshops" vaguely foreshadowed the later syndicalist ideal. Although no organized movement was created by Blanc, he had won wide support among the workers by 1848. His phrase "the organization of labor" was one of the most popular slogans of the revolutionary year.

Other thinkers who reflected the new and tougher outlook were Constantin Pecqueur, Auguste Blanqui, and Pierre-Joseph Proudhon. Pecqueur, a "socialists' socialist" whose influence was felt by other thinkers rather than by the mass of workers, began as a Saint-Simonian but ended with a doctrine somewhere between Marxism and modern Christian socialism. He advocated a kind of Christian collectivism, with the state owning the means of production and operating them in a democratic and humanitarian spirit. His system contained tinges of the corporative ideal, but it was also marked by the idea of class conflict and by an economic interpretation of history. Auguste Blanqui was the principal heir to the Babeuf tradition of direct revolutionary action, as carried down into the nineteenth century by that first of professional revolutionaries, Filippo Buonarroti. Blanqui refused to waste time blueprinting the new utopia: it would be enough, he argued, to seize control of the state and then to sweep away all barriers to reason, education, true enlightenment. Blanqui's repeated attempts at a coup d'état against monarchy, empire, and republic failed for lack of adequate planning and support; forty of his seventy-nine years were to be spent in the prisons of Louis-Philippe, Napoleon III, and the Second and Third republics.

Of all these mid-century theorists, Proudhon was clearly the most paradoxical. He called himself an anarchist; Marx labeled him a petty bourgeois utopian; some modern scholars have described him as a proto-fascist, others as a rugged individualist opposed to all tyrannies. Proudhon brought on most of the confusion by his refusal to knit his ideas together into a system and by his volcanic tendency to toss off striking epigrams. He created no organized movement, and his only attempt at practical reform—a free-credit system in 1848—failed completely. Yet his long-range impact was to exceed that of almost any other contemporary French social theorist; it can be argued that the French labor movement through most of its history has drawn as much of its inspiration from Proudhon as from Marx. Proudhon stated his anarchist position as a purely theoretical ideal, not as a practical possibility; he saw it as preferable to its theoretical opposite, an arbitrary and all-powerful state. The heart of his doctrine lay in its syndicalist and its pluralist aspects. As a forerunner of syndicalism, Proudhon rejected Marx's idea of a political revolution led by professional agitators; he held that the workers must depend on themselves and must resort to economic rather than political methods. As a pluralist, Proudhon rejected the idea that power in the hands of a new class or elite would be any less dangerous than power in the hands of the old vested interests. At the heart of his thinking was the conviction that all men are complex animals, capable not only of goodness and justice but also of evil and injustice; like Lord Acton a good many years later, he believed that power must always tend to corrupt its holders, no matter what their origin. His solution was "federalism," a scattering of power and property in such fashion that no power group could dominate all the others. Whether or not Proudhon's doctrine deserves the label "petty bourgeois socialism," it did prove attractive to the kind of workers who organized or joined the French trade-union movement in the Third Republic.

Not all of the social-reform ideas in nineteenth-century France came from the left. Just as in England during the same era, there was a current of conservative social thought, inspired in part by Christian principles and in part by a sense of humanitarian outrage at the abuses produced by laissez faire. Left-wing Catholics like Lamennais and Buchez did not belong in this current; they were, rather, isolated ancestors of modern Christian socialism. The true conservative reformers were essentially paternalists, moved by a sense of moral obligation or by a conviction that the principles of 1789 had atomized and destroyed society.

Frédéric Ozanam and his followers in the 1840's represented the moral impulse in pure form; they preferred to put their energies into social action rather than into theorizing. The shaping of a doctrine of conservative social reform was left to Frédéric Le Play during the Second Empire. Like so many other men of his time, Le Play's interest in social issues had been aroused by his youthful contact with the Saint-Simonians. During his lifetime of extensive travel as an engineer, Le Play developed the thesis that the family rather than the individual must be the ultimate unit in a healthy society. He pioneered the technique of sociological case studies of families and built upon his findings both a theory and an organized movement to propagate it. His goal was to substitute for the "unstable" family of the modern era a somewhat broadened and more tightly-knit family unit, dedicated to the common good and capable therefore of achieving happiness. His ideal of virtual self-sufficiency for such family groups could not, however, be adapted to the conditions of wage earners, whose fate inevitably depended on the employer group. Le Play's only remedy for the ills of the proletariat was a paternalistic one; he preached the obligation of employers to ensure their workers steady jobs and decent wages and to set them an example of hard work and probity. Le Play became a trusted counsellor of Napoleon III, and his ideas inspired the late nineteenth-century conservative school of social Catholicism in France.

✾✾✾✾✾✾✾✾✾✾✾✾✾✾✾

The transition from romantic utopianism to a tougher-minded mood was not confined to the social theorists of the 1840's. A similar transition was also in progress in the main current of French thought and culture and was preparing the way for the new mid-century *Zeitgeist* of materialism and realism.

A few forerunners of the new mood had appeared at the very height of the romantic era. Stendhal, whose masterpieces anticipated the psychological novels of the late nineteenth century, observed severely in 1821 that "imagination must learn to respect the iron laws of reality," and described his own work as "a mirror rambling along a highway." Honoré de Balzac, that gigantic figure who sought to portray in his hundred-volume *Human Comedy* every aspect of the society of his time, combined the romantic and the realistic moods much as Dickens was doing across the Channel. Friedrich Engels was to remark that he had "... learned more from Balzac than from all the works of the historians, economists, and professional statisticians of the period taken together"—this despite the fact that Balzac's politics were reactionary, though with a tinge of Saint-Simonianism.

But the real turning point in French thought and taste came in 1848. If the revolutionary upheaval was in part the product of romanticism, it was also the culmination of that movement; the tone and temper of literature, the arts, philosophy, changed drastically in the 1850's. Gustave Flaubert best reflected the new mood in literature; resisting a deep inner compulsion toward romantic self-expression, he drove himself to dissect in almost clinical fashion the characters and the society that he portrayed in objective if somewhat sordid detail. In painting, Gustave Courbet led the revolt against the dominant school of Delacroix and sought to reproduce real scenes and people with almost photographic accuracy. It was Courbet who first proudly adopted the label "realist" flung contemptuously at him by his rivals. In social theory, the positivist doctrines of Auguste Comte began to win wide acceptance in the decades after his death (1855). The romantic Michelet might still be the great national historian, but alongside his impassioned rhetoric a more rigorously scientific kind of history was winning readers. Renan's *Life of Jesus,* the sensation of the 1860's, represented this changing mood. In architecture, Napoleon III's builders chose an eclectic style in place of the pseudo-Gothic that remained so popular across the Channel and the Atlantic. Only in music did the romantic temper survive almost unchallenged right down through the nineteenth century. Offenbach and Meyerbeer, purveyors of the light romantic operetta, seemed even more representative of the rather gaudy and superficial gaiety of the Second Empire than did the native-born romantics Gounod and Bizet.

Frenchmen had not awaited the era of positivistic scientism to turn their talents to science and pure scholarship. As early as 1817 at least one American visitor found Paris to be not the literary and artistic but the scientific capital of Europe. For training in pure science and mathematics, few institutions anywhere could rival the École Polytechnique. Nor could many nations boast so remarkable a collection of creative thinkers and scholars as Ampère, Fresnel, Gay-Lus-sac, Laplace, Lamarck, Cuvier, Berthelot, Bernard, Pasteur, Champollion, Guizot, Michelet.

Taken as a whole, the half-century from 1814 to 1870 had been a brilliant one in the intellectual and cultural realms. Even though the achievements of Frenchmen did not lead the world in every field—the fine arts, literature, music, science, philosophy, political and social theory—it would be hard to name a rival nation whose citizens had done so much in so many activities of the mind and the spirit. If Frenchmen were guilty of a certain complacency, of a kind of cultural chauvinism, it was not entirely without justification. Even in retrospect, it is difficult to accept the caustic verdict of that English historian to whom the brilliance of the era was merely "the iridescence of decay."

# CHAPTER 16

# France, Europe, and the World, 1814–1870

For a nation that has known greatness and glory, there is no middle ground between maintaining its old prestige and slipping into complete impotence.

LUCIEN PRÉVOST-PARADOL *(1868)*

France, in the eyes of most Europeans during the first half of the nineteenth century, was the potential troublemaker of the Continent. It could hardly be otherwise, after a generation of French crusading for liberty or for conquest. Although defeated and chastened, the French were suspected of subversive inclinations that might lead them to aid liberal and national movements elsewhere; and they were suspected, too, of an ambition to recover the Rhine frontier. These apprehensions were kept alive by the fact that some Frenchmen over the years did keep urging an ideological or an expansionist foreign policy, and by the refusal of French patriots to forget their "humiliation" in the treaty settlement of 1815. The fears of the Europeans contributed eventually to their willingness to let Bismarck shift the balance of power against France by creating a powerful state in the heart of the Continent.

The curious thing was that French governments, from 1814 to 1852 at least, rarely behaved according to the European stereotype. They were inclined to walk softly and to carry a small stick. Caution, restraint, an avoidance of crusades of all kinds—these were the hallmarks of French policy until the accession of Napoleon III, and even Napoleon indulged in no rash attempt to restore French grandeur at any cost. Perhaps the French governments of the era were merely timid, unimaginative, even pusillanimous; perhaps, on the other hand, they contributed to the stability of Europe in its most peaceful century of modern times.

Throughout the Bourbon period the monarchy faced a double pressure for a more active policy; from the ultras on the one hand, from the liberals on the other. The ultras felt the need for a strong and colorful foreign policy to overcome the sentiment that the regime had been imported in the saddlebags of the conquering allies and dared not stand up for French interests. The ultras wanted a firm commitment to the Metternichean principle of antirevolution, with France leading the way as defender of continental stability. The liberals likewise urged an active foreign policy, but of quite the opposite sort: they wanted France to serve as symbol and sponsor of liberal movements everywhere. Ultras and liberals agreed on one point only: that French self-respect required a revision of the 1815 treaty settlement. A chauvinistic tinge was given to this campaign (and a word added to the language) by the agitation of such Napoleonic veterans as Nicholas Chauvin.

Both of the Bourbon kings and most of their ministers avoided either the ultra or the liberal line, preferring a cautious, noncommittal neutralism. For several years any other policy might have brought new foreign intervention; indeed, both the British and the Russians in 1816 privately exerted pressure to get the ultras out of office in favor of more moderate and restrained leadership. The return of the ultras in 1820 brought no real change, mainly because Villèle, strong man of the new government, was stubbornly opposed to adventures of any kind. Adventures might upset his program of financial stabilization and might bring trouble with England; Villèle's foreign policy was therefore limited to a single principle—to stay out of trouble.

The only important deviation from this line was France's expedition into Spain in 1823. Villèle had tried to evade ultra demands that France, acting on behalf of the Concert of Europe, go to the aid of the Spanish king against his liberal ministers. In an effort to frustrate the war hawks in his cabinet, he named Chateaubriand foreign minister; but Chateaubriand promptly switched sides and announced that a French army of a hundred thousand men would be sent into Spain. The venture seemed a foolhardy one, not only because the English were hostile to it, but also because no Frenchman could forget the reception that Napoleon's invading army had received in Spain. If France's greatest military genius had been unable to break Spanish resistance, how could a Bourbon-led army do so? The French liberals hopefully predicted disaster, and Villèle half believed them. Instead, the expedition developed into a triumphal military parade; Madrid fell within a month, with only a handful of French casualties. Bourbon prestige was reinforced, and so was the French army's loyalty to the regime; the soldiers revelled in the acclaim born of victory and in the promotions and decorations that followed it.

It was Chateaubriand, however, who deserved much of the credit for the triumph, and who claimed all of it. "My Spanish war, the great political event of my life" (he wrote in his memoirs) had done more to stabilize the regime than all the other politicians of France had managed to do in eight years. "The youth of France had come in a body to my side, and never afterward left me.... I could not step into the street without attracting a crowd."[1] The victory encouraged Chateaubriand to push ahead toward a new kind of French foreign policy, adventurous rather than cautious in spirit. The Spanish expedition he conceived as only the first step toward freeing France for action; his next move would be to secure an alliance with Russia, which would enable him to tear up the treaties of 1815 and to recover the Rhine frontier. But Villèle proved to be a shrewder political infighter than Chateaubriand. The rivalry between the two men produced a crisis in 1824, and Villèle got the furious foreign minister dismissed from office.

Not until Polignac's accession in 1829 was the policy of caution infringed again.[2] As an ultra-ultra, Polignac hoped for a great diplomatic victory that would restore the popularity of the regime. His aim was to sweep away the treaties of 1815 and to recover the Rhine frontier; and he could manage this only by getting Russian support. The scheme which he concocted was certainly one of the most remarkable in French diplomatic records. The partition of moribund Turkey was to furnish the occasion for a Franco-Russian agreement and for a complex series of territorial exchanges through which every nation would be bought off. Russia and Austria would receive sizable chunks of Turkish territory; Prussia would annex the Dutch Netherlands and Saxony; England would get the Dutch colonies; France would receive Belgium. The expropriated Saxon king would be transferred to a new state carved out of the Prussian Rhineland, while the Dutch monarch would rule a new Byzantine-Greek empire at Constantinople. Polignac tried out this fantastic scheme on the Russians, but it got a cold reception. As a substitute, he hit on the idea of an expedition against the Moslem ruler of Algiers. A long-standing economic and diplomatic controversy furnished an excuse for action, but British opposition to any European intervention in Algeria had led Polignac's predecessors to confine themselves to angry words. The expedition of 1830, which at the outset seemed as risky as the Spanish venture of 1823, proved to be an equally striking success. Algiers fell only three weeks after the French force landed, and news of the triumph encouraged Charles X to proceed with the domestic coup d'état of July that led to his overthrow. Polignac's active foreign policy thus contributed to the fall of the Bour-

---

[1] R. de Chateaubriand, *Mémoires d'outre-tombe* (Paris: Garnier, n.d.), IV, 284–85, 313.

[2] France's involvement in the naval battle of Navarino (1827) was not a very important exception, since the battle developed accidentally out of a Franco-British naval demonstration against the Egyptian fleet.

bons, and at the same time gave France an unintended dividend—the opportunity to acquire a new colonial empire in North Africa. For the Orleanist monarchy, after much backing and filling, chose to stay in Algiers and to conquer the vast hinterland as well.

❖❖❖❖❖❖❖❖❖❖❖❖❖❖❖

The wave of emotion that produced the revolution of 1830 was accompanied by an upsurge of nationalism and a demand for a more aggressive foreign policy. The moment seemed ripe for a change, for revolution spread through much of Europe in a kind of chain reaction, and the foundations of the 1815 settlement appeared to be seriously undermined. The revolt of the Belgians against Dutch administration encouraged those Frenchmen who wanted to recover the Rhine frontier, while Polish and Italian outbreaks against their Russian and Austrian masters offered tempting opportunities for crusades of liberation. Not only the republican left, but some of Louis-Philippe's supporters as well, urged action.

The new king faced a difficult choice. The great powers were tense, and hostile to the revolutionary usurper; a false move might bring disaster both to France and to his new dynasty, which had been received coolly by the other monarchs. Yet he dared not grovel too obviously because of the surge of patriotism among his own partisans at home. Discreetly, he announced a policy of nonintervention in the Belgian crisis, and resurrected Talleyrand as a special emissary to London, with instructions to work out a face-saving solution of the Belgian problem. Talleyrand's aim was an agreement dividing Belgium among all its neighbors; in the end, he had to settle for an independent Belgium, committed to choose its monarch from one of the minor royal families of Europe. The compromise disappointed the chauvinist element in France; and what followed infuriated them even more. The Belgians, ignoring instructions from the powers, invited one of Louis-Philippe's sons to become their king; Louis-Philippe, after some hesitation, sidestepped the opportunity for fear that it would lead to a confrontation with the other great powers. Meanwhile, his government was evading domestic pressure for an expedition to help the Poles, who had risen in revolt against their Russian masters. Several months of temporizing gave the Russians time to crush the insurrection. "Order reigns in Warsaw," announced the French foreign minister. Advocates of a strong policy on both left and right were beside themselves. The king's spineless conduct was contemptable, declared Chateaubriand: "Europe can spit in his face; he wipes himself, offers his thanks, and displays his royal certificate." The king's critics believed, both then and later, that an unparalleled opportunity had been missed in 1830. A vigorous French government, wrote Louis Blanc a decade later, could have made over the whole

Continent on liberal lines and could have raised France once again to the position of leader of Europe. The Belgians, he insisted, had been eager for annexation; in Italy, Poland, Spain, the liberals had needed only a French gesture to ensure victory; the Turks were looking for a patron and protector. France would have faced no serious opposition, according to Blanc, for the great powers were too preoccupied, or too hesitant, to interfere.

There is good reason to think that Blanc was much too sanguine both about the probable reaction of the powers and about the prospects of the central European liberals. Indeed, Louis-Philippe's "weak" foreign policy probably saved the dynasty from disaster, and it produced some constructive results in the process. If France failed to recover the Rhine frontier, it got the next-best thing: an independent and friendly Belgian state, whose new king shortly married a French princess. The establishment of Belgium also meant that France might hope for a gradual, peaceful revision of the 1815 treaties, which were thus infringed for the first time. And France secured, finally, a chance to try the experiment of an entente with England.

This Franco-British alignment was the most important aspect of Orleanist foreign policy, but it proved to be much less durable and useful than Louis-Philippe had hoped. Although it survived sporadically from 1830 to 1846, it lacked much substance after the first few years. No formal alliance was ever signed, despite a French effort in 1833 to negotiate a defensive pact. Some scholars believe that economic rivalries were responsible for its breakdown; that only a sharp reduction in French tariffs could have overcome British reluctance and could have given the diplomatic entente an essential base in economic collaboration. Others hold that trade rivalries and tariff conflict were merely contributing factors in the cooling of the new friendship. Much more basic, they argue, were such things as Palmerston's personal hostility toward Louis-Philippe and a series of Anglo-French controversies involving prestige rather than commerce, in areas ranging from Spain to the Pacific Ocean.

The Near East had been a potential source of tension from the outset. Turkey's defeat at the hands of Russia in 1829 suggested that the Ottoman empire might be on the verge of collapse. But Russian policy over the next generation was designed to bolster Turkey in order to make it a satellite state, while the British aimed to bolster Turkey for just the opposite reason—to make it an anti-Russian bulwark. Only the French showed an active interest in at least a partial dismemberment of Turkey. They were engaged in carving off Algeria (still theoretically subject to Turkish control); and they had built up special influence in the Egyptian province ruled by Pasha Mehemet Ali, who was challenging the sultan's suzerainty. The French sent officers to train Mehemet's army, granted him loans, and supported him when the sultan set out in 1839 to chastise him.

Unfortunately for France, British and Russian interests temporarily converged on one vital point: namely, their antagonism toward Mehemet Ali's pretensions to independence and conquest. Louis-Philippe might have been inclined to abandon Egypt had it not been for the pressure of public and parliamentary opinion in Paris, which drove him for a brief period to try a tough policy. Early in 1840 he appointed Adolphe Thiers head of the ministry. Thiers combined the qualities of a bantam rooster with a passionate interest in military strategy; he took an intransigent stand in support of the Egyptians. Once again, the French faced a general European coalition headed by England. Thiers rashly pushed ahead with a policy of bluff, apparently on the assumption that the powers would not really face war; but neither French opinion nor the French king was willing to run so great a risk. Thiers was dismissed late in 1840, and the way was opened for a revival of the English entente. The prospect of such a revival seemed especially good since Guizot, the new strong man of the ministry, wanted England's friendship and opposed foreign adventures.

But a whole series of plaguing issues kept the waters roiled during the 1840's. A conflict between British Protestant and French Catholic missionaries in Tahiti (the so-called Pritchard Affair) led to years of bickering, and resentment persisted even after a compromise settlement was arranged. The British blocked a French plan to intervene in Morocco and warned Paris against a projected Franco-Belgian customs union. But the incident that finally swept away the remnants of the entente occurred in Spain. Both the French and the British had been jockeying for position at the Spanish court, each one with a view to diplomatic and commercial advantage. Their rivalry came to focus upon the young queen, who was eventually to achieve well-earned notoriety as Isabella the Amorous. The French were eager to provide her with one of Louis-Philippe's sons as a husband; the British candidate was a German prince, a relative of Victoria's consort. After a long deadlock the French proposed a compromise: a Spanish duke would marry the queen, while Louis-Philippe's son would marry Isabella's younger sister. The British angrily denounced the plan as a clever French trick; they charged that the French had carefully handpicked an impotent husband for Isabella. Guizot pushed ahead with the scheme nevertheless and brought on the inevitable disruption of the entente. It was a sad commentary on Guizot's statesmanship that he considered the Spanish marriage plan his diplomatic masterpiece; even worse was the fact that French opinion also received it with enthusiasm. Perhaps Guizot had in mind the creation of a new alliance system linking France, Spain, the kingdom of Naples, and even Austria. Or perhaps his sole purpose was to win French applause for a successful finesse against England. Neither purpose would justify the price Guizot had to pay—the bitter hostility of the British.

The Orleanist era illustrates the difficulties involved in conducting a pacific, prudent foreign policy marked by the spirit of *juste milieu* and of compromise. It gave France a generation of peace, with some territorial gains and no territorial losses. Yet the policy contributed to the downfall of the regime, for it seemed weak and offered the opposition a handy stick with which to beat the government. Meanwhile, it won the monarchy no real friends abroad; by 1848 France was almost totally isolated. Critics of the regime both then and later argued that an ideological foreign policy would have been both more admirable and more profitable for France. The first and best chance was missed, according to them, in 1830; a second opportunity was developing after 1845, as serious unrest began to grow in Italy, Switzerland, and Poland. But the king and Guizot, instead of encouraging this liberal unrest, chose to collaborate with Metternich in a policy of repression. The door was left open for Palmerston to emerge as champion of liberal movements and to win for England the moral and diplomatic leadership that rightly belonged to France. At the very least, argue these critics, Paris ought to have expressed its sympathy with the liberals of the 1840's. Instead, Guizot concentrated his energies on the Spanish marriages and on controlling unrest in Europe. The Orleanist record in foreign affairs has sometimes been used as evidence that any foreign policy marked by caution and restraint, by a spirit of *juste milieu,* is bound to be flabby and futile. A fairer conclusion might be that such a policy requires extraordinarily shrewd and flexible leadership if it is not to end in general disillusionment.

❖❖❖❖❖❖❖❖❖❖❖❖❖

The 1848 revolution, even more than that of 1830, brought a wave of crusading fervor in France. Central Europe's insurrections were far more fundamental ones this time, and the prospect of renovating the whole Continent seemed far brighter. It is not surprising that the republican left wing put heavy pressure on the new provisional government to send armies of liberation marching across France's frontiers. Was this the great lost opportunity of the modern era? That question was later to obsess such eminent French Socialists as Jean Jaurès and Léon Blum. It has obsessed French historians as well. One of them asserts flatly that if Frenchmen had seized their chance in 1848 to wipe out feudalism in central Europe, they would have been spared the disasters of 1870, 1914, and 1940; and a British historian adds that the decision not to act marked the abdication of France as a great power.

The thesis is tempting, but its validity is open to at least some doubt. The provisional government of 1848 could not be sure that Frenchmen in general shared the activists' eagerness for a crusade on behalf of freedom. It knew that the interventionist current was offset by a strongly pacifist or isolationist stream, not only among the peasant masses but even among the Paris republicans. Perhaps the crusaders themselves would have been less enthusiastic if they had faced up to the possible consequences of their policy—the re-creation of the anti-French coalition of 1815 and a general war against the monarchs of Europe. It is true enough that the policy of inaction had unhappy results; the new regimes in central Europe were destroyed, and so was the French republic itself. It may be argued that a crusade could hardly have produced worse results. But it is unfair to ignore (as some historians have done) the hazards of a strong foreign policy in 1848, or to suggest that the provisional government's cautious line was nothing more than the product of blindness and class bigotry.

With Napoleon III came the first fundamental change since 1814 in the temper and conduct of French foreign policy. Although Napoleon announced just before the coup d'état of 1851 that "the Empire means peace," no ruler bearing his name was likely to rank peace higher than glory. Nor could any Napoleon fail to regard the treaties of 1815 as a humiliating *Diktat* that must be revised for the sake of national and dynastic prestige. One might think that the task of characterizing the Second Empire's foreign policy would be an easy one; yet quite the contrary is true. Napoleon's conduct of affairs aroused more controversy among contemporaries, and has been more diversely judged by historians, than any other phase in the foreign policy of nineteenth-century France.

To some historians, the emperor was a dreamer hypnotized by the principle of the rights of nationalities; a man whose idealism was not adequately balanced by a sense of realism, and who failed to understand how his dreams might impinge upon the interests of his country. To others, he was a calculating schemer concerned above all with prestige, aiming to dazzle the French people by his exploits, utilizing the nationality principle as a mere pretext to justify his meddling tactics. To still others, he was an admirably farsighted and intelligent statesman who foreshadowed the modern ideals of self-determination and European federation, who wanted France to lead Europe toward that brighter destiny. Finally, there are those who conclude that he had no clear aim at all; they see him as buffeted about by conflicting currents within France and concerned primarily to keep himself in power through shrewd manipulation.

Not only Napoleon's motives, but his alleged errors of judgment as well, have been subjects of continuing controversy. Some critics have charged him with focussing too narrowly on Italian questions, perhaps because his early experiences as a Carbonaro there left a kind of emotional residue. German scholars have accused him, rather, of a persistent determination to recover the Rhine frontier at almost any cost and to keep Germany weak enough to be subservient.

Other historians allege that he failed to raise his eyes from the European scene and to see that a vast colonial empire could be had for the taking. Still others believe that the emperor's central purpose was to build a great alliance system led by France, and that he bungled the task through his inability to choose among potential allies.

The controversy doubtless stems from Napoleon's complex and contradictory nature and from his habit of secretive, tight-lipped diplomacy. Probably the emperor was neither a rigid doctrinaire, nor an idealistic dreamer, nor an unprincipled opportunist. His interest in the rights of nationalities seems to have been genuine; but almost certainly it was not the core of his policy, the central aim for which he would sacrifice all else. He made no effort, for example, to push that principle in the Balkan region, where it would have interfered with his ambition to arrange an Austrian alliance. A reasonable conclusion might be that his central aim was a very broad and general one: to restore French prestige in Europe and to give his dynasty a solid base. Napoleon's revisionist attitude toward the treaties of 1815 was almost as fundamental as that of the Germans toward Versailles many decades later. Apparently the emperor had shaped no rigid program but intended to feel his way in pragmatic fashion toward a restoration of national prestige. His primary goal was neither territorial expansion nor European federation, but a balance-of-power system under France's diplomatic leadership.

During his first decade in power Napoleon sought to achieve this end through close collaboration with Britain. To win London to such a policy was probably his principal motive in entering the Crimean War of 1854–56; certainly French interests in the Near East offered no adequate justification for war with Russia. A non-hostile relationship with the British did develop for a time; the period brought the first use of the phrase "entente cordiale."[3] But the entente gradually cooled after 1860 as the result of a series of minor squabbles, in spite of the closer trade relationships made possible by the Chevalier-Cobden Treaty.

As a kind of substitute for the Anglo-French alignment, Napoleon turned to a device that had long attracted him: a revival of the European congress system of the Castlereagh era. The emperor's interest in diplomacy by conference (a practice for which there was little precedent in periods of peace) lends some plausibility to the thesis that he was a forerunner of the European federalists. He conceived of the congress system, however, much as Castlereagh had done—

---

[3] Napoleon tried to avoid conflicts with the British, even to the point of what might be called appeasement. For example, he gave little support to Ferdinand de Lesseps' company organized to build the Suez Canal, since he knew that the British opposed the project. If the canal was finally constructed the credit must go to De Lesseps rather than to Napoleon. P. Renouvin, *Histoire des relations internationales, le XIXᵉ siècle* (Paris: Hachette, 1954), I, 331–35.

as a mechanism for operating a balance-of-power system. His scheme got little support from the other powers, who usually evaded his invitations to settle problems around a table. Simultaneously during these middle years of the empire, Napoleon was embarking on a whole series of enterprises that aroused the suspicions of the rest of Europe and that produced division at home: aid to Piedmont in creating a north Italian federation, intervention in Mexico to establish a satellite empire, an expedition to Syria (1860) with the declared purpose of protecting Christians against Moslem persecution, penetration of Indo-China as a base from which to tap the Chinese market.

From 1866 onward the empire entered a third phase, during which Napoleon was increasingly preoccupied with the German problem. This was not to be the most brilliant phase of Napoleonic diplomacy; indeed, the disaster of 1870 was prepared in considerable part by the mistakes of the prewar years. The emperor seriously underestimated both Prussia's potential power and Bismarck's skill and ruthlessness. He even helped the Prussians get a treaty with Italy in 1866—a treaty that was essential to Bismarck's plans for an armed showdown with Austria. It is quite clear that he expected a standoff fight between Prussia and Austria, with France stepping in at the proper moment to mediate and to dictate terms. A few Frenchmen perceived the danger more clearly: Thiers, for example, who publicly warned the government on May 3, 1866. Napoleon ignored the warning; but even when the battle of Sadowa proved Thiers right, he failed to intervene while there was still time. After some hesitation, Napoleon gave up the idea of sending his army to the Rhine as a warning to Bismarck—probably because most French opinion was so vigorously and vocally hostile to the idea.

The fatal error of inaction in 1866 was compounded during the years that followed. Napoleon's clumsy efforts to get territorial compensation along the Rhine only played into Bismarck's hands. His attempts to negotiate alliances with Italy and Austria dragged on to an empty conclusion; and his desperate attempt to build up France's military power was defeated by an irritated public opinion at home. By the time of the decisive crisis in July, 1870, Napoleon seems to have let the power of decision slip almost entirely out of his hands—the result, at least in part, of chronic illness. It may be that the emperor saw the Prussian threat more clearly than either his advisers or his subjects during the last years before his downfall. But even if that was the case, he no longer showed the leadership and the determination required to conduct an unpopular but hard-headed policy. Napoleon's inadequacy as a crisis leader left the nation, at the end of his eighteen-year reign, reduced in prestige, isolated in Europe and threatened with demotion to the status of a second-rate power. Perhaps that decline was not entirely chargeable to him; perhaps the facts of geography, resources, and population were beginning to catch up with the French. But it would be futile to deny that Napoleon deserved an important share of the blame. Confronted by a rival as able and unscrupulous as Bismarck, the emperor's shortcomings as a shaper of foreign policy could no longer be concealed.

✸✸✸✸✸✸✸✸✸✸✸✸✸

European interest in empire-building reached its lowest point in the first half of the nineteenth century. France, like the other powers, showed only sporadic flashes of interest in colonial expansion during the years 1814–70. Yet the imperial impulse never died out entirely; on the contrary, a beginning was made toward creating a new overseas empire in place of that lost to the English in the eighteenth century.

The treaty of 1814 restored to France the scattered remnants of the old empire, consisting of little more than a few tropical sugar islands plus some trading stations on the west coast of Africa. The Bourbons were content with what they had; their one overseas expedition (to Algiers in 1830) was not intended as a colonial venture. Louis-Philippe absorbed the rest of Algeria, rather in spite of himself, and also added Tahiti and the Comoro Islands, off Madagascar. Napoleon III contributed Cochin-China, a protectorate over Cambodia, and control of the west African hinterland of Senegal. This scattered and incoherent list suggests that chance rather than any conscious goal governed these acquisitions. Only in the Second Empire were the first anticipatory signs of the new imperial age to be seen: national prestige, humanitarian drives, and economic motives seem to have been interwoven in Napoleon's mind.

If most Frenchmen had no clear idea of why (or whether) they wanted colonies, they were scarcely clearer on how to run an empire once they had gotten it. Until 1848 they fell back rather automatically into the mercantilist tradition of the old regime, according to which the colonies were mere appendages of the mother country, destined to contribute to France's well-being. The revolution of 1848 brought a brief experiment in humanitarianism a century ahead of its time. Napoleon III restored authoritarian control from Paris, but combined it with an unprecedented liberalism in the economic sphere, and capped all this with some rather ambiguous talk about building an Arab kingdom in Algeria.

The old colonies (like Martinique and Guadeloupe) continued to be run after 1814 by a planter class, set atop a population of slaves. Their trade, as mercantilist doctrine required, was completely monopolized by France. This system was already beginning to decay well before 1848 destroyed it. Colonial cane sugar was running into new competition from French beet sugar, developed on a large scale during the Napoleonic wars; the importation of slaves had been outlawed in 1815, and the institution of slavery itself was under rising attack. A farsighted policy in Paris would have broken the grip of mercantilism at the earliest possible date, in order to permit a gradual shift in the colonies from sugar plantations to new products adapted to the French or the world market. But the planters and, even more, powerful shipping interests in Bordeaux managed to block any change.

The acquisition of Algeria burdened the French with a brand-new problem, for which the old colonial system was in no way adapted. Here for the first time was a large indigenous population to be ruled; here, too, was potential space for French colonization on a large scale, at a time when France was threatened by overpopulation; here, finally, was an area whose agrarian products would compete with rather than supplement those of the mother country. France's conquest of Algeria was largely accidental. The Bourbons had no intention of empire-building in 1830; Charles X had apparently planned that a congress of European powers would decide the country's fate. Louis-Philippe kept troops in Algeria primarily because the British were so eager to get them out; he had knuckled under to England on the Belgian issue, and he had to resist British pressure somewhere to placate opinion at home. Then, having decided to retain a strip along the coast, the French were gradually sucked into a conquest of the hinterland as well in order to stop constant harassment by Algerian tribesmen. The cost of the conquest brought repeated complaints in the French parliament; it is likely that the critics would have had their way except for the prestige factor. By 1848 the conquest was complete except for the rugged Kabylia region; another generation of *razzias* (lightning raids, complete with burning and looting) was required before the Berbers there could be subdued. The process of colonization had already begun in the 1840's; by 1848 about a hundred thousand Europeans (only half of them French) had settled in Algeria. There was still no clearly conceived plan of development to govern such matters as the size of holdings or relationships between European and Algerian farmers.

The revolution of 1848 brought the most drastic change in the history of French colonialism. The republicans of that era, though not much interested in colonies, did have a clear-cut policy toward them. That policy was one of assimilation: it rested on the assumption that all men are free and equal, and that the overseas possessions ought to be integral, self-governing parts of France. One of the very first steps was to free the slaves, with a small indemnity to the owners. The ex-slaves were converted into citizens at once; and several of the old colonies were given the right to elect deputies to the Paris parliament. Northern Algeria was assimilated even more completely (in formal structure, at least); it was converted into three French departments complete with prefects and many of the formal appurtenances of departments in continental France. Most of the reforms of 1848 were to prove permanent, save for a partial interruption during the Second Empire. Economically, the reforms had a severe impact on the sugar islands, where the planters were already in difficulties. Production dropped sharply and did not regain the 1848 level for a generation. Gradually, however, the islands managed to convert to a new and healthier economic base. One further consequence of the 1848 upheaval was a new spurt of emigration to Algeria. After the National Workshops were closed, about twenty thousand settlers moved down with government aid; and the coup d'état of 1851 produced another important wave of emigrants. By 1860 the European population in Algeria had risen to two hundred thousand, and by 1870 to three hundred thousand.

Napoleon III's colonial policy, like almost every aspect of his reign, defies any simple description. In some ways, it foreshadowed the great age of European imperialism in the late nineteenth century; in other respects, it seemed tinged with the more humanitarian outlook of the twentieth. The idea of assimilation was promptly abandoned, and the colonies were restored to the status of political appendages governed from Paris. On the other extreme, the colonies gained a new freedom of trade when the emperor turned toward economic liberalism in 1860. Important new acquisitions were added to the empire in Indo-China and west Africa; but often they were not so much the product of conscious policy in Paris as of independent action by French army and navy officers on the spot. This was notably the case in Senegal, where French control of the hinterland was won by that remarkable soldier and empire-builder, General Faidherbe. It was less true in Indo-China, where the decision to intervene was made in Paris. A small force landed at Saigon in 1859 to protect Catholic missionaries and began a piecemeal conquest of Cochin-China. The real purpose was to get a naval base and to gain access, via the Indo-Chinese river valleys, to the supposedly fabulous Chinese market. At one point Napoleon was on the verge of withdrawing this expeditionary force, for there were rising protests in Paris about the cost involved, and his more important Mexican venture was running into difficulties. Pressure exerted by the clergy, by Bordeaux shipping interests, and by spokesmen for the French navy averted the withdrawal and committed France to a century of imperial activity in southeast Asia. Here was an early example of the complex blend of humanitarianism, prestige-seeking, and special interest that was to become so common in the new imperialistic age.

Napoleon's most curious overseas ventures were his Mexican expedition and his scheme to convert Algeria into an Arab kingdom under French protection. The excuse for intervention in Mexico (which began in 1861) was to force the Mexican revolutionary republic to honor certain debts owed to Europeans. The real reason appears to have been Napoleon's belief that Mexico might be turned into a kind of satellite state or sphere of influence of great economic value to

France. Perhaps he hoped also to appease the French clergy by breaking the power of the Mexican anticlericals and to please French patriots by a display of French energy. The venture proved to be, instead, an unmitigated disaster; Mexican resistance, United States warnings after the end of the Civil War, and the new Prussian threat across the Rhine forced a humiliating evacuation of Mexico in 1867.

Napoleon's Arab-kingdom plan bore at least a superficial resemblance to the projects of those twentieth-century French progressives who hoped for an autonomous multiracial Algeria. The emperor twice visited Algeria to study its problems on the spot and came away fascinated by the Arab people and Arab ways. For a time he stopped the flow of colonists into Algeria and talked of preserving the indigenous society with its feudal structure and leadership. The Algerian dream, like that of Mexico, ended in total frustration and was promptly abandoned by the Third Republic. Like so many other enterprises of the Second Empire, it can be used to buttress either of two theses about the emperor: Napoleon the humanitarian idealist, or Napoleon the well-meaning chaser of chimeras.

# CHAPTER 17

# The Varieties of History, 1814–1870

Historical controversy is a by-product of upheaval; agitated periods like the Great Revolution lend themselves to sweeping and doctrinaire interpretations. Controversy less often develops about periods of relative quiet, when changes occur in more gradual and undramatic fashion. There are clear-cut schools of thought about 1789 and its aftermath; there are only overlapping differences of opinion about the major trends of the early nineteenth century. Indeed, few historians have been tempted to examine those major trends for the period 1814–70, or even to see it as a coherent whole with its own distinguishing traits. More often they have preferred the piecemeal study of shorter segments of time— perhaps because the political chronology of the era lends itself so well to such subdivision. It is as though Frenchmen had thoughtfully sawed up their history like cordwood into lengths of fifteen to twenty years, in order to make them more easily manageable to the historian. What is lost in the process is continuity, and a sense of the overall significance of the times.

Some of the most useful studies are those that trace a single thread of development from 1814 to the present; they manage thus to reveal the continuity that is concealed beneath changes of regime. A solid example in the realm of political ideas is René Rémond's *Les droites en France*, in which the author dissects the right-wing tradition into three principal strands: traditionalist, conservative-liberal, and nationalist. Varying in strength, changing in character, they nevertheless persist from 1815 to the present. Rémond's analysis is now generally accepted, although it runs into some controversy when applied to the twentieth century. On the role of various social institutions, the position of the church and its relation to the state is treated by Adrien Dansette in his *Religious History of Modern France*. Dansette's central theme is the tension between the French church and "modern society," and the repeated frustration of attempts by progressive Catholics to bring the two into harmony. A more recent synthesis by Gérard Cholvy and Yves-Marie Hilaire, *Histoire religieuse de la France contemporaine*, is broader in scope and more solidly anchored in archival research; it extends to the minority religions as well as Catholicism, and to the lives of Catholic believers as well as to the church as an institution. On the role of the army, Raoul Girardet's *La société militaire dans la France contemporaine* traces evolving attitudes of Frenchmen toward the armed forces and of soldiers toward civilians and the state; he stresses the determined effort of the military to stay aloof from politics. The evolution of the educational system is soberly surveyed in Antoine Prost's *Histoire de l'enseignement en France, 1800–1967*.

Turning from institutions to social categories, Adeline Daumard's *Les bourgeois de Paris au XIXe siècle* is a pioneering investigation of the various strata that made up the bourgeoisie from 1815 to 1848; the emphasis is on their economic status and their system of values. Her work quantifies a mass of information dug out of notarial archives. On labor, a recent monograph by William H. Sewell, Jr., *Work and Revolution in France*, examines working-class culture in the early nineteenth century. Sewell shows that the rhetoric and the beliefs of artisans were shaped by a long heritage of *compagnonnage* activity as well as by the ideas introduced by the Great Revolution. A curious but stimulating monograph by Louis Chevalier, *Laboring Classes and Dangerous Classes*, sets out to portray what he calls the biological foundations of social history: the incidence of disease, crime, and prostitution in early nineteenth-century Paris. Chevalier traces the partial breakdown of law and order in that era to a pathological state induced by demographic change—notably by the rapid influx of population from the provinces, and the resulting lack of social integration. Class antagonisms became so bitter, he argues, that it was almost as though two hostile cultures were confronting each other in Paris. On the peasantry, Maurice Agulhon's chapters in volume 3 of the *Histoire de la France rurale* (Georges Duby and Henri Wallon, eds.) provide an up-to-date survey of conditions in the countryside. Agulhon's detailed study of one rural department in the south, showing its gradual conversion to republicanism, is a model of its kind (*The Republic in the Village: The People of the Var from the French Revolution to the Second Republic*). The beginnings of feminism from 1815 to 1848 have been traced by Claire G. Moses in *French Feminism in the Nineteenth Century*.

Many studies of France's economic development during the nineteenth century focus on the controversy over retardation: Was France's economic growth more sluggish that that of her industrialized neighbors, and if so, why? Two landmark articles by David S. Landes advanced the thesis that psychological and sociological factors were central in retarding modernization; it was the entrepreneurial spirit, he claimed, that was lacking ("French Entrepreneurship and Industrial Growth in the Nineteenth Century," and "French Business and the Business Man: a Social and Cultural Analysis"). Rondo Cameron, on the other hand, insists in his *France and the Economic Development of Europe 1800–1914* that talk of French backwardness belongs in the realm of "folklore." In fact, he says, until about 1880 France led the world in technical education and in the infusion of capital and technology into more economically retarded European countries. Several recent studies support the thesis that France's economic growth, although it fluctuated over time, compared quite favorably with that of other industrialized countries. François Caron, for example (in *An Economic History of Modern France*) rejects the thesis that French businessmen lacked the entrepreneurial spirit, and provides a useful summary of recent assessments of nineteenth-century economic growth.

France's position in Europe and the world from 1814 to 1870 has provoked less interest among historians. Aside from monographs of limited scope, there is only volume V of Pierre Renouvin's lucid and balanced synthesis, *Histoire des relations internationales: le XIXe siècle*.

Most specialists on nineteenth-century France have confined themselves to a single political regime. On the Bourbon monarchy, G. de Bertier de Sauvigny's *The Bourbon Restoration* stands almost alone. His account seeks to rehabilitate the much-criticized restored monarchy. Its shortcomings, he argues, were by no means fatal ones; indeed, he contends that its overthrow in 1830 inflicted an "irreparable wound" on the nation, for it destroyed the last chance of blending monarchical tradition with emergent democracy, on the British pattern. Some historians would find that argument more appropriate for Louis-Philippe's regime; it may be implicit in David Pinkney's recent *Decisive Years in France, 1840–1847*. The July Monarchy, Pinkney contends, brought the beginnings of a fundamental transformation of France. This was not a time of dull and stodgy conformity, he tells us; in a wide variety of spheres (industrialization, modern transportation, new social thought, artistic innovation) France in the 1840's was breaking out of her past into the modern age. Pinkney's challenge to orthodoxy will no doubt be challenged in its turn. For an analysis of the elites of the July

Monarchy, A. J. Tudesq's *Les grands notables en France, 1840–1849* is funda-mental. Tudesq shows that the label "bourgeois monarchy" is too simple; the notables who controlled society, economic life, and politics were a mélange of landowning aristocrats and rich businessmen—the ruling group of a society in transition, slowly evolving from a hereditary agrarian system toward modern capitalism.

The revolution of 1848 and the Second Republic have drawn much more attention from historians, and have inspired more argument. Karl Marx was the first to examine it in a work of "instant history": *The Class Struggles in France, 1848 to 1850* appeared in 1850, and has remained a touchstone for Marxist his-torians ever since. Marx and his followers have focused on socioeconomic factors and class relationships; they have traced the breakdown of the republic, with its pioneering social experiments, to the hypocrisy and greed of the bourgeoisie. The monarchy had fallen in 1848 because "finance capital" and "industrial capital" were at odds with each other; the social republic fell in turn because the capital-ists closed ranks to turn back the threat of social change. Roger Price's *The French Second Republic: A Social History* questions the Marxian interpretation on many points of theory and detail; Maurice Agulhon's *1848 ou l'apprentissage de la république* is an up-to-date and balanced synthesis, with mildly Marxian overtones.

A surprising development is a recent surge of interest in the later years of the Second Republic, from Louis-Napoleon's election as president to his seizure of power in 1851. Historians had been inclined to write off those years as little more than a warm-up period for Louis-Napoleon's coup d'état. Several re-visionist studies now argue that something important was going on in the provinces—namely, a strong resurgence of the republican left both in the towns and in the countryside. The rising strength of the "reds," it is argued, produced a wave of social fear among the elites, who saw the threat of a "red" victory in the 1852 elections. These elites therefore backed Louis-Napoleon's coup d'état and his ruthless repression of the thousands who protested against the coup. The protest movement, according to the revisionist view, was the greatest provincial insurrection of the nineteenth century. Repression did not destroy the left, but drove it underground; it was to emerge stronger than ever after 1870. Notable examples of this reading are Ted W. Margadant's *French Peasants in Revolt: The Insurrection of 1851*, and John M. Merriman's *The Agony of the Republic*. Their thesis has been challenged by Eugen Weber in his article "The Second Republic, Politics and the Peasant." According to Weber, the archives contain little evidence that the peasants were being politicized during the Second Re-public; that process, he believes, came a generation or two later.

The changing views of historians on Napoleon III's regime have been surveyed by Stuart L. Campbell in *The Second Empire Revisited*. The most striking shift in recent decades has been the turn from a negative to a positive image of Napoleon III. Written off by Karl Marx as "an old crafty roué" and by Victor Hugo as "Napoleon the Little," the emperor continued to have a bad press during the Third Republic. Recent biographers have been inclined to rehabilitate him, and even to exalt him as an admirable, farsighted statesman: for example, Albert Guerard's *Napoleon III*, and Jasper Ridley's *Napoleon III and Eugénie*. Some critics, however, remain unreconstructed: Henri Guillemin in *Le coup d'état du 2 décembre* reverts to the Hugo-Marx version, portraying Napoleon as an unprincipled schemer surrounded by a "band of racketeers." Alan Spitzer's lucid and ironic essay "The Good Napoleon III" is an excellent introduction to the historical debate about this enigmatic figure.

For the historian, the novel can sometimes be a source of understanding. Although resort to fiction has certain risks, there are times and places where it can illumine many obscure corners. Nineteenth-century France is clearly such a time and place. Perhaps the reason is that historians of modern France have left many glaring gaps which only the novelist has tried to fill; perhaps it is because French novelists have taken an especially lively interest in political and social issues; or perhaps (as Herbert Luethy puts it) "in France literature has taken the place of political economy, sociology, and statistics."[1]

It was Balzac, of course, who was the greatest practitioner of "imaginative sociology" through the novel. Karl Marx and Friedrich Engels claimed that Balzac's novels had taught them more about bourgeois society than any non-fictional source. One need not be a Marxian to share this opinion; Balzac's fascination with social relationships, and his habit of developing themes out of the actual events of the time, give his works a base in reality that has been tested and validated by several modern scholars. To choose among the ninety volumes of the Comédie Humaine is difficult, but surely any historian will profit by reading *Old Goriot, César Birotteau, Eugénie Grandet, Splendors and Miseries of Courtesans,* and *The Country Doctor.* Stendhal's works, which are more concerned with psychological than with sociological analysis, nevertheless use social satire to illumine the life and values of the Restoration elites—notably in *The Red and the Black* and in *Lucien Leuwen.* Gustave Flaubert's *A Sentimental*

---

[1] H. Luethy, *France Against Herself* (New York: Praeger, 1955), p. 72. "Literature," adds Luethy, "is the only possible and adequate social science of a society organized in innumerable groups held together by personal ties, each small enough to be surveyable by all its members and private enough to be impenetrable by outsiders; while in the mass their infinite divisions and subdivisions make them totally unsurveyable and incalculable."

*Education* contains a graphic (and unsympathetic) picture of the 1848 revolution and a remarkable panorama of Parisian bourgeois society under Louis-Philippe; his unfinished novel *Bouvard et Pécuchet* satirizes the passionate "scientism" that was beginning to fascinate Frenchmen. Eugène Sue's *Les mystères de Paris*, which appeared in newspaper serial form in 1842–43, strikes today's reader as overblown melodrama, yet much of it rested on serious documentation and observation of the Parisian underworld, and vividly contrasted life in the slums with that in the middle-class quarters. Victor Hugo's *Les misérables* is likewise melodramatic and sentimental, but it operated at the time to reinforce the guilt feelings of some bourgeois Frenchmen and to strengthen the current of social protest.

In a different genre, no one could claim a full appreciation of the period without some acquaintance with the caricatures of Honoré Daumier (who mercilessly satirized the ruling elite and the *bien-pensant* bourgeoisie of his time), and perhaps those of Henri Monnier as well. Monnier's character Joseph Prudhomme has gone down in French folklore as the epitome of obtuse petty-bourgeois pontificating ("That, gentlemen, is my opinion, and I share it.").

A Selective List of Readings About France 1814–1870

Agulhon, Maurice. *1848 ou l'apprentissage de la république.* Paris: Seuil, 1973.

Agulhon, Maurice. *The Republic in the Village: The People of the Var from the French Revolution to the Second Republic.* New York: Cambridge University Press, 1982.

de Bertier de Sauvigny, G. *The Bourbon Restoration.* Philadelphia: University of Pennsylvania Press, 1966.

Braudel, Fernand, and C.-E. Labrousse (eds.). *Histoire économique et sociale de la France* (vols. 3 and 4). Paris: Presses Universitaires, 1970–1982.

Cameron, Rondo. *France and the Economic Development of Europe, 1800–1914.* Princeton: Princeton University Press, 1961.

Campbell, Stuart L. *The Second Empire Revisited.* New Brunswick: Rutgers University Press, 1978.

Caron, François. *An Economic History of Modern France.* New York: Columbia University Press, 1979.

Chevalier, Louis. *Laboring Classes and Dangerous Classes.* New York: Fertig, 1973.

Cholvy, Gérard, and Yves-Marie Hilaire. *Histoire religieuse de la France contemporaine.* Toulouse: Privat, 1985.

Dansette, Adrien. *Religious History of Modern France.* New York: Herder, 1961.

Daumard, Adeline. *Les bourgeois de Paris au XIXe siècle.* Paris: Flammarion, 1970.

Duby, Georges, and Henri Wallon (eds.). *Histoire de la France rurale* (vol. 3). Paris: Presses Universitaires, 1976.

Girardet, Raoul. *La société militaire dans la France contemporaine.* Paris: Plon, 1953.

Guerard, Albert. *Napoleon III.* Cambridge: Harvard University Press, 1943.

Guillemin, Henri. *Le coup d'état du 2 décembre*. Paris: Gallimard, 1951.

Johnson, Douglas. *Guizot: Aspects of French History*. London: Routledge, 1963.

Kemp, Tom. *Economic Forces in French History*. London: Dobson, 1971.

Landes, David. "French Entrepreneurship and Industrial Growth in the Nineteenth Century," *Journal of Economic History*, IX (1949), 45–61.

Landes, David. "French Business and the Business Man: A Social and Cultural Analysis," in E. M. Earle (ed.), *Modern France*. Princeton: Princeton University Press, 1951.

Landes, David. *The Unbound Prometheus*. Cambridge: Cambridge University Press, 1969.

Margadant, Ted. *French Peasants in Revolt: The Insurrection of 1851*. Princeton: Princeton University Press, 1980.

Marx, Karl. *The Class Struggles in France, 1848 to 1850*. New York: International Publishers, 1964.

Merriman, John M. *The Agony of the Republic*. New Haven: Yale University Press, 1978.

Moses, Claire G. *French Feminism in the Nineteenth Century*. Albany: SUNY Press, 1984.

O'Brien, Patricia. *The Promise of Punishment: Prisons in Nineteenth Century France*. Princeton: Princeton University Press, 1982.

Pinkney, David. *The French Revolution of 1830*. Princeton: Princeton University Press, 1972.

Pinkney, David. *Decisive Years in France: 1840–1847*. Princeton: Princeton University Press, 1986.

Price, Roger. *The French Second Republic: A Social History*. Ithaca: Cornell University Press, 1972.

Prost, Antoine. *Histoire de l'enseignement en France 1800–1967*. Paris: Sirey, 1965.

Rémond, René. *La vie politique en France depuis 1789*. Paris: Colin, 1965–1969.

Rémond, René. *Les droites en France*, 4th ed. Paris: Aubier-Montaigne, 1982.

Renouvin, Pierre. *Histoire des relations internationales: le XIXe siècle*. Paris: Hachette, 1954.

Ridley, Jasper. *Napoleon III and Eugénie*. London: Constable, 1979.

Sewell, William H., Jr. *Work and Revolution in France: The Language of Labor from the Old Regime to 1848*. Cambridge: Cambridge University Press, 1980.

Spitzer, Alan. "The Good Napoleon III," *French Historical Studies*, II (1962), 308–329.

Tudesq, A.-J. *Les grands notables en France, 1840–1849*. Paris: Presses Universitaires, 1964.

Weber, Eugen. "The Second Republic, Politics and the Peasant," *French Historical Studies*, XI (1980), 521–550.

Wright, Gordon. *Between the Guillotine and Liberty: Two Centuries of the Crime Problem in France*. New York: Oxford University Press, 1983.

# III
# THE ROOTING OF
# THE REPUBLICAN SYSTEM
## *1870–1919*

# CHAPTER 18

# The Monarchist Republic, 1870–1879

If the Republic isn't the right system for France, the surest way to get rid of it is to establish it.

HENRI WALLON (1875)

The dramatic phases in a nation's history are not always the ones that do most to shape that nation's destiny. There was not much drama in the decade of the 1870's in France; it suffers by contrast with the somewhat meretricious glitter of the empire just before it and with the generation of political turmoil, crisis, and scandal that immediately followed. Yet it constitutes a vital and formative period in the political development of modern France. It saw the establishment of the governmental framework that served the nation for the next three-quarters of a century. It produced the beginnings of the modern party system and of the basic political divisions that were to harden and endure for decades. More fundamentally still, it brought the conversion of a majority of Frenchmen to the republican ideal. Republicanism, ever since the Great Revolution, had been a minority current in the country, though its size and strength could not be precisely measured. In February, 1871, not more than a third of the nation's votes were cast for declared republican candidates. But by the middle of the decade, and certainly by the end of it, that minority had become a permanent majority.

Such a transition to republicanism may seem quite normal to one who lives in the twentieth century. In the mid-nineteenth it was exceptional. No other major nation in Europe became republicanized so early as the French; the only existing republics on the Continent were Switzerland, Andorra, and San Marino. The reasons, therefore, deserve examination.

One shaping factor was negative in character: the monarchist majority that existed in 1870 helped to cancel itself out by its own internal rivalries. The three competing dynasties never quite managed to reconcile their differences; and obviously, as Thiers indelicately put it, there was not room on one throne for three backsides. But there was a positive factor at work, too; French republicanism in that decade seemed to be taking on a new look. From the outset in 1871 it was the moderate, libertarian wing that got control of the republican movement. In the past, whenever the French republicans had achieved power, this moderate element had been promptly challenged by a smaller, but noisier and more aggressive, egalitarian or Jacobin wing; and the challenge had usually produced a bloody clash between the two factions. So it had been in 1792–94, and so again in 1848. Any prospect that the radicals might get control would have terrified France's socially conservative elements, notably the peasants and the middle classes. They were reassured to find the republicans headed by a set of solid, stable, even stuffy men, who at the very outset met and mastered the left-wing activists. In that era at least, Thiers was surely right in his dictum that "the republic will be conservative or it won't be at all."

In the consolidation of the moderate republic, many men had a hand; but two of them played indispensable roles. One of these—Adolphe Thiers—was a late convert from the monarchist right; the other—Léon Gambetta—came over from the radical left. Rarely has France produced a pair of leaders so remarkable, and rarely have two men offered so striking a contrast. They shared a southern temperament and common birth. In almost every other respect, they were at opposite poles. Thiers was a patriarch of seventy-three, a veteran of four full decades of political life; Gambetta at thirty-two was a mere beginner who had barely had time to make his maiden speech in parliament when the empire fell. Neither man was made to understand the other; Thiers was to refer to his junior colleague as a "raging madman," while Gambetta labelled Thiers "that sinister antique." Yet the two careers converged in the 1870's to consolidate the new republic.

Thiers's role was to furnish leadership and stability at a critical moment, just after the disaster of 1870. His prestige had reached its peak in the country; and this lifelong monarchist put that prestige at the service of the provisional republic. The moderate republicans had other leaders as safe and sound as Thiers; but none was so widely respected or such a master of parliamentary tactics. Gambetta's role was to rally a sizable segment of the Jacobin left wing to the moderate, libertarian program, and thus to avert a potentially disastrous faction-fight among republicans over the nature of the republic. The irrepressible firebrand, the demagogic orator and patriot became the conciliator, the "opportunist," the practitioner of politics as the art of the possible.

❖❖❖❖❖❖❖❖❖❖❖❖❖❖

When the Paris crowd burst into the hall of the Corps Législatif on September 4, 1870, it was to Léon Gambetta that the rioters looked for leadership. He it was who led the revolutionists' march across town to the Hôtel de Ville, where, by long-established ritual, it had become customary to proclaim republics. He it was who promptly became the spark plug of the new provisional government, composed for the most part of deputies from Paris constituencies. In this Government of National Defense, Gambetta chose the key post of minister of interior. Because that ministry controlled the administrative bureaucracy and the police, Gambetta believed that he could use it to consolidate the republican victory. He promptly installed a new set of fervently republican prefects throughout the provinces and argued for postponing the election of an assembly until these new officials might have time to "prepare" the voters.

The immediate problem, however, was to expel the Prussian invader from the sacred soil of France. After the defeat at Sedan and the abdication of the emperor, Bismarck's troops had rapidly fanned out through northern and eastern France. Some members of the new government hoped at first that Bismarck might offer generous peace terms to the new republic, or that a European league of neutral states might put pressure on the Prussians to withdraw their forces. These vain hopes quickly evaporated. By September 23 Paris was surrounded and besieged by the Prussian forces. If France was to continue resistance, at least part of the government had to be transferred to the provinces. Gambetta volunteered; he took over the ministry of war in addition to his previous post, and on October 7 he and a friend dramatically escaped from beleaguered Paris via balloon. After a hazardous trip that saw the adventurers blown in the wrong direction almost to the Belgian frontier, Gambetta managed to make his way to Tours to organize some kind of armed force.

Over the next four months all his unbounded energy and powers of persuasion were thrown into the task of national salvation. His mind was suffused with the myth of Valmy, with the passionate conviction that an aroused nation in arms could throw back any invader. All Frenchmen, he proclaimed, must shelve political issues until the war was won. These were noble sentiments—a bit too noble, indeed, for Gambetta himself to accept without mental reservations. Military victory meant to him not only saving France from the Prussians but also rooting the republic in French affections. To evoke the myth of Valmy was one thing; to repeat the "miracle" of 1792 was another. Gambetta might measure up to Danton, but Danton had not been faced by a Moltke and a Bismarck. Within a few weeks Gambetta managed to patch together several makeshift armies, which engaged in several inconclusive skirmishes with the Prussians, but failed in an attempt to relieve besieged Paris. The futility of the enterprise grew increasingly clear to all but Gambetta and his loyal disciples. Europe would offer no aid; France's last trained army was lost when Marshal Bazaine, besieged in Metz, capitulated without a fight late in October; in Paris the threat of starvation and epidemic grew ominous. The provisional government's will to resist rapidly withered away. Besides, some members of the government had been growing suspicious of Gambetta's flamboyant activities in the provinces. Jealous of his rising popularity, they could easily persuade themselves that his goal was a kind of Robespierrist dictatorship. Late in January, over Gambetta's furious objections, Minister of Foreign Affairs Jules Favre approached Bismarck to seek an end to hostilities; and on the twenty-eighth, a three-weeks' armistice was signed. Some of Gambetta's entourage urged him to proclaim a dictatorship; he refused, but he angrily resigned his post in this government of capitulation.

The central purpose of the armistice, as both the French government and Bismarck saw it, was to allow time for a kind of plebiscite on the issue of war or peace. Orders went out at once to convoke the voters on February 8 for the election of a National Assembly, empowered to make peace in the name of the French people. The election proved to be the most curious one modern France has known. The campaign lasted only a week. Half the country was occupied by Prussian troops; public meetings were virtually impossible; mail service was in chaos; and any semblance of a nationally-organized campaign was out of the question. The electoral system of the Second Republic was resurrected for use; it provided for large multimember constituencies in which the voters would select a whole party list. Candidates had to be chosen hastily by impromptu local committees, often without informing the candidate that his name had been put up. The most eminent figures, or those best known locally, were usually chosen to head each ticket. One result was that Thiers was elected in twenty-six districts, Gambetta in ten.

More important still was the unique influence of local factors in the choice of candidates. That fact contributed to the election of a great many aristocrats; for in rural areas the *châtelain* was the man most generally known. But there was an added reason for this aristocratic resurgence: most of them ran on tickets ambiguously labelled "list of peace" or "peace and liberty," whereas their republican rivals were viewed by the electors as war hawks. As a matter of fact, most moderate republican candidates were also eager to end the war; but the Gambettist agitation for a bitter-end fight clouded the issue and aided the antirepublicans. Although few of the latter openly campaigned as advocates of a monarchical restoration, their tactics turned the election into a sweeping royalist triumph. When the new Assembly convened in Bordeaux a week later, it contained more than four hundred monarchists to only two hundred republicans and a handful of Bonapartists. Both Bismarck and the Government of National

Defense had correctly judged the country's temper. Everywhere except in Paris and a few scattered provinces, the nation had voted for peace on any reasonable terms. Whether the nation had voted for a monarchical restoration was, however, much more ambiguous.

❖❖❖❖❖❖❖❖❖❖❖❖❖❖

The Assembly's first obligation (and its only clearly defined duty) was to make peace. It acted with dispatch; Adolphe Thiers was chosen as provisional executive and was sent at once to negotiate with Bismarck. The Prussian terms were severe; Thiers fought hard to get them softened, but with slight effect. In the end he had to accept a preliminary peace that required France to pay a war indemnity of five billion francs, that provided for the occupation of eastern France until payment was complete, and that transferred all of Alsace save Belfort, and one-third of Lorraine, to Germany. On March 1 the Assembly reluctantly approved this settlement, whereupon Gambetta and his followers, together with most of the deputies from Alsace and Lorraine, walked out of the hall and handed in their resignations. Gambetta, thoroughly disillusioned, went into voluntary exile in Spain, his career apparently finished. Six months later, however, he was to be back in politics, a successful candidate in a by-election. The most colorful phase of his career was over, but the more important part was still to come.

The Assembly's choice of Thiers as provisional executive had seemed to be dictated by the results of the elections. His prestige, however, only half-explained his success; he had also played his cards with remarkable skill. Although a life-long Orleanist, he had carefully adopted a kind of neutralist position in politics after the fall of the empire, and he had cultivated friendships in all groups. When the Assembly convened, he seemed to stand above political divisions; and he encouraged this idea by urging the need for a political truce during the months of peacemaking and reconstruction. All groups therefore agreed unanimously to let him serve as a kind of combined president and premier. The monarchist majority reluctantly agreed to let the regime be called a provisional republic, partly because their plans for a restoration of the king were not yet quite mature, partly because they were relieved to let the republic be made responsible for signing a severe peace.

Early in March the Assembly voted to transfer the seat of government to Versailles, where the authorities would be less subject to public pressures than in Paris. Before the Assembly could reconvene in the new temporary capital, it found its authority repudiated by Paris and several other major cities, and it was drawn into a large-scale civil war. The seventy-two day episode of the Paris

Commune in 1871, bloodier than any other civil clash in modern French history, was to leave a lasting imprint on the nation. On the hill of Montmartre the exotic Byzantine bulk of the Church of the Sacré Coeur rises today to commemorate the Commune's victims; it was financed by nation-wide contributions collected in the 1870's by French conservatives as a kind of atonement for the nation's sins. In the cemetery of Père Lachaise, the "wall of the federals" (i.e., Communards) serves as a shrine to the Commune's martyrs, some of whom were executed there by government troops at the end of the revolt.

The bare facts of the affair are far simpler than the interpretations they have elicited. Paris since the armistice had been in a state of agitation that verged on collective neurosis. The excitement and tension of the siege culminated in an explosion of fury when the government suspended hostilities; and this sense of outrage was redoubled when the provinces voted massively for peace. Republican Paris also resented the monarchist character of the new Assembly, its decision to make Versailles the capital in place of Paris, and its brusque cancellation of such wartime emergency measures as moratoria on debts and rents and a daily dole to members of the National Guard. All of this dry tinder burst into flame on March 18 when Thiers, in a heavy handed move to get the city under control, ordered the army to haul away two hundred cannon that had been cast during the Prussian siege and had been paid for by public subscription. Angry mobs of Parisians drove off the Versailles troops and lynched two generals unfortunate enough to be caught in the vicinity. Thiers, instead of seeking to negotiate with municipal officials, evacuated the city in preparation for a siege and an eventual full-scale confrontation. Paris was left in the hands of various radical factions, whose leaders promptly called elections, organized the city as a self-governing "Commune" and called for the conversion of all France into a decentralized federation of such free municipalities.

This second siege of Paris, this time by Frenchmen, lasted for nine weeks. Thiers, whose troops were outnumbered at first by the Communards' National Guard, successfully appealed to Bismarck to release some prisoners of war to crush the rebellion. By May 21 Thiers had collected enough troops to strike. Sympathizers inside the city let the attackers through the outer fortifications, but the Communards dug in and fought back street by street. At the end of a week of bloody conflict, faced at last by imminent defeat, some Communard extremists set fire to many public buildings in the center of Paris: the Tuileries palace and the Hôtel de Ville were burned, the Louvre and Notre Dame were barely saved. Little mercy was shown by either side; the attackers summarily shot anyone caught with weapons, while the Communards executed a whole group of hostages, including the archbishop of Paris. Twenty thousand died in the repression of the Commune—several times as many as in the June Days, more than the total number of victims in the Reign of Terror. Fifty thousand others were tried, many of them being deported to the penal islands; thousands more escaped into exile.

A whole tissue of legend has grown up about the Commune. Some years ago a Soviet journalist visiting Paris asked a small boy in a working-class quarter what he knew about the Commune. "Do you mean what they teach you in school," asked the child, "or what papa says?" "Papa" no doubt followed the line first laid down by Karl Marx himself: this was the first proletarian dictatorship in history; the heroic Parisians "mounted an assault on the gates of heaven," and their brief triumph was "the glorious harbinger of a new society." Marx's thesis, abandoned after a time by Marx himself but then resurrected by Lenin, was to become an integral part of Marxist-Leninist doctrine in the twentieth century. Some Marxist historians claimed to find the origins of the Commune in a bourgeois conspiracy engineered by the Thiers faction: fearful of rising radical strength in Paris, the bourgeois establishment allegedly set out to provoke a revolt there in order to decapitate the radical movement.

Non-Marxian historians, on the other hand, are more inclined to find the Commune's origins in spontaneous combustion rather than conspiracy. Thiers was undoubtedly heavy handed, but was not necessarily moved by bourgeois hysteria and class hatred. One of his concerns was that negotiating with the rebels might look like appeasement, and might encourage the spread of rebellion to other cities, bringing on a nation-wide civil war. A second probable factor was more personal in nature. Thiers fancied himself something of a military genius, scarcely less brilliant than his hero Napoleon. His formula for mastering a rebellious Paris had long since been worked out; he had vainly proposed it to Louis-Philippe in February, 1848, and again to Cavaignac in June of that year. His plan called for prompt evacuation of the city, a tight siege until rebel enthusiasm began to dim, and then a lightning stroke by the armies massed around the outskirts. The Commune finally offered this frustrated strategist a chance to try out his recipe for victory. As for the severity of the repression that followed the victory, that too represented something more than bourgeois class hatred. Thiers almost certainly over-reacted to the Communards' execution of hostages and attempts to burn public buildings, as well as to the news that his own house, during the siege, had been pulled down stone by stone. No doubt a greater man than Thiers would have shown more mercy. After "bloody week" it is scarcely surprising that his name long remained anathema to Parisians; that he, almost alone among France's notable statesmen, never had a statue or monument raised to him in the city; that when the city council, after many decades, finally gave his name to a thoroughfare, it chose not a broad boulevard but a minor street one block long.

Non-Marxist historians also find little evidence for the view that this was a class-conscious proletarian rising, or that it was clearly socialist in inspiration. The Communards were drawn from a broad and complex cross-section of classes; rather like the sansculottes of 1793, their outlook was as much petty bourgeois as it was proletarian. Their leadership, as embodied in the 80-member elected body that governed the Commune, was likewise an ill-assorted mixture. About two-thirds were vaguely Jacobin or Blanquist in spirit: egalitarian, intensely patriotic and anticlerical, obsessed by the legend of 1793 with its memory of a strong centralized dictatorship. The other third were self-professed socialists, but mostly of the Proudhonian rather than the Marxist persuasion; they favored a decentralized federal system. Conflict within the Commune was unavoidable, especially when the caliber of its leadership was no better than mediocre. Toward the end, factionalism became severe, and inefficiency flagrant. It is scarcely surprising, given this internal conflict, that the Commune experimented with very few innovative social reforms. In retrospect, therefore, the episode appears as not the first modern proletarian revolution but rather the last in a long series of insurrections by the "little people" of Paris—the final catastrophe of the old romantic French socialism. Yet its durable impact was to be in its contribution to legend, as absorbed into one of the most powerful social myths of our age.

"The Commune," remarks one French historian, "is the key to our contemporary history." What he means, presumably, is that the experience left a kind of psychological scar; that it permanently divided French republicans, embittered the workers, and intensified class conflict. There is much truth in this view; the long-range effects were deep and severe. There is a striking parallel between the Commune and the June Days of 1848, which also exacerbated social tensions and encouraged the radical workers to justify the use of violence as a political weapon. Yet there is also a curious contradiction between these two episodes. The June Days contributed to the early overthrow of the Second Republic by a strong man; the Commune, on the contrary, did not wreck the Third Republic, and may even have helped it to survive for seventy years. To socially conservative Frenchmen, especially in the provinces, the government's victory suggested that the republic could be tough and effective and could handle serious threats to public order. Furthermore, republicanism was purged of its radical leaders by execution or exile and fell for a decade into the unchallenged grip of safe moderates. The rooting of the republic in the countryside was certainly made easier and swifter under such leadership. Perhaps the June Days might have had similar consequences if republican leadership after 1848 had been equal to that after 1871, and if there had been in 1848 no young and glamorous aspirant dictator on the scene, ready to take advantage of republican division and conservative fears. In 1871 Napoleon III was old and ailing, his son young and untried; and luckily for the republic, no other substitute turned up.

❖❖❖❖❖❖❖❖❖❖❖❖❖❖❖

It may seem strange that an Assembly dominated by a large monarchist majority had not moved without delay to restore the king. The most plausible explanation is that the monarchists were divided into roughly equal and completely irreconcilable factions, the Legitimists and the Orleanists, each with its own rival pretender. Still, both dynasties had been so long out of power that all but a few diehards were ready to seek a compromise. Furthermore, a solution lay naturally at hand. The Bourbon pretender, the Comte de Chambord, was aging and childless; the Orleanist Comte de Paris was young and prolific. Nothing seemed simpler than to unite behind Chambord as king, with the Comte de Paris as heir apparent.

The latter was willing, but Chambord brutally scuttled the plan. In July, 1871, he returned to France for the first time since 1830, and he issued a manifesto calculated to upset all but the most hard-shelled Legitimists. He would accept the throne, he declared, only on his own terms; and those terms implied a return to the pre-1830 restoration era, if not to the old regime itself. His statement said nothing of a responsible ministry; it placed much stress on a kind of quasi-feudal decentralization; and it bluntly ruled out the tricolor flag in favor of the fleur-de-lis.

The issue of the flag, insignificant in itself, stood as a symbol of Chambord's whole outlook. He failed to realize that the tricolor had taken root in French affections and could not be so easily replaced. But more important still, Chambord's apparent intention to restore arbitrary, paternalistic rule outraged even the great bulk of the monarchists themselves. Indeed, one reason they had not moved more impulsively toward a restoration was that the monarchist politicians wanted the king to return on their terms, not on his. Most of them wanted a British-type monarch, symbol of order and stability but subject to parliament's domination. For the time being, therefore, they suspended their planning and contented themselves with Thiers's provisional rule.

Only a few days before Chambord's manifesto, another severe blow had been dealt the monarchists. More than a hundred vacancies existed in the Assembly, thanks to multiple elections of certain candidates in January and to resignations since then. All these by-elections were held simultaneously on July 2, with startling results. Ninety-nine seats were won by republican candidates, twelve by monarchists, and three by Bonapartists. A more complete reversal in six months' time would have been hard to imagine. In reality, however, the result did not imply an overnight conversion of the nation from monarchism to republicanism. The most important factor was that since January the monarchists had lost their trump card: their demand for immediate peace. Indeed, the republicans managed to steal that card in July; they accused the monarchists of favoring an armed crusade to Italy to recover Rome for the Pope. The electoral outcome proved nevertheless that many Frenchmen were ready to accept a republic that existed and that was directed by a man like Thiers.

Thiers's position, meanwhile, had become almost unchallengeable. The period from 1871 to 1873 has sometimes been called "the reign of Adolphe I." It was one of the rare interludes in modern French history when the republic has possessed a strong executive; Thiers combined in his person the functions of president and of premier, much as General de Gaulle was to do in 1944–46. True, the Assembly had the right to replace Thiers at will, but in fact it dared not do so. His prestige in the country was too great, his skill as a parliamentary debater too awesome to encourage any critic to challenge him on the floor of the Assembly. Thiers was well aware of his strategic position and made the most of it. When the Assembly grew restive or balky, he talked of resignation and got his way. Thiers had spent a lifetime waiting to enjoy such untrammelled power; liberal in theory but authoritarian in temperament, he did not hesitate to use that power, and on the whole he used it well. He gave France almost two years of vigorous and effective leadership; if his "reign" redounded to his own glory, it also consolidated the emergent republic.

What Thiers managed to do was to restore some of the nation's shaken self-confidence and to convince Frenchmen that a republic could be safe and sane. He moved promptly to reorganize the army and to restore its morale. Within six months after utter defeat he was able to stage an impressive military parade through Paris; and within four years France's standing army was almost as large as that of Germany. He called on Frenchmen to restore the nation's credit by subscribing to two large bond issues; they responded by oversubscribing the first loan twofold, the second fourteenfold. By 1873 the indemnity was completely paid off, and French soil was liberated eighteen months ahead of schedule. Much more questionable were his actions in the economic and social sphere, where he beat back proposals for an income tax and took the first steps away from Napoleon III's experiments in free trade. Both decisions reassured the propertied classes but had regrettable social effects and long-term political results.

Thiers's vigorous leadership and domineering manner won him support in the country but lost him friends in the Assembly. Many deputies muttered privately against "the dictator," and monarchist suspicions were aroused by indications that Thiers was flirting with the republicans. They accused him of conniving with the latter in by-elections and of undermining monarchist chances by refusing to install good monarchists as prefects. It was clear enough that Thiers was becoming reconciled to a Thierist republic. In 1872 he said so openly, thus repudiating his initial promise to remain politically neutral. But if the republicans continued to win in by-elections, it was not so much through Thiers's connivance as through their own shrewd electoral tactics. Sensing the temper of the country, the republicans took care to choose moderate candidates; one of these even campaigned on the slogan, "I'm the biggest taxpayer in the district." They continued to accuse the monarchists of warmongering on behalf of the Pope and frightened voters by warning them of a subversive clerical conspiracy with its headquarters in the Vatican. So well organized was their whole campaign that it may suggest the existence of some kind of *sub rosa* republican central committee. If such a body existed, it is at least possible that Thiers was somehow in touch with it.

As the monarchist majority was steadily whittled away in by-elections, the angry and desperate monarchist faction decided that Thiers must be unseated and the king restored without further delay. Several months of planning and maneuvering went into the plot before they dared challenge the great man. Above all, they needed to have a substitute ready and willing to replace Thiers, and a candidate was not easy to find. They finally managed to persuade the commander of the army, Marshal MacMahon, to sacrifice himself for his country. In May 1873, they organized a devious scheme to clip Thiers' wings as president. When Thiers angrily resigned (as they expected), they hastily substituted Mac-Mahon before the latter could change his mind. One aspect of the change, scarcely noticed at the time, had long-range effects on the republic's political structure. Thiers had combined the functions of chief of state and prime minister; he had been a real presidential executive. MacMahon chose to confine himself to the role of chief of state and turned over the active task of forming and directing a cabinet to the ablest monarchist politician, the Duc de Broglie. This separation of formal from actual executive functions was to last as long as the Third Republic, and it was to reappear in the Fourth as well.

The monarchists' purpose, however, was not to perpetuate the republic, but to replace it without delay. This time they succeeded in arranging a meeting between the two pretenders and thought they had managed to work out a compromise on program and doctrine. So sanguine were they that they began to prepare the carriages in which King Henry V would enter Paris. Then, at the last minute, the Comte de Chambord again sabotaged the plan; once more he issued a kind of manifesto announcing that he would return only on his own terms, and under the fleur-de-lis flag. The monarchist leaders, convinced that the country would and should reject such a symbol of the divine right of kings, abandoned their plans in disgust. The only hope, they decided, was to wait until death removed this stubborn Bourbon. To give themselves an adequate margin, they voted MacMahon a seven-year term as president.

Chambord managed to furnish one more evidence of his quixotic temper when, late in 1873, he sought to carry out the restoration in his own way. Secretly he re-entered France and went to Versailles, hoping that MacMahon might be persuaded to appear with him before the Assembly and to call on the latter body to acclaim Chambord as sovereign. The marshal, to Chambord's indignation, refused to go along on the ground that such an act would be illegal. Chambord waited vainly for several days, then slipped back into exile with the bitter remark: "I thought I would be dealing with a Constable of France; instead, I found a captain of gendarmes." Thiers remarked that Chambord ought to go down in history as the French George Washington, the real founder of the republic.

Chambord's stubborn blindness has inspired a number of fanciful theories about his motivation. The most plausible explanation roots it in the curiously isolated life he had led since childhood. For thirty years he had lived in an Austrian chateau, surrounded by loyal émigré aristocrats who were nourished on illusions rather than reality. These retainers had convinced themselves and Chambord that the French masses still yearned in almost mystical fashion for their true sovereign. Chambord himself was marked by a deeply pious and mystical strain, a conviction that God would eventually open the eyes of Frenchmen. That such a man should have chosen to call himself Henry V was truly ironical; no one could have been more different from the last Henry, that sixteenth-century genius of flexible opportunism.

❖❖❖❖❖❖❖❖❖❖❖❖❖❖

The problem of giving France some kind of permanent or quasi-permanent political structure could not be postponed much longer. In 1873 the Assembly set up a committee to prepare a constitutional draft. It began in leisurely fashion by collecting and analyzing all republican constitutions of both past and present, in an effort to find those principles that ensured durability. But speedier action became essential as the trend in by-elections continued to flow toward the republicans.

Finding a majority for any draft was, however, not so easy; for already the Assembly's simple monarchist-republican-Bonapartist division was evolving into a more complex pattern of factions that foreshadowed a party system. Among the monarchists, two principal groups could be distinguished: (1) an extreme right-wing faction called the *chevau-légers* or "king's guards," rigid and stubborn supporters of the Comte de Chambord's ideals; (2) the Right-Center, larger, more flexible, and mainly Orleanist by tradition. On the republican side there were three subdivisions: (1) the Republican Union (popularly called "Radicals") on

the extreme left, led by Gambetta and marked by a Jacobin and egalitarian spirit;
(2) the Republican Left, containing the bulk of moderate bourgeois republicans
like Grévy, Ferry, Simon; (3) the Left-Center, a smaller faction of ex-Orleanists
like Thiers and Casimir-Périer who had recently crossed the line from monarchism. There was still a handful of Bonapartist deputies, but the death of
Napoleon III in 1873 had cut them adrift from any firm policy or leadership.
Thereafter they entered into an uneasy coalition with the monarchists.

The deepest line of cleavage no longer ran down the middle of the Assembly,
separating monarchists from republicans. More significant were those divisions
that set off the fanatical *chevau-légers* from the Right-Center, and (to a lesser
degree) the sectarian Radicals from the moderate republicans. In other words,
there was emerging a strong tendency toward a coalition of the center groups—
toward what the jargon of French politics was later to call a policy of *concentration*.
From the 1870's onward this often-frustrated impulse toward *concentration* was
to be one of the most marked and enduring aspects of French political life. Its
first product was to be the constitution of 1875, a curious compromise document
that was republican in name but monarchist in form. A patchwork affair, little
more than a framework of basic law, it established a two-house legislature, a
cabinet responsible to that legislature, and a presidency designed for easy conversion into constitutional kingship.

Some historians have argued that the compromise of 1875 was the product
of conscious and selfish scheming on the part of France's most powerful social
class—the well-to-do upper bourgeoisie that had risen to power and affluence
during the Great Revolution and had dominated politics and society through
the nineteenth century. These families, it is alleged, consciously or instinctively
spotted some of their leading representatives in both the monarchist and the
republican movements, so that the entrenched social elite could retain control no
matter what the form of government. The most intriguing bit of circumstantial
evidence was the link between monarchist Right-Center and republican Left-
Center factions in the Assembly; the parliamentary leaders of those two factions
had married sisters and lived in twin houses with adjoining gardens in Paris.
The thesis is plausible, however, rather than provable. Right-Center and Left-
Center were separated by a genuine difference in principle—the issue of monarchy
versus republic. Yet in practice, their common outlook could transcend that basic
difference. Both groups held firmly to the parliamentary system and to libertarian
ideals; no Machiavellian scheming was needed to show them that the kind of
regime they desired could exist in either monarchical or republican form.

The chief problem was how to bring the moderate Republican Left faction
into association with the two Centers; for without the moderates' votes, no
constitution could be adopted. That problem was easily solved, however, for the

moderates likewise wanted a parliamentary system operated in a libertarian spirit. The label "republic" attached to the constitution sufficed to win their adherence. More surprising and more important was the decision of Gambetta and most of his Radical supporters to rally to the constitution. Until 1875 the Radicals had steadily denied that this Assembly had any right to draft a constitution. Besides, they were vigorously opposed to the kind of constitution that the center groups would support. The Radicals' ideal was the constitution of 1793, concentrating all power in a one-house assembly rather than scattering authority through several balanced organs of government. Nevertheless, Gambetta refused in the end to embark on a course of intransigent (and probably sterile) opposition to the constitution of 1875. He persuaded most of the Radical group that the new system was the best they could get at the moment. At least it would continue to bear the republican label; and within it, the Radicals might continue to broaden their following until some day the system might be amended to fit the Radical ideal. Part of the Radical group resisted; led by Louis Blanc inside the Assembly and Georges Clemenceau outside it, this faction clung to its principles and denounced Gambetta as a turncoat. The Republican Union split permanently into factions labelled "Radical" and "Opportunist"; after some years the latter group gradually merged with the Republican Left of Grévy and Simon.

Gambetta's action astonished many Frenchmen who had thought of him as a noisy and dangerous demagogue, a kind of aspiring dictator. They had failed to realize that temperament often outweighs ideology. Gambetta, by origin and inclination, was a Jacobin and an egalitarian; but by temperament and instinct, he was a moderate and gradualist. Beneath his flamboyant language, there were deeper traits of flexibility or "realism." His enemies believed that his flexibility was mere hypocrisy, that he was a schemer ready to sell his principles in return for power. In fact, he was a man who liked to remark that "politics is the art of the possible," and who accepted the label "Opportunist" to illustrate his belief that each advance must await the opportune moment. Gambetta was convinced that the republic, if it was to endure, had first to be formally established and must not remain the subject of argument for a decade. He believed that it would have to be operated cautiously until the mass of voters were reassured as to its stability and balance. Only then could the ideal of equality be implemented, in gradual fashion. He was convinced that if the republicans remained deeply divided, if the Radicals boycotted the new system and sought to destroy it, the outcome would be disastrous; another Bonaparte or some other authoritarian substitute would find the way paved for him. By his new Opportunist line, Gambetta contributed as much as Thiers to the doctrine that the republic—at the outset, at least—must be conservative or must perish. It can be argued, too, that he contributed as much as Thiers to the consolidation of the Third Republic.

A different tactic might have led the republicans, like the monarchists, to cancel themselves out by internal division.

❖❖❖❖❖❖❖❖❖❖❖❖❖❖❖

Its work done at last, the National Assembly adjourned on the last day of 1875 to make way for the new constitutional system. Its members could look back on their five years of service with good consciences. Blind though they were to social and economic issues, they had achieved much in the political realm. Many of the Assembly's abler leaders were destined to play leading roles over the next two decades.

Four years still had to elapse, however, before the republicans could win full control of the new republic. The presidency was safely monarchist until 1880, when MacMahon's term was due to expire. The new Senate, as expected, was dominated by monarchists as a result of the system of indirect election designed for just that purpose. In each constituency, senators were chosen by an electoral college made up primarily of delegates from the various local councils (notably the municipal councils). Each municipality (or "commune") provided one delegate, no matter what its population; so Paris with two million inhabitants and St.-Jean-du-Doigt with a few hundred enjoyed a curious kind of equality. This system of weighting the vote in favor of small-town and village France ensured that the Senate would always be a rural body, inclined to check what rural France regarded as the dangerous passions and impulses of the cities. The system was also expected to ensure right-wing control of the Senate, since most rural towns and villages were traditionally administered by the local aristocrats or notables.

The republicans' best hope at the outset was to win control of the new lower house, elected by universal manhood suffrage. There had been no real nationwide test of public sentiment since 1871; even the most optimistic republican dared not be over-confident. Gambetta, in an effort to maximize republican chances, proposed that all republicans pool their strength by agreeing on a single candidate in each district. His proposal failed, and for a quite simple reason: any attempt to unify the republicans implied a leader, and the obvious leader would be Gambetta himself. He stood midway between Moderates and Radicals; he almost alone possessed a touch of charisma, the traits of popular leadership. Too many republicans, however, disliked this rumpled bohemian, or were jealous and suspicious of his demagogic flair. Rather than accept his leadership, the republicans chose to go to battle in three separate phalanxes: Moderates, Opportunists, and Radicals.

Perhaps Gambetta might have achieved his goal of republican unity, in spite of jealousy and suspicion, if the National Assembly had endowed the Third Republic with a different electoral procedure. One of the Assembly's final acts had been to set up the system used in most elections throughout the Third Republic: it provided for small single-member constituencies, with a run-off ballot if no candidate received a clear majority on the first ballot. The monarchists chose this scheme as likely to be profitable to them; it would give local notables a clear advantage. The republicans had tried unsuccessfully to retain the system used in 1849 and 1871, with large multimember districts and no run-off ballot. The latter system, if preserved, might have prevented the fragmentation of the republicans into rival factions at the very start and might thus have given modern France a quite different party structure. It might also have elevated Gambetta into the dominant role in the years after 1876.

In spite of their division, the republicans won a decisive victory in 1876; the new Chamber of Deputies contained 340 republicans and only 155 monarchists or Bonapartists. No one, it seemed, could any longer doubt the nation's conversion to the republican ideal. Gambetta, who had dominated the electoral campaign, was the logical choice to form the new regime's first cabinet; but Mac-Mahon refused even to call him in, choosing instead a colorless centrist named Dufaure. When Defaure was overthrown a few months later, MacMahon continued to ignore Gambetta, this time in favor of the Moderate Jules Simon. MacMahon's monarchist advisers acted thus with an ulterior motive: they hoped to anger Gambetta, split the republicans, and force Simon's moderate group to turn to the monarchists as partners in the new government. They underestimated their enemy. If Gambetta had been a small-minded man, moved by personal ambition and resentment, the scheme might have succeeded; but instead, he announced his loyal support of the Simon cabinet on major issues of policy, and he lived up to that promise.

The new premier's task was an almost hopeless one. Caught between a republican Chamber and a monarchist Senate, he could not avert serious friction on any important policy decision. Simon was well suited to the task; his flexibility approached the level of genius. For a few months he managed to straddle with great skill, but a whole series of pressing issues demanded action. The monarchists, for example, were urging a foreign policy of aid to the Vatican in its contest with the Italian state; and the republicans were agitating for legislation to unshackle the press. MacMahon's advisers began to urge him to find an excuse to unload Simon in favor of a good monarchist. A crisis was made more certain by the new constitution's ambiguities about the proper role of the president. MacMahon's conception of the presidential prerogatives was, on the whole, much like that of Charles de Gaulle eighty years later. The president, MacMahon believed, was intended to be the equal of parliament; he ought to be able to choose his ministers freely, without toadying to parliament's wishes; if a clash should occur, it would be his privilege to dissolve the Chamber and let the voters decide the issue. Only if the will of the people were made absolutely clear would the president be obligated to retreat. The republicans, on the other hand, held that the president was supposed to be a kind of formal figurehead; that he was obligated to appoint a ministry acceptable to the Chamber; that he had no right to set himself up as the rival and the equal of parliament. Both interpretations were plausible, since the constitution itself was so unclear; and there was no supreme court to decide the issue.

MacMahon grew increasingly irritated at Simon's straddling, and his monarchist cronies fanned that irritation. On May 16, 1877, he decided to act, as he believed he had a right to do: he sent Simon a sharply critical letter that virtually invited the premier's resignation. After a night's sleep MacMahon thought better of his impulse and sent a messenger to recover the letter before it reached the recipient. Unluckily, Simon had arrived at his office early that morning; he read the letter and immediately submitted his resignation.

The outcome was total deadlock between president and Chamber of Deputies. MacMahon nominated a monarchist as premier; the Chamber refused to approve him and announced that it would engage in a kind of sit-down strike until the president named an acceptable premier. MacMahon struck back by dissolving the Chamber (with the consent of the compliant Senate) and called on the voters to settle the dispute. But the president, prodded by his advisers, was not willing merely to state his case and let the voters have free choice. In the campaign that ensued, he used every kind of pressure to influence the outcome. He toured the country indefatigably as chief campaigner; his figure on horseback appeared on wall posters everywhere; he suspended or transferred seventy-seven of the eighty-seven prefects, substituting men of "correct" opinions; he accepted the active aid of priests and bishops who spoke from the pulpit in favor of monarchist candidates.

Whether MacMahon's activities helped or hurt his cause is hard to say. He was not an effective campaigner; indeed, his slow wit and bumbling comments made him an easy target for republican ridicule and quickly became part of France's political folklore. The church's unwise interference also boomeranged; republican orators frightened their hearers with predictions of a government run by the men in black. Furthermore, the campaign drove all republican groups together; for a few brief months France had its nearest approach to a two-party system. Gambetta stumped the country as chief spokesman; Thiers was put forward as the republicans' symbol and as MacMahon's putative successor. Thiers died midway through the campaign, but the republicans managed to use his prestige even in death; they staged a great public funeral for the grand old man, with the republican deputies, headed by Gambetta, walking bareheaded behind the coffin.

"We departed 363," Gambetta liked to declaim, "we will return 400." The republican victory proved to be less sweeping; indeed, their numbers fell from 363 to 320. But their margin in the Chamber and in the country was nevertheless clear-cut, and it had been won against the monarchists' best efforts. Some of MacMahon's counsellors urged him to call on the army to sweep away the republic; but his legal scruples were too great, and a number of monarchists shared those scruples. Gambetta summoned him to "give in or get out"; he gave in, accepted the republican interpretation of the president's proper role, and proceeded to name a premier acceptable to the Chamber. He was increasingly irritated, however, at his powerless role and at serving a regime that he detested. The final blow came in 1879, when partial elections to the Senate brought such sweeping republican victories that the latter achieved control of the upper house. This success was the most remarkable achievement of the decade, for it meant that the republicans had somehow infiltrated hundreds of small town and village councils and had taken control away from the older notables who had always run local affairs. Evidently some effective political activity had been going on at the grass-roots level through the 1870's; the result was, in the words of one historian, "a quiet village revolution."

Within a month MacMahon found an excuse to resign; "I've had enough toads to swallow," he remarked to friends. The republicans promptly chose as his successor the moderate Jules Grévy, an able but colorless career politician. That choice was consciously symbolic; one of Grévy's chief claims to eminence was the fact that in 1848 he had sat in the Constituent Assembly and had proposed that the Second Republic get along with no president at all. Such a man was unlikely to emphasize the potential prerogatives of his office.

The so-called *seize mai* crisis of 1877 has been called the decisive incident that converted the mass of Frenchmen to republicanism. Until that time a vote for a republican candidate might not mean very much of a commitment. But in 1877 the issues were clear, the chips were down; every voter had to choose between one course or another. Perhaps it would be more accurate to say, however, that the *seize mai* did not convert Frenchmen but rather furnished proof that the conversion had already occurred.

The long-range effects of the 1877 crisis are clear and can be easily summarized. It ended for many decades the attempt to make the presidency a powerful office capable of balancing parliament's authority. It weakened the cabinet as well as the president, for it deprived the premier of the important right to request the dissolution of parliament. Dissolution remained theoretically possible, but in practice it was never again used in France until 1955; MacMahon had poisoned it by giving it an odor of antirepublicanism. The crisis tended to weaken the parties as well, by contributing to the development of flabby and undisciplined groups. Without the use of dissolution, deputies were safely ensconced in their seats for four years and could not be brought in line by party whips threatening them with electoral retribution. In addition, the crisis further embittered France's religious feud; there followed almost immediately a showdown fight over church influence in education. A shorter-term effect of the *seize mai* affair was that it interrupted the parliamentary trend toward a *concentration des centres;* it drove a wedge between moderate monarchists and moderate republicans, who might otherwise have been inclined to collaborate in coalition governments. The old line of cleavage down the middle of the Chamber was deepened and broadened by the events of 1877; the effects were not to be fully overcome until the 1890's.

The year 1879 thus marked the end not only of a decade but also of an epoch in the Third Republic's history. In outward appearance and in social and economic structure, France had changed little in that decade. Yet a kind of divide had been crossed, irrevocably this time. The era of experiment and uncertainty was over; France was permanently a republic.

CHAPTER 19

# *The Opportunist Republic, 1879–1899*

> How beautiful was the Republic under the Empire!
>
> EDOUARD DURRANC

The abdication of MacMahon in 1879 completed the process of putting the republicans in control of the republic. For the next two decades, almost without a break, political power remained in the hands of the moderate or libertarian wing of republicans—the element then called Opportunists and composed of a fusion of the old Republican Left with the Gambettist ex-Radicals.

In retrospect, it is hard to resist the sentiment that the Opportunist era represents one of the great wasted opportunities of modern French history. The monarchists, except for brief periods, were no longer strong enough to threaten the regime; the Radicals on the other wing could not hope to dislodge the Opportunists but only to share power at best. Two things might have been accomplished by the Opportunist leaders, if they had been men of imagination and foresight. In the political sphere, they might have given the republic a backbone and sinews by developing a vigorous executive and a more stable party system; in the social-economic sphere, they might have taken at least some cautious steps toward social reform and economic modernization. The Opportunists did neither, and France ever since has been paying the penalty for their shortsightedness. Instead, the Opportunists wasted most of their energies in what might be called France's last religious war. That feud between clericals and anticlericals poisoned the atmosphere for a generation and left a heritage of bitterness that endured until the mid-twentieth century.

To some degree, the Opportunists' error was embedded in their view of man and the world, in their libertarian spirit and their somewhat arid rationalism. Their prejudices, their preconceptions, left little room for an understanding of the forces at work in France and Europe—forces that would require men to adapt their institutions to a more complex age. There were partial exceptions: Gambetta, for example, did recognize the need for an effective political system, with an executive that could act and with a majority that would support its action. His goal continued to be the fusion of all republicans into one large and coherent party that could defend the regime against its enemies; and he still thought that it could be achieved through the use of an electoral system based on multimember districts. But Gambetta also continued to be his own worst enemy; his political rivals were too jealous, or too suspicious of his aims, to adopt his electoral reform plan or to let him take power as premier. To some extent, it was a case of men without flair fearing and resenting one who possessed it; mediocrity, someone has said, tends to seek its own level. To a colorless and routine-minded politician like President Grévy, Gambetta's free and easy ways and flamboyant personality were anathema. Grévy's values were reflected in his comment to the director of the annual art exhibition, who had told him: "No extraordinary paintings this year, but a good average." "A good average!" responded the president, "Just what a democracy ought to have." Although Grévy posed as a do-nothing president, he was an old hand at manipulating affairs behind the scenes; he managed to keep Gambetta out of the premiership for almost three years and helped to block Gambetta's political program.

The need for governmental action in the social and economic spheres was even more alien to the Opportunist leaders. Gambetta quickly disappointed those workingmen who had expected him to be a social reformer. The idea of state action to alleviate misery, to correct inequities, or to modify the structure of the nation's economy collided head-on with the Opportunists' laissez-faire principles. Such heresies they associated with the name of Napoleon III, or with the gradually reviving "reds" on the left. Gambetta and his wing of the Opportunists did continue to exalt the little man as symbol and spirit of democracy; Gambetta proclaimed the emergence of what he called *les nouvelles couches*— new layers of society that deserved a share of power. But the little man to Gambetta was not the underprivileged and increasingly discontented proletarian but the small independent enterpriser—peasant, artisan, shopkeeper. To this kind of Frenchman, the threat of oppression came not so much from big business as from the state or, perhaps, from foreign competitors. His ideal, therefore, was high protection and invertebrate government.

The Opportunists were not alone in reflecting the prejudices of the little Frenchman; their Radical rivals were not much more profoundly committed to a program of social and economic action. The Radicals did advocate an income tax and laws to protect labor; but those possessed of a crusading zeal for reform were too few to have much impact. Most republican leaders of that era had only a superficial understanding of, or interest in, social or economic issues. Only the Catholic paternalists, the declining Bonapartists, and the emerging socialists took such problems seriously.

❖❖❖❖❖❖❖❖❖❖❖❖❖❖

These were the negative factors that explain why the Opportunists wasted their two decades in power. But there is another side to the problem. The political elite of the time underacted in the social and economic sphere; why did it over-act in the religious sphere? What produced its excessive, almost neurotic emphasis on the clerical problem as the fundamental issue of the age?

In a sense, the religious conflict was an almost inevitable product of France's past. Any country with an old and deep Catholic heritage, and with a church that once possessed a unique power role, must face severe stresses in a secular-izing age. Memories of the good old days were likely to attract some Catholics and to frighten most non-Catholics. But this factor alone does not suffice to explain the intensity of the conflict in the late nineteenth century. For a religious war there must be not one faith but two—faiths that are militant, hostile, and mutually exclusive. That kind of rivalry developed in France after the mid-nineteenth century; and each camp was dominated by a loud extremist minority too bigoted to think of compromise. Catholicism's rival in this era of conflict was the dogma that chose to label itself positivism.

Positivism's impact in France was first felt in the 1850's, but it arrived in full strength after 1870. The trend was not merely French; this was part of a general European movement toward materialism and scientism, one that spread as far eastward as Russia. But it took its most virulent form in France—perhaps because the founder of positivism was a Frenchman, perhaps as a reaction against the excesses of French romanticism, or perhaps because French republicans were most eagerly searching for a system, a doctrine, a faith. They found that system in Auguste Comte's teachings, with their vast panorama of human history mov-ing upward through successive stages of superstition to a utopian future. Comte taught the inevitability of progress as men managed to strip away those remnants of superstition called theology and metaphysics, and as they turned instead to a positive approach through science. Man, said Comte, was like any other animal the product of physical, chemical, and biological factors; and the laws of his behavior and of social organization could be discovered through scientific method.

There was little in all this that was really new; in most ways, it amounted to a restatement and elaboration of eighteenth-century ideas, with a touch of evolutionism grafted on. Its impact resulted from the fact that it came at just the right time to find a ready-made clientele. What French republicans found here was a consistent and complete set of ideas, a philosophical substructure, for their materialist and agnostic leanings. It supported their optimistic hope that men, through science, could remake the world. Most republican leaders, whether Opportunists or Radicals, absorbed some of it even when they did not swallow it whole. Gambetta expressed a generalized view when he declared soon after 1870, "What we propose to do is to apply positivism to the political order."

Positivism thus developed into a militant faith in brutal opposition to Catholicism. And like the latter faith, it had its organized arm, its militant counter-church, in Freemasonry. Until the mid-nineteenth century French Masonry had been relatively mild and tolerant in outlook; its spirit was deistic, not agnostic. The positivist temper produced a basic change; Masonry was rapidly converted into a crusading order dedicated to rooting out clericalism. The organization was never very large; estimates range from 24,000 to 50,000 members at the end of the century. But its rolls included an important proportion of republican politicians; by 1900 almost every Radical deputy was a Freemason. More crucial still, most local republican party officials, whether Radical or Opportunist, were members of a lodge.

The most eager converts to the new faith and its new church came from the white-collar strata: there were doctors, pharmacists, notaries, village schoolmasters in profusion. The classic caricature of the type appeared in Flaubert's *Madame Bovary;* his pharmacist M. Homais was the narrowest of bigots, whose prejudices were poorly concealed by a thin veneer of learning. Georges Clemenceau's father, a country doctor, was a representative figure; he used to tell his son: "Remember, Georges, there is only one thing worse than a bad priest—and that's a good priest." A lunatic fringe of anticlericals found Masonry too mild and organized Freethinkers' associations with chapters in many villages. On "so-called Good Friday," they arranged banquets at which they "avenged themselves on clericalism by stuffing themselves with sausage."

Religious wars, as earlier observed, require two rival sets of fanatics. So it was in France: a segment of Catholics in this era played into the hands of their critics, and the Vatican contributed to the strife. Pope Pius IX, after the revolutionary upheaval of 1848–49, was transmuted into the epitome of everything the positivist spirit execrated in the church; Vatican policy in his day took on a strongly intolerant and obstructionist cast. Meanwhile the Christian democratic current within the French church almost dried up after 1848; its importance had been temporarily exaggerated by the revolutionary crisis, and it returned to obscurity for several more decades. In place of these left-wing Catholics who had seemed to represent the new voice of the church in 1848, there emerged as a more influential spokesman one of the most fanatical and violent agitators French Catholicism has ever produced: the journalist Louis Veuillot.

Veuillot, a self-educated commoner, had been raised an unbeliever. Suddenly converted while still a young man, he became overnight a superheated zealot. In 1842 he became editor of the Paris newspaper *L'Univers,* and for the next forty years his voice thundered out from that lay pulpit. Veuillot was a rabid hater of the Christian democratic tendency in the church and of liberals and compromisers of all sorts. Absolutely intolerant of error, he "wielded the crucifix like a bludgeon, and mixed vitriol with his holy water." His only regret about the Reformation, someone remarked, was that John Huss had not been burned sooner, and Luther not at all. He crusaded vindictively against the republicans, all of whom he considered to be antisocial and fomenters of disorder. The idea of social reform was to him a dangerous delusion. "Some men," he wrote, "must work hard and live badly. Misery is a law of God to which they must submit. Society needs slaves." When the church won victories (as in the Falloux Law of 1850), Veuillot was rarely satisfied; what he wanted was not a partial but a complete success—in this case, complete and unrestricted control of education by the church.

Veuillot's campaigns served ideally to encourage the fears of the anti-clericals, who suspected that whatever churchmen might say, their real aim was to get a stranglehold on both education and politics. And unfortunately for French civil peace, the Vatican for a generation threw its weight behind the Veuillot faction. Such behavior confounded those liberal Catholics and mild anticlericals who hoped for a compromise, who sought some middle way between the spread of complete materialism on the one hand and a revival of a kind of medieval theocracy on the other.

Veuillot's influence was strengthened in the 1870's by the remarkable rise of a new religious order, the Assumptionist Fathers. This order, though founded in 1845, had been little heard of until after 1870; then it suddenly rocketed into prominence and played a first-rank role until expelled from France in 1901. Unlike older Catholic orders like the Jesuits and the Dominicans, the Assumptionists had no glorious past and produced no great thinkers; yet they left a deep mark on French Catholicism for two generations. Their spirit was mystical, emotional, fanatical; their purpose was to appeal to the masses through the more primitive emotions. Their remarkable success is not easy to explain. In part it grew out of the shock of national disaster in 1871; the Assumptionists called on Frenchmen to recognize that defeat was a natural product of seventy-five years of error and sin. They took the lead in a national campaign to collect funds for the building of the Church of the Sacré Coeur, as a sign of the nation's penitence. They turned, too, to mass action through modern methods. The practice of pilgrimages to holy places, moribund since the end of the Middle Ages, was resuscitated by them in the 1870's. Aided by the railway system (which was persuaded to grant special low rates to pilgrims), they were able to rally mammoth crowds from all parts of France. They moved also into popular journalism: they founded a daily called *La Croix,* to be sold at low cost and to be read by the common man. Its growth was phenomenal; soon it had over a hundred provincial editions and claimed a circulation of more than a half-million. Its tone resembled that of Veuillot's *L'Univers,* but its audience was far wider. To most parish priests in rural areas, it was the sole source of contemporary truth, as implicitly accepted on matters of politics as was the Vatican on matters of faith and morals.

This Assumptionist-led agitation of the 1870's was something new in scope and spirit; France had known nothing like it for a half-century at least. It was enough to frighten many good republicans, who in turn could use it to terrify the peasantry with threats that feudal privileges were in danger of being re-stored. All this was made still worse by the clerical extremists' efforts to influence French foreign policy. The republicans were convinced (or claimed to be con-vinced) that a powerful subversive group was seeking to get a stranglehold on the French state, with a view to using it in the service of a foreign potentate.

By no means were all French Catholics or freethinkers such bigoted ob-scurantists as Veuillot and Homais. Within the church both the tiny Christian democratic and the larger liberal Catholic current persisted, and both were appalled at the extremes of the new Assumptionist spirit. Thus the ablest mon-archist politician, the Duc de Broglie, refused to read *La Croix* or to join in Assumptionist-sponsored pilgrimages; he held that religion's place was in the heart and home, not in public places. Among republican freethinkers, too, there was an important moderate current. Some anticlerical republicans found them-selves dissatisfied with positivism and agnosticism and sought to fill their spiritual need by turning to Protestantism. A neo-Kantian revival led by the philosopher Renouvier asserted the idea that beneath the world of the senses there existed an ultimate reality, too deep to be comprehended by human reason and the scientific method. Still others, like Gambetta, remained freethinkers yet felt the need for some kind of reconciliation with Catholicism—a kind of peaceful coexistence, perhaps. They remained essentially anticlerical nevertheless, for they believed that the church should possess no special position in education or in the state.

But the extremists in both camps were louder and more aggressive; they looked on the moderates with suspicion as "soft," as fellow travellers of the enemy. Their mutual provocation was to dominate the political life of France from the 1870's to the end of the century, and to some degree even until the First World War. It is not surprising that the first years after the republicans' conquest of the republic were filled with a bitter squabble over church influence in education. Out of this controversy emerged a series of laws adopted piecemeal from 1879 to 1886, and usually called the Ferry Laws after their cabinet sponsor, Jules Ferry.

❖❖❖❖❖❖❖❖❖❖❖❖❖❖

France's educational system on the eve of the Ferry reforms consisted of two parallel sets of schools—Catholic and public—at every level from primary to university. In the Catholic system the primary schools were oldest and deepest-rooted; they had existed since pre-revolutionary times. In many villages the Catholic primary school had no competitor. At the secondary level Catholic *collèges* (high schools) had spread rapidly since their legalization by the Falloux Law in 1850; they now attracted almost half the male seondary students in France, and they almost monopolized secondary education for girls. Catholic universities, on the other hand, were new and weak; they had been authorized only in 1875, by one of the last legislative acts of the rightist National Assembly.

The more rabid anticlericals aimed at nothing less than the suppression of all church-controlled schools and the establishment of a state monopoly of education. They were convinced that Catholic schools were "mental incubators" designed to breed antirepublican and antimodernist ideas; and they further alleged that educational standards there were deplorably low. Ferry and most of the Opportunist leaders were not ready to go so far, at least in the foreseeable future. Their goal was not to outlaw Catholic schools but rather to expand the rival public-school system. They were determined, too, to secularize or "laicize" the public schools by rooting out religious teaching and clerical influence therein.

That influence had been strong since 1850 (except in the universities, the chief strongholds of positivism). In all public primary and secondary schools religious education was required by the Falloux Law; and in addition, parish priests were ensured a kind of ex-officio membership on local public-school boards. Even more important, many public-school teachers were members of the Catholic teaching orders, for the state simply did not recruit or train enough secular teachers to do the job.

The impact of the Ferry Laws was slightest at the university level; Catholic institutions of higher learning were merely denied the right to call themselves universities and had to be satisfied with the label "Catholic Institute" instead. It was the primary and secondary schools that felt the full force of the Ferry reforms. The new legislation outlawed religious training in the public schools and substituted civic education. It denied to members of Catholic orders the right to teach in public schools after a five-year transitional period, which would presumably give the state time to train replacements. The Chamber provided funds to build many new public schools, especially for girls, and to create vastly expanded facilities for teacher training. A normal school to prepare primary teachers was to be established in every department; and two advanced normal schools were set up in the suburbs of Paris to train those who would teach the teachers.

The impact of this new public educational system on French attitudes and behavior is not easy to estimate, but there is good reason to believe that it was a major shaping force over the next half-century. The centralized, standardized nature of the system tended to make for uniformity rather than variety—uniformity not only in teaching methods but also in teachers' attitudes. Catholics were convinced from the outset that the public schools would be consciously converted into mental incubators breeding materialism and positivism. Whether or not this was the conscious purpose, it was, in many cases, the result of the Ferry Laws. Village teachers, already inclined toward the positivist outlook, frequently became the self-appointed challengers of the village priests. Someone has described them, ironically but not inaccurately, as a "positivist priesthood," or as "the black hussars of the republic." Another consequence of the highly centralized teacher-training system was that it tended to indoctrinate each generation of elementary teachers with a kind of standard outlook. That first generation of 1885–1914 was militantly patriotic and infected the children in its charge with the same enthusiasm. The dominant attitude of the next generation of teachers, between the wars, was to be quite the opposite—pacifist and internationalist, skeptical and even cynical. The *instituteurs* of France both reflected the temper of their times and reinforced that temper in their students.

Although French Catholics feared that the Ferry Laws were only a first step toward complete suppression of church schools, no such action followed. Indeed, the state even failed to enforce all the provisions of the Ferry Laws. When the five-year transitional period ended, many Catholic brothers and nuns continued to teach in public schools; indeed, some were still there a half-century later. This lax enforcement may indicate a growing tolerance among republican leaders. But it also suggests that the republican politicians might have been wiser if they had drafted the laws in milder compromise form. The effect of the bitter debate over the Ferry Laws was to encourage the extremists on both sides, and thus to keep the religious war aflame.

❖❖❖❖❖❖❖❖❖❖❖❖❖

Although the school laws dwarfed other political issues during the early 1880's, two other significant episodes also marked those years. One was Gambetta's brief fling at the premiership; the other was Ferry's sponsorship of colonial expansion.

The Gambetta cabinet, though a complete fiasco, was notable as the last serious attempt to check the trend toward a weak executive and a flabby party system. If successful, Gambetta might have converted the Third Republic into something more like the parliamentary system of Great Britain. The republic was still new, and political habits not yet so deeply rooted as to resist all change. Gambetta's enemies, notably President Grévy, had managed to keep the great tribune out of power for almost three years after the republican triumph of 1879; but the parliamentary elections of 1881 forced their hand. The Opportunists won their greatest victory ever; with some three hundred and fifty seats, they possessed a clear majority in the Chamber. Monarchist strength was reduced to fewer than a hundred seats, while the Radicals on the left had almost the same number. Among the Opportunists there could be no doubt that Gambetta stood out as the most forceful leader, the only man of really national stature.

Gambetta's purpose, as he prepared to take power for the first time since 1870–71, was not to avenge himself on his jealous rivals but rather to win them over to his cause. He proposed to include every republican ex-premier, every important figure in political life, in his cabinet. He himself proposed to assume a new kind of role, as prime minister without portfolio; unlike his predecessors, he would not combine his post with the interior ministry or the foreign ministry but would undertake to direct and coordinate all governmental activities. In discussing his hopes with his friends, he revealed an even more ambitious goal; he hoped not only to give the republican system vigor and authority, but also to reconcile the deep divisions that marred France's heritage. Somehow, he thought, Frenchmen could be bound together into a real national unity: monarchists and republicans, Catholics and anticlericals, bourgeoisie and working men might be reconciled in a harmonious society and an effective state. Perhaps it was pure illusion to suppose that this could be done. Or perhaps it was a mark of real statesmanship to set up such a long-term goal. At least Gambetta had no illusions about the difficulties of his program; his plan, he said, was to *"sérier les questions"*—to take up one issue at a time, in the order of their urgency.

Gambetta's dream was clouded from the start. The various ex-premiers refused to join his cabinet—possibly because Gambetta had impulsively announced his plans to the press before explaining them to the politicians concerned, or possibly for less admirable reasons. Gambetta was forced, therefore, to form a cabinet of his own youthful disciples—many of them able men with brilliant futures in politics, but little known at the time save for their reputations as Gambetta's henchmen. The premier set out at once toward his goal of national reconciliation by appointing men of all political backgrounds to high posts in the administration, the army, and the diplomatic service. Such broad-mindedness offended many loyal Opportunists and increased their suspicions of Gambetta's motives.

The premier, sensing that his rivals were closing in for an early kill, chose to move rapidly and dramatically: he proposed a constitutional amendment to strengthen the government's authority. His plan was to reduce the power of the Senate so as to deny it the right to block legislation adopted by the lower house, and to write into the constitution a new electoral system that would, he thought, encourage the growth of fewer and stronger parties. An angry outcry followed; Gambetta was denounced as an incipient Caesar. He struck back with a remarkably prophetic speech on the dangers of drift and the need for effective government in a republic. But his enemies were too strong; in January 1882 he was beaten and overthrown after only two and a half months in office. With him disappeared the last real chance for the Third Republic to alter its constitution without abandoning republican principles.

If Gambetta had lived another twenty years, perhaps he might have gotten a second chance. But only a few months later he was dead, at the age of forty-four. Though some mystery and a great deal of rumor surrounded his death, the truth was less dramatic: he suffered a ruptured appendix.[1] The tragedy shocked even the enemies of the great tribune. All the republicans went into mourning and voted him a state funeral. Into his grave they poured earth from Alsace, smuggled across the frontier at night. His body was buried at Nice, his heart eventually extracted and placed in an urn in the Pantheon. The politicians were so shaken that as a kind of expiation they proceeded to adopt the electoral reform for which he had fought so vigorously. By a strange irony, it went into effect just in time to aid the enemies of the republic, resurgent in the elections of 1885.

Gambetta's death left Jules Ferry as the only first-rank moderate republican leader; and Ferry proceeded to give France three years of remarkable governmental stability. It began to seem that Gambetta's urgent call for constitutional reform had been premature, and that a stronger executive was emerging by natural processes. In fact, this period of stability was a kind of accident: it was made possible by the Opportunists' clear majority in the Chamber, and by the fact that Ferry was both able enough and colorless enough to keep that majority intact. If Ferry succeeded so well, it was precisely because he lacked Gambetta's popular appeal; rival politicians felt neither fear nor jealousy. Unlike Gambetta, he had no interest in popularity; he preferred to ignore the voters and to work behind the scenes with other professional politicians. Gambetta had hoped to

---

[1] Most of the rumors stemmed from the fact that Gambetta had accidentally shot himself in the hand ten days earlier. Many Frenchmen believed that he had been shot by an agent of the Jesuits or the Germans; or by an abandoned mistress; or even by his mistress *en titre*, Léonie Léon. Madame Léon's influence over Gambetta during their twelve-year liaison may have contributed heavily to his increasingly moderate views on the church and other issues.

strengthen the executive branch by linking it to the mass of citizens; Ferry further rooted the tradition of an executive dependent on parliament.

In other respects, too, Ferry was Gambetta's perfect opposite. Ferry had a curious way of doing things piecemeal; his reputation as one of the half-dozen ablest statesmen of the whole Third Republic was largely *ex post facto,* for the importance and coherence of his achievements could be seen only in retrospect. It would never have occurred to him to follow Gambetta's example: to lay out a clearly defined program, to go directly to the nation in search of support for that program, to regard political leadership as a process of educating the whole electorate.

Ferry followed his piecemeal technique in getting the school laws adopted; he used it again in laying the foundations for a new colonial empire. Ferry's chief claim to greatness, in the eyes of later generations, was that during his years in power France absorbed Tunisia, took over most of Indo-China, got a foothold in Madagascar, and moved out into the Sahara from bases along the coast. There is a powerful textbook legend that the whole enterprise was a kind of one-man operation conducted by Ferry; that he built an empire not only in spite of French public opinion, but behind France's back; that the bulk of Frenchmen were indifferent or hostile to colonies because their eyes were fixed on Alsace or on their own pocketbooks. Ferry was allegedly shrewd enough to recognize this fact and therefore cagily wheedled small sums from parliament by concealing his real aims. When the politicians and the country discovered what he had been doing, he was driven from office in disgrace.

Much of this standard account is certainly myth. Ferry was a late convert to colonialism; as an old republican of 1848 vintage, he was instinctively hostile to it. When the issue of sending a French force into Tunisia came up, he was one of the last members of the cabinet to agree to it. He initiated almost none of the colonial expeditions of the 1880's; most of them were the work of army officers or traders on the spot. If Ferry asked for small driblets of funds and never clearly laid out an imperial program, it was not so much because he feared parliamentary and popular opposition as because he habitually did things that way. If he was twice overthrown as premier on colonial issues, it was largely a matter of chance; in both cases his majority had been disintegrating, and he was due to fall on the first issue that might arise. When Ferry did fall, furthermore, his successors and critics continued what had been begun: there was no great revulsion in the Chamber or in the nation against colonial ventures.

Ferry has often been described as the conscious agent of powerful economic pressure groups whose imperialistic motive was sheer profit. Some colonialist pressure groups did exist, but it is difficult to gauge either their strength or the manner in which their influence was channelled into politics. The imperialistic drive in France seems to have been more often psychological and emotional than economic. The empire, someone has said, was built primarily by "bored army officers looking for excitement." Even Ferry himself appears to have been converted more for reasons of national prestige than in search of economic advantage.

✦✦✦✦✦✦✦✦✦✦✦✦✦✦

Jules Ferry's greatest shortcoming, as well as his greatest asset, was his utter lack of charisma. The dull grayness of his leadership contributed at least something to that first great challenge to the new republican system, the semi-comic-opera Boulanger affair. A general election occurred in 1885, shortly after the Ferry cabinet's fall, and that election produced one of the most startling reversals modern France has known. On the right, monarchists and Bonapartists more than doubled their strength and captured over two hundred seats; on the left, the Radicals made less spectacular gains but ended with more than a hundred seats. Opportunist strength fell to about two hundred seats; their formidable majority was wiped out. Few political experts had foreseen a shift so drastic. In retrospect, it seems to have been the product of a whole series of confluent factors, none of them very important if taken alone. One factor was the rising agitation of diehard patriots like Paul Déroulède—war hero, poet, professional chauvinist, exponent of *revanche*. Another was the rising dissatisfaction of the workers, who began to sense that they were the republic's forgotten men. The school squabble had deepened the hatred of monarchists and clericals for what they began to call *la gueuse*—that slut, the republic. And suffusing it all, there was the factor of sheer boredom with the regime's lack of color.

The Opportunists, incapable of forming a cabinet without either left or right support, turned by a kind of automatic reflex to their fellow republicans on the left; for the first time the Radicals entered a coalition government. They arrived in a chip-on-shoulder mood. Their gains had made them aggressive; they demanded, in return for their cooperation, two revolutionary changes—an income tax and a stiffer policy toward Germany. Few things could have frightened the Opportunists more than those twin scourges, war and the income tax. The Radical demand soon wrecked the coalition cabinet, and the Opportunists switched to a segment of the monarchist right as safer partners. This was not to be the last occasion when a center-left coalition, dictated by the outcome of an election, shortly gave way to a center-right coalition.

The new combination proved to be as shaky as its predecessor. Now it was the monarchists who expected to be paid for their support, and their price was a drastic revision of the Ferry school laws. Few good Opportunists were willing to abandon what they had just won. The Opportunists, condemned thus to operate a weak and unstable government under fire from both left and right, suffered a further blow by the untimely occurrence of a minor scandal in high places. President Grévy's son-in-law, a politician named Daniel Wilson, was found to have set up shop in the presidential palace as an influence-peddler; he sold decorations at prices ranging up to 100,000 francs, and had been unwise enough to solicit business on the presidential letterhead. Efforts to hush up the affair failed; the Opportunists persuaded the reluctant Grévy to resign and put an inoffensive politician named Sadi Carnot in his place.

Enough discontent of various sorts existed in 1887 so that the right chemical agent could easily crystallize it. That agent turned up in General Georges Boulanger. A newcomer to politics, Boulanger owed his rise to the support of prominent Radicals like Georges Clemenceau, who regarded him as one of the few true republicans in the officer corps. When the center-left coalition was formed in 1885, the left had insisted that Boulanger be included as minister of war. He would protect the republic, they said; and he would stand up to Bismarck as well.

It is clear in retrospect that the Radicals did not really know their man. As war minister, he made himself a national hero almost overnight. He won the army's affection by instituting a whole series of reforms in barracks conditions, food, weapons; he won the general public by restoring the custom of military parades and by riding at the head of the troops on a handsome black horse; he won the businessmen by sending troops to control a strike; he won at least some workers by ordering the soldiers to share their rations with the strikers; he won all patriots by issuing a public challenge to Bismarck. An orgy of personal publicity accompanied all these acts; by 1886 Boulanger was the most popular figure in France.

Boulanger's tub-thumping behavior contributed to the breakdown of the center-left coalition; the Opportunists were not only nervous about his popularity but also frightened at his warmongering. When the cabinet fell, the new government reassigned him to an obscure provincial command. By this time many of his original Radical sponsors like Clemenceau had lost their illusions about the general. Other Radicals, however, were more enthusiastic than ever. Here, they thought, was the man who might rescue the republic from the impotent lawyers, and might give it vigor and color. They kept him informed of the rise of discontent in Paris and continually urged him to take up the crusade.

Boulanger reacted cautiously at first; but the Wilson scandal finally encouraged him to come out of the wilderness. Although he listened to his old Radical backers, he began listening also to new voices on the right. Some of the more rabid monarchists, and some Bonapartists as well, had decided that Boulanger might be their man and might pave the way to a restoration. Boulanger, in disguise, visited Switzerland and talked to both pretenders; he secretly accepted their money to conduct a political campaign. His new sponsors got him a campaign manager who had learned electoral tactics in the United States. Beginning in 1887 Boulanger's name began to be entered in a series of by-elections; and almost always he was triumphantly elected. The government sternly warned him that a soldier on active duty could not run for office; Boulanger blandly replied that his name had been put up without his permission and pointed out that after each election he had promptly resigned. It was clear, nevertheless, that a piecemeal plebiscite was under way.

The government was convinced that Boulanger was directly involved, but it was unable to uncover his tracks. In an effort at punishment, the cabinet put him on the retired list. Nothing could have been more unwise; for now he was free to campaign actively and openly. He issued a program marked by calculated vagueness: it called for a sweeping revision of the constitution, though without indicating the nature of the projected changes. He sought and got support from a mixture of left and right elements; in many cases Boulangism was strongest in the areas that had been strongly Bonapartist. But in one notable respect Boulanger differed from Napoleon III: his program included no social or economic reforms. He continued to run for the Chamber in a series of by-elections, but his real aim was to build up support for the general elect'ons of 1889. His plan was to enter a list of candidates in every district, with h.s own name at the head of each list. He would then presumably take over as the beneficiary of a kind of national plebiscite. Some of his backers urged him to more rapid action—to a coup d'état without delay. Boulanger resisted their pressure and chose to try for power through the forms of legality.

The shaky center-right coalition meanwhile collapsed again, and the desperate Opportunists turned back to the anti-Boulangist Radicals for help in saving the republic. In January, 1889, a few months before the scheduled general elections, a by-election occurred in Paris; and government leaders challenged Boulanger to a contest there. They believed that a victory over the general in this oldest of republican strongholds would burst the Boulanger bubble. Boulanger accepted the challenge; he took on the strongest candidate the republicans could find and defeated him badly. The moment appeared to be ideal for a coup d'état; the regime would have been hard pressed to resist a determined challenge. But Boulanger chose once more to stay within the forms of legality; in a few months, he believed, the voters would sweep him into power.

The government had been given a reprieve by Boulanger's inaction, but its chances of winning the coming general elections seemed slight. Some desperate republican politicians wanted to steal Boulanger's thunder by revising the constitution at once. Others, more cynical and certainly more realistic, argued that the best course would be to discredit the general personally. Somehow they had detected the real nature of the man and the real psychology of the movement.

Minister of Interior Ernest Constans managed to trick Boulanger into believing that the government had evidence of his treason to the republic, and that he would shortly be put on trial before the Senate. The plan succeeded: Boulanger fled to Belgium and announced lamely that his political enemies had planned to railroad him into prison.

Few political bubbles have ever burst so completely or so quickly. In the elections six months later, only 38 declared Boulangists (including the novelist Maurice Barrès) managed to win seats. Some of the general's disillusioned followers began to tell the inside story; soon his secret dealings with both monarchists and Bonapartists came into the open and the remnants of his prestige disintegrated. Two years later he committed suicide at the grave of his mistress in Brussels. Clemenceau proposed as his epitaph: "Here lies General Boulanger, who died as he lived—like a second lieutenant."

The surprising fact, in view of the brevity of the episode and the mediocrity of its leader, is that Boulangism had deep and enduring consequences. The short-term effect was to give the beleaguered Opportunists a new lease on life; they were ensured another ten years in office, almost unchallenged. Their Radical rivals were divided and discredited; the monarchists and Bonapartists also lost prestige by having involved themselves in such an adventure. Some monarchists decided to make the best of a bad business and converted themselves into conservative republicans. These converts shortly got encouragement from the Vatican, when Pope Leo XIII through a spokesman recommended the policy called *ralliement,* or acceptance of the republic.

More striking still were the long-term results of the Boulanger affair. The most obvious of these was the deepened neurosis of republicans with respect to strong men in politics and to the reinforcement of the executive. The libertarian ideal of negative government henceforth had greater charm than before; even immobility seemed better than adventure. Less clear, but perhaps just as important, was the effect of the episode on the temper of the right wing in politics. For almost a generation the dominant current within the right wing had been moderate and parliamentarian in spirit, peaceable and compromising in foreign policy, mainly rural in its support. An English-type conservatism had seemed to be emerging in France in place of the older traditionalist right. But the Boulanger episode either produced or reflected the rise of a quite different kind of rightist group—more authoritarian, more violent, more demagogic and emotional in nature. Its militant spirit was accompanied by a new chauvinism; the right henceforth took over from the Jacobin left the tradition of superheated patriotism and blind confidence in the army. This new right also found its strongholds in the cities rather than the rural districts. Until Boulanger's victory in the Paris by-election of 1889, Paris had always been considered the "reddest" city in France; henceforth it was to remain predominantly right-wing in politics. The existence of this new variety of rightist doctrine, a permanent current in twentieth-century France, was bound to have a significant impact on French political life. Perhaps it would have arrived without Boulangism as its midwife; perhaps such a movement is an unavoidable product of the mass age throughout the Western world. But that Boulangism speeded its emergence and helped to shape its character in France can hardly be denied.

✳✳✳✳✳✳✳✳✳✳✳✳✳✳

The decade of the 1890's, seen in retrospect, stands out as an era of political transition, a time of general shifting of political forces. Party labels changed, and so did party attitudes. Gambetta's term "Opportunists" took on unpleasant connotations and gradually gave way to "Moderates"—a term that has endured ever since as a generic name for mildly conservative bourgeois republicans. More fundamental than the change in name was a kind of reversal in attitude: the Moderates showed a growing tendency to look toward the right rather than toward the left for their political allies. Heretofore, during the first republican generation, the standard slogan had been "no enemies to the left"; each crisis found all republicans joining in defense of the regime. By the end of the 1890's, however, the Moderates were more inclined to form coalitions with a segment of the ex-monarchist right. It was, according to one historian, "... the most significant political realignment that occurred between the 1870's and the First World War."

The Moderates' new outlook derived in part from changes on the right; a good many monarchists became ex-monarchists during the 1890's. It is tempting to assume that the Vatican's new line, the policy of *ralliement,* was responsible for the conversion of the right. Superficially at least, the facts do not support this theory; most monarchist politicians, most prominent Catholics in France, rejected the idea of *ralliement,* openly critized it in their press, and ignored the Vatican's suggestion that Catholic politicians seek a merger with the Moderates to form a large and solid conservative party. The only Catholic politician who tried to carry out the Pope's plan—Albert de Mun—failed dismally in the attempt. So bitterly did many rightists resent the Vatican's shift of policy that some of them swallowed rumors of an alleged kidnapping of the Pope by Freemasons. The plotters (so went the story) had imprisoned Leo XIII in the Vatican dungeons and had put up an impostor to issue false instructions to the faithful.

Beneath the surface, however, the *ralliement* was much more effective than it seemed to be. Catholic leaders might say "no" to the Vatican, but Catholic voters proceeded to say "yes." Through the 1890's Catholic electoral support steadily drained away from monarchist candidates to the advantage of Moderate republicans, who were regarded as a more effective barrier against the rise of the left. As the monarchist bloc in parliament declined, the Moderate republicans no longer saw it as a grave danger. Indeed, as Moderate deputies came to draw more and more of their support from these ex-monarchist voters, they naturally developed a greater sympathy with conservative and Catholic ideas. The *ralliement* may have failed as a formal policy, but it succeeded in a more important sense; it hastened the erosion of the old barrier between republican center and monarchist right. The trend of the 1890's foreshadowed the decline of the church question as a critical political issue; France's religious war might have lost much of its intensity had it not been revived in the late 1890's by the Dreyfus Affair.

The Radicals, it is true, refused to abandon their suspicions of clerical motives. They warned that the church, unable to win in an open fight, had returned to tactics of infiltration in an effort to recover its lost influence in politics and education. Clemenceau called the *ralliement* a Vatican trick, and warned his colleagues against trying to do business with Rome: "You say that the Catholics have held out a hand to you. Put your own in it; it will be so firmly held that you can never draw it back.... You will be the prisoner of the church."

Although the Radicals clung stubbornly to their anticlerical convictions, in other ways they, too, showed signs of a changing outlook in the 1890's. Many of them were watering down their egalitarian and Jacobin heritage; if they still gave lip service to the old Radical program of political and social reform, they no longer took it very seriously. More and more, they were becoming the heirs of the Gambetta tradition, with its opportunism and its commitment to defend the little Frenchman. A more intransigent wing, revolted at this softening of the doctrine, broke away and chose the label "Socialist Radicals"; its members still prided themselves on their Jacobin heritage and clung to the principle "no enemies to the left." Even after the two wings fused again into a single group (called henceforth the Radical and Radical-Socialist party), they continued to look in opposite directions for political allies. The party was able to bear these internal tensions only because its discipline was so lax; the Radicals had almost no central organization, and they remained "less a party than a state of mind."

The 1890's brought not only change in the old parties, but the emergence of a potentially powerful new force—socialism. Its rise was still another factor that turned the Moderates toward the right; they began to fear a new threat to the established order, a graver threat than that posed by declining monarchism.

Socialism's roots in France were old and deep, but as an organized political force it was relatively recent in origin. The repression of the Commune in 1871 had set back its growth for a decade; but the repression also had the curious effect of strengthening the Marxian variety of socialism at the expense of other native-grown kinds. Most of the Commune's leaders had been non-Marxians Proudhonians or Blanquists, for the most part. With the ground pretty well cleared of these rival socialist movements, Marx's disciples could step into the vacuum and seize the initiative in evangelizing the working class. When the first "socialist workers' congress" met in 1879, the fanatically Marxian convert Jules Guesde was able to take the leading role and shape the doctrine of the French Workers' party that emerged.

This is not to suggest that Guesde had a clear field. His party, like all socialist movements, soon ran onto the shoals of doctrinal controversy and shattered into several mutually antagonistic fragments. Some adherents found Guesde's party too rigid, others not rigid enough; some wanted to admit any sympathizer, others insisted on proletarian purity; some favored orthodox Marxism, others wanted to fuse it with the Blanquist tradition. Despite these conflicts, a few socialist candidates won seats in the Chamber in the 1880's; and in 1893 the number jumped suddenly to about forty. They represented, however, five different organized socialist parties as well as an unorganized collection of "independent socialists" like Jean Jaurès with vaguely egalitarian and humanitarian ideas. The principal goal of the next decade was to be the fusion of all these factions into one large unified party; it was eventually accomplished in 1905, thanks largely to the work of Jaurès.

❖❖❖❖❖❖❖❖❖❖❖❖❖

Both the rise of socialism and the general shifting of political forces in the 1890's were hastened by that fragrant episode known as the Panama Scandal. Ferdinand de Lesseps, the builder of the Suez Canal, had organized the Panama Company in 1880 to dig a canal through the isthmus. Frenchmen rushed to invest in a firm headed by one of France's national heroes; but mismanagement and poor planning soon got the company into hopeless difficulties. The promoters, in a desperate effort to mobilize new capital, sought the consent of the Chamber to issue a lottery loan. In 1888 agents of the firm bribed enough politicians to get the scheme approved and paid off enough journalists to get favorable press publicity. The loan nevertheless failed dismally, and the company collapsed.

Embittered shareholders set up a cry for an investigation. In 1892 a poison-pen journalist named Edouard Drumont took up their cause in an effort to prop up his sagging newspaper. Anti-Semitism was his stock in trade, and Drumont therefore concentrated his fire on two Jewish agents of the company who had allegedly bought off the politicians: Baron Reinach and Dr. Cornelius Herz.

His two victims had a falling-out, and each one privately began to feed information to Drumont in the hope of buying protection from the latter's attacks. At the height of the agitation, Reinach committed suicide; and the scandal reached such proportions that parliament had to set up an investigating committee. Eventually the committee recommended that the directors of the company, together with ten deputies who were seriously compromised, be tried for bilking the public and accepting bribes. The trial ended in 1893 with an almost complete whitewash. A verdict of guilty against the directors was promptly quashed on a technicality; and all of the accused deputies were acquitted save one who was imprudent enough to confess.

Superficially, the political consequences of the affair might seem to have been slight. Most of the deputies tainted by the scandal were re-elected in 1893; the one notable exception, Georges Clemenceau, was beaten for other reasons. The Moderates who had dominated politics throughout the period of the scandal continued in power through the rest of the decade. Some Anglo-Saxon purists have concluded that Frenchmen have no ethical standards in politics and take graft to be a matter of course. French monarchists offer a somewhat related thesis: the republic, they assert, had corrupted the country's morals and had implanted the doctrine that anything goes if one can get away with it.

The effects of the scandal in fact went much deeper than appeared to be the case. Many of the leading Moderate politicians, though re-elected to parliament, prudently withdrew into the background to let the dust settle. In their places there emerged a new generation of Moderates: young men, untouched by the scandal. This renewal of personnel in turn strengthened the tendency of the Moderates to make political alliances with the right. Unlike their predecessors, the new men were too young to remember the heroic struggles of the 1870's when all republicans had stood together to save the regime. The memory of the *seize mai* had been a powerful emotional cement, binding together the center and the left; that memory meant little to the new generation.

The scandal contributed also to the shift of rural France toward the left. It reinforced the old provincial suspicion that Paris was a sink of corruption, and that even the most honest provincial deputies could rarely resist that fetid atmosphere for very long. Common sense, therefore, seemed to call for a frequent change of deputy, and normally a change toward the left—since the chances of remaining pure were believed to be greater on the left margin of the political spectrum. Panama thus speeded the leftward trend that was a steady undercurrent throughout the Third Republic. That the republic survived the crisis without much trouble was in part a matter of luck; the enemies of the regime, still divided and staggering after the Boulanger episode, could not yet put together a serious threat to the system. A few years earlier or later, Panama might have had far more disastrous results.

❖❖❖❖❖❖❖❖❖❖❖❖❖❖

The republic was not to enjoy a very long breathing spell. From 1896 until the end of the century France was sucked into the vortex of an almost unprecedented crisis—a crisis that deserves the name of a bloodless but no less intense civil war. This was the Dreyfus case; or, in French usage, simply *l'Affaire.*

Few fictional thrillers are more complex than this real-life case of alleged treason. So many of the basic facts remain in dispute that even a summary of the actual events is open to challenge. In 1894 an unsigned letter apparently destined for the German military attaché in Paris (and probably filched from the attaché's wastebasket) came into the possession of the French army's counter-intelligence unit; it listed several secret military documents which the author was prepared to deliver to the Germans. After a brief investigation, suspicion fell on a French staff officer, Captain Alfred Dreyfus. Arrested by the army and privately pressed to confess, Dreyfus indignantly asserted his innocence. Handwriting experts failed to agree as to whether Dreyfus had actually written the incriminating letter, and army investigators failed to uncover any persuasive supporting evidence. The case might have been dropped had not that professional anti-Semite, Edouard Drumont, heard rumors of the affair and raised a public outcry. Drumont (whose best-selling book *Jewish France* [1886] has been called "the first great explosion of modern anti-Semitism") charged that wealthy Jews were trying to buy the freedom of a traitor who had been caught red-handed.[2] Army authorities decided, therefore, to proceed with a court-martial from which the public was excluded. The verdict of guilty, it later turned out, rested heavily on a secret dossier presented to the court but never shown to Dreyfus or his attorney. Dreyfus was sent to Devil's Island for life, while Frenchmen applauded the army's efficiency and toughness. The Socialist Jean Jaurès even commented in the Chamber that if Dreyfus had not been a bourgeois and an officer, he would have been shot. Efforts by the Dreyfus family to get the case reopened aroused no support.

Military secrets nevertheless continued to flow to the German Embassy. In 1896, two years after the original trial, the new chief of counter-intelligence, Colonel Picquart, reexamined the Dreyfus file for leads to possible collaborators in treason. Astonished and dismayed by what he found, Picquart concluded that Dreyfus had not written the original letter, and his suspicions turned to another officer, Major Esterhazy, known to be of dubious character and habits. Picquart reported his findings to his superiors, and urged that the Dreyfus case

---

[2] The Jewish community in France at this time was small—about 80,000, of whom 50,000 lived in Paris. Most of them had been quite thoroughly assimilated.

be reopened; when he persisted, they transferred him to a post in the Tunisian desert. But something of what he knew began to leak out to the press, and a few newspapers (notably Georges Clemenceau's) launched a crusade for a new trial. Meanwhile another counter-intelligence officer, Major Henry, fed bits of anti-Dreyfus information to Drumont and other journalists, so that the controversy grew increasingly public and bitter. Looking to the future, Henry also took the precaution of forging some new documents for the Dreyfus file in order to strengthen the case against him. Army authorities steadily resisted all demands for a reopening of the case—the more so because they resented civilian inter-ference in a matter of military justice. At last, in an effort to end the matter once and for all, the army staged a court-martial of Major Esterhazy (January 1898); he was triumphantly acquitted. Two days later the novelist Emile Zola published in Clemenceau's newspaper a long article headed *"J'accuse,"* openly charging the army's top commanders with conniving at deliberate injustice. Zola was promptly arrested, tried, and sentenced to a year's imprisonment. Rather than serve his term, he departed into English exile.

By this time (1898) virtually the entire educated elite of France was com-mitted to one side or the other. Families were split; there were frequent clashes in the streets, and duels were fought daily. Most intellectuals became vociferous Dreyfusards; but a smaller group of intellectuals joined the monarchists and right-wing Catholics to resist a new trial for Dreyfus. The Assumptionist organ *La Croix* leaped into the fray and campaigned for stripping all Jews of citizen-ship. Most politicians still tried to quiet the storm and to stay aloof from any commitment; but there were notable exceptions like Clemenceau, Jaurès, and the Alsatian Senator Auguste Scheurer-Kestner who held that party interests should give way to the overriding principle of justice for the individual citizen. Even Jaurès, that dedicated apostle of human rights, had been slow to come out for Dreyfus; many of his Socialist colleagues remained reluctant until the end.

A major break in the case came suddenly in August 1898, when a new counter-intelligence officer accidentally detected Major Henry's forgeries in the Dreyfus file. Henry confessed, and a day later cut his throat in his jail cell. Esterhazy fled to England, where he gave out conflicting stories about his role in the case. The anti-Dreyfus faction still insisted, however, that Dreyfus was the culprit, and that there were top-secret documents in the files of counter-intelli-gence to prove it if they could only be made public without causing a war. The army could no longer resist a new trial. In August 1899 Dreyfus was brought back from Devil's Island to face a second court-martial, public this time. In a curious verdict, the military judges found him guilty, but with extenuating circumstances. He was promptly pardoned by the president of the republic and was fully vindicated by a civilian court several years later.

There are enough gaps and contradictions in the evidence to leave the affair still partially shrouded in uncertainty. Only a few Frenchmen still believe that Dreyfus was guilty and was saved by Jewish influence and money. Some think that there may have been two traitors—Esterhazy and a second officer who, to avoid discovery, continually fed in false leads to distract the pursuers. Still others suggest that there may have been no traitor at all; that Esterhazy, for somewhat obscure reasons, had been ordered by his superiors to write the note of 1894 to the German attaché. The list of hypotheses is almost endless.

More important, however, was the impact of *l'Affaire* on French political life and the enduring myth that it left behind. Its immediate effect was to bring the Radicals into power and to keep them there almost steadily until the Great War. The Moderates were badly split over the Dreyfus issue and were mainly concerned with keeping the lid on; the Radicals profited by the opportunity to come out on the winning side when victory for the Dreyfusards had become almost certain. They convinced themselves, and a great many voters, that they had saved the republic from a clerico-monarchist plot, and that they must be kept in office to protect the republic. The new Waldeck-Rousseau cabinet (1899–1902), though headed by a Moderate, was dominated by Radicals and supported by Socialists; it was a kind of popular front ahead of its time, cemented by the presumed right-wing threat to the regime.

*L'Affaire* also sharpened the suspicions of French leftists toward both the army and the church. A new wave of antimilitarism and anticlericalism followed at once; steps were taken to republicanize the officer corps and to weaken church influence. Both the general staff and certain elements in the church had blundered badly in their handling of the Dreyfus controversy; their behavior naturally fed the republicans' suspicions. The general effect was to deepen existing divisions within France and to set back the growth of something like national consensus.

Like most great emotional upheavals, this one was significant mainly for the mythology it inspired. Most French republicans saw the Affair as a contest between the forces of righteousness and progress on the one hand and those of bigotry and obscurantism on the other. The Dreyfus camp asserted the principle of justice for every man, even though the institutional foundations of society and the state might be temporarily shaken. The anti-Dreyfus factions stood for the principle of *raison d'état,* in which the end justifies the means; they rejected the idea that the individual citizen possesses any sacred rights transcending those of the state. To some degree, the controversy *was* rooted in this fundamental conflict in values, and the victory of the Dreyfusards did reinforce a certain view of human rights. But the case was also heavily encrusted with less admirable motives of political advantage and bigoted loyalty; and in large part the story was one of fallible human beings sucked into the maelstrom without quite knowing how they got there. One curious by-product was the strengthened self-image, and popular image, of intellectuals as incorruptible men of virtue, unsullied by prejudice and able always to detect the right and just cause. Along with it went the legend of honesty and fairness as characteristics of the left, and selfishness and bigotry as qualities of the right. Both illusions were of strictly limited validity and were to produce some unfortunate consequences in twentieth-century French political life. Thus the complexities of the case itself were hardly greater than the complexities of the heritage left by it. One might epitomize *l'Affaire* as "the shame and the glory of modern France." And one might ask whether a Dreyfus Affair could have occurred anywhere except in France.

# CHAPTER 20

# The Radical Republic, 1899–1914

Radicalism: no term so necessary to comprehend if one is to understand contemporary France; no term whose comprehension is so difficult.

MAURICE SORRE

When René Waldeck-Rousseau took office as premier in 1899, the Third Republic reached a major political turning point. Waldeck himself was a Moderate, of the same stripe as the men who had been governing France for twenty years (though superior to most of them in ability). A wealthy lawyer of austere temperament, who fixed on his colleagues "the cold eye of a jellied fish," he was one of the few surviving representatives of the *haute bourgeoisie* in politics. What distinguished his cabinet from its predecessors was that the key posts were held by Radicals, and that it even contained one Socialist, Alexandre Millerand. Henceforth the Radicals were to replace the Moderates as the fulcrum of republican politics; from 1899 to 1940 they were rarely out of power (usually in coalition with a segment of the Moderates), and for most of that time they were the largest group in the Chamber. Their conquest of the Senate followed more slowly, but no less surely; after the First World War, the upper house was to become the Radicals' chief fortress.

The transition from Moderate to Radical rule, however, brought no sharp change in the republic's structure or spirit. There had been a time when the Radicals were ferociously Jacobin and egalitarian, but they had been gradually drifting away from that heritage. The source of Radical strength, which had once been urban, was coming to be mainly rural and small-town in character; the party had come to represent the interests of the little independent producer or trader, the village pharmacist or schoolmaster, who might still be strongly egalitarian in theory but who was much more inclined to be libertarian in practice.

One development that helped to reshape the Radical outlook from the 1890's onward was the rise of socialism. As the Radicals found themselves outflanked on the left by a more dynamic and aggressive faction, they began to feel that segments of the Moderate group were more congenial neighbors. This turn toward the right was also strengthened by the Radicals' accession to power after 1899. The responsibilities of office had their customary effect; and in addition, success brought a new batch of more conservative recruits into the party. Many aspiring young politicians who might have chosen to be Opportunists or Moderates a generation earlier now found the Radical label to be the best guarantee of electoral success. These "immigrants" had little in common with the generation of intransigent doctrinaires that had denounced Gambetta for his opportunism. Yet the Radical party—or a large segment of it, at any rate—never shook off a kind of nostalgic yearning after its lost virtue. The party still prided itself on its leftist character; many of its members were never quite reconciled to the idea of collaborating with the Moderates and almost instinctively hoped that somehow the old slogan "no enemies to the left" might be rejuvenated. Thus the party remained an ambiguous, loose-jointed organization, still deeply anticlerical, still theoretically egalitarian, yet no longer attracted to any social reform more drastic than the income tax—and, indeed, no longer sure that this ancient Radical panacea would be quite safe.

The Radical temper was both reflected in and reinforced by the writings of their favorite philosopher-journalist, the man who called himself Alain (Emile Chartier). His epigrams were widely quoted and savored. "Obey, but resist—there is the whole secret," wrote Alain. "Anything that destroys obedience is anarchy; anything that destroys resistance is tyranny." Basic in Alain was a fear and suspicion of leadership, a conviction that the good citizen is not the one who conforms and cooperates, but the one who resists authority. To him, the function of the deputy was "to represent the ordinary undistinguished citizen against the eternal conspiracy of the strong, the rich, the powerful"—those who have been corrupted by power and success.[1] The function of the cabinet minister, likewise, was not to govern but to keep a watchful eye on the bureaucrats. Alain's disciples gradually infiltrated the teaching profession and, after the Great War, taught the new generation to distrust all leaders, to regard patriotism as the last refuge of a scoundrel, to scoff at talk of sacrifice or discipline as sheer hypocrisy, to see as the highest symbol of civic virtue the gesture of thumb-to-nose. If ideas

---

[1] P. Williams, in J. M. Wallace-Hadrill and J. McManners (eds.), *France: Government and Society,* p. 229.

and attitudes shape human events, there is much to be said for the thesis that the doctrines of Alain had a grave demoralizing effect in twentieth-century France. His brand of libertarianism—negative, desiccated, ungenerous—brought to a sad culmination that admirable current of ideas that had done so much to free men in an earlier age. That it was the natural, the inevitable culmination of liberal thought is, however, a dubious thesis.

❖❖❖❖❖❖❖❖❖❖❖❖❖❖

The left-wing coalition of Radicals, Socialists, and Waldeck Moderates welded together by the Dreyfus crisis gave the republic an almost unique experience in stability from 1899 to 1905. Five and a half years with only two cabinets (and those two almost identical) constituted an all-time record; some Frenchmen even began to believe that a cure had been found for the disease of governmental weakness. The new stability, however, proved to be no more than an interlude, and the system soon reverted to type. From time to time a strong premier backed by a fairly coherent majority could temporarily reinforce the executive branch, but the institutional framework went on unchanged, and the republic's political mores were not seriously altered. Indeed, the coalition of 1899–1905 lacked even the vigorous centralized authority essential for an effective functioning of the cabinet system; for behind the premier, and restricting all his acts, hovered a permanent steering committee called the *Délégation des Gauches,* representing the various component parties in the coalition. Policies were made by this unofficial body operating behind the scenes and reaching decisions through a kind of diplomatic negotiation; premier and cabinet had only to execute policies handed down to them.

When the coalition took office France appeared to be on the verge of civil war. For several months the regime seemed constantly in danger; then, suddenly, with Dreyfus' pardon, the agitation faded away as though by magic. A few diehards on both sides continued to bicker, but they quickly found themselves isolated; *l'Affaire* disintegrated with astonishing speed. The explanation, François Goguel suggests, is that the agitation of 1898–1900 had not been based on a hard substratum of economic discontent. Once the fate of the man Dreyfus was decided, the one crystallizing factor in the conflict was gone.

Yet in a deeper sense the Dreyfus crisis faded out much less quickly; indirectly, it pervaded political life for most of the next decade. Such passions had been aroused that either side, if victorious, was likely to abuse its victory. The new governing coalition was determined to hobble and punish those groups that had threatened the republican regime and the ideals that it represented. The chief offenders, as the coalition saw it, had been the army and the church; the government was determined to republicanize the one and to hamstring and isolate the other.

The new minister of war, General André, set out to destroy the army's right to run its own affairs (and also, perhaps, hoped to avenge himself on those fellow officers who had long cold-shouldered him for his republican views). André reformed the system of promotion by taking it out of the hands of the officer corps and vesting it in the ministry of war. He set up a kind of private espionage system to keep track of officers' opinions and habits: Freemasons in many cases served as volunteer agents, sending their reports to the central Masonic head-quarters in Paris, whence they went to the war ministry. A card file indicated the officers who attended Mass and who expressed their antirepublican views too freely. Eventually the details of this amateur spy system leaked out and produced such an uproar in parliament that André had to resign. Although he had not completed his task of republicanizing the general staff, enough was accomplished so that by 1914 the high command was no longer a solidly mon-archist-clerical stronghold.

The Dreyfus upheaval and its aftermath contributed to reshaping the officer corps, but the cost was high. Army prestige and morale, which had reached their peak during the generation after 1871, fell to a new low after 1900. Applications for entrance into Saint-Cyr military academy fell by half; a great many officers resigned their commissions or retired. In part, the change in mood resulted from dissatisfaction at the army's long inactivity, at the low levels of pay, at the slow-ness of promotion. The challenge of constant tension, the hope of imminent revenge against Germany, had begun to disintegrate by 1890. The officer corps gradually slipped again into a rut of inertia and conformity. If this mood had lasted until 1914, the German onslaught might have brought a repetition of 1870. Luckily for the nation, however, the resurgence of national spirit that set in after 1910 was to be reflected in the army. A new vigor and toughness pervaded the officer corps just in time to prepare it for the great test; although unaccompanied by any increase in imagination or by fresh strategic thinking, the revival of morale enabled the army to survive the shock of the German attack.

The Waldeck government's second target was the church. Unfortunately, many priests and members of religious orders had plunged into the Dreyfus con-troversy, even though no basic issue of faith or morals had been involved. The left's bitterness was focussed on certain congregations like the Assumptionists, who had crusaded most violently against Dreyfus, and the Jesuits, who had always been fair game when the church came under fire. Dreyfusards were per-suaded that a clerical-military plot lay behind the whole Dreyfus affair; they believed that most of the officer corps had been educated and consciously cor-rupted in Catholic schools. Waldeck-Rousseau himself favored rather mild measures of repression; he proposed to exile only those orders that had gone to fanatical extremes during the Affair. But the Chamber was far more intransigent; it amended Waldeck's bill to provide for the expulsion of all orders save those that might be granted special authorization by parliament. In practice, few authorizations were granted; thousands of monks and nuns set off into exile in Spain, the United States, and elsewhere.

The reprisals against the church were intensified after Waldeck voluntarily retired from the premiership in 1902 and suggested as his successor Senator Émile Combes. Waldeck evidently misjudged his man; Combes shared none of Waldeck's spirit of moderation but was a dedicated fanatic who saw clerical plots and intrigues everywhere. As a young man, Combes had almost completed his training for the priesthood when he lost his faith and turned to medicine instead. This "heretic theologian" made the works of Voltaire his new Bible and embarked on a single-minded campaign against the church. As a one-time seminarist, he could claim a special insight into Catholic intentions. "Raised in the harem," he used to say, "I know its inner secrets."

Combes' total achievement in his two and a half years as premier (1902–5) was to continue and expand the anticlerical program begun by Waldeck. He evicted most of the remaining religious orders; he engaged the Vatican in a series of jurisdictional disputes over the appointment and disciplining of bishops. His purpose was to drive the Pope into denouncing the Concordat (which quickly became, as someone has put it, a Discordat). In the end it was his own patience that gave way first, and in 1905 he requested the French parliament to denounce the century-old agreement. By the separation laws that followed, all ties between church and state were severed. Priests and bishops were taken off the state payroll; title to all church property was transferred to the state; committees of Catholic laymen were to administer church affairs in each parish.

Most Catholics bitterly resented this treatment and feared its effects on the church in France. The unilateral denunciation of the Concordat struck them as a calculated insult to the Vatican. They were disturbed at the problem of finding private financial support for the church establishment; since clerical salaries were certain to drop, the recruitment of new priests might become almost impossible. Nevertheless, most bishops were convinced that they had no choice, and that they had better make the best of a bad business. A few liberal churchmen even found a silver lining in the cloud, foreseeing a new era of vigorous growth for a free church, untrammelled by official bonds. But the French hierarchy was promptly overruled by the Vatican. The Pope issued strict orders that Catholics should resist the new legislation and should refuse to participate in the new parish committees of laymen. At the same time he excommunicated every deputy who had voted for the separation laws.

For a year or two France again faced a threat of generalized violence. In the

Chamber the more rabid anticlericals welcomed the Vatican's intransigence and wanted to seize the opportunity for a showdown fight with the church. If Catholics refused to set up laymen's committees, they argued, then Catholics had no legal right to function as an organized group or to use the churches for worship. They insisted that the government proceed at once to take inventory of its new properties, as provided by an apparently inoffensive clause in the new laws. But the civil servants sent to "count the chandeliers," as Clemenceau put it, met violent resistance from the embattled congregations. In some rural areas Catholics guarded their churches with shotguns; in remote hill regions they set wolf traps or even chained a wild bear at the church door. Several were injured, and at least one killed in the scuffles that followed. Luckily, neither parliament nor the bureaucracy was dominated by anticlerical extremists. The renegade Socialist Aristide Briand, who became minister of cults in 1906, relaxed the enforcement of the new church legislation. Ignoring anticlerical protests, he authorized extralegal arrangements that permitted parish priests to lease church buildings and equipment from municipalities for a nominal sum. Gradually the new system rooted itself in French mores.

The impact of separation on the church was quite as severe as Catholics feared it might be. Heretofore, the average priest's income had made him slightly better off than most of his parishioners; now, except in a few rich parishes, he was near the very bottom of the scale in economic status. Recruiting became much more difficult; within a few years the number of young men entering the priesthood had dropped by half. Catholic schools were hard hit, too, for contributions now had to go to support the church itself, and often no money was left to operate a school. In a short time the number of children in Catholic primary schools fell by more than a third; in secondary schools, by a quarter. Separation also speeded up the process of de-christianization that was already well under way in the working-class suburbs and some rural areas. The impact was especially great on the peasants, in whose minds Catholic observances had often come to be matters of custom or habit rather than an expression of genuine faith. So long as the church was linked to the state, it retained a kind of official prestige; in 1905 that prestige was suddenly destroyed. An example of the effect may be found in the Limoges area, where the proportion of nonbaptized children rose from two to forty per cent between 1899 and 1914, and the number of civil marriages from fourteen to sixty per cent.

At the same time the church did gain something from the separation. A greater liberty of action was one such gain. The state could no longer intervene in church affairs; it could no longer cut off an offending priest's salary, or deny priests the right to exert active pressure in elections, or protect a bishop against the Vatican's disciplinary action. Separation thus wiped out the last feeble remnants of the Gallican tradition. A second long-range gain was in the character of the priesthood. After a decade of drastic decline recruiting gradually rose again to the previous level in quantity and attained a much higher level in quality. Young men who entered the church henceforward could no longer hope to find there a relatively soft berth carrying official status; if they entered now, it was by fervent conviction. Here was a case where pruning the tree had certainly rendered it healthier. Finally, separation opened the way to the possibility of harmonious coexistence of Catholics and freethinkers in France. The clerical threat gradually lost most of its potency after 1905, not only because some members of the new generation were beginning to drift away from positivism, but also because even positivists found it harder to believe that the men in black were about to take over the country. The old feud was slow in dying; indeed, remnants of it still survive to plague present-day politicians. Certainly, however, the separation of 1905 hastened its decline.

**************

Meanwhile, the long era of stable coalition government had broken down in 1905, when the Socialists withdrew their support. Many Socialists had been urging such a withdrawal ever since the end of the Dreyfus crisis. Once that battle was won, they argued, the Socialists had nothing to gain by giving their votes to a bourgeois cabinet—especially to one that had no interest in social reform. It had taken all the persuasive powers of Jean Jaurès, the party's ablest spokesman, to keep his group in line behind the Waldeck and Combes cabinets. Behind the scenes, in the *Délégation des Gauches,* his influence over the government had exceeded that of any other man.

Republican France has produced few political leaders more remarkable or more appealing than Jean Jaurès. Almost every French town has a street or square named for him; every leftist party quotes him or claims him as an ancestor. Jaurès was a man of the south: a warm, expansive personality, a spellbinding orator. Some skeptics believed that he was inclined to inebriate himself with his own rhetoric and to dazzle his hearers more often than he enlightened them. He was nevertheless a man of brilliant mind, and the lucidity of that mind was further sharpened by exposure to the best training offered by the French educational system. In his class at the École Normale Supérieure—a kind of forcing-ground for the best intellects in France—his only serious rival had been the philosopher Henri Bergson. He taught philosophy briefly in the south; but the lure of politics had soon tempted him out of the classroom. In 1885, at the age of twenty-five, he became the youngest member of the Chamber of Deputies.

Jaurès entered politics as an Opportunist whose political heroes were Gambetta and Ferry. In a sense, that was what he always remained. He was at heart no doctrinaire but a humanitarian—a liberal idealist who believed in the essential goodness of man, and who was persuaded at first that a bourgeois elite could and should lead the way toward social justice. He suffered some disillusionment when his bourgeois backers, irritated by his passionate appeals for the alleviation of human misery, helped to defeat him in the 1889 elections. But a man so intensely optimistic by nature could never become really disillusioned. His rival, Clemenceau, a convinced cynic, once snorted: "Do you know how you can always recognize a speech by Jaurès? All the verbs are in the future tense."

In the nineties Jaurès began calling himself an Independent Socialist, and he returned to the Chamber in 1893 on the rising Socialist tide. Though he had been reading Marx and henceforth called himself a Marxist, he never really succumbed to the master's system or dogma; always he sought to reconcile it with his own liberal idealism. His socialism, such as it was, sprang from the heart rather than the head.

When Jaurès entered the Socialist movement, he found it split into six competing segments: five organized parties, plus a number of Independent Socialist deputies like himself. From the outset he was convinced that unity was essential if the proletariat were to use what he called "the revolutionary instrument of universal suffrage" to bring about the new era. In addition, he believed that socialism must set out to attract as many bourgeois sympathizers as possible. It took him more than a decade to accomplish Socialist unity, so deep were the schisms within the movement. Jaurès' chief rival was Jules Guesde, founder of the first Marxian party in France. The contrast between the two men could hardly have been more complete. They shared intelligence and sincerity; but Guesde was dogmatic and doctrinaire, intensely suspicious of the bourgeoisie (from which he himself had come), cold and austere in temperament. Jaurès was robust and earthy; generous, impulsive, naively optimistic; as careless in dress and personal habits as a four-year-old child. Guesde was "the ferocious sectarian, sharp-featured and bilious," whose piercing eye and long beard made him resemble (as a contemporary put it) "either Christ or Alphonse Daudet." In those early years of socialism in politics Jaurès and Guesde clashed on almost every major policy decision: on whether to commit the movement to the Dreyfusard cause, on whether to support Waldeck-Rousseau in 1899, on whether to let a Socialist enter that cabinet, on whether to abandon the apocalyptic vision of eventual class violence. Yet the two men did in the end reach an accommodation that permitted the creation of a united Socialist party. And there survived in both men a powerful residue of patriotism, despite the Marxist dogma that the worker has no country.

On the issue of supporting the Radical-dominated cabinets of 1899–1905, however, Guesde never became reconciled to Jaurès' views; indeed, his antagonism increased with the passage of time. Guesde insisted that the Socialists would get nothing in return for their support; that the Radical politicians were concerned only to harass the church and not to aid or protect the proletariat. He steadily argued for an ultimatum to the cabinet: either real social reforms or an end to the coalition. Jaurès could not deny the fact that the workers had gotten little from the Waldeck and Combes governments, but he continued to insist that his strategy would produce long-range results. He contended that once the Radicals had completed their anticlerical program thanks to Socialist support, they would be willing to turn to social reforms—both because they would have no program of their own left to accomplish, and because they would have learned to trust the Socialists through long experience in collaboration.

It would be pleasant to believe that Jaurès' program, if continued for a few more years, might have brought an enduring coalition or even a merger of Radicals and Socialists into a broadly-based leftist party like the British Labour party. But his strategy rested on some shaky assumptions. It took for granted that the Radicals, once their own program was accomplished, would naturally turn to the left for allies and a program. Jaurès failed to see that the Radicals were sliding toward the center and were coming to share much of the Moderate outlook. In any event, his tactics never reached the point of being tested, for in 1904 Guesde finally managed to force Jaurès to abandon the bourgeois coalition. Guesde won his victory by carrying his fight to a higher authority, the Socialist International, at its Amsterdam congress in 1904. There the two French spokesmen publicly argued the case: could a Socialist party cohabit with bourgeois politicians without losing its virtue? In the end, it was the powerful German delegation that decided the issue in favor of Guesde; for the German party was already committed to a Guesdist line at home. Jaurès almost carried the day by his eloquence, arguing that what was good for the German Socialists was not necessarily good for other national groups. In France the party could find some really dependable allies among the progressive bourgeoisie, and together they could get control of parliament and of the state itself. In Germany a different strategy was quite proper, since the Reichstag was so weak and the bourgeoisie so uncooperative that the prospect of attaining real power via elections was slight.

Jaurès took his defeat at Amsterdam in good spirit; he obediently put an end to Socialist support of the Combes cabinet. He was convinced that proletarian unity was all-important, and that it could at last be achieved in France if he would knuckle under. He was right: in 1905 the Guesdist and Jaurèsist factions were merged into the unified Socialist party, henceforth called the S.F.I.O. From 1905 to 1936 (save for a *pro forma* interruption during the Great War) the party clung doggedly to its policy of nonparticipation in "bourgeois" cabinets. In that sense, Guesde's influence dominated French socialism for a generation. But it was the spirit and outlook of Jaurès that steadily pervaded the party in the years after Jaurès' defeat at Amsterdam. On almost every major party issue that arose down to 1914 the reformist, antidoctrinaire faction triumphed. French socialism developed into a constitutional party, the advance guard of the democratic groups, and not into a dogmatic class-bound revolutionary movement. Its gains were steady; its percentage of the popular vote rose in every prewar election, until in May, 1914, it emerged as the second-largest single group in parliament with one-sixth of the nation's votes and one-sixth of the seats in the Chamber. One did not have to be a Jaurèsian optimist to conclude that France's future lay in socialism.

❖❖❖❖❖❖❖❖❖❖❖❖❖

The new Socialist line brought an end to the post-Dreyfus era of cabinet stability. Henceforth the Radicals were driven to collaborate with the Moderates, which most of them did without reluctance. For the next generation, from 1905 to 1936, France was governed by a kind of permanent though shifting coalition; sometimes the premier was a Radical, sometimes a Moderate, sometimes a hybrid like Aristide Briand, with friends in all camps.

Curiously, the two most notable Radical premiers in the prewar decade—Georges Clemenceau (1906–9) and Joseph Caillaux (1911–12)—could hardly have been more atypical of the Radical temper. Indeed, only a loose-jointed and amorphous group like the Radical party could have contained such a maverick as Clemenceau for so long. In a sense, he was the last survivor of an earlier phase of radicalism, when the leaders had been tough-minded, doctrinaire zealots, filled with Jacobin patriotism and egalitarian convictions. The party's trend toward libertarian views, toward flexibility and compromise in politics, had left Clemenceau untouched. By temperament he had always been harshly authoritarian, and this trait grew more marked with advancing age. His specialty in political life had been the destruction of cabinets, which gave him his sobriquet "the Tiger." No other politician possessed a sharper tongue or sword; Clemenceau counted his duels by the dozen.

The aging Jacobin got his chance at last in 1906. The record of his premiership contained little that was consistent with the older Radical tradition. His initial program did call for several measures of social reform, but they remained stillborn. The period was marked, rather, by the most severe labor unrest France had ever known, culminating in an attempted general strike in 1909. Clemenceau, who insolently described himself as "France's number one cop," ruthlessly repressed the disorders by using troops. Such behavior cost him some of his support; but his caustic tongue irritated even more of his partisans. This abrasive quality finally brought him down in 1909, barely short of Waldeck-Rousseau's record of three years in office. Most Frenchmen concluded that Clemenceau's first chance at power would also be his last. One thing was certain: the Radicals would no longer mistake him for one of theirs.

Joseph Caillaux, premier in 1911–12, was even less representative of his party. Frustrated ambition had led him to defect from the Moderate camp, but he remained a Moderate in all but name. A financial expert of strictly orthodox economic views, his ties were mainly with influential banking circles. Only a few weeks after joining the Radicals he had become their party leader; a few more weeks and he was head of a Radical cabinet. Like Clemenceau, Caillaux was a man of authoritarian temper; but he outdid the Tiger in personal vanity, and he lacked any trace of Clemenceau's savagely Jacobin patriotism.

Caillaux's soft line toward Germany infuriated Clemenceau, but another trend of the epoch irritated the Tiger even more. This was the growth of antimilitarism and antipatriotism on the left. The spread of Marxism contributed to this trend, and so did the Dreyfus Affair. But the spearhead of the antimilitarist campaign was to be found in the labor movement, with its syndicalist tradition, its antipolitical outlook, and its stress on violence. Soon after the turn of the century a *lycée* professor named Gustave Hervé began a vindictive crusade in the trade-union press. Hervé denounced the officer corps and scoffed at the ideal of patriotism; he called on French soldiers to throw off their shackles, to rip the flag from the barracks and plant it on the nearest dunghill. Some segments of the Radical party were gradually pulled into this campaign, though in a milder way. Radical politicians soon learned that their peasant and small-town voters disliked military service and retained an old prejudice against the officer class. Since re-election often seemed to depend on catering on these views, most of the Radical deputies from rural districts began to denounce the army and to support a reduction in the term of military service.

The change in mood that set in about 1911 was primarily the product of European tensions, and it was stimulated by what most Frenchmen took to be the aggressive and unreasonable behavior of the German government. The nationalist revival in France of 1911–14 pervaded almost every segment of French society—the political elite, the army, the bureaucracy, the urban bourgeoisie, even the labor movement. The Moderates, whose ancestors had been horrified at Boulanger's jingoism, shared the new temper as strongly as anyone; so did many Radical politicians, though the bulk of the Radicals lagged behind the trend simply because their home districts in rural France were less quickly affected. That rural lag was reflected in the last prewar elections (April-May 1914), when the country chose a Chamber whose majority was committed to a reduction in military service and a pacific foreign policy. Meanwhile, however, the nationalist revival had swept Caillaux and the Radicals out of office in favor of a more intransigent Moderate government headed by the Lorraine patriot

Raymond Poincaré; and a year later (1913) had carried Poincaré to the presidency of the republic. It had also bolstered the sagging morale and prestige of the army and had given the officer corps a new sense of confidence and purpose at a moment when that was desperately needed.

❖❖❖❖❖❖❖❖❖❖❖❖❖❖❖

Two new political movements, small in numbers but in both cases durable and significant, were added to the existing parties during the prewar decade in France.[2] One was the Action Française; the other, the Christian democratic Sillon.

Action Française, a tiny group of intellectuals founded in 1898 as a weapon to fight the Dreyfusards, was quickly taken over by one of its members, a young critic and essayist named Charles Maurras. Under his inspired leadership, the organization developed into an intensely nationalistic and authoritarian movement of the extreme right, dedicated to saving France from such un-French elements as the Protestants, the Freemasons, and the Jews. Maurras soon grafted both monarchism and Catholicism onto his movement, on the ground that both institutions were needed in order to restore national unity and to rebuild a solidly structured society. Though membership remained relatively small, the impact of the organization was far out of proportion to its size. It attracted an active and vocal group of intellectuals and young people: the historian Jacques Bainville, the journalist Léon Daudet, the novelist Paul Bourget were among them. Its newspaper was brilliantly written and scurrilously shocking; its young activists kept Paris in an uproar by battling Socialists in the streets and persecuting unpatriotic professors at the Sorbonne.

Though the movement in many ways foreshadowed later fascist groups, its doctrine as defined by Maurras contrasted with those of later irrationalist leaders. Maurras thought of himself as the purest of rationalists and positivists, as a defender of France's true Greco-Roman heritage against the corrupting influence of Teutonic mysticism. His goal was to restore traditional institutions and mores, those that France had known before the disaster of the Great Revolution; it was not to go forward by disintegrating the old society and establishing a new elite, in modern totalitarian fashion. Yet despite his purposes and the disclaimers of his later disciples, it is clear that the product of his agitation was a

---

[2] The Dreyfus Affair crystallized a whole series of political parties and movements, some of which had existed as amorphous factions without much organizational structure. Thus in 1901 the Radical-Socialist party was given nationally organized form for the first time, and the Moderate faction gave birth in 1901–2 to two organized parties: the Democratic Alliance (which supported Waldeck's coalition with the left) and the Republican Federation (which opposed it).

proto-fascist mood. Maurrassism reinforced the rabid right-wing temper that had emerged from the Boulangist agitation, and ensured its persistence in France. While Alain was desiccating the outlook of many young Frenchmen on the left, Maurras was corrupting an important part of the right. In the wealthy, well-born, right-thinking classes that dominated industry, the upper bureaucracy, the army and navy, Maurras had a large and attentive audience. He indoctrinated them with a violent contempt for the masses as degenerate, for the republic's leadership as rotten; he persuaded this segment of the French elite that the nation faced catastrophe unless "the real country" could seize control from "the legal country." Thanks in part to Alain and Maurras, "...the masses distrusted those who might have led, and the classes hated and despised those who might have followed."[3]

Catholics in the old Veuillot and Assumptionist tradition welcomed the Maurrassian agitation. Another segment of Catholics found it nauseating. They found their apostle in young Marc Sangnier, a crusading idealist who in 1894 brought together a little group of fellow students eager to find a way to live as well as to practice their faith. From a discussion group the Sillon (Furrow) turned to social action; it attracted a small but devoted band of young laymen and parish priests. In 1907 Sangnier began to convert the Sillon into a political movement and to put up candidates for the Chamber. The organization was frankly committed to a reconciliation between church and republic; its leaders rejected control by the hierarchy and opened their ranks to all well-wishers, whether Catholic or not. In that era the enterprise was far too daring to achieve success. Both Catholics and freethinkers remained warily aloof; yet the Vatican (influenced, possibly, by Action Française advisers) viewed it as potentially dangerous. In 1910 Pope Pius X issued a virtual death warrant, in which he described the Sillon as "that miserable tributary of the great stream of apostasy." Sangnier submitted and liquidated the organization. But its small elite continued to work through other less vulnerable agencies; after the Second World War, many of them (including Sangnier) were to see their dream of a great Christian democratic movement become reality.

---

[3] P. Williams, in J. M. Wallace-Hadrill and J. McManners (eds.), *France: Government and Society*, p. 242.

# CHAPTER 21

# Economy: Structure and Trends, 1870–1914

A huge factory isn't my idea of the model for a perfect society.

"ALAIN" (1907)

Frenchmen since the Great War of 1914–1918 have been inclined to look back on the prewar years as *"la belle époque"*—roughly translatable as "the good old days." Some of this sentiment springs from simple nostalgia; almost any past era eventually takes on an attractive quality in retrospect. As an ironic Frenchman once remarked, people are rarely able to conjugate the verb "to be happy" in the present tense. Yet the generation that lived from the 1890's to 1914 may have come closer to that fortunate state than has any other in modern French history.

During the half-century of peace that intervened between the Prussian war and the 1914 conflict, the nation enjoyed a remarkable combination of political and social stability and sporadic economic expansion. The old France survived, yet alongside it a new France was obviously emerging. Industrial output tripled between 1870 and 1914; total national income probably doubled; French investments abroad increased sixfold. The process of urbanization continued steadily, though not fast enough to destroy the older village and rural society. In 1870, 52 per cent of the active population was engaged in agriculture; in 1914, the figure still exceeded 40 per cent. Living standards, though difficult to measure, were on the rise for the bulk of the population; on the average, Frenchmen by 1914 were probably better off than any other Europeans except the English. Although housing conditions (both urban and rural) remained antiquated and uncomfortable for most people, levels of consumption steadily rose, and real wage rates in industry increased by something like half between 1870 and 1914.

Most of the peasants, after surviving a period of serious stress from the mid-seventies to the mid-nineties, came to be better off too. Average crop yields improved a little, farm prices began to rise again, and a slow drift to the cities combined with a rapid drop in the birth rate to cut the pressure of population on the land. The only statistics that were beginning to disturb Frenchmen were those in the demographic realm. Whereas the population had grown by 32 per cent from 1801 to 1850, it rose by only 14.6 per cent from 1850 to 1914. Even before the carnage of the Great War, France as a nation was falling behind its more prolific neighbors, and the population pyramid was beginning to show the first signs of a middle-age bulge.

A graph of French economic activity from 1870 to 1914 would reveal a jerky pattern of economic growth. Until about 1883, expansion continued at about the same rate as during the latter part of the Second Empire—that is, a rate somewhat slower than that of 1840–1860, but respectable nevertheless. Then, from 1883 to 1896, came a period of virtual stagnation; prices dropped sharply, industrial growth was slowed, while agriculture found itself in almost constant difficulties caused by the competition of overseas imports and by the disastrous impact of a vine disease called phylloxera that destroyed a third of France's vineyards. In the mid-nineties the upturn came, and developed into a real boom after 1905, almost as impressive as that of the 1850's. From 1896 to 1914 prices rose again by 40 per cent, foreign trade increased by about 75 per cent, and the national income made its most phenomenal growth since the days of Napoleon III. The pace of industrial growth after 1905, according to a recent study, amounted to about 4.5 per cent annually. By almost every statistical measure, the French outdid the British during the prewar decade.

The reasons for the shift from slackness to boom about 1896 are complex and somewhat debatable. To some degree, the pattern in France merely reflected a European-wide trend: the eighties and early nineties had been a time of slackness and declining prices everywhere, and the upturn was general from the mid-nineties. But some special factors seem to have been operative in France to make the boom there even greater than in Britain. One such factor was the opening of the vast Briey iron-ore fields in French Lorraine. The Germans had drawn the 1871 frontier between French and German Lorraine in such a way as to annex most of the known iron deposits of the area, but what they had taken proved to be the outcroppings of a huge subterranean deposit, the bulk of which lay on the French side of the frontier. The Lorraine ore, though rich, contained impurities that made it almost unusable until English experiments developed a new smelting process in 1878. French engineers began at once to drill in the area and shortly made a rich strike in the Briey basin, only four miles from the German frontier. Technical difficulties interfered for a time with the exploitation of the new ore, but these were solved shortly before 1900, and the iron and steel industry of the region expanded at a remarkable rate. By 1914 there were twenty iron and steel works in French Lorraine, producing more than two-thirds of France's total pig iron and steel. In addition, large quantities of raw ore and pig iron were sold to Germany and Belgium; France became the world's largest exporter of iron ore.

A second factor, much more controversial in its impact on economic growth, was France's decision in 1892 to adopt a high-tariff policy on both industrial and farm products. Napoleon III's turn toward freer trade had never been widely popular with the French business class, though it had forced much of French industry to modernize itself during the sixties. The revulsion against the empire after 1870 provided an added reason for a return to higher tariffs, and so did the general European trend toward protectionism beginning in the seventies. When Napoleon's low-tariff treaties expired, the Opportunist politicians re-established duties on many industrial products; but it was not until the so-called Méline Tariff of 1892 that all-out protectionism was adopted. The Méline rates were boosted again in 1910, making French tariff rates the fourth highest in the world.

Whether the Méline Tariff marked a return to good sense or the beginning of French decadence is an issue that has divided Frenchmen ever since. Its defenders assert a direct causal relationship between the tariff law and the boom that followed shortly after; they point out that protectionist France after 1900 enjoyed a more rapid rate of growth in production and foreign trade than did free-trade Britain. They argue also that the Méline Tariff, by setting up duties on imported foodstuffs, enabled France to preserve a "healthy" and "balanced" economic and social structure. French farmers, instead of being driven off the land as in Britain, managed to survive and, in some cases, to prosper. France was able to remain 90 per cent self-sufficient in foodstuffs and to keep third rank among the wheat-producing nations of the world. Furthermore, according to the defenders of the tariff, this large farm population constituted a steady home market for French industrial goods.

Critics of the Méline Tariff deny that it contributed very much to the subsequent boom, which, they say, was the product of European and world-wide economic trends. They admit that the tariff enabled many French producers to survive, but at a heavy cost to the economy and to society as a whole. France continued to raise much wheat, for example, but at a cost twice that of more efficient countries. The rate of economic growth after 1896, the critics insist, could and should have been much faster than it was; without tariffs, exports might have been expanded far more rapidly, and a bigger and healthier domestic market might have been developed. They believe that the long-range effect of the tariff was to produce a stagnant rather than a vigorous economy. Inefficient factories and farms could survive without having to modernize; the cost of production remained high, consumption levels low, and France's competitive trade position bad.

This debate has hinged largely on the kind of society preferred by the two camps. If the central goal is a system built around small independent producers and distributors—if the aim is a kind of Jeffersonian social stability rather than a technocratic social fluidity—then the Méline policy was wise and healthy. If, on the contrary, the goal is a vigorously competitive economy, capable of adapting and keeping up with other nations in a fluid world, then the Méline Tariff certainly had long-range results that have weighed on France ever since. It was not that the Méline Tariff rendered impossible the modernization and expansion of French factories and farms; some industrialists and agrarians undertook such modernization voluntarily. The trouble with the tariff was that it encouraged the tendency of most businessmen, peasants, and politicians to avoid changes in the established routine, and strengthened their conviction that France had attained a beatific state of perfect harmony and balance. The effect of the republic's tariff policy was to reinforce the division of modern France into two sectors: a dynamic, modern, efficient sector that increasingly dominated the nation's production figures, and a static, backward, unadapted sector that scarcely changed at all and that continued to dominate the nation's political machinery.

The survival of this large static sector in France nevertheless raises some important questions. Other nations also turned protectionist in the late nineteenth century, yet they saw their static sectors rather thoroughly squeezed out by dynamic competitors. Indeed, this latter process was so rapid in the United States that antitrust laws were finally adopted to check the trend toward monopoly. France needed no such laws. Two factors there blocked what might seem to be a natural trend: one of them was political, the other psychological.

Politically, most of the Third Republic's leaders consistently tended to favor the little man—both by necessity and by choice. A successful politician could hardly avoid such an attitude in a country with so many voters who were little men. But it was a genuinely appealing attitude as well, for it fitted the honest prejudices of most French politicians, the bulk of whom were themselves of middle- or petty-bourgeois origin. The Opportunists and Moderates, with their conservative social philosophy, saw the small producer and distributor as the source of social stability. The Radicals were even more deeply committed to defending the little man, by doctrine and interest as well as by family background.

But the survival of static France was ensured also by a psychological factor. Most of the efficient industrialists and farmers in France were not strongly impelled to expand production, to corner the market and to destroy their small competitors. Perhaps they restrained themselves because they thought it wise to preserve a large buffer element of small producers and distributors as a sort of "social umbrella" beneath which their own power and profits could be dissembled. Or perhaps they saw here a simple device for keeping their profit margin high. By permitting prices to stay at a level that would keep the small inefficient producer in business, the dynamic manufacturer or farmer could enjoy the pleasant condition of operating without much risk or effort, and could count on a comfortable income from a limited but stable market.

These factors kept the new dynamic sector of the economy from overrunning and crushing out the static sector. Yet they could not prevent a gradual erosion of static enterprise and a steady concentration of economic power, especially in the industrial sphere. By 1914 more than half of the total output of many items was being produced by four or five firms, and small marginal enterprises were steadily dropping in number. Even so, small firms did survive in far larger proportion than in other western nations. In 1914 one-third of France's industrial workers were still employed in shops with no more than ten workers each, and more than half were still in plants with no more than a hundred employees. The survival of the static sector was even clearer in agriculture, where the excessively slow drift to the cities (amounting to about one per cent of the rural population per year) left far too many marginal farms operating, and where most peasants had no easy access to capital for improvements. French agriculture increasingly became a museum with exhibits ranging from the medieval to the ultra-modern.

In a sense, the most remarkable successes of French businessmen after 1870 were achieved outside the frontiers of France. From mid-century onward, French bankers and engineers had been playing an active part in the industrial development of the rest of the European continent. Already, between 1850 and 1870, French investments abroad had risen from two billion to fifteen billion francs; by 1914 the total had reached forty-five billion francs, two-thirds of which had been placed in Europe or in the Mediterranean basin. The largest single recipient was Russia, with 25 per cent of the total; the French colonial empire, in contrast, attracted only 10 per cent. Almost one-third of France's available liquid capital had gone into foreign investment by 1914—a proportion higher than that of England. Most of these funds were funnelled abroad through powerful new investment banks founded during the generation after 1870: the Banque de Paris et des Pays-Bas (1872) was the best known. Along with French cash, French technicians were also items of export. According to the American historian Rondo Cameron, French firms "accounted for the greater part of railway construction in every country on the Continent outside Germany and Scandinavia."[1]

Whether this foreign activity benefited or harmed the nation is a controversial issue, the answer to which depends partly on the perspective of the viewer.

---

[1] R. Cameron, *France and the Economic Development of Europe* (Princeton: Princeton Univ. Press, 1961), p. 101.

Frenchmen after 1914 would undoubtedly have been better off if most of this exported capital had been invested at home—especially since so much of it was lost through Russian default after 1917. On the other hand, Frenchmen before 1914 probably gained more than they lost by foreign investment, which brought them higher returns in interest than they could have earned through domestic use of the funds. In the short run, the national income and standard of living were increased thereby.

In the years before 1914 few Frenchmen believed that the nation had been following the wrong economic path during the nineteenth century. They possessed stability, prosperity, a solid currency, and a balanced budget; what more could they want? If the per capita income of Frenchmen lagged behind that of Englishmen and was only half that of Americans, it was probably higher than anywhere else on the Continent. They could observe with pardonable pride that the German epigram to describe an idyllic existence ran thus: "to live like God in France." Yet even in that pre-1914 era a few French businessmen and economists were beginning to express less sanguine views, and to talk ominously of French decadence—talk inspired largely by the astonishing industrial growth of Germany next door. Some labor leaders, too, complained of the sluggishness of the French economy and the lack of dynamism displayed by many French entrepreneurs. American employers, they observed, might be just as hostile to the labor movement as French employers, but at least they were men of imagination and energy whose productive drive might eventually benefit the workers. Besides, they argued, the Americanizing of the French business group would have another value: aggressive and ruthless bosses might strengthen the feeble trade-union movement by shaking the French worker into a more active class-consciousness.

Another full generation was to elapse, however, before Frenchmen in large numbers would critically re-examine their nation's economic record in the pre-1914 era. When they did so, in the 1930's and especially after the Second World War, some of them concluded that the decline of French power in the twentieth century was not merely the product of two disastrous wars but was deeply rooted in *la belle époque* itself. Growth and prosperity between 1870 and 1914, they now decided, had concealed from contemporaries a relative decline that was dramatic. In 1870 France had still been the world's second industrial producer and trading nation; by 1914 it had fallen to a poor fourth in both respects. The French share of world industrial production had dropped meanwhile from almost 10 to only 6 per cent. And as the population curve had levelled off, the French domestic market had shrunk in comparison to that of other nations.

It was this mood of gloomy self-criticism that stimulated much of the post-1945 debate between the so-called "coal-men" and "culture-men." Both camps agreed that Frenchmen since the nineteenth century have failed to compete successfully with the most dynamic industrial nations; they differed as to the reasons.

One school argued that the French did about as well as they could with what they had; that the nation's structural and technical shortcomings were simply too great to permit effective competition with rival states better equipped by nature for the industrial age. The chronic shortage of coal—especially of good coking coal for blast furnaces—was one such handicap; another was the deep-rooted tradition of luxury manufacture that hampered easy conversion to production-line methods. The second school argued that the principal factor hampering France's economic growth, before as well as after 1870, was the lack of real entrepreneurial spirit. They observed that other nations had managed to find ways to compensate for their lack of essential raw materials, or had succeeded in uprooting an older manufacturing or farming tradition in favor of a new. They pointed out that France no longer lacked liquid capital after mid-century, but that French investors preferred to invest it in "safe" foreign government bonds rather than in more venturesome domestic enterprise. They pointed to the persistence of the family firm in France—to the stubborn conviction of many businessmen that no outsider should even be permitted to invest in the enterprise, and that the owner's family duty was to protect and pass on his patrimony to his sons rather than risk losing it in an effort to double its size. They noted the French inclination to take smallness as an ideal—an inclination deeply rooted in French mores, business or otherwise. "Mon verre est petit, mais je bois dans *mon* verre" ("My cup may be small, but I drink from my own"): few French maxims are more revealing of a generalized attitude toward life.

The "culture-men" argued, in addition, that French entrepreneurship continued to be hampered by the old heritage of social values—a heritage that was generally uncongenial toward the ideas of business expansion and monetary success. Even after 1870 there were still remnants of the traditional attitude that the way to attain status was to escape from business, not to succeed within it. The escape route, which in the ancien régime had led into the aristocracy, now led into politics or the professions. For those who failed to escape, there was what David Landes has called "a genteel pattern of entrepreneurship," whose "... ideal model is that of the businessman as a 'rounded,' civilized individual, not enslaved by his wealth, but master thereof to spend it in the fashioning of an elegant, cultivated existence." The values contained in this ideal of the good life were the values of an aristocratic precapitalist age; and there is reason to believe that this ethos kept much of its appeal in France well into the twentieth century. It provided a certain self-justification for French business men as they saw themselves being outstripped by crassly materialistic rivals in "less civilized" societies.

If one were to accept the thesis of the "culture-men" that lack of a dynamic entrepreneurial spirit in the business community held back industrial growth in France, it would be only fair to add that the politicians of the time shared some of the responsibility. The Third Republic's political elite was largely un-trained and uninterested in economic problems, and adopted a kind of narrowly protective attitude toward the business world. Someone has pointed out that no statesman of the Third Republic left his name attached to a significant piece of legislation in the economic sphere. There are two possible exceptions to this generalization—Méline and Freycinet—but whether their contributions were posi-tive or negative is open to debate.[2] On the whole, the politicians of the era prob-ably did more to retard than to promote economic growth. But if that was the case, they were surely not being unrepresentative of their electors. Like most suc-cessful politicians of all eras, they shared the mores of their time and place.

Two final remarks ought to be added, even though they will further compli-cate an already complex problem. First, the "cultural" argument that Frenchmen lacked entrepreneurial drive does not properly explain the periods of rapid and dynamic economic growth—notably 1840–1860 and 1905–1914. Nor does it explain why Germany, with an even stronger aristocratic and precapitalist value-system, did see the rise of an unusually dynamic entrepreneurial group. Second, in our day even many non-Frenchmen have begun to weigh the virtues of economic growth against other values—those values that go to make up that vague but important entity called "the quality of life." When they do so, the record of *la belle époque* begins to take on a new attractiveness. François Crouzet reminds us that if France fell from second to fourth rank in total industrial output between 1870 and 1914, the nation continued to compete successfully with almost all rivals in *per capita production* (which, to many economists, is a better and fairer test of economic progress). It can be argued, adds Crouzet, "that nineteenth-century Frenchmen sacrificed long-term economic growth to social stability and to the individual's independence and right to happiness. They were the only western people to sacrifice population growth for an increase in living standard. And ... the crafts-man of Paris or the peasant of Auvergne was, quite likely, happier than the Lancashire cotton-mill operative, or the proletarianized Prussian rural journey-man."[3] His argument, though controversial, bears serious reflection. Perhaps the real problem of *la belle époque* was not sluggish growth but fairer distribution of the product of reasonable growth.

---

[2] Méline's achievement was the tariff of 1892; he is the patron saint of agrarian protectionists in France. The Freycinet Plan (1879) laid out an elaborate program of state-subsidized railway construction, confined to secondary lines in areas still remote from the completed trunk system. It has often been criticized as a costly piece of pork-barrel legislation that gave France a largely useless network of uneconomic lines at heavy cost to the taxpayer.

[3] F. Crouzet, "French Economic Growth in the 19th Century (1815–1914): Data and Inter-pretations" (unpublished essay).

# CHAPTER 22

# Society: Structure and Trends, 1870–1914

Here we find once more the national character: the collective pursuit of equality, the individual pursuit of privilege.

ALFRED SAUVY

The Third Republic, a lover of paradox might say, was created by the aristocracy, administered by the upper and middle bourgeoisie, governed by the lower bourgeoisie, and dominated by the peasantry.

The interrelationships between social realities and political mechanisms or forces are never easy to untangle, save perhaps in the kind of system that the Germans call a *Ständesstaat,* where social categories are pretty much fixed and functions are rigidly defined. In a modern social system of relatively open and fluid character, however, even its component categories, strata, or "classes" defy clear definition. Throughout modern French history these categories merge and overlap, so that commonly used terms like "bourgeoisie" and "proletariat" may mislead more than they enlighten. Even more ambiguous is the relationship between rural and urban dwellers in a changing society. The practice of lumping together the whole rural population under the collective label "the peasantry" lacks validity; yet an attempt to assimilate farm laborers with urban factory workers, or proprietors of small farms with the urban middle classes, runs into important contradictions. These complexities will help to explain why scholars disagree on class relationships in modern France.

Of all social categories in late nineteenth-century France, the aristocracy is most easily dealt with, for it was the smallest, the most clearly defined, and the least important group. The decade of the 1870's represented its last brief resurgence in politics. Since 1830 most of the old Legitimist families had been sulking in domestic exile; they had lived on their country estates or in the Saint-Germain quarter of Paris and had ostentatiously disdained official society and politics. The newer aristocracy created by Louis-Philippe had been out of power only since 1848 and had been less inclined to turn its back on the system. Many Orleanist notables had remained active in business during the Second Empire, and some had re-entered politics as well—usually as members of the liberal opposition. The fall of the empire brought both groups flooding back into dominant roles in national as well as local politics; but their triumph was short. By 1879 they had been dislodged from one position of strength after another, and their subsequent attempts to recover influence only reaffirmed their permanent eclipse as an important organized group. For a time the sons of aristocrats continued to enter the diplomatic service and the army in disproportionate numbers, but those services, too, had become rather thoroughly republicanized by 1914. In the church hierarchy, the aristocrats' grip had long since been broken; as early as 1889 eighty-six of the ninety bishops and archbishops were of humble origin. The voters of a few rural areas in western France stubbornly continued to send aristocrats to parliament throughout the period of the Third Republic, and even into the Fourth. On the whole, however, aristocratic titles in the twentieth century had taken on an archaic and anachronistic flavor. Better than any historian, the novelist Marcel Proust in his vast novel *Remembrance of Things Past* caught the spirit of that decaying society in the generation before 1914.

❊❊❊❊❊❊❊❊❊❊❊❊❊

In France, as in all the Western world, the nineteenth century was the era of the bourgeoisie; and the Third Republic represented its ultimate triumph. But its steady growth in size and power made both the label and its content harder than ever to define. "Vast and multiform as the nation itself," the bourgeoisie ranged from a millionaire banker like Henri Germain to the village druggist or postal clerk of Claquebue. A common denominator, either economic or psychological, is difficult to find here. If there was such a thing as a bourgeoisie, presumably its members should have shared a way of life or a set of values. Various efforts have been made to identify this bourgeois spirit, but none seems quite satisfactory. The political scientist André Siegfried once proposed to define the bourgeois as "a man who has something in reserve"; in somewhat the same spirit, the historian Pierre Sorlin argues that "the bourgeois is one who has more money than he needs for bare subsistence, and who considers the excess indispensable to maintain a certain social position."[1] Siegfried has also suggested

---

[1] P. Sorlin, *La société française 1840–1914* (Paris: Arthaud, 1969), p. 128.

that bourgeois status embodies a state of mind, a particular set of mores, a type of behavior. Perhaps at bottom the bourgeoisie is bound together in a negative way; its members define themselves as distinct from either the aristocracy or the workers.

Within this amorphous conglomerate, there are clearly several sub-strata. André Siegfried has proposed four or possibly five categories: *grande, haute, moyenne, petite,* and (perhaps) *très petite.* Some other scholars have tried to escape the ambiguities by abandoning the term "bourgeoisie" entirely and substituting "middle classes," with the emphasis on the plural form of that term. In the confused state of the question, historians may as well be content with a loose-joined analysis that uses the terms "middle classes" and "bourgeoisie" interchangeably. If scientific precision is unattainable, one can at least try for consistent usage.

In the early years of the Third Republic the political and economic elite of the regime was drawn for the most part from the upper middle classes: from Siegfried's *grande bourgeoisie* (old, wealthy families like the Rothschilds) and, even more commonly, from the *haute bourgeoisie* (men like Thiers, Casimir-Périer, Henri Germain). Most of them were Orleanist by tradition, though a few had rallied to Napoleon III. After 1870 they proved more flexible and adaptable than the aristocracy; most of them, like Thiers, were converted to republicanism during the first decade and retained important roles in economic and political life. Politically they straddled the center, and it was from this strategic position that they were able to help shape the constitution of the new republic. After 1880, however, few members of the *haute bourgeoisie* remained in parliament. Their political influence henceforth was exercised indirectly, through the action of pressure groups like the Comité des Forges (an iron and steel makers' trade association, set up in 1864) or through personal contacts with prominent politicians. Moderate premiers like Maurice Rouvier, Radical premiers like Joseph Caillaux, were linked closely to Parisian bankers of the *grande* and *haute bourgeoisie*. Intermarriage was common within this social group, and the world of banking and business took on a kind of clannish character through the development of what some historians have called "bourgeois dynasties," or a "business aristocracy." One aspect of this trend was a slowing of upward social mobility after the mid-nineteenth century; rare indeed were the poor boys, or even the sons of middle bourgeois, who now managed to climb into the upper bourgeois ranks.

Although their ancestors had been Voltairean anticlericals in the eighteenth and early nineteenth centuries, most members of the upper bourgeoisie had by now reconciled themselves to the church as a respectable and necessary institution. If many of them were still religious skeptics, they were willing to see their wives go to Mass and their children to Catholic schools. A powerful minority of the upper bourgeoisie, however, was Protestant; and that group had always clung more fervently to its faith. The role of what the French call the "H. S. P." (*haute société protestante*) in industry, banking, politics and journalism was far out of proportion to its size.[2] For one brief period there was even a Protestant majority in the cabinet.

The *moyenne bourgeoisie,* numbering perhaps in the two or three millions, was much more varied in character. Its members were not newcomers to economic affluence and social status. Most of them had become solidly established in business or in the professions during the early nineteenth century; they were well-to-do, well-educated, and respected citizens. Most of the republican leadership in 1848 had come from the middle bourgeoisie; many of its members had also done well in business and in the governmental bureaucracy under Napoleon III. But its apogee was still to come. Economically, many of its members were shrewd enough to profit both by the era of falling prices in the eighties and nineties and by the boom that followed. During the first phase they piled up savings and got control of much of the nation's liquid wealth, while during the second phase they invested abroad or participated cautiously in business expansion.

Politically, the triumph of the middle bourgeoisie was even clearer. From about 1879 onward its representatives dominated parliament and cabinet, although after the turn of the century they began to be edged out of this dominant role by men of lower social origin. The middle bourgeoisie got an even firmer and more durable grip on the higher posts in the civil service; efficient and well-trained, these middle bourgeois officials went on quietly administering the republic long after political power proper had shifted downward in the social scale. From the middle bourgeoisie there also came an influential group of lobbyists or intermediaries between the worlds of business and politics: *politiciens d'affaires* they were called, in the curious French phrase. Their nebulous activities occasionally emerged out of the shadows into public view, as during the Panama Scandal, and clouded the reputation of the regime. The contrast between the pure, romantic, even naive spirit associated with the 1848 republic and the unscrupulous affairism that came to be much too common in the political life of its successor impressed and disturbed many Frenchmen.

If the era of the Third Republic brought any really fundamental social change in France, it was the active emergence into roles of political and social importance of the lesser bourgeoisie—*petite* and even *très petite.* These were the elements whose rise Gambetta had foreseen when he spoke of *les nouvelles couches* that would soon be demanding recognition. They were the "little Frenchmen" *par excellence:* the small shopkeepers, clerks, white-collar employees, school-

---

[2] In 1866 there were approximately 850,000 Protestants in France: i.e., just over 2 per cent of the total population. Most of them were clustered in Alsace, the Rhône-Cévennes-Nîmes region in the southeast, and the Paris area. By 1965 the proportion had fallen slightly to about 1.6 per cent.

masters, petty civil servants of city, town, and village. Already before 1870 they had begun their ascent into the middle classes; the first and essential step in this process of upward mobility had come when their peasant or artisan fathers had put aside enough money to give them a secondary education. No other social group had so many fervent disciples of the revolutionary tradition—and especially of its Jacobin, Robespierrist phase. Ferociously egalitarian, positivist, anticlerical, and patriotic, their theoretical utopia was a republic purged of "superstition" and dedicated to the protection of the little man. Although their rise into the middle classes was recent, few members of this petty bourgeoisie had much comprehension of social issues. They wanted equality of status and careers open to talent, not equality of condition or state action to protect the weak and "lazy." If they had a social program, it was summed up in a moderately progressive income tax and the expansion of mutual-aid societies.

It was the lesser bourgeoisie that flooded into both Opportunist and Radical ranks from the seventies onward, and that got an unshakable grip on the Radical movement by the end of the century. Its greatest strength was in local politics; its members, fervent and dedicated men, became the active militants of the Radical party and of Freemasonry—the ward heelers, town councillors, village mayors, and members of electoral committees that chose candidates for parliament. The ablest of them began to rise into national politics as well; by 1914 a large proportion of the Radical deputies came of petty bourgeois origin. These (along with the members of the *moyenne bourgeoisie*) were the new notables of the regime, the men who dominated political life in the middle years of the Third Republic, and who continued to constitute the bulk of the political class down to the collapse of 1940. The eventual decline of the republic, as some scholars see it, was intimately associated with the shortcomings of this political class after 1918—in particular, its stubborn and narrow-minded inability to adapt to changing times. If the Third Republic, then, may properly be called a bourgeois democracy, that phrase tends to hide a steady evolutionary process within the middle classes themselves: a gradual downward shift in the locus of political power, from *haute* to *moyenne* to *petite* bourgeoisie.

❖❖❖❖❖❖❖❖❖❖❖❖❖

Aristocracy and bourgeoisie combined made up only a small fraction of the French population before 1914—no more than 15 or 20 per cent in all. Alongside them, or below them, was the great mass of workers and peasants, sometimes lumped together as *les classes populaires*—ill-defined, poorly organized, and only vaguely class-conscious. Between them and the bourgeoisie the line of separation was indistinct. It was not an economic boundary, for there were workers and peasants who were better off than some of the lesser bourgeoisie. Perhaps the clearest distinction by this time was educational: the "popular classes" had no more than an elementary education (if they received any at all), while the bourgeois was the product of a secondary school, either *lycée* or *collège*.

Within this mass the peasantry was in steady but slow decline, and the industrial workers in constant numerical progress. In 1870, 52 per cent of Frenchmen had made their living by agriculture, while only 23 per cent were industrial workers or artisans. By 1914 the farm population had dropped to a little over 40 per cent, and the number of urban workers had risen to 39 per cent. Another 10 per cent of Frenchmen in 1914 were commercial employees, and 6 per cent were civil servants. Thus the peasantry, by a narrowing margin, still formed the largest single element; and in addition, the unequal distribution of population gave the peasants an outright majority in more than half the departments of France. The potential political power of this rural mass is obvious; some scholars have concluded from it, with at least the appearance of validity, that the Third Republic may have been operated by the bourgeoisie but was in fact dominated by the peasantry.

The truth is somewhat more complex, largely because the peasantry was too heterogeneous to constitute a solid bloc. For one thing, the number of independent farmers in 1870 was balanced by an almost equal number of farm laborers, whose outlook did not necessarily coincide with that of owners and operators. Furthermore, the independent farmers were subdivided into owners, tenants (*fermiers*), and sharecroppers (*métayers*), and their holdings ranged from several hundred acres to miniscule plots too small to support a family. Finally, in some parts of France the peasants lived clustered together in villages or even sizable towns, while in other sections they were isolated in separate farmhouses scattered through the countryside. Such diversity virtually ruled out any common outlook, except perhaps a set of negative attitudes—a deep-rooted suspicion of the city-dweller and a desire to be left alone by the tax collector and the army recruiter.

Although peasant diversity did not grow less between 1870 and 1914, the period did see the beginnings of gradual change that foreshadowed a kind of rural revolution in the twentieth century. Until about 1890 the dominant nineteenth-century trend continued; a steady subdivision of the land increased the number of farms until the figure reached an all-time peak of 5.7 million. This trend was the product of rural overpopulation; in many regions population growth was still not being offset by the drift to the cities. Land hunger remained intense; peasants scraped and saved to buy bits of large estates or to develop new marginal land. While the independent peasantry thus reached its maximum size about 1890, the cost of that process was heavy, for most of these small farm operators were primitive in their methods and marginal in their standards. Their precarious state furnished a good argument to the proponents of the Méline Tariff in 1892—although in fact most peasants sold little or nothing on the market and stood to lose more than they gained by high tariffs on farm products.

Sometime in the nineties came a reversal of the trend; the number of farms operated began to drop, and it has continued to decline almost without interruption ever since. From 5.7 million in 1890 it fell to 5 million in 1911, 4 million in 1929, 2.5 million in 1946, and 1.5 million in 1970. This trend may seem to reinforce the Marxian thesis that sooner or later big capitalist enterprise ruthlessly drives the little farmer off the soil. In certain limited areas of France (notably in the wheat and sugar-beet country that extends from the Paris basin to the Belgian border), there were real signs of such a tendency toward capitalist concentration both before 1914 and after the war. But for most of France, the post-1890 process was rather one of gradual consolidation of dwarf holdings into middle-sized family farms in the 25-to-100 acre class. The rural exodus at last offset rural population growth; many small-owners, or sons of small-owners, began to sell or rent their bits of soil to a neighbor or, in some cases, let it go back to nature. This process presaged the rise of a healthier and more prosperous peasantry, although there continued to survive a great many of the older marginal farms too small and too poorly equipped to furnish more than a meager subsistence.

A second healthy trend was the spread of education and an increase in rural permeability to outside contacts. In 1870 probably a third of the peasants were still illiterate; by 1914, thanks to the Ferry school laws, almost all could read and write. In 1870 the inhabitants of three out of four rural communes still lived in almost total isolation from the outside world; by 1914, thanks to improved rail and road communication and the growing use of the bicycle, most peasants had come to know something beyond their own villages. It was an era, too, of continuing political education in the countryside. In the elections of 1871 many peasants still were uncertain about the use of the ballot; they fell back on voting for, or accepting the guidance of, the local notables—the châtelain or the curé. That habit persisted in 1914 in a few areas like the Vendée; but in most of France the peasantry had long since gained at least an elementary degree of political sophistication. Republican prefects and subprefects had their share in this educational process; so did returning country boys who had gone to the cities to work or had served in the army; so did urban newspapers, as they began to penetrate the countryside. But most important of all was the action of republican militants —the village school teacher who challenged the local curé to doctrinal combat; the village politician, whether doctor or pharmacist or veterinarian or notary, who labored assiduously to indoctrinate the peasants and to line up the vote. Few French peasants by 1914 had learned much about economics, or agronomy, or the importance of organization; but they had learned to listen to the new notables in place of the old, and they had discovered that most politicians were dependent on peasant votes to stay in office.

❖❖❖❖❖❖❖❖❖❖❖❖❖❖

If France had a forgotten man in the pre-1914 era, it was surely the urban worker. The expansion of the working class since 1870 had brought rising unrest and violence but not very much in the way of social gains. In 1884 trade unions had at last been formally legalized; in 1900 women and children were restricted to a ten-hour day; in 1906 Sunday rest was made obligatory; in 1910 an optional social insurance plan was established. This was not a very impressive record of reform; almost no other industrial state in those years granted so little to its labor force.

Bourgeois and peasant shortsightedness was partly responsible for this lack of progress. Neither middle classes nor farmers had developed much of a social conscience; they clung to the doctrine of laissez faire and to the ideal of the lowest possible tax bill. Together, these two segments of society formed a solid phalanx in parliament against which labor demands could beat in vain. Almost the only signs of interest in social problems in the later nineteenth century turned up on the extreme left, among the Socialists, and on the extreme right, among Catholics and Legitimists. Even the Comte de Chambord, for all his obtuseness in political matters, had some inkling of the need for social reform. The attitude of these rightists, however, was naively paternalistic. Efforts by such Catholic conservatives as Comte Albert de Mun to develop what they called "social Catholicism" ran up against the incomprehension of most French employers and the suspicious hostility of the working class.

But labor shared at least some responsibility for its failure to get more from the politicians. Much of its potential influence as a pressure group was wasted by the workers' reluctance to join trade unions, and by the antipolitical bias of the unions that did exist. The Confédération Générale du Travail (C.G.T.), although it was by far the largest union organization, had several rivals; and five million out of the six million industrial workers in 1914 still preferred no union at all. In part, labor's resistance to organization may have derived from the excessive individualism that is supposed to be typical of French workers (and of Frenchmen in general). But a more important factor was the character of French industry, so much of which remained small and semiartisanal in structure. In shops with only a dozen employees, *patron* and laborer remained both physically and temperamentally close; class-consciousness sprouted slowly there. Furthermore, even large enterprise had a special character in France; 40 per cent of

French workers were still employed in the textile and clothing trades in 1914, and more than half of these worked at home rather than in factories. Such a labor force was far more resistant to organization than a mass of production-line workers in vast impersonal plants.

Labor discontent was blunted, too, by a slow, uneven upward trend in living standards during the nineteenth century. Although price and wage statistics for the period are not very dependable, virtually all studies agree that the average workingman was better off in 1914 than he had been in 1870. One economist's estimates of real wages (which conceal many variations within the working class as well as year-to-year zigzags, but which roughly suggest the worker's buying power) run approximately thus (base year 1900 = 100) :[3]

| 1840 | 60 |
| 1865 | 70 |
| 1880 | 80 |
| 1890 | 90 |
| 1900 | 100 |
| 1913 | 102 |

Recent studies of property inventories made in connection with inheritances generally confirm the fact of slow improvement in the worker's economic status during the nineteenth century.[4] Statistics can, however, be misleading. In this instance they leave aside the really underprivileged groups: the old, the sick, the unemployed, for whom little protection was provided, and whose misery has gone unrecorded. They leave aside the widespread sense of frustration and injustice: "In a society completely oriented toward the exaltation of individual success, one dramatic aspect of the workingman's world was the lack of any prospect of a better future, for oneself or for one's children."[5] Finally, the statistics leave uncertain the question of "relative immiseration": was the working class getting its fair share of the benefits from French economic growth? On the whole, probably not. But even if labor's slice of the cake was getting smaller, the cake itself was obviously getting larger. Therefore no sense of desperate urgency drove the mass of workers to join a union or to become active militants in the Socialist movement. Even though the incidence of strikes increased after 1900, there was actually less labor violence in France than in the United States or Britain during that era.

---

[3] J. Lhomme, "Le pouvoir d'achat de l'ouvrier français au cours d'un siècle: 1840–1940," *Le Mouvement Social*, no. 63 (1968), p. 46.

[4] A. Daumard, "L'évolution des structures sociales en France à l'époque de l'industrialisation (1815–1914)," *Revue Historique*, no. 502 (1972), p. 336.

[5] Daumard, *loc. cit.*, p. 342.

Paradoxically, however, this was a time when the leadership and the official doctrine of the trade union movement reached a peak of radicalism. The C.G.T., organized in 1895, promptly adopted an ideology known as revolutionary syndicalism; it called for direct action through strikes, sabotage, and boycotts, and a refusal to participate in the normal political process. Some of the C.G.T.'s founders had been influenced by the ideas of Proudhon and the anarchists; long before Georges Sorel proposed the general strike as a "social myth" to galvanize labor's energies, they had developed the thesis of the general strike as the ultimate weapon. Political action, they held, was futile and corrupting; "to send workers into parliament," asserted one union leader, "is to act like a mother who would take her daughters into a house of prostitution."[6] The C.G.T. refused to become a kind of trade-union branch of the Socialist party; in its Amiens Charter of 1906 the union asserted a rigorously antipolitical position that it was to retain (in theory at least) for forty years. The trade union movement and the Socialist party thus functioned as jealous rivals for the workingman's support. The C.G.T.'s extremist doctrine and propaganda line probably helped to keep it small; its numerical weakness in turn helped to keep the doctrine extreme. Labor leaders without many troops could easily fall back on the romantic thesis that a small but militant vanguard would one day lead the unorganized mass of workers in a spontaneous movement to achieve its proletarian destiny.

Although the doctrine of revolutionary syndicalism remained the C.G.T.'s official line until 1914 (and the apolitical stance survived even longer), there is reason to doubt that the mass of workers was ever attracted to its apocalyptic dogma. Even when the revolutionary activists had their strongest grip on the movement (from 1900 to about 1908), most workers went to the polls to vote for Socialist candidates, and some C.G.T. officials even stood for office themselves. The myth of the general strike was counterbalanced by the attractions of collective bargaining, parliamentary labor legislation, and wage-hour gains as immediate goals. The crusading antimilitarism of the revolutionary syndicalists was also being challenged by a current of revived patriotism that affected many workers as well as other Frenchmen. When the Great War arrived, it should have been no surprise that the idea of a general strike was swept away by another far more powerful social myth—the myth of the nation.

❖❖❖❖❖❖❖❖❖❖❖❖❖❖

If the worker in late nineteenth-century France was the forgotten man, women continued to constitute the disadvantaged sex. The coming of the Third Republic did, however, bring with it the growth of an organized feminist movement and

---

[6] Quoted in V. Lorwin, "Labor and Economic Development in France."

the beginnings of change in the traditional mores that had exalted woman's status as *mère de famille* at the cost of denying women the possibility of self-fulfillment outside the family unit. That traditional status, buttressed by the influence of the Catholic church, was challenged mainly by certain anticlerical republicans and by a few crusading female activists, most of them of bourgeois origin.

The pioneers in this movement were Léon Richer and Maria Deraismes, who collaborated from the late 1860's until the 1890's in a sustained campaign to convert the republic's political leaders to the cause of women's rights. Richer founded a feminist organization and for twenty years published a weekly newspaper that preached the need for legal equality and educational opportunities for women. Maria Desraismes, an effective and tireless speaker, proselyted for a transformation of the dominant mores that had rigidly confined French women to a separate and subordinate social role. In 1889, the centennial of the Great Revolution, the two leaders sponsored in Paris an international congress on women's rights which stimulated a burst of activism. New organizations and new leaders emerged to carry on the campaign—notably Marguerite Durand, who in 1897 founded a daily newspaper called *La Fronde,* staffed entirely by women and concentrated on the women's cause. A wide variety of feminist groups emerged in the 1890's, ranging from a small faction of Catholic feminists to several rival socialist clans.

Most of the early French feminists had avoided the sensitive issue of woman suffrage—in the belief, apparently, that the church's hold on women was still too strong to risk entrusting them with the right to vote. One vigorous activist, Hubertine Auclert, did set out from about 1880 on a lonely campaign for woman suffrage and the right of women to hold office, but she attracted more ridicule than support until after the turn of the century. Although she began to get a hearing after 1900, the fears of the anticlerical Radical politicians combined with the traditionalism of the Catholic conservatives to blunt any reform. Woman suffrage was not to be achieved until 1945.

Access to higher education and to the professions was also slow in coming; the barriers were broken down mainly by the piecemeal efforts of individuals with an urge to achieve. In 1861 a young woman named Julie Daubié, who had studied at home with her brothers, showed up for the *baccalauréat* examination and passed with honors. The baffled authorities refused, however, to grant her the diploma that would have permitted access to a university. Napoleon III's minister of education, Victor Duruy, did authorize a kind of back-door entry for women into the Sorbonne, and during the 1870's this access became a bit easier. By 1880 a handful of women had achieved medical doctorates. The upward trend was slow but steady; by 1914, 10 per cent of university students were women. A few were now practicing medicine or law, and large numbers were moving into the teaching profession, especially at the elementary level.

In the labor force generally, the proportion of women began to rise slowly after a low point in the middle third of the nineteenth century. This trend stemmed in part from the growth of the so-called tertiary sector of the economy, which opened new clerical and service jobs that attracted women applicants. By 1906 women made up 37 per cent of the total work force—a proportion higher than that in most European countries. Most of them, however, were confined to sectors that had long been, or were coming to be, regarded by society as constituting "women's work": domestic service, textiles, the garment trades, clerical jobs, and elementary teaching (where they gradually displaced men after the 1880's). Wages for women before 1914 averaged about half that paid to men for similar work; they were to rise sharply during the Great War, only to fall again during the interwar years to about 70 per cent of men's wages. The major trade unions held out until 1935 against even the principle of equal pay; in practice it has not yet been fully achieved today. Few women became members of trade unions before 1914, and not many more between the wars. Some did join the Socialist party, which professed a commitment to equal rights but confined itself mainly to lip service. The number of women Socialists was much lower than in Germany, and their influence in the party markedly less—perhaps because, unlike the Germans, they lacked a separate women's organization attached to the party, or perhaps because the energies of French Socialist leaders were diverted into factional struggles.

Despite the growth of the feminist movement, the status of French women had not changed dramatically by 1914. Parliament did legalize divorce in 1884, but it was so hedged about as to be little used, and it was at any rate a reform advocated as much by men as by women. A few minor reforms in women's legal status followed after 1900, but they were marginal in nature. The goal of real equality thus remained elusive during the *belle époque,* and was to remain so still when the Third Republic collapsed in 1940.

# CHAPTER 23

# The French Mind and Spirit, 1870–1914

Science is, then, a religion. . . . Science alone can resolve for man those eternal problems for which his nature imperiously demands the solution.

ERNEST RENAN

Frenchmen in the decade before 1870 had already entered upon a new phase in their intellectual evolution. The formidable figure of Victor Hugo still loomed up to overshadow all rivals as the symbol of French cultural achievement; but, although he lived on until 1885, he had become a kind of gigantic anachronism, an object of mixed admiration and tolerant cynicism. The time had passed when the romantic mood was congenial to men's spirits; this was a harder, less frankly emotional age, attuned to the rise of science and materialism. Science alone, wrote the chemist Marcellin Berthelot in the sixties, possesses ". . . a moral force powerful enough to bring about without delay the blessed era of equality and fraternity." "The trend of the times is toward science," added Émile Zola; "we are driven in spite of ourselves toward the exact study of facts and things." This change of mood that set in after mid-century was, of course, not uniquely or even especially French; it was shared with the rest of the Western world. Yet as always, when refracted through French minds and adapted to the French cultural heritage, it took on a special coloration.

Three men stand out as the high priests of that first republican generation from 1870 to 1890: Auguste Comte, Hippolyte Taine, and Ernest Renan. Comte had died in 1855, but it would be hard to exaggerate the impact of his ideas; rarely in history has a thinker of such indifferent talent managed to indoctrinate so thoroughly the whole political class of the next generation. This success was due not so much to Comte's originality as to his talent in systematizing and modernizing the doctrines that had sprung up during the Enlightenment era. These ideas he wove together into a coherent world-view; and that world-view rested on the faith in science and inevitable progress that was burgeoning throughout the West. This ideology was produced at just the moment to catch on, for the anticlerical republicans of France were seeking a doctrine, a philosophy, upon which to build their new world. By 1870 Comte's positivism had become the quasi-official world-view of almost every republican, whether Opportunist or Radical; and many monarchists like Thiers were influenced as well. Comte's dedicated disciple Émile Littré (most celebrated as compiler of a dictionary) devoted a lifetime of pamphleteering to the task of indoctrinating the educated French elite.

Ernest Renan, though he refused to call himself a positivist and though he was only a late and reluctant republican, was another powerful inspirer of the new generation in France. Like the positivists, he preached and practiced the cult of reason and science. A devout Breton by birth, he had almost completed his training for the priesthood when he lost his faith and left the church. His *Life of Jesus,* published in 1863, brought him overnight fame (or infamy, depending on the point of view); it was a brilliant and unprecedented attempt to write the life of Christ as a human being, through the use of the most rigorous methods of scientific research. Renan spent a lifetime crusading for the introduction of German scientific methods into French education; he traced the disaster of 1870 in part to France's backwardness in this sphere, though he found it also in the excesses of universal suffrage and in racial degeneration. As late as 1889 he published a book called *The Future of Science* (written forty years earlier) that was a hymn to reason and progress: "Science," he declared, "is a religion."

Renan represented a deep-rooted tradition in the French outlook: the spirit of skepticism. His contemporary, Hippolyte Taine, literary critic and historian, epitomized an equally ancient heritage: the rationalist or Cartesian cast of French thought, with its stress on order, clarity, and logic. In a book published in 1870, Taine denounced metaphysical speculation as futile and proclaimed it man's duty to study facts alone. Alongside the natural sciences Taine set what he called the "moral sciences"; he advocated the use of similar methods to seek laws in history and in human behavior. The same attitude was reflected in his literary criticism: books were to him, like any other product of the human spirit, the outgrowth of race, milieu, and moment, while "vice and virtue are products like vitriol and sugar." As a true Cartesian, Taine had a passion for formulas, for reducing ideas to their essentials; every man and every book, he remarked, could be summarized in three pages, and every three pages in three lines. A mathematical theorem seemed to him the ideal of perfect beauty. Like Renan, Taine after 1871 set out to analyze the reasons for the nation's disgraceful military failure; he found the origins of French decadence in the ideological abstractions and the revolutionary myth that had seduced the nation since 1789. There is considerable irony, therefore, in the fact that both Taine and Renan were so admired and lionized in the new republic, and that both men had so deep an impact on the mood of that republican generation.

The dominant mood of positivism and scientism in the 1870's and 1880's was revealed in literature almost as clearly as in philosophy and politics. In literature, two major currents stemmed from Renan and Taine, respectively, and ran parallel until the end of the century. Renan's skepticism pervaded the work of such novelists as Anatole France; Taine's Cartesian rationalism was reflected in the novels of the naturalistic school headed by Émile Zola. Anatole France, perhaps the most widely-read literary man of the era, was a kind of mild successor to Voltaire—a master of wit and irony, "a humanitarian dilettante with a choice style and no very deep convictions." Perhaps his skepticism went so deep that in the end it left him a total agnostic; yet underlying France's gentle mockery of human foibles there persisted a deep though vague attachment to the principles of 1789, to the ideals of liberty and justice. That attachment brought him eventually to a kind of humanitarian socialism, best reflected in his own ironic comments on bourgeois institutions. "I have pondered the philosophy of law," remarked his protagonist Monsieur Bergeret, "and I recognized that all social justice rests on these two axioms: theft is reprehensible, the product of theft is sacred." In the same spirit was France's comment that "the law in its majestic impartiality forbids the rich as well as the poor to sleep under bridges, to steal purses and to beg for bread."

Zola, the greatest and most representative figure of the naturalistic school, sought quite frankly to apply the scientific method to fiction. Like Taine, he saw men as products or playthings of powerful forces beyond their control; a pessimistic determinism pervaded his works. Zola believed that the novelist should attack his subject with the objectivity of a chemist in his laboratory. Massive research went into his books, for he believed that novels, like histories, should be written from documents. Almost annually, beginning in 1871, he produced a volume in his massive Rougon-Macquart series, examining in vast detail the degeneration of a family in mid-nineteenth-century France. His concentration on the seamy side of human existence only added to the brutal power of his works. Many readers thought that they found here a kind of untouched photograph of life beneath the false surface of bourgeois society.

Some cultural historians believe that scientism had its effect in even such unlikely realms as poetry and the fine arts. The evidence here is considerably less persuasive. It is true that the school of Parnassian poets, led by Leconte de Lisle, did react against the excesses of romanticism, and did seek to depict real episodes from history or real natural phenomena as accurately and objectively as possible. But their temper seems to have been more neo-classical than scientistic; their emphasis was on poetic form, on the use of cool, unemotional, perfectly structured verse. Somewhat more convincing is the thesis that the vogue of positivism was reflected in the work of certain artists after 1870. That band of individualists grouped together under the label "impressionists" (Manet, Monet, Degas, Renoir, and a number of others) did show at least superficial interest in recent advances in the science of optics as it revealed more accurately the nature of light. But most of them sought to apply that knowledge in intuitive rather than scientific fashion; their emphasis on spontaneity, on fleeting visual effect, ruled out careful analysis and studied technique. Their world remained personal and subjective, their method empirical rather than truly scientific. Only a tiny group of so-called neo-impressionists led by Pierre Seurat pushed on to what might be called impressionism's outer limits; they began with painstaking studies of color theory, then tried by the use of carefully calculated color contrasts and rigorously measured brush strokes to catch on canvas the flickering effect of light and shadow. Their enterprise proved to be a dead end; art resisted absorption into the world of pure science.

A positivist age ought properly to reveal itself not only through the impact of science on thought and the arts, but also through a heightened interest and more rapid advances in science itself. Such was the case in France in this era; in pure science, and even in many of its applied branches, Frenchmen competed successfully with almost every rival nation. Their achievements were all the more striking in light of the inadequate resources available to them; university laboratories were meager and primitive, industrial research almost nonexistent. A full catalogue of names would be of little use, save perhaps to indicate the variety of French interest in the sciences. Among the eminent scientists of the time were Louis Pasteur in medicine; Marcellin Berthelot in chemistry; Pierre and Marie Curie and Henri Becquerel in physics; Jean Charcot (Freud's predecessor and briefly his teacher) in psychopathology; and Henri Poincaré in mathematics. Frenchmen began to pioneer also in the newer social sciences and to apply the spirit and even the methods of science to such humanistic disciplines as history and literary criticism.

❖❖❖❖❖❖❖❖❖❖❖❖❖❖❖❖

Yet even at the height of the age of positivism and scientism, contrary trends persisted from a past era, and premonitory signs of a new mood began to appear. If the year 1879 brought the first novel of Anatole France, it also brought the first work of Pierre Loti, whose lush and exotic romanticism clashed strangely with the temper of the times, but whose books found a wide public for several decades. The new republican class might find its inspiration in Comte's arid positivism, but it could never escape its youthful impregnation with Michelet's passionately romantic version of French history. Flaubert and Zola might pride themselves on confronting life with cold detachment, yet even these giants of realism and naturalism could not always manage to repress their own subjective impulses. Good republicans might denounce the "superstitious obscurantism" of the church, yet some of them were repelled by total agnosticism and sought a compromise in conversion to Protestantism or in a return to Kant as a substitute for Comte.

Alongside these surviving currents from the past, new ones of even greater import began to emerge in the 1880's and 1890's. In 1886, at the very height of the positivist age, the new school of symbolist poets began to attract a few avant-garde readers. In 1889 the conservative writer Paul Bourget, in his best-selling novel *Le Disciple,* challenged all the basic assumptions of the era and began to preach a traditional ethic based upon authority, the family, and social order. In his didactic preface Bourget warned young Frenchmen of his generation against the twin temptations of "brutal positivism" and "disdainful sophism," and be-moaned the corrupting influence of universal suffrage, "the most monstrous and iniquitous of tyrannies." Over the next two decades Bourget and Anatole France were to engage in an impassioned fictional debate involving every major political issue as well as the rival doctrines underlying those issues. It was in 1889, too, that the young philosopher Henri Bergson produced his first book, *Time and Free Will,* little noticed at the time but a harbinger of real intellectual revolution. There was a kind of symbolism in the fact that the two remaining high priests of the scientific age, Renan and Taine, disappeared from the scene in 1892 and 1893 respectively. New idols, new sources of inspiration took their place; from the mid-1890's onward Bergson and Maurice Barrès became the standard-bearers of the revolt against positivism and scientism.

Barrès, a brilliant young Lorrainer whose first novel appeared in 1888, spoke out passionately for a repudiation of the stultifying doctrines that had dominated republican thought. He called for a return to "the sources of national energy" and sought to found a cult of the self, of the soil, of *la patrie.* An "integral na-tionalist" (a phrase that he borrowed from Charles Maurras), a life-long repub-lican who preached authoritarianism, a mystical unbeliever who deeply admired the church, a spokesman for the extreme right who advocated a kind of socialism, Barrès epitomized in his person many of the complexities and contradictions of the new era and of the new twentieth-century right wing in politics. A fervent supporter of General Boulanger, he was elected to parliament just as Boulangism disintegrated; and over the next two decades he remained an isolated but in-fluential voice in politics. That influence, however, defies precise analysis; it was always curiously diffused rather than focussed. Barrèsism did not become embodied in a formal, enduring organization; rather it infiltrated the ideas and emotions of a whole generation. Few men did so much to consolidate the new mood of chauvinistic authoritarianism on the extreme right; few men found such a devoted following among young intellectuals; few men have written novels that so successfully reflected a vital aspect of their times. "Without Barrès," a French scholar has remarked, "it is impossible to study France's domestic history from 1880 to 1914."

The influence of Bergson, though it developed more gradually, proved in the end to be both broader and deeper than that of Barrès. His ideas "powerfully shaped not only the thought but the sensibility of a whole generation of Frenchmen"; he has even been called the Descartes of the modern era. Bergson undermined the very foundations of positivist thought and offered a new set of doctrines to take its place. He attacked the determinism and the scientific dogmatism of the age; he shifted attention to man's non-rational drives, to intuition as the proper path to truth. In his phrase *élan vital* (vital urge), he characterized the creative force that, according to him, makes some men and nations great. Our real selves, Bergson taught, are not represented in our clear ideas, the product of rational reflection; they lie buried in those subconscious tendencies that rarely emerge from the depths. Bergson's full impact came after the publication of his best-known work, *Creative Evolution,* in 1906; by 1910 Bergsonism had become a kind of new gospel. His lectures at the Collège de France were social events where serious students and the *beau monde* competed for classroom space; his ideas penetrated almost every intellectual discussion in prewar Paris. As Taine's ideas recurred in the work of Zola and Renan's in that of Anatole France, so Bergson's may have had their literary reflection in Marcel Proust. The first volume of Proust's massive novel *A la recherche du temps perdu,* however, went almost unnoticed in 1913; his appeal, like that of Bergsonism generally, was to reach its climax in interwar France.

The literary and artistic revolt that accompanied Barrèsism and Bergsonism had begun even before the impact of these men was felt. The poets Verlaine and Rimbaud led the way in the seventies, and inspired the school that chose to call itself the symbolists. This school, led by Stéphane Mallarmé, reacted strongly against the materialism and scientism of the nineteenth century; its adherents rejected the ideal of aloof objectivity in favor of intense and highly personal self-expression. Even more than the French romantic poets, who had retained something of neo-classicism's clarity and logic, they broke away from traditional forms to make way for fantasy and fluidity. The symbolist poet sought to invent a special language—words, images, suggestions—that would express his private sensations and emotions; his purpose was not to express clear ideas, or even to evoke precise images, but merely to give verbal form to the confused sentiments arising from the subconscious. The effects of poetry were thought to be like those of music: an appeal to sense impressions rather than to rational reflection. It is not surprising that symbolist influence was felt also in music; composers like Claude Debussy and Maurice Maeterlinck were in close touch with Mallarmé's circle. Although the movement had only a brief existence, its powerful liberating and renovating effect lasted for a long time. Some of the most notable writers of the new generation—Paul Claudel and André Gide, for example—passed through a symbolist phase as young men; so did a number of innovative composers. Symbolism had no obvious parallel in the realm of painting; but a similar resurgence of subjectivism did mark most of the new artistic schools that proliferated in Paris after 1890. As neo-impressionism withered away, more vigorous competitors such as cubism and fauvism swept into view; these painters had no desire to be mere scientific observers of life, but were driven by an urge to express on canvas their own deeper emotions and subconscious drives, or to reproduce a symbolic equivalent of nature rather than nature itself. Some looked to the Dutchman Van Gogh or the Frenchman Gauguin for inspiration; more of them looked to Paul Cézanne as the great innovator who had moved from impressionism to something far more powerful and promising, and had freed the artist from the restrictive conventions of the past.

Even in political and social theory, the Bergsonian outlook had its impact in the work of that curious figure Georges Sorel. Sorel was a retired engineer who, after a brief Marxist phase, came under the influence of Bergson's teachings as he sought a new path to salvation for the worker and for society. His doctrine, which was somewhat misleadingly called syndicalism, represented a partial return to nineteenth-century anarchist ideas, but gave those ideas a new irrationalist foundation. Direct action alone, he argued, could save the proletariat; political activity and theoretical palaver were mere diversions, a waste of time and energy. No great movement in history, he asserted, had ever succeeded without an inspiring social myth; and the myth that will grip and inspire the working class is the general strike—an apocalyptic moment out of which will emerge a new society built and run by heroic leaders. Sorel attracted few proletarian readers; when a leading trade union official was asked by friends whether his ideas were derived from Sorel, he answered wryly: "No, I read Alexandre Dumas." Indeed, the French labor movement had no need to borrow a doctrine from Sorel; in a sense, it was the C.G.T.'s existing doctrine of revolutionary syndicalism that Sorel borrowed and systematized, after attaching to it some effective slogans. His ideas, in the long run, were picked up by right-wing activists like Mussolini rather than by workers. Even so, his concept of the social myth as a drive to action, and his stress on heroic leadership, clearly reflected the turn to irrationalism that was beginning to alter the climate of the age.

But if the prevailing mood in thought, in literature, and in the arts under-went a sharp change after 1890, the grip of positivism and scientism remained almost unshakable in the educational establishment, and probably among most of the literate population as well. The prewar years therefore brought a widening gulf between an intellectual avant-garde on the one hand and the world of scholarship, business, and politics on the other. Not until after the Great War did the avant-garde revolt against rationalism and science spread out through other social and intellectual strata. To most prewar Frenchmen, the symbolists and similar literary coteries were "decadents," the new schools of painters were unbalanced exhibitionists, the ideas of Barrès and Bergson were curious ex-crescences of right-wing thought. Anatole France continued to be the literary idol of the republican left; positivism persisted as the quasi-official doctrine. In the universities the great names were those of Emile Durkheim in sociology, Vidal de la Blache in human geography, Fustel de Coulanges and Ernest Lavisse in history—all of them men who sought to apply the most rigorous scientific method to the study of human affairs. The impact of Durkheim's thought was especially great, since it reinvigorated and modernized Comtean positivism, and spread out through the human sciences generally. That impact was, however, somewhat paradoxical. For while Durkheim's constant goal was to create a genuine science of human behavior, and while he rejected what he called the "renascent mysticism" of the time, the content of his scholarship challenged some of the fundamental concepts of the positivist age. Central to his thought were such conservative ideas as the primacy of society over the individual, the organic nature of that society, and the essential role of religion in the shaping of moral law. "...A liberal by political choice and action..., his sociology constitutes a massive attack upon the philosophical foundations of liberalism."[1] That aspect of Durkheim's thought, however, remained for a long time hidden beneath his methodology—and it was the methodology that pervaded both universities and secondary schools for another generation or more.

Since the republican political class remained committed to positivism, one might presume that the post-1890 intellectual revolt should have found its special following among the antirepublican monarchists and Catholics of the right. On the whole, that was the case; yet some of the loudest exponents of the new irra-tionalism claimed to be republicans (Barrès and Sorel, notably), while some of the sharpest resistance to the irrationalist mood appeared on the extreme right and within the church. Charles Maurras, founder of the neoroyalist Action Française, professed the greatest contempt for the antirationalist outlook and claimed as his intellectual master none other than Auguste Comte. Maurras persuaded himself that his doctrine had been worked out in Comtean fashion,

---

[1] Robert A. Nisbet, *Emile Durkheim* (Englewood Cliffs, N. J.: Prentice-Hall, 1965), p. 28.

through a rigorously scientific study of the facts; his attempt to harness his new authoritarian nationalism to the monarchy and the church was not the product of emotional fervor but of hard-headed analysis, of "political science." Where Maurras went wrong was in assuming that his doctrines and his methods would appeal to other Frenchmen through their rational rather than their emotional force. In fact, Maurras encouraged the very mood he professed to abhor.

An even more serious kind of opposition to the new irrationalism was beginning to develop meanwhile within the church, in the form of neo-Thomism. Intellectually speaking, the nineteenth century had not been a brilliantly creative age for French Catholicism; there had been some remarkable pioneer ventures in the sphere of social action but little innovation in the realm of thought. The education of priests had grown narrow and routine-minded; fresh ideas, if they appeared, were viewed with suspicion. Toward the end of the century this stagnancy began to be stirred by several new currents. One group of "modernists" sought to reconcile church doctrines with the positivist, rationalist outlook. Another group of "fideists" turned in the opposite direction, arguing that religion should be separated completely from science and should be quite frankly rooted in purely irrational faith. But far more influential (and more acceptable to the Vatican) was the return to the doctrines of St. Thomas Aquinas that centered in France from the 1880's onward. The Thomists, following Aquinas, refused to accept the view that faith and reason were irreconcilable; and they sought to buttress the validity of the Catholic position by appeals to Aristotelian metaphysics. In 1906 the conversion of a young freethinker named Jacques Maritain (partly through the preparatory influence of Bergson's teaching) brought to neo-Thomism its most lucid and prolific exponent. By 1914 this was to be the most vigorous intellectual current within the church, with an even more notable future before it.

The rich variety and individuality of French intellectual life still made it possible, too, for paradoxical figures like Charles Péguy to appear and to resist inclusion in any school or category. Poet, essayist, and editor, Péguy began as a Marxian Socialist and ended as the most fervent of Catholic converts. He denounced the republican politicians with the intensity of a Maurras, yet steadily defended democratic processes and the republican system. An intense nationalist and a sincere admirer of the army, he crusaded ardently against nationalists and army during the Dreyfus case and died as a front-line soldier at the Marne. No Frenchman of his generation so thoroughly embodied the irrational spirit of the era; both his faith in God and his passionate patriotism were those of a mystic. He belongs somewhere in that long Catholic tradition that runs from Pascal to Emmanuel Mounier, and that makes of French intellectual history an especially complex mosaic.

# CHAPTER 24

# France, Europe, and the World, 1871–1914

To forget is as impossible as to pursue revenge.

D'ESTOURNELLES DE CONSTANT *(1913)*

The inception of the Third Republic found French prestige in Europe and the world at its lowest point since 1815. On the Continent, France was without friends or allies; overseas, France possessed only scattered remnants of a once-great empire. The contrast in 1914 was striking. France had become the keystone of one of Europe's principal power blocs and had brought under the tricolor the world's second largest colonial empire. In the light of this record, the historian Maurice Reclus may be right when he remarks that if a king or an emperor had ruled France between 1870 and 1914, it would be considered one of the great reigns in the nation's history.

The era was obviously one of notable achievement in foreign and imperial affairs. There is special irony, therefore, in the fact that few Frenchmen had any real interest in either foreign policy or colonial expansion in those years. Neither topic was an important issue in electoral campaigns; parliament rarely debated problems of foreign policy or empire; cabinets almost never fell on such an issue. Most politicians and most citizens had their minds fixed on such domestic problems as the church-state conflict or the Dreyfus controversy. This widespread indifference left a fairly free field of action to those few politicians and those specialized interest groups that looked beyond France's frontiers. The roles of such men as Ferry, Delcassé, Caillaux, and Poincaré therefore take on special significance.

French policy throughout the period 1871–1914 has often been described as dominated by a single passion: the thirst for revenge against Germany, the determination to recover Alsace-Lorraine. French diplomacy, according to this legendary view, was simply the story of a slow, steady, single-minded effort to break out of the isolation imposed by Bismarck and to encircle Germany for the final reckoning by force. Much has been made of the black crepe in which Parisians after 1871 veiled the statue of Strasbourg in the Place de la Concorde; and of the pathetic appeal of Daudet's classic story "The Last Class;" and of the Paris Opera's refusal to stage Wagner from 1870 to 1891; and of Gambetta's pungent phrase, "Never speak about it, always think about it." The *revanchard* thesis was perpetuated in many of the histories of diplomacy written after 1918; it was buttressed also by the tone of postwar French schoolbooks, which were inclined to see the Great War as the inevitable climax of a kind of Greek drama.

A variant form of this simple legend was the thesis advanced by the monarchist historian Jacques Bainville. To him, the Third Republic's political leaders were divided into heroes and villains: on the one hand, farsighted patriots; on the other, weak-kneed appeasers. The men in the former group—Delcassé, Clemenceau, Poincaré—courageously faced the fact that permanent coexistence with a dominant Germany was impossible, and that a new war must come eventually; they concentrated on building up French strength so that the disaster of 1871 would not be repeated. Bainville's second category, the appeasers, included most of the republic's prominent leaders: Thiers, Gambetta, Ferry, Hanotaux, Waldeck-Rousseau, Rouvier, Caillaux. These men, according to Bainville, lacked either courage or vision and were prepared to see France sink into the role of second-class state or even German satellite.

The story of French foreign policy was in fact more complex than either of these theories would suggest. France's feud with Germany over Alsace was not the only issue of importance, or even the central issue, in that era; and French political leaders cannot be so easily separated into heroes and villains. A. J. P. Taylor has suggested that the whole record of European diplomacy in the prewar years resembles a quadrille more than a tug-of-war; and his metaphor is well adapted to the role of French diplomacy.

The legend nevertheless contains at least a kernel of truth. For one thing, Alsace-Lorraine was the only important issue that never disappeared from the minds of French policy-makers from 1871 to 1914. It persisted, however, as an irritant rather than as a poison; it affected policy, but it was not the key to an understanding of all French attitudes and actions. If most Frenchmen never really forgave the Germans after 1871, the idea of *revanche* had clearly lost most of its appeal by the nineties, and even before that time references to the lost provinces had taken on a character that was often more ritualistic than passionate. Black crepe on the statue of Strasbourg, a special color for Alsace-Lorraine on maps—these manifestations were enough to soothe the injured pride of most Frenchmen. What persisted was a refusal to forget the two lost provinces, to accept their loss as final and unalterable. That refusal weighed on French policy-makers and narrowed the choices open to them. But it did not produce the kind of national psychosis that has sometimes been attributed to the French in those years.

There is a kernel of validity in the Bainville thesis too. If French political leaders cannot properly be divided into patriots and appeasers, they can be separated into exponents of two different methods in seeking some kind of co-existence with Germany. Alongside the Delcassés and the Poincarés, who doubted the Germans' willingness to tolerate a France of equal strength and prestige, there existed an almost unbroken series of politicians who hoped that a real reconciliation with Germany might be possible. A few of these men (although they dared not admit it publicly) were prepared to write off the lost provinces, if only the Germans would grant the Alsatians real autonomy or would return a strip of Lorraine as a kind of gesture. Some of them advocated schemes of economic collaboration—notably the development of Franco-German banking consortia for joint investment in Africa. Some of them—notably the rising Socialist leaders—were impressed by the size and apparent power of German socialism and foresaw as an imminent reality the friendly coexistence of several proletarian states in western Europe. If all of these hopes for reconciliation failed, that failure probably resulted more from the erratic and shortsighted policies of the German government than from the persistence of irreconcilable anti-German feeling in France. There is some reason to believe that a more receptive and imaginative attitude in Berlin might have pulled France into the German power bloc.

❖❖❖❖❖❖❖❖❖❖❖❖❖

For the first twenty years after 1871 French diplomatic isolation remained complete, and no leader or group made any real effort to break out of that isolation. While both Thiers and Gambetta hoped for an eventual understanding with either Britain or Russia, no good opportunity for such a rapprochement occurred. The price of an entente with Russia would have been a French promise of support to the Russians in their conflicts with Britain in the Middle East and the Far East; the price of an entente with the British would have been similar support in reverse. In both cases the risks seemed out of proportion to possible French gains. Besides, neither Russia nor Britain appeared very receptive, and the French themselves were not agreed as to which of these two potential allies they preferred. For ideological reasons, part of the monarchist right was inclined toward Russia, and the constitutional monarchists plus most of the Radical left toward Britain.

A third possible alternative did exist even then, in the form of a reconciliation with Germany. The price in this case, however, was far too high; France would have been required to renounce Alsace-Lorraine and to accept the status of client or veiled satellite, after the fashion of Austria-Hungary. The surprising thing is that the principal Opportunist leaders of the period nevertheless did toy with the idea of seeking some sort of understanding with the Germans. Gambetta, in spite of his intransigence in 1871 and his general reputation as a fire-eating patriot, went so far in 1878 as to consider a secret meeting with Bismarck, but gave up the idea as premature. Ferry went even farther; he was prepared to accept occasional collaboration with Germany on precise and limited issues. Ferry, like every other Frenchman of his day, could not accept the loss of Alsace-Lorraine, but as a hard-headed realist he declared that it would be senseless for France to keep its whole attention fixed on "a wound that will never stop bleeding." He was ready to divert some French strength to overseas expansion—not because Bismarck urged such a diversion, but in spite of the fact that Bismarck urged it. When Bismarck in 1884 hinted that he might welcome a Franco-German alliance aimed against Britain, Ferry ignored the feeler, probably because he quite rightly distrusted Bismarck's motives. Even if Bismarck had been sincere in wanting an alliance, it is unlikely that a formal reconciliation would have been possible so soon after 1871 unless the Germans had been remarkably generous. An active and vocal minority of Frenchmen remained intransigent toward Germany; indeed, the *revanche* idea really emerged in organized form at just this time, with the formation of Paul Déroulède's League of Patriots in 1882. This upsurge of chauvinism contributed to Ferry's downfall and to the Boulanger craze that followed. But if Frenchmen—politicians as well as common citizens—were still unwilling to accept anything that looked like renunciation of the lost provinces, most of them were no more enthusiastic about an armed crusade to recover them; and so Boulanger promptly followed Ferry into political oblivion.

If a reconciliation with Germany was still beyond the reach of the Opportunists, an entente with Britain seemed to be a more attainable alternative. The idea of forming a bloc of liberal states had an ideological appeal to most Opportunists even though, like Frenchmen generally, they were inclined to distrust the British. But any real hope of a Franco-British entente was destroyed for a generation by the emergence of an almost accidental conflict over Egypt. British forces landed there in 1882 to repress nationalist disorders and to protect British lives and property. Once there, they stayed, much to the irritation of the French political world. Frenchmen in general—both common citizens and business groups with interests in the eastern Mediterranean—seem to have been largely indifferent to the Egyptian imbroglio, but the Paris politicians somehow persuaded themselves that the nation had lost face. Over the next two decades French cabinets wasted much effort in a policy of pinpricks vainly intended to dislodge the British from Egypt. Repeated attempts to find a solution never quite succeeded; it was not until 1904 that this "absurd impasse" was resolved in the negotiations that led to the Entente Cordiale. The most ironic aspect of the whole affair was the fact that the British had landed in 1882 at the suggestion of French Premier Gambetta, and that Gambetta's purpose had been to use joint intervention as a first step toward creating an Anglo-French entente. After his fall from office the Chamber refused to vote funds for French participation in the landings, and somehow the device that was intended to produce an entente turned into a trap that postponed one for a generation.

Meanwhile, the French had embarked on their new course of imperial expansion in Africa and Asia. Jules Ferry, who usually gets the credit or the blame, has often been described as the political spokesman for business groups that were beginning to see vast potential markets and investment possibilities in the underdeveloped areas. Some colonialist pressure groups did exist in that era, but it is difficult to gauge either their strength or the manner in which their influence was channelled into politics. For the most part, the new imperialism of the 1870's and 1880's seems to have reflected noneconomic motivations: the hope of Christianizing and "civilizing" backward peoples, the desire to rebuild French prestige by proving the nation vigorous and virile.

Ferry evidently came to share these psychological and emotional drives, and used the economic argument mainly as an ex post facto justification. When he first took office as premier in 1881, he lacked interest in colonial expansion; and his decision to take over Tunisia in 1882 was reached rather reluctantly, under pressure from certain foreign ministry and army officials who had been preparing the action. Once converted, however, Ferry became a consistent and enthusiastic expansionist. During his second ministry (1883–85) he pushed a whole series of expeditions that had already been launched on a small scale by French traders, explorers, or army officers. The French foothold in southern Indo-China was expanded northward into Tonkin; de Brazza's acquisitions in the Congo were further extended; Djibouti on the Red Sea was annexed as a coaling station; the first steps were taken toward the conquest of Madagascar.

Ferry was probably ahead of both public and parliamentary opinion. Yet succeeding cabinets abandoned none of his acquisitions; and the process of absorbing bits and pieces of Africa and Asia continued, mainly through the autonomous action of traders and soldiers on the spot who pushed ahead without awaiting instructions from Paris. In the 1890's imperialism began to win broader popular support. Probably it was not mere chance that the same decade brought a rapid decline in the appeal of *revanche,* though which was cause and which effect is not clear. New and more vigorous pressure groups began to emerge: notably the Committee on French Africa in 1890 and the Colonial Union in 1895. These organizations were backed by textile exporters and investment banking groups as well as by the older colonialist elements in the church, the armed forces, and the patriotic societies. The economic factor thus assumed a steadily growing importance in French expansionism, even though it probably remained secondary throughout. General public interest, however, was still relatively slight and superficial when compared with British enthusiasm in the last years of the century. Jules Ferry, strolling past a lurid side show at the Paris Exposition of 1889, remarked bitterly: "There's all *they* know about the empire—the belly dance." Yet despite this indifference and the continued hostility of much of the left, the building of the empire was almost complete by the turn of the century.

The economic impact of empire on France was not very great in the pre-1914 era, for the French neither put much into their colonies nor got much out of them. Most of the colonial budget went for the salaries of administrators and for support of the army; public expenditure on public works, schools, and so on was meager. Private capital also shied away from the colonies; only 10 per cent of France's overseas investments went there, as compared to 25 per cent to Russia alone. Although the French reserved most of the imperial trade for themselves, the total remained small because most of the colonies were still so underdeveloped. The empire took only 13 per cent of France's exports, and it furnished little in return except foodstuffs. A few French companies and banks made handsome profits (notably in Indo-China); but for Frenchmen as a whole, the golden age of imperialism was largely gilt.

❖❖❖❖❖❖❖❖❖❖❖❖❖❖

In the midst of all this overseas activity, the French had achieved a major victory in Europe itself: a political accord signed with Russia in 1891 ended their long period of diplomatic isolation. The principal author of this pact, someone has said, was not a Frenchman at all, but the German foreign-office expert Baron von Holstein, on whose recommendation the Germans had abandoned their secret tie with Russia in 1890. But even before that date tensions between Germany and Russia had been growing, and French policy-makers had been moving to take advantage of this change. When Bismarck closed the German money market to the tsar's government in 1887, French lenders had stepped in as substitutes; and this flow of private funds, approved and encouraged by the French government, gradually thawed the tsar's frigid hostility toward the republic. More important still, the Russian government after 1890 began to fear that the Germans might decide to court France, and thus leave Russia in total isolation. In 1891 the tsar reluctantly approved a Franco-Russian agreement that was really nothing more than a friendly entente; the two nations agreed to consult together to maintain the peace of Europe and to take joint action if either party were attacked. French policy-makers set out at once to add a more precise military agreement, to which the tsar acceded only after long hesitation. A pact was drafted in 1892, but the tsar was so upset by reports of the Panama Scandal that he sought to restore the old tie with Germany instead. German obtuseness, however, drove the Russians back into French arms, and the military pact was signed in 1894. Although neither party used the word "alliance" for several years, an alliance in fact existed; and for the next decade it was to be the cornerstone of French foreign policy.

In France the Russian pact was welcomed enthusiastically by almost everyone except the left-wing Radicals and the Socialists. Over the next few years, however, some of its initial popularity ebbed away, for the Russian government showed little inclination to back French diplomatic action either on the Continent or in Africa. Some Frenchmen who wanted to take a stronger line in dealing with Germany felt that the Russian pact actually hampered them more than it helped them, for the Russians wanted no trouble with the Germans. The French, in turn, had no enthusiasm for supporting Russian ambitions in Turkey, where French investors held 60 per cent of the state debt, or in the Balkans, where the French had nothing to gain if their allies stirred up a crisis. Nevertheless, in 1899 Foreign Minister Delcassé decided to tighten France's rather lax ties with Russia. His motives were somewhat obscure; apparently he was concerned that the possible disintegration of Austria-Hungary might shift the European balance and threaten France's interests in the Mediterranean. In any case, he went to St. Petersburg and negotiated an additional accord that committed the two parties to collaborate in maintaining not only peace but also the balance of power in Europe. The new terms implied that France would back Russia if the Balkan *status quo* were upset, and they also implied that Russia would help France recover Alsace-Lorraine if the Central Powers sought to upset the European balance. The pact also added a provision for joint action if either party were attacked by the British. Without this reinforcement of the Franco-Russian alliance in 1899, the pact might have disintegrated before 1914.

The weaknesses of the Franco-Russian alliance during the 1890's kept two alternative schemes alive in Paris—an entente with Britain, or a reconciliation with Germany. Each of these alternatives is supposed to have had its vigorous proponent in the French foreign ministry: Gabriel Hanotaux for the pro-German orientation, Théophile Delcassé for the pro-British. Certainly both of these men had a remarkable opportunity to shape French policy; Hanotaux served as foreign minister from 1894 to 1898 with only one brief interruption, while Delcassé broke all durability records by holding the post from 1898 to 1905. They enjoyed other advantages too: the pattern of European power relationships was still some-what fluid, and the French political world was so preoccupied with domestic problems that both men had a fairly free hand in foreign affairs.

Hanotaux, according to some of his admirers, came nearer than any other French statesman to settling the old quarrel with Germany. He supported a scheme to challenge British power in Egypt by dispatching a French expedition across Africa to the upper Nile, consciously ignoring British warnings that this would bring trouble. Meanwhile, he avoided clashes with the Germans and was even on the verge of accepting a German proposal to collaborate against British expansion in Africa when he fell from office in 1898. Some historians conclude that Hanotaux's fall was a disaster that led eventually to the 1914 war; for he was replaced, they say, by a vindictive faction of Germanophobes, headed by Delcassé, who spent the next few years preparing the encirclement of Germany.

This thesis, though simple and appealing, has never been supported with adequate proof. There is no evidence that Hanotaux was systematically pro-German; indeed, at least twice he ignored German feelers for active collaboration against the British in South Africa. As for the Marchand expedition to challenge Britain in the upper Nile, Hanotaux was not its only or even its principal sponsor. Although Hanotaux's real aims have never been fully clarified, it seems probable that his policy resembled that of Jules Ferry: he was willing to consider occasional collaboration with Germany on precise issues but not a general reconciliation on German terms. Perhaps what he wanted was just enough Franco-German cooperation to frighten the British into letting France expand in Africa and Asia.

The traditional view of Delcassé's role after 1898 is even more controversial. His critics see him as the warmonger who took office with a single-minded pur-pose—to build an alliance system that would isolate Germany and open the way to revenge. Some of his admirers accept the same view but justify it: "France's answer to Bismarck," one of them has called him. Indeed, some of Delcassé's closest collaborators later lent support to this thesis by drawing a direct line from his aims in 1898 to the victory of France in 1918. Yet it is by no means clear that Delcassé was a single-minded *revanchard*. He seems to have been as much anti-British as anti-German before he took office; and his resentment toward Britain was intensified when his first act as foreign minister was a humiliating retreat before British threats in the upper Nile. The Marchand expedition, which had arrived at the town of Fashoda on the Nile, was ordered home in order to avoid possible war with Britain. "Fashoda," wrote the German ambassador in Paris triumphantly, "has made Frenchmen forget Alsace-Lorraine." It is true that Delcassé is supposed to have said privately: "As long as the Germans remain at Strasbourg and Metz, France will have but one permanent enemy: Germany." Yet several of his actions between 1898 and 1901 suggest a continuing suspicion of British aims and a willingness to collaborate with Germany in a kind of continental league against Britain. How far he would have been willing to go in this direction cannot be guessed, as the Germans failed to seize the opportunity. The only certainty is that by 1902 Delcassé had definitely decided to play the British rather than the German card and to prepare a Franco-British entente that finally materialized in 1904. German leadership, he had concluded, was so unstable that it would probably force France into a war sooner or later. This view of Delcassé would suggest that the British entente was not the central goal of his whole career, but simply one move in a complex chess game whose only goal was to strengthen France's diplomatic position in Europe.

Whatever the truth about Delcassé, he did solidify France's rather amorphous foreign policy into a pattern that was to endure for the next decade. Delcassé himself lost control of that policy in 1905 when German pressure forced him out of office. His error had been to push France along too far and too fast toward a set of commitments that involved serious risks, without making sure that the nation was ready either morally or materially to assume such risks. When the threat of war came, and Delcassé insisted on facing it, France's unreadiness emerged with disastrous clarity. Even the cabinet to which he belonged voted unanimously against him.

How responsible Delcassé was for bringing on that 1905 crisis is again unclear and controversial. For several years the French had been preparing to absorb Morocco, the last rich territory still open to domination in north Africa. One great power after another was bought off or gave its consent; even the British finally approved in 1904, as part of the Entente Cordiale arrangements. When the French took steps to move in, however, the German government intervened by sending Emperor Wilhelm II on a state visit to Morocco. Delcassé's critics contend that he had consciously sought to insult Berlin by buying off every power except Germany. His defenders reply that he had sounded out the German ambassador in Paris as early as 1901 and had been assured of German indifference toward Morocco. They see him as puzzled and upset by the Germans' sudden interference, but as willing to placate them by offering such assurances as the maintenance of the open door for German trade. When it became clear that they were not willing to be placated, but aimed to use the crisis as a lever to disrupt the new Franco-British entente, Delcassé grew angry and stubborn and insisted that France face Germany down.

Delcassé believed (or professed to believe) that the Germans were merely bluffing, and insisted that the British had given him oral assurances of military aid if it came to war. His cabinet colleagues were unwilling to take the risk, and in this they were probably right. War in 1905 would have been, as D. W. Brogan puts it, "deeply unpopular and certainly disastrous"; the nation was still seriously divided by the Dreyfus Affair and the church-state controversy, and army morale had reached its lowest point for decades. Ten years later a remarkable national and military revival had set in, and the chance of victory was much more real.

Most of Delcassé's work survived, despite his fall. Premier Maurice Rouvier, who took the lead in forcing him out of office, had not intended that the Delcassean system should continue. Rouvier not only feared that war would bring defeat, but he hoped that war might not be necessary at all; his ambition was to achieve a reconciliation with Germany through developing financial collaboration between French and German investment groups. An ex-banker himself, Rouvier remained in close touch with certain Paris banking circles that favored the creation of a Franco-German consortium to develop Africa and Asia. His hopes quickly evaporated, however; the German government proved much more difficult to deal with than he had expected. Berlin rejected his proposal of direct negotiations to liquidate the crisis and insisted on a full-scale international conference to exploit its diplomatic victory. Within six months Rouvier had concluded that France's security required the maintenance of Delcassé's alliance system. Neither he nor his immediate successors as premier made any attempt to carry out a diplomatic revolution. The most striking case was that of Clemenceau, premier from 1906 to 1909. The Tiger had been, ever since 1891, one of the bitterest critics of the Russian alliance. Once in power, though, he made no attempt to undermine the Russian pact, but rather approved its expansion into the Triple Entente in 1907. He sought also to reinforce the Entente Cordiale by urging the British to build up an army to go with their fleet. He and other Frenchmen feared that an armyless Britain in case of war might sink the German navy and let the French fight the rest of the war alone. On the other hand, the Clemenceau cabinet refused to expand its support of Russia to the point of risking war on behalf of the Russians in the Bosnian crisis of 1908–9.

Although the Delcassé policy was maintained by a series of Radical-led cabinets, the idea of reconciliation with Germany never died out. Its appeal was strongest among the left-wing parties. The Socialists were dazzled by the strength of the German Socialists, by far the largest Marxian party in Europe; and they continued to despise Russia as the heart of reaction. One segment of the Radical party also clung to the idea of reconciliation, mainly through the device of Franco-German financial collaboration in underdeveloped areas. Just as Maurice Rouvier had been spokesman for this viewpoint in 1905, now Joseph Caillaux sought to move toward the same end. Caillaux, a former treasury official turned politician, had kept many close ties with Parisian banking circles. His purpose, when he became premier in June, 1911, was to reduce Franco-German tensions through business collaboration. Some British diplomats at the time suspected him (probably unjustly) of aiming at a real diplomatic revolution that would jettison the Entente Cordiale and substitute a similar pact with Germany.

If Caillaux really hoped to carry through a major change in foreign policy, his plan was disrupted at the very outset. On the day that he took office a new Franco-German crisis over Morocco began; the German gunboat *Panther* arrived at Agadir to protect the lives and interests of German nationals (none of whom, incidentally, lived anywhere near Agadir). This German action was in fact a clumsy protest against a French move (ordered by Caillaux's predecessor) to convert Morocco into a protectorate. Several months of tension followed; eventually Caillaux, behind the back of his own foreign minister, tried a kind of appeasement by ceding a large slice of the French Congo to Germany in return for a free hand in Morocco. Perhaps he hoped that this might be a first step toward a broader rapprochement with Berlin. Instead, it produced just the opposite result. The angry Chamber of Deputies ratified the cession of the Congo strip but then overthrew the cabinet. A wave of anti-German feeling swept across the country; and partly in response to it, the politicians replaced Caillaux with Raymond Poincaré. This rigid and rather narrow Lorrainer, widely respected for his personal integrity, was to be both symbol and spokesman of the nationalist revival of 1911–14.

Both the origins and the character of this nationalist revival have been disputed. Was it aggressive or defensive in spirit? Was it the product of German saber rattling or of some native-born chauvinistic hysteria? Recent studies of the phenomenon (by German and American as well as French scholars) strongly support the view that it was primarily defensive; that it was the patriotic reaction of politicians and citizens who were baffled, upset, and increasingly resentful at the behavior of Berlin. This was not merely a revival of the *revanchard* chauvinism of the previous generation, the mood of Déroulède, Barrès, and Boulanger. The importance of the new spirit was that it affected precisely those kinds of Frenchmen who a generation earlier had opposed the chauvinists and had hoped for some kind of peaceful coexistence with Germany. Poincaré was not the political heir of Déroulède but rather of the Ferrys and the Gambettas— of those middle-of-the-road republicans who had been hostile to Boulanger's tub-thumping. And while the nationalist revival impinged most strongly upon the Moderates, it also affected a considerable segment of the Radicals, and even a few maverick Socialists.

It would be easy to conclude that the leaders in France's nationalist revival, whatever their motivation, contributed directly to the outbreak of war in 1914 by their intransigence, their chip-on-shoulder attitude in every international crisis. Poincaré especially, in his post as premier in 1912–13 and then as president of the republic, has often been denounced as a warmonger, a practitioner of what a later generation of Americans came to call "brinkmanship." The full evidence suggests a much less damning conclusion. There is very little proof indeed that Poincaré and the men around him were eager for an armed showdown with Germany; but they believed that it was likely to come, and they were determined to build up France's material, moral, and diplomatic strength so that out of war might come victory. They strengthened the standing army in the only way still open to them—by keeping draftees under arms for three years rather than two. They sought to persuade the British to accept more precise commitments and managed to get at least a little satisfaction. They took steps to reinvigorate the sagging Russian alliance by promising to support Russian diplomatic action in the Balkans. This did not involve goading the Russians to adopt a positive Balkan policy; rather, it meant abandoning direct attempts to restrain Russia there. As the Poincaré group saw it, the greatest danger facing France was not that Russia might drag France into an unnecessary war, but that Russia might desert France and rejoin Germany. Such a diplomatic revolution, French leaders believed, would leave France no alternative but to accept the role of a dependent power, subject to the unreasonable whims and dictates of an almost incomprehensible German governing elite.

This Poincaré policy would be open to serious criticism if there had existed at the time a sound and workable alternative. Some Frenchmen of that era did believe that such an alternative existed, and many historians have sided with them in retrospect. It was Caillaux who continued to be the chief representative of a softer policy of reconciliation. Caillaux retained most of his influence in the left-wing parties and managed to regain a cabinet post late in 1913. After the victory of the Radicals and Socialists in the parliamentary elections of April-May 1914, he ought to have been in line for a return to the premiership. His restoration to power would presumably have meant a reversal of the Poincaré policy of preparedness and tightened alliances, and a renewed effort at a Franco-German rapprochement. The experiment might have been forced on President Poincaré save for two assassinations: that of a Parisian editor by Madame Caillaux in March, that of the Archduke Franz Ferdinand at Sarajevo in June. Madame Caillaux's rash act temporarily clouded her husband's political chances; the archduke's death produced general war. Whether the Caillaux policy could have succeeded at that point in history is an unanswerable problem. One thing only is sure: its success would have depended more on men and moods in Berlin than on choices and attitudes in Paris.

# CHAPTER 25

# "The Grandeur and Misery of Victory," 1914–1919

When a man dies, I suffer. When fifteen hundred thousand die, that's statistics.

PHILIPPE BERTHELOT

No historian has yet managed to measure the effects of the First World War— "the Great War," as Frenchmen still call it—on the French nation. It is easy to cite statistics of physical damage or loss of life or decline in industrial production; it is much harder to assess the moral and psychological impact of this vast calamity, its permanently debilitating results, its traumatic effect on large parts of the population. Nations, like the individual human beings that compose them, are remarkably resilient things; history furnishes many examples of their vigorous recovery from periods of disaster. Perhaps that very resilience tends to conceal some of the deeper effects that endure beneath the surface of the system and that surprise observers by their long-range consquences. Such lesions are more likely to be concealed when a nation seems to triumph over disaster— when the long strain of war ends in what men call victory. Nations that are beaten undergo long examination and self-examination; the effects of the war may even be exaggerated to the point of producing a kind of national neurosis. Nations that triumph are generally assumed to be, and assume themselves to be, healthy organisms that have somehow been spared by the plague.

The real significance of the Great War for the student of French history lies not so much in the dramatic details of the military effort or the tensions of wartime politics as in the total impact of the experience on the France of the next generation. That impact can hardly be overrated. More often, it has been underrated—especially during the interwar era, when it seemed that France had survived the crisis almost unchanged, had emerged even stronger than before, and had recovered its position as the dominant power of Europe. Some of the effects of this misconception will be examined in succeeding chapters.

The test of war presents any democratic system with difficult and paradoxical problems: problems that are intensified when no one has foreseen a long war and when the fighting occurs on the nation's own soil. That the French republic survived this kind of test is in some ways astonishing. The fact of victory in 1914-18, contrasted with disastrous defeat in 1870-71 and 1939-40, suggests some intriguing problems of comparison. One explanation would find the difference in the realm of national morale: in the fact that Frenchmen in 1914 were more united, more enthusiastic, more determined than in 1870 or 1939. This was probably the case at the outset, and it contributed much to France's success in checking the initial German drive; but as the Great War dragged on, disunity and defeatism did grow to serious proportions without producing military collapse. Another explanation might trace the difference to the realm of equipment and manpower: to the fact that in 1914 France was better prepared materially and was less heavily outnumbered than in the earlier and later wars. It is probably true that in relative numbers of men under arms the French were somewhat better off than they had been in 1870, in spite of the fact that population trends had favored the Germans. Universal military service and the three-year service law had partially redressed the balance. But the most notable advantage the French possessed in 1914 was that only in that war could they count on Russian manpower to divert much of Germany's striking force.

Still a third explanation would attribute France's success in the 1914 war to better military leadership, to the vigor and imagination of French generalship, which proved more than a match for that of the enemy. Such a thesis is both highly controversial and difficult to test. There had undoubtedly been a notable current of rejuvenation and of new energy in the French high command just before 1914, and this current surely contributed to the victory. But there is not much evidence of imaginative thinking or of strategic genius in the army's planning just prior to the war. Plan XVII, in effect when the war broke out, was no better adapted to the times than was the French war plan of 1940; it involved an immediate offensive into Alsace and Lorraine and left Paris exposed to a German drive through Belgium. French intelligence reports about German strength and plans seem to have been little better or worse than those of 1940 (though certainly better than those of 1870). The high command had shown little inclination in the prewar years to experiment with new kinds of weapons; advocates of more heavy artillery were brushed off by those who considered the smaller, more mobile 75mm. cannon adequate for all purposes—"the Father, Son, and Holy Ghost of warfare," as someone put it. To the extent that new ideas about strategy and tactics had affected the army, they tended to be the wrong ones for the kind of war that was impending. The most vocal and vigorous faction in the officer corps had been preaching the virtues of all-out attack by masses of infantry unencumbered by any other equipment than a rifle and a mood of exaltation. The *furia francese,* these doctrinaires contended, would more than offset the enemy's superior numbers. A good many French soldiers were sacrificed to this religion of the offensive during the Great War; but luckily, the dominant faction in the high command viewed it with some skepticism and was flexible enough to adapt its strategy to the needs of a stalemated defensive war.

The army's commander-in-chief, General Joffre, belonged to that new group of republican (and perhaps Freemason) officers elevated to top command posts after the Dreyfus Affair. The Radical cabinet of 1911 had chosen him in preference to such officers as Philippe Pétain, a freethinker who was reputed to be a monarchist, and Ferdinand Foch, a fervent Catholic with Jesuit training and a Jesuit brother. Joffre's interest was the army, not politics; and if he lacked imagination and flair, he had the kind of stolid, imperturable temperament that adapted him well to a dragging defensive war. Although his Plan XVII put the French armies at an initial disadvantage, Joffre was far less deeply committed than the Germans to a single recipe for victory. When the German forces drove through Belgium into France, Joffre acted in time to shift troops back to Paris, where they successfully checked the German attack at the Marne River in September. Joffre and the French high command undoubtedly deserved much of the credit for this decisive success; but they were aided by the fact that the German army's former commander General Schlieffen had endowed the attackers with a dangerously risky plan. If superior French generalship was partly responsible for victory in the Great War, it was mainly because German military leadership fell so far below the standards of 1870 and 1940.

At the outset of war both politicians and public in France had temporarily abdicated into the hands of the high command; the country was ruled for the first few months by a tacit military dictatorship. The war of 1914 has been called the last popular war in history. Many (though certainly not all) Frenchmen greeted its outbreak with enthusiasm—partly because it came as a kind of emotional release after a long period of pent-up tension, partly because none of them foresaw its scope and duration. Even the antimilitarists, so vocal in past years, forgot their suspicions of the army. The spirit of *union sacrée,* while it lasted, was intense. On the floor of the Chamber of Deputies, Edouard Vaillant, a Communard in 1871, and Albert de Mun, an officer in Thiers's army that repressed the Commune, shook hands for the first time in their political careers. The cabinet was broadened to include every group; it ranged from the Socialist Jules Guesde to the conservative Denys Cochin, "the first qualified representative of Catholic interests" to enter a French cabinet since MacMahon's day. Prewar plans for the preventive arrest of a thousand trade union and extreme-leftist leaders were cancelled as unnecessary. The laws exiling the religious congregations were suspended, permitting many Jesuits and Assumptionists to return for army service.

Joffre's success at the Marne temporarily strengthened the high command's authority and enabled him to keep the post of commander-in-chief until 1916. As the months passed, however, the politicians gradually recovered their voices and began to chip away at the high command's power. Some of the friction that developed between Paris and Joffre's headquarters was political in character; it derived from a conflict between Joffre and his subordinate Albert Sarrail, "the Jacobin general," hero of the more doctrinaire Radicals and the Socialists for his vigorously leftist views. A personal conflict between the two men, caused by Sarrail's ambitious intrigues and Joffre's jealousy, led to Sarrail's demotion in 1915. The parliamentary left thought that it smelled a reactionary plot; the incident almost turned into a crisis and seriously shook the "sacred union" for the first time. Other complaints by the politicians were better founded: they were inspired by growing dissatisfaction with Joffre's conduct of the war. His "nibbling policy" of limited attacks on the German trenches bled the army without producing much in the way of results. Meanwhile his refusal to strengthen the defenses of the great fortress city of Verdun, based on his conviction that the Germans would not attack there, also brought rising criticism. When the Germans did strike early in 1916 and overran most of Verdun's outer defenses, Joffre proposed to abandon the city and retreat to a shorter defense line. The politicians openly rebelled against this scheme on the ground that it might lead to disintegration of the army's and the nation's morale. The formidable task of saving Verdun was turned over to the sector commander, General Pétain, who managed to blunt the German offensive in perhaps the most critical action of the whole war. It was clear that Pétain's victory owed little to Joffre. Late in 1916 the accumulated dissatisfaction in Paris led to Joffre's transfer to a desk job in the war ministry and his replacement by a junior general named Nivelle.

Joffre's fall marked the end of the long struggle between military and civilian authorities that had gradually eroded the initial predominance of the high command. From late 1916 to late 1917 the politicians were in the saddle; the Chamber and Senate exercised direct and constant control over both headquarters and cabinet. Nivelle was parliament's man; his vigor and charm had impressed touring politicians at the front, and his plan for an all-out series of coordinated attacks to win the war at once appealed to men who were growing war-weary. Unfortunately Nivelle overlooked one essential factor: to succeed, his plan needed large reserves of manpower, which in the spring of 1917 simply did not exist. The so-called Nivelle offensive was a bloody fiasco and was followed by a near collapse of morale in parts of the French army; whole companies "mutinied" in the sense that they refused orders to go over the top.

The disaster led to the substitution of Pétain for Nivelle. Pétain got the mutinies in hand by a policy of mixed repression and generosity. He immediately cancelled any further offensive actions and decided to mark time until large-scale American aid could arrive. "Squat, do little, and keep the losses small"—such was his doctrine. But if the French army had reached and survived its low point in the spring of 1917, behind the front the nadir was still to come. By the autumn of 1917 there was a serious current of defeatism in Paris and rising pressure for an immediate white peace. This sentiment was strongest among the Socialists and left-wing Radicals. The outbreak of the war had led the entire left to rally solidly to the nation's defense; the Socialist deputies had voted un-animously for war credits, and some of them had gone off to the front to die at the Marne. In 1915 came the first few defections, and from that time onward defeatism grew steadily. By 1916 the white-peace advocates within the Socialist party were almost strong enough to control the organization; only the influence of men like Guesde kept the Socialist delegation in parliament from going into open opposition. The events of 1917—the Russian upheaval and general war-weariness—played into the hands of the defeatists, but it was not until the party congress of July 1918, that they got control of the Socialist party machinery and policy. By that time the moment had passed when they might have done serious damage to the French war effort.

The potential symbol and spokesman for the defeatists was not a Socialist, however, but the Radical Joseph Caillaux. The ex-premier was still convinced that the war might have been averted had he been in power in 1914. During several wartime trips abroad he allegedly made contact with German agents to discuss the possibility of a negotiated peace. Meanwhile, Caillaux's friend Jean-Louis Malvy, minister of interior, fed secret subsidies to defeatist newspapers in Paris. Even Aristide Briand, after his overthrow as premier early in 1917, apparently had "fugitive contacts" with German agents in Switzerland.

By the autumn of 1917 there was grave doubt of France's ability or willing-ness to fight on toward victory. Squabbling had become so bitter, suspicion so widespread, that President Poincaré faced a dramatic choice: either a Caillaux government that would presumably try for a white peace at once, or a Clemen-ceau cabinet that would stand for a fight to the finish. For three years Clemenceau in his newspaper had been denouncing with equal vehemence the defeatists and the leaders of France's war effort—including Poincaré himself; but Poincaré's resentment was outweighed by his revulsion against Caillaux's defeatism. When the shaky Painlevé cabinet was overthrown in November 1917, the president promptly called Clemenceau to the premiership. Abruptly, the period of parliamentary domination ended; France entered upon a kind of civilian dictatorship, or the nearest thing to it that the republic had known since the days of Gambetta in 1870.

Clemenceau was the last survivor of the old Jacobin tradition that had once been the hallmark of the Radicals. He and his old political colleagues had long since parted company; his support in 1917 came almost solidly from the parties of center and right. Clemenceau angered the left by his prompt and brutal suppression of defeatists of all kinds; he made no distinction between disreputable German hirelings like the journalist Almereyda and idealists or imprudent schemers like Caillaux and Malvy. The latter were both arrested, though they were eventually acquitted of the charge of illegal contacts with the enemy. Even Briand was threatened with prosecution unless he retired into the background. Many leftists never forgave Clemenceau; their chance for revenge was to come in 1920, when they helped to defeat the Tiger for the presidency.

Clemenceau's harsh obstinacy, much like that of Winston Churchill in a later war, injected a new spirit into the nation; morale stiffened just enough and just in time to allow France to survive the great German spring and summer offensives in 1918. Once again the enemy reached the Marne, not far from Paris. At the critical moment Clemenceau managed to win over his allies to the principle of a single command for all allied forces in the west; and it was largely his decision that gave this assignment to General Ferdinand Foch rather than to Pétain. The Tiger's feelings about Foch had always been mixed; he disliked the general's Jesuit connections, yet he was attracted by Foch's gamecock qualities and was put off by Pétain's defeatist tendencies. Within an hour after Foch had been named general-in-chief of the Allied armies in France, he and Clemenceau were engaged in a bitter controversy, and serious friction continued to mark their relationship throughout the last months of the war. Clemenceau repeatedly tried to give Foch suggestions or orders; Foch answered sharply or, worse still, ignored the premier entirely. The infuriated Clemenceau became persuaded that Foch and Poincaré had entered into a conspiracy against him. Yet to his credit, the Tiger let Foch have his way and backed him till the end. Undoubtedly, part of the explanation for France's victory in 1918 must be found in the kind of leadership France got at the critical moment. Probably a Clemenceau and a Foch would not have been enough to turn the tide either in 1870 or in 1940; but if there had been no Clemenceau and Foch in 1918, the outcome of the war might have been quite different.

❖❖❖❖❖❖❖❖❖❖❖❖❖

Victory, like champagne, produces a certain temporary delirium in those who savor it. Not all Frenchmen resisted that delirium in 1918 and after; no people can easily endure such an ordeal, emerge victorious, and face the dismaying fact that they are worse off than before the war began. One effect of the conflict was to reassure Frenchmen about their governmental system. Before 1914 it had been widely criticized as ineffective and unstable; yet it had survived and beaten the great autocracies and had managed to turn up abler leadership than did the authoritarian regimes. The republic's greater flexibility quite rightly proved to be a virtue; the regime had managed to adapt itself to changing wartime circumstances. Unfortunately, it was easy to carry this reassurance too far and to conclude that critics of the system had no valid case whatsoever. The republic had admirably survived the terrible test of a long war, but it was destined to be less effective in facing the domestic problems of an industrial age.

Although many Frenchmen and foreigners assumed that France would now play the dominant role in Europe, taking the place of Bismarck's Germany, there were some who sensed that France could probably never again face another crisis like this one. No other warring nation had suffered such high proportionate manpower losses: of the eight million men mobilized, five million were killed or wounded. The dead alone amounted to 10 per cent of the active male population, and even more were partially or totally incapacitated. No nation could less afford such losses, especially when they were concentrated in the middle years of the male population. The demographic problem, already grave, threatened to become insoluble. Material losses were less critical, yet exceptionally severe; a large segment of France's best industrial and agricultural territory had been devastated. Industrial production, despite the building of new war plants, dropped to 60 per cent of the prewar figure; in later retrospect, it was estimated that French economic growth had been set back by almost a decade.

Still another war-born problem was that of public finance. From one of the world's most solid currencies in 1914, the franc was suddenly transformed into one of the most unstable. So long as the war lasted, depreciation reached only 15 per cent, but within a year after victory it had passed 50 per cent. Wartime governments had preferred borrowing or inflation rather than a pay-as-you-fight policy; the tax yield during the war years scarcely exceeded the prewar level. True, parliament finally adopted an income-tax law in 1916, but the rates were too low to produce much revenue. In addition to the heavy load of domestic and foreign debt in 1918, France had lost much of its overseas investment, including the huge sums sunk in tsarist Russia. France's condition was by no means hopeless at the end of the war; the nation remained rich enough to recover financial stability if its leaders and citizens had seen the problem clearly and had acted with vigor and dispatch. But the financial impact of war plus postwar policy errors did turn the financial problem into a major source of French weakness during the interwar era.

In many ways the war did not so much alter basic trends in France as speed up trends already under way. Such was the case, for example, in the demographic sphere and in the nation's social and economic evolution. The wartime experience did profoundly transform France's industrial structure—more profoundly, indeed, than any other experience of war or depression in modern times. These changes derived not only from the army's need for war material, but also from an enforced shift in industrial location. Because the area that included most of French heavy industry was overrun and occupied, a new heavy industry had to be created in Paris and in central and southern France. For the first time Paris became a major center of large industry; until now it had been mainly small plants that had clustered around the capital. At the same time there occurred a rapid shift from textiles to metallurgy. In 1906 the balance had been three to one against metallurgy in percentages of industrial workers employed; by 1920 metallurgical workers outnumbered those in textiles. This change meant not merely new products, but a new kind of labor force—more concentrated, more unskilled, more inclined to radicalism. The war brought a million new members into the trade unions; most of them were fresh immigrants from rural districts, without the individualistic tradition of workers who came of artisanal backgrounds. The metallurgical workers became the most radical segment of labor, and the red belt of industrial suburbs around Paris became the chief Communist stronghold between the wars.

The effect of the war on the industrial ownership group is harder to assess. The army's insatiable need for munitions and supplies opened up easy avenues to men of enterprise; the number of millionaires sharply increased, for profit controls were inadequate to check the rise of great wealth. Yet there is not much evidence that the war stimulated the growth of a new kind of business elite. No significant group of self-made men rose to industrial prominence; rather, it was the established families of the upper bourgeoisie that profited by the opportunities offered. Perhaps that was because only the older families had ready access to credit for building new plants or converting to war production; perhaps it was because their political connections put them in touch with the government offices that controlled war contracts. At any rate, there was neither a notable broadening of the business elite nor a real change in the outlook of that elite. The cautious, conservative attitude typical of French business continued dominant into the postwar era.

The war's impact on the peasantry was clearer and more profound. No other segment of society was so hard hit by mobilization; few peasant boys were deferred, whereas a fair proportion of factory workers and miners had to be excused from duty at the front. It has been estimated that half of France's war casualties were peasants. Among those who survived, many had had a taste of city life and refused to go back to their isolated rural existence. On the other hand, peasants who stayed on the land during the war years attained a temporary prosperity such as they had never known. Many farmers paid off old mortgages and bought more land; many marginal farms were enabled to survive for an additional decade. Yet the long-range result of the war was to inject a new spirit of questioning and discontent—not only among those whom the army had uprooted, but also among those who stayed behind. The peasantry "went into the war docile and resigned; it came out resentful and ready to complain."

On the whole, then, the war's effect on France's social and economic structure was to shake it up without producing really revolutionary or fundamental changes. The country emerged still a curious blend of dynamic and static elements; the upheaval and its aftermath produced no large rootless element of *déclassés,* or "marginal men," as it did in Germany. The long-range effects seem to have been strangely mixed: on the one hand, an increased stability approaching the point of stagnation; on the other hand, a growth in stresses and tensions within this rigidified social and economic structure. Perhaps the upheaval was both too great and not great enough for a nation faced with the problem of converting itself to twentieth-century conditions.

❖❖❖❖❖❖❖❖❖❖❖❖❖❖

France's role at the Paris peace conference forms a necessary addendum to any account of the war. At the time, and during the interwar years, the Anglo-Saxon world was inclined to view that role critically: France was seen as a kind of narrow-minded Shylock determined to get its pound of flesh and indifferent to the disastrous consequences of such an attitude. Hitler's aggressive career tended to reverse this view; during the Second World War the French began to seem the misunderstood heroes of the Paris conference, who alone had clearly perceived the German threat and had urged the creation of solid barriers on the Rhine and in eastern Europe. These fluctuating estimates tend to conceal the essential fact that the real errors of Western statesmen were committed not at the conference itself but during the two postwar decades, and that these mistakes did not grow inevitably out of the nature of the peace settlement. It can be argued, as a theoretical proposition, that if the French had been more generous and reasonable in 1919, a peaceful democratic Germany might have emerged and endured. It can be argued likewise that if the French had been allowed to write a really severe treaty, perhaps Hitler could have been stopped in time. Treaties, however, are less important for what they contain than for how they are applied; the effectiveness of either a soft or a severe treaty would have depended on the wisdom of interwar statesmanship. As it turned out, Western leaders were incapable of administering a compromise treaty like Versailles; there is no reason to suppose that they would have done much better with any other kind.

At the outset of the peace conference Clemenceau's program included the following essential points: the creation of one or several buffer states on the west bank of the Rhine, permanently occupied by French troops or linked with France; the establishment of strong new states on Germany's eastern border (notably a Poland *"forte, forte, et très forte,"* in Clemenceau's words); the payment of reparations by the Germans to cover the cost of restoring all war damage (the word "damage" being broadly interpreted). French negotiators were also determined to secure a share of the German and Turkish colonial empires, as provided by wartime secret treaties.

Not all Frenchmen were agreed on this program. Some of them (notably on the left) regarded it as too severe and likely to destroy the hope of building a new harmonious European order. Some of them thought it too soft: they favored the permanent dismemberment of Germany into several states and total disarmament of these states. As the conference proceeded, however, the bitterest criticism came not from those who had opposed the Clemenceau program but from those who had initially approved it, and who believed that the Tiger was sacrificing too much of it without a fight. These critics—men like Foch, Poincaré, Barrès—later argued that if Clemenceau had stood intransigently on his original demands, the British and Americans in the end would have accepted them, since both those nations had already achieved their war aims: control of the seas in the one case, national security in the other.

Clemenceau, however, at no time believed it possible for France to dictate the peace terms. He was aware that the French had not won the war alone; indeed, he was aware that France's victory had been in some ways a kind of lucky accident. Without British and American aid, the disaster of 1870 might have been repeated; and American aid had come not through clever French diplomacy, or even through French righteousness, but through German blundering. Neither did Clemenceau believe, deep down, that the permanent repression of Germany was possible. His anti-German epigrams have too often been taken as examples of a bigoted extremism: "There are twenty million Germans too many"; "The more Germany is split up, the better I'll like it." Less well known, but more revealing, were his remarks before the French Senate during the subsequent debate on treaty ratification: "Today, we are masters. Nevertheless, if we want conciliation in the interests of our children, we must use this superiority with moderation.... I do not want to run after their [the Germans'] good will— I don't have the proper feelings for that. Still, sixty million people in the center of Europe will take some room, especially when they are men of science, of method."

The division among Frenchmen over the peace settlement was most clearly revealed when the Versailles Treaty came before the Chamber of Deputies for ratification. The debate was no mere formality; it dragged on, interspersed with other business, for six full weeks between August and October 1919. Criticisms were showered on Clemenceau from almost every side of the Chamber; from *Père la Victoire,* said the wits, he had been transmuted into *Perd la Victoire.* The Socialists took the line that the treaty was too harsh for the new democratic and peaceful Germany; French policy, they argued, ought to be based on collaboration with that Germany and on active participation in the League of Nations. But the center and right critics took exactly the opposite position and, by their skepticism toward both the new Germany and the League, revealed a deep strain of inferiority and defeatism. The treaty, they charged, contained no real guarantee against German recovery or rearmament and no assurance that the Germans would ever pay reparations. The American and British aid treaties were of doubtful value and would probably be repudiated by the Americans anyway. Only the annexation or indirect control of the Rhineland-Saar area would have provided security, they asserted. A few of these critics, more farsighted, complained also of the string of weak states set up in eastern Europe. "In reality," warned one of them, "you have Balkanized eastern Europe. If this continues, you may see them Bolshevized tomorrow."

Clemenceau himself sat grimly silent through most of the debate, while his younger lieutenants offered the government's rebuttal. The error of these spokesmen was that they went too far in defending the treaty as an almost foolproof instrument. They insisted that the critics' fears of German evasion or of future allied weaknesses were groundless; they argued that if the Americans should repudiate Wilson's military-aid treaty, France would be legally authorized to seize the Rhineland by force. What they failed to do was to face up realistically to any of the difficult problems, such as how Germany could pay large reparations without first getting a grip on much of world trade, and how France could checkmate German power if the wartime coalition disintegrated. The effect of their presentation was to mislead many Frenchmen both within and outside parliament about the impending problems of the postwar era.

Clemenceau alone sought to inject a more realistic note, when he rose to speak at the very end of the debate. "What you are about to vote on today," he told the Chamber, "is not even a beginning, but the beginning of a beginning." His critics were right, he asserted, when they found the treaty full of imperfections; they had missed the real point. "M. Louis Marin [a right-wing deputy] went to the heart of the question when ... he said with a touch of despair: 'Your treaty condemns France to eternal vigilance.'" That, said the Tiger bluntly, was exactly and unavoidably the case. "Peace is only war pursued by other means.... I see life as a perpetual conflict in war and in peace...; that conflict you cannot suppress." Like Winston Churchill a generation later, Clemenceau was offering his countrymen blood, toil, tears, and sweat, but in this case he was doing so just at the moment of triumph, when most Frenchmen desperately wanted to relax behind some puncture-proof barricade. If the Clemencist spirit, hardheaded yet not inflexible, had been widely shared by Frenchmen at the time and over the two decades to follow, the course of French and European history might have been quite different. But it would have required more than Clemenceau's valedictory speech to offset the illusions already implanted about the treaty and to alter the mood of the times. The interwar era was already committed to indulgence in wishful thinking and the propagation of myths. Perhaps, after such a war, nothing else could have been expected.[1]

---

[1] Three years later, a young admirer called on Clemenceau as the latter sat in embittered retirement. "Everything I have done has been wasted," growled the old Jacobin. "In twenty years, France will be dead."

CHAPTER 26

# The Varieties of History,
# 1870–1919

The Third Republic stands out as the Methuselah of modern French regimes—the only one since 1789 that has lasted longer than a generation (though the Fifth is now bidding to become a second exception). One might expect historians to grapple with that fact, in an effort to explain both the general pattern of instability and the particular exception that was the Third Republic. Yet surprisingly few of them have tried to do so in any serious and sustained way. Perhaps historians tend to overlook the big and obvious questions, the kind that occur to nonspecialists; or perhaps they prefer to leave them open, for students to wrestle with in seminar discussions or on examination papers. At any rate, truly interpretive works that view the Third Republic as a whole, and that try to place it within the broader context of modern France's development, are rare.

One of those exceptions is David Thomson's *Democracy in France since 1870* —a sophisticated analysis of the political and social dynamics of the system. Thomson argues that the Third Republic, by combining conservative institutions with revolutionary ideas, was "the first successful attempt to reconcile the conservative and revolutionary traditions in France." He believes, however, that a turning point came about 1905, when the regime's assets gradually turned into liabilities. The new problems of an industrial age could no longer be handled by a political system that was little more than "a mirror or a photographic negative—reflecting or reproducing accurately the conflicts of social and political forces" in the nation.

François Goguel's *La politique des partis sous la IIIe république* remains a solid reference for those who would understand how the political system worked.

The core of French political life, according to Goguel, was an enduring conflict between two rival "political temperaments"—that of "Movement" and that of "Established Order." These categories he considers more fundamental than André Siegfried's older right-center-left classification, for on major issues, he contends, the right and center always joined to defend the Established Order. This schema is probably too rigid to embrace all the complexities of the republic's history, but it offers a useful base from which to develop alternative models.

D. W. Brogan's *France Under the Republic, 1870–1939*, remains a kind of minor classic. Brilliant, witty, erudite, Brogan roams through the thickets of French politics with consummate ease, leaving the reader somewhat bewildered but more often dazzled and informed. His book, like that of another British expert, Alfred Cobban (*A History of Modern France*, vol. 3) advances no general thesis about the Third Republic, but both studies represent the views of urbane and perceptive British liberals toward their puzzling cross-Channel neighbor. More difficult to classify is a blockbuster by Theodore Zeldin: *France, 1848–1945*. Again, his work is not bound together by any overarching theme, except perhaps the thesis that France is too complex for any kind of confident generalization. Zeldin surveys in almost microscopic detail a wide variety of unorthodox as well as standard topics: from politics and society to values and mores, from taste and cuisine to "worry, boredom, and hysteria." The effect is kaleidoscopic, but the book sparkles with original insights and esoteric discoveries.

Eugen Weber's *Peasants into Frenchmen* is, on the other hand, a book with a clear thesis, and one that challenges orthodox beliefs. He argues that a clear sense of nationhood did not arrive in rural France (which was then most of France) until the last decades of the nineteenth century, and that it emerged thanks mainly to some of the Third Republic's innovations—an improved network of railways and roads, a system of universal education, and universal military service. Accompanying this central argument is a colorful description of nineteenth-century manners and morals in the provinces. Weber's concept has been disturbing to those Frenchmen who have always believed that the sense of Frenchness is old and deep, dating back at least to the Great Revolution (or even, in subliminal ways, to the Middle Ages). Still, his thesis may help to explain why the Third Republic survived so long when previous regimes had been so short-lived.

❖❖❖❖❖❖❖❖❖❖❖❖❖

Most of the topical studies mentioned in chapter 17 carry on their particular threads through the Third Republic. To supplement them, a vast library of monographs and biographies is available, but only a few notable examples will be mentioned here. Michael Howard's *The Franco-Prussian War* is a magisterial account of the conflict that gave birth to the Third Republic. Karl Marx's *The Civil War in France* (on the Paris commune) remains a classic of "instant history" and has continued to inspire his followers as they re-examine the episode. Recent evaluations of the Commune range from orthodox and revisionist Marxian versions (Jean Bruhat et al., *La Commune de 1871*; Henri Lefebvre, *La proclamation de la Commune*) to more balanced accounts such as Stewart Edwards's *The Paris Commune 1871*. The Dreyfus Affair has provoked a constant flow of books (several of them excellent) that attempt to untangle its mysteries and to explain its significance; perhaps the most readable and thorough account is that of Jean-Denis Bredin, *The Affair*. On political leaders and movements, Eugen Weber's *Action Française* and Harvey Goldberg's *The Life of Jean Jaurès* stand out. Weber's book not only assesses the importance of Maurras's movement (its influence lasted for three generations and, some think, exceeded that of any rival force except Marxism) but also illumines bourgeois society and right-wing politics generally in the pre-1914 era. Goldberg shows why Jaurès remains the greatest figure in France's pantheon of left-wing leaders, and in the process provides capsule summaries of the growth of the Socialist party as well. Zeev Sternhell's controversial study *La droite révolutionnaire 1885–1914* finds in the Action Française and in the thought of some other doctrinaires of the time the emergence of a genuine French fascism.

The position of Frenchwomen in the later nineteenth century has recently been transformed from a neglected field into the scene of intensive cultivation (mainly by Americans). Bonnie G. Smith, in *Ladies of the Leisure Class*, portrays the lives and values of middle-class Frenchwomen in the industrial north. Stephen C. Hause and Anne R. Kenney, in *Women's Suffrage and Social Politics in the Third French Republic*, show that a large and active feminist movement existed in that period. Patrick K. Bidelman, in *Pariahs Stand Up!*, introduces the founding generation of feminist leaders. Charles Sowerwine, in *Sisters or Citizens?*, explains the limited appeal of the Socialist movement to Frenchwomen, and of feminist ideas to those women who *were* Socialists.

Labor history is enriched by such works as Michelle Perrot's massive account of strike activity (*Les ouvriers en grève: France 1871–1890*); Joan W. Scott's *The Glassworkers of Carmaux*; Donald Reid's *The Miners of Decazeville* (which ranges through the history of a mining town from its founding in the 1820's to the closing of the mines in the 1960's); and Kathryn Amdur's *Syndicalist Legacy* (a study of rival currents within the trade union movement in two French cities in the early twentieth century).

On foreign policy there are two weighty monographs on France's relations with Germany and Russia: Raymond Poidevin's *Les relations économiques et financières entre la France et l'Allemagne de 1898 à 1914,* and René Girault's *Emprunts russes et investissements français en Russie, 1887–1914.* The motives and methods of colonial expansion are examined by Henri Brunschwig (*French Colonialism 1871–1914: Myths and Realities*) and Jacques Thobie (*La France impériale, 1880–1914*). Brunschwig seeks to refute the economic interpretation of French imperialism, while Thobie reasserts its importance.

Intellectual and cultural developments are clarified by Claude Digeon's classic study *La crise allemande de la pensée française, 1870–1914,* and by Roger Shattuck's *The Banquet Years: The Arts in France, 1885–1918.* Digeon shows the impact of the defeat by Prussia on the national self-image, and the way in which that self-image continued to be strongly affected by the French view of Germany as rival, enemy, or model. Shattuck's lively essay deals with the avant-garde writers and artists who broke with tradition to foreshadow the dominant cultural mood of the twentieth century.

For the years of the Third Republic, as for the earlier nineteenth century, novels provide a rich supplement for historical understanding. Émile Zola's works are indispensable; Zola set out to chronicle his own times, and documented his novels with all the care of a superior journalist. His Rougon-Macquart series, though set in the time of Napoleon III, draws mainly on episodes of the early Third Republic. *The Debacle* is a commentary on the Franco-Prussian War; *Germinal* contains an unforgettable picture of life in the northern coal-mining area, and describes a great strike that occurred at Anzin in 1884; *The Dram Shop* is a grim study of slum life in Paris. Maurice Barrès's trilogy *Le roman de l'énergie nationale* portrays, from a right-wing point of view, the intellectual and political scene in Paris in the period 1880–1900. Paul Bourget's *The Disciple* was the didactic manifesto of the resurgent conservatives against the dominant positivist and secular mood of the time; Anatole France's four-volume series called *Contemporary History* was a kind of sustained answer to Bourget from the left, with the political crises of the Dreyfus decade as its subject matter. France's *Penguin Island* is an amusing, broad satire on French history, poking fun at the church and culminating in a thinly disguised parody of the scandals of the 1890's. Roger Martin du Gard's *Jean Barois*, though not a work of great literary merit, is of unique value to the historian for its portrayal of the conflict of ideas in France between 1890 and 1914. Marcel Proust's vast fresco of a vanishing world of Parisian society—*Remembrance of Things Past*—attracts readers both for its literary qualities and for its evocation of an age.

Jules Romains's twenty-eight-volume *Men of Good Will* is a less-successful attempt to do for the France of 1907–33 what Balzac had done for his time. The volume entitled *Verdun* stands out for its evocation of trench warfare in that crucial battle in 1916.


A Selective List of Readings About France 1870–1919

Amdur, Kathryn. *Syndicalist Legacy.* Urbana: University of Illinois Press, 1986.

Auspitz, Katherine. *The Radical Bourgeoisie: The Ligue de l'Enseignement and the Origins of the Third Republic, 1866–1885.* New York: Cambridge University Press, 1982.

Barrows, Susanna. *Distorting Mirrors: Visions of the Crowd in Late Nineteenth-Century France.* New Haven: Yale University Press, 1981.

Bidelman, Patrick K. *Pariahs Stand Up! The Founding of the Liberal Feminist Movement in France, 1858–1889.* Westport, Conn.: Greenwood, 1982.

Bredin, Jean-Denis. *The Affair: The Case of Alfred Dreyfus.* New York: Braziller, 1986.

Brogan, Denis W. *France Under the Republic, 1870–1939.* New York: Harper, 1940.

Bruhat, Jean et al. *La Commune de 1871.* Paris: Ed. Sociales, 1970.

Brunschwig, Henri. *French Colonialism, 1871–1914: Myths and Realities.* New York: Praeger, 1966.

Burns, Michael. *Rural Society and French Politics: Boulangism and the Dreyfus Affair, 1886–1900.* Princeton: Princeton University Press, 1984.

Cobban, Alfred. *A History of Modern France* (vol. 3). Baltimore: Penguin, 1965.

Digeon, Claude. *La crise allemande de la pensée française, 1870–1914.* Paris: Presses Universitaires, 1959.

Edwards, Stewart. *The Paris Commune 1871.* London: Eyre and Spottiswoode, 1971.

Girault, René. *Emprunts russes et investissements français en Russie: 1887–1914.* Paris: Colin, 1973.

Goguel, François. *La politique des partis sous la IIIe république.* Paris: Seuil, 1946.

Goldberg, Harvey. *The Life of Jean Jaurès.* Madison, Wis.: University of Wisconsin Press, 1962.

Hause, Steven C., and Anne R. Kenney, *Women's Suffrage and Social Politics in the French Third Republic.* Princeton: Princeton University Press, 1984.

Howard, Michael. *The Franco-Prussian War.* London: Collins, 1967.

Johnson, Douglas. *France and the Dreyfus Affair.* New York: Walker, 1967.

Keylor, William R. *Academy and Community: The Foundation of the French Historical Profession.* Cambridge: Harvard University Press, 1975.

Lefebvre, Henri. *La proclamation de la Commune.* Paris: Gallimard, 1965.

Lévy-Leboyer, M. (ed.). *La position internationale de la France: aspects économiques et financières.* Paris: Ecole des Hautes Etudes, 1977.

Marrus, Michael. *The Politics of Assimilation.* Oxford: Clarendon, 1971.

Marx, Karl. *The Civil War in France.* Moscow: Progress Publishers, 1974.

Mayeur, J.-M. et al. *Histoire du peuple français: cent ans d'esprit républicain*. Paris: Nouvelle Librairie de France, 1965.

Merriman, John M. *The Red City: Limoges and the French Nineteenth Century*. New York: Oxford University Press, 1985.

Miller, Michael B. *The Bon Marché: Bourgeois Culture and the Department Store, 1869–1920*. Princeton: Princeton University Press, 1981.

Mitchell, Allan. *The German Influence in France after 1870*. Chapel Hill: University of North Carolina Press, 1979.

Nye, Robert A. *Crime, Madness, and Politics in Modern France*. Princeton: Princeton University Press, 1984.

Offen, Karen. "Depopulation, Nationalism, and Feminism in Fin-de-Siècle France," *American Historical Review*, 89 (June 1984), 648–676.

Perrot, Michelle. *Les ouvriers en grève: France 1871–1890*. Paris: Mouton, 1974.

Poidevin, Raymond. *Les relations économiques et financières entre la France et l'Allemagne de 1898 à 1914*. Paris: Colin, 1969.

Reid, Donald. *The Miners of Decazeville: A Genealogy of Deindustrialization*. Cambridge: Harvard University Press, 1985.

Renouvin, Pierre. *Histoire des relations internationales: le XIXe siècle, de 1871 à 1914*. Paris: Hachette, 1955.

Rothney, John. *Bonapartism after Sedan*. Ithaca: Cornell University Press, 1969.

Scott, Joan W. *The Glassworkers of Carmaux*. Cambridge: Harvard University Press, 1974.

Shattuck, Roger. *The Banquet Years: The Arts in France, 1885–1918*. New York: Harcourt, 1958.

Shorter, Edward, and Charles Tilly. *Strikes in France 1830–1968*. London: Cambridge University Press, 1974.

Smith, Bonnie G. *Ladies of the Leisure Class: The Bourgeoises of Northern France in the Nineteenth Century*. Princeton: Princeton University Press, 1981.

Sowerwine, Charles. *Sisters or Citizens? Women and Socialism in France since 1876*. New York: Cambridge University Press, 1982.

Sternhell, Zeev. *La droite révolutionnaire 1885–1914: les origines françaises du fascisme*. Paris: Seuil, 1978.

Thobie, Jacques. *La France impériale, 1880–1914*. Paris: Mégrelis, 1983.

Thomson, David. *Democracy in France since 1870.*, 5th ed. New York: Oxford University Press, 1969.

Weber, Eugen. *Action Française*. Stanford: Stanford University Press, 1962.

Weber, Eugen. *Peasants into Frenchmen: The Modernization of Rural France, 1870–1914*. Stanford: Stanford University Press, 1976.

Weber, Eugen. *France: Fin de Siècle*. Cambridge: Harvard University Press, 1986.

Weisz, George. *The Emergence of Modern Universities in France, 1863–1914*. Princeton: Princeton University Press, 1983.

Zeldin, Theodore. *France 1848–1945*. Oxford: Clarendon, 1973. (Also published in five paperback volumes.)

# IV
# CONTEMPORARY FRANCE:
# CRISIS AND RECOVERY
## 1919–1986

# CHAPTER 27

# The Quest for Normalcy, 1919–1931

France contains two fundamental temperaments—that of the left and that of the right; three principal tendencies, if one adds the center; six spiritual families; ten parties, large or small, traversed by multiple currents; fourteen parliamentary groups without much discipline; and forty million opinions.

JACQUES FAUVET

The Third Republic, as seen in retrospect by observers of our day, seems to have passed through three distinct though interconnected phases: the heroic age from 1871 to about 1900, during which the republicans fought off all challenges and consolidated the regime; the stable era from 1900 to about 1930, when the system appeared to have won a degree of popular consensus unequalled by any of its predecessors; the period of disintegration that began about 1930 and ended in collapse a decade later.

If this broad pattern has any validity, it might seem logical to assume that something disastrous happened about 1930 to disrupt a popular and generally successful regime. That disaster, one might conclude, was the great economic crisis that not only created grave tensions within France but also opened the way for the rise of aggressive enemies across the Rhine and the Alps. Probably it is true that the Third Republic would have endured—by force of inertia, if nothing else—if spared the impact of depression and war. Yet the real test of any regime is how well it can face up to crisis. A nation that collapses as quickly as France did in 1940, a nation where consensus disintegrates when confronted with the economic and social stresses of a depression decade, is clearly suffering from some deeper sources of weakness. Something was wrong well before the depression hit France—though just what was wrong is a complex and controversial question.

It has sometimes been argued that the source of the trouble can be traced to the Great War of 1914–18, with its terrible drain on French manpower, resources, and emotions. The remarkable economic recovery of the 1920's and the factitious hegemony of France in postwar Europe would then be seen as a plastering over of the fatal cracks in the edifice. Others have held that the sources of weakness really went far deeper, into the character of the French political and social system itself. The Third Republic, a Frenchman once remarked, was a system of government well adapted to "an independent, rich, and happy people"—but not to a nation in crisis. So long as it faced nothing more complex than the theoretical and doctrinal problems of the later nineteenth century, it worked reasonably well. But an essentially negative instrument of government, designed to prevent abuses rather than to get things done, was scarcely adequate for an era of rapid and profound change. The trouble with the Third Republic (according to this line of argument) was that it succeeded in taking root in French affections just at the moment when it was beginning to be outmoded. Frenchmen clung to it after 1900, just as most of them clung to a social structure and a cluster of attitudes that belonged to the nineteenth century. As a result, they entered the new industrial age—an age of mass production and mass rule—psychologically unprepared and politically unarmed. For such a nation, the cumulative effect of the Great War and the Great Depression was likely to prove overwhelming.

During the first postwar decade, however, these weaknesses could easily be ignored. Frenchmen, like Americans in the same era, were eager to recover what the Americans called "normalcy." Victory seemed to prove that France needed no fundamental change, that it would be enough to repair the damage and resume the upward trends of the pre-1914 years. By the end of the 1920's the devastated regions had been reconstructed, as nearly as possible on the prewar model; rebuilt factories had raised industrial production well above the 1914 level; the manpower gap left by the war had been filled by the immigration of two million foreign workers.

Politically, too, the republican system survived the war unaltered. A restless parliament promptly shook off Clemenceau's wartime dictatorship and reasserted its prewar ascendancy over the executive. But if the structure of the system emerged intact, within this old framework the postwar era brought both new forces and new men. The most striking change, superficially, at least, was an apparent shift in the political center of gravity toward the right. Since the inception of the Third Republic the trend had been almost steadily leftward; power had shifted from the monarchists to the Opportunists to the Radicals, and on the eve of the war it had begun to seem that the Socialists' turn would be next. Suddenly, in the elections of November, 1919, this trend appeared to be reversed: Frenchmen chose their most rightist Chamber since 1871, giving the Moderates and the conservative right more than two-thirds of the seats.

This startling reversal in parliament did not, however, reflect a major shift of opinion among the voters. In 1919 the left-wing parties actually increased their popular vote over the 1914 figure, and during the next two decades the left won every election except that of 1928. The rightist victory just after the war was a kind of fluke, made possible by the new electoral system adopted in that year. It provided for large multimember electoral districts in place of small single-member constituencies; it gave a clear advantage to those parties that could organize electoral coalitions. The various Moderate and conservative groups managed to do so in 1919, under the label Bloc National; the leftist parties fought each other instead. The Socialists by now were in the throes of a bitter internal conflict; one powerful faction was attracted to Moscow and wanted the party to join Lenin's new Third International. Most Radicals were unwilling to link their fate with a party that might be on the verge of embracing Leninism. So it was that the left cancelled itself out, even though the Radicals won as many votes as in 1914, and the Socialists won more.

If the rightist victory had any real significance, it was to show the declining intensity of the religious issue in French politics. For the Moderates to form electoral coalitions with strongly clerical conservatives represented a sharp change since prewar days. Time and the wartime *union sacrée* had done their work; the extreme right had accepted the secular republic, the Moderate right-center was prepared to meet it halfway. The renewed political influence of the Moderates between the wars was traceable in large part to the fading impact of clericalism as a vital issue. To please the new Chamber of 1919 (the first since 1871 to contain a majority of practicing Catholics), the government quietly restored diplomatic relations with the Vatican and exempted Alsace from the separation laws of 1905.[1]

On the whole, however, the right's victory produced no major change in policy or mood. If the Moderates were willing to ally with the conservative right for electoral purposes, many of them preferred to govern in combination with their Radical neighbors just to the left. The old impulse toward *concentration,* toward collaboration of right-center and left-center groups, became stronger than ever before. From 1899 to 1919 the Radicals had usually dominated such coali-

---

[1] When Herriot's Radical cabinet tried in 1924 to revive the clerical issue by extending the separation laws to Alsace, the effect was to consolidate the center and right rather than to rally the left around the old anticlerical banner. The hierarchy encouraged the creation of a pressure group called the National Catholic Federation that effectively influenced parliament and the *bien-pensant* public. Since large segments of the left were indifferent, the cabinet soon abandoned its anticlerical program, though pools of hostility toward the church survived. The one remaining issue that threatened to reawaken the old anticlerical spirit was the question of state aid to church schools; Catholics began to advance this idea in the mid-1920's.

tions; from 1919 to 1936 it was more often the Moderates. But since the same fluctuating alliance continued to govern the country, the interwar period proved to be a political prolongation of the prewar era. Even when the left-wing parties managed to recover control of the Chamber (as in 1924 and 1932), their failure to cooperate among themselves, combined with the Socialists' steady refusal to enter any cabinet, always led to a restoration of the Radical-Moderate alliance, with the Moderates usually shaping policy and holding the key positions.

Since the fulcrum of politics lay in the shadowy zone where Radicals and Moderates met, the most likely candidate for the premiership would be a man with a foot in both camps—a man better adapted to compromise than to vigorous, forthright action. There could hardly have been a more fitting aspirant than Aristide Briand, who had already headed six cabinets before and during the war, and who broke all records by forming five more during the 1920's. Briand's political background was strangely variegated. As a young man he had flirted with Boulangism and anarchism; then he had joined the Socialist party of Jaurès, only to leave this group in 1906 in order to accept a cabinet post. His first act on becoming a minister, it is said, was to send an aide to the Bibliothèque Nationale to destroy the violent articles he had once written in an anarchist newspaper. Since then he had hovered between or above parties, maintaining his contacts and friends in all camps. France has rarely produced a more flexible politician; indeed, Briand's favorite maxim was "life is made of rubber." His admirers said that, like an insect, he possessed invisible antennae that enabled him to operate by "feel." It is likely that he had no deep convictions, no doctrine, nothing beyond a highly developed politician's instinct. Yet his personal charm, his oratorical skill, and his adaptability made him in many respects the most successful and the most representative French political figure of the era.

Briand's only serious rival for leadership in the postwar decade was the Moderate Raymond Poincaré, who broke precedent by returning to active politics after his presidential term ended in 1920. Both men headed coalition cabinets of much the same kind, yet they could hardly have been more different in temperament. Where Briand was devious and improvising, Poincaré was rigid and intransigent. A wit of the day remarked that "Briand knows nothing and understands everything; Poincaré knows everything and understands nothing." If few of his fellow politicians liked Poincaré, most of them respected him for a personal honesty so scrupulous as to be unusual in the world of politics. As a young minister in prewar days, he had astounded his secretary by sorting out his personal letters from his official correspondence and buying his own stamps for the former kind. His reputation as a financial expert and as a dedicated patriot adapted him for leadership at a time when the two critical issues were the problem of the franc and the enforcement of Versailles. Poincaré's cabinets, unlike

Briand's, were few but durable; he held the premiership from 1922 to 1924, and again from 1926 to 1929.

Alongside these older leaders whose political careers had begun before the turn of the century, a younger generation of politicians was beginning to emerge into prominence in the 1920's. On the right, the most notable new figures were André Tardieu and Pierre Laval; on the left, Edouard Herriot and Léon Blum. All four were to play first-rank roles during the crisis decade of the 1930's. Tardieu, scion of an old family of the middle bourgeoisie, was one of the few native Parisians to rise high in a political world monopolized by provincials. After a brilliant prewar career as civil servant and journalist, he had entered the Chamber in 1914 and had risen to prominence as Clemenceau's right-hand man at the peace conference. As arrogant as he was able, Tardieu's contempt for lesser men and for public opinion hampered his political career and led him eventually to repudiate the parliamentary system in favor of an authoritarian republic. Laval, son of a village innkeeper and butcher from the remote hill country of central France, had a career that resembled that of his idol Briand. A Socialist of the most rabidly leftist variety before 1914, he left the party shortly after the war and underwent a gradual and rather obscure conversion that eventually turned him into a nonparty Moderate. A shrewd and unscrupulous manipulator of men, Laval took it for granted that a politician ought to appeal to man's baser motives. In the 1930's he was to become Briand's successor as the most remarkable political manipulator in parliament. However, he lacked Briand's oratorical skill and his sense of timing.

Edouard Herriot emerged in the 1920's as the new spokesman and standard-bearer of the Radical party. Son of a career army officer, brilliant graduate of the École Normale, professor of literature in a Lyon *lycée*, he had been drawn into politics during the Dreyfus Affair and had entered parliament in 1912 as France's youngest senator. Herriot was a talented if rather rhetorical orator, a man who managed to combine the realist's flexibility with the idealist's respect for doctrine. Twice, after the left's electoral victories in 1924 and 1932, he was to serve briefly as premier at the head of a shaky left-wing coalition.

In the Socialist party it was Léon Blum who sought to fill the gap left by the assassination of Jaurès in 1914 and the aging of Guesde (who died in 1922). Blum was another ex-Normalien, the son of Jewish bourgeois parents whose forebears had come to Paris from Alsace. A brilliant student of esthetic tastes and subtle mind, he had become politically conscious during the Dreyfus uproar and had become a dedicated disciple of Jaurès. After the victory of the Dreyfusards he had returned to his original career as journalist, literary man, and high civil servant (in the Conseil d'État); but Jaurès' assassination and the outbreak of war brought him back to an active role in the party. By the end of the war he was leader of the Socialists' center faction, and in 1919 he won election to the Chamber. Like Jaurès, Blum was a humanitarian socialist for whom Marxism was a method of analysis rather than a dogma. Blum neither sprang from the working class nor had any direct acquaintance with it; his intellectual tastes, his somewhat effeminate voice and manner, made him seem the least likely candidate for the leadership of a proletarian party. Still, French socialism had never been led by proletarians, and during the interwar years it was to become more and more a party of white-collar workers, intellectuals, and elements of the lower middle class. If Blum lacked the personal magnetism and the robust earthiness of Jaurès, he won the genuine respect of his party followers as a subtle theoretician and as a remarkable spokesman for humanitarian ideals.

Blum's first task as party leader was to prevent French socialism from slipping into the Moscow orbit. Since 1917 the Bolshevik experiment had exerted a powerful pull, not only on the new unskilled proletariat in war production plants, but also on many old-time Socialists of the Guesdist wing. This group persuaded itself that Lenin's communism was basically not much different from Western Marxian movements: "Socialism with Tartar sauce," one of them ironically called it. But some Guesdists, together with most of the heirs of Jaurès, were more dubious; men like Blum detected in Leninism something new and ominous, and they managed to block the pro-Moscow element for a time. At the party congress of Tours in December, 1920, however, they were swamped by a three-to-one vote in favor of joining the Third International. Blum preferred secession to unity on Lenin's terms; he led the minority group out of the congress hall, leaving almost everything—party machinery, newspaper, membership—in the hands of the majority that promptly renamed itself the French Communist party.

At the outset the Socialists' prospects seemed gloomy; the very survival of the party, except perhaps as a tiny splinter group, appeared doubtful. Communist membership in 1921 outnumbered that of the Socialists by 140,000 to 30,000; the Communist organ *L'Humanité* outsold the new Socialist daily *Populaire* by 200,000 to 5,000. But the next few years were to justify Blum's determination to go it alone. By 1924 the Socialists' dues-paying membership exceded that of the Communists; by 1932 there were one hundred thirty-one Socialist deputies as compared to the Communists' ten; by 1936 the Socialists had become France's largest party, and Blum took over the premiership. This remarkable recovery stemmed in part from Blum's determined and intelligent leadership. He refused to permit the party to become a new version of the Radicals, but clung instead to the policy of nonparticipation in bourgeois cabinets and to the doctrine of revolution rather than gradualist reform. If such a doctrine was unrealistic and in some ways misleading, it did preserve the Socialist party as a haven for disillusioned Communists and for proletarian idealists. More of the credit, however, should probably go to those lesser party officials and local militants who, at the grass-roots level, worked doggedly at the task of party reorganization. And perhaps the major credit must go to the Communists themselves, for their policies contributed heavily to the Socialist revival. French communism's record during the twenties was one of chronic dissension and division. At the outset its members were united by little more than a romantic enthusiasm for the Russian experiment. They had accepted Lenin's twenty-one conditions in order to gain admittance to the Third International, but most of them had not taken very seriously the prospect that Moscow would insist on dictating party policy within France. A kind of resurrected Gallican spirit marked the outlook of the early French Communists; their aim was formal allegiance to Moscow without domination by Moscow.

Through the 1920's a steady stream of telegrams and investigators poured into France from Russia as the Soviet leaders sought to discipline the French party. One faction after another was expelled, or angrily resigned. By 1923 it was estimated that two-thirds of the original members had left the party, and many of these deserters found their way back to the Socialists. But if Moscow's policy was temporarily disastrous, it was potentially effective. By the end of the decade what was left of the French Communist party had been thoroughly Bolshevized. A new generation of younger leaders, tougher and more Leninist in spirit, more truly proletarian in origin, had replaced the older group—men like the miner's son Maurice Thorez, the metallurgy worker Jacques Doriot, the veterans' organizer and ex-pastry cook Jacques Duclos, the onetime naval petty officer André Marty. These men, untouched by French socialism's deep-rooted humanitarian and libertarian heritage, were dedicated to Leninist doctrines of organization and action. From its low point in the mid-twenties the Communist party began to make slow but steady progress at the polls. Most of its strength remained concentrated in the red belt of workers' suburbs surrounding Paris; but the party was already experimenting with new propaganda appeals destined to attract the largest French voting groups—the petty bourgeoisie, the artisans, the poorer peasants, the intellectuals. By the end of the decade the Communists had forged a small but reliable weapon for use in times of stress or crisis.

Communism was not the only new force in politics that emerged in the postwar decade. Other movements of the center and right, though smaller, also foreshadowed future trends. One of these was Christian democracy, which burgeoned in the 1920's in a whole series of forms. The prewar Sillon, after its condemnation by the Vatican, had left behind a small nucleus of militants dedicated to the idea of reconciling their faith with the ideals symbolized by the Great Revolution. Many of them had turned to social rather than political activity, and they worked through the lay organization called Catholic Action. After the war they founded a whole series of new specialized branches of Catholic Action aimed at young people: the Young Christian Workers (J.O.C.), the Young Christian Farmers (J.A.C.), and so on. Some of the ex-Sillonistes also helped to organize a new Catholic trade-union movement, the C.F.T.C., in 1919; and in 1924 they re-embarked in politics when they founded the Popular Democratic party. Between the wars Christian democracy remained a minor current; the Popular Democrats managed to elect only about a dozen deputies, mainly in strongly Catholic provinces like Alsace and Brittany. The old religious feud, though no longer so intense, still tainted men's minds and emotions; neither Catholics nor freethinkers quite trusted a party like this one. But the foundations for expansion were being laid by training a new Catholic elite in the youth movements—an elite that in time of crisis would prove its dedication to the republic's ideals.

On the extreme right, too, there were signs of effervescence during the 1920's; several small but noisy movements emerged, most of them traditionalist and authoritarian in spirit, but tinged in some cases by the new fascist mood emanating from Mussolini's Italy. The earliest of these new antiparliamentary leagues, created in 1924, was Pierre Taittinger's Jeunesses Patriotes. Four years later came the Croix de Feu, a nonpolitical organization of decorated veterans at first, but one that was marked by an authoritarian temper and by a growing tendency toward political action. Rivalling these new groups was the older Action Française of Charles Maurras. Its rabid nationalism, its refurbished traditionalism, and its arrogant elitism appealed to young activists in much the same way that Leninism attracted another segment of youth. Several eminent literary figures lent intellectual respectability to the movement; and in addition, it offered a chance for action and excitement through participation in a kind of private army called the Camelots du Roi. In 1919 the Action Française managed to get its spokesman into the Chamber of Deputies: Léon Daudet, son of the distinguished novelist and wielder of the most scurrilous and venomous pen in Parisan journalism.

French monarchism had been almost moribund until Maurras came along to revive it. The king's cause was brought to life again by all this agitation; but the pretender was not at all sure that he wanted such unorthodox and dangerous champions. Many Catholics, too, were disturbed at the violence and the brutal cynicism of the Maurrassian doctrine; some of them suspected (quite properly) that Maurras's aim was not to serve the church but to use it for his own purposes. After many years of hesitation the Vatican concluded that young Catholics were being corrupted by an amoral and dangerous ideology; in 1926 Catholics were instructed to abandon the movement and to give up reading its newspaper. Some years later the royal pretender followed suit and repudiated Maurras. Although many Catholic laymen openly refused to follow the Vatican's directive, the Pope's action proved to be a major blow to the Action Française. The clergy generally submitted; Maurrassism was pruned out of Catholic schools and universities, leaving Catholic youth to be exposed to a different set of intellectual leaders. When the crisis decade of the 1930's arrived, the Action Française found itself quickly outdistanced by newer authoritarian groups. Yet the insidious doctrines of the movement had made their way into the minds of an important minority of the French elite and had softened up that element for fascist or proto-fascist agitators. After 1930 the republic would once again be faced by vigorous and unscrupulous enemies on the far right.

Between the extremes of right and left, the old political groups clung to their prewar habits without much change. The Radicals (still technically named the Radical and Radical-Socialist party) remained a kind of loose confederation of libertarian, petty-bourgeois individualists bound together by little more than tradition and electoral interest; party discipline was weak, party policy more negative than positive. On most important votes in the Chamber, the Radicals divided three ways: yes, no, and abstention. Radicalism had long since shifted from an urban to a small-town and rural base, with its greatest strength in the economically static southwest. Through most of the interwar period the Radicals had the largest single organized group in the Chamber, and they attained an even firmer grip on the Senate, largely because they had gotten control of so many municipal and departmental councils in rural France. The Moderates remained divided into several rather loose party groups, of which the Democratic Alliance and the Republican Federation were the largest and most durable. The line of separation between Moderates and Radicals continued to be obscure; one of the most effective parliamentary groups of this era, the misnamed "Radical Left," profited from this obscurity by frankly straddling the gap and furnishing ministers to all kinds of cabinets. On the whole, the Moderates had outgrown their anticlericalism more rapidly than the Radicals, and they were more inclined to reflect the interests of large-scale business, while the Radicals responded to the pressures of small enterprise.

One of the few political novelties of the postwar decade was the emergence of fairly sizable and influential organized interest groups. Only a few such organizations had existed in prewar days—the steelmakers' Comité des Forges, for example, and the coal industry's Comité des Houillères. There had also been such loose groups as the Union of Economic Interests, set up shortly before 1914 to provide an electoral slush fund for center and right-wing politicians, and the so-called Mascuraud Committee, which from the late 1890's had financed the election of Radical candidates, and which drew its funds mainly from small business firms. All of these groups continued to function after the war; the Union of Economic Interests even expanded its activities and allegedly subsidized more than half the successful candidates for the Chamber in the 1920's. What was new in the postwar era was the proliferation of important interest groups representing almost every segment of society and of the economy. Businessmen established the first national employers' confederation (C.N.P.F.) in 1919. In the same year a much less successful National Agricultural Confederation sought to group the farmers; it was quickly outpaced by a whole series of specialized associations representing the wheatgrowers, the sugar-beet producers, and so on. Labor, which needed its own pressure group more desperately than did any other social stratum, continued to divide its strength. To the old C.G.T., which still tried to turn its back on politics, there were now added the Catholic C.F.T.C. and the Communist C.G.T.U. Probably the most effective interest groups of the period were those representing war veterans. Here again, however, diversity rather than unity was the rule: the Union Fédérale and the Union Nationale des Combattants, which had almost a million members each, were only the largest of a half-dozen groups. Although they were hampered by division, most of the interest groups quickly learned that the French political system was ideally suited to their needs. The decision-making process was widely diffused through parliament and the bureaucracy; there existed no powerful and stable executive authority to speak for the nation as a whole and to resist demands for special privilege. During these last years of the Third Republic the lobbyist became an increasingly familiar and influential figure in the committee rooms of parliament and in the offices of high civil servants.

In that era of recovered normalcy that extended from 1919 to about 1931, Frenchmen once again could believe—as they had before 1914—that politics was less a serious matter than a kind of game, passionately interesting, perhaps, but not of vital importance. The journalist Robert de Jouvenel had written of his compatriots in prewar days: "France is a happy land, where the soil is generous, the artisan ingenious, and wealth widely shared. Politics one can take or leave, according to individual taste: it is not the decisive factor in Frenchmen's lives."[2] The novelist-diplomat Paul Morand was later to add, with a touch of irony, that the practice of politics had been brought to its ultimate refinement by Frenchmen, who had made of it "a pure indigenous art." Such epigrams contained a disturbing germ of truth. Although most Frenchmen refused to recognize the fact, the time was at hand when politics could no longer be viewed as little more than a game, a spectacle, a career. For good or ill, it was rapidly becoming the overwhelming factor that would really shape the condition of men's lives.

---

[2] R. de Jouvenel, *La république des camarades* (Paris: Grasset, 1914), p. 4.

# CHAPTER 28

# The Era of French Hegemony, 1919–1933

France victorious must grow accustomed to being a lesser power than France vanquished.

JULES CAMBON (1918)

For more than a decade after the victory of 1918 France appeared to be the undisputed mistress of the Continent. With Russia disrupted, Germany reduced and disarmed, and Britain inclined to return to its tradition of island aloofness, it did not seem remotely possible for any European nation to challenge the preeminence of France. Yet by 1939 the French position had disintegrated completely; France had lost its military superiority, diplomatic predominance, even independence of action. Such a disastrous reversal suggests a failure of effective leadership in France; yet it may also suggest that France's hegemony in the 1920's was more factitious than real, and that outside factors partially beyond French control were more important than internal weakness in destroying the French position.

Throughout the interwar years French foreign policy had a double focus: on relations with Britain and on relations with Germany. The prewar entente with the British barely survived the victory; within a year the relationship had taken on a bittersweet flavor. Late in 1919 Clemenceau, a lifelong exponent of cooperation with Britain, remarked privately: "England is the lost illusion of my life! Not a day passes that I do not receive from one of our agents abroad reports indicating veritably hostile acts. I had hoped that the fraternity of arms ... would suppress the old traditional prejudices. Not at all. The evil is without remedy."[1]

---

[1] A. François-Poncet, *De Versailles à Potsdam* (Paris: Flammarion, 1948), p. 65

Clemenceau almost certainly exaggerated the case, yet his remarks reflected a revived and widespread Anglophobia in those postwar years, inspired by friction in the Near East and over the German reparations settlement. Across the Channel most Englishmen reciprocated this suspicion and hostility. Their outlook was deeply influenced by John Maynard Keynes's best-selling book *The Economic Consequences of the Peace,* which denounced the Versailles settlement as the product of France's unreasoning thirst for revenge. They were skeptical, too, about the sincerity of French motives in demanding large reparations payments from Germany; the French purpose, many Britishers believed, was not so much to restore war-ravaged France as to keep the Germans permanently on their knees.

In fact, the overriding goal of almost every Frenchman was neither revenge nor hegemony, but simply security; and even with several decades of hindsight, it is still not easy to say how they might best have achieved it after 1919. One possible course, advocated at the time by part of the French left, would have been to commit France's future to the new League of Nations and to such collective security arrangements as might be developed around the League. A second alternative was to construct a new alliance system to replace that of prewar days. The small new states of eastern Europe, however, offered a rather shaky substitute for Russia, the keystone of the old Triple Entente. Even if the French had been able to pour into those states as many francs as they had invested in prewar Russia, they probably could not have created a solid bulwark. In any case, such an effort was well beyond France's postwar capacity. Only the active collaboration of Britain in this alliance system might have made the eastern states strong enough to survive and to serve as a barrier against future aggressors. French statesmen tried repeatedly to convince the British of the wisdom of such a commitment. They pleaded for a British promise to guarantee the security of the little east European states; the British consistently refused. Lloyd George told Briand frankly in 1921 that Britain had little interest in eastern Europe: "The British people felt that the populations in that quarter of Europe were unstable and excitable; they might start fighting at any time, and the rights and wrongs of the dispute might be very hard to disentangle."[2]

If the French were not strong enough to construct a solid continental alliance themselves, and if they could not persuade the British to help construct one, there remained very few alternatives indeed. One theoretical possibility might have been to abandon eastern Europe as indefensible against a resurgent Germany or Russia; to leave the Poles and Rumanians and Czechs to their inevitable fate and to fall back on a kind of isolationist "fortress France" policy. Such a

---

[2] Foreign Office (Great Britain), *Papers Respecting Negotiations for an Anglo-French Pact* (Cmd. 2169) (London: H. M. Stationery Office, 1924), pp. 112–13.

plan would have required a bigger and better Maginot Line, extended all the way to the Channel. Or, alternatively, the French might have chosen from the beginning to put all their eggs in the British basket; to abandon the initiative in foreign policy to the British, in return for a binding guarantee of British aid if France were attacked. Such a policy would have involved writing off eastern Europe, scaling down German reparations, and relaxing controls on Germany, as the British wished. Toward the end, in the late 1930's, the French were to arrive at something very much like this position; but its wisdom a decade earlier would have depended on the farsightedness of British foreign-policy makers in that era. Still another possibility might have been an attempt to develop a close Franco-German entente, with a view to channelling the resurgent power of Germany into some sort of western European alliance or federation.

If all of these alternatives were theoretically open to French leaders after 1919, they were not all feasible in practice. Like policy-makers everywhere, those of France were limited by their own prejudices and by those of the nation they represented, as well as by the mood of the nations with which they had to deal. In the early postwar years an intimate rapprochement with Germany was inconceivable; so was a frank abdication of initiative into the hands of the British, or a wholehearted gamble that the League of Nations would bring a new era. Frenchmen emerged from the war divided over the proper course of foreign policy, and that division was increased by the peace settlement and the events of the early 1920's. It is not surprising that the behavior of French statesmen during their years of hegemony seems groping and ineffective, or that their policy appears to have been shaped more by improvisation than by farsighted planning.

❖❖❖❖❖❖❖❖❖❖❖❖❖

At the peace conference Clemenceau had abandoned France's demand for control of the Rhine and had won, instead, a promise of American and British treaties guaranteeing aid if France should be attacked. When the United States Senate repudiated the American guarantee, the British government withdrew its offer as well. Some French nationalists held that France would now be legally justified in seizing the Rhineland by unilateral action; but even a heavily rightist Chamber was unwilling to take such a risk. The government turned, instead, to constructing a military alliance system that eventually came to include Belgium, Poland, Rumania, Czechoslovakia, and Yugoslavia. The idea of adding a line of fortifications along the Franco-German frontier was still several years in the future; the Maginot Line was not begun until 1929.

Meanwhile the problem of setting a German reparations figure (entrusted by the peace conference to an interallied commission) was creating serious friction between France and Britain. The deadline for a decision was finally met early in 1921, but the figure set was resented by both the British and the Germans as unreasonably high and by the French as unjustly low. The critical problem of transfer from the Germans to the victors was evaded rather than settled; part of the payment was to be in specified raw materials, but large-scale financial transfers would be possible only if the Germans cut their living standards drastically, or if they were encouraged to flood world markets with German exports, or if they could borrow large sums from some broad-minded lender. The French apparently assumed that the Germans, as loser, ought to choose the first alternative —that they should resolutely swallow the bitter medicine of defeat and face several years of marginal existence. French spokesmen pointed out quite logically that for the victors to bear the cost of reconstruction while the vanquished went largely unscathed would be a gross inequity. The gap between logic and equity on the one hand, and the hard realities of national attitudes and international relationships on the other, has rarely been so great. Most Germans, rightly or wrongly, were unwilling to behave as the French thought they should; and the British and Americans were increasingly convinced that the French, not the Germans, ought to retreat. No German was likely to resist the temptation to profit by the disintegration of the victors' coalition.

By the end of 1921 French leadership faced a simple choice: either to agree to a drastic scaling down of reparations, or to go it alone in an effort to call the Germans' bluff. Premier Briand, who had been an advocate of rigorous treatment of the Germans, adapted himself to what seemed to be necessity; in a private session with Lloyd George, he agreed to cut reparations in return for a British guarantee of military aid if France should be attacked. The news leaked out before Briand could try to charm parliament into accepting his policy; his cabinet was overthrown, and Poincaré was restored to power in January, 1922. A tenacious legalist, Poincaré stood on the letter of the agreements in force; he made it plain that if Britain would not cooperate, France would have to act alone. Yet even Poincaré hesitated for a year before taking drastic action; it was only in January, 1923, that he ordered French troops to occupy Germany's Ruhr valley, on the legally valid ground that the Germans had chronically evaded and postponed payments due.

It was a divided France that occupied the Ruhr. Almost the entire left vigorously opposed the action; Marshal Foch himself, when consulted by the cabinet, had advised against it. Poincaré evidently had serious doubts about the wisdom of acting in defiance of British and world opinion, and he took the plunge only because neither he nor his cabinet could face the alternative—a major retreat to suit German demands. If the purpose of the occupation was to seize reparations in kind that the Germans had refused to supply, the action failed badly. France's reparations collections in 1923 were scarcely higher than they had been in 1922, and the cost of collecting them was higher than the value of the goods. If the hidden purpose was, as many of Poincaré's enemies alleged, to seize and keep the Ruhr and Rhineland area by encouraging the growth of a native separatist movement there, it failed just as completely. Some Frenchmen did take the opportunity to encourage separatist activity, but the movement never attained serious proportions. Only if the purpose was to call the German bluff—to ensure that the Germans would stop evading and delaying—can it be argued that the Ruhr occupation succeeded; for by the end of 1923 the new Stresemann cabinet in Berlin abandoned passive resistance and agreed to resume payments.

The victory, however, was a costly one at best—not only for its economic and psychological effects on the Germans, but perhaps even more for its impact on French minds. It marked the end of a really independent French policy in Europe; never again during the interwar years was a French government willing to act on its own, in defiance, if necessary, of world opinion. French power remained great enough to permit such action for another decade at least, and probably as late as 1936; but the French were henceforth reluctant to move without British support. Such a change of attitude in Paris might have had merit if this had been an era of wise and constructive British leadership; coordinated Franco-British action of a farsighted character might have shaped a healthy future for all of Europe. But Paris gained little by grudgingly abdicating the initiative to a series of British cabinets that meant well but lacked the qualities of tough-mindedness and foresight.

The apparent success of Poincaré's policy of enforcement did not impress French voters. They were struck much more by the fact that the government had to raise taxes by 20 per cent to cover the costs of the Ruhr expedition. Still, the elections of 1924 probably would have turned Poincaré out in any case, for the left-wing parties had learned from the last elections that dispersing their strength was a costly error. This time the Radicals and Socialists succeeded in forming an electoral alliance under the label *Cartel des Gauches;* and even though the Moderates and the conservative right managed to poll 51 per cent of the popular vote, the leftist coalition was swept into control of the Chamber. A Radical cabinet under Herriot took office, with Socialist support but without Socialist ministers; and this new government participated in an international conference that worked out the new Dawes Plan, scaling down German reparations payments. Some months later Briand became minister of foreign affairs, a post that he was to hold almost without interruption from 1925 to 1932. Never since Delcassé had there been such continuity at the foreign office, such an opportunity for a man to put his stamp on the whole course of French foreign policy. The so-called Locarno era of the late twenties may quite properly be called the era of Briand.

Yet to crystallize in words the spirit of that era is not as easy as it might seem. Briand, who knew how to attune himself to changing moods, talked much about disarmament, about his faith in the League of Nations, about his self-chosen role as "the pilgrim of peace"; his record as foreign minister was peppered with pacts and schemes like the Locarno Treaties, the Kellogg-Briand Pact, the projected United States of Europe. He set out frankly to appease Stresemann's Germany; indeed, it was Briand who first used and popularized the word *apaisement*. He brushed aside evidence that the Weimar Republic had been evading the Versailles controls on its rearmament. Briand told Foreign Minister Stresemann that he had received "kilos of documents" proving Germany's illegal armament; "I threw them in a corner, I refused to waste my time with these trifles." At a private meeting with Stresemann in 1926, he proposed a sweeping across-the-board settlement of all outstanding Franco-German problems, including an immediate end to the occupation of German soil, the return of the Saar Basin at once, and a lump-sum settlement of reparations. This proved to be too much for either the French cabinet or parliament to swallow. But Briand did accept Stresemann's Locarno scheme for "freezing" the Franco-German frontier; he abandoned France's right to keep military inspectors in Germany; and he withdrew the last French occupation troops in 1930, five years ahead of schedule.

Perhaps the most surprising aspect of Briand's reconciliation policy was that Poincaré's return to the premiership in 1926–29 did not interrupt it. Both Poincaré and his Moderate successors kept Briand at the foreign office; outwardly, it almost seemed that a kind of bipartisan unity had been achieved on policy toward Germany. Poincaré had not changed his mind, but he had lost some of his faith in a tough independent line, and he knew that the temper of the voters required a continuation of Briandism. Besides, since 1925 Germany had been paying reparations without quibble or delay, thanks to the booming prosperity of the era and to copious American loans.

There was another reason, however, for Poincaré's willingness to keep Briand in office. He was aware that Briandism and Poincarism were not so contrary as they seemed; that the difference between them was one of mood and emphasis, not of goal or of fundamental conviction. Briand's appeasement had its limits. He was determined to maintain the French army as the largest in Europe and to preserve the French alliance system. Indeed, it was Briand rather than Poincaré who negotiated new treaties with the Poles and the Czechs tightening France's obligations to those two partners. Though Briand never precisely defined his aims, he seems to have based his reconciliation policy on two hopeful assumptions: (1) that the new Germany, more democratic and peaceful in spirit than that of 1914, would reconcile itself to a secondary role in Europe if treated with generosity; (2) that the British, even though refusing any formal commitments to France or eastern Europe, would intervene in case of a major crisis to prevent France from being overrun. On the second point, time was eventually to prove him right, even though British aid in 1940 turned out to be inadequate to save France from defeat. On the first point, Briand apparently began to develop some qualms after Stresemann died in 1929, for no one of Stresemann's quality and force appeared in German politics to carry on his work. Perhaps that is why, in 1929–30, Briand began to talk in rather vague terms about a United States of Europe; perhaps his concern was to integrate the resurgent power of Germany with that of the rest of Europe before that power could get out of hand.

The wisdom or unwisdom of the Briand experiment in the late 1920's produced a continuing debate during the years that followed. Hitler's rise to power in 1933 led some French rightists to denounce Briand as the appeaser whose concessions had opened the way to the Nazis. If he had not withdrawn French occupation forces from the Rhineland ahead of schedule, ran the argument, they would have been on the spot in the years after 1933 and could have choked off Hitler's preparations for aggression. An American historian has added more recently that Briand, by falling back on the hope of British aid rather than continuing Poincaré's independent policy, made France the prisoner of Britain and took "the first step on the road to Munich."

Briandism is easy to criticize, for it did fail in the end. Yet even in retrospect, it is not easy to suggest a workable alternative for that period, except the old Poincaré policy of independent action in the face of world opinion and even of much French opinion. Even if perpetuated, the Poincaré policy could not have endured much longer simply because France's dominant position in Europe was artificial and temporary and was not based on the solid realities of geopolitics. In truth, France by the late 1920's was caught in an almost insoluble dilemma. Whatever the French might do, their fate depended on the nature of German and British leadership; and they could no longer exert much influence over the decisions of German and British policy-makers, if indeed they had ever been able to do so when French strength was at its peak.

The French may have missed one last chance during the early years of the Great Depression to shape the future by heading off the rise of Hitler in Germany. The impact of the economic crisis on the Weimar Republic was severe. Chancellor Heinrich Bruening, who took office in 1930, argued that a generous loan from the prosperous French, or a German diplomatic victory such as a customs union with Austria or a revision of the Versailles settlement to permit German rearmament, might give him time to ride out the storm. But the French balked at both the customs union and the idea of rearmament, while the loan negotiations failed to work out for lack of real understanding on both sides. Bruening came to Paris to ask for help, but was unwilling to pay for French aid by making any reciprocal commitments. The French, in turn, talked of floating a large French-British-American loan, but only if the Germans would agree to a kind of mortgage on their economy and a firm commitment to respect the *status quo* in Europe for a decade. A partial breakthrough finally came in June 1932, when an interallied conference at Lausanne virtually cancelled further German reparations payments; but by that time it was too late to save the Weimar regime. Briand, an old and sick man, had already been replaced at the foreign ministry. Whether a full dose of Briandism in the years 1929–32 might have saved the German republic is impossible to say; yet in retrospect, it would probably have been worth trying as a kind of calculated risk.

❖❖❖❖❖❖❖❖❖❖❖❖❖❖❖

France's policies toward the chain of smaller states extending from the Baltic to the Balkans were determined by French relationships with Germany, Italy, and the new Soviet regime. Poland, largest of all in size, population, and standing army, became the anchor of the French alliance system in eastern Europe. French military aid to the Poles helped them to survive their critical war with Russia in 1920–21, when for a time it seemed that Poland might be overrun and converted into a Soviet satellite. France also acted as a kind of sponsor to the so-called Little Entente, made up of countries carved out of the old Austro-Hungarian empire and dedicated to averting the return of the Hapsburgs. Some French aid was extended to these states in the form of loans and expert military advice, but the flow remained relatively small. French commercial relationships with eastern Europe were also not very highly developed; only in Yugoslavia was French private capital to be found in sizable amounts, mainly in the copper-mining industry there. French policy-makers made sporadic efforts in the late 1920's and early 1930's to fuse parts of eastern Europe into a tighter bloc; their favorite scheme was a Danubian federation that might be strong enough to serve as a barrier against both a resurgent Germany and an adventurous Italy. But internal divisions in the Danube valley combined with hostile pressures from Rome, Berlin, and London to keep the French plan in the blueprint stage.

Although some Frenchmen were tempted by the idea of restoring the old tie with the Russians or the wartime alliance with the Italians, both projects ran into ideological opposition. Herriot's Radical government did recognize the Soviet Union in 1924, and then sought to negotiate a payments agreement on the tsarist debt to French bondholders. The attempt broke down even before the return of the Moderates to power; relations thereafter grew steadily worse, as the Soviet government sought to use its Paris embassy for purposes of propaganda and espionage. The Communists' hostile line toward the French Socialists blocked the growth of broad left-wing sympathy for a Franco-Soviet tie.

Franco-Italian friendship cooled during the Paris peace conference of 1919, and it suffered a further setback when Mussolini took power in 1922. Although the extreme right in France welcomed the new Italian regime and campaigned actively for a Latin bloc, the left and much of the center remained skeptical or hostile. Most of Italy's antifascist émigrés fled to Paris, where they carried on active agitation against Mussolini's regime and provoked repeated diplomatic protests from Rome. Continuing friction over the status of the large Italian minority in Tunisia provided another irritant; the French refused to grant this minority equal status unless its members would become French citizens. Fascist designs on parts of the French colonial empire and fascist intrigues in the Danube valley added to the suspicion in Paris. Not until the rise of Hitler did the threat of German power begin to overshadow the differences separating what some Frenchmen liked to call the Latin sisters.

❖❖❖❖❖❖❖❖❖❖❖❖❖❖

In the realm of overseas empire, French power reached its peak during the years between the wars. To the old colonies absorbed two centuries earlier and the vast areas added in the pre-1914 generation, victory in the Great War brought important new acquisitions: a sizable share of the German empire in Africa and the Turkish empire in the Near East. President Wilson's insistence at Paris forced the French to agree that the new territories would be mandated areas supervised by the League of Nations; but the limitations on French control proved to be slight. France's overseas possessions now totaled four and a half million square miles—twenty times the area of the homeland, with a population almost double that of France. Patriots began to claim proudly that there were now a hundred million Frenchmen under the tricolor.

But if Frenchmen took pride in their imperial strength, most of them still had no real interest in, or understanding of, the empire. With a few exceptions, the colonies were not adapted to large-scale European settlement, even if the French as a people had been inclined to emigrate. The vast stretches of French Equatorial Africa, for example, never attracted more than about five thousand Frenchmen, most of them colonial officials rather than settlers or businessmen. Only Algeria, and to a lesser extent Tunisia and Morocco, had European minorities of any size. French investment in the empire was not much more extensive than French emigration. Public expenditures on railways, harbors, schools, social services, remained relatively meager after the Great War; private capital preferred other outlets, though some banks and enterprises did invest in mining and large-scale agriculture in Indo-China and Morocco. Most of the old colonies survived like outmoded ghost towns from another era; the vast new ones slumbered on without much change, save for a gradual improvement in public health through the control of endemic and epidemic diseases. These vast underdeveloped areas provided only a meager market for French goods and furnished little except foodstuffs in return. In 1929 only 15 per cent of France's foreign trade was with the empire. A few politicians in the 1920's began to advocate a program of planned economic development (*mise en valeur,* they called it) and contended that private capital could not do the job alone. Some of them even proposed that the colonies be freed from the rather rigid embrace of the French tariff system so that they might buy and sell on the world market. None of these campaigns produced significant results; and the Great Depression was to undermine the slight progress that had been accomplished. As foreign markets for French exports shrivelled up, French businessmen were jolted into a new awareness of the value of a closed imperial market. By the mid-1930's almost one-third of France's exports were going to the empire—more than the French could now sell to their three best European customers combined. These figures, however, concealed the fact that the colonial market had simply shrunk less rapidly than the foreign market.

In the broader realms of political and cultural relationships, it scarcely occurred to any Frenchman that paternalistic and bureaucratic rule from Paris might not be the wisest way to run an empire. True, the older policy labelled "assimilation," which aimed to convert the colonized peoples into completely acculturized Frenchmen, was being abandoned in favor of "association," sponsored initially by the French left. But the new doctrine involved no very fundamental change; its goal was to acculturize only a small native elite, which would then share with Frenchmen the task of governing vast populations sunk in primitive barbarism. The idea of a real decentralization of decision-making, a real trend toward autonomy and federalism, was simply outside the mental horizons of French leaders of that era.

For a time after 1918 French politicians seriously discussed extending the military conscription law to the overseas possessions, so as to draw on what they called an "inexhaustible reservoir of men" to supplement France's own dwindling manpower and to shorten the conscription period. About a half-million colonial soldiers (most of them volunteers) had served in France during the Great War; the temptation was great to extend the practice. Even those Frenchmen who favored the idea, however, would not consider racial integration of French and colonial troops or a grant of citizenship to those who served. In the end parliament rejected general conscription, partly on the ground that it would divert native manpower that might be needed for colonial economic development. Some limited conscription did persist, but it varied in different colonies and affected only a few men.

If Frenchmen were guilty of the sins normally associated with colonial rule, their brand of imperialism continued to be more cultural than economic. It was easy to cling to their illusory paternalistic practices so long as the subject peoples remained passive and unorganized; and until the 1930's that was the case almost everywhere. Only in the Near Eastern mandated area of Syria was there an aggressive nationalist movement that threatened French control and that had to be checked by force. In 1925–26 a revolt of the Riff hill tribes under Abd el Krim spilled over from Spanish into French Morocco; but it resembled the American Indian wars rather than a modern nationalist movement. Elsewhere, the premonitory signs of nationalist discontent already detected by men like Lenin remained too feeble to attract the serious notice of politicians in Paris or colonial officials in the field. Small nuclei of activists existed in Indo-China and Tunisia and were to grow rapidly in the 1930's; elsewhere, it was easy to believe throughout the interwar years that the native populations had no higher ambition than to remain French subjects.

# CHAPTER 29

# Economy and Society
# in the Postwar Decade, 1919–1931

In the meantime Penguinia gloried in its wealth. Those who produced the things necessary for life, wanted them; those who did not produce them had more than enough. "But these," as a member of the Institute said, "are necessary economic fatalities."

ANATOLE FRANCE

A wealthy country chronically on the verge of bankruptcy: such is the impression given by France in the interwar years. War and reconstruction had left the state with a heavy burden of public debt, owed both to foreign nations and to its own citizens—a burden that, if assumed without postponement, would have skimmed off much of the nation's wealth and would have imposed a policy of strict austerity on a whole generation. But French leaders of the era, responsive to the pressures of French citizens generally, took the understandable if shortsighted position that if anybody's wealth were to be skimmed off, it should be that of Germany and not of France. No American can properly criticize this French failure to face up to hard and painful facts in the postwar decade, for Americans scarcely did better in that respect. The difference was that France's problem was bigger and more urgent. It needed to be faced without delay, while French wealth and resources were still adequate to meet it without large-scale external aid.

The French failure to take prompt and adequate action was the product of several convergent factors. One of these was lack of experience with a shaky currency and a serious deficit in the public treasury. For decades the franc had been solid as a rock, and the state budget had been steadily balanced despite the failure of French governments to modernize their ramshackle and antiquated tax structure. The "myth of the franc"—the illusion that even major catastrophes like wars, revolutions, and depressions could not shake its value—had a powerful grip on French minds, and it could not be dissipated at once when circumstances changed. A second factor was the persistence of a social structure that made any major change in the tax system politically difficult. In an economy dominated by a few giant firms, a parliament responsive to the voters can presumably get the bulk of its revenue from large enterprise, which controls few votes. In an economy based in considerable part on a huge mass of small private operators, the problem of raising tax levels or redistributing the tax burden becomes much more severe. France's parliament did finally adopt an income-tax law in 1916, but its rates were so low and its loopholes so large that it worked no revolutionary change in public finance. During the interwar years less than a quarter of the government's total tax revenue came from the income tax; the rest was produced by the so-called four old taxes on real property and by various indirect levies such as the business turnover tax adopted in 1920. Still a third factor was the economic illiteracy of most French politicians. Those who were lawyers by profession had been exposed to a highly abstract and outmoded kind of economics in the law schools, while the nonlawyers in parliament had only private business experience and a set of deep-rooted prejudices to guide them. Not one French leader at the end of the Great War was both able and willing to try to educate the electorate in the economic problems that faced the nation. Clemenceau had the courage to do so, but he prided himself on his ignorance of economics. Poincaré probably had the requisite knowledge, but he clung to his legalistic illusion that since "the Boche" ought to pay, he *would* pay. In the early postwar years a curious double-budget device lulled the voters into security; alongside a regular budget that was not merely balanced but showed a surplus, an "extraordinary budget" almost three times as large was devoted to war and reconstruction costs, with no provision for receipts except as the Germans might pay reparations.

So long as the war had lasted, interallied controls kept the franc from depreciating by more than 15 per cent. Within a year after the armistice its value had fallen by more than 50 per cent; and the downward trend continued, more slowly and spasmodically, in subsequent years. A series of reconstruction bond issues were floated and sold to French citizens, in order to finance the rebuilding of the devastated areas without delay. In addition, some of the wartime bonds began to come due, and the government chose to replace them with new issues bearing even higher interest rates. The treasury thus borrowed more from French citizens during the early 1920's than it had borrowed from them during the war itself; and the interest burden piled up in ominous fashion. French suggestions that the United States write off American war loans to France got a cold reception in Washington; eventually, and reluctantly, that burden had to be shouldered, too, though a payments agreement was not worked out until 1926.

It was obvious to everyone—even the politicians—that taxes had to be increased, but until 1923 every proposal to that end was defeated. Most deputies were willing to vote additional taxes; they simply could not agree as to which Frenchmen should pay them. Meanwhile, governments managed to operate by resorting to a disguised form of inflation; the treasury was supplied with steadily larger advances from the Bank of France, which in turn put more currency into circulation. The left wing's victory at the polls in 1924 only made matters worse. The two major parties of the left clashed sharply on financial policy, the Socialists favoring a capital levy and a reduction of the interest rate on government bonds, the Radicals rejecting both ideas as dangerously confiscatory. Many Radical voters possessed a small nest egg of capital, often in the form of a few government bonds. Another factor also operated against the left. The Bank of France, controlled by large private banking interests, began to balk at further advances to the treasury; its directors had little enthusiasm for a government that might be tempted to try a capital levy. A flight of capital set in after 1924, leading to a new and more rapid decline in the franc and a new record for cabinet instability—six cabinet crises in the space of only nine months.

This state of almost permanent crisis, with the franc down to less than one-tenth of its prewar value and threatening to collapse entirely, forced the Radical leadership to make a decisive choice: either to adopt the Socialists' drastic program, or to abdicate power to the Moderates. Most of them preferred the second alternative; Raymond Poincaré was called back to the premiership in 1926, and the Radicals assured him of their support. Poincaré they trusted as scrupulously honest, a dedicated republican, and a lifelong anticlerical. His broadly-based cabinet (which included some Radical representatives) checked the crisis with remarkable ease, and without either foreign borrowing or really fundamental reforms at home. The impact was primarily psychological, through a restoration of confidence that the government would neither "soak the rich" nor let the franc collapse. Taxes were sharply increased (perhaps too sharply, indeed), though without altering the distribution of the tax burden; drastic cuts were made in government expenditures. But what really counted was the return of capital from hiding or from safe havens abroad, to be reinvested at home or to be used to buy government bonds. The franc suddenly rose so rapidly that the government had to step in and check it at about 20 per cent of its prewar value (the equivalent of four cents in place of twenty). The Paris daily *Le Temps* (which reflected the outlook of its industrialist owners) labelled the premier "Poincaré the Well-Beloved" and asserted that "one would have to go back to Saint Louis to find such popular enthusiasm for a sovereign."

Over the next several years the franc seemed to have recovered the stability of prewar days, and the chronic financial problem appeared to be solved at last.

True, the franc had not been restored to its full prewar value, in the fashion of the British pound; therefore many Frenchmen (holders of wartime bonds, for example) lost 80 per cent of their original investment. But rather than sulk over this loss, most of these Frenchmen were inclined to congratulate themselves that they had not been wiped out completely, as had many German investors during the 1923 inflation. The French solution to the war's financial burden—an inflation that was checked short of disaster—fell midway between that of the Germans and that of the British and was probably healthier than either. It was, however, a solution that was more empirical than planned.

France's inflationary experience, nevertheless, had serious long-range results. For one thing, it left the French with a kind of neurosis about the franc. After 1926 they suffered from a nagging fear of another decline and developed a kind of psychological block against any tampering with the currency. Some years later, when the depression drove nations everywhere to abandon the gold standard and to devalue their currencies, the French clung to the "Poincaré franc" with disastrous results. A second serious consequence of the episode was to consolidate the legend that a greedy band of capitalists had used its financial power to destroy the left-wing coalition of 1924-26, thus frustrating the will of the voters. The big bankers, it was alleged, had erected a *mur d'argent* (barrier of money) against the left's reform program by refusing further advances to the treasury from the Bank of France. The legend contained a little truth; but at least an equal share of responsibility for the left's downfall was traceable to the left's own voters. Thousands of little investors cashed in their government bonds or withdrew their savings from French banks in order to send it abroad or buy easily hoarded gold. Rarely had there been a clearer example of André Siegfried's hackneyed law of politics that even though Frenchmen's hearts might be on the left, their pocketbooks remained on the right. The legend of the *mur d'argent* persisted nevertheless; it contributed to the later rise of the Popular Front (which was bound together in part by its denunciations of the "two hundred families" that controlled the Bank of France) and to the eventual nationalization of the major French banks in 1946.

❖❖❖❖❖❖❖❖❖❖❖❖❖❖❖❖

When one looks behind the problem of public finance to the state of the French economy as a whole, the impression of crisis and instability disappears in favor of a sense of steadily expanding wealth and well-being. By 1929-30 all production and trade figures had reached record levels. Industrial production, which had fallen during the war to 57 (base year 1913 $= 100$), was up to 140, whereas the British figure still lagged behind the prewar level. Foreign trade had attained 166. Only agriculture remained relatively stagnant, with total production up barely 3 per cent over the 1913 figure. These gains resulted only in part from the recovery of Alsace with its textile mills, Lorraine with its iron ore and its steel plants, the Saar with its temporary supply of coal. The improvement also derived from the destruction of much outmoded French industry in the north and its replacement by modern factories. There was a general increase in productivity as well, and a slow but steady modernization of a broad sector of French enterprise.

Agriculture lagged behind as the weakest sector of the economy, but this fact reflected a world-wide condition in the 1920's. As a whole, French farming was becoming more efficient; total production increased even though the number of people on the land continued to decline. By 1929 the average yield of wheat per acre, for example, was 30 per cent higher than during the prewar decade. But much of this improvement was concentrated in a limited area in the northeast, the wheat and sugar-beet country, where large-scale mechanized farming was taking over. Most of rural France dragged on with scarcely altered methods and at a marginal standard. Economists calculated that the 35 per cent of Frenchmen who still lived by agriculture were receiving only 18 per cent of the national income. At the time almost no French farmers knew of these statistics, nor were they aware that some of the same sort of disproportion between agriculture and industry existed in every country. But they were beginning to sense acutely that many peasants were worse off than the city population and that the days of farm prosperity during the war were definitely over. The drift to the cities, temporarily checked during the war years, became more rapid than ever before. And the peasants' growing discontent opened a wide gap for the activities of agitators of both left and right, particularly in the 1930's.

Although the economy as a whole seemed to be prosperous and expanding in the 1920's, it can be argued that far more might have been done, and that France may have missed a golden opportunity for really fundamental modernization and economic resurgence in that boom era. It is true that French recovery was far more successful than British, but the rate of economic expansion was sharply below the world rate in the postwar decade. Indeed, it had been falling behind the world rate since 1910 at least. One reason was that postwar France failed to invest enough in modernizing its productive plant. This was not because French capital was again flowing abroad; Frenchmen after the war were investing outside France only one-twentieth as much as they had before 1914. Rather, it was because so large a slice of France's national income had to go for paying for the recent war and policing Europe against a new one. Reconstruction, pensions, and the army were absorbing ten per cent of the national income. Another cause of lagging investment was the nervousness of holders of capital and the resulting periodic flight of funds. And more basic still was the survival of so many small plants that failed to make enough profit either to allow self-financed expansion or to attract outside funds. Their existence produced an apparent stability that approached stagnation; their chief economic impact was to keep French price levels inordinately high.

It is true that in some circles during the 1920's France experienced a real drive toward the rationalizing of industry, toward more modern and efficient methods. A current of Saint-Simonianism or Americanism, stronger than at any time since the days of Napoleon III, set in during the boom years after 1925. The most typical representative of this spirit was André Citroën, an automobile manufacturer who had worked for a time in Detroit and who had become inspired by the example of Henry Ford. Citroën was a new industrialist who got his chance during the war years and made the most of it. He adopted production-line methods and large-scale marketing devices aimed at encouraging mass consumption; he even advertised by skywriting and by illuminated signs on the Eiffel Tower. Unlike traditional French enterprisers, his ambition was to undersell competitors and dominate the market rather than to share a limited market through cartel procedures. In politics, the leading exponent of the same renovating spirit was André Tardieu, whose experience as wartime purchasing agent in the United States had convinced him of the virtues of American industrial methods. This new spirit took organized form in 1925 when a group of rightist politicians, industrialists, and bankers of somewhat technocratic outlook formed a pressure group called Redressement Français (French Resurgence). Its suggestive symbol was a reproduction of the Roman statue "The Dying Gaul"; its program called for a tougher, more vigorous political system (notably a stronger executive) and a new entrepreneurial spirit in the business world (emphasizing a really competitive laissez faire ideal).

This revival of Saint-Simonianism, however, affected only a limited minority in the French business and political worlds. Far larger and more powerful was the older group of industrialists, content with the tradition of limited production, high profit margins, and market-sharing through cartel agreements. Most of France's basic production (e.g., of steel, chemicals, etc.) remained in their hands; the innovators appeared primarily in the conversion or finished-goods industries, where they were seriously hampered by the high cost of their basic materials. Besides, the new entrepreneurs were far more vulnerable to the impact of a major economic crisis. Thus the postwar recovery era merely accentuated the division of the French economy into two increasingly divergent sectors: the dynamic and the static. That division coincided in part—but only in part—with the differentiation between large and small enterprise and between urban and rural areas. Within limits, there was also a gradual tendency toward geographical differentiation—the dynamic enterprises clustering in the northeastern quarter of France, from Paris to the Belgian and German frontiers, the static element holding doggedly to its habits in the central and southern half of the country. Economically and socially, two Frances were emerging within this long-unified nation, the one superimposed on the other as in a double-exposure photograph.

One much debated issue of the postwar decade—an issue with both economic and social implications—was the demographic problem. France emerged from the Great War seriously short of manpower; in the 1920's active campaigns to recruit foreign labor were undertaken by the large steel firms, coal mines, and mechanized farms. Two million immigrants arrived during that decade from almost every part of Europe; France replaced the United States as the world's melting pot. The newcomers were not, however, easily assimilable. Four-fifths of them were men, unmarried or with families left at home; and French regulations restricted most of them to the less desirable types of work and to relatively isolated mining towns or large farms. Some of the immigrants also took over abandoned farms in the south, as tenants or sharecroppers. Only about one in four became a naturalized citizen.

Many Frenchmen had come to accept immigration as a logical necessity to solve a population problem far older than the war. But the population question promptly got entangled in politics. The trade unions and the left wing generally were skeptical about any planned immigration policy or any scheme to stimulate the birth rate through bonuses to large families; they suspected the capitalists of seeking devices to get cheaper labor or the Catholics of plotting to recover control of France. The unions looked without enthusiasm on experiments with family allowances undertaken in the 1920's by some Catholic employers. Not until after the Second World War did the left become fully aware of the deleterious economic effects of an aging population and of the social justice of some redistribution of income in favor of larger families. After 1945 family allowances were to become an essential part of the French social security system, with labor's hearty consent.

If the French working class in the 1920's showed an excessive tendency to be suspicious and resentful toward both employers and politicians, at least it had much justification for such an attitude. Already in the prewar boom era labor had failed to get its full share of the nation's expanding prosperity; in the postwar period of expansion the workers' gains from rising productivity continued to lag behind those of other urban groups. During the 1920's the wage-earners' buying power (based on 1914 = 100) fluctuated between 100 and 120. Only the small peasantry profited less from economic growth. Labor did win one major victory immediately after the war, when Clemenceau in 1919 legalized the eight-hour day in an effort to forestall a major strike wave. That reform, however, had proved to be the end of labor's gains rather than the first step in a whole series of improvements, as the trade unions had hoped. The C.G.T., bolstered by the influx of a million new members during and after the war, embarked on a series of strikes in late 1919 that culminated in May 1920, in an attempt at a general strike. The undertaking had been poorly prepared, and it was met head-on by the right-wing majority in the new Chamber. The collapse of the strike was disastrous to the unions; within a year two-thirds of the C.G.T.'s members had abandoned the organization. Through the rest of the decade, and down till 1936, ninety per cent of French workers remained unorganized. And to make matters worse, those who remained union members were divided among three rival organizations—Communist, Catholic, and nonpolitical syndicalist.

This division of the workers and their resistance to organization sterilized the proletariat as a pressure group; it meant that labor could exert little influence on parliament to offset that of big business, small enterprise, or even those farm producers who learned at last during the 1920's that organization pays. Yet even if French labor had been unified and organized, it would doubtless have been frustrated in its demands. Parliament, by the nature of the electoral system and the social composition of the electorate, remained dominated by small-town and rural France, and these voters were steadily reluctant to tax themselves to help the urban workers. Furthermore, most French employers showed little sign of social conscience; their central interest in the 1920's seemed to be to secure the repeal of labor's single gain, the eight-hour day, on the ground that it was responsible for the high cost of production in France.

Undoubtedly, labor gained a little from the general growth of production in the postwar decade—though more in increased leisure than in improved living standards. The urban workers also gained, in the short run at least, by the perpetuation of wartime rent controls; in an era of inflation, rents were held at so low a level that they eventually absorbed only 5 to 7 per cent of the worker's budget. In the long run, however, this advantage boomeranged against both workers and lower bourgeoisie. Rents were too low to permit proper maintenance by landlords, so vast areas in the cities rapidly deteriorated into noisome slums, sometimes concealed behind façades that remained externally impressive. There was no longer any incentive for low-cost housing construction, which dried up completely except for a few municipally-financed projects. By the end of the interwar period France was facing a critical housing emergency. Rent controls, a sop to the voters by the politicians, ended by breeding a whole series of social problems; and these in turn fed proletarian resentment toward a society that would permit such evils to exist.

If a doctrine or mystique was needed to reinforce these unpleasant facts, it was provided by the Soviet example. "Just as a new generation was beginning to forget the Paris Commune [Val Lorwin tells us], the Russian Revolution added its spell. In no country did this great twentieth century myth make a deeper impression than in skeptical France; among no group a greater impression than on the workers who had never made a successful revolution of their own."[1] The new mystique combined with an old and brooding sense of injustice to prevent a lessening of social tensions even in a time of prosperity. Through the years of normalcy the active minority of French labor remained alienated from the republic, indifferent to its fate and hostile to its leadership. The consequences in an era of depression and crisis were to be disastrous.

[1] V. Lorwin, "Labor and Economic Development in France."

# CHAPTER 30

# Depression Politics, 1931–1936

A governing class in decline lives by half-measures, from day to day, always postponing the examination of vital questions until tomorrow.

IGNAZIO SILONE

From 1926 to 1931 France experienced what seems in retrospect to have been a kind of Indian summer. *La belle époque* had apparently returned; a stable franc, a booming economy, a brilliant culture coincided to produce a wave of euphoria and a new sense of confidence. Paris once more could regard itself as the capital of Europe, or even of the world. The reconstruction of the war-torn areas was complete; German reparations payments were arriving on schedule; the "Locarno spirit" seemed to promise a long era of relaxation and harmony in Europe. Not only was the governmental budget balanced annually, but an impressive surplus was piling up in the treasury. It was beginning to attract so many demagogic politicians that in 1929 Premier Tardieu proposed a great five-year spending program to devote the surplus to public works and economic expansion.

As the repercussions of the New York stock market crash spread throughout the world, France seemed more and more like a protected island in a stormy sea. The boom continued through 1930 and well into 1931; only after two full years of world crisis did the French dikes begin to break down. But more important than the late arrival of the depression in France was the fact that when it came, it stayed; it developed into the longest and deepest economic crisis France had known for a century. The downswing was not checked until the end of 1935, much later than in other nations; and when recovery did set in, the upswing was slower than in almost any other country.

Until 1931 some Frenchmen reacted to their good fortune with a certain smugness; the advantages of France's economic and social structure, they argued, were being proved over those of societies that claimed to be more dynamic. Much was made of the healthy balance between farm and factory, between large and small enterprise; such an economy was held to be less susceptible to the great economic swings of modern capitalism. Defenders of the French system pointed out that the small producer or trader, the little polycultural farmer, was better able to adapt himself to stringent times than was the big operator with a large overhead and a constant need for a mass market. They pointed, too, to the merits of the cautious and conservative business approach of Frenchmen, whose prudence had protected them against the wild speculative gambling of business men elsewhere. Now Frenchmen could gloat a bit and enjoy the fruits of their virtue.

This case was not entirely invalid. A less dynamic economy is likely to survive a long crisis better than an advanced, highly complex system dependent on a stable world with freely-flowing trade currents. France's archaic small farms served as a kind of cushion to absorb the shock of the crash; the peasants could fall back on even more complete self-sufficiency than usual, and they could feed part of the urban unemployed who returned to the farm to sit out the crisis. In heavy weather, a raft is more seaworthy than a speedboat.

But if the nature of the French economy and of French business psychology helped to soften the impact of the depression once it arrived, other factors were responsible for postponing that impact. The crisis came late to France because of a series of lucky accidents. For one thing, the franc had been stabilized in 1928 at a relatively low level—probably too low to reflect its real exchange value at the time. France thus became a cheap country for foreign buyers and visitors; a large backlog of orders poured in, carrying French producers along into 1931 without much slackening in production. A second factor was the steady flow of gold back into France, attracted because the franc remained stable and business good. The French gold supply therefore continued to rise after 1929 and gave the illusion of wealth that tended to conceal the crisis for months after the first danger signs began to appear. Still a third factor was a lucky turn in the weather in 1930; a bad harvest postponed until 1931 the problem of agricultural surpluses that had plagued the rest of the world since the crash.

The unfortunate consequence was that French governments did almost nothing until 1932, and not very much more until 1935, to work out a consistent crisis program. What actions they did take were of a piecemeal, opportunistic nature, fitting into no kind of long-range policy or plan. In part, this immobility derived from the fact that in a divided country, with a weak executive power, agreement on vigorous economic measures of any kind is hard to reach. But it also derived from the conviction of many Frenchmen that there was no French crisis at all; that a healthy France was simply unlucky enough to be caught in a world of sick nations. That doctrine suggested that France needed only to seal itself off from the rest of the world in order to keep out the germs of disease.

The primary aim during the early 1930's, therefore, was to isolate France behind a tariff wall, and behind that wall to prevent any changes in the French economy. Above all, French governments sought to keep the French price level from dropping, even if that might mean a loss of foreign markets and a sharp reduction in the size of the domestic market. When world prices fell so low that foreign farm products began to spill across the high tariff wall, the French added a system of quotas as well. Within this closed area, meanwhile, governments let industry take care of itself through domestic cartel arrangements. Participating producers agreed to cut production, share the shrinking home market, and keep prices at the predepression level. Government and industry cooperated to avert any serious unemployment problem; thousands of foreign workers were sent back to their countries of origin, while many French workers voluntarily returned to their ancestral farms. French unemployment figures even at the worst moment in the depression decade never rose much above a half-million—a total lower by far than that of any other industrial nation. Most small farmers and shopkeepers of the precapitalist type also took care of themselves by the simple process of belt-tightening, aided by only a little governmental action. The government's help was primarily negative and took the form of a kind of legalized tax exemption. Whereas 700,000 farmers had paid an income tax in 1927, the figure dropped to 97,000 in 1935.

For the more dynamic sector in agriculture—the large capitalist farms or the smaller, one-crop producers, dependent on the market—the problem of adjustment to the depression was much more serious. Successive governments had to step in with a system of controls to limit production or to bolster the prices of such items as wheat and wine. Although these schemes often functioned badly and aroused much criticism, they worked their way into the habits of the farm population and became quasi-permanent aspects of French agricultural policy. Since the depression a free market system has never been restored for certain important farm products. One particular group of specialized farmers did take care of itself—too well, indeed, for the welfare of the nation as a whole. The sugar-beet growers, few in number but prosperous and shrewd, managed to organize a kind of producers' cartel that limited acreage effectively. Far more important, however, they learned to operate as a political pressure group. By recruiting the support of the winegrowers, whose voting power was far greater than their own, they persuaded parliament to authorize purchase of all excess sugar-beets and wine at a favorable price. These products were then distilled into alcohol, which the government either stored, sold at a loss, or mixed into the gasoline supply that automobile owners then had to buy at double the regular gasoline price. This arrangement, once adopted, became a kind of inviolable vested interest even after the economic emergency ended. "Alcohol," remarked the French demographer Alfred Sauvy twenty years later, "makes two kinds of lunatics: those who drink it and those who pay for it."

In industry as in agriculture, the dynamic sector was harder hit than the static sector by the depression. One traditional indirect advantage of old-style "panics" had been their function of cutting away economic deadwood; hard times forced many inefficient enterprisers out of business or drove them to modernize and rationalize their methods. That purpose was not served by the French depression of the 1930's. If anything, the effect was just the opposite: it was the least fit that tended to survive. This happened in part because the government took measures to help the weak, and in part because the static industries kept each other afloat through cartel arrangements. Those who went under (and there were some resounding crashes) were often the most vigorous and imaginative entrepreneurs—those in the uncartelized sector of the industrial system. The most notable case was that of André Citroën. His spectacular career had won him the ironic sobriquet "King of Paris," but it had brought him few friends among the traditional industrialists and bankers. When trouble came Citroën proposed to meet it not by retrenching but by capturing the market with a new front-wheel-drive model. As the crisis deepened, he borrowed money to retool his entire plant; but before the conversion process was complete, disaster struck. His creditors closed in and refused his pleas for a ninety-day extension to get his new car on the market. In 1934 his empire crashed into bankruptcy; and shortly afterward Citroën carried his symbolic Americanism to its ultimate conclusion by failing to survive an operation for ulcers.

❖❖❖❖❖❖❖❖❖❖❖❖❖❖❖

During the early depression years the political machinery of France remained in the hands of the Moderates. Poincaré's successful stabilization of the franc, and the years of prosperity that followed, had enabled the right-center groups to triumph in the 1928 elections. Again there was no important shift in the popular vote, but a return to the traditional electoral system of small single-member districts benefited the center parties. Illness forced Poincaré to abandon the premiership in 1929, but his prestige enabled his Moderate friends to retain control of the cabinet until the 1932 elections. The key figure of the period was André Tardieu, who headed three cabinets between 1929 and 1932. A brilliant man of overbearing and cynical temper, Tardieu for years seemed to be on the verge of becoming one of the republic's really first-rank statesmen, yet never quite lived up to his promise. The economic crisis reinforced his conviction that the French political and economic system must be transformed in the direction of either the British or the American model. Political reform, he believed, was the essential first step toward economic rejuvenation; what France needed was a two-party system with a strong and stable executive.

Tardieu's plan for modernizing the Third Republic was not a new one; it consisted of introducing the Anglo-American electoral system of electing representatives by simple plurality, without a second run-off ballot. Such a plan, he believed, would force all parties to fuse into two major political movements; and he was convinced that the bulk of the Radicals in such case would be driven to join the Moderates, thus ensuring a clear right-center majority. At his urging, the Laval cabinet in 1931 managed to get this electoral reform adopted by the Chamber, but it was rejected in the Radical-dominated Senate. The Radicals much preferred the run-off ballot, which enabled their candidates to ally with either left or right and thus maximize their chances.

Beaten by the politicians, Tardieu sought to sell his program to the country at large. He had no illusions about the wisdom of the man in the street; "public opinion," he remarked privately, "is a harlot that must be driven with a whip." But he had no choice; and so he led the Moderates into the 1932 elections, preaching the virtues and the necessity of reform. In spite of an almost unprecedented slush fund furnished by Tardieu's business friends, the voters failed to respond. By this time the impact of the depression was being clearly felt, and the parties in power suffered the natural consequences. The Moderate groups were beaten, and Tardieu angrily withdrew from active political life, devoting himself henceforth to an increasingly bitter one-man press crusade against the shortcomings of the invertebrate republic.

The left's electoral victory in 1932 brought the Radicals back into power. They outnumbered the Socialists in the new Chamber, even though for the first time the Socialists emerged as France's largest party as measured by popular votes. The Communists, still isolated by choice and badly split by internal dissension, lost votes for the first time since the party was founded. The Socialists, faithful to the non-participation doctrine of Guesde as revised and elaborated by Léon Blum, refused to enter any coalition cabinet which they could not dominate; but as in 1924, they promised to support a Radical government without participating in it. Once again Herriot became premier; and once again France entered upon a two-year period of governmental instability that had been equalled only in 1924–26. Six cabinets in twenty months was the dismal record. The source of the trouble was once again the inability of the Radicals and Socialists to agree on an economic program and particularly on that essential question, who should bear the cost of recovery?

This chronic instability, combined with the steadily worsening economic situation and the ominous growth of Nazism across the Rhine, led many Frenchmen and foreigners, too, to conclude that the republic was on the verge of complete disintegration and that some sort of authoritarian regime had become almost inevitable. Whether France really skirted the edges of fascist revolution in those years is a controversial question that has been debated ever since. In the opinion of one school, a carefully planned fascist coup was barely averted in 1934 and was thwarted thereafter only by the organization of a Popular Front alliance that fused the strength of the entire left. A second school holds that the threat has been much exaggerated; organized fascism in France was relatively small and weak, it made no serious attempt to seize power, and it would probably have failed if it had tried to strike. According to the exponents of this second view, the experience of the 1930's proved that France was virtually immune to fascism, except as it might be imported by a foreign conqueror. The controversy hinges in part on varying definitions of "fascism," and in part on varying views of what really happened in 1934 when the attempted coup d'état allegedly took place.

The depression decade did encourage the growth in France of a whole series of movements or "leagues" that were loosely labelled "fascist" by their enemies. Some of them professed an affinity with the doctrines and systems of Mussolini and Hitler: for example, Marcel Bucard's Francistes, Major Jean Renaud's Solidarité Française, and Eugène Deloncle's Comité Secret d'Action Révolutionnaire (popularly called the Cagoulards or hooded men) of the later 1930's. Although some of these groups were subsidized by wealthy extremists like the perfumer François Coty, they failed to attract mass support. No dependable membership figures exist, but probably none of them enrolled more than fifty thousand real activists, and some had only a few hundred. The one exceptional case was Jacques Doriot's Parti Populaire Français (P.P.F.), which eventually attracted a half-million disciples. Until 1934 Doriot had been one of the top figures in the Communist party and was viewed by many as the potential Stalin of France. Increasingly, however, it became clear that he saw the party as an agency to serve his own ambitions. Like Mussolini before him, he was an opportunist and an activist rather than a fanatic and a doctrinaire; his goal was power rather than utopia. After his expulsion by the Communists in 1934 he tried for a time to compete with them for the labor vote, then followed Il Duce's example by shifting abruptly to the extreme right. It is not surprising that Mussolini secretly subsidized his movement after 1936; what *is* surprising is the fact that so many old-fashioned French conservatives were misled by the traditionalist phrases that partially concealed Doriot's totalitarian aims. If Doriot had founded the P.P.F. earlier and had been ready to strike in 1934–35 when the republic's defenses were down, his movement would have been a formidable threat to the regime.

All of the aforementioned leagues were truly fascist—or, to use a less ambiguous word, totalitarian. They were revolutionary in spirit; they aimed to uproot the old system completely and to overturn all traditional institutions; they proposed to create a new elite and not to restore or confirm the power of the old traditional elites. They were marked by a kind of distorted neoromanticism in their stress on change and on action for action's sake. They truly represented that twentieth-century current called the radical right.

But alongside these totalitarian groups there emerged a number of more ambiguous movements that attracted much wider support, and that belonged more properly in the older French tradition of the authoritarian nationalist right. The largest by far was the Croix de Feu movement of Colonel de La Rocque; the most durable was that hardy perennial the Action Française of Maurras. Such organizations deserved the fascist label only in the loosest sense of the term. Their leaders were not right-wing radicals but conservatives or reactionaries. They yearned not for upheaval and the creation of a new elite, but for order, stability, authority, and a return to the old elites. They favored not the totalitarian ideal that would create a monopoly of power, but a more pluralistic and decentralized system that would respect the nation's deep-rooted institutions. Some men of totalitarian temper were attracted to these groups for a time, but most of them withdrew as soon as they detected the lack of revolutionary spirit there. Many of Doriot's P.P.F. adherents, for example, were dissatisfied deserters from the Croix de Feu, and the Cagoulard conspiracy was composed mainly of impatient ex-members of the Action Française.

The Croix de Feu, founded in 1928 as an organization of veterans decorated for valor, was gradually converted into a political movement after Colonel de La Rocque became its president in 1931. By 1933 it had between forty and sixty thousand members; by 1935 it claimed several hundred thousand. Its appeal depended in part on its amorphous vagueness; any patriot who wanted strong government and disliked communism could feel at home here. It was in a sense (as René Rémond puts it) a political boy-scout movement for adults. Its most massive growth was to come after 1936, when it was suppressed along with the other leagues and re-emerged at once as a regular party—the Parti Social Français or P.S.F. Its claim of three million members in 1938 was certainly exaggerated, but its following just as certainly exceeded that of all the radical-right groups combined.

That most Frenchmen of the right preferred a La Rocque to a Doriot or a Bucard may not prove that France was immune to fascism; it may prove only that "France found a Mosley, but not a Mussolini." Still, the record does seem to suggest that France was more resistant to the totalitarian germ than were some other nations. It might be argued that a greater degree of political maturity, a longer experience with free government, explains the difference. Or perhaps the essential factor was the lack in France of the essential sociological and psychological base for fascism's success. Totalitarian movements have a special attraction for *déclassé* groups, for a broken or threatened middle class and a large mass of unemployed workers; and that attraction is reinforced in a period of social upheaval and national frustration. Although France in the 1930's suffered from growing social stresses, French society on the whole remained stable, and there was no widespread sense of frustrated nationalism to increase the degree of discontent.

There remains a second question of highly controversial nature: Did the republic's enemies (whether totalitarian or merely authoritarian) try to destroy it by violence during the riots of February 6, 1934? For French leftists, it has always been an article of faith that a coup was tried and thwarted. A parliamentary investigating committee in 1947 even concluded that there could be "...no room for doubt. It was not a question of a spontaneous demonstration but of a genuine insurrection, minutely prepared." Yet every rightist involved in the riots of that day has steadily denied that there was a planned coup, even though some of them might normally be expected to boast of a plot to smash the hated republic.

The 1934 riots grew out of a scandal, much like the Panama affair of the 1890's, that reflected on the honesty of a number of politicians and on the purity of French justice. Serge Stavisky, a second-rate confidence man with connections in high places, had a long police record for shady financial schemes, but had never been brought to trial on any of the charges. Trial dates had been set repeatedly and had been repeatedly postponed through the influence of powerful friends. His last venture was to establish a municipal pawn shop conveniently located near the Biarritz gambling casino, and to sell unlimited issues of stock in this enterprise. The ramshackle edifice collapsed late in 1933, and a great outcry went up from the bilked investors. Rumors spread that Stavisky had been abetted and protected by leading Radical politicians, including even a cabinet minister. The outcry grew worse when Stavisky was cornered in an Alpine hideout and reportedly committed suicide to avoid capture. It was widely believed that the police had shot him on orders from the besmirched politicians, in order to prevent a damaging confession.

The whole affair was minor compared to Panama, or even to a number of other earlier scandals. But it came at just the right moment to crystallize the nation's growing discontent and to furnish good copy for the right-wing press. For several weeks there were small street riots almost every evening, and the politicians' attempts to restore order only made things worse. Late in January Edouard Daladier organized a new and presumably tougher cabinet and dismissed the Paris prefect of police who had allegedly favored the rioters. All of the extremist papers, along with certain veterans' organizations, responded by calling on their followers to gather on the evening of February 6 for a massive demonstration against the corrupt regime. If anyone was really planning an insurrection, the planners were incredibly inept. There was apparently no coordination of the protesting groups; each chose its own route of march and its own destination, and none struck at such obvious targets of a coup as the railway stations and the public utilities.

In the huge Place de la Concorde, just across the river from the Chamber of Deputies, a mob of demonstrators and curious sightseers milled about through the late afternoon, hemmed in by mounted policemen. The Croix de Feu, operating independently, marched on the Chamber from the rear but was diverted by a police barricade; its columns gradually disintegrated, and many members went home. The Communists, not to be outdone, called out their small veterans' organization to march in the Champs Élysées. In the Place de la Concorde, meanwhile, tensions were building up to the verge of spontaneous revolution. The crowd, spearheaded by members of the right-wing veterans' organization called the Union Nationale des Combattants, tried several times to break through police cordons on the bridge, only to be beaten back by fire hoses and bullets. By midnight the scene resembled a battlefield; there were fifteen dead and fifteen hundred injured on the two sides. Not since the Commune of 1871 had so much blood been shed in Paris. Soon after midnight, nevertheless, the mob broke up as its members rushed to catch the last subway train home.

If this was really "a genuine insurrection, minutely prepared," it disintegrated with surprising speed. The aim of the demonstrators was almost certainly a more modest one; they sought not to topple the regime but to force out the Radical cabinet in favor of a more rightist combination. This at least they achieved; Daladier's cabinet resigned the next day to make way for a broad "national union" ministry under ex-President Gaston Doumergue, an aged wheelhorse politician resurrected from rural retirement to save the republic. Although the cabinet included such symbolic figures as Tardieu and Marshal Pétain, it also included some Radicals and a majority of Moderates; it stood for the existing republic rather than for the authoritarian revolution desired by the right. Yet the rioters seemed to be satisfied with this "Doumergue experiment"; the disorders of February 6 were not renewed in the days that followed.

The Radicals were not reluctant to abdicate power at such a moment; they preferred to let the Moderates wrestle with the worsening crisis. They had abdicated to Poincaré in the same way in 1926, and Poincaré had succeeded admirably. But Doumergue was no Poincaré, nor was his problem any longer quite so simple. The new premier, "a vain and complacent antique," let his temporary prestige go to his head, and developed a mild version of a messiah complex. Since he lacked interest in economic problems, he turned his attention to the political problem: how to give France stable government. Perhaps he was influenced by La Rocque, as the left suspected; more probably he listened to Tardieu, who urged him to bolster the executive power. There was nothing shocking about Doumergue's reform proposals, the core of which was to re-invigorate the premier's authority to dissolve parliament. But the manner in which he tried to achieve reform was unwise. He embarked on a program of direct radio talks to the nation, over the heads of the politicians, and he aroused suspicion among the Radicals by failing to take them into his confidence. A series of resignations shook his ministry in the autumn, and by November the Radicals felt it safe to bring down the government by withdrawing their ministers. Thus the much publicized Doumergue experiment collapsed after only nine months, leaving behind it a record of futility.

❖❖❖❖❖❖❖❖❖❖❖❖❖

If 1934 had been the year of Doumergue, 1935 was that of Pierre Laval. This shrewd parliamentary manipulator, this disciple of Briand who had by now completed his migration from left to right, was the strongest figure in the government throughout the year, though he became premier only in June. After several months of significant activity as foreign minister, Laval turned his attention to the nation's domestic problems. Industrial production had fallen by about a quarter since 1929, foreign trade by half; the unemployment figure was approaching a half-million. Whatever Laval may have lacked in wisdom, he at least showed courage; for the first time a French cabinet made a really coherent and systematic attack on the economic crisis. Laval's program called for severe deflation in an effort to get the French price level down to the world level. The Chamber, impotent to take action itself, empowered him to legislate by decree, and Laval used or abused that power to cut state expenditures dras-tically. He hoped that this example would have wide repercussions in private enterprise as well.

The effects of the Laval experiment have been disputed ever since. His defenders point out that during the year from June 1935 to June 1936 (when the Popular Front took office), the curve of industrial production at last hit bottom and started upward again. They insist that recovery would have con-tinued at an increasing rate if the Popular Front had not scuttled Laval's pro-gram. Laval's critics, on the other hand, believe that the industrial upturn of 1935–36 was misleading and inadequate; that by every statistical measurement except that of industrial production, France's economy continued downward or remained stagnant. They argue that far more drastic action would have been needed to make the deflationary plan succeed; a severe wage cut, a devaluation of the currency, and a ruthless clearing away of the barbed-wire entanglement of laws and exemptions protecting the static sector of the economy. Without these measures, they believe, French production costs were doomed to remain high, and French prices well above the world level. Worst of all, say the critics, was the psychological impact of the Laval experiment, for it seemed to require the mass of little Frenchmen to bear the burden of recovery. At any rate, the rising resentment of many voters led the Radicals to withdraw from Laval's cabinet in January 1936, and to wreck the Laval experiment.

The Radicals' repudiation of Laval was linked with their decision to turn back toward the left and to join the new Popular Front. For the first time since the Dreyfus era the entire left wing consolidated its strength with the declared purpose of defending the republic against its enemies both at home and abroad. The Popular Front was, in a sense, the product of the alleged coup d'état of February 6, 1934, but it was by no means an automatic reflex resulting from that day of bloodshed. Several months went by after the riots before the Socialists and Communists could agree on even an embryonic alliance, and it was not until January 1936 that Radical adherence made the Popular Front complete. Complex and arduous negotiations were required to reconcile the differences among the leftist groups, and most of those differences were in fact side-stepped rather than resolved. The heart of the problem was the curious role that the Communist party had played since 1920 and the well-founded skepticism of many Socialists and Radicals about the Communists' sincerity in suddenly changing their tactics.

Until the Popular Front era the Communists had clung stubbornly to a policy of isolated political action. Indeed, their most vindictive epithets had been reserved for the leaders of the non-Communist left; as late as December 1933, Comintern instructions declared that the principal task of Communist parties everywhere must be to disintegrate social democracy by unremitting attacks on its leaders. As for defending the bourgeois republic, Communist spokesmen had always made it plain that they were uninterested in its renovation or its survival; they alleged that it differed from fascist regimes only in form, not in fundamentals. On the day of the 1934 riots Communist demonstrators had echoed many of the slogans of the rightist mob. The French Communists appeared to be patterning their action on that of the German Communists in the last months of Weimar, when Nazis and Communists had collaborated in the great Berlin traffic strike against the regime.

Immediately after the February riots the first faint signs of a reversal appeared. The Socialists and the C.G.T. called for a symbolic general strike on February 12 as a warning to the republic's enemies, and the Communists ordered their followers to participate—perhaps because they felt it dangerous to resist the wave of energy that swept through the working class. But for several months thereafter the party continued its denunciations of Socialist leadership and its efforts to detach the Socialist rank and file. A sudden though slight softening of tone occurred in June 1934, and opened the way to a cautious "unity of action" pact with the Socialist organization. The real switch came in the spring of 1935, when the Communists began to push hard for "organic unity," or a complete merger with the Socialist party. Still another obstacle was removed in May, when Stalin publicly announced his interest in the strengthening of France's military power; three days later the French Communists leaped aboard the patriotic band wagon. The Communist trade-union movement, the C.G.T.U., was shortly merged with the older and larger C.G.T.

A few Radicals like Edouard Daladier and Pierre Cot were already seeking to pull their party into the common front, and they finally got their way in January 1936. A vocal minority of Socialists had meanwhile picked up the Communist cry of working-class unity and was campaigning for a complete merger of the two Marxian parties. But the dominant Socialist group around Léon Blum was more cautious; and besides, the problems that emerged in working out a common program for the Popular Front showed that unity was a long way off. The Socialists and the C.G.T. wanted a precise, coherent, and sweeping plan of economic and social renovation; both the Radicals and the Communists preferred ambiguous generalities, with the emphasis on blocking fascism rather than on reforming the republic. The program that emerged in January 1936 contained no provisions for substituting even partial socialism for capitalism; but it did include a set of demands in the economic and social sphere that added up to a real new deal. It was enough to frighten the orthodox and to send a wave of hope through a working class that had never before been offered so much as a reward for its electoral support.

The electoral campaign of 1936 was dominated by slogans and emotions rather than by rational discussion of party programs. Yet it would be a serious mistake to underestimate the significance of that campaign or the depth of the passions it aroused. Not since the great contest of 1877 between MacMahon and Gambetta had any election been so bitterly fought. The outcome closely resembled that of 1877: again the left won a narrow but clear cut victory. As usual there was no great shift of voters from right to left; what happened, rather, was a hardening of existing attitudes and a sharp polarization of the vote around extremes of right and left at the expense of all the center groups. Areas that had traditionally voted to the right simply moved farther to the right, while leftist areas moved farther left. The Socialists emerged as not only the nation's largest party but also as the largest group in the Chamber, with 146 seats. The Radicals slipped sharply to second place with 116 seats. But the Communists' gains were the most dramatic: their popular vote doubled, and their parliamentary representation rose from 10 to 72 seats. No other group benefited so greatly from the coalition tactics imposed by the Popular Front agreements. To Frenchmen of the time, the elections of April-May 1936 seemed to mark the end of an era and the beginning of a wholly new phase in the Third Republic's history. Hopes and fears coalesced into an impassioned sense of expectancy.

CHAPTER 31

# Crisis and Collapse, 1936-1940

When a country hasn't an army that fits its policies, it must have policies that fit its army.

RAYMOND RECOULY (1936)

"At last—the difficulties begin!" So wrote a leading Socialist intellectual in June 1936, as his party prepared to take power in France for the first time. Only twice in the history of the party had a Socialist participated in a cabinet, and then only in token fashion. Socialists in several other European nations had become full partners in "bourgeois" coalitions between the wars, but the French party had clung doggedly to Blum's doctrine that it must not take office unless it could dominate the coalition.[1] Now at last, as the largest group in parliament and as the axial party in the Popular Front alliance, the Socialists were marked out to form a government. "Go to work!" Blum was urged by one of his bourgeois friends. "France is ready for you. She awaits you nervously, but her nervousness is that of a young bride."

Yet it took only a year for the Blum cabinet to be overthrown by the Popular Front-dominated Chamber of Deputies, and only two years for the Popular Front itself to disintegrate completely. Few episodes in modern French history have generated such passionate initial enthusiasm or such rapid dis-

---

[1] A number of prominent Socialists who chafed at the party's refusal to let them enter cabinets broke away in 1933 to form the Neo-Socialist group. One segment of the secessionists, led by Pierre Renaudel, eventually returned to the Socialist party, but a second faction, headed by Marcel Déat and Adrien Marquet, showed a rising interest in fascist doctrine and tactics. After 1940 Déat was to become a leading exponent of collaboration with Hitler's Germany and a one-party system for France.

370

illusionment; few have so promptly crystallized into durable and influential myth. There is a good deal of irony in the fact that in working class circles this abortive experiment left behind it a legend of hope, derived from the deep conviction that the workers had never been so close to victory, and that success had been snatched away by the self-seeking capitalists. Ever since, nostalgia for the Popular Front has been a powerful force within the French working class. That nostalgia, however, does not extend to the bourgeois left.

The Blum cabinet proved to be narrower in composition than the Popular Front coalition that produced it. Despite Blum's appeals, the Communists agreed to support the government but not to join it. Thus they succeeded to the role played by the Socialists for a generation, combining the advantages of power with those of irresponsibility. Socialists and Radicals therefore shared most of the key ministerial posts, and the old problem of reconciling their basic differences on social and economic issues promptly reappeared. In retrospect, Blum might have been wiser to try a more daring venture in 1936, by forming a homogeneous Socialist cabinet that could have struck out vigorously on a path of consistent reform. Such a government would have been based on only a minority in the Chamber, but the mood of the moment might have forced both Radicals and Communists to support its program. Had they opposed it and brought down the cabinet, at least they would have been forced to assume open responsibility for blocking vigorous reforms. Blum's motives in refusing such a gamble were admirable ones; he was determined to preserve the *élan* of the Popular Front and to give his government the broadest possible democratic base. But in the end his decision blunted his government's action, diffused responsibilities for its failure, and produced general disillusionment. Most of the Popular Front's reforms turned out to be more spectacular than effective, in part because they remained incomplete. Social reforms proved to be easier to accomplish than were the economic measures required to give them a solid foundation.

The Blum cabinet's social reforms could not have been postponed—both because they were already long overdue, and because any delay might have produced violent insurrection or civil war. A week after the April-May elections a wave of sit-down strikes inundated the country; when the new cabinet took office almost two million workers had seized control of their plants in the Paris region alone, to the fury and despair of owners and managers. France had known no social upheaval of such proportions since 1848. It was a curious aftermath to a left-wing electoral victory, for it seemed more like the kind of action that might have followed a leftist defeat. The workers had never resorted to such methods against previous governments that had been far more indifferent to labor's interests. It was widely alleged at the time that Communist agitators, convinced that the revolutionary moment had arrived, had stirred up the strikes. In fact, the outbreak was almost certainly spontaneous—the product of a cluster of longstanding grievances and of the emotions aroused during the election campaign. The Communists actually tried to restrain the strikers until restraint proved impossible. As for the trade unions, the head of the C.G.T. first heard of the strikes when he was informed of them by telephone.

This effervescence forced the new government into rapid action, more improvised than planned. Blum brought together labor leaders and representative employers and persuaded them to accept a series of agreements that provided for immediate wage increases averaging 12 per cent and the introduction of generalized collective bargaining. During the next two weeks the cabinet rushed through parliament several other notable reforms, including the forty-hour week in industry, paid vacations for workers, and (later) compulsory arbitration of labor disputes. Certain other measures were products of the Popular Front's demonology concerning bankers and munitions-makers. The Bank of France, for example, was brought under state control, and some aircraft plants were nationalized. In the political sphere, the antiparliamentary leagues like the Croix de Feu were dissolved—though most of them promptly reappeared as political parties, with new labels. An effort was made to raise and stabilize farm prices by setting up a Wheat Office.

Some of Blum's ex post facto critics have argued that his fatal mistake was his failure to go far enough on the road to reform in June 1936. The outcome of the elections and the quasi-revolutionary situation produced by the strikes, they believe, had stunned the business community and had offered Blum an unparalleled chance to carry through a drastic but peaceful social revolution. This thesis is a plausible one, yet it is easier to assert than to prove that the country would have accepted more sweeping reforms at the time. A more valid criticism can be directed at Blum's failure to supplement his initial social reforms with the kind of economic measures needed to support the new social program and to revitalize the economy. The Popular Front's economic doctrines were, on the whole, rather primitive; it operated on the pump-priming theory that if purchasing power could be put into the hands of the masses, prosperity would follow automatically. In the proper circumstances, so simple a device can be effective; but it was not effective in the conditions existing in France in 1936. Industrial production, which had stood at 87 just before the elections (base year 1928 = 100) fell to 76 in August 1936, then rose to 91 in December and remained at about that level throughout 1937. When the Popular Front finally disintegrated in 1938, industrial production had dropped again and was lower than it had been when Blum took office.

Meanwhile the governmental deficit continued to rise; prices jumped rapidly and soon wiped out much of labor's gains from wage increases; unemployment stubbornly refused to decline. In desperation, the government finally devalued the franc late in 1936, after having proclaimed for months that it would never take such action. A devaluation carried out several years earlier might have stimulated the French economy; but it now came too late to have any significant effect. Economically speaking, as one French expert has brutally put it, "the Blum experiment was a total failure."

Defenders of the Popular Front have always insisted that the experiment of 1936–38 was consciously sabotaged by its enemies on the right. Business men and investors, they have charged, sent their capital to safe havens outside the country, refused productive investment in home enterprise, and cut production by running their plants only forty hours a week—all this with the aim of wrecking the Popular Front. The thesis undoubtedly has some validity. Many French capitalists were frightened by the Popular Front's program and by the electoral oratory of its more demagogic spokesmen—more frightened, indeed, than they were hurt by the Popular Front in action. A serious flight of capital did occur, thanks to the government's reluctance to set up exchange controls until too late to stop the hemorrhage.

Yet not all the responsibility for economic failure can be attributed to the business group. Labor itself contributed to that failure by focussing narrowly on its own interests, without much reference to the question of national interest, and by failing to work toward some kind of joint action by capital and labor to reinvigorate the economy. In too many cases, as one critic ironically put it, the forty-hour week came to mean four hours of work plus thirty-six hours of discussing the rights of labor. Still another share of responsibility for failure must be assessed against the government for its lack of expertise in economics, which produced a series of fundamental mistakes both in the original conception of the Popular Front's program and in the implementing of that program.

In Blum's defense it ought to be added that perhaps no one could have done much better, given the long postponement of many of the problems his government had to tackle, given the deep class antagonisms that had developed in the nation, and given the divisive impact of international tensions on France in those years. Perhaps Blum's social reforms were, as he later claimed, inescapable—the only alternative to civil war. A few of these social gains did prove permanent, and in that sense the Popular Front experience was not a total failure. Never again was French labor to be so badly off as it was before 1936. Nevertheless, to some of those who had hoped for a new era in 1936, the shortcomings and the prompt disintegration of the Popular Front produced intense disillusionment. Such Frenchmen concluded that no true reform in France could be achieved without a prior revolution to shake up the country's basic structure. The Popular Front's limitations therefore pushed many workers and intellectuals into the arms of the Communist party. On the other slope of politics, the episode also strengthened extremism at the expense of moderation.

The emotions aroused in 1936 made many moderate rightists more receptive to antidemocratic slogans and drove them to support authoritarian or totalitarian movements like those of La Rocque or Doriot. In a significant sense, therefore, the Popular Front boomeranged against the republic.

In defense of the Popular Front, it should also be pointed out that it made a serious attempt to carry out a wide variety of reforms designed to clean up long-standing abuses. For example, a bill was introduced to create a healthier and purer press by tightening the libel laws and publicizing newspaper ownership. Measures were also projected to liberalize French colonial policy by broadening the rights of the colonized peoples, notably in Algeria and Syria-Lebanon. These proposals, however, bogged down in parliament and were still pending when the Popular Front fell apart. On the other hand, Blum made no attempt to clear away the barbed-wire entanglement of restrictions and privileges that protected the static sector of the economy and that prevented any rapid invigoration and modernization of French enterprise. On the contrary, the Popular Front added even more barbed wire; laws were adopted, for example, to block the expansion of chain stores and *prisunics* (the French equivalent of five-and-ten cent stores). Such measures reflected the fact that the Popular Front rested not only on the votes of factory workers but also on those of many small enterprisers, marginal survivors of a past economic era, typical representatives of "static France."

The Blum cabinet was overthrown by the Radical-dominated Senate in June 1937, when at last it sought to introduce such real economic restrictions as controls on foreign exchange. Leadership in the Popular Front passed to the Radicals, who were satisfied with a policy of drift rather than action. In 1938, after a second Blum cabinet far more brief and futile than the first, the Popular Front was formally buried. As in 1924 and 1932, a left-wing victory at the polls ended two years later in a return of the center or right-center groups to power. Once again the Radicals executed their standard pirouette from left to right and accepted as their new partners a segment of the Moderate group.

The new prime minister, Edouard Daladier, was a onetime protégé of Edouard Herriot, but he had risen to be Herriot's rival for leadership of the Radical party. A southerner by origin, he had been a *lycée* professor of history before entering parliament in 1919. Daladier had been one of the first Radicals to advocate a Popular Front, but he had quickly lost his enthusiasm for collaboration with the Communists. Somehow he had acquired a misleading reputation for vigor and firmness; events were to show that he possessed more intelligence than character. As premier, Daladier was preoccupied mainly with matters of foreign policy and national defense; in domestic affairs, the dominant figure in his cabinet was Paul Reynaud, a Moderate who stood out in French politics as one of the rare exponents of genuine laissez-faire philosophy. Reynaud shared with the rest of the center and right a dislike for the Popular Front's tendencies toward state intervention in the economy; but in contrast to his political colleagues, he believed also in clearing away the barrier of privileges and exemptions that prevented real competitive enterprise. Reynaud's aim was to reinstill confidence in the business community and to encourage large-scale private investment and expansion. He urged the cabinet to lower taxes on business enterprise, to modify the 40-hour week, and to offer business men guarantees against spoliation if they would bring their capital back from abroad. The Radicals balked for a time; they were just as horrified as they had been when the Socialists had talked of a capital levy. At last, however, they reluctantly agreed to try the Reynaud plan.

The announcement late in 1938 of what Reynaud called "the last experiment in liberalism" threatened to produce a social upheaval as serious as that of 1936. The unions, in protest, resorted to their rarely used ultimate weapon—the general strike. Its failure was complete. The cabinet took a tough line, utilizing its special emergency powers to mobilize many of the strikers for continued service on their regular jobs. But more important still was the apathy of the workers, who failed to respond with enthusiasm to the strike call. The euphoria of the Popular Front victory had long since been dissipated. In the springtime mood of 1936, trade-union membership had grown in almost incredible fashion; the C.G.T. had jumped from one to five million members in a few months. By 1938 about half of the new members had already abandoned the C.G.T., and the failure of the general strike produced a further hemorrhage. For example, the building-trades union, which had boasted a membership of six hundred thousand in 1936, had fallen by 1939 to a mere sixty thousand. Cynicism, bitterness, apathy marked labor's outlook at the end of the decade.

The Reynaud program, though it lacked much concern for social justice, at least had vigor and coherence. The failure of the general strike and the government's repression of the strikers served as psychological stimuli to ensure the program's temporary success. Capital flooded back into France; industrial production, still at 83 in October 1938 (1928 = 100) rose to 100 in June 1939, for the first time since the depression struck France. The franc, which had been slipping ever since 1936, tended to stabilize in value, and prices at last levelled off. In the short run, Reynaud's program was clearly an economic if not a social success.

There were still grave weaknesses, however, in the French economy. Figures on production, national income, population level, all indicated that France in 1939 was still about where it had been in 1913; a quarter-century had gone by with no real progress at all. Such figures suggested a condition of pernicious anemia in an era of rapid world economic expansion. Furthermore, the crisis decade of the 1930's had aggravated the disease. The economy became even more rigid and less adaptable; the crisis was prolonged by many of the measures taken to combat it. Economists calculated, furthermore, that between 1929 and 1939 there had been a net disinvestment in France; that the nation's productive capacity had actually gone backward during the depression decade. In the realm of public works and housing, the record was meager; Great Britain, dominated by the Conservatives, built six times as many housing units as France in the 1930's. The Daladier-Reynaud regime took no direct steps to rationalize and modernize the economy, but relied on the prospect that the free winds of competition would accomplish that end over the years. Possibly a decade or two of Reynaudism might have accomplished such a change; but at best it was likely to be a slow process, given the traditional outlook of the French business community and the powerful hold of static France on the political machinery. In any event, the experiment was scarcely begun when it was interrupted by the outbreak of war.

❖❖❖❖❖❖❖❖❖❖❖❖❖❖

The Third Republic's record during the crisis decade was even more dismal in foreign than in domestic policy—though perhaps there was more excuse for failure in the international sphere. The disintegration of France's power position in those years was rapid and dramatic. In 1930 France was still the dominant state on the Continent; by 1940 the country's strength and morale were gravely undermined, and any real independence of action had been lost. The nation's alliance system had crumbled; its military establishment was overshadowed by that of Germany; its unity and determination were dubious. Even in retrospect, there is no simple explanation for this disastrous record, though a good many easy answers have been suggested. Leaving aside for the moment the question of personal or party responsibilities, one might single out three approaches to a general explanation. Each one contains at least a little validity, though none offers a really satisfactory answer.

The root of the trouble, according to one thesis, was France's ideological disunity in face of the fascist threat. The right wing, traditionally most intransigent toward Germany and most thoroughly committed to a strong and independent foreign policy, gradually abandoned this position during the 1930's; many rightists sought an accommodation with Hitler's Germany or Mussolini's Italy, or both. Exponents of this thesis point out that certain aspects of fascism appealed even to the nonfascist elements of the French right, which allegedly (though in fact rarely) adopted the battle cry, "Better Hitler than Blum!" Meanwhile part of the French left—notably the Communists—underwent an opposite evolution, from traditional pacifism to a stance of belligerent hostility toward the Nazis; but that change was offset by the division and doubt produced by the right's new role.

A second thesis centers attention not on French disunity but on the fundamental issue of French morale. Most Frenchmen, it is argued, were permanently scarred by the traumatic experience of the Great War; whatever their ideological preferences, they desperately sought a way to evade a new clash at almost any cost. Wishful thinking encouraged their effort to escape from their commitments to their eastern allies, in order to retire to safe isolation behind the Maginot Line. No great nation, however, could embark on such a policy of weakness without an adequate excuse; and the French allegedly sought that excuse by abandoning the initiative to the British, who they knew would insist on the appeasement of Hitler. If the French repeatedly received unwise counsel from London, asserts the British historian Sir Lewis Namier, they had no real cause to complain; "...for they would not have sought British advice, whose character they could gage beforehand..., had it not answered their own unavowed inclinations."[2]

Still a third thesis views the French as more to be pitied than censured; it holds that they were the victims of other nations' errors and of almost inexorable circumstances. According to this view, French leaders recognized the Nazi threat more clearly than did those of any other nation, but they were also realistic enough to recognize France's weakness and inability to act alone. Above all, France needed the support of Britain. Throughout the decade, therefore, French governments constantly sought to alert London to the danger threatening the West, and in failing to awaken the British, they were dragged unwillingly into the futile line of appeasement.

All three of these strands, along with many other lesser ones, were intertwined in the story of French diplomacy during the crisis decade. Perhaps a more stable regime or a more forceful set of leaders might have slowed or prevented the disintegration of France's position. More probably, the combination of circumstances in interwar Europe—the psychological aftermath of the Great War, the disruptive impact of the depression, the widespread hold of certain political myths, the generalized tendency to wishful thinking—would have made the task of even the ablest of French statesmen impossible.

During the first three years of the Hitler era (1933–36) there was fairly broad agreement in France on the question of Nazi Germany. Only a few intellectuals were attracted by the dynamism of the new regime across the Rhine; some of them joined such fringe groups as Fernand de Brinon's France-Germany Committee to work for collaboration. The appeasers of these early years included a curious mixture of rightists attracted to Hitler's authoritarianism,

---

[2] L. B. Namier, *Europe in Decay* (London: Macmillan, 1950), p. 5.

of neo-Socialists more interested in planning than in democracy, and of leftists attached to the pacifist ideal that no people would be aggressive if treated fairly. No first-rank political figure was involved; the bulk of the right, center, and left-center favored a stiff policy of bolstering France's alliance system and military strength, while most of the Socialists contended that fascist aggressors ought to be stopped by measures of collective security through the League of Nations.

The League, however, was already a feeble reed by 1933. The French foreign ministry therefore turned back to a frankly avowed policy of independent French action. Worked out by Alexis Léger, the top career official at the Quai d'Orsay from 1933 to 1940, this program proposed to tighten France's alliances with the eastern European states, to bolster the military strength of those allies, to add pacts with the Soviet Union and Italy, and to seek once more a British commitment to an eastern Locarno that would fence in the Nazis on both their frontiers. Léger was a former protégé and collaborator of Briand, but the threat of Hitler converted him from the Briandism of the 1920's to something more like the old Poincarist line. The new policy was further invigorated early in 1934 when Louis Barthou, one of Poincaré's closest political associates, took office as foreign minister. Barthou made a series of visits to France's eastern allies, opened negotiations with Moscow and Rome, and seemed well on the way to encircling Hitler with a ring of steel. Only the Socialists, the Communists, and the few pro-Nazis in France resisted the Barthou policy. But in October 1934, Barthou was assassinated along with King Alexander of Yugoslavia, who had just arrived on a state visit. Perhaps that was a fatal turning point in French diplomatic history; or perhaps the Barthou experiment rested on a faulty foundation that would have wrecked it eventually. At any rate, his successor as foreign minister, Pierre Laval, approached the problem in a somewhat different spirit.

It is true that outwardly at least, Laval continued the Barthou policy. He visited Rome and came to an understanding with Italy, though possibly at an exorbitant price. He travelled to Moscow to sign the mutual aid pact with the Soviet Union that Barthou and Léger had initiated. But Laval was much more devious than Barthou in carrying out these moves. Reports got out that he had bought Mussolini's support by secretly handing over Ethiopia to the Italians. Proponents of the Soviet pact noted that Laval, after signing it, kept postponing its presentation to the Chamber for ratification. Late in 1935 rumors spread in Paris that Laval was privately undercutting the Barthou policy by seeking some kind of understanding with Hitler. Laval angrily denied this charge; and there is no reason to believe that he was lying. The available evidence does not suggest that Laval at that time was either attracted to Nazism or convinced that France was too weak to resist Hitler. It does suggest that Laval, true to his own character, was more sinuous and opportunistic than Barthou in shaping French foreign policy, more willing to play a complex double game. Such devious behavior doubtless helped to confuse the French public and to undermine the nation's "multipartisan" firmness in the face of the German menace.

Until 1936 pro-Nazi or pro-appeasement sentiment remained rare in France, even on the right. Indeed, during those years the right's record of firmness had been at least as good as that of the left. When Hitler openly announced conscription in 1935, most right-wing Frenchmen denounced him; when French cabinets asked for credits to expand the armed forces, they gave their support. The Socialists, on the other hand, came around slowly and reluctantly to the need for national defense and voted against military credits until 1936. Their pacifist dogmas hampered their adaptation to the age of aggressors, while their Marxist schema clouded their understanding of the true character of twentieth-century fascism, a movement that transcended economic or class interests. As for the Communists, their sudden right-about-face in 1935 to vociferous support of national defense and a democratic crusade against fascism contributed more to confusion and suspicion than to French unity.

The first serious signs of pro-appeasement sentiment on the right appeared during the winter of 1935–36. Two causative factors were involved: the loss of Italian friendship, as a result of the Ethiopian conflict, and the formation of the Popular Front in France. Together, these two factors raised a new bogey that to many rightists seemed at least as bad as the Hitler threat. Italy's support, as these rightists saw it, was a vital necessity now that France had decided to ally itself with the Soviet Union. Without Italy as a makeweight, they feared that the alliance might be converted from a realistic anti-Hitler bloc into an ideological coalition devoted to furthering the Communist cause. The formation of the Popular Front seemed to intensify this latter danger. Rightists were frightened into believing that France itself might soon be taken over by a left-wing coalition sympathetic to Moscow's interests, and that such a government might let control of the alliance slip out of French into Russian hands. In an important sense, therefore, the formation of the Popular Front and the Russian pact weakened France's resistance to fascism more than they strengthened that resistance. While the antifascist forces were broadened by the adherence of the Communists, they were weakened by the tendency of many Frenchmen of the center and right to be driven even farther toward the right and toward appeasement.

The first precise indication of this changing attitude on the right came in February 1936, when the Soviet mutual aid pact was at last brought up for ratification. A year earlier most of the right had openly supported such a pact. Now, only a few rightists like Paul Reynaud and P.-E. Flandin joined the left in arguing and voting for it. Ratification came by a bare majority; and the military staff conversations needed to implement the pact were repeatedly postponed by succeeding French governments. Even when the Popular Front took office,

Soviet requests for such conversations were evaded, mainly because of Radical and Socialist skepticism about Moscow's motives.

It was thus a divided France that faced the challenge of Hitler's first great gamble: his military occupation of the Rhineland in March 1936. That act violated not only Versailles but also Locarno; Hitler's excuse was that France had just torn up Locarno by ratifying the Soviet pact. A year or two earlier the French might have reacted sharply to such a challenge; now the growing divergence between right and left, combined with the fact that France was on the threshold of an election campaign, made the government hesitate. The cabinet, a weak interim coalition headed by the Radical Sarraut, met at once and called on the general staff for technical advice. Commander-in-Chief Gamelin disclaimed authority to make a policy recommendation, but told the cabinet that only two paths were open: either all-out action involving total mobilization against the Germans, or no action at all. The army had prepared no plans for a limited police operation, and such an operation was impossible to improvise with an army of draftees. Faced by such a choice, only a handful of ministers favored an open challenge to Hitler by France alone.

The cabinet postponed its decision, however, until an effort could be made to get British support. Foreign Minister Flandin was sent to London to argue the case for action. Whether either Flandin or the cabinet really thought that Britain might help is a highly controversial question; it is conceivable that they were only seeking an excuse for their own inaction. At any rate, the British government urged caution and refused any commitment; Flandin's discouraging report on his return to Paris made it certain that the cabinet would accept the accomplished fact. Some Frenchmen believed then, and many more have argued since, that France should have moved unilaterally; they hold that the British would then have given reluctant support and the German bluff would have been called. Yet it is worth stressing that both French and British public opinion were strongly opposed to military action in 1936. It would have required a really unified and courageous cabinet to move in the face of the public mood and at a time of serious division in the country. Besides, it is by no means certain that the use of force would have brought quick success.

Nevertheless, the failure to act had grave consequences. It marked the collapse of the Poincaré-Barthou policy of independent French action to keep Germany hemmed in by a ring of bayonets. It meant the sterilization of France's alliance system, for the guarantees of French aid to the Czechs and the Poles would become largely meaningless as soon as Hitler could fortify the Rhine. It converted France into a kind of undeclared British satellite, dependent on prior British consent for any important foreign policy action. Italy had already been lost in 1935; the Soviet tie had been rendered almost useless; the British still boggled at any binding commitments to block German aggression.

As the French examined the alternatives that were still theoretically open to them after March 1936, they could not be very sanguine. Most rightists seized upon the idea that winning back the Italians would solve the problem. Many of them harbored serious illusions about both Italian strength and Italian aims; they convinced themselves that Mussolini would be a dependable ally, and that recovering his help would redress the European balance. Buttressing this idea was the right's growing tendency to find some virtues in Mussolini's brand of fascism; to conclude that it had brought order, authority, and social peace, uncorrupted by ambitious designs of European aggression.

A growing minority in France, however, now began to be infected by sheer defeatism. Flandin, after his unsuccessful mission to London, was the clearest example. He had favored action against Hitler in March 1936; now he saw no hope for France except in renouncing an independent role and abandoning any pretensions to great-power status. He and others like him proposed to make the best possible arrangement with Hitler, on the theory that France could then retire to secure isolation behind the Maginot Line. Still a third alternative was to accept totalitarianism as the wave of the future; to junk the Third Republic and join the Axis. Such was the doctrine preached by Doriot's P.P.F. and by several lesser extremist groups. There remained, finally, one other path: to patch together what remained of the Barthou encirclement policy by maintaining France's commitments in eastern Europe, refusing any further retreats before Hitler's menace, and gambling that if aggression did come, both the British and the Russians would be driven by self-interest to aid France before it was too late. Such was the policy preferred by most of the center and left-center politicians and by a few maverick rightists like Reynaud and Georges Mandel. Since clear proof of Hitler's aims was not then available, it is easy to see how risky and almost irresponsible this firm policy seemed to many contemporaries.

It is just as easy to see why French policy from 1936 onward seemed then, and seems in retrospect, so groping, fumbling, and flabby. Every one of the alternatives still open to France was either risky or potentially disastrous. Frenchmen were therefore quite naturally tempted to slip into a mood of wishful thinking; to avoid choosing any one of these evils and to hope that, after all, Hitler might be reasonable in spite of all appearances to the contrary. Even the leading figures of the Popular Front were affected by this mood. Although they were loudly and unanimously antifascist, in fact they were divided into two camps: those who held that any concessions would be dangerous, and those who hoped that Hitler might behave if given a little rope.

The central foreign policy problem of the Popular Front era was the Spanish civil war, which broke out just after Blum came to power. It was natural for a Popular Front government in Paris to want to help its sister regime in Madrid. Yet within a few weeks French aid in arms and volunteers was cut off, and

Blum reluctantly accepted a policy of nonintervention by the great powers. Blum's defenders have always argued that his hands-off attitude was dictated by the British, and that Blum accepted it because he clearly recognized France's overriding need of British friendship. But more important, probably, were the Popular Front's own internal divisions over the Spanish issue. Many of the Radicals were reluctant to risk active aid, and if Blum had pushed ahead, the coalition probably would have collapsed. Blum was tempted to resign rather than "betray" his Spanish comrades, but was persuaded to stay in office by the Spanish government, which wanted a friendly regime in Paris even more than it wanted arms.

Blum's decision on Spain has often been branded the worst foreign policy error of the Popular Front period. Superficially, the case of the critics is strong; for the Axis powers evaded their nonintervention pledges, while the *élan* of the antifascist forces in France was weakened by what seemed to be a craven attitude. It is too easy to conclude, however, that bold French intervention would have saved the Spanish republic, and that it would have consolidated the European forces committed to stop naked aggression. In fact, what Hitler had in mind in 1936–38 was a dragging, spreading war in Spain that would involve Britain and France against Italy and would thus give him a free hand to strike toward the east.

By the spring of 1938, when the spotlight shifted from Spain to central Europe, the Popular Front had virtually disintegrated, and the making of French policy had passed into new hands. Alexis Léger was still at the foreign ministry as secretary-general, but diplomatic decisions were now shaped mainly by Premier Edouard Daladier and Foreign Minister Georges Bonnet. Both men played a highly controversial role during the last two years of peace. Some have seen them as weak men, appeasers by choice and conviction; others reply that they reluctantly succumbed to unrelenting British pressure. In fact, Bonnet seems to have deserved the first description and Daladier the second, though neither was an absolutely clear-cut case. Certainly Daladier was a much less willing appeaser than his British colleague Neville Chamberlain; and the evidence is clear that he was subjected to continuous British pressure all through the period that culminated in the Munich settlement in September 1938. Bonnet was a much more pliable and vacillating figure. For a time after he took office he seems to have balanced between appeasement and resistance, but he soon came to incline strongly toward the former course. Daladier privately admitted that he had absolutely no confidence in Bonnet, yet felt compelled to put up with him as foreign minister in order to keep the pro-Bonnet faction of the Radical party behind the cabinet. It would be hard to imagine a more unhealthy state of affairs at a time when firmness and unity were essential.

Hitler's first blow in central Europe, the annexation of Austria in March 1938, had been foreseen and written off in advance by both the French and the

British. But the pressure on Czechoslovakia that began at once and increased through the summer months could not be absorbed so nonchalantly. France had binding commitments to the Czechs; and besides, it was clear that once the Czech bastion was destroyed, there would be only a dim chance of checking further Nazi expansion to the east. Until the French archives are opened, no one can be sure whether Daladier made a really serious and sustained effort to persuade the British government to support the Czechs. But it is quite clear that the attitude of the Chamberlain government would almost certainly have made such a French effort futile; for Chamberlain was determined to force the Czechs to accept a compromise satisfactory to Hitler. Bonnet bowed to this British pressure early; even Léger accepted the idea of enforcing a Czech retreat on the ground that France could no longer go it alone and must keep Britain friendly at all costs. The four-power agreement signed at Munich on September 30, 1938, forced the Czech government to hand over the Sudeten provinces to Germany, and stripped Czechoslovakia of effective defenses against Hitler's future pressures. This western capitulation, though welcomed by the bulk of French opinion and approved by the French parliament, was the direct product of British rather than French policy; the Daladier government was essentially an accomplice before the fact. Daladier himself had no illusions; he was thunderstruck at the triumphal reception given him by Parisians on his return from Munich, and privately he expressed the conviction that Munich had been a disastrous setback for the West.

During the six months after Munich the idea of winning back Italy from the Axis to the Western camp entered its most active phase, with Chamberlain as its most active proponent. The French right also urged an all-out effort to court Mussolini; and Foreign Minister Bonnet even sent a private emissary to Rome to explore the ground. The scheme had not the least chance of success; Mussolini was privately contemptuous of the soft Western democracies, and remarked to his son-in-law Count Ciano that France was a nation "ruined by alcohol, syphilis, and journalism." Besides, the British and French could not agree on the bait to be used in attracting the Italians; each government wanted the other to foot the bill through colonial concessions. The sole effect of all these initiatives was to deepen the distrust between Paris and London and to divert attention from the desperate need to prepare for war. The French, meanwhile, were seeking a further accommodation with Germany; in December 1938, Foreign Minister von Ribbentrop came to Paris for conversations with Bonnet, out of which came a Franco-German agreement for mutual consultation, similar to the one signed by Britain and Germany as a by-product of the Munich conference. It was subsequently alleged that Bonnet had privately encouraged Ribbentrop to turn German power eastward; these charges Bonnet vigorously denied.

The false illusions produced by the Munich settlement were given a rude jolt in March 1939, when Hitler found an excuse to absorb the rest of Czechoslovakia. Frenchmen were less surprised than Britishers by this cynical act, and they could more promptly draw the consequences of the failure of appeasement. The bulk of Frenchmen on both left and right now rallied to a policy of firm resistance and a last-ditch attempt to fence Hitler in by a pact with the Soviet Union. Even the conservative Catholic daily *La Croix* came out for reinforcing the Soviet tie. There were important exceptions, like the outright fascists and the Flandin-type defeatists, joined now by such new converts as Pierre Laval. The phrase of the neo-Socialist Marcel Déat, "Why die for Danzig?" became the keynote of the defeatist campaign.

From March until August, French policy-makers sought to pull the rather reluctant British government in the direction of a tight East-West pact against aggression. French leaders shared British skepticism about the effectiveness of the Soviet army as a fighting force and about the sincerity of the Kremlin. They took the position, nevertheless, that something would be better than nothing to divert part of Germany's striking power to the east; and they believed that the possibility of Russian duplicity had to be accepted as a calculated risk. They urged the British, therefore, to accept Soviet terms no matter how unreasonable they might seem; and they began to exert pressure on their Polish allies to authorize Soviet troops to enter Polish territory in case of war. Disturbing reports reached Paris of *sub rosa* negotiations between the Russians and the Germans, but the French government discounted these as baseless.

The news of Stalin's pact with Hitler in August 1939 struck Paris with staggering effect. Daladier remarked privately that France's position had been rendered almost hopeless; that if Hitler now attacked Poland, France alone would have to face the combined power of Germany and the U.S.S.R., for Poland could not resist for more than two months, while Britain would not be armed short of two years. As Hitler had expected, his diplomatic coup stunned Frenchmen, many of whom concluded that it would now be folly to fight for Poland. But contrary to his expectation, Daladier and the resisters managed to keep their grip on the government, against the efforts of the defeatists. Foreign Minister Bonnet sent a personal agent to Rome in an effort to arrange a second Munich, but the French cabinet as a whole repudiated the idea. Most responsible Frenchmen, though dubious about the chances of victory, concluded that another Munich would turn France into a German satellite. They preferred to accept the formidable risks of war.

❖❖❖❖❖❖❖❖❖❖❖❖❖

France's long-standing pact with Poland, as revised in May 1939, committed the French to furnish active military aid no later than the sixteenth day after an attack on the Poles. No one, however, had foreseen the tempo of the Nazi blitzkrieg. After sixteen days of war Poland had been half overrun and was on the verge of collapse even before the Soviet armies struck from the east on September 17. The French furnished almost no help at all to their Polish allies. A few border raids into the Saar provided no real diversion; and French appeals for British air strikes against the Ruhr were rejected by London. By the end of September all Polish resistance had ceased.

Formally, the *casus foederis* had disappeared; France could no longer fight for Poland when no Poland existed. Many Frenchmen reasoned thus, and Hitler sought to appeal to their prejudices by offering peace on a forgive-and-forget basis. The appeal was strengthened by a widespread and panicky sentiment in Paris that Germany, supported by the Soviet air force, would turn at once on isolated France, and that the British would stand by across the Channel ready to make peace after France had succumbed. Premier Daladier and Secretary-General Léger at the foreign ministry were subjected to intense pressure from leading politicians to withdraw from the war at once. Both men, despite their gloom about the chances of victory, resisted the pressure and chose to face the risk of an armed showdown with Hitler. Some French critics later denounced their decision as a grave error, inspired by bravado and shortsightedness rather than courage. Such an argument, however, ignores the consequences of an unresisted Nazi conquest of all Europe. It was a kind of minor miracle, nevertheless, that the French government did manage to stick to its guns in October 1939.

The winter of 1939–40, variously labelled the "phony war" and the *drôle de guerre,* was replete with false alarms of German attacks, with persistent and bitter squabbles between the French and British, and with efforts to expand and reorganize the Western military forces so that they might hold off a German blow. The German threats were real enough, and they failed to materialize as attacks only because weather conditions interfered; but repeated alerts produced some feeling in France that perhaps Hitler was only bluffing, and that he would never really dare to strike. The controversies with London, produced both by clashes of personality and by differing concepts of warfare, interfered with the smooth operation of the alliance. The heart of the difficulty was a hard core of mutual distrust. French political and military leaders became convinced that Britain would refuse to commit more than a token force of men and aircraft to the continental front and would stand silently by while the French carried the brunt of the coming attack. The British, meanwhile, concluded that the French were eager to devise a plan of action in some distant theater of war, as far as possible from French soil and as dependent as possible on British naval and air power for success. Nazi psychological warfare took advantage of these differences to encourage suspicion on both sides of the Channel.

Meanwhile both French and British desperately sought to remedy the long-standing deficiencies in their armed forces. France at least possessed a large and well-trained land army, which was still believed by many to be the world's best in equipment and morale. All through the 1930's French military leaders like Marshal Pétain and Generals Weygand and Gamelin had resisted pressures for fundamental change in the direction of greater mechanization or increased air power. Their fault was not lack of loyalty to the republic, but lack of imagination and foresight; they clung to their memories of the First World War and anticipated another long defensive struggle of the same type. "For an army," remarked one disillusioned Frenchman, "perhaps a victory is harder to overcome than a defeat." A few unorthodox officers like Colonel Charles de Gaulle, and a few politicians like Paul Reynaud, had been campaigning for years for a new conception of warfare that would convert the French armies from an essentially defensive instrument into a maneuverable weapon for lightning offense or for roving defense. Their doctrine called for the concentration of tanks and armored vehicles in several mechanized divisions supported by tactical aircraft, and for a shift of emphasis away from a mass of conscripted troops toward a smaller long-term professional army. Perhaps their chief error lay in combining these two reforms; for the idea of a small professional army frightened and irritated good republicans and blurred their understanding of the real advantages of mechanization. In consequence, neither reform was adopted, and reformers like de Gaulle were shunted off into obscurity.

Preparedness had suffered further during the 1930's because of the persistent hold of pacifism on both politicians and public. The warmongering armament-maker and the saber-rattling soldier came to be legendary ogres in the folklore of the French left, as they did in most democracies in the same era. This sentiment made it easy for Hitler to seize the initiative in armaments and to gain a lead of two or three years over the Western powers. The Popular Front's accession to office in 1936 introduced a further diversion, for it focussed attention on social reforms and a shorter work week at a moment when an all-out productive effort was vital. Blum showed no more understanding of the need for a new military doctrine than did most other politicians of the decade. However, Vichy's later charge that the Popular Front, either deliberately or through its fumbling incapacity, sabotaged French preparedness and opened the way to defeat was a blatant distortion.

A much more important factor in French unpreparedness was the government's adoption in 1938 of a plan to modernize the air force by converting to new models of aircraft. This essential change came so late that the outbreak of war caught France in the midst of the conversion process. In September 1939, the French had fewer than 500 first-line planes available, as compared to the Germans' 4000. Great Britain's contribution of 1100 first-line planes fell far short of making up the difference.[3] In a desperate effort to remedy this imbalance, Premier Daladier in November 1939, made a dramatic and pressing plea to the American government to come to France's aid by building 10,000 planes at once for sale to the French. The cost, he declared, was immaterial; with some hyperbole, he declared his readiness to mortgage France or sell the palace of Versailles if that should be the Americans' price. It was a hopeless appeal; President Roosevelt feared to challenge American isolationist opinion in such a brusque fashion, and Daladier sank into a kind of moody spirit of defeatism.

Meanwhile the French army was making belated efforts to adapt itself to the kind of warfare inaugurated in the Polish campaign. The army had some 2300 modern tanks along the eastern frontier to match the Germans' 2700, but when the war began they had been parcelled out in small packets to support a large number of infantry divisions.[4] Steps were taken during the winter of 1939–40 to group them into a few highly mobile armored divisions, but the conversion process was only half complete when the German attack finally came. Six months proved far too short a time to create an effective mobile force. Furthermore, the French high command still clung to its blind confidence in the superiority of French troops and equipment and to its conviction that Hitler's blitz tactics would be too risky to succeed in the West. Half of the French eastern frontier was impregnably protected by the Maginot Line; the other half, from Sedan to the Channel, was only lightly fortified. Proposals during the 1930's to extend the Maginot Line to the sea had bogged down because of the cost, and because French governments hesitated to alienate the Belgians by leaving them outside France's defensive frontier. The Franco-British war plan of 1939 called for a massive swing of Allied troops across the frontier into Belgium, pivoting on the northern end of the Maginot Line. This move was to begin only if and when Belgium and the Netherlands should be invaded by Hitler, and it was predicated on the assumption that the Allied forces would have several days to reach advanced defensive positions along the Meuse River. Arguments over the wisdom of this plan continued right up until May 1940.

Still another serious problem during the phony-war winter was the state of

---

[3] By May 1940, French and British production had narrowed the gap somewhat. France now had 1300 first-line planes (of which 300 were based in North Africa); Britain had an estimated 1350; and the Germans had more than 5000, plus 1000 transport planes. (Lt. Col. J. Le Goaster, "L'Action des forces aériennes," *Revue d'histoire de la deuxième guerre mondiale,* III [June 1953], 137–40.)

[4] Whether the French possessed as many tanks as the Germans in 1940 has been much disputed. According to one careful study, the French armies that were actually engaged in the critical phase of the German attack (May 10 to June 1) had only 1520 tanks as compared to the Germans' 2683 used during that operation. By June 11, however, the French had brought into action a total of 2262 modern and 540 obsolescent tanks. (Major A. Wauquier, in *Revue d'histoire de la deuxième guerre mondiale,* III [June 1953], 163–64.) .

civilian morale. Some Frenchmen were lulled into security by the repeated postponement of Hitler's attack; others persisted in a quasi-public campaign in favor of a negotiated peace. Dissension was increased by the curious role played by the Communists. From 1935 to 1939 they had spearheaded the antifascist crusade and had denounced the appeasers who had sacrificed Czechoslovakia and were allegedly scheming to sacrifice Poland. The Nazi-Soviet pact in August 1939 converted the Communists overnight into advocates of neutrality; "brave little Poland" suddenly became "Poland, that monstrous bastard of the Versailles treaty." The Daladier government, naturally but unwisely, outlawed the party as soon as the war began and interned many of its leaders. Communist agitation against the war nevertheless continued, especially in the trade unions, and contributed to doubt and defeatism. Morale was further injured by the persistent Franco-British squabbles over the conduct of the war and by a resurgence of parliamentary factionalism. Daladier's rivals sought to displace him as premier and also to substitute a more vigorous commander-in-chief for the scholarly but indecisive Gamelin.

These domestic feuds finally produced a cabinet crisis in March 1940. Daladier was overthrown, in part because he had failed to help Finland resist Soviet attack. Paul Reynaud replaced him as premier, introducing a new mood of energy and optimism in place of Daladier's moody doubts. The balance of political forces, however, forced Reynaud to keep Daladier in the cabinet as war minister; and a kind of political cold war between the two rivals ensued, to the further detriment of effective leadership. This conflict produced a new cabinet collapse on May 9, but before the press could even announce the news, Hitler struck at last into the Low Countries, and the shaky Reynaud government had to be left in office to face the emergency. Winston Churchill's personal representative, General Spears, who arrived in Paris at about this time, was appalled by what he described as "the slimy mess of disastrous incompetence" that passed for leadership in France. His savage comment was manifestly exaggerated and unfair. Yet it is clear that in this new emergency France turned up neither a Clemenceau, nor a Foch, nor a Poincaré. Even if men of this caliber had been available, it was doubtless too late to improvise an effective defense.

Within a week after the attack the French lines had been pierced near Sedan, and an armored German spearhead was swinging to the right toward the Channel, disrupting French communications and dividing the Allied armies into two isolated segments. The French and British had moved up into Belgium on schedule, but faulty intelligence had led them to underestimate the speed with which the German panzer divisions could advance. Gamelin left a weak covering force at the Sedan hinge, on the assumption that this area would be protected by the rugged Ardennes forest region in southern Belgium. Once the initial breakthrough occurred, the result was spreading chaos. Headquarters could no longer communicate with the various command posts; each unit had to fall back on its own initiative. Stunned by the attack and unprepared for improvised action, much of the army disintegrated as a fighting force. Roads choked with thousands of fleeing refugees further disrupted the war zone. In desperation, Reynaud called General Weygand back from Syria to take over direction of the French armies; and he pleaded passionately with the British government to send the bulk of the Royal Air Force from England to join the fight. Both steps were futile. Weygand, almost as soon as he arrived, concluded that the fight was hopeless. He refused to adopt a plan advocated by General de Gaulle that called for a fighting retreat to a redoubt in Brittany and the eventual transfer of both government and armed forces to North Africa. When the second phase of the German offensive got under way after the battle of Dunkirk, France's capacity for armed resistance had virtually disappeared. On June 10 the government left Paris for the south, arriving finally in Bordeaux; the Germans occupied the capital city without a fight. On the sixteenth a majority in the cabinet voted to ask the Germans for armistice terms; Reynaud submitted his resignation at once and recommended that President Lebrun appoint Marshal Pétain as premier. A week later, on June 22, the capitulation was signed in Compiègne Forest, in the same railway car that had sheltered the signers of the 1918 armistice. Pending a final peace settlement, two-thirds of France (north of the Loire valley, plus all of the Atlantic coast) was to be occupied by German troops, and France was to pay all costs of the occupation. Most of the French army was to be demobilized, and the Navy immobilized in French or North African seaports. Never before in modern history had France been so prostrate, so stunned and broken in spirit. Defeat the French had known, in 1814, 1815, 1871. But this was far more than defeat: it was utter humiliation, almost too deep for any Frenchman to comprehend.

# CHAPTER 32

# Bifurcated France, 1940–1944

There are times when one must have the courage to bet on two possible winners.

EX-PREMIER CAMILLE CHAUTEMPS

The years from defeat to liberation—described by Alexander Werth as "the strangest and most complicated in the whole history of France"—constitute a curious interlude in the record of the nation. For the second time since 1815 the parliamentary system gave way to an authoritarian regime. But alongside that regime, and challenging its legality, there emerged a rival government-in-exile. On June 18 General Charles de Gaulle, who had fled from Bordeaux to London in a British plane, issued a call for continued resistance and set up a Free French movement that was eventually to attain the status of a *de facto* government. Meanwhile the Third Republic's last regularly appointed cabinet headed by Marshal Pétain was transferring its temporary center of operations to Vichy and was embarking on its own attempt to purge and renovate the nation.

Parliament, whose sessions had been suspended during the invasion, was convoked at Vichy (in the unoccupied southern part of France), on July 9–10 to consider Pétain's plans for a new order. Most of the deputies and senators managed to make their way to the meeting in the Grand Casino, though there were two dozen notable absentees who had left Bordeaux for North Africa on June 21 in a vain attempt to set up a government-in-exile there. Among them were such figures as Edouard Daladier, Georges Mandel, and Pierre Mendès-France. Their departure (along with that of President Lebrun) had been approved initially by Pétain, but Pierre Laval and others had persuaded the marshal to abandon the idea. Lebrun remained in France; Mandel and his colleagues, when they sought to land in Casablanca, were arrested by French army authorities acting on orders from Bordeaux, and were charged with plotting against the security of the state.

Pétain's support among the politicians at Vichy (as among Frenchmen in general in July 1940) was virtually unanimous. The nation had not yet emerged from the numbing shock of the disaster, which had struck with the startling power of an avalanche. That shock produced an intense desire for vigorous leadership and an equal revulsion against the men and the system that had failed to avert the debacle. Almost every parliamentarian was ready to entrust France to Pétain at least for the immediate future, and many were prepared to see a permanent shift to a more authoritarian system.

Just what the marshal had in mind for France was not, however, fully clear. The character of his entourage gave a strong hint, but nothing more precise than that. His first cabinet contained a curious mélange of politicians, bureaucrats, and army and navy officers. Most of the politicians were rightists who had been appeasers before September 1939, and defeatists since, though there were one or two notable exceptions. Most of the "technicians" from the civil service and the armed forces were more or less open critics of the parliamentary republic; their sympathies were generally authoritarian rather than fascist. But the man who was already assuming the dominant role in the cabinet was Vice-Premier Pierre Laval, to whom Pétain entrusted the task of drafting and presenting to parliament a program of reform.

Although most of Laval's adult life had been spent as an astute and successful parliamentary politician, the events of 1940 had destroyed the last remnants of his loyalty to the parliamentary system. Perhaps he was moved by nothing more than sheer opportunism—by an instinctive and catlike reaction that led him always to land on his feet. Much more probably, he was motivated by personal resentment against the regime that had shunted him into the background since 1936, and by an overhasty conviction that fascism had proved itself the wave of the future. In later retrospect, his defenders were to argue that he had merely accepted the inescapable fact of defeat and had devoted himself to protecting France against its full consequences. His comments at the time, however, suggested a quite different mood: "Parliamentary democracy has lost the war. It must disappear and give place to a hierarchical authoritarian regime, national and social."[1]

Laval's purpose was to persuade parliament to abdicate its power into the hands of Marshal Pétain, and he proceeded with characteristic shrewdness and skill. In the end, however, he had to accept a degree of compromise. While the

---

[1] R. Aron, *Histoire de Vichy, 1940–1944* (Paris: Fayard, 1954), p. 130.

parliamentarians were ready for temporary abdication to Pétain, a vocal minority was determined to put the question of a permanent new regime "on ice" for the duration of the war. Laval, by a combination of threats, promises, and concessions, managed to avert this postponement; on July 10 a joint session of parliament approved by a vote of 569 to 80 his revised plan for vesting Pétain with power to draft a new constitution without delay. Laval agreed, in return, that the new system would be referred to the voters by referendum, and he allegedly promised that members of the moribund parliament would meanwhile continue to enjoy their privileges and salaries. Not a single party voted solidly against this grant of virtually unrestricted powers to Pétain. The Socialists furnished the largest single bloc of opposition votes, but even the remnants of their solidarity were destroyed by the events of 1940.

The original mélange of Third Republic politicians, idealistic patriots, Catholic personalists and integrists, Maurrassians, protofascists, and sheer opportunists that surrounded Pétain at the outset quickly disintegrated through internal strife. The politicians were the first to go; all of them except Laval were dropped from the cabinet within three months. The fascist sympathizers departed also, disillusioned with the reactionary traditionalism of the men closest to Pétain. Most of them (Doriot, Déat, Deloncle) went to German-occupied Paris, where through press attacks and intrigue (aided by German subsidies) they carried on a kind of political guerrilla warfare against Vichy. Those who remained around Pétain were either disciples of Maurras, authoritarians in the Croix de Feu tradition, or men of technocratic temper—civil servants, bankers, or business men. This inharmonious mixture reminded one observer of a café he had once seen in the Midi, bearing the sign "Aux Anciens Romains et aux Nouveaux Cyclistes."

During the early months of Vichy, it was the traditionalists who had Pétain's ear. The Marshal praised Charles Maurras as "the most French of Frenchmen," substituted the P.S.F. slogan "Travail, Famille, Patrie" for the old republican trilogy "Liberté, Egalité, Fraternité," and proclaimed the arrival of what he called a "National Revolution." There was much grandiloquent talk about a return to the soil, about a decentralized structure based on the old pre-Revolutionary provinces, about a corporative system. Several new agencies of a corporative nature were set up during the first year or so: a state-controlled labor organization, a Peasant Corporation, and a series of Organization Committees for various branches of industry. But these piecemeal measures never coalesced into a coherent system, so that the "National Revolution" remained more slogan than reality. The ineffective nature of traditionalist leadership and the bankruptcy of their policies—especially in a time of stress such as the years of German occupation—soon became obvious; the "Anciens Romains" were gradually edged out by the "Nouveaux Cyclistes"—the technocrats from business and the bureaucracy. They too wanted a national revolution, but of a different sort: their goal was a modernized, efficient France run in authoritarian fashion by a technical elite. Their most brilliant representative, Jean Bichelonne, found a kindred soul in Hitler's confidant, Albert Speer; from 1943 onward the two men joined forces in an effort to build up France into a major industrial power within Hitler's Europe. Many of the Vichy technocrats were to survive the postwar purge and, after a brief period of disgrace, would reappear as key figures in the economic renovation of the country.

One of Pétain's declared goals was political stability—an end to the corridor politics and collapsible cabinets that had marked the Third Republic. Yet Vichy soon developed most of the same ailments in aggravated form. Factions and cliques engaged in constant subterranean or open warfare; men and groups followed one another into office and out again with bewildering frequency. Vichy came to resemble (as Alfred Cobban puts it) "a ramshackle copy of an eighteenth century court" over which Pétain presided as a more or less benevolent autocrat, guided more by whims than by principles. If the period had any continuity, it lay in the passionate fear of social upheaval that gripped most Vichyites, and the persistent efforts of most Vichy leaders to win the Germans over to the concept of collaboration. An understanding with Hitler seemed not only expedient but also essential, if the growing threat to social order embodied in the resistance movement were to be held in check. The Vichy leadership refused to face the fact that Hitler had no real interest in a policy of collaboration with France. Until almost the very end, therefore, they continued to chase this will-o'-the-wisp.

Pierre Laval, Pétain's first vice-premier, set out at once toward this elusive goal. In October 1940, he was granted a personal audience with Hitler at the village of Montoire, and was able to arrange a "summit" conference between Hitler and Pétain a few days later. Although the meeting was inconclusive, Laval was encouraged; he arranged a meeting with German Foreign Minister von Ribbentrop, at which he hoped to get the bulk of the French prisoners of war in Germany released and the German occupation costs reduced by half. It may have been the prospect of this Laval-Ribbentrop meeting, and the fear of some Vichyites that Laval might offer to bring France into the war against Britain, that triggered the fall of the vice-premier in December 1940. Several other factors, however, were involved. There was much jealousy and personal dislike of Laval in Pétain's entourage. Indeed, Pétain's own attitude toward Laval was ambiguous; his behavior toward the vice-premier and his comments about him contained irreconcilable inconsistencies. The most plausible explanation of their uneasy relationship is that Laval thought of Pétain as a successor to the presidents of the Third Republic, dignified but powerless, while Pétain thought of Laval as a chief of staff, whose role was to obey orders from his commander-in-chief. At any rate, Laval was summarily dismissed, and after a brief period of house arrest departed for Paris, where from 1940 to 1942 he developed a close relationship with Hitler's ambassador to France, Otto Abetz.

Pétain meanwhile chose another politician of the Third Republic, P.-E. Flandin, as Laval's successor. The Flandin interlude was brief, however; he arrived with the illusion that Vichy was an independent government, and Berlin quickly disabused him of his error. In February 1941 he was replaced by Admiral François Darlan, a naval officer with a passion for politics and a talent for intrigue. Darlan, as active head of the government and Pétain's new heir-apparent, lasted for fourteen months. Though shrewd and ruthless, his efforts to persuade Hitler that France should be accepted as Germany's closest ally failed to produce results. One German official later remarked that "when we asked Laval for a chicken, he gave us an egg; when we asked Darlan for an egg, he gave us a chicken." Darlan's stance toward Britain has been described as "all hostility short of war"; he was even willing to commit France to military collaboration in the colonies against British troops, but as he failed to secure anything tangible from Berlin in the way of concessions, his influence gradually deteriorated. It was during his year in power that the technocrats rose to the top at Vichy, and that the myth of "la Synarchie"—an alleged secret cabal of technocratic elements—became widely diffused.

The entrance of the United States into the war, however, shook the confidence of the technocrats; their business acumen made them well aware of the weight that the Americans could throw into the scales. Their retreat toward a policy of *attentisme* (fence-straddling) combined with Darlan's shrinking prestige to bring a new change of leadership in April 1942. This time it was Laval who returned triumphantly to a post that he was to retain until Vichy collapsed. It was a somewhat different Laval, though, from the Laval of 1940. Then he had been convinced of an imminent German victory, and had sought to win for France a favored place in the New Order. Now the outcome of the struggle was no longer sure, and his altered purpose was, by dissembling and delay, to evade German exactions and to preserve some semblance of French autonomy. Toward the end he even nursed the illusion that he could manage a peaceful transition from Vichy to a restored Third Republic. Laval played this new role until August 1944, with considerable skill and cunning, though with steadily decreasing power to shape the course of events.

Laval returned to office just at the moment when German pressures began to intensify sharply. The terrible drain of the war in Russia plus Germany's shortage of manpower brought a demand for the requisitioning of French labor for work in Germany. Laval's efforts at evasion eventually failed, and he ended by agreeing to conscript workers for the Germans in return for the freeing of some French prisoners of war. By 1944 seven hundred thousand French workers had been recruited or impressed into service in Germany. Many potential conscripts preferred, however, to take to the hills in central and southeast France and to join armed bands of resisters called the *maquis*. The Germans also stepped up pressure for the arrest of Jews. Again Laval sought to negotiate and delay, then finally agreed to turn over all foreign-born Jews in return for a German promise to spare French Jews.[2] As the anti-German underground in France grew more active, the Germans declared their intention to seize and execute hostages as a deterrent to underground sabotage. Again Laval sought to soften the repression by offering to do the job for the Germans; he set up a special corps of French police and special courts empowered to arrest and punish "terrorists." The effect was to free some of Germany's overburdened security police and SS agents for service in other parts of occupied Europe.

That Laval played a double game after 1942, assuring the Germans of his undying allegiance but in fact evading their exactions, seems likely. Whether in the long run the policy was a wise and justifiable one is much more questionable. Laval believed that in accepting lesser evils he was sparing his countrymen greater ones: that it was better for the Vichy police to shoot ten resisters than for the Germans to shoot a hundred hostages. He believed that the Germans' confidence in him made him the last remaining barrier to the appointment of a gauleiter in France—a German bureaucrat, or a Doriot or Déat, ready to do Hitler's will. He believed that the alternative to his tortuous leadership was the "Polonization" of France, with mass deportations and the liquidation of anti-Nazis. "If my policy succeeds," he told a friend in 1942, "there won't be enough stones in France to put up statues of me; if it fails, I'll be hanged. But that doesn't bother me—I will have done it for my country." Yet even if "Polonization" was really the alternative to Laval's rule, it might have been no worse for France in the long run; the limited protection provided by Lavalism was won at the cost of grave division and confusion within the nation. For even if Laval successfully misled the Germans (which is doubtful), he also misled many of his own countrymen. And whether Laval liked it or not, France became Germany's most important supplier of war materials and (except for the U.S.S.R. and Poland) of manpower during the occupation years.

Laval has had his defenders since 1944; Pétain has had even more defenders, and these have been more successful in influencing the opinions of postwar Frenchmen. The Pétainists hold that it was the marshal who was the real master of the double game; that he played it from the very outset, and that it was he who saved the nation from "Polonization." He was France's shield (the thesis

---

[2] After the war, Vichy's Commissioner-General for Jewish Affairs, Xavier Vallat, asserted that 95 per cent of all French Jews survived the occupation period, whereas only 5.8 per cent survived in seven other occupied countries. His statistics have never been verified; and his testimony carefully avoids such embarrassing facts as the spoliation of French Jews and the role of Vichy police in rounding up and deporting non-French Jews to concentration camps in eastern Europe.

goes) while de Gaulle was the sword; *la patrie* needed both. Pétain's role is, in fact, not easy to assess. His excessive secretiveness, his talent for dissembling, his contradictions of word and action, are almost impenetrable barriers to understanding. His closest advisers were third-rate figures like his personal physician, Dr. Ménétrel. His own behavior seems to have been more impulsive than carefully calculated; his venerable appearance and charismatic aura seem to have concealed a shallow mind, a kind of peasant cunning, and a deep-seated vanity. There is little evidence to support the Pétainist claims that he hoodwinked the Germans, or that he seriously and consistently sought a secret *modus vivendi* with the British, or that he sent Admiral Darlan to North Africa in 1942 with secret instructions to turn the area over to the Allied invaders. Pétain's role had some meaning and even some grandeur until November 1942; it lost any meaning whatsoever when he remained in office after the Allied landings in North Africa and the resultant occupation of all France by the Germans. At eighty-six he was doubtless too old to leave for Algeria at that critical moment; but he was tempted for a time to put himself at the head of France's tiny armistice army and to offer token resistance to the Germans as they flooded in to occupy southern as well as northern France. Such an act, however quixotic, would have ended "the Franco-French War," and it might have prepared the way for a broader unity of Frenchmen in the postwar era. Pétain no longer had any real function after November 1942. His tragedy was not his decision to take power in 1940 but his failure to realize when he and the regime he headed had outlived their usefulness.

✲✲✲✲✲✲✲✲✲✲✲✲✲

Alongside Vichy stood a second wartime France—one committed from the outset to what seemed a quixotic determination to continue the war, but one destined to grow in strength until at last its leaders and its ideals would emerge to shape the restored republic. Some kind of government-in-exile was almost certain to emerge from the collapse; but that Charles de Gaulle should lead it was something of an accident (unless one believes, like de Gaulle, in the force of destiny). As the youngest general (aged forty-nine) in the French army, he was outranked by dozens of better-known officers; and at first he was prepared to follow the orders of any of his superiors if they would carry on the fight. But none spoke out in the moment of crisis, and no well-known political figure managed to escape abroad to serve as rallying point. De Gaulle stepped promptly into the vacuum, and just as promptly found the task of leadership of the Free French movement much to his liking.

De Gaulle was no ordinary professional officer. His offbeat views on strategy during the interwar years, when he preached the new doctrine of mechanized warfare, won him some notoriety if not very much support. He was a voracious reader, something of a military philosopher, an author of essays distinguished by an elegant, almost classical style. His views on the nature of leadership, contained in a volume with the unlikely title *The Edge of the Sword* (and dedicated to Marshal Pétain), accurately reflected de Gaulle's own self-image and foreshadowed in almost uncanny fashion his own conduct over the quarter-century that followed. His books betrayed a fervent patriotism, a touch of mysticism, an austere and mainly humorless integrity, a serene conviction of destiny. The personal traits of such a man were sure to shape the character of the movement that he led.

Free France at the outset was an ill-assorted collection of accidental exiles bound together by nothing more than a common response to de Gaulle's rallying cry of June 18. There were few prominent figures among them, and in some cases their loyalty to the republican ideal seemed uncertain. Indeed, de Gaulle's own political views remained unclear for a time; his declarations were fervently patriotic, but what he talked of restoring was France, not the republic. In the end he followed the counsel of his legal adviser, who urged him to take the position that the Third Republic remained France's legal government, and that it had been destroyed by the unconstitutional machinations of the men of Vichy. Over the next two years, however, de Gaulle's contacts with the emergent French underground showed him that the resistance leaders wanted neither the prewar system nor an authoritarian substitute, but rather a new and purified republic. In 1942 de Gaulle responded by issuing a call for the restoration of France's traditional liberties, and thereafter he began to talk openly of a fourth republic. That commitment was necessary if there was to be a merger of Free France in exile with the underground movement at home.

Within de Gaulle's organization there was never perfect harmony. The general had little sympathy for palaver and compromise; meetings of his quasi-cabinet, the French National Committee, resembled briefings by a commander more than discussions of policy. But the fault was not all de Gaulle's; his makeshift organization contained more than the usual quota of prima donnas and mediocrities. Some members resigned and took to denouncing de Gaulle as an incipient dictator surrounded by fascists. Much criticism centered on the man who called himself Colonel Passy, an ex-officer who headed the Free French intelligence service. His enemies accused him of operating a small scale Gestapo office in London, complete with dungeons for the uncooperative. Eventually de Gaulle was driven to replace Passy with a civilian director, the young anthropologist Jacques Soustelle. There were accusations, too, that de Gaulle aimed to establish a one-party system in postwar France. To offset these fears, Gaullist agents in France were eventually ordered to stimulate the revival of the prewar parties, some of which had disintegrated completely since the collapse. The long-range effect of this decision was to render more likely the restoration of a multiparty parliamentary system after the war, rather than the two-party presidential system favored by many Gaullists. On the other hand, it gave de Gaulle a broader base for his claim to represent all French resisters and helped him to push aside rival aspirants to leadership.

There was serious friction, too, with the British, almost from the outset. Although Churchill's government supported Free France with loans and grants and furnished office space and broadcasting facilities, de Gaulle quickly concluded that British policy, "malevolent and scheming," was designed to undermine his influence in France and to absorb most of the French empire. A series of clashes brought repeated threats that de Gaulle might move his headquarters to Brazzaville. A disastrous Franco-British sortie against Dakar in September 1940 added to the mutual resentment. The whole bittersweet relationship inspired one of Churchill's most celebrated witticisms: his remark that the Cross of Lorraine (de Gaulle's symbol) was the heaviest cross he had to bear.

Within France, meanwhile, there was springing up in almost spontaneous fashion a whole series of tiny and uncoordinated underground movements, dedicated to restoring French morale and rebuilding the will to resist the German conqueror. They were usually the work of a single individual or a handful of men; the first of these grouplets appeared within two months after the 1940 collapse. In the unoccupied southern zone the underground was predominantly leftist in composition, for most Frenchmen of right-wing leanings there were committed at first to the Pétain experiment. In the German-occupied north, where Pétain's hold was weaker, the membership was more broadly recruited from right as well as left. In organizational structure, too, south and north differed somewhat. The southern groups were fewer, but larger and better articulated; by 1942 three organizations called Combat, Libération, and Franc-Tireur dominated the resistance movement in the south. The northern groups were smaller, more isolated, more activist. To function under the noses of the Germans required great daring; frequent arrests kept the northern movements small and tough. Of the northern groups, the best known were the Organisation Civile et Militaire or O.C.M. (rightist in tone), Libération-Nord (mainly Socialist), and Défense de la France (composed largely of Parisian students).

Only one movement straddled the two zones from the outset: this was Front National, founded by Communist activists in 1941. There had been some individual examples of Communist resistance to the Germans before Hitler attacked the Soviet Union in 1941; but the party's official line until then had continued to be one of "revolutionary defeatism." After June 1941, the party sprang enthusiastically into a type of activity for which no other group in France was so well prepared. Individual Communists joined most of the leading resistance groups, but they held all the key posts in Front National. The party's purpose seems to have been to make Front National the capstone of a united or federated resistance movement that would absorb all other groups and would thus be in a position to shape postwar France.

It was not the Communists, however, who managed to weld the underground into a nation-wide federation. Instead, Gaullist agents smuggled in from London accomplished that difficult task. De Gaulle's hopes for building a new France in the postwar era depended on his ability to fuse and win over the resistance movement. He believed that both British and American intelligence agents were out to forestall him by offering the underground arms and money. As soon as possible, therefore, a Free French representative was parachuted into France with the mission of uniting the underground and committing it to de Gaulle. That representative was Jean Moulin, a young career prefect who had been dismissed by Vichy for his resistance activities.

Moulin's task was not easy. By 1942 there were many personal rivalries to overcome, as well as conflicting conceptions of both organization and aims. Many resistance leaders preferred to remain independent of London; some hoped to set up their own central organization and then to negotiate with de Gaulle as his equal. In the end, however, Moulin got his way—thanks in part to the arms and money he could distribute and in part to the growing prestige of de Gaulle as national symbol. In May 1943, the underground agreed to the creation of a National Resistance Council under Moulin's presidency, representing not only the major resistance groups but also the principal parties and trade unions. The underground paramilitary forces were also united under a single command and were shortly given the label French Forces of the Interior (F.F.I.). These guerrilla units were already beginning to play an effective role, especially in railroad sabotage.

Moulin's personal triumph was brief. In June 1943, an informer led the Gestapo to a conclave of resistance leaders near Lyon; Moulin was arrested and so brutally "interrogated" that he died a few days later. The National Resistance Council, instead of waiting for de Gaulle to designate a new president, seized the initiative and promptly chose its own: Georges Bidault, a professor of history and a leading Christian democrat. Sporadic friction between the underground and de Gaulle's headquarters continued during the last year of the German occupation, but it never reached the point of a major clash. Further stresses resulted from the Communists' tendency to play a semiautonomous role within the federated underground, and from Communist complaints that de Gaulle's agents discriminated against their *maquis* units in parachuting arms.

De Gaulle, meanwhile, had transferred his headquarters from London to Algiers, in order to be on "French" soil. The Allied landings in North Africa in November 1942 had produced several months of severe tension between the Free French and the Anglo-Americans; for de Gaulle had neither been informed in advance about the expedition nor invited to participate in it. The general's sense of grievance was aggravated when the Allied command, finding Admiral Darlan on an unexpected visit to Algiers, made a pragmatic arrangement with him to call off French resistance to the landings. Still more irritating was the fact that the Americans, who had been misled into thinking that de Gaulle's influence in North Africa would be meager, had smuggled a rival general out of France to serve as symbol and leader of the French African war effort: Henri Giraud, a war hero who had dramatically escaped from a German prison.

After some complex negotiations all parties agreed that de Gaulle would go to Algiers to join Giraud as co-president of a new French Committee of National Liberation. Only a few months were needed to prove Giraud's total incompetence as a political leader and his almost complete lack of popular appeal. By the end of 1943 de Gaulle had skillfully elbowed him into the shadows and had firmly established his leadership of the French resistance movement both underground and overseas. The only remaining issue was the question of formal recognition by the great powers, which would enable de Gaulle to assume governmental powers as soon as the Allied armies should land in France. The British were prepared to grant such recognition well in advance of D-Day, but President Roosevelt, still suspicious of de Gaulle's motives and of the genuineness of his popular support, refused even *de facto* recognition until July 1944, and *de jure* recognition until October.

During the final months at Algiers, de Gaulle and his advisers had worked out the procedure by which liberated France would be governed pending the creation of a new republican framework. The general's own temperament, and the fashion in which he had dominated the government-in-exile, fed the fears of his critics that his real aim was some kind of authoritarian regime. His plan for the postliberation era only partially alleviated these fears. It provided that the French people would determine their future by a free election, but only after the country could be cleared of the Germans, and only after two million French war prisoners and conscripted workers could be brought back from Germany. During the interim months a provisional government headed by de Gaulle would rule with virtually unrestricted authority. The Communists (and many other leftists as well) suspected that de Gaulle would prolong this interim arrangement as much as possible, with a view to getting Frenchmen accustomed to strong-man rule. Their suspicions were to prove unfounded; but on the eve of D-Day, 1944, not even de Gaulle's closest confidants could be sure of his real intentions.

When one considers the wartime stresses and strains between Free French and Anglo-Americans, and between de Gaulle and the underground movement, one has some right to be surprised that the actual process of liberation of French soil went off so smoothly. True, D-Day (June 6, 1944) came near producing an open breach between de Gaulle and Churchill, for the British informed de Gaulle of the invasion only after it had actually begun. De Gaulle's furious reaction so aroused Churchill that the latter allegedly wrote (but did not send) a letter breaking off all personal relations and ordering de Gaulle off British soil. The crisis passed; during the next few weeks Allied forces moved in from the Normandy beaches (and up from the Riviera) in close coordination with the F.F.I. guerrilla forces. Fortunately, Allied headquarters abandoned plans to set up an Anglo-American military government in France, and the liberated areas were promptly turned over to de Gaulle's representatives. In some parts of France, German troop withdrawals left a vacuum that was promptly filled by self-appointed resistance leaders, many of them Communists. De Gaulle moved rapidly to appoint his own regional representatives with orders to take over from these local committees. Some Communists wanted to resist and to strike for power, but they were overruled by the party leaders who permitted the Gaullist agents to take over with no more than a mild protest. Paris itself was liberated on August 25, when de Gaulle made his triumphal entry, marching afoot down the Champs-Élysées, flanked by the members of the National Resistance Council, while Parisians roared their enthusiasm and hunted down the last remaining Vichyite snipers on the rooftops.

Recent French history contains few episodes so dramatic and so heroic as the resistance era. Thousands of Frenchmen, moved by a vague but generous idealism and by a sense of patriotic duty, risked or gave their lives with a courage worthy of the highest cause. There were many late adherents, of course—"resisters of August 32nd," the French called them—and the great majority who practiced *attentisme* or fence-straddling till the very end. But more than a hundred thousand suffered deportation to concentration camps, from which only forty thousand returned; and the story of the underground is replete with accounts of real heroism.

It has sometimes been suggested, nevertheless, that the whole episode was little more than a futile and quixotic gesture; that the destiny of France would scarcely have been altered if there had been no Free French movement, no active underground at all. Such an assertion is not easy to test. It is true enough that much of the wartime idealism soon curdled; that resistance dreams of a wholly new era, a *république pure et dure,* were quickly shattered; that the Fourth Republic as a political system turned out to be not very much different from the Third. Yet it can be argued that the resistance movement, by pulling together the active elements in the nation and creating at least a temporary consensus in liberated France, did at least ensure a quick and peaceful transition from Vichy to the new republic. It may even be true that the consolidation of a single underground movement "spared France a civil war in the liberation period."[3]

Much more important were the broader or deeper consequences in the postwar era. Any nation's morale can easily disintegrate, its outlook can become badly distorted, if at moments of crisis it fails to discover within itself a civic-minded elite possessed of deep convictions and courageous enough to fight for them. There are powerful arguments for the easier road of *attentisme;* for a national policy of "rolling with the punch" or waiting for outside salvation. Still, a France totally committed to *attentisme* in those critical years might have left a heritage quite different from that derived from the resistance mystique. There is something to be said for the thesis that if France since 1945 has shown some healthy trends and signs of renewal, they are to be traced for the most part neither to Vichy nor to the straddlers, but to the men, the action, the ideals of the wartime resistance.

---

[3] H. Michel, *Histoire de la résistance* (Paris: Presses Univ., 1950), p. 126.

# CHAPTER 33

# The Life and Death of
# the Fourth Republic, 1944–1958

France is not ungovernable. It can be ruled by skill and dissimulation.
*Attributed to* PREMIER EDGAR FAURE

"From resistance to revolution"—so ran the masthead slogan of a leading Paris newspaper of the liberation era. To those Frenchmen who had led the fight against Vichy and the Germans, and to a considerable number of *attentistes* as well, the time had come for a drastic overhaul. The prewar Third Republic retained few supporters; its inefficacy had been proved during the depression decade and the humiliating collapse of 1940. The fiasco of Vichy had shattered the prestige and self-confidence of the traditionalist right. The advocates of rejuvenation and reform seemed to have a clear field; and the mood of the nation appeared to guarantee their success. The flame of the resistance had seemingly fused together the great mass of patriotic Frenchmen, producing a degree of unity the nation had not known for a generation or more. The National Resistance Council's program of reforms for the postwar era had the approval not only of the underground leaders but also of spokesmen for the major prewar parties, from left to right. Charles de Gaulle as provisional president was acclaimed with such enthusiasm that there was no need of a plebiscite to buttress his authority; his was a temporary dictatorship by general consent.

This mood of euphoria was dismayingly brief. Only sixteen months after the liberation of Paris, de Gaulle angrily resigned his post and left the task of rejuvenation to lesser men. Soon after, the political leaders agreed on a new constitution for the Fourth Republic, but it was greeted with indifference or hostility by a majority of Frenchmen. The hope and enthusiasm of the liberation era had already given way to a mood of cynical apathy and increasing resentment. Perhaps one should be surprised that the new republic endured until 1958, considering the problems it faced and the load of unpopularity it carried.

And yet, viewed in retrospect, the period of the Fourth Republic was by no means empty of accomplishment. It was a time when France inaugurated the world's first experiment in national economic planning by a democracy; a time when France moved into the welfare-state era by creating an extensive social security system; a time when the downward population trend of the past century was dramatically reversed; a time when France took the lead in bringing Germany back into the European community. Midway through the Fourth Republic's brief existence, France entered on a period of economic growth more impressive than the nation had known in a century. And in foreign and colonial affairs, painful but important steps were taken toward readjusting France's role to the new realities of its position in Europe and the world. Perhaps even more might have been done; perhaps the accomplishments of the period were not the work of the Fourth Republic's political elite, but were achieved in spite of the regime and its leaders. In any case, there is an ironic contrast between the Republic's poor public image, both then and now, and the record of constructive change that coincided with its existence.

❖❖❖❖❖❖❖❖❖❖❖❖❖

In a precise sense, the Fourth Republic was not established until October 1946, when its constitution was narrowly approved by the voters via referendum. It is convenient, nevertheless, to view the period of provisional government from August 1944 to late 1946 as a preliminary chapter in the Republic's history, when the new institutions were shaped and the new political class emerged. Indeed, some historians see that period as decisive, molding the whole future of the regime.

De Gaulle's dictatorship by consent lasted from the liberation of Paris until October 1945, when Frenchmen elected a Constituent Assembly. De Gaulle's appointed officials quickly fanned out through the country to take over from the deposed agents of Vichy; in some areas there was friction with local resistance groups (notably where the Communists were strong), but the Gaullist authorities everywhere emerged on top. Some of de Gaulle's wartime followers had hoped that after the liberation he would organize and lead a broad new centrist party, perpetuating the underground coalition against the Germans and providing a solid base for a governmental majority. But the general quickly blighted any such hopes; refusing to lend his name or prestige to any party, he chose a position above parties so that political currents might swirl and eddy far beneath him. Whether he missed a chance to build a powerful Gaullist party in the euphoria of the liberation is, in any case, open to question; the unity of the wartime resistance was more apparent than real, and fundamental cleavages began to emerge almost at once. To weld these disparate elements into a single party would have required a leader with all of de Gaulle's strength but without his tactical inflexibility.

Some Frenchmen hoped that even without de Gaulle's leadership, a broad new left-of-center political movement might emerge. The Socialist party, partially rejuvenated by its role in the resistance, appeared to be the natural pole of attraction around which other groups might coalesce. Such groups included, notably, those Christian democrats who had effectively opposed Vichy, and a considerable number of newcomers to politics whose taste for civic action had been whetted by their wartime experience. But by the end of 1944, the Christian democrats decided to strike out on their own path as a party of Catholics without the Catholic label: the new Mouvement Républicain Populaire (M.R.P.) was headed by Georges Bidault, who had been president of the National Resistance Council. Its program of social reform and a partially state-managed economy suggested the leftist bent of its leaders; but mutual distrust on the part of both Catholics and Socialists blocked the kind of fusion which for a time had seemed possible. A second disappointment soon followed. A sizable group of ex-resisters organized themselves into a new Union Démocratique et Socialiste de la Résistance (U.D.S.R.), and in 1945 sought fusion with the Socialist party. Despite strong support from Léon Blum (who had meanwhile returned from detention in Germany), the effort failed; old-guard Socialists refused to water down the party's verbal heritage of Marxism, and insisted that new converts, whatever their resistance record, must work up from the bottom in the party's hierarchy. By mid-1945, therefore, the fragmented political pattern of the Third Republic was beginning to reappear.

To the right of center, meanwhile, there was a temporary vacuum. Many of the most prominent rightists had compromised themselves at Vichy and were either working their passage home or were facing trial before special purge courts. The Radicals, whose profoundly individualistic tastes now made them seem anachronisms, had been almost destroyed by the collapse of the Third Republic; a few ghostly survivors now found themselves wandering uncomfortably through the empty reaches of the right. Since Frenchmen of conservative temper had nowhere else to go, many of them turned to the M.R.P. as the least of evils, thus inflating the size of this new party and giving it an ambiguous character ("a red head and a white tail", someone remarked). Several years were to pass before either the Radicals or the traditional right recovered their self-confidence and reasserted their influence in postwar France.

On the far left, the situation was quite different. The Communist party, shaken and divided by its sudden plunge into revolutionary defeatism in September 1939, had made a dramatic recovery during the resistance era. Whether its members really outdid all other Frenchmen in courage and self-sacrifice may be debatable, but at least the party had managed to create a powerful legend by 1945. No other group had so many martyrs, or used them so effectively. The new prestige of the Soviet Union gave added glamor, and they profited as well by the general trend of opinion toward the left. De Gaulle helped to remove the stigma of unpatriotic conduct when he authorized the return of Communist leader Maurice Thorez from Moscow despite the latter's desertion from the French army in 1939. De Gaulle's visit to Moscow at the end of 1944, and his signature of a twenty-year alliance with the U.S.S.R., seemed further guarantees that Communists were to be regarded as good Frenchmen. At the same time, de Gaulle stubbornly resisted Communist pressure for certain key ministries in his postliberation cabinet, through which the party hoped to get control of foreign policy, the armed forces, or the police. The party line, especially after Thorez's return from Moscow, was moderate and ultra-patriotic; Thorez urged his working-class followers to avoid strikes and increase production. By 1945 the Communists had at last gained outright control of the major trade-union confederation, the C.G.T.; they were winning converts in almost every segment of society. A considerable number of Frenchmen were persuaded (as a British journalist put it) to board the train for 1984 in the belief that it was bound for 1848. Still, the real destination was not entirely clear in that postliberation era, nor is it beyond debate even in retrospect.

De Gaulle, meanwhile, was governing France without much interference from the politicians or the public. The liberation of eastern France was not completed until the end of 1944, after which French forces shared in the invasion and defeat of Germany. This task of liberation and conquest ranked highest on de Gaulle's priority list; above all, he believed, the nation's morale and prestige had to be re-established. Elections were deferred until the return of the prisoners of war, political deportees, and labor conscripts in Germany (2½ million in all). Pending that time, the most pressing domestic issues were mainly economic in nature.

It was in this economic sphere that de Gaulle's decisions were most short-sighted. France emerged from the German occupation a stripped and debilitated country, desperately short of raw materials, consumer goods, and food supplies. Transportation was paralyzed; industrial production had fallen to 40 per cent of the 1938 level; a generalized black market had replaced the usual channels of trade; a disastrously inflated monetary system (the result of the Germans' legalized pillage based on exaggerated occupation costs in the 1940 armistice) threatened to bring the whole economy down into chaos. Some of these problems could not be tackled until final victory over the Axis; others—notably the monetary problem—called for immediate and drastic action. Minister of National Economy Pierre Mendès-France strongly urged such action; he recommended drastic reduction of the volume of inflated currency and its replacement with new bank notes and the adoption of a stringent austerity program. De Gaulle considered but finally rejected these recommendations, which were regarded by more cautious Gaullist advisers as a risky challenge to those Frenchmen who, legally or otherwise, had salted away large quantities of the old currency. The spiralling inflation that followed, the lack of effective controls in a time of severe scarcity, exacerbated social tensions and hampered economic recovery for several years.

A second source of dissension during the early postliberation months was the purge of Vichyites and collaborators. For many ex-resisters, the demand for swift and severe justice took top priority. Some of them quite understandably sought revenge; but their stronger motive was to renovate France by sweeping away the old elites. Special purge courts were quickly set up, but even before establishment of these courts the purge process had begun in more informal fashion. The liberation was accompanied by a good deal of vigilante justice, some of which involved a settling of personal or political scores. Vichy sympathizers soon began to circulate rumors that the new masters of France had outdone Robespierre's reign of terror; their body count went as high as 120,000. A more likely estimate would be 10,000, though the exact number will never be known. Official records show that the purge courts sentenced 39,000 persons to prison terms, 40,000 to loss of civic rights for varying periods, and 2000 to death; but fewer than 800 of the death sentences were carried out. That of Marshal Pétain was commuted by de Gaulle to life imprisonment; but Pierre Laval went before a firing squad after his attempt at suicide was barely frustrated. The number of Frenchmen arrested and punished was proportionately far lower than in liberated Belgium or The Netherlands. For ex-Vichyites, the purge was nevertheless seen as excessive; for many ex-resisters, as far too lenient. It did, however, help clear the decks for a new political and administrative elite born of the resistance.

By the autumn of 1945 most of the prisoners and deportees had been repatriated, and the initiative could pass to the voters. The Constituent Assembly elected in October, with French women enjoying the suffrage for the first time, reflected the powerful leftist surge of the postwar era. Never had a French legislature been so heavily weighted toward the left: Communists, Socialists, and M.R.P. combined drew almost three-fourths of the votes. The Communists, with 26.6 per cent of the ballots cast, emerged as France's largest party; their strength had doubled since 1936, and their support was far broader both sociologically and geographically. The surprising new M.R.P. ran second with 25 per cent, while the Socialists, who had been expected to rank number one, managed only 24 per cent.

The outcome gave added proof that most Frenchmen wanted change. But it soon became clear that they were by no means agreed on the kind of change to be accomplished. In one camp were those who held that the times called for a stronger executive, on the British or even the American model. An opposite camp urged a system of government by assembly: they wanted an all-powerful one-house legislature that would govern through a kind of executive committee and would not be restrained by checks and balances. The former plan was said to be favored by de Gaulle, the latter by the Communists; and both were suspected of ulterior motives. As the Socialist patriarch Léon Blum put it, the Communists were "a party of foreign nationalists" rather than true Frenchmen, while de Gaulle "stood for democracy but did not embody it." Between the two extreme solutions, there was virtually no place to go except back to a system resembling the Third Republic, with its essentially negative machinery of checks and balances. In the end, after five months of haggling, the Assembly arrived at such a compromise. Its constitutional draft was presented to the voters for approval in May 1946.

Many voters, however, were by now disillusioned and suspicious. Spokesmen for the M.R.P. (as well as the few Radicals and rightists who were back in politics) charged that the draft embodied the Communist program of government by assembly; the Socialists, they alleged, had been taken in by a false appearance of checks and balances that would not really restrain legislative tyranny. They warned also that the constitution did not adequately guarantee property rights or the integrity of the French empire. The M.R.P.'s vigorous campaign contributed heavily to the defeat of the draft in the May referendum; and the whole weary process of constitution-making had to begin once more. In the second Constituent Assembly elected in June the M.R.P. moved ahead of the Communists to become the largest party, but once again the third-ranked Socialists held the balance of power. This time the Socialists and M.R.P. worked together to salvage what they could of the rejected draft; they sought only to write some safeguards into the system. More effective checks and balances were introduced and the refurbished French empire (rechristened the French Union) was given a tighter structure in order to head off secessionist movements. The changes were slight enough to permit the Communists in the end to support the new draft. A new referendum was scheduled for October 1946.

This time it was General de Gaulle who suddenly emerged from political hibernation to lead the fight against the constitution. For the first time de Gaulle publicly stated his own constitutional views; his speech at Bayeux closely foreshadowed the constitution that he was to promulgate a decade later as the basic law of the Fifth Republic. The referendum thus turned into a two-way struggle:

on the one hand, the three big leftist parties; on the other, de Gaulle buttressed by the reawakening right. The outcome was claimed as a victory by everyone, and satisfied no one. Thirty-six per cent of those entitled to vote accepted the constitution; 32 per cent voted against it; and 32 per cent refused to vote at all. The Fourth Republic had its basic law at last; but the country's mood had shifted in two short years from passionate idealism and hope to skeptical cynicism and indifference.

This is not to suggest that nothing constructive had been accomplished during those two years. A system of responsible government had been restored, despite the fears of those who had seen de Gaulle as an apprentice dictator. A rejuvenated French army had participated in the last stage of the war, thus bolstering French pride and ensuring France a share in the occupation of Germany. Most Vichy legislation had been repealed, though some of Pétain's lesser reforms were quietly retained by the republic. A spate of new daily newspapers had sprung up out of the resistance movement, seeming to give promise of a purer and more vigorous press. An important segment of the economy—coal, gas, electricity, the four largest deposit banks, most of the insurance companies—had been nationalized by the coalition government that succeeded de Gaulle in 1946. France had been given the most extensive social security system it had ever known. Labor won at least the possibility of a voice in plant management through works committees. The first step toward national economic planning had been taken by the creation of a Planning Commission, headed by Jean Monnet, with authority to lay out a four-year plan of investment in key branches of the economy. A new day was heralded for the overseas empire when all the overseas possessions were given representation in the two Constituent Assemblies and were thus allowed to share in shaping the new French Union. France had rarely experienced so much change in any biennium in its history. Even so, given the special conditions of the liberation period, an opportunity to do still more was missed.

✳✳✳✳✳✳✳✳✳✳✳✳✳✳✳

The republic's new institutions went into operation early in 1947. Not many months passed before the cynics began to remark that the Fourth Republic was already dead—it had been replaced, they said, by the Third. Although the constitution contained a number of gimmicky provisions designed to correct the weaknesses of the prewar system, they turned out to be largely ineffective. Tradition and habit quickly reasserted themselves. Cabinets, on the average, fell every six months; power, instead of being balanced between the executive and legislative branches, was concentrated once more in the lower house of parliament, now renamed the National Assembly. The postliberation trend toward a new party pattern of fewer but more disciplined parties gave way to a partial return to the older pattern of loose and shifting parliamentary groups. The decentralizers who had hoped to transfer some power away from Paris to the regional and local units of government, thus revivifying local democracy, abandoned the task as futile. Most of the resistance-born newspapers failed or were bought out by powerful economic groups; the liberation effort to purify the press, to turn it into a quasi-public service rather than a commercial enterprise, was quietly buried.

Still, this reversion to custom and habit had its limits; the Fourth Republic never became a mere carbon copy of its predecessor. The differences were revealed not so much in the mechanisms of government as in the substructure of politics: in the evolution of social and economic forces, and in the changing attitudes and values of Frenchmen. But even in the strictly political realm, there were some differences as well. The reversion toward the old multiparty structure of loose, amorphous parliamentary groups was checked halfway—partly because the Fourth Republic's electoral law (a modified version of proportional representation) gave an advantage to large organized parties, and partly because the size and discipline of the Communist party forced some degree of discipline on the other parties if they wished to compete. There emerged, in consequence, a kind of hexagonal party system: Communists, Socialists, M.R.P., Radicals, Independent-Peasants, and, more sporadically, some kind of right-wing protest movement (Gaullists, Poujadists).

A second important contrast between the Third and Fourth Republics was the increased size and influence of interest groups. With a few exceptions, these had been weak and ineffective before 1940 (at least in comparison to other modern democracies). But now, a whole congeries of professional associations emerged to speak for the interests of labor, employers, farmers, small businessmen, white-collar elements, veterans, and so on. Some observers contended that they had become more powerful than the parties themselves, and that a kind of *de facto* corporatism was emerging in France, much more effective than the version created from above by Vichy. In a political system where authority is dispersed through parliament rather than concentrated in a powerful executive, special interest groups can more easily find paths of effective access to power. The Fourth Republic in this respect differed from the Third in degree rather than in kind; but differences in degree can be important.

One apparent novelty that marked the Fourth Republic was a steady shift of the political center of gravity toward the right—a reversal of the long-term trend that occurred during the Third Republic. For a time after 1945, the parties that called themselves leftist (however dubious their real claim to that label) had attained an unchallengeable monopoly, far greater than they enjoyed even in the post-Dreyfus or the Popular Front era. The first break came when the Communists were ejected from the governing coalition in 1947; the new "Third Force" government was made up of Socialists, M.R.P., and Radicals. In 1951 the Socialists in turn withdrew into the opposition, leaving control in the hands of the Radicals, the M.R.P., and the newly organized bloc of moderate rightists (Independent Republicans and Peasant party). The Socialists reentered the coalition in 1956, but as a fourth participant; the fulcrum did not really move back toward the left. This jerky rightward evolution, however, was less novel than it seemed. It produced a pattern of government by a shifting, heterogeneous centrist coalition; and this was painfully reminiscent of the Third Republic. If there was a difference, it lay in the increased strength of the parliamentary republic's critics on the far left and among the authoritarian right. In view of that strength, a centrist coalition with all its weaknesses seemed to be the only barrier against a threat to the republic itself.

The nature of the threat posed by the Communists remains a sharply debated issue. It can be argued that their purpose after 1945 was to get a grip on key positions in the state, and eventually to carry out the kind of quasi-legal coup by which Czechoslovakia in 1948 came under Communist control. It may be that the massive strike waves of 1947 and 1948 were seen by the Communists as weapons to destroy the Fourth Republic and to substitute a "people's democracy." The evidence is mixed and incomplete. At any rate, there was widespread suspicion in France that the party had some such goals in mind; and this suspicion wrecked any prospect of a stable left-wing coalition that might have governed with more effectiveness and clearer purpose than the flabby centrist cabinets. Yet so long as centrist governments failed to achieve significant social and economic reforms, the Communist grip on a quarter of the electorate was unlikely to be shaken. The circle was classically vicious.

The Fourth Republic's problem was complicated by the intermittent challenge posed by powerful protest movements on the right: Gaullism from 1947 to 1953, Poujadism during the mid-50's. De Gaulle reentered politics in 1947 when he organized the Rassemblement du Peuple Français (R.P.F.)—a movement that quickly attracted over a million members, far exceeding that of any rival group. In the 1951 elections the R.P.F. won more than a hundred seats in the National Assembly, and would have done even better if the Third Force majority had not altered the election laws to favor centrist alliances. But this was the high point of Gaullism; within a year, the general lost control of his followers in parliament. Many of them were attracted by the image and the program of a new premier, Antoine Pinay, a conservative in the old Poincaré tradition. Despite de Gaulle's angry orders to oppose any cabinet of the Fourth Republic, most R.P.F. deputies abstained or voted for Pinay. The general, in a fury, soon disowned the movement: "They've chosen to guzzle at the trough," he said bitterly. A small remnant of loyalists, led by Jacques Soustelle in the National Assembly and Michel Debré in the Senate, continued to carry the Gaullist torch; but the R.P.F. as a mass movement was dead.

The Poujadist episode represented a different kind of right-wing challenge to the parliamentary republic. Pierre Poujade, a small-town shopkeeper who had fought in de Gaulle's Free French forces during the last months of the war, first won notoriety in 1953 when he rallied a group of merchants in his home town to resist the government's new tax brigades sent out to check the common practice of tax evasion. He promptly organized a regional and then a national Association for the Defense of Shopkeepers and Artisans, whose mushroom growth (especially in the smaller towns and rural areas) indicated the depth of the fears and discontent of "static France" confronted by the beginnings of a modernization process. That growth also suggested to Poujade the possibility of moving from tax resistance to active politics. Shortly before the 1956 parliamentary elections he converted his movement into a party and entered candidates in almost every district.

Poujade's agitation got under way just in time to attract some ex-members of the R.P.F. who were seeking a new channel for their discontent. But Poujadism and Gaullism were fundamentally different in temper and, for the most part, in membership as well. The R.P.F. had appealed not only to malcontents and antiparliamentarians but also to right-wing and even some left-wing advocates of drastic change: men who were contemptuous of the Fourth Republic's *immobilisme,* and who wanted to restore France's greatness through modernization and expansion. Something of the same temper had marked Louis Napoleon's supporters in the early years of the Second Empire. The Poujadist appeal was of just the opposite character; it was a desperate protest by marginal self-employed people ("independents," as the French call them) against the threat of change. Poujade argued (with much validity) that tax evasion and legal loopholes were essential to the survival of the small businessman and farmer, since their margin was so slim; and he appealed unashamedly to their special interests. Among his spiritual ancestors, a French observer pointed out, was that Radical "philosopher" of an earlier generation, Alain.

The 1956 elections gave the Poujadists a startling success. Almost three million votes were cast for his amateur and unknown candidates; more than fifty Poujadists won seats in the Assembly. But the disintegration of Poujadism was as rapid as its growth. Poujade himself, though a demagogue of talent, showed not the slightest capacity for leadership; and his movement contained (as a critic put it) "as much intellectual content as a scream." During the next two years more than half of the Poujadist deputies deserted to other right-wing parties; Poujade himself was crushed when he ran in a Paris by-election; the organization simply fell apart as its leaders groped blindly for slogans and for allies and gave vent to anti-semitism and ultra-nationalism. But the discontent that had generated the movement continued to smolder just beneath the surface.

Throughout all this, successive centrist cabinets continued to fend off the threats from left and right and to keep the republic going, though without much momentum. The general strikes of 1947 and 1948 were contained through tough measures improvised by the Socialist minister of interior, Jules Moch. The centrist parties were enabled to maintain a narrow but clear majority in the Assembly thanks to the election law of 1951, which offered a bonus to parties that would agree to combine their votes. The old Radical party, seemingly moribund after the liberation, made a modest comeback; many of its prewar leaders were experts at the parliamentary game, and levered themselves into key cabinet posts or even the premiership. The heirs to the old Moderate tradition made an even more remarkable recovery; they organized two new parties (the Independent Republicans and the Peasants) which spoke respectively for prosperous businessmen and small independents, and which merged during the 1950's to become one of the strongest groups in parliament. The M.R.P. steadily participated in every coalition, but its electoral strength had been badly eroded since 1945–46; many of its conservative supporters had switched to Gaullism or to the Independents. In principle the party retained its Christian democratic ideals, but in practice lost much of its crusading zeal; some saw it as embodying the new political Establishment, much as the Radicals had done in the Third Republic.

*Immobilisme* became the hallmark of the system, for almost any crucial issue was sure to split the governing coalition and bring down the cabinet. Only once during the Fourth Republic was there a dramatic effort to interrupt the process and to transform the system. That came in 1954, when Pierre Mendès-France was raised to the premiership. Mendès-France, a Radical whose views were not typical of that invertebrate laissez-faire party, had for some years been playing a kind of Cassandra role in parliament, warning the politicians and the nation that continued evasion of difficult issues would in the end be fatal to the republic. France, he kept insisting, had too many grave problems and too few resources; it was essential to make hard-headed choices, to set painful priorities, to tackle problems one by one.

By 1954 Mendès's constant hammering began to have its effect. His opportunity came when France was confronted by the prospect of defeat and withdrawal from Indo-China. Nationalist sentiment in Indo-China had begun to build up even before the Second World War; according to some estimates, there were as many as 10,000 political prisoners there during the 1930's. The conquest of the entire peninsula by the Japanese in the course of the second world war undermined French prestige and strengthened nationalist sentiment. After Japan's defeat, the northern half of the area was occupied by Chinese Nationalist forces, the southern half by a British occupation army. In the south, the British facilitated the return of French administrators and troops, but the north quickly came under the control of nationalist rebels led by a Communist who called himself Ho Chi-Minh. Through most of 1946 Ho and the French engaged in elaborate negotiations designed to create an autonomous state of Viet-Nam loosely linked to France. That attempt broke down at the end of 1946, and a long, gruelling guerrilla war followed. Ho Chi-Minh's remark to a French acquaintance in 1946 showed remarkable foresight: "If it is necessary for us to fight we shall fight. You will kill ten of our men, but we will kill one of yours and it is you who will end by wearing yourselves out." Ho received some support from Mao's regime in China after 1949 (despite Viet-Namese distrust of Chinese intentions), while the French turned increasingly to the United States for supplies and financial aid. But the long struggle increasingly divided French opinion and poisoned the political atmosphere in Paris. Early in 1954 Ho's forces besieged a French garrison at Dien-Bien-Phu and, after several bloody weeks, won a major victory. French officials had pleaded for massive American air support in the crisis—"clouds of bombers," and perhaps tactical nuclear weapons—but in the end President Eisenhower refused the appeal. The war-weary French decided to seek a negotiated settlement; Mendès-France was called to office as premier, with liquidation of the war as his principal task.

Although the cabinet lasted for only seven months, its temporary impact on political life was profound. Many Frenchmen—especially younger ones—were shaken out of their cynical apathy; a kind of *Mendèsiste* cult emerged. Not only was an Indo-Chinese settlement worked out at a nine-power conference in Geneva, but the first long steps were taken toward Tunisian and Moroccan independence, thus averting potential rebellions in those protectorates. At home, Mendès was able to wrest control of the Radical party from the older leadership, and set out to transform it into a vigorous, disciplined political movement with a program of Keynesian economic reform.

The experiment quickly failed. Once Mendès had extricated France from the Indo-China swamp and turned to economic action at home, he ran into a blizzard of opposition in parliament. Early in 1955 his cabinet was overthrown, and a more old-fashioned Radical took his place at the head of an orthodox centrist coalition. The Radical party disintegrated into internal feuds; Mendès-France was deposed from his leadership post, and eventually left the party. A small band of disciples continued to preach his doctrine, but the prospect of achieving a major change of direction seemed more hopeless than ever. The failure of the Mendès-France experiment, though no doubt predictable, contributed to a mood of bitter disillusionment among young reformers that helped to open the way three years later to the return of another reformer—Charles de Gaulle.

Although the Socialists rejoined the coalition in 1956 and saw their leader,

Guy Mollet, elevated to the premiership, not much was really changed. A four-party combination was even more unwieldy and immobile than a tripartite one; Mollet clung to power for sixteen months (a record for the Fourth Republic), but only because there seemed to be no workable alternative, and because Mollet was content to tread water. When he finally proposed some limited measures to appease his labor supporters, he was promptly overthrown and replaced by the usual Radical who was always waiting conveniently in the wings.

In quiet times this sort of makeshift government might have carried on indefinitely; for France suddenly found itself prosperous, booming beyond the memory of any living Frenchman. Poujadist discontent persisted, but it was doomed in the long run by economic growth and modernization. Chronic inflation persisted, too, and weak governments were unlikely to risk painful correctives; but inflation is a condition that many nations have learned to accept. The decisive factor in the destruction of the Fourth Republic was not internal but external; the regime fell victim to its colonial wars.

Since the end of 1946 French forces had been engaged almost constantly in efforts to repress major rebellions in some part of overseas France. The war in Indo-China had dragged on from 1946 to 1954, ending in humiliating defeat at Dien-Bien-Phu and a face-saving settlement at Geneva. Only a few months later, revolt had broken out in Algeria and had steadily gained strength despite French efforts at repression. Mendès-France prevented its spread into Tunisia and Morocco by according quasi-independence to those states. But Algeria was different; by a legal fiction it was an integral part of France, and, more important still, it contained a million European *colons* many of whose forebears had been there for generations. When the Socialist Guy Mollet became premier in 1956, he seemed inclined to seek peace through negotiation; but when he visited Algiers the angry *colons* bombarded him with overripe tomatoes and demanded that Algeria remain forever French. Mollet then gave way completely and switched to a hard line, sending almost a half million troops (the largest French expeditionary corps since the Crusades, it was said) in a futile attempt to corner the much smaller guerrilla army of the rebels. Terrorism and atrocities by the Algerians brought counter-atrocities by the French; the conflict grew steadily more bitter and bloody. The use of conscripts in Algeria (a risk the government had not dared to take in Indo-China) brought this war home to many French families. By 1958 the nation's morale was sagging badly. A few Frenchmen began to speak out for a negotiated peace; a larger number admitted privately that the struggle was hopeless; the rest (probably a majority) insisted that Algeria must remain French no matter what the cost.

It is not surprising that the revolution of 1958 began in Algiers, or that the French army played a major role. For the army to throw its weight in a political crisis was almost without precedent in modern French history; by long tradition, the officer corps had remained aloof from politics and had loyally served each successive regime. Most French officers would probably have preferred to carry on in that tradition. But years of defeat, of courageous but futile effort, had gradually produced a state of intense neurosis. Some French soldiers had been fighting almost without interruption since 1939, and had known almost no victories. Many of them had been posted in Africa or Asia for almost two decades, and had lost touch with civilian society in France. It was easy for them to believe that the weak and scheming politicians and the unpatriotic intellectuals in Paris had sacrificed the army by giving it a whole series of difficult assignments but refusing it the material and moral support needed to do the job. Given this mood, the right kind of appeal at the right moment might convert the army into a revolutionary force.

Plots against the regime had been simmering for some time, both in Paris and in Algiers. The schemers—some of them serious men, some of them fanatics or eccentrics—were for the most part civilians or ex-soldiers; but a few active officers had indicated their sympathy. Some leaders of the disaffected element looked to de Gaulle as symbol and savior (though de Gaulle, quietly engaged since 1953 in writing his memoirs at his country house, gave them no real encouragement). Other dissidents (notably those with a Vichyite heritage) were bitterly anti-Gaullist and hoped that an army coup d'état would culminate in some kind of military dictatorship or army junta. There was no widespread public sentiment for a change of regime or resort to a strong leader. In an opinion poll conducted early in 1958, only 13 per cent of those questioned expressed a desire for Charles de Gaulle's return to power.

The opportunity for action came unexpectedly, while the plans of the dissidents were still maturing. The Mollet cabinet had fallen in 1957; its successor in turn fell in April 1958, and a month passed before a new coalition (scarcely different from the old) could be patched together. The long interregnum encouraged uncertainty and unrest; the new premier, Pierre Pflimlin of the M.R.P., was rumored to be in favor of negotiating with the Algerian rebels. On May 13, when Pflimlin was scheduled to present his cabinet before the National Assembly, extremist leaders in Algiers organized a mammoth street demonstration designed to frighten the deputies in Paris into refusing to confirm the cabinet. The demonstration grew into a riot; the main government building in Algiers was invaded and sacked; a revolutionary government was proclaimed, headed by a Committee of Public Safety.

The crisis in Algiers had immediate repercussions in mainland France. Throughout the second half of May, the country seemed on the verge of violent revolution or civil war. The anti-Gaullist rebels wanted an open break with the Paris government and a paratroop attack on the capital as well as on other major cities. Gaullist agents preferred to use the crisis to achieve a bloodless change of regime; they hoped that the Fourth Republic's leaders would be forced to call on de Gaulle as savior. The general himself adopted an aloof and ambiguous position; on May 15 he announced his willingness to serve if called upon, but made it plain that he would refuse to return to power either through a violent coup d'état or through the slow and cumbersome processes of the constitution. His tactic was to negotiate with leading politicians, and to persuade them to abdicate voluntarily, without strings on his authority.

In the end de Gaulle and his agents proved to be the cleverest maneuverers. In Algiers, they won over some key generals (notably Salan and Massu) and elbowed their way into control of the Committee of Public Safety. In Paris, de Gaulle met secretly with a number of parliamentary notables and presented himself as the only alternative to civil war. Pressure on the regime was increased when Gaullist sympathizers on May 24 seized Corsica in a successful coup; Premier Pflimlin was unable to get the insurrection in hand, despite his best efforts. There were rumors (not entirely empty) that Algiers had set a date for a paratroop attack on Paris, coordinated with an advance on the city by army units in the provinces. President René Coty, working desperately against time to stave off civil war, finally managed to persuade Pflimlin and his cabinet to resign in favor of de Gaulle, while de Gaulle in turn compromised to the point of accepting the premiership via the normal constitutional route (designation by the president, approval by the National Assembly). On June 1 the general appeared before the Assembly, and was confirmed in office by a vote of 329 to 224.

De Gaulle took power as the last premier of the Fourth Republic. In reality, however, that regime went into limbo on June 1, for the National Assembly voted the new government full powers for six months, then adjourned *sine die,* never to reconvene. De Gaulle was authorized to draft a new constitution for approval by popular referendum. If this was a revolution, it was an unusual sort—bloodless, like that of 1870. But if there is any historical parallel for the events of 1958, it may be found not in 1870 but in 1940. There was some irony in the fact that de Gaulle arrived in power in much the same fashion as Pétain—by the abject surrender of the members of parliament, a kind of suicide of the regime. In both cases, there was little popular opposition or even protest; the Fourth Republic, like the Third, died almost without mourners. But the parallel cannot be carried too far. When Pétain took power, his goal was to destroy the flabby republic in favor of an openly authoritarian regime that would repudiate much of the heritage of 1789. De Gaulle's aim, on the contrary, was to renovate the republic by changing its structure and demonstrating to Frenchmen that strong leadership was compatible with the principles of the Great Revolution. For some of his countrymen, a hopeful new era had begun; for others, more cynical in temper, it was likely to be a temporary interlude.

# CHAPTER 34

# De Gaulle's Republic, 1958–1969

Frenchmen, when they are in the depths of anguish or on the heights of hope, instinctively cry "Vive de Gaulle!"

**CHARLES DE GAULLE**

For more than a century now (save for the brief Vichy interruption), France's normal form of government has been the parliamentary republic. But this apparent continuity, Stanley Hoffmann reminds us, conceals a political pattern that is somewhat more complex: a zigzag alternation between what he calls the game-model and the savior-model of politics.[1] Most of the time since 1870, normalcy has meant the game-model: politics, like professional football, was a kind of spectator sport played by experts, followed with passionate interest by many aficianados, but ignored or viewed with contempt by the bulk of citizens whose lives were scarcely touched by the heroics and histrionics of parliament. On occasion, however, severe crises threatened the breakdown of the system and forced the politicians to call on a strong leader—Clemenceau in 1917, Poincaré in 1926, Doumergue in 1934—who could hold things together till tension eased. Then, as quickly as possible, they reverted to normalcy.

Twice in recent times—in 1940 and in 1958—the resort to a savior has implied a more profound and permanent change in the system itself. Pétain quite frankly intended to institutionalize the savior-model; de Gaulle's purpose was not quite so clear. True, de Gaulle's public statements for more than a decade had revealed a venomous contempt for the parliamentary republic—that "regime of mediocrity and chloroform," that system "floating on the surface of France like scum on the sea." There was some reason to believe that the general's long years

---

[1] Stanley Hoffmann *et al.*, *In Search of France* (Cambridge: Harvard Univ. Press, 1963), p. 50.

of self-exile ("the crossing of the desert," Gaullists were to call it in retrospect) had reinforced his authoritarian tendencies and might lead him to establish a kind of revived Bonapartism. Instead, de Gaulle moved quickly to reassure his critics; time and experience, if they had not mellowed his character, had at least taught him the wisdom of flexibility. He did not remind Frenchmen of his long campaign against the Fourth Republic, nor did he sweep away the old political personnel in favor of a purely Gaullist elite. His first cabinet included only a few inner-circle Gaullists like Michel Debré, Jacques Soustelle, and André Malraux; alongside them were such game-model experts as Guy Mollet and Antoine Pinay, plus a number of nonpolitical "technicians" from the higher civil service.

The task of drafting a new constitution was entrusted, for the first time in French republican history, to an appointed committee rather than an elected assembly. Its chairman, Michel Debré, set out to institutionalize the governmental ideas of de Gaulle himself. Yet the new constitution embodied less drastic change than many Gaullists had anticipated. It perpetuated the parliamentary republic in revised form, strengthening and stabilizing the executive branch but leaving the cabinet still responsible to the legislature. The National Assembly's right to overthrow cabinets was sharply curtailed, and the duration of its sessions limited to six months a year. The head of government would now be called prime minister, a more prestigious title than the old président du conseil des ministres (or "premier"). The head of state would continue to be the president of the republic, but he would henceforth be elected not by parliament but by a nation-wide college of some 80,000 electors chosen in the main by local units of government. His prestige would clearly be enhanced by this arrangement, but his constitutional powers were not made notably broader than in previous republics. It was the prime minister who would shape and conduct state policy; the president would remain above politics and would represent the permanent interests of the nation. All this was reassuring to the traditionalists. Still, the relationship between president and prime minister remained ambiguous. If the president happened to be named de Gaulle, could he keep his hands off the decision-making process? If tension developed between them, which one would go? Some critics professed to see a resemblance to the July Monarchy, when Louis-Philippe chafed at the restrictions on his role, and felt an urge to govern as well as reign. As things turned out, these critics were good prophets.

De Gaulle had promised to submit his new constitution to the voters for approval. Their response in the referendum of September 1958 was overwhelming: almost 80 per cent of those who cast ballots gave their consent, despite a vigorous opposition campaign by the left. It was clearly a vote of confidence in de Gaulle's personal leadership rather than in the mechanisms of the new system. De Gaulle pushed on promptly to erect the new institutional framework. A reorganized two-house parliament (National Assembly and Senate) was elected;

de Gaulle, without serious opposition, was chosen president for a seven-year term; and he in turn designated Michel Debré as the first prime minister. In the process, the political elite of the Fourth Republic was decimated; only one out of four deputies in the new Assembly carried over from the old regime. Almost half of the seats went to loyal Gaullists, who had hastily banded together in a new party called the Union for a New Republic (U.N.R.). The left parties suffered a disaster: the Socialists fell from 97 to 44 seats, the Communists from 149 to 10. A revised electoral law was partly responsible for this holocaust, but there was also a massive shift in the popular vote; the Communists lost one-third of their electors.

The winds of change were felt not only in continental France but in the overseas possessions as well. The populations there were also called to participate in the constitutional referendum; and de Gaulle announced that a "no" majority in any territory except Algeria would mean immediate independence for that territory. A "yes" vote, on the other hand, would open various alternatives—among them, autonomous status within a new French Community. De Gaulle's offer temporarily checked the surge toward separatism that had been developing in many parts of the empire; only one territory, French Guinea, chose independence. The others ratified the constitution by majorities even greater than that in continental France; and during subsequent months, most of them opted for autonomy within the French Community. But this taste of self-government quickly whetted their appetite for more. By 1960 the new African republics were already pressing for full independence; and the government in Paris, reluctantly but realistically, acceded to this final demand. The French Community thus vanished into the shadows almost as soon as it was born. Yet it left an important residue, thanks to de Gaulle's acceptance of the *fait accompli,* and to his offer of generous economic and technical aid to the newly-independent ex-colonies. Indeed, the relationship between Paris and the Black Sub-Saharan republics in Africa was to become warmer and closer after independence than it had been in the days of empire.

The most serious overseas problem, however, still defied solution. In Algeria the guerrilla war dragged on, increasingly poisoning the atmosphere both there and in France. French "doves" had hoped that de Gaulle's enormous prestige might permit some sort of face-saving compromise and a quick exit from Algeria. French "hawks" counted on him to reinforce the French military effort and to ensure French sovereignty in Algeria. They were cheered by his initial words on visiting Algeria in June 1958: to a huge crowd of European settlers, he declared, "Je vous ai compris." But as the months went by, it became clear that the famous phrase had two possible meanings (one of which was, "I've got your number"). De Gaulle carefully avoided using the right-wing slogan *Algérie française,* and began to talk instead of an *Algérie algérienne.* Behind the scenes, he sought a compromise, but the Algerian rebel leaders were stubborn. They had passed the point of no return in their drive for independence, while the *colons* (as the European settlers were called) saw negotiations of any kind as a betrayal.

In January 1960 the *colon* extremists again took to the streets in Algiers in an open challenge to de Gaulle. The army wavered but finally remained loyal, and the rebellion collapsed. But the crisis grew steadily worse. In Paris, many prominent left-wing intellectuals came out openly in support of the Algerian cause and published evidence of the use of torture by the French army. On the other extreme, many right-wing politicians plus some of de Gaulle's earliest disciples (notably Jacques Soustelle) broke with him and demanded victory at any cost. Between Scylla and Charybdis, de Gaulle pushed ahead with his effort to end the war. In the spring of 1961, the Algerian leaders agreed to begin peace talks at Evian.

This development converted right-wing dissidence into open subversion. In Algiers, a group of generals headed by Raoul Salan and Maurice Challe formed an *Organisation armée secrète* (O.A.S.) committed to keeping Algeria French by any methods. In April they launched a military putsch, seizing control of Algiers and calling for an insurrection in France. De Gaulle invoked his emergency powers under the constitution, appealed to the nation for support, and prepared for possible civil war. After three tense days, the coup collapsed; the forces of the left and center in France rallied around the government, while most of the conscript soldiers in Algeria refused to obey their subversive generals. The peace talks opened on schedule in May, and continued sporadically through the rest of the year. Meanwhile the Algerian struggle rose to a final paroxysm. The O.A.S. turned to unrestricted terrorism in the major Algerian cities and in Paris. Bombings and assassinations were daily occurrences; de Gaulle himself survived at least two near-misses. But the peace talks went on, and in March 1962 the Evian accords were signed, granting full independence to Algeria (with safeguards for French settlers and their property). For a time, the O.A.S. terrorists still kept up their senseless effort; toward the end they turned to a scorched-earth policy of sheer destruction. Before it was over, the O.A.S. orgy produced a toll of some 12,000 victims. But most Frenchmen were long since sick of the killing; in April 1962 more than 90 per cent of them approved the Evian accords by referendum. For a time, a torrent of *colon* refugees poured out of Algeria to safety in France— 800,000 of them, mostly destitute and profoundly embittered. But de Gaulle had met his most important challenge; he had extracted France from the Algerian quagmire while preserving the country from outright civil war.

Meanwhile, the Gaullist leadership had been wrestling with a second major problem inherited from the Fourth Republic—the financial crisis. The inflationary spiral that had set in once again after the mid-1950's had been too much for weak coalition cabinets to handle; as prices rose, French exports fell sharply, gold drained out of the country, the stability of the franc was threatened. When de Gaulle took office, French gold and foreign exchange reserves had fallen to a critical low, and the treasury deficit was alarming. De Gaulle's economic advisers recommended a drastic remedy—deflation and austerity. Taxes were increased, governmental expenditures reduced by such painful measures as suspension of veterans' pensions and abolition of the state subsidies that had held down food costs. A lid was clamped on wages and prices; the franc was devalued; import controls were relaxed in an effort to let foreign competition reinvigorate the domestic economy.

Deflation soon produced encouraging results. By 1960, exports were rising significantly; capital flowed back into the country; gold and foreign exchange reserves made steady gains. Through most of the Gaullist decade, Frenchmen enjoyed greater financial stability and healthier economic growth than they had known since 1914. The gross national product increased at about 5 per cent a year; foreign exchange reserves reached a record level; the franc seemed solid. As in the case of Algeria, a strong and self-confident government had apparently succeeded in doing what weak coalition cabinets simply could not do. Yet the Gaullist achievement had another less impressive side. The benefits of stabilization and modernization were not equally shared by all strata of Frenchmen. Indeed, the gap between prosperous and underprivileged elements probably became wider during the de Gaulle era. To some degree that was doubtless unavoidable in a country with a large static sector, as modernization squeezed out the marginal and the weak. But the stresses were made worse by government policies on taxes, housing, social benefits, expansion credits that improved the lot of the more prosperous strata at heavy cost to the others. In addition, the Fifth Republic after the first couple of years was only relatively more successful than the Fourth in resisting inflationary pressures and the demands of various special-interest groups. As time went by, a deep sense of grievance persisted and grew among those who believed they were paying the price of building a bankers' and technocrats' paradise, and among those social reformers who viewed Gaullist economic policy as one of "short-sighted archaic liberalism." In the midst of booming prosperity, opposition on the left therefore made quiet but steady gains.

✤✤✤✤✤✤✤✤✤✤✤✤✤✤✤

The end of the Algerian war opened the way to a new chapter in the Fifth Republic's history. Already, the pressure of events combined with de Gaulle's own monarchical temperament had skewed the regime in the direction of presidential government. De Gaulle had let it be known that he viewed certain aspects of public policy—notably foreign affairs and Algeria—as a "reserved sector" in which he rather than the prime minister would make the decisions. By his actions he made clear that a constitutional role aloof from active politics was not to his taste; "inaugurating chrysanthemum shows," he remarked scornfully, was not in his line. Shortly after the war ended he gave another stretch to the constitution by asking Michel Debré to resign as prime minister, and substituting his close collaborator Georges Pompidou.

This strong trend toward presidentialism reinforced the desire of the pre-Gaullist politicians to challenge de Gaulle as soon as possible. Heretofore they had restrained their irritation; they needed de Gaulle to end the war and to overawe the right-wing extremists. Now it seemed that the day of the savior was over, and that they might return to the game-model once more. Parliamentary elections were due in 1963; if they could regain control there, they might be able to revise the constitution and give de Gaulle the MacMahon treatment: give in or get out.

But the general was too shrewd for them. Seizing the initiative, he proposed a constitutional amendment that would consolidate the trend toward presidentialism; it called for election of the president by direct universal suffrage. France had tried such an experiment only once before, in 1848; and the result had been the election of a Bonaparte. French republicans were disturbed at the precedent, but they were even more outraged by de Gaulle's decision to submit the amendment to popular referendum rather than to parliament (thus violating his own constitution of 1958). The party leaders responded by voting a motion of censure, which was supposed to bring down the Pompidou cabinet. But again de Gaulle overrode the challenge; he dissolved the Assembly, and kept Pompidou in office. The voters, he said, would choose between him and the politicians.

The referendum campaign that followed was bitterly contested: de Gaulle and the U.N.R. on one side, all of the other parties, along with the trade unions and most of the press, on the other. De Gaulle won the day, but narrowly; the "yes" vote dropped to only 62 per cent. He saw this as a kind of moral defeat, and thought for a time of abdicating once more—then changed his mind and decided to push on. In the parliamentary elections that followed (November 1962), he campaigned actively on behalf of the U.N.R., and won an impressive victory. The U.N.R. increased its strength in parliament, and with the support of other pro-Gaullist deputies, now enjoyed an unshakeable majority. The election completed the sequence of events that had begun with the constitutional amendment; it "blew up the road back to the Fourth Republic," and gave the Fifth a new character. Ten years later, a leading French commentator was to describe the 1962 amendment as "the most important and no doubt the most enduring change in the nation's political life since the foundation of the Third Republic."[2]

In retrospect, the middle years of the 1960's appear as the Gaullist golden age. France was at peace and master of her own destinies, for almost the first time since 1939. The republic was stable: Georges Pompidou broke every endurance record by remaining prime minister for six years. Frenchmen could turn their attention from "the poisons and delights" of politics to the challenges of economic growth and the fruits of prosperity. Only the opposition leaders and some intellectuals complained that the nation was being "depoliticized," or even anesthetized, by de Gaulle's paternalistic rule. The president loomed majestically over the scene, enjoying his chosen role as elective monarch, greeting the foreign dignitaries who streamed to Paris for audiences, presiding over subdued cabinet meetings where ministers reported to the chief but rarely discussed issues, asking counsel only of himself in the "reserved sector" of foreign policy, intervening at will in domestic policy as well, and reporting semi-annually to the nation at carefully-staged press conferences.

Stability and prosperity gave de Gaulle his chance to rebuild France's prestige as a great power. "France cannot be France without greatness," he had declared in his war memoirs. Yet it was obvious that a nation of France's small size and limited resources could scarcely hope to rank with the super-powers. The president's solution was to assert France's leadership of a bloc of European and Third World states, strong enough to mediate between the U.S.S.R. and the U.S.A. and to hold the balance. His policy of generous aid to the ex-colonies in Africa contributed to this end; the Francophone republics there repaid him with diplomatic support, and gave credence to the cherished thesis that French was not a European regional but a world language. In the Middle East, where the French had long supported the cause of Israel, de Gaulle quietly switched sides and undertook to build a pro-French clientele among the Arab states. In Europe he talked grandiosely about continental unity "from the Atlantic to the Urals," holding out the prospect that France was destined to restore fruitful collaboration between east and west. To reinforce the French claim to great-power status, de Gaulle continued and expanded the Fourth Republic's atomic energy program. He placed central stress not on peaceful uses of atomic power but on what he called the *"force de frappe"*—an independent nuclear striking force whose impact would be more diplomatic than military. It was designed to ensure France membership in the "nuclear club" and to reinforce France's influence in times of crisis. But its cost was heavy, and its possible benefits uncertain.

Still more complex was the problem of France's proper role in a federated western Europe and in the North Atlantic alliance. The Fourth Republic had

---

[2] Pierre Viansson-Ponté, *Histoire de la république gaullienne* (Paris: Fayard, 1970–71), II, 44.

already committed France to membership in both NATO and the European Common Market (EEC). De Gaulle before 1958 had caustically condemned both organizations; they were, he believed, destructive of French independence and, in any case, doomed to futility. On attaining power, however, he found it politic to mute his hostility a bit. NATO was the more vulnerable target, now that Frenchmen no longer feared a Soviet invasion of western Europe. De Gaulle at first demanded that NATO be run by a triumvirate of Britain, France, and the United States. When his proposal was ignored, he moved step by step to withdraw French forces from the NATO command, and finally (1967) invited NATO to remove itself and all its installations from French soil. This tough line won him points in French public opinion, thirsty for a little national self-assertion as against what de Gaulle called *les Anglo-Saxons.*

A challenge to the newly-created Common Market involved greater risks, for it had considerably more support than NATO among Frenchmen. Idealists were attracted by its federalist mystique, realists by the prospect that it would provide a market for French agricultural surpluses. De Gaulle belonged to the latter category; and besides, he thought that by converting it into a confederation of sovereign nations under French leadership, he might use the EEC for his own purposes. Persuaded as he was that national sentiment is the ultimate reality in international affairs, he was determined to head off the growth of an artificial supranationalism. His consistent goal was to limit the autonomy of the EEC "technocrats" in Brussels, and to coordinate the foreign policies of the six member states. Twice—in 1963, and again in 1967—de Gaulle brusquely vetoed bids by Great Britain to join the Common Market; he saw Britain as a dangerous rival for EEC leadership, and claimed to believe that the Americans would use Britain as their "Trojan horse in Europe." Although de Gaulle failed to line up the EEC nations in support of French foreign policies, he did bull through some important decisions at Brussels on economic policy. During discussions of agricultural policy in 1965, he ordered French officials to boycott EEC policy-making operations for six months, and finally imposed a settlement highly favorable to his view of EEC decision-making: multinational rather than supranational. This hard-nosed tactic, however, caused considerable alarm in France both among idealists and realists; the latter feared the loss of the Common Market outlet for farm surpluses. Threatening EEC proved to be far less popular than baiting NATO. A more successful foreign policy move by de Gaulle was his dramatic rapprochement with Germany. A treaty negotiated with Chancellor Konrad Adenauer provided for periodic consultation between French and German leaders and for cultural and student exchanges on an unprecedented scale. The old Franco-German hostility had already been dissipating before de Gaulle took power; the process was now speeded, and seemed likely to transform attitudes on both sides of the Rhine.

On the domestic political scene, two episodes interrupted these golden years and somewhat tarnished their glitter. In 1965 de Gaulle's term as president ended, and he had to choose between seeking reelection (at age 75) or retiring to bask in the admiration and gratitude of his fellow citizens. Many years earlier, de Gaulle had criticized his old patron Marshal Pétain for clinging too long to power: "Old age is a shipwreck; no man should let himself grow old in office."[3] When reminded of the advice, he saw no reason to apply it to his own case; so he announced his candidacy once more. A serious challenge to his reelection seemed unlikely; the only effort to build up a rival candidacy had collapsed when the Socialist Gaston Defferre was unable to put together a coalition of the parties that lay between Gaullism and Communism. But once the campaign opened, two other rivals shot into prominence: François Mitterrand and Jean Lecanuet. Mitterrand claimed to speak for the new "living forces" of politics—the political clubs that had proliferated since 1958, and that sought to renovate the old party structure; he appealed for, and got, both Socialist and Communist backing. Lecanuet, a centrist senator, relied on the appeal of youth against age and conducted a Kennedy-style television campaign that piqued wide interest. De Gaulle, to his great chagrin, won only 44 per cent of the votes cast, and was forced into a runoff election two weeks later. Even after vigorous campaigning his margin over Mitterrand was only 55–45; the close race dimmed his prestige considerably. Two years later came another disappointment; in elections for a new National Assembly, the Gaullist bloc lost some 40 seats, and retained only a bare majority. The parties of the left meanwhile continued their steady resurgence.

Still, these setbacks appeared minor, and did not suggest that the regime or its leader was in any real danger. De Gaulle felt confident enough to continue his abrasive conduct on the world stage, lecturing the Americans about their Viet Nam policy and embarking on a quixotic campaign in behalf of Canada's French-speaking province: "Free Quebec!" His New Year's day message in 1968 contained this complacent remark: "Amid so many countries which are being shaken by so many upheavals, our own country will continue to offer an example of effectiveness in the conduct of its affairs." Yet only four months later, France was suddenly disrupted by a social-political upheaval that came within an ace of destroying the regime. "The events" *(les événements)* of May-June 1968 (to use the common French euphemism for this episode) began modestly enough, as a culmination of months of student unrest in universities of the Paris region. A confrontation between students and police at the Sorbonne on May 3 led into a period of guerrilla warfare in the streets of the Latin Quarter; students and their sympathizers built barricades in the old Paris tra-

---

[3] J.-R. Tournoux, *Secrets d'état: Pétain et de Gaulle* (Paris: Plon, 1964), p. 347.

dition, and were besieged by squadrons of armed police using every weapon short of gunfire. The government zigzagged between conciliation and repression; the conflict only grew worse, and spread to provincial universities as well. Toward mid-May many workers began to join in; strikes (often of the sit-in variety) closed down one factory after another, until by May 20 at least 7 million workers had laid down their tools. Public services came to a halt; transportation broke down; the country was virtually paralyzed. In the Latin Quarter, the huge Sorbonne building was occupied and converted into the world's biggest commune; radical grouplets proliferated, and sought to win over the workers to a program of common action. From university protest and labor discontent, the wave of dissent seemed to be moving toward political action. The chant "Ten years—that's enough!" began to be heard in the streets.

De Gaulle, baffled by this violent and "incomprehensible" outburst, tried to get things in hand by a personal appearance on television in which he promised a referendum on workers' participation in industry. His performance was a lamentable failure; he seemed a querulous old man who had been by-passed by events. Pompidou had meanwhile stepped into the breach and had initiated talks with the trade union leaders, hoping that concessions to labor would end the strike. A generous agreement was finally arrived at, but the trade union rank-and-file repudiated its leaders and rejected the settlement. In the last days of May, the regime seemed to be tottering and French society itself seemed to be disintegrating. Two left-wing notables, François Mitterrand and Pierre Mendès-France, stepped forward to propose a provisional government under their leadership. The Communist high command, which until now had attempted to restrain the revolt and had denounced the student radicals as woolly-minded anarchists, reluctantly decided that since power was about to fall into someone's lap, the party had better prepare to share it. All the predictions of doom seemed to be confirmed when de Gaulle, on May 29, suddenly cancelled a cabinet meeting and left Paris by helicopter for an unknown destination. It was widely believed that he had gone to Colombey and would shortly announce his resignation.

But his design was quite the opposite. Sensing an imminent change in public sentiment as disorder deepened and the threat of chaos loomed, he carefully planned a *coup de théâtre*. Returning to Paris the next day, he let it be known that the army was prepared to restore order if necessary, then spoke to the nation by radio, this time with enormous effect. France, he declared, faced two alternatives: de Gaulle or chaos. He accused the Communists of plotting to take power, called for the support of all right-thinking citizens, and announced the dissolution of the National Assembly with elections to follow at once. His followers, silent and disheartened until now, rallied enthusiastically. The Communists issued a mild protest but made it plain that they preferred the ballot box to civil war. The strike ended, and France began to grope its way back to normalcy. In the June elections, the country swung massively behind de Gaulle: his Union des Démocrates pour la République (the rebaptized U.N.R.) scored the greatest landslide in French republican history. Even without Gaullist fellow-travelers, the U.D.R. now had a massive majority of 291 seats, and could steamroller any parliamentary opposition. As for the country, it was tired and shaken, with little taste for a renewal of disorder. The workers were pacified by wage increases and broadened bargaining rights; the rebellious students were promised drastic university reforms.

De Gaulle had, to all appearances, scored one of the most remarkable triumphs of his remarkable career. Single-handed, through excellent timing and the use of his charisma, he had saved the regime and shattered its enemies. Yet the reality was somewhat less brilliant. The events of May had seriously shaken de Gaulle's prestige. He had so obviously lost control during the crisis; his government had blundered so badly in the early stages; and the disaffection in the country had welled up so strongly, that the myth of the Gaullist republic was largely dissipated. Furthermore, the concessions that had been made to labor threatened to undermine the financial stability in which the regime took such pride. Finally, de Gaulle found himself for the first time confronted by a serious rival within his own system. Prime Minister Pompidou seemed to have met the test more effectively than his chief; he had carried the burden of round-the-clock negotiations with labor; he had managed the triumphant U.D.R. election campaign; he had given an impression of strength when de Gaulle had lost his bearings. It is little wonder (except for those who believe in gratitude) that de Gaulle's first act after the election was to ask for Pompidou's resignation, and to substitute the more colorless Maurice Couve de Murville.

For ten more months de Gaulle remained president; but it was a sad postscript to a distinguished career. Renewed inflation gravely threatened the franc; a new devaluation seemed inevitable, and was staved off only when de Gaulle vetoed the idea as unacceptable. The universities were reopened, but limped along in a state of confusion as they attempted to carry out drastic reforms imposed by Minister of Education Edgar Faure while at the same time coping with the flood of students that swamped their inadequate facilities. Unrest spread downward into the lycées and threatened new disruption. In parliament, the powerful U.D.R. bloc grumbled and bickered over Faure's reform plans and over issues of law and order generally. De Gaulle found it prudent to modify his stance a bit in foreign policy; his public statements were less abrasively assertive than before.

In spite of all this, de Gaulle's position seemed unshakeable. His term as president would run for four more years, and his parliamentary support was overwhelming. He needed only to sit tight and to avoid risky ventures. But for de Gaulle, that was unthinkable. He chafed at the decline in his public support, and at the fact that Pompidou was openly putting himself forward as the presidential successor. It was evidently in an effort to reassure himself, and to prove that his hold on French affections was as deep as ever, that he embarked on the most ill-advised and unnecessary of his appeals to the people. Once again, he proposed a constitutional revision to be approved by referendum.

His proposal involved two changes: an increase in regional autonomy, and a restructuring of the Senate to make it a kind of corporative body, representing various economic and social interest groups. De Gaulle had toyed with both ideas for a long time, but neither one represented a fundamental change or responded to a pressing need. Nevertheless, he made the referendum into a test of France's constancy to him; he demanded that the voters give a single yes-or-no response to the reform package, and staked his own continuance in office on the outcome. For opposition groups of every color, this was an incredible windfall; they could fuse all of the country's discontents, most of which had little to do with the proposed amendments. When the returns came in, the referendum failed by a margin of 53-47; and de Gaulle immediately abandoned office without formally resigning or even issuing any public statement. For many of his countrymen, it was impossible to believe that so shrewd a leader could have made so colossal an error of judgment; they speculated that de Gaulle must have planned it all thus, in order to escape the burdens of office and to make a dramatic exit. More probably, it was a case of pride, age, and self-deception doing their work. In any case, he retired into total silence and seclusion at Colombey, and resumed the writing of his memoirs. Death took him in the midst of this task, in November 1970.

Throughout his dramatic career, de Gaulle had been a figure of controversy. His death changed that: it inspired a surge of deep emotion and respect, both in France and abroad. World leaders gathered for his funeral in Notre Dame cathedral, and for his burial in the humble village cemetery of Colombey. Even those among his countrymen who had most bitterly opposed him, and who had charged him with being a man of the past rather than of the future, now joined the chorus. They sensed, no doubt, that whatever may have been de Gaulle's faults, he had stood out above all other Frenchmen of his time, and had achieved world stature. In his youth, de Gaulle had arrived at the belief that destiny had chosen him to lead France in a time of crisis. Destiny—or chance—had done its work; de Gaulle had indeed led his country, and had left an enduring mark on its history.

# CHAPTER 35

# France Since de Gaulle, 1969–1986

> In the depths of their historic unconscious, the French believe that a president of the right is more legitimate than a president of the left.
>
> **MAX GALLO**

President de Gaulle's abdication of office in 1969 brought the so-called de Gaulle era to an abrupt end. But would the system that he had installed survive him? The constitution of the Fifth Republic had been tailored to his measure; the Gaullist party that had provided stability from the start was held together by little more than its leader's charisma. Would that party, the U.D.R., now splinter into fragments? And if it did hold together, was there anyone of sufficient stature to take de Gaulle's place? These were the questions that occupied the minds of Frenchmen during the months that followed.

The initial answer was that the Gaullist movement would indeed hold together, at least for a time; and that Georges Pompidou would be seen as the natural candidate for the succession. His election prospects depended in part on the strategy of the opposition parties: could they agree on a single candidate, and thus consolidate the victory they had won in the referendum? To that question the answer was negative; personal and political rivalries were too great to permit unity. Each party of the center and left therefore entered its own candidate, splitting up the opposition vote so that Pompidou won easy election. With his authority further buttressed by the Gaullists' control of parliament, Pompidou could count on the regime's stability. He proclaimed his intention to preserve the Gaullist heritage intact.

Yet it soon became evident that Gaullism without de Gaulle would not be quite the same. Pompidou's personality and style introduced a new tone into public life—and such personal qualities, in a quasi-presidential system, are likely to affect the functioning of the regime. Pompidou's style was quite different from de Gaulle's: in place of the rigid, aloof, autocratic soldier-statesman, France was now led by a *bon vivant* whose career had included stints as professor of French literature and executive of the Rothschild bank. Some fervent Gaullists complained privately that Pompidou had been a late adherent to the general's crusade, and that he had no wartime resistance record. The new president shortly adopted a more moderate and flexible attitude in foreign policy matters; there was less talk of French grandeur, none at all of such things as "free Quebec." De Gaulle's veto of Britain's admission to the Common Market was quietly abandoned. In the domestic sphere, Pompidou favored classical laissez-faire doctrine, in keeping with the ideas of his friends in the business and banking world. When his prime minister Jacques Chaban-Delmas pushed too strongly for a mildly technocratic policy of state intervention in the economy (in line with de Gaulle's leanings), Pompidou brusquely requested his resignation and substituted a more docile minister.

Pompidou's drift toward a more conservative business-oriented line not only caused some dissension within the U.D.R., but also encouraged a gradual revival of the political left. The left parties had been badly shattered by the upheaval of May-June 1968; in the parliamentary election that followed the crisis, only the Communist party had retained a solid foothold, with about 20 per cent of the popular vote. But now the moribund Socialist party began to show surprising signs of renewed life. In 1971 François Mitterrand, leader of a small left-center party, engineered a merger of several minor leftist groups with the old but hidebound Socialist party of Jaurès, Blum, and Mollet. As head of the renovated party, Mitterrand promptly embarked on negotiations with the Communists and the left-wing Radicals; in 1972 a "Common Program" was worked out, providing for cooperation in future elections and setting forth a kind of platform for an eventual coalition government of the left. Cooperation paid handsome dividends in the parliamentary election of 1973; the left parties made impressive gains at the expense of the Gaullists, who lost 89 seats in the National Assembly. Encouraged by this shift in the public temper, the leftists set their sights on the presidency; Pompidou's term was due to end in 1976.

Their opportunity came earlier than expected. Pompidou, who had been suffering from cancer, died suddenly in April, 1974, without having named his preferred successor. This time Gaullist unity broke down in the face of personal and factional rivalries. The U.D.R. caucus nominated Jacques Chaban-Delmas, but a considerable minority of party leaders broke ranks and threw their support to Valéry Giscard d'Estaing, candidate of a smaller conservative party called the Independent Republicans. This split within the center-right coalition that had backed de Gaulle and Pompidou was not echoed on the left; Communists, Socialists, and Left Radicals rallied solidly behind Mitterrand as their sole candidate. In the first round of balloting, Mitterrand led the field, while Giscard beat out Chaban-Delmas for second place. In the run-off that followed (a clear majority was required), Giscard barely edged out Mitterrand by a 51–49 margin. The Gaullists emerged from the campaign divided and embittered. For the first time since 1958 they had lost the presidency; and although they remained the largest party in the National Assembly, decline and disintegration seemed their likely fate.

Giscard's relative youth and energetic, informal style reminded Frenchmen of John F. Kennedy, who was much admired in France. The new president, despite his aristocratic heritage and his ties to the business world, announced his intention to transform France into what he called "an advanced liberal society." His program included progressive tax reform and measures designed to satisfy young people (the vote at age eighteen), women (relaxed controls on contraceptives and abortion), and the growing ecology movement. Some Frenchmen doubted the depth of Giscard's commitment to social and economic change. But a true test of his intentions was blocked at the very start by the worldwide recession brought on (or made worse) by the oil crisis of 1973—the sudden and drastic increase in the price of Middle Eastern oil, on which France depended heavily. For the first time in twenty years, industrial growth slowed down sharply; unemployment emerged as a serious problem, and with it a rising rate of inflation that confronted the government with a painful choice between jobs and financial stability.

These difficulties quickly undermined Giscard's initial popularity, and played into the hands of the left-wing opposition. Opinion polls showed a steady rise of support for the left, with the resurgent Socialist party enjoying most of the gains. By 1977, the polls foreshadowed an almost certain victory for the left in the parliamentary election due in 1978; and within the left, the Socialists enjoyed a percentage lead of 35 to 20 over their Communist allies. Giscard's problems were made still worse by a challenge from within his own center-right coalition. He had chosen as prime minister a forceful young politician named Jacques Chirac, who had led the Gaullist dissidents in backing Giscard for the presidency and who seemed destined to be Giscard's loyal lieutenant. But Chirac's restless ambition soon began to show; he openly sought to assert himself as the real leader and spokesman of France's conservative forces, and as the only man who could beat off the rising electoral challenge of the left. By 1976 the tension between Giscard and Chirac had reached a breaking point; Chirac angrily resigned and was succeeded as prime minister by a nonpolitical "technician," the economist Raymond Barre.

Chirac moved quickly to strengthen his personal power base, from which he might challenge Giscard for the leadership of the fight to save France from what he called the menace of collectivism. He persuaded the divided and discouraged

Gaullists to transform the U.D.R. into a more disciplined and dynamic Rassemblement pour la République (R.P.R.) and to elect him its president; then he ran successfully for the recently revived post of mayor of Paris, beating Giscard's candidate in the process. These unseemly squabbles among the conservatives seemed to ensure what had already appeared likely—a leftist victory in the parliamentary election, to be followed by a confrontation between a left-wing National Assembly and a centrist president with shaky conservative support.

Suddenly and dramatically, the leftist threat collapsed; in September, 1977, the Socialist-Communist coalition broke apart and the two main partners fell to open feuding. On the face of it, the argument concerned a revision of the Common Program of 1972, demanded by the Communists and opposed by the Socialists. But for many observers, what the Communists really wanted was to break off the alliance. Since 1972, the balance of forces on the left had changed. At the outset, the Communists had been the stronger partner, and could expect to dominate a coalition government; but now it was clear that the Communists would play second fiddle to the Socialists in such a coalition. To the party's leadership, such a prospect probably seemed worse than the continuation of conservative rule. In any case, many voters were alienated by these squabbles on the left, and switched their support to Giscardian candidates, thus ensuring the left's defeat. Giscard's personal position was greatly strengthened, for his backers, grouped in a loose center-right coalition called the Union pour la Démocratie Française (U.D.R.), won almost as many seats as Chirac's R.P.R. Giscard could now look forward with some confidence to reelection as president when his seven-year term ended in 1981.

That prospect was clouded, however, by the persistence of economic problems: industrial slowdown, inflation, unemployment. Prime Minister Barre imposed tough austerity measures, cutting governmental expenses and freezing wages and prices, but his program was more painful than effective in the short run. Meanwhile Giscard's public image was tarnished by a series of minor scandals—notably his evasive attempts to explain a gift of diamonds from the disreputable Emperor Bokassa, ruler of one of France's ex-colonies in central Africa (the Central African Empire, formerly part of French Equatorial Africa) —and by a growing impression that the president was both indecisive and pretentious. Nevertheless, opinion polls until the very eve of voting continued to predict Giscard's reelection.

The outcome, therefore, came as a stunning surprise to most of the public. In the first round of balloting, Giscard held only a narrow lead over the perennial Socialist candidate Mitterrand, while Chirac and the Communist leader Georges Marchais lagged behind in third and fourth position. In the run-off between the two top candidates, the swing to the left was confirmed: Mitterrand triumphed by a 52–48 margin. Ninety per cent of the Communist voters had switched to his support, while many of Chirac's followers had refused to rally to Giscard. For the first time in a generation, the conservatives' grip on power had been broken. France, declared the pundits, was about to enter a new era.

❖❖❖❖❖❖❖❖❖❖❖❖❖

The unexpected nature of Mitterrand's victory, even among most voters on the left, produced a wave of euphoria. When the returns were announced, thousands of citizens (most of them young) congregated at the Place de la Bastille in a quite spontaneous celebration. At last, they believed, everything in France was going to change. The new president, hoping to profit by that euphoria and to consolidate his victory, promptly dissolved the National Assembly and called new parliamentary elections. This time the leftist triumph grew into a landslide; the conservative majority was swept out, while the Socialists alone won a clear majority of seats in the Assembly. Only once before in French republican history (in 1968, when the Gaullist landslide occurred) had a single party gained such a majority. The Communists, as well as the conservatives, suffered sharp losses. Thus the Socialists, in full control of both executive and legislative branches, were now free to carry out their plans for transforming France.

Although President Mitterrand had been an active politician for thirty-five years, he remained something of an enigma to his compatriots. His background (family and early education) was Catholic, but as a young man he had turned toward a more secular and democratic-socialist set of beliefs. During the Second World War he had escaped from a German prisoner-of-war camp and had played an active role in the resistance. That experience had drawn him into politics; he joined a small left-center party, the Union Démocratique et Socialiste de la Résistance (U.D.S.R.), organized by ex-resisters, and won election to parliament in 1946. He had kept his seat there with only one short interruption, and had also served eleven times as a cabinet minister during the Fourth Republic. It was only in 1971 that he had joined the Socialist party and had become its president and renovator. Mitterrand was admired for his political skills and his intellectual qualities (unlike many politicians, he both read and wrote books), yet an aura of deviousness and opportunism clung to him. He had opposed de Gaulle's institution of a strong presidency, but now he found the prospect of its power congenial. "Force tranquille" (quiet strength) had been his campaign slogan; and in his new role he set out to justify that slogan.

As party leader, Mitterrand had advocated what he called "French-style socialism," more revolutionary than social democracy but more respectful of individual liberty than the Soviet version. The party's electoral platform had promised to implement these general ideas by a long list of social reforms, while at the same time tackling the economic recession by Keynesian emergency measures. Barre's austerity program was to be replaced by deficit spending, designed to reinvigorate industry and to soak up unemployment. The new leadership hoped that other industrial nations would fall in line with the French initiative, and that worldwide recovery would follow. To accomplish these goals, Mitterrand chose as prime minister a longtime Socialist militant, Pierre Mauroy. The cabinet, mainly at Mitterrand's insistence, included four Communists—a move that outraged the conservatives and was sharply criticized by some of France's Atlantic allies. The president's purpose, however, was not to repay the Communists for their electoral support, but to neutralize their potential opposition to the government's program and, in the longer run, to undermine still further the Communists' support in the country. The future was to show that these were shrewd calculations.

The new team moved promptly to convert the party's promises into law. The first year brought an impressive yield of emergency measures and longer-term structural reforms. In the latter category, the most sweeping changes involved the nationalization of a considerable slice of the nation's economy, and a decentralization of power from Paris to regional and local authorities. The list of nationalized firms included several of France's biggest industrial conglomerates and virtually all of the country's private banks; experts estimated that about 30 per cent of France's industrial production, and almost the totality of credit facilities, would now be in the public sector. Decentralization, which had been talked about for decades but never enacted, involved the strengthening of elected regional councils which would now choose their own executives, and a transfer of authority from the centrally appointed prefects to regional and municipal officials. The complexity of this reform ensured that it would take years for full implementation; the hope was that it would breathe new life into local democracy.

Other social reforms proliferated. The minimum wage, family allocations, and old-age pensions were increased, and a wealth tax was imposed on the rich to help pay these social costs. Industrial workers were accorded a series of new rights: a shorter work week, expanded use of shop-floor committees, protection against factory layoffs by requiring prior governmental approval. France's large population of immigrants, many of whom had entered illegally, were given new rights of permanent residence. In criminal justice, the law-and-order stance of the previous government was reversed. The death penalty was abolished despite the angry protests of its defenders and the contrary view of the general public; and prison overcrowding was relieved by the release of a quarter of the inmates. Along with these social changes, short-term measures were taken to cope with the economic recession: emergency funds were allocated to create new jobs in both the public and the private sector.

Most of these actions, of course, were bitterly opposed by the conservative opposition and by the interests which it represented. A flight of capital to safe havens abroad became so serious that the government was impelled to impose strict exchange controls. Even more serious, however, was the evidence that other industrialized nations would not be following the French lead in a common effort to grapple with the world recession. On the contrary: they were turning in just the opposite direction, toward conservative belt-tightening remedies. The Socialists' program was unlikely to succeed if France had to go it alone. And besides, as a British scholar reminds us, "Periods of economic recession are not especially propitious for the pursuit of redistributive economic and social justice."[1]

By the end of the government's first year, euphoria was already giving way to skepticism. The economy remained sluggish; inflation and unemployment had risen; the budgetary deficit and the foreign trade imbalance were alarming. To make matters worse, some of the newly nationalized industries such as Sacilor (steel), Rhone-Poulenc (chemicals) and Thomson (electronics) were turning out to be albatrosses rather than golden geese; they required large state subsidies to keep going. Midway through 1982, therefore, the government took a first step backward toward austerity, freezing wages and prices and trimming some expenses. A much more drastic second step followed in 1983; prices for public utility services were raised, a special surtax on income was imposed, and strict limits were placed on the amount of money French tourists could carry abroad. For many Socialists, the party had abandoned its ideals and had returned to the hated austerity of Raymond Barre. Opinion polls showed a serious decline in public confidence.

Further signs of malaise appeared in 1984. On the extreme right, Jean-Marie Le Pen's National Front emerged from obscurity to win some municipal elections and to score a surprising 11 per cent of the vote in the election of deputies to the European parliament. Le Pen's line was violently xenophobic and racist: he seized on the immigrant problem, accusing the government of letting foreigners take jobs away from Frenchmen, and demanded a return to tough law-and-order measures. Le Pen's demagogy won over some conservatives and, more surprisingly, many Communist voters as well. New discontents were added by an ill-timed government move to reform the educational system. The bill, under study for two years and repeatedly revised, called for integrating private primary and secondary schools (mostly Catholic) into a national public school system. The conservatives, with strong Church backing, mounted a highly emotional crusade to protest what they saw as a threat to the independence of Catholic schools; it culminated in a monster rally of over a million people in the streets

---

[1] Vincent Wright, *Continuity and Change in France* (London: Allen and Unwin, 1984), p. 74.

of Paris. Mitterrand sought to limit the damage by withdrawing the school bill and by dismissing Prime Minister Mauroy. In his place the president chose Laurent Fabius, the youngest prime minister France had seen for more than a century.

Fabius, a "technocrat" who was little known to the public, diverted the tide of criticism for a time by adopting a tough non-ideological stance. "Modernization" was his keynote; he promised increased investment in industry to make France competitive with foreign rivals, and warned that inefficient enterprises must be allowed to go under even though jobs would be lost. Such a program had its appeal in certain quarters, but its results could only be long-range, and it involved some painful adjustments. The Communists, who had already been critical of the Socialists' turn toward austerity, now chose to drop out of the government and to return to the more comfortable stance of opposition. While sharing governmental responsibility, their public support had continued to decline, as Mitterrand had shrewdly calculated.

Already, politicians and voters were riveting their attention on the parliamentary election scheduled for early 1986. The conservatives were savoring in advance the prospect of victory that was promised by the opinion polls. Mitterrand, in an effort to improve the Socialists' chances, pushed through a change in the electoral system, replacing the traditional form of single-member districts by proportional representation. The government also drew attention to the first encouraging results from its austerity program: inflation had fallen to the lowest point in eighteen years, the foreign trade deficit had been sharply reduced (partly due to the drop in world oil prices), and some of the ailing nationalized industries were beginning to show a profit. Unemployment, on the other hand, had continued to rise, reaching almost 10 per cent. Other concerns too fed public discontent. There was a resurgence of terrorist attacks in the streets of Paris, carried out by small far-left groups or by agents of radical Middle Eastern factions. And the curious "Rainbow Warrior" affair cast further discredit on the government. A group of ecologists called Greenpeace had planned a voyage to protest a French nuclear test in the south Pacific; their small ship was sunk in a New Zealand harbor. The local police arrested two French secret agents in the vicinity; Paris authorities disclaimed all responsibility, but soon had to admit complicity; the minister of defense and other high-level officials were forced to resign. Few Frenchmen condemned the act of sabotage, justifying it on grounds of "national security"; but many were furious at the evidence of bungling, and the government lost face.

March 1986 brought the crucial test. The Socialists' last hope was that rivalries among the conservatives might split the opposition so that the left could stay in power. Those rivalries were more personal than ideological; pitted against one another were Giscard, Chirac, and Barre, each of whom hoped to be recognized as leader of the anti-Socialist forces. Although the three rivals were known for their mutual dislike, they managed to put together a partial coalition to improve their electoral chances. The strategy succeeded: the conservative bloc won 286 seats, while the Socialists were cut back to 212. Communist strength was reduced to only 35 seats, exactly matching the number won by Le Pen's National Front on the extreme right. The Socialists' only consolation was that they had done better than the polls had predicted, and that Mitterrand's term as president still had two years to run. For the time being, however, the Socialist era was clearly over.

The interlude of Socialist rule from 1981 to 1986 had potentially mixed consequences for the Fifth Republic's future. On the one hand, the hopes and illusions of many Frenchmen that a left-wing government would transform the country into a land of harmony, prosperity, and social justice were, if not destroyed, badly tarnished. Something in the way of change had indeed been accomplished, but it fell far short of expectations; and many of the Socialists' reforms would soon be swept away. On the other hand, the experience had largely dissipated the myth that only the conservative parties could be safely entrusted with governmental power. It was now clear that an alternation between left and right in office was both possible and healthy. The exclusion of almost half of France's citizens from access to the levers of power had unduly narrowed the base for a solid democracy. That exclusion had lasted for almost a generation; now it no longer seemed likely to be repeated. Thus an important step had been taken toward consolidating the Fifth Republic as a regime worthy of the loyalty of all Frenchmen and Frenchwomen.

In the course of the election campaign, one central question had over-shadowed all others: if the conservatives won, would "cohabitation" work? Could the Fifth Republic function, and avoid deadlock, with a left-wing president and a right-wing National Assembly? De Gaulle's constitution had left the question open; it had remained open because every president until now had been able to count on an Assembly majority. But the curious quasi-presidential system, in which the prime minister was named by the president but had to be confirmed in office by the Assembly, contained a built-in booby trap. If the Assembly were to stonewall the president's choice, his only recourse would be to dissolve the Assembly and appeal to the voters. And if the voters then backed the Assembly majority, the president's alternatives would be (as Gambetta had once said of MacMahon) to "give in or get out." Such an outcome might inaugurate a return to the weak presidency of the Third and Fourth republics.

Mitterrand made no attempt to evade the verdict of the voters; he named as prime minister the head of the largest conservative party, Jacques Chirac. Evidently he aimed to show his compatriots that he would respect their wishes and would play a strictly constitutional role. Chirac put together a cabinet drawn from all groups of the center and right; his rivals Giscard and Barre were not included, but the danger of open conflict among the conservative leaders and factions was averted. As for cohabitation between president and prime minister, it seemed about to get a fair trial. The relationship between Mitterrand and Chirac was, however, more in the nature of an armistice than a peace treaty. Both men moved warily, with an obvious eye to advantage in the 1988 presidential election campaign.

The new prime minister had sobered and matured since his first term in that office (1974–76). Though still dynamic and assertive, he had learned to control his temper and to soften his abrasive manner. Chirac had won respect for his effectiveness as mayor of Paris (a post which he continued to hold), and he had developed an impressive oratorical style that evoked memories of de Gaulle. A "technocrat" by training (he was still another graduate of the elite École Nationale d'Administration), he had deep family roots in the back country of central France, from which he had been repeatedly elected to parliament. An imposing figure—at six feet five he stood an inch taller than de Gaulle—his capacities were matched by his ambition. Whether this latter-day Gaullist represented the general's true heritage was debatable; like his rival Mitterrand, he possessed a streak of opportunism. But his energy and intelligence were formidable qualities.

The conservatives had promised during the campaign to undo most of what the Socialists had done. They turned to the task at once. Using the constitution's emergency powers at times to avoid long parliamentary debates, they pushed through a series of repeal measures. "Privatization" was the new catchword: it involved the return to private ownership of the industries and banks that had been nationalized since 1981, together with the sale of one public television channel. The complex process of transferring ownership was scheduled to take five years. Along with privatization went deregulation: wage and price controls were lifted, and factory layoffs were no longer subject to governmental authorization. The wealth tax was abolished, effective in 1987, and income tax rates were reduced at the upper levels. Chirac also pushed through an electoral reform designed to strengthen conservative chances: proportional representation was replaced by the traditional system of single-member districts in elections to the National Assembly. On the other hand, some of the Socialists' social reforms were quietly retained: notably the process of decentralizing power to the regions and cities, the thirty-nine-hour work week, the increased minimum wage, and the broadened powers of shop-floor councils in large industries.

Throughout this retreat from socialism, Mitterrand remained aloof from day-to-day affairs, intervening only rarely to impose some limits by tactical moves and warnings. He was aware from opinion polls that the public wanted cohabitation to work, and in case of breakdown they would be likely to blame the person deemed responsible. The effect of the president's restrained conduct was dual: his standing in the opinion polls rose sharply (while Chirac's declined somewhat), but his power was clearly reduced, for it was soon obvious that Chirac rather than Mitterrand was in charge. Cohabitation did not rest on an explicit power-sharing arrangement between president and prime minister; it worked because Mitterrand chose to retreat into a position above the battle, accepting for a time a more restricted interpretation of the presidential role. It worked also because in the sector where presidents heretofore had claimed special authority—foreign and defense policy—there were no serious differences between Mitterrand and Chirac. Both men favored the maintenance of strong armed forces, with nuclear weapons central to defense planning. Both were prepared to intervene in Africa, with military force if necessary, to bolster the governments of France's ex-colonies. Both were determined to maintain French influence in the Middle East through friendly ties with the Arab states. And both were inclined (with slight variations) to favor the presence of United States troops and missiles in Europe. In foreign policy, then, what might be called the Gaullist stance survived in modified form despite the swings between right and left since de Gaulle's time.

On the domestic front, however, the conservative government soon ran into stormy weather. Partisans of the left resented Chirac's use of constitutional emergency powers to ram his program through parliament. Then, beginning in autumn 1986, came a series of unsettling developments. A new outbreak of bloody bombings, attributed to Middle Eastern extremists, spread panic in Paris for a time and shook confidence in Chirac's promises that he would ensure public security. Next came student protests, reminiscent of the events of May 1968 though on a lesser scale. In November, students organized massive street demonstrations to denounce as "undemocratic" a proposed government reform of the universities; they objected to such ideas as limiting admissions and allowing individual universities to award their own degrees. The demonstrations turned into violent clashes with the police; there were many injuries and one death. Chirac sought to limit the damage by withdrawing the reform, but his government was denounced for excessive brutality at the outset and for capitulation in the end. Serious strikes by the labor unions soon followed. Encouraged perhaps by the students' success, the railway engineers struck in December over wages and working conditions. Transportation was disrupted throughout the country, and the strike soon spread to the Paris subway and the electrical power workers. The government stood firm, and the strikers eventually went back to work; but the crisis further eroded public confidence in Chirac's leadership. Polls showed a corresponding rise in the standing of President Mitterrand and of Raymond Barre, both of whom were happily free of responsibility for day-to-day decision-making. Mitterrand also scored points by expressing sympathy with the students and the strikers. Chirac seemed well enough entrenched to prevail over his critics, but his attention was bound to be increasingly diverted by the presidential election looming ahead in 1988. And that election, along with the campaign leading up to it, gave promise of being a donnybrook.

CHAPTER 36

# A New France?
# Economy and Society Since 1945

Alas! is it not the usual tendency of Frenchmen, whatever their occupation, to clamor for progress while hoping that everything will remain the same?

CHARLES DE GAULLE

Frenchmen, a German observer remarked some fifty years ago, are basically hostile to the twentieth century. At the time, he was undoubtedly right. Indeed, until at least the end of the Third Republic, most Frenchmen would have felt more at home in the nineteenth century, and did their best to preserve its essential traits. Change came to France nevertheless; and out of the conflict between change and resistance came a curious hybrid that Stanley Hoffmann has christened the stalemate society—a blend of the feudal-agrarian past, the industrial present, and the variegated world of commercial enterprise that straddles the two.[1] Static and dynamic elements were combined in a delicate equilibrium which, by tacit consent, all groups (except a sizable segment of the working class) had grown accustomed to protect. Keeping the balance was made easier by the nature of the pre-1940 political system; a weak and negative regime like the Third Republic was ideally suited to freeze the status quo, or at least to limit change to the speed of glacial action.

One of the sharpest differences between pre-1940 and post-1940 France has been the breakdown of the old consensus on socioeconomic issues and the emergence of a powerful urge on the part of many Frenchmen to "marry their century" (the phrase was de Gaulle's). This impulse has not been universal, of

---

[1] Hoffmann et al., In Search of France, pp. 3–4.

442

course; at times there have been severe tensions between the neo-Saint-Simonian exponents of modernization and the beleaguered defenders of traditional ways. The process of transition out of the stalemate society would no doubt have been easier for Frenchmen if they had not waited so long to "marry their century," or if geographical isolation had allowed them to make the change more gradually. But the facts being what they are (another of de Gaulle's favorite phrases), France after 1945 could not escape a harsh choice: rapid transformation or creeping decadence. An American observer put it thus: "...the urgent, the critical dilemma hangs over France today: To change and, in changing, die; or not to change, and risk a swifter death."[2]

Even before 1940, some Frenchmen had begun to doubt the blessings of the stalemate society. The great depression initially shook their confidence; in the mid-thirties, well after other nations had begun to recover, France was still floundering in the morass. Economists pointed out that the gross national product in 1938 had grown by only 6 per cent since 1913; thus a whole quarter-century (which, to be sure, included over four years of terrible war) had been devoted to almost standing still. The demographic factor added another cause for concern. The birth rate, in decline for more than a century, dipped below the point required for the population to reproduce itself; France in the 1930's became the first great power to enter upon a period of absolute population decline. Such a prospect seemed more dismaying then than it does to us today; the idea of zero (or zero minus) population growth was widely viewed as a symptom of decadence, a trend that would produce both national insecurity and economic stagnancy. Its psychological impact was therefore severe.

The defeat of 1940 dealt an even more shattering blow to French complacency, and the vampire-like effects of the German occupation left the nation economically debilitated and psychologically exhausted. After this series of shocks, one might have expected Frenchmen to crawl back into their shells, to prefer repose to strenuous effort and renovation. Yet the nation struck out on the opposite path; during the quarter-century that followed, France was to experience the most sustained economic growth and the most rapid social transformation in its entire history. For the first ten years after the war this pattern was not yet clear; both French and foreign diagnosticians were given to cautious and pessimistic predictions. They wrote despairingly of a nation "dedicated to the survival of the unfit," of "France, the sick man of Europe." Even after the point of economic takeoff in the mid-fifties, they hesitated for several years before admitting their mistake. But by 1960 it was clear that something important

---

[2] David Landes, "French Business and the Businessman: a Social and Cultural Survey," in E. M. Earle (ed.), *Modern France* (Princeton: Princeton University Press, 1951), p. 353.

had really happened—that perhaps it was not an exaggeration to speak of "a new French revolution."

*Why* it had happened now became the question for debate; and several different explanations were put forward. One undeniable factor seemed to be the population explosion of the postwar years; the downward curve was suddenly reversed, and the French birth rate zoomed upward to become for a time one of the highest in Europe. The national motto, a wit remarked, had been rephrased to read "liberté, égalité, maternité." By 1968 there were 50 million Frenchmen, as compared to 40 million just after the Second World War. True, the growth rate has slowed again since the mid-sixties. Even so, twenty years of rapid increase had done their work; the old structures could not contain this burgeoning population of youngsters who continually required more schools, more social services, more jobs. Economic expansion, and the new set of expectations that it dictated, were forced on Frenchmen whether they liked it or not.

A second factor, some observers believed, was the reform program achieved during the liberation era: the nationalizing of basic sectors of the economy, the state's venture into economic planning, the turn toward a welfare state. The government, it was argued, had given itself new power to act: it funnelled large investments into both the public and the private sectors. State planning had not only ensured the most efficient use of French investment capital, but had drawn large numbers of businessmen, farm leaders, and labor officials into the work of the planning commission, and had thus spread the gospel of productivity among the nation's economic elite. Broadened social security was seen as a factor in increasing the birth rate (mainly because it provided allocations to large families), and as a factor in reconciling the working class to a more enlightened capitalism. Thus it was argued that the postwar wave of social reform, far from being a costly extravagance that weighed down the French economy, had been an important force contributing to the economy's growth.

A third stimulant was occasionally mentioned: namely, the impact of American economic aid in the postwar years. The Marshall Plan, inaugurated in 1947, channelled several billion dollars' worth of goods and services into the French economy at a crucial moment, mostly as outright grants, and it was followed by other American aid programs providing not only loans and equipment but American specialists and training courses for French managers and technicians. Measuring the effect of this aid was, however, a delicate and perhaps impossible task. Neither Americans nor Frenchmen could be entirely objective in their assessments, nor could they know just how different the scenario might have been without such an infusion of resources. Foreign aid seems inevitably to involve some waste, some misdirected effort, some mutual irritation that reduce its effectiveness. Yet common sense and economic theory both suggest that French recovery would have been considerably slower without American aid at that moment. But it was the French ability to utilize grants, loans, and technical assistance that were as critical as the aid itself.

A fourth possible stimulant of French economic growth was the turn toward European economic cooperation and integration. France in 1951 entered into the six-nation European Coal and Steel Community, and in 1957 helped organize the much more important European Economic Community or Common Market. Both steps aroused exaggerated hopes and fears among Frenchmen, many of whom were skeptical of France's ability to compete successfully with its neighbors. Those fears were soon dissipated by the general rise in steel and coal production during the early years of ECSC, and by the impetus given to French industrial and agricultural expansion when a broader free market was created.

These various explanations of the great postwar boom failed to satisfy some diagnosticians. They argued that the turn to state economic planning could not have been all that important, since the Planning Commission enjoyed only limited power to dictate investment patterns, to impose techniques, or to set production targets. They observed that broadened social security did not really explain the baby boom, since the birth rate rose as fast in comfortable bourgeois families as in those of workingmen, who gained most from the welfare state. Something deeper seemed to underlie all of the obvious explanations; and that something was almost certainly psychological in nature. The sequence of upheavals through which this generation of Frenchmen had lived—depression, defeat, occupation, penury, loss of empire—had severely shaken their self-confidence, their complacent belief that the France of tradition was not only the best-loved and most-admired of nations, but the nearest approach to a balanced and harmonious society as well. Something had obviously gone wrong; and unlike the Germans after 1918 (many of whom had sought a scapegoat for their disasters), a considerable number of Frenchmen indulged their penchant for sharp and even brutal self-criticism in an effort to find a rational answer. During the war years, this mood of self-examination emerged both at Vichy and in the resistance movement; the two camps differed in their solutions, but both factions challenged one or another aspect of the stalemate society. After the liberation, "structural reform" became one of the bywords of the new elite; for a time, no change seemed too drastic to contemplate. If the resistance leaders oversimplified the complexity of the task, if they failed in the end to smash all the bulwarks of the old order and to place reformers in all the seats of power, they did give voice to the widespread urge for constructive change, and they did dislodge many old-guard politicians, bureaucrats, and managers in favor of younger men with a new outlook. More than any other factor it was this new mood, this psychological change, that provided the foundation upon which the new France was built.

Still, just how new was this new France? Even after a quarter-century of remarkable change, skeptics could still be found. In 1969 Prime Minister Chaban-Delmas himself still chose to describe France as "une société bloquée"—i.e., a stalemate society. "Such a society," added an influential French sociologist, "doesn't fail to talk constantly of change, but in spite of its revolutionary appearance, it refuses to envisage the least bit of real change, and one of its essential weapons is its extraordinary ability to hide or fuzz up reality...." The new power elite, he asserted, still clings stubbornly to old ways—to a rigid bureaucratic structure, mentality, and style of human relations that act as powerful brakes on change.[3] Other critics offered reminders that a great deal of continuity always underlies change; that even after the most profound of revolutions, men gradually become aware that much of the old order has survived. Perhaps, by the 1970's, Frenchmen were beginning to sense that the era of chronic upheaval through which they had lived for four decades was coming to an end; perhaps a kind of Restoration mentality was emerging—a mentality marked by a partial reversion to the outlook and values of the classic stalemate era. But if this was the case, it also seemed clear that the return to the past would not be complete. What had happened in France since the 1930's was in large part irreversible. Values, expectations, life styles had been profoundly altered. Some Frenchmen would never again be reconciled to the traditional system of their fathers and grandfathers, and would go on struggling to destroy its remnants; an even larger number favored a compromise that would unfreeze the system, would make it more easily and quickly adaptable to changing times, would somehow manage to reconcile tradition with modernity. Whether such a reconciliation was really possible, time alone could tell. In its favor is the fact that logical consistency has rarely been a hallmark of human social or political structures—even in that homeland of reason and logic, France.

✤✤✤✤✤✤✤✤✤✤✤✤✤

When one narrows the focus from society as a whole to its various sectors, some more precise patterns and trends of change emerge. Paradoxically, the most drastic transformation of all seems to have occurred in the social group that was rooted most deeply in traditional ways—the peasantry.

When the war ended in 1945, there was little sign of this impending transformation. The great bulk of the peasantry, which still constituted more than one-third of the active population (a proportion far higher than in any other

---

[3] Michel Crozier, *La Société bloquée* (Paris: Seuil, 1970), pp. 20, 77.

advanced western country), had remained a bulwark of that ferocious individualism so well expressed by Alain, and had scarcely changed its traditional techniques. Only a small minority of specialized farmers (mainly in the north and the Paris basin) had moved into the modern era of mechanization and professional organization for self-defense. But the unsettling impact of two world wars plus the great depression had begun the slow process of converting the peasantry into an active, self-conscious social force. Vichy catered to rising peasant self-consciousness by preaching the rural virtues and sponsoring a back-to-the-land movement, but even more by setting up a virtually compulsory Peasant Corporation as a first step toward a corporative state. The experiment was brief, but not without impact; among other things, it brought to the surface local peasant leaders in many parts of France. Many of these soon reappeared in the new national farmers' organization established after the liberation. This National Federation of Farmers' Unions (F.N.S.E.A.) promptly came under the control of the large mechanized growers and the more prosperous family farmers, who combined conservative political views with a cautious interest in modernization.

A social sector so variegated as the peasantry could not be adequately represented by its "kulaks" alone. French agriculture, remarked one expert, resembled "a museum with exhibits from every period since the Middle Ages"; the life style of a great many peasants had not changed substantially since the days of Balzac. But they were becoming more and more conscious of their isolation and their relative deprivation, and were beginning to listen to advocates of change or even violent protest. A small agrarian activist movement had already emerged in the 1930's, led by a barnyard demagogue named Henri Dorgères; similar bursts of resentment stirred the countryside from time to time after 1950, taking the form of tractor roadblocks on the highways or avalanches of unsold potatoes dumped in the entryway of tax offices. More significant in the long run, however, was the organized rural action of two groups: the Communists and the Christian democrats.

The Communists had already won some scattered peasant recruits before 1940. During the liberation period, they intensified their rural effort and considerably expanded their centers of strength (mainly in central and southwestern France). For a time the party hoped to win a strong foothold or even outright control of the F.N.S.E.A.; but when that organization fell under conservative domination, the Communists focused increasingly on the most backward stratum of the peasantry—the small family farmers (owners, tenants, sharecroppers) of the west, center, and south. Their program did not call for restructuring and modernizing French agriculture, with a view to converting these marginal peasants into prosperous Danish-style farmers; rather, it appealed to their more primitive prejudices and fears as they faced the threat of the modern age. That appeal was effective enough to win the Communists a solid nucleus of rural support in the small-farming regions; but the broader effect was to put another brake on the slow process of rural change.

The impact of Christian democratic activism after 1945 was quite the opposite. The Church had always shown a special interest in rural France, but in the past its major concern had been to preserve traditional ways and values as a bulwark of Catholic influence. One of the most striking novelties of the postwar era was the forward surge of a progressive current within Catholicism —a current that was a century old, but that until now had been of marginal importance. The turmoil of the 1930's and 1940's gave it a new impulsion; many young Catholics took an active part in the wartime resistance, and emerged with a strong commitment to help build a new and purer France. Some entered politics (mainly via the M.R.P.), others turned their energies to rejuvenating the somewhat stagnant Catholic youth movement. Within this movement, the branch designed for young peasants (the Jeunesse Agricole Chrétienne or J.A.C.) grew most rapidly and had the greatest impact. By the end of the 1950's, a new generation of J.A.C. graduates was beginning to move into positions of influence. During the next decade they gradually won control of the F.N.S.E.A., embarked on a variety of experiments in the modernization of techniques and even group farming, and won election to town councils and mayoralties in hundreds of villages. Their goal was not only to modernize agriculture, but to transform the peasant mentality, to convert the rural population from a negative into a positive force in the nation's affairs, and to reduce the gap in living standards between country and city.

Support for their enterprise came from those "technocratic" civil servants and agricultural specialists who saw the old peasantry not as a stabilizing social force but as a dead weight hampering France's effort to move into the twentieth century. Reinforcement came too from the basic long-term trends of the age; for the exodus from farm to city that had begun'many decades earlier grew more rapid in the 1950's, and reached the proportions of a flood. Between 1945 and 1980 the proportion of farmers in the active population fell from approximately 35 per cent to 8 per cent; more than three million peasants left the land, and the trend showed no sign of slackening. Marginal farms went out of production as their aging owners died or entered precarious retirement. The prospect of a France without peasants (in the traditional definition of that term) was an imminent reality. Yet agricultural production climbed higher than ever before in French history, thanks to mechanization and modern methods.[4] France had become a major agricultural exporter to its Common Market partners; French

---

[4] The number of tractors in use on French farms, for example, rose from 26,800 in 1929 to 1.1 million in 1967.

farmers were increasingly dependent on that broader market for their stability and prosperity.

Rural France thus seemed to have crossed the divide into the twentieth century. Even so, the process was still incomplete, and the remaining tensions painful. Some 400,000 old-fashioned subsistence-type farms remained, and the cost of modernizing the middle-sized farms weighed heavily on the public treasury, on France's Common Market partners, and on those younger farmers who had mortgaged their future in order to mechanize. Partly because of these transitional problems, and partly because French farmers rarely controlled the marketing of their produce, rural living standards continued to lag behind those of the city populations. The real income (buying power) of the average farmer had risen slowly but steadily during the 1960's, but from 1973 onward it slipped into decline. In addition, the drive for change in the countryside had lost its edge. The young Catholics who had led that drive were aging now; their dynamism and commitment had to some degree burned itself out, and their successors, although more professional now, appeared to be more concerned with individual success than with transforming the peasant world. Much had been done to integrate rural France into the national society, but part of the job was still ahead.

One other social category, the industrial workers, had slightly outnumbered the peasantry when the postwar period began. Shrinkage occurred there too, but it was far less dramatic than in the case of the farm population. By the 1980's, the industrial labor force still made up 34 per cent of the active population, as compared to the 8 per cent in agriculture. And alongside the industrial workers, those in the so-called tertiary sector of the economy—commerce, transportation, services—had experienced explosive growth; by the 1980's, they numbered more than 57 per cent of the active population. Industrial workers might still consider themselves to be the elite of the working class, but their dominance of the labor movement was no longer secure.

Labor emerged from the Second World War with increased prestige and renewed hope for an effective voice in society and the state. Many workers had proved their heroism in the resistance movement; the liberation mood favored social reform; the business community was temporarily embarrassed by its Vichyite connections. Membership in the C.G.T. soared for a time to the record figure of over 6 million, and that of the Catholic C. F. T. C. to a more modest 750,000. Welfare-state measures adopted in 1945–46 gave the workers greater security than they had ever known. Once again, however, labor's hopes of a new era were soon dimmed. One reason was the resurgence of the business group after its brief postliberation period of disgrace. A second factor, though, was labor's own mistakes—its chronic inability to use what potential influence it possessed. In 1945 the Communists wrested control of the C.G.T. from the older syndicalist leadership, and set out to use the organization for partisan ends. After three years of severe internal strife, the anti-Communist wing broke away to form a rival organization called Force Ouvrière with syndicalist leanings and unofficial Socialist ties. Conflict between these two groups and with the Catholic federation weakened the effectiveness of all three; before long, two-thirds of the union members had dropped out. Although membership figures fluctuated thereafter, they remained low; by 1986 it was estimated that no more than 12 per cent of French workers belonged to a union.

Labor's interests were further hurt by the recovery of the conservative parties. Throughout most of the Fourth Republic, governments were dominated by the center and right, which represented the interests of the bourgeoisie and the more prosperous farmers. De Gaulle's Fifth Republic, in the view of most workers, brought little improvement. Labor spokesmen complained that the state bureaucracy was dominated by "technocrats" whose sole concern was alleged to be efficiency rather than social justice. De Gaulle's sporadic expressions of interest in structural reform—notably in the shape of what he called "participation," or workers' profit-sharing in industry—they regarded with suspicion, as a trap to mislead gullible proletarians. The scope and intensity of labor discontent were dramatically revealed during the May 1968 crisis. A wave of wildcat strikes surged through the factories, despite efforts by the C.G.T. leadership to damp down these "anarchistic" actions. Furthermore, the C.G.T. found itself outflanked on the left by the former Catholic trade union confederation, which in 1964 had dropped the word "Christian" from its title in favor of "Democratic," in a shrewd move to broaden its appeal beyond the ranks of practicing Catholics. The rechristened Confédération Française Démocratique du Travail (C.F.D.T.) remained smaller than its older rival, but it adopted a more aggressive stance in pressing for labor's demands, both during the 1968 events and in the years that followed.

While a chronic sense of grievance continued to mark the outlook of many workers throughout the postwar period, this mood was softened by the gains achieved through economic growth. Real wages by 1960 surpassed the previous French record, and the level continued to rise (though much more slowly) even after recession and inflation set in after 1973. By now, upper-echelon workers had grown used to enjoying the fruits of relative affluence: automobiles, refrigerators, better housing, vacations at resorts that had once been the preserves of the bourgeoisie. The old contrasts in life style were slowly eroded, at least with respect to those external manifestations that had distinguished the workers from the middle classes. Attitudes, too, were in the process of partial change. Some workers were becoming less suspicious of technocratic talk about efficiency and productivity as goals from which all would benefit. There were signs of the emergence of what certain observers called a new working class—those employed in the most technically advanced plants, where specialized training was essential. Workers there appeared to be losing interest in traditional trade union militancy or political activism; they looked inward to the individual factory, where they sought to secure a voice in policy-making and a share of the gains from higher productivity.

In that sense, France was plainly moving into the post-industrial age. But even clearer evidence of that transition was the massive growth of the non-industrial working class—the white-collar *employés* in the tertiary sector. By the 1980's, this category of wage earners far outnumbered the industrial workers. Although many white-collar workers were unionized within the major labor confederations, they were less vocally class-conscious and more inclined to support moderately reformist political parties (notably the Socialists). Workers in the tertiary sector also included a large and growing proportion of women, who were traditionally less inclined to union membership and militancy. By the 1980's, women constituted 43 per cent of France's total work force.

The transition to the post-industrial age had the effect of blurring still further the indistinct line between working class and middle classes. In life style, self-image, and attitude toward other groups, many workers in the tertiary sector resembled the lesser bourgeoisie rather than their fellow wage earners in industry. A further obscuring of class lines has resulted from the emergence of the so-called *cadres moyens* (middle-level supervisory personnel). This managerial category was small and unimportant a generation ago; it is now estimated at 13 per cent of the active population. Its members, like other workers, depend solely on their salaries and have no policy-making functions, but in out-look and life style they have more in common with the bourgeoisie than with the industrial work force. They have refused to join the major trade unions, preferring to organize their own Confédération Générale des Cadres. Along with the "technocrats" of the governmental bureaucracy, they form a kind of technological elite. Some observers suggest that middle-class leadership is likely to shift from the older sectors of the bourgeoisie to this more vigorous and self-confident managerial stratum. But if so, the shift is still in its early stages.

One further development within the working class has been the recent appearance of a new sub-proletariat of foreign immigrants, who have taken on the more onerous tasks of society. An earlier wave of immigrant workers had arrived in the 1920's, when wartime losses had left France short of manpower. Many of those immigrants remained, and their children were gradually integrated into French society. The new wave, from the mid-1950's to the mid-

1970's, was much larger and more varied; about half came from Portugal, Spain, and Italy, the rest from Africa or Viet Nam. By the mid-1970's, they numbered more than 4 million, or 8 per cent of the country's population. Their presence undergirded the great economic boom of the postwar years; they took over most of the manual or routine jobs, leaving native-born Frenchmen to move upward into skilled or white-collar employment. But their presence also brought some social costs. Poorly paid, miserably housed in urban or suburban slums, and in most cases separated from their families who remained in the homeland, the foreign workers constituted a segregated and almost unassimilable minority, in the nation but not of it. Their arrival in such large numbers also brought out a latent and almost unsuspected racism in many Frenchmen; some violent racial incidents followed. New tensions resulted from the rise of unemployment after the mid-1970's. Although the Socialist government in 1981 took action to protect immigrants' rights, even that government was eventually forced to backtrack and to encourage foreign workers to return home.

The social sector that has put its special stamp on France in the modern era is the one commonly labelled the bourgeoisie. For a century it has provided most of the nation's political and bureaucratic personnel, and almost all of its business leadership. Frenchmen and Frenchwomen, despite their deep theoretical attachment to the principle of equality, had long been accustomed to living in a structured society that permitted but scarcely encouraged upward mobility. Children of farm or factory parents might work their way up the social ladder in two or three generational steps, but rarely in one leap. Most of them did not even presume to try.

One by-product of France's experience in the Second World War was a reinforcement of the equalitarian ideal. Men and women of every social origin had worked together in the underground and had learned to judge one another as individuals rather than as representatives of a class. For a time after 1945 there was much talk of opening up the system to permit the free rise of talent. Plans were laid for a democratized educational system that would no longer separate the children of workers from those of the bourgeoisie, and that would ensure fully equal rights to women. In business, the grip of the old "bourgeois dynasties" was shaken by the nationalizing in 1945–46 of a number of industries and banks. Even in privately owned plants, workers were to be given a voice through the new Works Councils.

The reality, as usual, fell short of the dream; France soon reverted to a pattern that preserved much of the past. The old bourgeois families recovered both their social influence and their economic power. The Works Councils proved to be ineffective as devices to achieve industrial democracy. Although the educational system was partially restructured to give all children a theoretically equal chance, most of those who survived the rigorous competition and rose to the top continued to be the sons and daughters of the bourgeoisie. A renewed cry for democratized education arose during the May 1968 upheaval; the protestors pointed out that though all lycée graduates were entitled to enter a university, only 16 per cent of those who actually did so came from blue-collar workers' or farmers' families. True, the proportion of such students had been rising before 1968 and has continued to do so since then; but many young Frenchmen were beginning to realize that a university degree was no longer a sure passport to an elite job, as had once been the case. There were simply not enough elite jobs to go around for the expanding numbers of university students. The desirable positions were monopolized, therefore, by the graduates of the *grandes écoles*—those highly selective training schools such as the Polytechnique and the Institut d'Études Politiques that had long dominated access to the upper bureaucracy in government and business. Nor did the postwar reforms alter the system of ferociously competitive state examinations that ensured intellectual quality but also tended to perpetuate the power of the bourgeois elite. Indeed, the creation of a new École Nationale d'Administration in 1945 increased the grip of that elite on the levers of power in France; for the so-called "Enarchs" (graduates of the E.N.A.) have almost monopolized the top positions in government and even in some sectors of business. Social mobility in postwar France, therefore, has not increased very much over that of prewar times.

Within that heterogeneous category called the bourgeoisie, however, the postwar era did bring some significant change, though more in attitudes than in structure. In the business world, the old tradition of cautious secretiveness came under sharp attack from those neo-Saint-Simonian reformers who charged that French enterprisers had in fact been among the western world's most benighted non-enterprisers. A new gospel of aggressive entrepreneurship was preached by the technocratic civil servants who emerged from the wartime resistance movement, by American advisers in the Marshall Plan era, by a ginger group of young businessmen, and by such crusading publicists as J.-J. Servan-Schreiber. Their ideas gradually caught on in the upper echelons of the business community, producing changes that would have stunned their bourgeois ancestors. The modernizers, after some hesitation, supported France's entry into the Common Market; they began to put venture capital into new plants and products; they sent their sons to American business schools; and they financed the establishment of their own managerial training institutes on the American model.

There remained, of course, static elements committed to preserving traditional ways. Most middle-level and small businessmen, grouped in their own organization, were mainly concerned with survival, and used their considerable political clout in a spirit of narrow self-protection. Most fearful and vocal of all were the small shopkeepers and artisans—that urban and small-town petty bourgeoisie that had played such an important role ever since the Revolution. They formed the hard core of Pierre Poujade's protest movement in the 1950's, and of a succession of similar movements thereafter. But their complaints could only slow the process a little; the number of small shops continued to decline as villages decayed and as chains of *supermarchés* won French consumers away from their ancient habits.

❖❖❖❖❖❖❖❖❖❖❖❖❖

Continuity and change are always interwoven in history. Looking back from the 1980's over the past four decades, it would seem that change has been the dominant leitmotif. France has become an urban nation: more than half of all Frenchmen now live in communities of over 10,000 population—12 million of them in the swollen conurbation of Paris alone. French values, habits, life styles have been extensively modified. The bonds of family, the domination of the young by their elders, have been relaxed (though by no means broken). Population growth has slowed; the divorce rate has risen, as has the number of single-parent families. A growing number of urban citizens, both old and young, live alone. Frenchmen and Frenchwomen have changed their tastes; they spend proportionately less on food and more on health, housing, travel, vacations, and education. They have become easier spenders, too; installment buying for the first time is common, household appliances have become necessities rather than luxuries, the new superhighways are jammed on weekends with carloads of pleasure-seekers. Urbanites have developed a passionate urge for a "second residence"—a house at the beach or in some country village to which they can escape on weekends or during the August vacation. Measured per capita, far more Frenchmen than Americans own such hideaways. Living the good life seems to have replaced politics as the Frenchman's favorite off-the-job avocation. And the good life is plainly better, and more widely shared, than was the case in France a generation ago. A five-fold increase in the gross national product since 1950 has produced, among other things, the highest living standard the French have ever known. From 1960 to 1983, the buying power of the average Frenchman doubled.

Does it follow that France in the 1980's is a happier, healthier, more stable nation than it used to be, even in the fabled *belle époque* before 1914? On that question, the French themselves would probably find cause for vigorous debate. Charles de Gaulle, ruminating in self-exile during the last months of his life, made this judgment: "Despite ... the material progress of the French people ..., social relationships were still marked by suspicion and bitterness. . . . Everyone resented what he lacked more than he appreciated what he had."[5] And a prominent sociologist added that in his view, France remained fundamentally unchanged, unreconstructed in its basic values, locked into a traditional bureaucratic system resting on a mutually suspicious style of human relationships: a nation that "simply can't tolerate authority, yet at the same time . . . considers it indispensable."[6]

Such judgments may be excessively severe, reflecting a deep-seated French tendency to denigrate not only foreigners but, even more virulently, each other. Certainly the gains registered in many spheres since the disasters of 1930–45 are impressive ones, for which both political and business leaders and ordinary citizens can claim part of the credit. True, some problems remain only partially solved. For example, statistics suggest that while economic growth has brought increased affluence to most Frenchmen, it has not reduced the spread between rich and poor. A recent study shows that the top 10 per cent of French families own 57 per cent of the nation's wealth.[7] Indeed, France leads most of its northern European neighbors in inequality; and an unprogressive tax system does little or nothing to correct such imbalance. Poverty persists in the midst of affluence; to find it, one must go to a remote backwoods village, or to the urban slums where immigrant workers are crowded into converted garages and warehouses. Old-age pensioners, on the other hand, have had their condition eased recently by more generous government grants.

Advocates of women's rights can also claim that some injustice persists. Although women did at last get the suffrage in 1945, along with a constitutional guarantee of absolute equality of rights, the speed of change since then has been less than dazzling. On the credit side, a handful of women have regularly sat in parliament, and a great many more in municipal councils throughout the country. Women have been regularly named to cabinet posts since the mid-1970's; Pierre Mauroy's cabinet in 1982 included five women. There were two women candidates for the presidency in 1981. Some new legislation has responded to women's needs: abortion was legalized (with some restrictions) in

---

[5] Charles de Gaulle, *Memoirs of Hope: Renewal and Endeavor* (tr. Terence Kilmartin) (New York: Simon and Schuster, 1971), p. 342.

[6] Crozier, *La société bloquée*, p. 130.

[7] A similar study of the distribution of wealth in the United States suggests even greater inequality here than in France: the top 10 per cent of American families own 84 per cent of the nation's wealth.

the 1970's, and the phrase "head of the family" was deleted from the law on parental authority over children (now shared by both parents). Nine million women now hold jobs outside the home; this represents 72 per cent of all women aged 25–49, and 43 per cent of France's total work force. The proportion of women in the professions, however, remains relatively small; likewise the number who have attained executive or managerial positions. A vigorous but small feminist movement continues to be active, but it confronts a deeply entrenched conservatism not only among men but among women as well.

One other source of discontent that has emerged in recent years is regional in nature. Certain ethnic groups around the fringes of France—notably the Bretons and the Corsicans—have spawned active autonomist movements that have turned at times to violence. Although the old Alsatian autonomist movement has been quiescent in recent years, agitation of an unexpected sort has emerged in the southwest, where partisans of a quasi-mythical Occitanie have drawn some attention, and where French Basques have lent some support to their brethren in Spain. These regionalist groups complain that their areas have been neglected by the centralized bureaucracy in Paris, and the Bretons have also demanded official recognition of their language alongside French. These developments run counter to the standard French belief that all residents of "the hexagon" since the Great Revolution have thought of themselves as Frenchmen and Frenchwomen first and foremost. But the trend hardly presages a serious disintegration of national unity; the sense of Frenchness remains profound.

It is tempting at times to think that something in the French cultural heritage feeds an anarchistic and contentious mood, rendering Frenchmen constitutionally unable (as one of them once said) to conjugate the verb "to be happy" in the present tense. More probably, however, the sources of discontent are simpler and more straightforward. When an old country encrusted with tradition and heavy with history enters upon a period of rapid economic and social change, sharp stresses and strains are the price that must be paid to secure the benefits desired. Social justice, and the conviction that such justice is being done, are elusive goals in quiet times; how much more so, then, when a partially new France is in the process of gestation.

# CHAPTER 37

# French Thought and Expression, 1919–1986

Can man alone create his own values? That is the whole problem.

**ALBERT CAMUS**

"We civilizations now know that we are mortal.... We see that the abyss of history is large enough for everyone. We feel that a civilization is as fragile as a life." So mused the noted poet-essayist Paul Valéry in 1919, in the lengthening shadow left by the Great War. Valéry's somber soliloquy reflected the fact that twentieth-century France shared with the rest of the western world a widely generalized malaise of the mind and spirit. That this should be so was hardly surprising, for Frenchmen from 1914 onward lived constantly in or near the edge of crisis. The shattering experience of the Great War left the nation shaken and unsettled even during the postwar decade of quasi-normalcy. There had scarcely been time to settle back into old habits when the Great Depression brought new social and psychological tensions, quickly intensified by the disaster of 1940 and its complex aftermath.

But France's malaise, like that of the West generally, had origins older and deeper than the series of post-1914 crises. Its harbinger had been the new intellectual generation of the 1890's, as it challenged and undermined the dominant mood of the positivist age. By 1914 an avant-garde was in full revolt against the optimistic and confident premises of the Enlightenment in its revised nineteenth-century form. French thinkers and writers after 1890 had been among the major contributors to this revolt against rationalism and scientism, though no French spokesman—not even Henri Bergson—could rival Sigmund Freud for pervasive long-term influence.

The noisiest and best-publicized iconoclasts of the 1920's were such fringe groups of artists and poets as the Dadaists and the surrealists. The Dada movement, founded in Switzerland during the war by a band of angry young men from various parts of Europe, transferred its postwar headquarters to the more congenial atmosphere of left-bank Paris. Its campaign of "calculated nonsense" was the product of a passionate revolt against orthodox bourgeois standards; it rejected as false the sensible pretensions of an actually senseless world. In origin an emotional protest against such human folly as the Great War, the Dada movement pushed on to develop its own esthetic theory, frankly antirational in nature. For a time its art exhibits and festivals (a later generation would have called them "happenings") gave the movement a *succès de scandale*. The novelty soon wore off, but Dadaism seen in retrospect did have a considerable impact. It began the process of liberating art and literature from formal rules and the confines of logic; it "freed the imagination from the control of reason." And from it emerged an even more influential successor, the surrealist movement, that managed to "organize the destructive frenzies of Dadaism."

Surrealism's founder, the poet André Breton, drew on the writings of Freud to preach his version of esthetics: true art should express deep-buried subconscious drives by stripping away the repressive crust of reason. One of Breton's manifestoes exalted those human traits and experiences that foster the creative impulse, but that had long been restrained by bourgeois culture: "... the dream; the subconscious; love, freed from all moral or social fetters; revolutionary fervor; flamboyant atheism." Although the surrealists produced only a few enduring masterpieces of painting, poetry, or cinema, many of France's most innovative young artists and writers passed through a surrealist phase and remained marked by it. Surrealism, says the critic Henri Peyre, "proved to be the great force which, even more than Symbolism in 1890, almost as much as the Romanticism of 1820–1830, launched young creators on their careers." But if it had a powerful liberating effect on French cultural expression, it also gave voice and encouragement to the rising irrationalist mood.

The major figures of the 1920's, however, belonged to none of the self-conscious literary or artistic schools; they went their own independent ways. Yet independence did not mean that they were unaffected by the pervasive mood of their time. In different fashions, both Marcel Proust and André Gide (the two literary giants of the epoch) reflected and encouraged that mood. Someone has said that in a period of uncertainty and drift, when men seem to have lost their trust in a set of rigorous standards and beliefs, they are inclined to turn either outward to the transcendental limits of sensibility, or inward to that only sure reality, the self. It was this latter course that attracted both Proust and Gide.

Proust's many-volumed masterpiece *A la recherche du temps perdu* had begun to appear in 1913, but most of it was a product of the 1920's. Not since

Rousseau's *Confessions* had any French literary work revealed such minutely introspective probing into the most remote crannies of an exceptionally complex mind. Proust was one of the pioneers of the stream-of-consciousness technique in modern literature, yet he rigorously channelled that stream so that his novel possessed an overall architectural design that was almost Cartesian in its balanced perfection. The beauty of Proust's language and his rich and haunting gallery of characters gave the work much of its distinction; but the trait that made Proust representative of his time was his absorbing interest in the realms of the subconscious and the marginally conscious. At the same time, however, Proust was a penetrating observer of a disintegrating social world—the world of the Parisian aristocracy in the early decades of the twentieth century. His blend of shrewd social satire with keen psychological sensibility made his work unique.

Gide was an equally complex and contradictory figure. A man of bourgeois origin and Calvinist heritage, but tormented by the passionate drives of his own ambiguous nature (like Proust, he was a homosexual), he sought throughout his literary career to find an ethic broad enough to reconcile these opposites. "Nostalgic for the previous century's world of secure middle-class values yet forced against his will into opposing those values and declaring new ones,"[1] Gide engaged in a lifetime of introspective wrestling with conscience and instincts that reflected many of the ambiguities of his age. Man, as Gide saw him, was cast into the world without divine guidance or predetermined destiny but with "innumerable possibilities of becoming." In one of his early novels, *Les Caves du Vatican,* he toyed with the Bergsonian concept of the "gratuitous act" —the action that is performed spontaneously, without forethought or motive. Gide seemed to suggest that only such an unplanned act, lacking in both purpose and calculated result, could be the action of a free man; for all of man's "rational" decisions are forced on him by society or by his previous education and training. Yet Gide was no nihilist; along with his revolt against conventional mores and hypocrisy went a painful search for an ethic in harmony with the needs of twentieth-century man.

It would be surprising indeed if, even under the stress of chronic crisis, the educated elite of a country like France were to embrace a doctrine of pure irrationalism. The Enlightenment heritage, the long tradition of rationalist humanism in France, constitutes a powerful barrier against the surge of man's darker (some would say deeper and purer) impulses. For a century the French educational establishment had been stressing the Cartesian process of logical deduction as the proper path to knowledge and truth, and had placed the highest premium on reason, order, and clarity. Some required reading in Pascal may have qualified the Cartesian influence in a few sensitive minds, but Pascal's mystical and

---

[1] H. Stuart Hughes, *Consciousness and Society* (New York: Knopf, 1958), p. 360.

irrationalist leanings ("I believe because it is absurd") were usually treated as the curious aberrations of a great stylist. The impact of nineteenth-century positivism and scientism had shifted the educational emphasis slightly toward more empirical and inductive methods; but Cartesian rationalism remained the core of French mental training, just as the literary classics remained the essential fare of the cultivated man.

The French educational system remained highly resistant to reform in the twentieth century, and thus acted as a kind of brake on any rapid change of mood. If the new spirit of irrationalism crept into the universities via Bergson and a few others, it was more than counterbalanced by the survival of a dominant positivist and rationalist tradition. Durkheim's influence in the social sciences prevailed during the interwar years; from its prewar stronghold in higher education, it seeped down even into primary education and reinforced the positivist outlook for another generation. Bergson might be the admired and respected luminary of contemporary French thought, but Descartes was still The Philosopher. The writing of history remained, by and large, in the scientistic tradition, although tinged by Michelet's passionate romanticism and modernized by the leavening influence of such creative synthesizers as Marc Bloch and Lucien Febvre. Literary and artistic criticism, at least in the serious journals, remained essentially traditionalist through most of the interwar era, though the more venturesome *Nouvelle Revue Française* (powerfully influenced by Gide) brought increasing prestige to literary experimenters.

Alongside the rebels and the self-analysts, therefore, a major segment of the French literary and artistic world continued to work in a more traditional vein and to attract the bulk of the reading public.[2] Probably most Frenchmen of the interwar years regarded as the literary masterpieces and milestones of the era the massive *romans-fleuves* of Georges Duhamel, Jules Romains, and Roger Martin du Gard—social chronicles, in each case, of the evolving fortunes of a French bourgeois family. Paul Valéry, the dean of French poets, managed to combine the symbolist heritage with a formidably austere intellectualism. The satirist Marcel Aymé continued the skeptical and ironic tradition of Anatole France (though without the latter's social conscience), combined with a lively sense of fantasy; the prewar Catholic novelists and poets had their successors (far more sophisticated and tinged with the gloomier mood of their time) in François Mauriac, Paul Claudel, and Georges Bernanos. The essayist Julien Benda, in his widely discussed pamphlet *La trahison des clercs* (1927), struck back vigorously at all those thinkers (Bergson the chief among them) who had turned to intuition or dialectics as substitutes for pure Cartesian rationalism.

---

[2] Perhaps the breadth of that reading public can be roughly judged by a survey carried out in 1978, which found that 43 per cent of French adults had not read a book in the preceding three months.

Modern intellectuals, he charged, had abandoned their true role by descending into the arena of passion and controversy rather than standing aloof on the heights of objectivity and pure reason. All of these writers clung, in their separate ways, to the long French tradition of rationalist humanism—to an attempt to grapple with the enduring tensions between man and society, and to a sympathetic concern for the dignity of the individual.

But as the "normalcy" of the 1920's turned into the chronic crisis of the 1930's, the cultural climate too showed signs of change. Those who defended the old values and practiced the traditional methods found themselves shaken in their certainties, and were thrown onto the defensive. On the other hand, those who had turned to intense subjectivism were suddenly jostled into a painful awareness that the material world around them would not leave them alone to indulge their introspective fantasies. The Proustian temper seemed increasingly outmoded in the upheaval of the 'thirties; neither pure craftsmanship nor the sensitive probing of man's psychic depths was any longer very satisfying. More and more, French writers and thinkers turned (as did those of other western nations) from psychological to social and political concerns, from a narrowly elitist culture to one that sought a broader audience. Even Gide developed a sudden interest in politics, and indulged in a brief love affair with communism.

More representative of the new mood, however, were such rising stars as André Malraux and Louis-Ferdinand Céline. Malraux, esthete and adventurer, plunged into a career of quixotic activism in Indo-China and Spain, and wove his own experiences in the civil-ideological wars of the period into a series of brilliant novels. He too (like so many intellectuals of the 'thirties) developed a lively sympathy for communism as a movement that was sure of its purposes and committed to activism in a polarized world. Malraux's neoromantic taste for heroic action and his desire for clear-cut solutions to human problems were later to lead him, by a kind of natural progression, to a command-post in the wartime *maquis* and eventually to prominence in the Gaullist regime as cabinet minister and semiofficial doctrinaire.

The man who chose the pen name Céline represented a quite different response to the era of crisis. A doctor by profession, a wounded veteran of the First World War, Céline turned to literature as an outlet for his essential nihilism, a way to vomit forth his loathing for so-called civilized society and for the beast called man. His was "a satanic vision of the godless world, rolling helplessly through space and infested with crawling millions of suffering, diseased, sex-obsessed, maniacal human beings."[3] Céline's first novel, *Voyage au bout de la nuit* (1932), won him wide notoriety through its uninhibited language, its black

---

[3] John Weightman in *The New York Review of Books,* June 5, 1969, p. 25.

humor, and its pioneering use of an antihero as central figure; but thereafter he slipped rapidly into the swamp of scurrilous antisemitism and general paranoia. The postwar charge that he had collaborated with the Nazis during the occupation was probably unfair; Céline's rage and hate did not discriminate in favor of Hitler. But for some promising young writers of the 1930's, fascist ideology did have a strong appeal. Robert Brasillach and Pierre Drieu la Rochelle, for example, found in the Nazi movement a heroic ideal of action, of commitment to a cause and rejection of a decaying bourgeois world, that was to make them enthusiastic collaborators after 1940.

Fortunately, commitment to action could follow other channels than those of fascism, communism, and neoromanticism. The deepening crisis of the 1930's stirred a new interest in social and political theorizing among Paris intellectuals, especially those of the younger generation. Discussion groups and little magazines pullulated on the left bank, in much the same way that social thought had flourished in Paris during the decade before 1848. Among these intellectual movements of the 1930's, the most influential in the long run was that led and inspired by a youthful Catholic thinker, Emmanuel Mounier. A Sorbonne drop-out (he had been repelled by the desiccated intellectualism of the French university system), Mounier developed a quasi-philosophy which he called personalism, and founded the magazine *Esprit* to carry his message. While Mounier's thought was tinged with the cultural pessimism that had been infiltrating European minds, he refused to succumb to the temptation of despair. Unlike the existentialists, he held that men are not isolated atoms in an absurd world. What he called "the established disorder" of our time can be replaced, he believed, if men will reject both individualism and collectivism in favor of a true sense of community. It was Mounier who developed what he called the philosophy of personalism, and who first used and popularized the concept of *engagement*—of commitment to the cause of community, seen as the high obligation of the intellectual and especially of the Christian. Mounier's early impact was confined to a small coterie, but it was to be felt strongly in the postwar era. Symbolically, *Esprit* was the only new magazine of the 1930's to survive the war.

❖❖❖❖❖❖❖❖❖❖❖❖❖

The shocks of the Second World War broke up not only the French army and the Third Republic, but also the contours of French thought; and out of the jumbled wreckage new forms and patterns were slow to take shape. One immediate effect, however, was to reinforce the impulse of intellectuals toward *engagement,* toward commitment to political and social action. Those who had been drawn into the discussion groups of the 1930's were natural recruits for the resistance movement (though in some cases—as with Mounier, for example —they first went through a brief flirtation with Vichy in its early "National Revolution" phase). From the resistance they emerged into the turmoil of post-war politics and journalism: author-philosopher Camus for a time edited a leading newspaper, novelist and essayist Sartre tried to found a new left-wing party, Malraux attached himself to the Gaullist cause, Mounier redoubled his effort to build a bridge between the Communists and Catholic (as well as other secular) reformers. In this sense, the decade after the war represented a kind of prolongation of the activist 1930's.

These were the years when French thought was powerfully affected by the new intellectual movement called existentialism. Not since the days of the sur-realists had any self-conscious school of thought had such impact; not even the surrealists had won such general notoriety. Existentialism's chief French exponent, the brilliant young philosopher, novelist and essayist Jean-Paul Sartre, had been exposed to the new doctrine at the University of Berlin during the early 1930's. Before the war, however, existential thought had produced no echo in France, and Sartre's own interests had remained purely intellectual and intro-spective; he was so apolitical that he refused to vote in the Popular Front elections of 1936. His first novel, *La nausée* (1938), reflected his prewar mood (and, no doubt, the malaise of at least some of his contemporaries). Its central character drifted aimlessly through an empty existence in a dull provincial city, alienated to the point of physical repulsion. Only at the end of the novel did this antihero experience a kind of awakening; through commitment to the task of literary creation, a way opened before him that would give meaning to his life.

The collapse of 1940 somehow impelled Sartre in a new direction: toward political activism rather than escape, toward political art rather than purely esthetic creation. As he reshaped existentialist doctrine and embodied it in his novels and essays, it became a kind of cry of defiance by lonely man confronting an incomprehensible universe. What man is, whence he comes, where his destiny may lie—these were questions that the existentialists held to be unanswerable. Man could know nothing more than the fact of his existence and his freedom to make choices, to shape his own life, to "make himself." Freedom to act and choose in an absurd, irrational universe was admittedly a lonely and painful privilege or duty, a burden that few men would be strong enough to bear; but Sartre and his disciples nevertheless preached the necessity for such self-commit-ment. Existentialism has been called "the Counter-Enlightenment come at last to philosophical expression." Few Frenchmen ever grasped its highly technical philosophical substructure; its appeal was the frame of mind, the attitude, the mood that it represented. In a sense, it contained in capsule form all of the disillusionment, anxiety, even despair that had been building up in Europe for two generations, and that reached a climax in an exhausted continent wrecked by war. The product of a time of crisis, it took on faddist qualities for awhile and was even successfully commercialized by the operators of left-bank tourist traps.

Existentialism's rapid decline in the 1950's stemmed in part from postwar recovery, which dissipated much of the crisis mood. But it stemmed also from Sartre's inability to develop a satisfying existentialist ethic, and his decision to substitute for it an existentialist politics by allying himself with the Communists. Neither in theory nor in practice did this alliance work smoothly; Sartre failed to win many French intellectuals to the idea that existentialist and Marxist ideas can be blended, and skeptics continued to ask why, if the world was really absurd and irrational, Sartre's free choice of ethical standards and goals was any more valid than those of, say, an anarchist or even a member of Hitler's SS. Sartre's long-promised book on existentialist ethics failed to appear, some of his best-known allies fell away, and existentialism by the mid-1950's began to seem an artifact of intellectual history rather than a living force. Even so, it surely left some residue, for its overtones of pessimism and despair still persisted in the mood of western Europe.

As existentialism declined, new intellectual movements emerged to offer proof that French imagination and creativity had not become sterile. Although Paris failed to recover its onetime preeminence in the fine arts (a kind of chauvinistic traditionalism seemed to stifle new experiments in painting, music, and the ballet), a so-called "new wave" of cinema directors, novelists, and critics gave luster to the city's reputation as a cultural center. The literary spotlight was seized for a time by exponents of the so-called "new novel"—Michel Butor, Natalie Sarraute, Alain Robbe-Grillet. Their hyperintellectual and often baffling experimental "anti-novels" and cinema scripts (of which the best known were for Alain Resnais' films *Last Year at Marienbad* and *Hiroshima Mon Amour*) inspired impassioned debate; in book form they attracted only a restricted circle of readers, but as films they reached a large and enthusiastic clientele. Much of their work was deeply marked by a Kafkaesque view of the world: plot and characterization often disintegrated completely; the very existence of the blank and nameless antihero was sometimes unclear; the reader might be left to choose among several partial and contradictory versions of the same events. In *Last Year at Marienbad* the distinctions of time—past, present, future or even non-happening—were deliberately blurred. Whatever else it signified, the new novel certainly represented a sharp reaction against the long period of *engagement* and a swing back toward the more aloof, highly elitist, self-consciously experimental writing of the 1920's.

Further evidence of this pendulum-swing toward a more intellectualized culture, toward *dégagement* in place of *engagement,* was given by the rise of structuralism as the dominant intellectual fashion of the 1960's. The fading of existentialism opened the way for some new synthesizing principle that might serve as base for a world-view, a "philosophy" in the loose sense of the word. Structuralism, to some French intellectuals, seemed to provide such a base for understanding man and the world. The word and the concept had been developed a generation earlier by pioneers in the new science of linguistics, who had given it a limited and precise meaning. For them it was an analytic technique by which to understand the form and function of languages. After the Second World War, the idea was taken over and broadened by France's leading ethnologist, Claude Lévi-Strauss, who sought to use it to understand all human cultures through time. For Lévi-Strauss, the traditional idea of cultural evolution from "primitive" to "advanced" was misleading; to him, all societies rest on a few simple structures that are internally coherent and that resemble each other closely. The impact of Lévi-Strauss's writings after 1960 was rapid and widespread; structuralism was seized upon and adapted to various purposes by a number of leading French psychologists, philosophers, and literary critics. Even the work of certain historians carried overtones of the structuralist view—notably the members of the so-called *Annales* school, who scoffed at narrative treatment of the past ("eventish" history, they called it) and stressed slow underlying changes over centuries of time. From a scientific methodology, structuralism showed a tendency to develop into an ideology and even a kind of cult—one that challenged the basic tenets of both existentialism and rationalist humanism. Man, the structuralist ideologues seemed to say, can neither make history nor "make himself." Man is the object, not the subject; the idea that his initiative can bring about change is pure illusion. Basic structures are decisive; history and human endeavor become largely irrelevant.

As structuralism's novelty faded in the 1970's, it was replaced by a more varied assortment of ideas loosely grouped under the label "post-structuralist." Rival clans of Parisian intellectuals clustered around such *maîtres-à-penser* as the psychoanalyst Jacques Lacan, the literary critic Roland Barthes, the Marxologist Louis Althusser, the intellectual historian Michel Foucault, and the philosopher Jacques Derrida. Within the tight little intellectual world of left-bank Paris, these clans engaged in intense forensic battles, and relegated all skeptics to the ash heap of outmoded beliefs. The skeptics in turn dismissed the whole thing as "a glorious cerebral game," and declared that simple ideas dressed up in unintelligible jargon remained nothing more than simple ideas. By the mid-1980's, most of the post-structuralist mandarins as well as their most notable predecessors had passed from the scene, leaving a kind of intellectual vacuum for the first time in a generation. The influence of Foucault and Derrida seemed most likely to endure for awhile, though probably more strongly abroad than in France. On American university campuses, for example, Foucault became a cult figure, while Derrida's "deconstructionist" method was seized upon by literary critics and some philosophers. But in Paris itself, the intellectual world appeared to be entering upon a period of taking stock, with no major new *maîtres-à-penser* in sight; instead, there was a revival of interest in less esoteric theories and less exotic experimentation in the creative arts. Still, while the excitement lasted, France had once again proved itself to be one of the world's most heated incubators of pure intellectualism.

Throughout the postwar years, however, many French thinkers, writers, and citizens kept their distance from these hyperintellectual debates; they preferred to cling to their long heritage of rationalist humanism. One branch of that tradition survived in the Voltairean or skeptical form; another, in Marxist materialism, especially the revisionist variety; and still a third in the shape of Christian humanism, embodied in the teachings of Emmanuel Mounier and others. The most notable spokesman for that tradition was surely the novelist and essayist Albert Camus. "Probably no European writer of his time," says an eminent critic, "left so deep a mark on the imagination and, at the same time, on the moral and political consciousness of his own generation and the next."[4] Camus had been close to Sartre until the two men parted company in 1952 over Sartre's support of the Soviet line; his early novel *The Stranger* seemed to reflect the existentialist outlook, and he retained a strong sense of the world's absurdity and man's tragic condition. Camus was intensely aware of the enduring dilemma between means and ends—a dilemma that becomes more acute in times of stress. He found no solution for that dilemma, but sought one patiently until the end. Receiving the Nobel prize for literature in 1957, he described himself as the voice of his generation of Europeans—a generation whose lives had been spent in political and social chaos, but whose members refused to succumb to the mood of cultural despair. Purposeful action, Camus insisted, can have meaning, both for oneself and for the world. That world may seem absurd, and man more often than not irrational; but this should be no excuse for abandoning the fight against the absurd and the irrational, or for seizing upon the most convenient form of *engagement* merely to give one's own life meaning. Not all causes, he argued, are equally valid; the true test is their respect for the one trait that binds all men together—the trait of common humanity. In proposing an ethic for his generation, Camus exalted what he called "the rebel": the man who fights back not only against tyrants but also against fanatics, self-appointed saviors, men who see themselves as substitutes for God—and against the pervasive absurdity of the human condition.

Camus belongs to an old moralistic tradition that stretches back through several centuries of France's intellectual life, and that embodies much of the Enlightenment spirit that has so powerfully marked modern France over the

---

[4] Conor Cruise O'Brien, *Albert Camus* (New York: Viking Press, 1970), p. 103.

past two centuries. That tradition has been subjected to sharp challenge in recent decades, and some consider it outmoded as the twentieth century moves toward its close. Yet so long as the various currents of rationalist humanism continue to run among Frenchmen, and so long as they bring us from time to time a voice as compelling as that of Albert Camus, one can believe that there is hope for France—and for man.

# CHAPTER 38

# The Varieties of History, 1919–1986

Those who write the history of the very recent past take special risks. "Who follows truth too closely at the heels may have his brains kicked out." In France until the last couple of decades, historians have been inclined to treat modern history as though it ended in 1914, and even to label the nineteenth century "contemporary history" (a label almost, though not quite, as damning as "current events"). The immediate past was therefore left to the journalists and to certain less fastidious Anglo-Saxon scholars. Now, however, times have changed; French historians in considerable numbers have been moving into this formerly neglected realm. Indeed, what the French call "l'histoire immédiate" may be in process of transformation from an underdeveloped to an overcultivated area. On the other hand, works that are likely to outlast their decade are still few; historians' judgments of the recent past tend to be quickly outmoded.

Two general interpretations of contemporary France have come from social scientists, but their ideas have found wide currency among historians. Stanley Hoffmann's essay "Paradoxes of the French Political Community" (in Hoffmann et al., *In Search of France*) sets out to explain the country's transformation since the Second World War. The Third Republic, he argues, represented a political compromise that was based on what he calls a "stalemate society." The political system allowed for gradual but narrowly limited change; it successfully protected the vested interests and the shared value-system of the dominant social groups—most of all, of the bourgeoisie and the small landowning peasantry. But beginning with the 1930's, a series of powerful shocks originating outside the borders of France hit the country one after another: depression, military defeat, foreign occupation undermined the habitual consensus. The psychological impact of these shocks led the new postwar leadership to question the traditional system and to embark on a program of drastic change. The stalemate society's foundations were undermined, despite the dogged resistance of its defenders. One result was to alter Frenchmen's values and semi-sacred beliefs, and to shatter much of the old complacency that had led them to see their political and social structures as a guarantee of safety, stability, and national greatness. Hoffmann's analysis (dating from the early 1960's) was marked by a cautious optimism about the long-run effects of this changed outlook, and his subsequent writings (notably his collection of essays entitled *Decline or Renewal? France Since the 1930's*) have reiterated that cautious hope. His thesis of pre-war stalemate giving way to postwar dynamism has won wide acceptance, though some French critics see the contrast as too black and white.

A more jaundiced view of main trends in postwar France comes from sociologist Michel Crozier. The title of his book *La société bloquée* is the French equivalent of "stalemate society"; its theme is that stalemate persists despite all the evidence of postwar changes. Underlying those changes, traditional values and attitudes survive; no real transformation will occur unless the leaders of politics and opinion take vigorous action to alter basic human relationships in France. Crozier's earlier book *The Bureaucratic Phenomenon* probes into those relationships through a microanalysis of two governmental agencies, to show how French bureaucracy functions. From there, he proposes the thesis that the bureaucratic structure both shapes and reflects national attitudes and behavior. The bureaucracy, he argues, is rigid and inefficient, yet it helps to resolve the dilemma between the Frenchman's urge for personal autonomy and his awareness that total autonomy would breed chaos. Bureaucratic officials are vested with some authority over their subordinates, but they are also restricted by a set of elaborate rules; the superior is forbidden to intrude upon the tiny independent realm marked out and fiercely defended by each of his subordinates. The system, says Crozier, prevents any real sense of community; each individual, jealous of his turf and fearful of face-to-face relationships, relies for protection on the bureaucratic rules and feels no impulse to join formal or informal primary groups, either social or professional. When Frenchmen join together, they are more likely to do so in the negative and self-protective fashion of the school-boys' "delinquent community" (as described by the sociologist Jesse Pitts in Hoffmann et al.'s *In Search of France*). Given this model, Crozier believes that gradual change through give-and-take is almost impossible—that change can come only through a general crisis that disrupts the entire system. In the intervals between such crises, the system reverts to stalemate; to transcend it will require the creation of a new pattern of human interaction. Although both

Crozier's and Hoffmann's analyses are now somewhat dated, they continue to provide useful parameters within which one can seek to follow the processes of change in contemporary France.

❖❖❖❖❖❖❖❖❖❖❖❖❖❖

Selecting representative books on France's recent history is more chancy than was the case for earlier periods. A complete annotated bibliography would outrun the available space, while singling out a few specimens is bound to be somewhat arbitrary. The latter risk seems preferable, even though it means omitting many solid specialized works.

There have been few recent attempts to reexamine the interwar years as a coherent unit. A good brief exception is Claude Fohlen's lucid essay *La France de l'entre-deux-guerres*; a more traditional account may be found in volumes 5–7 of Jacques Chastenet's *Histoire de la troisième république*. Charles S. Maier's massive study *Recasting Bourgeois Europe* argues that the dominant elites of western Europe managed to reassert their control after 1918 despite the upheaval of war and postwar pressures for social change. Several recent monographs draw on newly opened archives to advance a revisionist view of French aims and conduct at the 1919 peace conference and during subsequent years: Walter A. McDougall's *France's Rhineland Diplomacy 1914–1924*, Marc Trachtenberg's *Reparation in World Politics*, and Stephen A. Schuker's *The End of French Predominance in Europe*. All three authors replace the older negative view by a more sympathetic understanding of France's dilemmas in postwar Europe.

On the 1930's there are two notable biographies of Léon Blum, one by Joel Colton, the other by Jean Lacouture, and there is an authoritative account of France's foreign policy by the leading French diplomatic historian, J.-B. Duroselle; *La décadence, 1932–1939*, and *L'abîme, 1939–1945*. Duroselle is the first scholar to have enjoyed full access to the French foreign office archives for the period; his judgments of French policy-makers of the time are devastating. On the military defeat of 1940, much has been written in retrospect, but the most thoughtful assessment is still Marc Bloch's brief contemporary essay *Strange Defeat*. Bloch, an eminent historian who served in the army in 1939–40 (and was shot by the Germans in 1944), lays bare the weaknesses of leadership and of public morale that contributed to the debacle.

For the Vichy period, Robert Paxton's *Vichy France: Old Guard and New Order* is a severe but persuasive indictment of the men who surrounded Petain; so is *Vichy France and the Jews* by Michael Marrus and Robert Paxton. Both volumes draw on German archival sources, and shatter the legend that the Vichy leaders were merely French patriots seeking to protect their compatriots against the conquerors. On the resistance movement, there is a good survey by H. R. Kedward (*Resistance in Vichy France*) and a multivolume work by Henri Noguères et al., *Histoire de la résistance en France*. Charles de Gaulle's war memoirs are of course indispensable, as is Jean Lacouture's remarkable new biography of de Gaulle (two volumes published to date).

On the Fourth Republic, Philip Williams's microscopic analysis *Crisis and Compromise* is generally regarded as the standard work. The Algerian war which brought down that regime has found two fine historians: Alistaire Horne (*A Savage War for Peace*) and John E. Talbott (*The War Without a Name*). France's retreat from empire, viewed from a neo-Marxist perspective, has been skillfully analyzed by Jacques Marseille in *Empire colonial et capitalisme française: histoire d'un divorce*. The Fifth Republic for the most part remains in the province of the journalists. Good examples of their work include Pierre Viansson-Ponté's *Histoire de la république Gaullienne*; John Ardagh's *France in the 1980s*; and Serge July's *Les années Mitterrand*. The crisis of May 1968 brought a proliferation of "instant history"; that by Raymond Aron (*The Elusive Revolution*) has some durable interest because of its author's intellectual eminence, while Bernard E. Brown's *Protest in Paris* benefits from a slightly longer perspective.

On particular topics, there are important studies of France's adoption of economic planning (Richard F. Kuisel's *Capitalism and the State in Modern France*), of postwar foreign policy (Alfred Grosser's *Affaires extérieures*), of the Communists' role in the labor movement (George Ross's *Workers and Communists in France*), and of the transformation of agriculture (Henri Mendras's *The Vanishing Peasant*). On rural France, four accounts of village life deepen our understanding of French values and mores: Laurence Wylie's *Village in the Vaucluse*, André Burguière's *Bretons de Plozevet*, Pierre-Jakes Hélias's *The Horse of Pride*, and Emilie Carles's *Une soupe aux herbes sauvages*. Wylie's book was the product of a year's stay in a southern village in 1950–51, with short return visits thereafter; it shows that profound changes have not been confined to the cities. Burguière synthesizes the studies and observations of dozens of social scientists who used a Breton village as their laboratory; his book combines historical depth and immediacy. Hélias and Carles recount their own experiences while growing up in remote rural communities—the former in Brittany, the latter in the Alps.

❖❖❖❖❖❖❖❖❖❖❖❖❖

For the student of history who resorts to novels as a source of understanding, the period since the First World War lacks the variety of choice offered by that golden age, the nineteenth century. One finds no Balzac, Flaubert, or Zola—and only a pale shadow of Anatole France. Proust's later volumes, though published in the 1920's, continued to portray a vanishing prewar world. So did Roger Martin du Gard's *The Thibaults* (which evoked the mood of 1914 in remarkable fashion). The greatest literary figures of the interwar years—André Gide, François Mauriac, André Malraux—either preferred psychological to social analysis, or (in Malraux's case) set their novels of war and revolution in Asia or Spain. Jules Romains's massive epic *Men of Good Will* carries his protagonists through the 1920's, but it has a rather dated and lifeless quality when read today. Yet a few novels of the period *are* helpful, either because they consciously deal with social or political issues, or because they reflect the mood of their time.

The Great War produced no outstanding work of imaginative literature in France; but the traumatic impact of that experience can be sensed in L.-F. Céline's cynical and nihilistic *Journey to the End of the Night*, and in Henri Barbusse's *Under Fire*. Georges Bernanos's *Diary of a Country Priest* affords remarkable insight into the tensions and frustrations of provincial life; Bernanos wrote as a fervent though idiosyncratic Catholic. Gabriel Chevallier's *Clochemerle* verges on the category of sleazy literature, but beneath its racy satire some have seen a crude but faithful portrait of small-town life and politics during the later Third Republic. Marcel Aymé's *Travelingue* is satire, too, of a more mordant sort; his targets are the leaders of the 1936 Popular Front. Jean-Paul Sartre's *Nausea* (1938) was the first important existentialist novel, foreshadowing the mood that was to have its full impact just after the war. Sartre's postwar trilogy *The Roads to Freedom* carried his intellectual antihero from apathy to commitment under the stress of events from the Munich conference to the 1940 collapse.

The occupation years and the resistance movement have inspired a number of topical novels. Albert Camus's *The Plague* is the most impressive, though it is plainly much more than a mere parable of France under German occupation. Simone de Beauvoir's *The Blood of Others* concerns the exploits of the anti-German underground, while Jean Dutourd's *The Best Butter* satirizes those opportunists who did well under Vichy and switched sides just in time. Few novels have dealt explicitly with the political or social issues of the years since 1945. One exception is Simone de Beauvoir's *The Mandarins*—a thinly veiled fictional account of Parisian postwar intellectuals, notably Sartre and Camus, and their brief unsuccessful venture into politics. Sartre's postwar plays and Camus's last novel *The Fall* attempt to grapple with some of the eternal human dilemmas that transcend time and place. As for the younger school of the "new novel" that emerged in the 1950's, its practitioners ostentatiously turned their backs on the issues of the day. The student of France's contemporary history may thus be compelled to resort to more traditional sources of understanding, or perhaps to turn from the novel to its modern successor, the film.

Not all of France's film classics, of course, are useful for the student of history, but there are some exceptions. Three recent releases deal with events of the revolutionary-Napoleonic era: Ettore Scola's *La nuit de Varennes* (1983) (on the king's failed attempt to escape abroad in 1791); Andrzej Wajda's *Danton* (1983); and Abel Gance's monumental epic *Napoleon* (1926; re-released 1981). Marcel Carné's *Les enfants du paradis* (1945) portrays the world of the theater and the Paris boulevards in the era of Louis-Philippe. René Clément's *Gervaise* (1956) is drawn from Zola's novel *The Dram Shop*; it depicts Parisian working-class life in the 1860's and reflects Zola's theories about the fatal grip of heredity. Jean Renoir's *La grande illusion* (1937) focuses on a group of French prisoners of war in Germany during the Great War; it suggests the futility of war, and the importance of class loyalties as opposed to national loyalties. (This may explain why the film was banned in Hitler's Germany, and again in liberated France after 1944.) Georges Rouquier's *Farrebique* (1946) and Jacques Becker's *Goupi-Mains-Rouges* (1943) are graphic portrayals of peasant life before the onset of modernization. The Vichy era has recently attracted a number of film-makers; the most notable example is Marcel Ophuls's *Le chagrin et la pitié* (1969), a powerful documentary and retrospective commentary. Costa-Gavras's *Section spéciale* (1975) dramatizes a real courtroom episode that occurred in Paris in 1941; it poses the painful dilemma of greater versus lesser evil. Louis Malle's *Lacombe Lucien* (1973) is a controversial attempt to delineate a young French collaborator; and Michel Mitrani's *Les guichets du Louvre* (1974) deals with the roundup of the Jews in Paris in 1942. Aspects of France's war in Algeria provide the subject matter for another Ophuls documentary *Français, si vous saviez* (1975) and for Gilles Pontecorvo's *Battle of Algiers* (1961); the latter dramatizes, from a pro-Algerian viewpoint, one of the war's crucial episodes, using as actors some of the actual participants. Alain Resnais's *L'année dernière à Marienbad* (1961), with script by the chief spokesman for the "new novel," Alain Robbe-Grillet, transposes to the screen the somewhat confusing world-view of that esoteric literary movement.

A Selective List of Readings About France 1919–1986

Ardagh, John. *France in the 1980s*. New York: Penguin, 1983.
Aron, Raymond. *The Elusive Revolution*. New York: Praeger, 1969.
Bloch, Marc. *Strange Defeat*. New York: Oxford University Press, 1949.
Brown, Bernard E. *Protest in Paris*. Morristown, N. J.: General Learning, 1974.

Burguière, André. *Bretons de Plozevet*. Paris: Flammarion, 1975.

Cairns, John C. "Along the Road Back to France, 1940," *American Historical Review*, LXIV (1959), 583–603.

Carles, Emilie. *Une soupe aux herbes sauvages*. Paris: Simoën, 1977.

Chastenet, Jacques. *Histoire de la troisième république* (vols. V–VII). Paris: Hachette, 1952–1963.

Colton, Joel. *Léon Blum: Humanist in Politics*. New York: Knopf, 1966.

Crozier, Michel. *The Bureaucratic Phenomenon*. Chicago: University of Chicago Press, 1964.

Crozier, Michel. *La société bloquée*. Paris: Seuil, 1970.

Duroselle, J.-B. *La décadence 1932–1939*. Paris: Imprimerie nationale, 1979.

Duroselle, J.-B. *L'abîme 1939–1945*. Paris: Imprimerie nationale, 1982.

Fohlen, Claude. *La France de l'entre-deux-guerres*. Paris: Casterman, 1966.

de Gaulle, Charles. *The Complete War Memoirs*. New York: Simon and Schuster, 1964.

Grosser, Alfred. *Affaires extérieures: la politique de la France 1944–1984*. Paris: Flammarion, 1984.

Hélias, Pierre-Jakez. *The Horse of Pride*. New Haven: Yale University Press, 1978.

Hoffmann, Stanley, et al. *In Search of France*. Cambridge: Harvard University Press, 1963.

Hoffmann, Stanley. *Decline or Renewal? France Since the 1930's*. New York: Viking, 1974.

Horne, Alistaire. *A Savage War of Peace*. New York: Viking, 1978.

Jäckel, Eberhard. *Frankreich in Hitlers Europa*. Stuttgart: Deutsche Verlags-Anstalt, 1966.

July, Serge. *Les années Mitterrand*. Paris: Grasset, 1986.

Kedward, H. R. *Resistance in Vichy France*. Oxford: Oxford University Press, 1978.

Kemp, Tom. *The French Economy 1913–1939: The History of a Decline*. London: Longmans, 1972.

Kriegel, Annie. *The French Communists: Profile of a People*. Chicago: University of Chicago Press, 1972.

Kuisel, Richard. *Capitalism and the State in Modern France*. Cambridge: Cambridge University Press, 1981.

Lacouture, Jean. *De Gaulle* (2 vols published to date). Paris: Seuil, 1984–

Luethy, Herbert. *France Against Herself*. New York: Praeger, 1955.

Maier, Charles S. *Recasting Bourgeois Europe*. Princeton: Princeton University Press, 1975.

Marrus, Michael R., and Robert Paxton. *Vichy France and the Jews*. New York: Basic Books, 1981.

Marseille, Jacques. *Empire colonial et capitalisme français: histoire d'un divorce*. Paris: Albin Michel, 1984.

McDougall, Walter A. *France's Rhineland Diplomacy 1914–1924*. Princeton: Princeton University Press, 1978.

Mendras, Henri. *The Vanishing Peasant*. Cambridge: M.I.T. Press, 1970.

Milward, Alan S. *The New Order and the French Economy.* Oxford: Clarendon Press, 1970.

Noguères, Henri, et al. *Histoire de la résistance en France de 1940 à 1945* (5 vols). Paris: Laffont, 1967–1976.

Paxton, Robert. *Vichy France: Old Guard and New Order.* New York: Knopf, 1972.

Peyre, Henri. *French Novelists of Today.* New York: Oxford University Press, 1967.

Ross, George. *Workers and Communists in France: From Popular Front to Euro-communism.* Berkeley: University of California Press, 1982.

Schuker, Stephen A. *The End of French Predominance in Europe.* Chapel Hill: University of North Carolina Press, 1976.

Soucy, Robert. *French Fascism: The First Wave, 1924–1933.* New Haven: Yale University Press, 1986.

Talbott, John E. *The War Without a Name.* New York: Knopf, 1980.

Tavernier, Yves, et al. *L'univers politique des paysans.* Paris: Colin, 1972.

Trachtenberg, Marc. *Reparation in World Politics.* New York: Columbia University Press, 1980.

Viansson-Ponté, Pierre. *Histoire de la république Gaullienne.* Paris: Fayard, 1970–1971.

Williams, Philip. *Crisis and Compromise: Politics in the Fourth Republic.* London: Longmans, 1964.

Wohl, Robert. *French Communism in the Making, 1914–1924.* Stanford: Stanford University Press, 1966.

Wright, Gordon. *Rural Revolution in France.* Stanford: Stanford University Press, 1964.

Wright, Vincent (ed.). *Continuity and Change in France.* London: Allen and Unwin, 1984.

Wylie, Laurence. *Village in the Vaucluse.* New York: Harper, 1964.

# Index

The content of the four bibliographical chapters is indexed by general topics rather than by authors and titles. A few authors whose work has been especially influential, or whose interpretations are discussed in these four chapters, are also indexed.

Front reforms, 372; Peasant Corporation, 392; "silent revolution" after 1945, 446–49; exodus to cities, 448; and E.E.C., 448–49; influence in Fourth Republic, 450; books about, 203, 205, 207, 208, 320, 323, 324, 471, 474, 475

Pecqueur, Constantin, 184

Péguy, Charles, 294

Père Lachaise cemetery, 216

Périer, Casimir, 112, 116, 153, 165, 168

Persigny, Jean Gilbert, Duc de, 146, 147

Pétain, Marshal Philippe, 397, 418, 427; in World War I, 309–12; in Doumergue cabinet, 365; opposes military reforms, 386; premier 1940, 389–91; heads Vichy regime, 392–94, 398; estimate of, 395–96; death sentence commuted, 407; survival of some reforms, 409; compared to de Gaulle, 427

Peyre, Henri: quoted, 458

Pflimlin, Pierre, 416–17

*Philosophes*, 19, 25–32, 36, 40, 57, 86, 87

"Phony war", 385–88

Pichegru, General Charles, 63

Picquart, Colonel Georges, 249–50

Piedmont, 71, 143, 197

Pinay, Antoine, 411

Pitt, William, 65

Pius VI, Pope, 48

Pius VII, Pope, 69, 71, 73

Pius IX, Pope, 137, 138, 143, 220, 221, 233

Pius X, Pope, 257, 265

Pius XI, Pope, 334

Plan XVII, 308–9

Planning Commission, 409, 444–45

Poincaré, Henri, 289

Poincaré, Raymond, 411, 418; elected president, 263–64; attitude toward Germany, 295–96, 380; premier, 305; policy of preparedness, 305–6; in World War I, 311–12, 388; Paris peace settlement, 316; postwar political role, 330–31; Ruhr occupation, 340–41; accepts Briand's German policy, 342–43; financial policy, 349; "savior of the franc", 350, 360, 365

Poland, 73, 132, 194, 338, 395; revolt of 1831, 191–92; Paris peace settlement, 316; French alliance, 339, 342, 344; Nazi threat, 380, 384; German conquest, 384–85, 387; Communist attitude toward, 388

Police, 74, 130–31, 395, 406

Polignac, Jules de, 109, 112, 190

Pompadour, Madame de, 12

Pompidou, Georges: prime minister, 422–23, 427–28; rival to de Gaulle, 429; president, 430–31

Pontecorvo, Gillo, 473

Popular Democratic Party, 334

Popular Front, 362, 366; organized, 367–68; program, 368; electoral victory 1936, 368–69; in power, 370–74; foreign policy, 379,

381–82; social and economic policies, 371–75; military policy, 386

Population: growth 1750–1850, 14–15, 175; crisis of 1846–51, 176; rural overpopulation, 171; problem of demographic decline, 176, 267, 271, 375, 443; effects of World War I, 313, 354; after World War II, 404, 444, 445, 454

Portugal, 73

Positivism, 139, 186, 264; influence during Third Republic, 232–33, 235–37, 278, 286–89, 290, 293–94, 460; decline, 259, 291, 457

Post-structuralism, 465–66

Poujade, Pierre, 412–13

Prestwich, M.: quoted, 8

Prévost-Paradol, Lucien, 181; quoted, 188

Pritchard affair, 193

"Privatization", 439

Proletariat. *See* Workers

Protestants, 118, 154, 159, 170, 235, 264, 290; role in modern France, 276–77, 277n

Proudhon, Pierre-Joseph: doctrines, 184–85; influence in Paris Commune, 218, 247; influence in labor movement, 283

Proust, Marcel, 275, 291, 322, 458–59, 461, 472

Provençal language, 7

Prussia, 190; war with France, 51, 53, 72–73, 76; in 1848, 131; war of 1870–71, 148–49, 167, 213–15

Public finance: before 1789, 9, 11, 15, 36–37, 39; during Great Revolution, 48–49, 64; under Napoleon, 70, 96–97; during July Monarchy, 154; during Third Republic, 220; effects of World War I, 313, 348–51; Laval's deflation, 366; Popular Front, 372–73; Fourth Republic, 421–22; Fifth Republic, 422

Purge of collaborators (1944), 407

Quebec, 426, 431

R.P.F. (Rassemblement du Peuple Français), 410–13

R.P.R. (Rassemblement pour la République), 433

"Race": as factor in shaping modern France, 5–7

Radicals, 222–25, 230, 284, 412, 431; program, 231–32, 233; in Boulanger affair, 241–44; growing moderation, 246; division and reunification, 246; effects of Dreyfus Affair, 251; years of dominance, 253–65; change in outlook, 253–54; post-Dreyfus reform program, 255–59; rapprochement with Moderates, 261–62; antimilitarism, 263; economic policy, 269; petty-bourgeois base, 278; foreign policy, 298, 301, 304, 305; election victory 1914, 306; in World War I, 309–12; in postwar politics, 328–30, 231; social and eco-